Short Stories

Stories

for Students

National Advisory Board

Short Stories for Students

Presenting Analysis, Context, and Criticism on Commonly Studied Short Stories

Volume 9

Ira Mark Milne, Editor

GALE GROUP

Detroit
New York
San Francisco
London
Boston
Woodbridge, CT

Short Stories for Students

Staff

Editorial: Ira Mark Milne, *Editor.* Tim Akers, Angela Y. Jones, Michael LaBlanc, Polly Vedder, *Contributing Editors.* Dwayne D. Hayes, *Managing Editor.*

Research: Victoria B. Cariappa, *Research Team Manager.* Cheryl Warnock, *Research Specialist.* Corrine A. Boland, Tamara Nott, Tracie A. Richardson, *Research Associates.* Timothy Lehnerer, Patricia Love, *Research Assistants.*

Permissions: Maria Franklin, *Permissions Manager.* Margaret A. Chamberlain, Kimberly Smilay, *Permissions Specialist.* Kelly Quin, *Permissions Associate.* Sandra K. Gore, Erin Bealmear, *Permissions Assistants.*

Production: Mary Beth Trimper, *Production Director.* Evi Seoud, *Assistant Production Manager.* Stacy Melson, *Production Assistant.*

Imaging and Multimedia Content Team: Randy Bassett, *Image Database Supervisor.* Robert Duncan, Michael Logusz, *Imaging Specialists.* Pamela A. Reed, *Imaging Coordinator.*

Product Design Team: Cynthia Baldwin, *Product Design Manager.* Pamela A. E. Galbreath, *Senior Art Director.* Gary Leach, *Graphic Artist.*

Copyright Notice

Table of Contents

Why Study Literature At All?

Short Stories for Students is designed to provide readers with information and discussion about a wide range of important contemporary and historical works of short fiction, and it does that job very well. However, I want to use this guest foreword to address a question that it does *not* take up. It is a fundamental question that is often ignored in high school and college English classes as well as research texts, and one that causes frustration among students at all levels, namely—why study literature at all? Isn't it enough to read a story, enjoy it, and go about one's business? My answer (to be expected from a literary professional, I suppose) is no. It is not enough. It is a start; but it is not enough. Here's why.

First, literature is the only part of the educational curriculum that deals directly with the actual world of lived experience. The philosopher Edmund Husserl used the apt German term *die Lebenswelt*, "the living world," to denote this realm. All the other content areas of the modern American educational system avoid the subjective, present reality of everyday life. Science (both the natural and the social varieties) objectifies, the fine arts create and/or perform, history reconstructs. Only literary study persists in posing those questions we all asked before our schooling taught us to give up on them. Only literature gives credibility to personal perceptions, feelings, dreams, and the "stream of consciousness" that is our inner voice. Literature wonders about infinity, wonders why God permits evil, wonders what will happen to us after we die. Literature admits that we get our hearts broken, that people sometimes cheat and get away with it, that the world is a strange and probably incomprehensible place. Literature, in other words, takes on all the big and small issues of what it means to be human. So my first answer is that of the humanist—we should read literature and study it and take it seriously because it enriches us as human beings. We develop our moral imagination, our capacity to sympathize with other people, and our ability to understand our existence through the experience of fiction.

My second answer is more practical. By studying literature we can learn how to explore and analyze texts. Fiction may be about *die Lebenswelt*, but it is a construct of words put together in a certain order by an artist using the medium of language. By examining and studying those constructions, we can learn about language as a medium. We can become more sophisticated about word associations and connotations, about the manipulation of symbols, and about style and atmosphere. We can grasp how ambiguous language is and how important context and texture is to meaning. In our first encounter with a work of literature, of course, we are not supposed to catch all of these things. We are spellbound, just as the writer wanted us to be. It is as serious students of the writer's art that we begin to see how the tricks are done.

Seeing the tricks, which is another way of saying "developing analytical and close reading skills," is important above and beyond its intrinsic literary educational value. These skills transfer to other fields and enhance critical thinking of any kind. Understanding how language is used to construct texts is powerful knowledge. It makes engineers better problem solvers, lawyers better advocates and courtroom practitioners, politicians better rhetoricians, marketing and advertising agents better sellers, and citizens more aware consumers as well as better participants in democracy. This last point is especially important, because rhetorical skill works both ways—when we learn how language is manipulated in the making of texts the result is that we become less susceptible when language is used to manipulate us.

My third reason is related to the second. When we begin to see literature as created artifacts of language, we become more sensitive to good writing in general. We get a stronger sense of the importance of individual words, even the sounds of words and word combinations. We begin to understand Mark Twain's delicious proverb—"The difference between the right word and the almost right word is the difference between lightning and a lightning bug." Getting beyond the "enjoyment only" stage of literature gets us closer to becoming makers of word art ourselves. I am not saying that studying fiction will turn every student into a Faulkner or a Shakespeare. But it will make us more adaptable and effective writers, even if our art form ends up being the office memo or the corporate annual report.

Studying short stories, then, can help students become better readers, better writers, and even better human beings. But I want to close with a warning. If your study and exploration of the craft, history, context, symbolism, or anything else about a story starts to rob it of the magic you felt when you first read it, it is time to stop. Take a break, study another subject, shoot some hoops, or go for a run. Love of reading is too important to be ruined by school. The early twentieth century writer Willa Cather, in her novel *My Antonia*, has her narrator Jack Burden tell a story that he and Antonia heard from two old Russian immigrants when they were teenagers. These immigrants, Pavel and Peter, told about an incident from their youth back in Russia that the narrator could recall in vivid detail thirty years later. It was a harrowing story of a wedding party starting home in sleds and being chased by starving wolves. Hundreds of wolves attacked the group's sleds one by one as they sped across the snow trying to reach their village. In a horrible revelation, the old Russians revealed that the groom eventually threw his own bride to the wolves to save himself. There was even a hint that one of the old immigrants might have been the groom mentioned in the story. Cather has her narrator conclude with his feelings about the story. "We did not tell Pavel's secret to anyone, but guarded it jealously—as if the wolves of the Ukraine had gathered that night long ago, and the wedding party had been sacrificed, just to give us a painful and peculiar pleasure." That feeling, that painful and peculiar pleasure, is the most important thing about literature. Study and research should enhance that feeling and never be allowed to overwhelm it.

Thomas E. Barden
Professor of English and
Director of Graduate English Studies
The University of Toledo

Introduction

Purpose of the Book

The purpose of *Short Stories for Students* (*SSfS*) is to provide readers with a guide to understanding, enjoying, and studying short stories by giving them easy access to information about the work. Part of Gale's ''For Students'' Literature line, *SSfS* is specifically designed to meet the curricular needs of high school and undergraduate college students and their teachers, as well as the interests of general readers and researchers considering specific short fiction. While each volume contains entries on classic stories frequently studied in classrooms, there are also entries containing hard-to-find information on contemporary stories, including works by multicultural, international, and women writers.

The information covered in each entry includes an introduction to the story and the story's author; a plot summary, to help readers unravel and understand the events in the work; descriptions of important characters, including explanation of a given character's role in the narrative as well as discussion about that character's relationship to other characters in the story; analysis of important themes in the story; and an explanation of important literary techniques and movements as they are demonstrated in the work.

In addition to this material, which helps the readers analyze the story itself, students are also provided with important information on the literary and historical background informing each work.

This includes a historical context essay, a box comparing the time or place the story was written to modern Western culture, a critical overview essay, and excerpts from critical essays on the story or author. A unique feature of *SSfS* is a specially commissioned overview essay on each story by an academic expert, targeted toward the student reader.

To further aid the student in studying and enjoying each story, information on media adaptations is provided, as well as reading suggestions for works of fiction and nonfiction on similar themes and topics. Classroom aids include ideas for research papers and lists of critical sources that provide additional material on the work.

Selection Criteria

The titles for each volume of *SSfS* were selected by surveying numerous sources on teaching literature and analyzing course curricula for various school districts. Some of the sources surveyed include: literature anthologies, *Reading Lists for College-Bound Students: The Books Most Recommended by America's Top Colleges; Teaching the Short Story: A Guide to Using Stories from Around the World,* by the National Council of Teachers of English (NTCE); and ''A Study of High School Literature Anthologies,'' conducted by Arthur Applebee at the Center for the Learning and Teaching of Literature and sponsored by the National Endowment for the Arts and the Office of Educational Research and Improvement.

Input was also solicited from our expert advisory board, as well as educators from various areas. From these discussions, it was determined that each volume should have a mix of "classic" stories (those works commonly taught in literature classes) and contemporary stories for which information is often hard to find. Because of the interest in expanding the canon of literature, an emphasis was also placed on including works by international, multicultural, and women authors. Our advisory board members—current high-school teachers—helped pare down the list for each volume. Works not selected for the present volume were noted as possibilities for future volumes. As always, the editor welcomes suggestions for titles to be included in future volumes.

How Each Entry Is Organized

Each entry, or chapter, in *SSfS* focuses on one story. Each entry heading lists the title of the story, the author's name, and the date of the story's publication. The following elements are contained in each entry:

- **Introduction:** a brief overview of the story which provides information about its first appearance, its literary standing, any controversies surrounding the work, and major conflicts or themes within the work.

- **Author Biography:** this section includes basic facts about the author's life, and focuses on events and times in the author's life that may have inspired the story in question.

- **Plot Summary:** a description of the events in the story, with interpretation of how these events help articulate the story's themes.

- **Characters:** an alphabetical listing of the characters who appear in the story. Each character name is followed by a brief to an extensive description of the character's role in the story, as well as discussion of the character's actions, relationships, and possible motivation.

  Characters are listed alphabetically by last name. If a character is unnamed—for instance, the narrator in "The Eatonville Anthology"—the character is listed as "The Narrator" and alphabetized as "Narrator." If a character's first name is the only one given, the name will appear alphabetically by that name.

- **Themes:** a thorough overview of how the topics, themes, and issues are addressed within the story. Each theme discussed appears in a sepa-

rate subhead, and is easily accessed through the boldface entries in the Subject/Theme Index.

- **Style:** this section addresses important style elements of the story, such as setting, point of view, and narration; important literary devices used, such as imagery, foreshadowing, symbolism; and, if applicable, genres to which the work might have belonged, such as Gothicism or Romanticism. Literary terms are explained within the entry, but can also be found in the Glossary of Literary Terms.

- **Historical and Cultural Context:** This section outlines the social, political, and cultural climate *in which the author lived and the work was created.* This section may include descriptions of related historical events, pertinent aspects of daily life in the culture, and the artistic and literary sensibilities of the time in which the work was written. If the story is historical in nature, information regarding the time in which the story is set is also included. Long sections are broken down with helpful subheads.

- **Critical Overview:** this section provides background on the critical reputation of the author and the story, including bannings or any other public controversies surrounding the work. For older works, this section may include a history of how story was first received and how perceptions of it may have changed over the years; for more recent works, direct quotes from early reviews may also be included.

- **Sources:** an alphabetical list of critical material quoted in the entry, with bibliographical information.

- **For Further Study:** an alphabetical list of other critical sources which may prove useful for the student. Includes full bibliographical information and a brief annotation.

- **Criticism:** an essay commissioned by *SSfS* which specifically deals with the story and is written specifically for the student audience, as well as excerpts from previously published criticism on the work.

In addition, each entry contains the following highlighted sections, if applicable, set separate from the main text:

- **Media Adaptations:** where applicable, a list of film and television adaptations of the story, including source information. The list also includes stage adaptations, audio recordings, musical adaptations, etc.

- **Compare and Contrast Box:** an "at-a-glance" comparison of the cultural and historical differences between the author's time and culture and late twentieth-century Western culture. This box includes pertinent parallels between the major scientific, political, and cultural movements of the time or place the story was written, the time or place the story was set (if a historical work), and modern Western culture. Works written after the mid-1970s may not have this box.

- **What Do I Read Next?:** a list of works that might complement the featured story or serve as a contrast to it. This includes works by the same author and others, works of fiction and nonfiction, and works from various genres, cultures, and eras.

- **Study Questions:** a list of potential study questions or research topics dealing with the story. This section includes questions related to other disciplines the student may be studying, such as American history, world history, science, math, government, business, geography, economics, psychology, etc.

Other Features

SSfS includes "Why Study Literature At All?," a guest foreword by Thomas E. Barden, Professor of English and Director of Graduate English Studies at the University of Toledo. This essay provides a number of very fundamental reasons for studying literature and, therefore, reasons why a book such as *SSfS*, designed to facilitate the study of literature, is useful.

A Cumulative Author/Title Index lists the authors and titles covered in each volume of the *SSfS* series.

A Cumulative Nationality/Ethnicity Index breaks down the authors and titles covered in each volume of the *SSfS* series by nationality and ethnicity.

A Subject/Theme Index, specific to each volume, provides easy reference for users who may be studying a particular subject or theme rather than a single work. Significant subjects from events to broad themes are included, and the entries pointing to the specific theme discussions in each entry are indicated in **boldface.**

Entries may include illustrations, including an author portrait, stills from film adaptations (when available), maps, and/or photos of key historical events.

Citing Short Stories for Students

When writing papers, students who quote directly from any volume of *SSfS* may use the following general forms to document their source. These examples are based on MLA style; teachers may request that students adhere to a different style, thus, the following examples may be adapted as needed.

When citing text from *SSfS* that is not attributed to a particular author (for example, the Themes, Style, Historical Context sections, etc.) the following format may be used:

> "The Celebrated Jumping Frog of Calaveras County." *Short Stories for Students.* Ed. Kathleen Wilson. Vol. 1. Detroit: Gale, 1997. 19-20.

When quoting the specially commissioned essay from *SSfS* (usually the first essay under the Criticism subhead), the following format may be used:

> Korb, Rena. Essay on "Children of the Sea." *Short Stories for Students.* Ed. Kathleen Wilson. Vol. 1. Detroit: Gale, 1997. 42.

When quoting a journal essay that is reprinted in a volume of *Short Stories for Students,* the following form may be used:

> Schmidt, Paul. "The Deadpan on Simon Wheeler." *The Southwest Review* XLI, No. 3 (Summer, 1956), 270-77; excerpted and reprinted in *Short Stories for Students,* Vol. 1, ed. Kathleen Wilson (Detroit: Gale, 1997), pp. 29-31.

When quoting material from a book that is reprinted in a volume of *SSfS,* the following form may be used:

> Bell-Villada, Gene H. "The Master of Short Forms," in *Garcia Marquez: The Man and His Work* (University of North Carolina Press, 1990); excerpted and reprinted in *Short Stories for Students,* Vol. 1, ed. Kathleen Wilson (Detroit: Gale, 1997), pp. 90-1.

We Welcome Your Suggestions

The editor of *Short Stories for Students* welcomes your comments and ideas. Readers who wish to suggest short stories to appear in future volumes, or who have other suggestions, are cordially invited to contact the editor. You may write to the editor at:

Editor, *Short Stories for Students*
The Gale Group
27500 Drake Rd.
Farmington Hills, MI 48331-3535

Literary Chronology

1799: Alexander Pushkin is born on May 26 (June 6, modern calendar) into an aristocratic family.

1830: Alexander Pushkin's "The Stationmaster" is published as one of the *Tales of the Late Ivan Petrovich Belkin*.

1837: Alexander Pushkin is killed in a duel with his brother-in-law at the age of thirty-seven.

1842: Ambrose Bierce is born in Ohio.

1843: Henry James is born in New York.

1873: Ellen Glasgow is born in Richmond, Virginia.

1875: Thomas Mann is born on June 6 in Lubeck, Germany.

1899: Ernest Hemingway is born on July 21 in Oak Park, Illinois.

1899: Jorge Luis Borges is born in Buenos Aires, Argentina, on August 24.

1903: Kay Boyle is born in St. Paul, Minnesota.

1905: Jean-Paul Sartre is born in Paris.

1908: Henry James's "Jolly Corner" is published in *The English Review* and is collected later in 1909 in volume 17 of the definitive New York edition of James's work.

1908: Richard Wright is born on September 4 near Natchez, Mississippi.

1909: Ambrose Bierce's "The Boarded Window" is published in the second edition of the twelve-volume *Collected Works of Ambrose Bierce*.

1909: Eudora Welty is born on April 13 in Jackson, Mississippi.

1911: Naguib Mahfouz is born in Cairo, Egypt.

1912: Thomas Mann's "Death in Venice" is published in German as *Der Tod in Venedig* in the journal *Rundschau*.

1914: Ambrose Bierce dies on January 11, 1914, perhaps in Mexico.

1916: Henry James dies.

1917: Peter Taylor is born in the small northwestern Tennessee town of Trenton.

1918: Alexander Solzhenitsyn is born on December 11 in Kislovodsk, Russia.

1923: Ellen Glasgow's "The Difference" is published in both *Harpers Magazine* and the short story collection *The Shadowy Third and Other Stories*.

1932: Ernest Hemingway's "A Clean, Well-Lighted Place" is published in *Scribner's Magazine* and collected in *Winner Take Nothing* in 1933.

1935: Kay Boyle's "The White Horse of Vienna" is published and wins the O. Henry Award for best short story of the year.

1935: Ellen Gilchrist is born in Vicksburg, Mississippi.

1937: Jean-Paul Sartre's "The Wall" is published and in 1939 is collected in the volume *The Wall and Other Stories*.

1940: Peter Taylor's "A Spinster's Tale" is published in *Southern Review*.

1941: Jorge Luis Borges's "The Garden of Forking Paths" is published under the Spanish title *"El jardin de senderos que se bifurcan."* This also served as the title of the collection of stories in which it appeared.

1941: Eudora Welty's "Why I Live at the P.O." is published in *Atlantic* magazine and is also included in her first collection of short stories entitled *A Curtain of Green* of the same year.

1941: Ellen Glasgow receives the *Saturday Review of Literature* award for Distinguished Service to American Literature, and later this year receives the Pulitzer Prize for Fiction for her novel *In This Our Life*.

1945: Ellen Glasgow dies in this year.

1947: Ann Beattie is born in Washington, D.C.

1952: Amy Tan is born in Oakland, California.

1954: Ernest Hemingway is awarded the Nobel Prize for Literature.

1955: Thomas Mann dies in Switzerland.

1960: Richard Wright dies in Paris at age 52.

1960: Richard Wright's "The Man Who Was Almost a Man" is published in the collection *Eight Men*. An earlier version appeared in *Harper's Bazaar* under the title "Almos' a Man".

1961: Ernest Hemingway dies by suicide.

1962: Alexander Solzhenitsyn's "One Day in the Life of Ivan Denisovich" is published in the leading Soviet intellectual magazine *Novy Mir* (*New World*).

1970: Alexander Solzhenitsyn wins the Nobel Prize in literature.

1980: Jean-Paul Sartre dies in this year.

1984: Ellen Gilchrist's "Victory over Japan" is published as the title work in Gilchrist's second collection of short stories, *Victory Over Japan*.

1985: Ann Beattie's "Janus" is published in the *New Yorker* and appears later in the 1986 collection *Where You'll Find Me*.

1986: Jorge Luis Borges dies in Geneva, Switzerland.

1988: Naguib Mahfouz wins the Nobel Prize for Literature in 1988.

1989: Naguib Mahfouz's "Half a Day" is published in Arabic as part of a short story collection *The False Dawn*. It is included in the 1991 English language collection *The Time and the Place* .

1989: Amy Tan's "Two Kinds" is published in *Atlantic* in February, and then appears as the last story in the second of four sections of Amy Tan's successful first book, *The Joy Luck Club*.

1994: Peter Taylor dies in this year.

Acknowledgments

The editors wish to thank the copyright holders of the excerpted criticism included in this volume and the permissions managers of many book and magazine publishing companies for assisting us in securing reproduction rights. We are also grateful to the staffs of the Detroit Public Library, the Library of Congress, the University of Detroit Mercy Library, Wayne State University Purdy/Kresge Library Complex, and the University of Michigan Libraries for making their resources available to us. Following is a list of the copyright holders who have granted us permission to reproduce material in this volume of *Short Stories for Students (SSfS)*. Every effort has been made to trace copyright, but if omissions have been made, please let us know.

COPYRIGHTED MATERIAL IN *SSfS*, VOLUME 9, WERE REPRODUCED FROM THE FOLLOWING PERIODICALS:

America, v. 152, April 27, 1985. © 1985. All rights reserved. Reproduced with permission of America Press, Inc., 106 West 56th Street, New York, NY 10019. *American Imago,* v. 26, Summer, 1969. Copyright 1969 by The Association for Applied Psychoanalysis, Inc. Reproduced by permission of The Johns Hopkins University Press. *American Literature,* v. XLII, March, 1970. Copyright © 1970 Duke University Press, Durham, NC. Reproduced by permission. *Arizona Quarterly,* v. 35, 1979 for "Henry James's 'The Jolly Corner': The Writer's Fable and the Deeper Matter" by Jesse Bier. Copyright © 1979 by the Regents of the University of Arizona. Reproduced by permission of the publisher and the author. *College Literature,* v. 24, June, 1997. Copyright © 1997 by West Chester University. Reproduced by permission. *Essays in Literature,* v. VI, Spring, 1979. Copyright 1979, Western Illinois University. Reproduced by permission. *The Explicator,* v. 40, Spring, 1982. Copyright 1982 by Helen Dwight Reid Educational Foundation. Reproduced with permission of the Helen Dwight Reid Educational Foundation, published by Heldref Publications, 1319 18th Street, NW, Washington, DC 20036-1802. *The Henry James Review,* Vol. 13, Winter, 1992. © 1992. Reproduced by permission of The Johns Hopkins University Press. *The Hudson Review,* v. XXXVIII, Summer, 1985. Copyright © 1985 by *The Hudson Review,* Inc. Reproduced by permission. *Kansas Quarterly,* v. 9, Spring, 1977 for "The Vagaries of Taste and Peter Taylor's 'A Spinster's Tale'" by Jan Pinkerton. © copyright 1977 by the *Kansas Quarterly.* Reproduced by permission of the publisher and the author. *The Mississippi Quarterly,* v. 49, Spring, 1996. Copyright 1996 Mississippi State University. Reproduced by permission. *Modern Fiction Studies,* v. XI, Summer, 1965. Copyright © 1965 by Purdue Research Foundation, West Lafayette, IN 47907. All rights reserved. Reproduced by permission of The Johns Hopkins University. *Mosaic: A Journal for the Interdisciplinary Study of Literature,* v. XVIII, Spring, 1985. © Mosaic 1985.

Acknowledgment of previous publication is herewith made. ***The New York Times Book Review,*** September 23, 1984. Copyright © 1984 by The New York Times Company. Reproduced by permission. ***Philosophy and Literature,*** v. 14, April, 1990. © 1990. Reproduced by permission of The Johns Hopkins University Press. **San Jose Studies,** v. 9, Winter, 1983 for "The Importance of Food in One Day in the Life of Ivan Denisovich" by Alfred Cismaru. © San Jose State University Foundation, 1983. Reproduced by permission of the publisher and the author. ***Slavic and East-European Journal,*** v. 21, Spring, 1977. © 1977 by AATSEEL of the U.S., Inc. Reproduced by permission. ***The Slavic Review,*** v. 30, December, 1971. Copyright © 1971 by the American Association for the Advancement of Slavic Studies, Inc. Reproduced by permission of the publisher. ***Soviet Studies,*** v. XVI, July, 1964. © 1964 The University of Glasgow. All rights reserved. Reproduced by permission of Taylor & Francis Ltd. ***Studies in Short Fiction,*** v. XI, Spring, 1974; v. 23, Fall, 1986; v. 25, Winter, 1988; v. 29, Fall, 1992. Copyright 1974, 1986, 1988, 1992 by Newberry College. All reproduced by permission. ***University of Hartford Studies in Literature,*** v. VI, 1974. Copyright © 1974 by the University of Hartford. Reproduced by permission.

COPYRIGHTED MATERIALS IN *SSfS*, VOLUME 9, WERE REPRODUCED FROM THE FOLLOWING BOOKS:

Debreczeny, Paul. From ***The Other Pushkin: A Study of Alexander Pushkin's Prose Fiction.*** Stanford University Press, 1983. © 1983 by the Board of Trustees of the Leland Stanford Junior University. Reproduced by permission. Green, Mary Jean. From ***Fiction in the Historical Present: French Writers and the Thirties.*** University Press of New England, 1986. © 1986 by Trustees of Dartmouth College. All rights reserved. Reproduced by permission. Hardy, Barbara. From "'The Jolly Corner'" in ***Henry James—The Shorter Fiction : Reassessments.*** Edited by N. H. Reeve. St. Martin's Press, Inc., 1997. © Barbara Hardy 1997. All rights reserved. Reproduced by permission of Macmillan, London and Basingstoke. In North American by St. Martin's Press, LLC. Pohl, Frederick. From "One Day in the Life of Ivan Denisovich" in ***Censored Books: Critical Viewpoints.*** Nicholas J. Karolides, Lee Burress, John M. Kean, eds. The Scarecrow Press, Inc., 1993. Copyright © 1993 by Nicholas J. Karolides, Lee Burress, John M. Kean. Reproduced by permission. Rudy, Stephen. From "The Garden of and in Borges' 'Garden of Forking Paths'" in ***The Structural Analysis of Narrative Texts.*** Edited by Andrej Kodjak, Michael J. Connolly, and Krystyna Pomorska. Slavica Publishers, Inc., 1980. Copyright © 1980 by each author for his or her article. All rights reserved. Reproduced by permission of the author. Yarrow, Ralph. From "Irony Grows in My Garden: Generative Processes in Borges's 'The Garden of Forking Paths'" in ***The Fantastic in World Literature and the Arts: Selected Essays from the Fifth International Conference on the Fantastic in the Arts.*** Edited by Donald E. Morse. Greenwood Press, 1987. Copyright © 1987 by Donald E. Morse. All rights reserved. Reproduced by permission of Greenwood Publishing Group, Inc., Westport, CT.

PHOTOGRAPHS AND ILLUSTRATIONS APPEARING IN *SSFS*, VOLUME 9, WERE RECEIVED FROM THE FOLLOWING SOURCES:

Beattie, Anne, photograph by Jerry Bauer. © Jerry Bauer. Reproduced by permission.

Bierce, Ambrose, photograph. Corbis-Bettmann. Reproduced by permission.

Borges, Jorge Luis, photograph. The Library of Congress.

Center of Rottendam, Holland, 1940, photograph. AP/Wide World Photos. Reproduced by permission.

Child at piano, photograph, photograph by Robert J. Huffman/Field Mark Publications. Reproduced by permission.

Children playing on Saline School playground, Ford Rouge Plant is in the background, photograph by Millard Berry. Reproduced by permission.

Cornet Wilkin of the 11th Hussars, 1855, during the Crimean War, the Crimea, Russia, photograph by Roger Fenton. CORBIS. Reproduced by permission.

Gilchrist, Ellen, photograph by Jerry Bauer. Reproduced by permission.

Glasgow, Ellen, photograph. Library of Congress.

Gondola and bridge of sighs, Venice, Italy, photograph by Susan Rock. Reproduced by permission.

Hemingway, Ernest, photograph. Archive Photos, Inc. Reproduced by permission.

James, Henry, photograph. The Library of Congress.

Kahl, David, illustrator. From the cover of If I Should Die Before I Wake, by Han Nolan. Harcourt Brace & Company, 1994. Cover illustration copyright © 1994 by David Kahl. Reproduced by permission of David Kahl.

Kuhlman, Gilda. From a cover of Labyrinths: Selected Stories & Other Writings, by Jorge Luis Borges. Edited by Donald A. Yates and James E. Maurois. New Directions, 1964. Copyright © 1962, 1964, renewed 1992 by New Directions Publishing Corporation. Reproduced by permission of New Directions Publishing Corporation.

Log cabin homestead, Arches National Park, Utah, photograph by Robert J. Huffman/Field Mark Publications. Reproduced by permission.

Mahfouz, Naguib, 1984, photograph. AP/Wide World Photos. Reproduced by permission.

Mann, Thomas, photograph. The Library of Congress.

Map of Russia and Siberia, illustration by XNR Productions. Gale Research.

Mushroom cloud rising from atomic bomb, 1945, Nagasaki, Japan, photograph. National Archives and Records Administration.

Pushkin, Alexander, photograph of a painting. The Library of Congress.

Russian slave laborers building the ''Stalin Canal,'' photograph. Archive Photos. Reproduced by permission.

Sartre, Jean Paul, photograph. AP/Wide World Photo. Reproduced by permission.

Solzhenitsyn, Alexander, photograph. AP/Wide World Photos. Reproduced by permission.

Tan, Amy Ruth, photograph. Archive Photos, Inc. Reproduced by permission.

Temple, Shirley, photograph. Corbis-Bettmann. Reproduced by permission.

The original Colt's Revolver, photograph. Corbis-Bettmann. Reproduced by permission.

Times Tower, photograph, Archives Photos. Reproduced by permission.

Two drunken men passed out on sidewalk, photograph. Archive Photos/Lass. Reproduced by permission.

Two men with pack mule, photograph by S. J. Morrow. National Archives and Records Administration.

View of Nagasaki in the aftermath of the Atom Bomb, Nagasaki, Japan, 1945, photograph. UPI/Corbis-Bettmann. Reproduced by permission.

Wright, Richard, photograph. AP/Wide World Photos. Reproduced by permission.

Contributors

ANDREWS HENNINGFELD, Diane. Associate professor of English at Adrian College in Michigan; has written extensively for a variety of educational and academic publishers. Entries: ''The Garden of Forking Paths'' and ''Janus.''

BERNHEIMER, Kate. Received her M.F.A. in fiction writing from the University of Arizona and is the author of *Mirror, Mirror on the Wall: Women Writers Explore Their Favorite Fairy Tales* (Anchor Books, 1998). Commissioned Essay for Entry: ''Two Kinds.''

BRENT, Liz. Ph.D. in American Culture, specializing in cinema studies, from the University of Michigan. Teacher of courses in American cinema, freelance writer and editor. Entry: ''Half a Day.'' Commissioned Essay for Entries: ''The Boarded Window,'' ''The Difference,'' ''Janus,'' and ''Two Kinds.''

DEIGNAN, Tom. Teaching Assistant in American Cultural Studies at Bowling Green State University. Entry: ''A Spinster's Tale.''

DELL'AMICO, Carol. Ph.D. candidate in the Program of Literatures in English at Rutgers, The State University of New Jersey. Entry: ''A Clean, Well-Lighted Place.'' Commissioned Essay for Entry: ''Half a Day.''

DEWSBURY, Suzanne. Has taught English and American Studies at Wayne State University. Entry: ''Victory over Japan.''

GOLDFARB, Sheldon. Has a Ph.D. in English and has published two books on the Victorian author William Makepeace Thackeray. Commissioned essay for Entry: ''The Boarded Window.''

JOHNSON, Kendall. Teaches American literature at the University of Pennsylvania where he recently received his Ph.D. Entries: ''Death in Venice'' and ''Jolly Corner.''

KILPATRICK, David. Is a freelance writer and editor. Entry: ''The Stationmaster.''

KORB, Rena. Freelance writer and editor with a master's degree in English literature and creative writing. Entries: ''The Boarded Window,'' ''The Difference,'' and ''The Wall.'' Commissioned Essay for Entry: ''Half a Day.''

MADSEN HARDY, Sarah. Ph.D. in English literature from the University of Michigan, freelance writer, and editor. Entry: ''The Man Who Was Almost a Man.'' Commissioned Essay for Entry: ''Janus.''

PIEDMONT-MARTON, Elisabeth. Teaches American literature and directs the writing center at Southwestern University in Texas; writes frequently about the modern short story. Entry: ''Two Kinds.'' Commissioned Essay for Entry: ''The Difference.''

SAUER, James. Has taught poetry and drama at Eastern College in Pennsylvania. Entry: ''One Day in the Life of Ivan Denisovich.'' Commissioned Essay for Entry: ''Victory over Japan.''

The Boarded Window

Ambrose Bierce
1909

To contemporary audiences, Ambrose Bierce is known for his writings—journalism, essays, and short fictions—for his cynicism and his misanthropy, and for his famous disappearance into revolution-torn Mexico in 1913, an adventure from which he never returned. His literary reputation, however, rests primarily on his short stories of the Civil War and the supernatural. In both of these genres, Bierce explores his interest in bizarre forms of death and the horror of existence in a meaningless world. Shortly before his disappearance, Bierce also took on the monumental task of organizing his body of work into the twelve-volume *Collected Works of Ambrose Bierce*. In the second volume of this work, amongst the gripping Civil War tales which perhaps have brought him his greatest renown, Bierce chose to included the slight ''weird tale'' ''The Boarded Window.''

''The Boarded Window'' is not a popular story; that is, reviewers rarely discuss it and reference to it among Bierce scholars is almost nonexistent. Critics who have paid it attention have generally commented on its surprise and sudden ending. The story deals with a turning point in a man's life, one which has the ability to completely change his future. Murlock believes that his seemingly dead wife has returned as a ghost and as fear immobilizes him, she actually does die a most horrific death. While Bierce artfully reverses the supernatural element of the plot, the story still contains the essence of its enigmatic author. Though masquerading as a ghost

story, ''The Boarded Window'' conceals within its words an even greater mystery of the relationship among its characters. This mystery is one to which Bierce proposes no easy answers.

Author Biography

Ambrose Bierce was born in Ohio in 1842. He lived in the Midwest during his childhood, but he attended the Kentucky Military Institute in 1859. When the Civil War broke out, he enlisted in the Union army. He fought bravely in the battles of Shiloh and Chickamauga and participated in Sherman's March to the Sea. After the war ended, Bierce traveled with a military expedition to San Francisco, where, in 1867, he left the army.

Bierce's poetry and prose began appearing in the *Californian* magazine around that time. In 1868, he began to work as the editor of the *News Letter* for which he wrote his famous ''Town Crier'' column. He quickly became an important figure in California literary society, establishing friendships with Mark Twain and Bret Harte. In 1872, however, Bierce left the United States for a three-year stay in England where he wrote for several magazines. In England, he acquired the nickname that has stuck with him to this day—''Bitter Bierce.'' During this period as well, his first three books of literary sketches were published.

After returning to California, Bierce worked in the editorial departments of several magazines. In 1887, he began writing for William Randolph Hearst's *San Francisco Examiner.* In his regular column, he published many short stories, essays, and epigrams. Many of these pieces were later published in his short story collections.

When publishers lacked the enthusiasm for *Tales of Soldiers and Civilians,* Bierce's friend, the merchant E.L.G. Steele, paid for its publication himself. The volume then came out in England the following year—1892—under the title *In the Midst of Life.* Steele also brought out another story collection, *Can Such Things Be?* (1893). Many of the stories in the first collection draw on Bierce's civil war experiences, while the majority in the second are tales of the supernatural.

During this period, Bierce kept busy writing and acquiring a group of ''pupils''—fledgling writers who wrote to him for advice and criticism. However, at the beginning of 1900, Bierce decided to move to the East Coast, where he spent his last years. He continued pursuing his journalism and consolidated his literary position, particularly through his own management of his *Collected Works,* a 12-volume work that took him four years to produce.

In 1913 Bierce left for Mexico, intending to join Pancho Villa's revolutionary forces as an observer of the Mexican civil war. From there he expected, if possible, to go to South America. He wrote to friends of the possibility that he might never return. Indeed, his last know whereabouts were Ojinga, Mexico, where he was seen going into battle in January 1914. After this event, Bierce was never heard from again. No one knows how or when he died, but noted biographer and scholar M.E. Grenader believes that he died in that battle on January 11, 1914. One of the rebel officers heard later that an ''old gringo'' had been shot during the fighting.

Plot Summary

The story opens with an unnamed narrator recalling years past, back in 1830, when the area around Cincinnati was almost unbroken forest. A man named Murlock lived alone in a small log house. Murlock kept to himself, making his living by bartering animal skins. The most noted aspect of the house was a window, directly opposite the front door, that was boarded up. Nobody could remember a time that this window was not boarded, yet no one knew why, except for this narrator, who learned Murlock's story from his grandfather.

At the time of his death, Murlock was about 50 but looked decades older. Murlock had come to the frontier while still a young man. He lived in his cabin with his wife. It would appear that the couple lived happily, for Murlock's life after her death was that of a lonely, burdened man.

One day when Murlock returns home from hunting, he finds his wife sick with fever. As they have no neighbors or nearby physician, Murlock tries to nurse her back to health. His efforts are unsuccessful, however, and she falls into a state of unconsciousness and apparently dies without ever recovering awareness.

Murlock thus sets about preparing her body for burial. He conducts this task stoically, and it occurs to him that he should be more saddened at the loss of his wife. He tells himself that after he buries her, he will miss her; for the present moment, he must convince himself that things are not as bad as they seem. The narrator supposes that Murlock, who had no experience with grief, was experiencing a sort of numbing at his wife's death.

After he finishes preparing the body, Murlock sits down feeling utterly tired. Through the open window he hears an unearthly sound, perhaps a wild animal, but perhaps it is a dream, for Murlock is already asleep. A few hours later he is suddenly awakened. He listens intently, wondering what woke him up. Then he hears, or thinks he hears, a soft step—it sounds like bare feet walking upon the floor. Terrified, Murlock neither cries nor calls out. Instead, he waits in the darkness. He tries to speak his wife's name but finds no sound will come. Then he hears something even more dreadful—the sound of some heavy body throwing itself against the table upon which his wife lay. He hears and feels something fall on the floor so heavily the whole house shakes. Next he hears the sounds of a scuffling. Murlock places his hands on the table, but is horrified to discover his wife is not there.

At this point, his terror turns to madness, which drives him to action. He springs to the wall and grabs his loaded rifle. He shoots the rifle without even aiming. In the flare of the gunpowder, he sees a giant panther dragging his dead wife toward the window by the throat. Suddenly, Murlock loses consciousness.

When he awakens the next day, he sees his wife's body near the window where the cat dropped her before fleeing. She lies in disarray. Underneath her collects a pool of wet, runny bloody from the wound on her throat. Her hands are clenched. Between her teeth is a piece of the cat's ear.

Characters

Murlock

Murlock is the protagonist of this brief story. He is first introduced to the readers by the narrator after his death as a lonely, prematurely aged man, one who scarcely had a personal connection to anyone in his community. He lived the life of a recluse in his cabin in the forest. Yet, years and years ago, Murlock had been an optimistic young

Ambrose Bierce

man, forging a new life in rural Ohio. His world changes one night when his wife falls grievously ill and lapses into a coma-like state. Murlock believes she is dead and feels guilty because he experiences little grief or even any emotional reaction. However, his wife is not yet dead, and she ends up dying a particularly horrible death that night; it is most horrible because Murlock can never know the true extent of his role in her death. After this wrenching event, Murlock draws within himself and lives the rest of his days in apparent misery.

Murlock's Wife

Murlock's wife died when she was a young woman. The narrator supposes her to have been ''in all ways worthy of his [Murlock's] honest devotion'' and one who ''shared the dangers and privations of [Murlock's] lot with a willing spirit and a light heart.'' The wife falls dangerously ill with fever and falls into a coma-like state, but Murlock believes her to be dead. He prepares her body for burial, including binding her wrists. However, as Murlock learns, she is not dead. That night, a panther creeps into the cabin and grabs her by the throat. Apparently, she fights back. When Murlock discovers her dead body the next day—seemingly she died from the wound to the throat—she has a piece of the panther's ear between her teeth.

The Narrator

The unnamed narrator never meets Murlock, but learns of his sad tale from his grandfather. As a boy, the narrator, aware of the rumors of a ghost haunting Murlock's cabin, ventures near it and throws a rock at it. Little else is known about the narrator, particularly his relation to Murlock or why he concerns himself with the story or knows its details.

Themes

Death

Death is one of the most important themes in "The Boarded Window." When Murlock's wife falls into a comalike state, he mistakenly believes she is dead. In fact, she is not dead, but Murlock turns out to contribute to, if not actually cause, her death. His unconscious wife is attacked by a panther while Murlock sleeps. He awakens and views the horrible sight of the great cat dragging what he believes to be his dead wife's body. When he immediately loses consciousness, Murlock loses any chance he might have had of stanching the flow of blood from her wound and thus saving her life.

The idea of death, and the effect it has on the living, can also be seen throughout the story. Murlock's frenzied action in shooting the rifle stems from the knowledge that his dead wife is not where he left her on the table. He seems to believe that her ghost has returned, though the story is so brief that such a theory is only hinted at, not explored.

Murlock also suffers a symbolic death after the real death of his wife. He ages rapidly, keeps to himself, and isolates himself from the rest of society. In essence, he ceases to live in the real world. His suffering can most likely be attributed to his guilt at his role in his wife's death.

The Supernatural

Bierce is known for excelling in what S.T. Joshi has called the "weird tale," which can be loosely defined as a tale that has a certain atmosphere of unexplainable dread coming from unknown forces, as well as the hint that somehow events have transformed the fixed laws of nature. Joshi further notes that of Bierce's weird tales, the majority fall under the subset of supernatural horror tales. Certainly, parts of "The Boarded Window read like a ghost story. Murlock's fear when he wakes in the middle of the night reflects his feeling that something supernatural is taking place. He hears what seem to be bare feet on the floor, yet he knows this is not possible. His utter terror can only stem from his belief that his wife has risen—as a ghost. The language Bierce employs also points to this analysis: Murlock had previously heard an "unearthly cry" and now he hears a "confusion of sounds impossible to describe." Ironically, there is nothing supernatural taking place. The sound he heard earlier was most likely the shrill cry of the panther, and the scuffling sounds are clearly his wife attempting to get away from the cat. Yet, Murlock's wrenching fear and belief in the supernatural contribute to the demise of his wife.

Loneliness

The prevailing mood in "The Boarded Window" is that of utter loneliness. Murlock's abandoned cabin is "ruined," distant from any neighbors, and surrounded by a gloomy, silent forest. Murlock had formerly cleared the land, but now it is covered with decaying tree stumps and is in the midst of being overtaken by wild plants. Murlock himself had never been seen to smile "nor speak a needless word." Only the occasional hunters who pass by the cabin see evidence of Murlock's enjoyment of life as he sits on his doorstep enjoying the sunshine. He dies alone in his cabin, to be found later by some unnamed person. He is buried near his cabin, doomed to spend eternity in that barren, forsaken place.

Murlock also seems to have little capacity to understand what loneliness means. When his wife dies, he is not struck by grief. He is surprised by his own inability to cry. The narrator shares his belief that to some people grief comes "as the blows of a bludgeon, which in crushing benumbs," and hypothesizes that is the grief that later befalls Murlock. However, the story strongly suggests that it is not actually the loss of his wife but his role in her death that turns him into a reclusive curmudgeon.

Style

Narrator and Narration

The narration of "The Boarded Window" raises significant questions: Who is this unnamed narrator? More importantly, what is his relation to Murlock? Why is he so interested in Murlock? How does he know so many details about the night in

Topics for Further Study

- Conduct research to find out more about the opening of the American frontier in the early 1800s, particularly such aspects as settlement patterns and economic trends. Do the comments of the narrator in ''The Boarded Window'' aptly reflect what you have learned?

- Read some supernatural horror stories, such as those of Edgar Allen Poe or H.P. Lovecraft. How do true ghost stories compare to ''The Boarded Window''?

- Study gothic-type paintings such as Henry Fuseli's ''The Nightmare'' (1871). What elements of the supernatural do these works contain? What kind of mood is conveyed by them?

- Analyze Murlock's reaction to his wife's apparent death from a psychological standpoint. Con-

sult psychology reference books or textbooks as needed. Then write up a psychological profile of Murlock.

- Read samples of Bierce's journalism from the 1890s. Then imagine that Bierce were writing a newspaper column about the events portrayed in ''The Boarded Window.'' Write the piece as if you were Bierce, utilizing both his style and his outlook on life.

- Bierce's literary reputation has often been questioned throughout the 20th century; he is constantly being ''rediscovered'' by a new generation of critics who claim his readership is not as large as it deserves to be. Do you think ''The Boarded Window'' adds to his literary reputation? Why or why not?

---

question? Bierce answers none of these questions in this brief tale.

The narrator, as he tells the reader, grew up near Murlock's cabin. As a boy—knowing of the ghost that haunted the spot—he visited the ruined cabin and threw a stone against its outer wall. His only other association with Murlock is the distinction of being one of the few people to know the secret of the boarded window, which his grandfather related to him. Other than these details, the reader finds out little about the narrator.

The beginning of the narration sets up the background, providing sketchy details of the region, Murlock, his marriage, and his ultimate death after having become a prematurely aged man. Once the narrator ventures into Murlock's story, however, he generally resides in the man's head, though at times he does make outside observations. The narrator, however, imagines himself privy to thoughts only Murlock could know, such as what he says to himself as he prepares his wife's body and the terror he feels when he awakens in the night. The narration stops abruptly upon Murlock's discovery of his

dead wife on the floor. The narrator, who has been so willing to commit himself to exposing Murlock's private thoughts, makes no comment about how the man now feels, though he has earlier hinted at the devastation that would so radically alter the man's life.

Setting

The setting of ''The Boarded Window'' plays a key role in the development of the terror plot. Murlock's cabin is situated far away from neighbors in the middle of a great forest where wild beasts—such as the panther—lurk. Murlock and his wife live in solitude. Because of this, when she falls ill, Murlock must care for her alone. His isolation—along with his wife's supposed death—contribute to his great terror when he hears strange noises in the night.

Further, the narrator paints a picture of a bleak and desolate area. The forest that surrounds Murlock's cabin is characterized as one of ''gloom and silence.'' Indeed, most of the people, according to the narrator, who first settled the region quickly moved on westward. These details foster the psychological setting of emptiness and detachment, characteristics shared by Murlock, who dies the lonely man's solitary death.

Structure

Structurally, the story is divided into two parts. The first part provides the readers with relevant background information. Readers learn about the region and who settled there, as well as a few specific details about Murlock's cabin and his life: when Murlock came to Ohio filled with optimism and plans, how he built a cabin, cleared the surrounding land, and loved his spirited young wife. This part of the story also gives the end, telling of how Murlock changed and died a recluse.

The second part of the story presents the connecting event that turned the hopeful young man into a prematurely old man. In this part of the story, the narration is firmly fixed on Murlock, presenting his thoughts, worries, and fears. This section reads profoundly differently from that which came before it. The unnamed narrator takes little part here, and indeed the narration is rooted in concrete, specific details, rather than abstract vague ones. This section is also a mini-story in itself, complete with a beginning—the wife's illness and apparent death; middle—Murlock's fear at the strange sounds he hears; and end—his wife's real death.

Historical Context

The Lure of the Frontier

The first pioneers crossed the Appalachian Mountains and moved into the Ohio River valley in the 1750s. These settlers found large stands of oak, maple, and hickory and forests full of wild game such as turkey and deer. The soil was rich, and they began to clear land for farming. Despite the promising conditions, movement to the region was slow, and settlements generally remained small and isolated. In the next decade, however, as the British victory in the French and Indian War reduced white people's concerns about Indian raids, settlers began crossing the Appalachians in greater numbers. Despite a proclamation in 1763 that banned further colonial settlement west of the Appalachians, settlers continued to come both to farm the land and trade in goods.

The Battle for the Frontier

By the late 1700s, enough Americans had settled in the region that today consists of Ohio, Indiana, and Illinois that Native Americans, fearing they would lose their land, tried to push them back. In 1790, an Indian confederation went to battle against U.S. troops. Despite early victories, the Native Americans were eventually defeated. The ensuing peace treaty formally ceded much of present-day Ohio and part of present-day Indiana to the United States. This treaty opened up the area even further for rapid white settlement. Soon whites had expanded into lands that were not included in the peace treaty. Throughout the early 1800s, thousands of Americans poured into the Northwest Territory.

Britain, however, continued to post soldiers in the region. The British also armed Native Americans, who then used these weapons against American settlers. The British presence in the Northwest Territory was a major cause for the American declaration of war against Britain. The United States won the ensuing War of 1812, which guaranteed the U.S. government control of the Northwest Territory.

Connecting the Frontier

Developments in transportation helped connect the frontier to markets back east. In 1814, construction began on a road that went from Cumberland, Maryland, to Wheeling, West Virginia, a town on the Ohio River. In the 1830s, this road was extended to Columbus, Ohio, and within a few decades it reached all the way to Illinois. Completed in 1825, the Erie Canal, which stretched from Buffalo, New York, on Lake Erie, to Albany, New York, also opened up the nation's largest port city. The Erie Canal encouraged settlement and also allowed Americans in what was then considered the Middle West to get their goods to eastern consumers and import supplies in a more expedient fashion. These improvements in transportation made their lives easier and induced more people to move west.

Life on the Frontier

Despite the availability of amenities, in the mid-1800s, life on the frontier differed greatly from life back east. People often lived in sparse log cabins. Many supported themselves as farmers, growing wheat and corn, and raising hogs. Farmers found their work growing increasingly easier and more productive. The Industrial Revolution had led to greater technological advances, and by the middle of the century, farmers' toil was greatly improved by such inventions as the steel plow and the

Compare & Contrast

- **1820s:** There are fewer than 10 million people living in more than 1.7 million square miles of the United States. This averages to fewer than six people for every square mile.

  1990s: The U.S. population is about 250 million on just over 3.6 million square miles of land. This averages to about 70 people for every square mile.

- **1820s:** The United States is comprised of land stretching from the Atlantic Ocean to the Rocky Mountains. The land making up present-day Oregon and Washington is claimed by both Britain and the United States, while most of the West and Southwest is Spanish territory.

  1990s: In addition to the 50 states, the United States holds the territories of Puerto Rico, the Northern Mariana Islands, American Samoa, Guam, the Federated States of Micronesia, the Republic of Palau, the U.S. Virgin Islands, as well as some smaller Pacific islands.

- **1830s:** John Deere begins work on a steel plow

to make plowing the soil easier, and Cyrus McCormick begins to develop a mechanical reaper to cut down wheat quickly and efficiently. These inventions allow midwestern farmers to plant and harvest huge wheat fields cheaply and quickly.

1990s: Farming in the 1990s is made easier by machines that do much of the work planting and harvesting crops. Breeding programs, crop technologies, and food-processing techniques also assist farmers.

- **Early to mid-1800s:** Cincinnati is chartered as a city in 1819, and the completion of the Erie Canal and the coming of the railroad help it to develop into one of the largest cities in the United States by 1854.

  1990s: With a population of about 346,000, Cincinnati is the third-largest city in Ohio. It still remains one of the largest inland coal ports in the United States.

---

reaper. More and more merchants continued to arrive in the Middle West. They sold manufactured goods that they brought or imported from the East Cost and opened stores to satisfy the needs of the Middle West consumers.

Critical Overview

"The Boarded Window" saw its first major publication in 1909, when it was collected, along with most of the stories from 1891's *Tales of Soldiers and Civilians,* in the second volume of the *Collected Works of Ambrose Bierce,* a 12-volume set. The majority of stories in the book, which had been republished in 1892 under the new title *In the Midst of Life,* concerned the Civil War, with the notable exceptions of the otherworld fantasies "An Inhabi-

tant of Carcosa," "Haita the Shepherd," and "The Middle Toe of the Right Foot." In putting together his collected works, however, Bierce omitted any overtly supernatural tales from volume 2, placing them instead with other like stories in volume 3. At the same time, he added "The Boarded Window," which hints at the supernatural but does not truly involve it. Bierce scholar S.T. Joshi is one of the few to note this significant rearrangement on Bierce's part. He contends that such shifting is "of vital importance to Bierce's aesthetic of horror, for the dominant motive at work is the segregation of his supernatural and nonsupernatural tales."

When volume 2 of The Collected Works was published in 1909, Bierce again drew critical attention. A reviewer for *The Athenaeum* wrote that "this collection of short stories might fitly have borne the name of one of them, 'A Holy Terror.'"

Example of a log cabin.

The reviewer believes that the difficulty Bierce had in originally publishing the book in 1891 (it was published through the donation of funds from an individual) stemmed from the more sedate literary tastes of that day. The reviewer finds that most of the stories are ''a study of the workings of fear. . . . Perhaps 'The Boarded Window' reaches the outer limit of the terrible.''

Again, in 1918, *In the Midst of Life,* which now included ''The Boarded Window,'' saw a new edition. A reviewer from *The Nation* asserted that ''the four or five among these [Civil War] tales which are touched with tragic pity and terror are compromised by their enforced fellowship with stories which are mere gruesome inventions.'' Although ''The Boarded Window'' is not specifically mentioned, the reviewer's statement that ''the tales rest their effect too much on the surprise ending which Bierce, before 'O. Henry,' somewhat overemployed'' certainly would seem to apply.

''The Boarded Window'' has rarely drawn critical notice. One of the rare instances of its inclusion in discussion of Bierce's some 100 short stories can be found in Walter Blackburne Harte's ''A Tribute to Ambrose Bierce'' published in 1924's *The Biblio.* '''The Boarded Window,''' he wrote, ''holds one in a thrill of expectation; but the climax,

told so tersely, comes with the shock of sudden horror.''

Indeed, Bierce's reputation rests more on war fiction, such as ''An Occurrence at Owl Creek Bridge,'' which delves into the psychological state of a man as he is being hanged, or ''Chickamauga,'' which depicts a young boy crawling among a battlefield strewn with the bodies of dead and dying soldiers. The noted supernatural writer H.P. Lovecraft, however, in his 1939 essay *Supernatural Horror in Literature*, pointed out that little distinction between Bierce's war fiction and weird fiction existed; they have a similar overarching effect on the reader. Bierce's ''artistic reputation must rest upon his grim and savage short stories,'' Lovecraft wrote. ''Virtually all of Bierce's tales are tales of horror; and whilst many of them treat only of the physical and psychological horrors within Nature, a substantial portion admit the malignly supernatural and form a leading element in America's fund of weird literature.'' Lovecraft also quotes the poet and critic Samuel Loveman, who was also a personal acquaintance of Bierce's: ''In Bierce the evocation of horror becomes for the first time not so much the prescription or prevention of Poe and Maupassant, but an atmosphere definite and uncannily precise. Words, so simple that one would be prone to ascribe them to the limitations of a literary hack, take on an unholy terror, a new and unguessed transformation.''

Indeed, an entire body of Bierce's ''weird tales''—tales which deal with unknown, dread-inspiring forces and rely on the reversal of the fixed laws of nature—do exist. In his introduction to *The Weird Tale*, Joshi categorizes most of Bierce's weird tales as ''supernatural horror,'' but a few fall under the category of ''quasi science fiction.'' The main difference between these two types is that the former take place ''where the ordinary world of our daily lives is presupposed by the norm,'' and the latter provide a rational explanation for the ''''impossible' intrusions.'' Bierce also dabbled in ''nonsupernatural horror.'' Joshi contends that a close reading of Bierce's weird tales ''will show that in almost every case he provides sufficient clues to point to a supernatural or nonsupernatural resolution.''

Criticism

Rena Korb

Korb has a master's degree in English literature and creative writing and has written for a wide variety of educational publishers. In the following essay, she discusses the many mysterious elements inherent in ''The Boarded Window.''

Ambrose Bierce is a well-known literary figure for many reasons. He was a man out of time; his pessimistic, cynical writings were oddly out of place in a period dominated by optimist thought; he introduced psychological studies into a literary world that valued realism and naturalism. He is the author of the brutal and realistic Civil War short stories ''Chickamauga'' and ''An Occurrence at Owl Creek Bridge'' and the witty, ironical Devil's Dictionary. During the 1890s, he was one of America's most famous newspaper columnists. Bierce's flight to Mexico in 1913, to join up with Pancho Villa's revolutionaries, and his subsequent disappearance, only added fuel to the legend of ''Bitter Bierce.'' Today Bierce is also well known as an adventurer, with his apparent death in Mexico one of the most celebrated among the literary-minded. While Bierce has not always enjoyed a wide body of readers, he consistently had a fierce and loyal readership who compared his writings to the likes of such masters of short fiction as Edgar Allen Poe and Guy de

Maupassant. Indeed, Bierce's fame is deserved. One thing he is not known for, however, is his short story ''The Boarded Window,'' which the author included in volume 2 of his *Collected Works*.

''The Boarded Window'' falls into the genre of the weird tale, thus defined by the supernatural writer H.P. Lovecraft: ''The true weird tale has something more than secret murder, bloody bones, or a sheeted form clanking chains according to rule. A certain atmosphere of breathless and unexplainable dread of outer, unknown forces must be present; and there must be a hint, expressed with a seriousness and portentousness becoming its subject, of that most terrible conception of the human brain—a malign and particular suspension or defeat of those fixed laws of Nature which are our only safeguard against the assaults and the daemons of unplumbed space.'' At the turn of the century, many reputable writers, such as Mary E. Wilkins-Freeman and William Dean Howells, tried their hand at the weird tale. Thus Bierce was not alone in his exploration of the supernatural—and in seeing its manifestation in the everyday world—yet his mixture of the psychological with the supernatural distinguish him. As H.E. Bates writes in his study *The Modern Short Story*, ''In Bierce, . . . two forces were in incessant conflict: spirit against flesh, normal against normal. This clash, vibrat[es] in his work from beginning to end, keep[s] the slightest story nervous, restless, inquisitive.'' Bierce's short pieces, both the war fiction and the weird tales, overlap in their exploration of the horror of life.

''The Boarded Window'' indeed hints of the supernatural but does not actually involve it. It is a relatively short tale, describing a man who lives alone in the sparsely settled forests outside of Cincinnati, Ohio. The man, Murlock, once had a wife, a farm, and an optimistic outlook on the future. After the death of his wife, however, Murlock became a recluse and died a solitary death. The story is related by an unidentified narrator, and the man's relation to Murlock is as mysterious as the events that lead to the wife's death. In essence, Bierce has written a weird tale that works on two levels: that of the incident itself, and that of the role of the narrator.

Bierce infuses the second part of the story, the section that relates Murlock's sad tale, with hints of the supernatural. Bierce paints a convincingly eerie atmosphere, one that would encourage ghostly presence. Murlock's cabin is in the midst of a great forest that is filled only with ''gloom and silence.'' Murlock's sleeping mind registers an ''unearthly

What Do I Read Next?

- The third volume of *The Collected Works of Ambrose Bierce* (1910) contains the majority of Bierce's supernatural and weird tales.

- Turn-of-the-century author Mary E. Wilkins-Freeman was mainly noted for her regional fictions. Yet, in 1903's *The Wind in the Rose Bush* she collects her own assortment of weird tales.

- In *The Deerslayer* (1841), James Fenimore Cooper explores the frontier culture developing as more whites settle in the western lands.

- Nathaniel Hawthorne's short story "Young Goodman Brown" (1835) depicts a pious man in Puritan New England who believes he sees a group of townspeople gathering in satanic worship. This startling event has a profound effect on Goodman Brown.

- Carlos Fuentes's award-winning novel *The Old Gringo* (1985) is an imaginary account of what happened to Bierce after he disappeared in Mexico in 1913.

- Willa Cather's novel *My Antonia* (1918) portrays the hardscrabble life on the Nebraska plains.

- *The Fall of the House of Usher* (1839) by Edgar Allen Poe tells the twisted and perverse story of a family and its members descent into madness.

- Charlotte Perkins Gilman's short story "The Yellow Wallpaper" (1891) mixes psychological realism and Gothic fiction in its depiction of a woman who is losing her mind.

- Henry Miller creates an atmosphere of sinister evil in *The Turn of the Screw* (1898), a Victorian ghost story. The author tells the tale of the influence of two dead servants over their young charges.

---

cry." He awakens to a state of "black darkness by the side of the dead." He hears "sounds of bare feet upon the floor" and waits "there in the darkness through seeming centuries of such dread as one may know." Then he hears a scuffling "and a confusion of sounds impossible to describe." All of these details lead the reader to believe what Murlock believes: that his dead wife has risen as a ghost.

In his utter terror at finding that his wife's body no longer rests upon the table, Murlock grabs for his rifle and shoots into the darkness. There, by the flash of the gunpowder, he sees an enormous panther dragging his wife toward the window. In his shocked state, Murlock loses consciousness. The next day when he awakens, he sees his dead wife's body lying on the floor. Apparently, she had not died of the illness but rather died later in the night from the wound the panther's teeth sunk into her throat, for underneath her is "a pool of blood not yet entirely coagulated." If that is not enough to demonstrate that his wife in fact was alive "[B]etween

the teeth was a fragment of the animal's ear." Thus does Bierce do away with the idea of the supernatural tale. Bierce provides the answers to the sounds that scared Murlock in the night: the strange cry was the panther's call, the sounds of the bare feet were the panther's, and the scuffling was his wife desperately battling the great cat. In his fear, Murlock missed any chance at saving her life after the panther's attack.

During the night, before the panther incident, Murlock experiences a psychological state of alienation. So shocked is he by his wife's supposed death that he is unable to accept it and process it. He does not weep over his wife's passing, feeling "surprised and a little ashamed" by his own reaction. He speaks aloud, comforting himself: "[S]he is dead, of course, but it is all right—it *must* be all right, somehow. Things cannot be as bad as they seem." While preparing her body "through his consciousness ran an undersense of conviction that all was right—that he should have her again as before, and everything explained.'' Such an understanding of Murlock's psychological state helps explain his instant belief that his wife has returned as a ghost. In refusing to accept his wife's death, he leaves open the possibility for her return.

Murlock's project of distancing himself only deepens after his wife's death. The man who once cleared his land lets the forest retake it. He ages prematurely, becoming a ''burden bearer.'' He lives in extreme isolation with only the occasional hunter seeing him outside of his cabin. When he dies, he is alone. Indeed, although nothing supernatural occurred to take his wife from this earth, Murlock lives out the rest of his days as a haunted man. However, he appears to be haunted by the role he played in his wife's death. He is haunted by guilt, not by a ghost.

Yet while Bierce competently solves one mystery, ''The Boarded Window'' hides another, one that is not so easily solved: the relation of the narrator to Murlock. The narrator presents himself as having an authorial voice, thus, what he says should be taken as truth. He first demonstrates this authority through his depiction of the frontier region in the early 1800s, when Murlock's tale unfolds. With only a few words he describes the surrounding and sets up the scene as one that is fairly isolated and little inhabited. He also knows a bit about Murlock's background, for instance, that the man lived alone for years but that he had come to the country ''young, strong and full of hope.''

The words he chooses to share, however, prove the narrator to be unreliable. He constantly contradicts himself, thus subverting his own authority. He says that ''every well-informed boy'' knew Murlock's cabin to be haunted by a ghost, but he doesn't say how this knowledge—which would imply that others in the region knew of what had taken place there—came to be universal. In actuality, any neighbors had little knowledge of the wife. As the narrator states, she had ''preceded'' her husband in death ''by so many years that local tradition had retained hardly a hint of her existence''; in fact, there was no longer even any ''known record of her name.'' The narrator also repeatedly emphasizes the mystery of the evening in question, declaring of the boarded window of Murlock's cabin, ''nobody could remember a time when it was not [boarded up]. And none knew why it was so closed.'' Almost immediately thereafter he confesses, ''I fancy there are few persons living to-day who ever knew the secret of that window, but I am one,

> Readers are left with the question: What is the narrator's relation to Murlock?''

as you shall see.'' Finally, he reveals how he came to be privy to the information: ''But there is an earlier chapter—that supplied by my grandfather.'' Thus essentially ends the role of the narrator. The rest of the story focuses on Murlock's sad tale, and indeed ends without ever returning to the narrator.

Readers are left with the question: What is the narrator's relation to Murlock? How does he come to know this information that no one else knows. While the narrator proposes an answer to this question—that his grandfather ''had known him [Murlock] when living near by in that earlier day''—this answer is far from satisfactory. For the narrator has already described the land upon which Murlock lived as ''surrounded on all sides by the great forest.'' Indeed, when his wife fell ill, her care rested solely upon him because there ''was no physician within miles, no neighbor.'' How then, is the reader to believe that this man who elected to live, and die, in such isolation would choose to reveal his horrible story to a seemingly random person? It seems unlikely that he even has a neighbor.

A reader could likely conjecture that the narrator's grandfather is in actuality Murlock: the narrator is privy to facts, details, and knowledge that it would appear no other living soul has, not only about the night of the panther, but about Murlock's feelings and thoughts. The narrator explains Murlock's lack of reaction to his wife's death as due to the fact that ''[H]e had no experience in grief; his capacity had not been enlarged by its use. His heart could not contain it all, nor did his imagination rightly conceive it. He did not know he was so hard struck; *that* knowledge would come later, and never go.'' Of these statements, only the last could be construed from the life that Murlock went on to lead. Clearly, Murlock was devastated by the death of his wife, otherwise he would not have retreated into his isolated state. The narrator, however, presents no plausible explanation for his knowledge about how Murlock deals with grief. He even emphasizes his illogical authority when he says, "We may conceive Murlock to have been that way affected. . . (and here we are upon surer ground than that of conjecture)." The mystery of the narrator's relation to Murlock is never answered in any satisfactory fashion. Readers are left to form their own opinion, based on a brief text and insubstantial evidence.

Alfred Kazin has noted of Bierce's short stories, "There is invariably a sudden reversal, usually in a few lines near the end, that takes the story away from the reader, as it were, that overthrows his confidence in the nature of what he has been reading, that indeed overthrow's his confidence." This statement certainly applies to the ending of Murlock's tale, as the reader discovers that the wife did not die a natural death as Murlock thought, but at the teeth of the panther. Kazin's assertion also applies to the narrator in general, however, the noted lack of confidence comes not at the end but is instead pervasive throughout the story. As he has done so many times, in "The Boarded Window" Bierce presents a compelling story, one that is not at all what it seems.

Source: Rena Korb, for *Short Stories for Students*, The Gale Group, 2000.

Sheldon Goldfarb

Goldfarb has a Ph.D. in English and has published two books on the Victorian author William Makepeace Thackeray. In the following essay, he discusses the cryptic aspects of "The Boarded Window" and examines its treatment of reclusiveness.

In her 1984 study, *The Experimental Fictions of Ambrose Bierce*, Cathy Davidson says that some of Bierce's stories create a sense of "perceptual confusion" in the characters or the readers or both. There is a sense of mystery or "indeterminacy," sometimes with two different views of events being presented, so that it is hard to know what actually happened. Or, as in a story like "The Death of Halpin Frayser," everything is so uncertain that the reader is left utterly baffled.

Bierce's point in creating such bafflement may be to suggest that the world is a mysterious place that cannot be fully understood, and this may be what he is suggesting in "The Boarded Window." Certainly, the ending of that story raises all sorts of baffling questions. At first, in fact, it is hard to understand exactly what has happened, even on the most literal level, leaving aside its deeper significance.

A reclusive man named Murlock (at least, that is "said to be" his name: even this point is uncertain) has been nursing his sick wife. She dies. At least, she "apparently" dies. Her husband, totally isolated from civilization, makes the burial preparations himself, just as he previously had nursed her by himself. Before he buries her, however, on a night when she is still in their cabin, lying on a table, something enters through the window. A scuffle ensues. Murlock fires his rifle and sees by the glare of its discharge that a panther has his wife by the throat and is dragging her away. He falls unconscious. When he awakes, he sees his wife's body by the window: some still unclotted blood has come from her throat, her hands are clenched, and in her teeth is part of the panther's ear.

The ending contains a surprising twist, somewhat akin to the surprise endings of O. Henry, but with a sense of horror more reminiscent of Edgar Allan Poe. Mostly, though, there is a sense of confusion. What has happened? Was the wife not really dead? Was she just in some sort of coma, and when the panther attacked her, did she revive and fight back?

To S.T. Joshi in *The Weird Tale* this is what probably happened, because otherwise blood could not have flowed from the wife's throat. Also, how could she have bitten off the ear if she was truly dead? Joshi in general plays down the element of ambiguity in Bierce's work, saying in particular that it is almost always clear in Bierce's stories whether the supernatural is involved. However, Bierce does write stories in which corpses act like living people and the laws of nature are defied, so without further evidence how do we know that the wife was only in a coma? This could be one of Bierce's corpses-come-to-life tales. Or it could be the sort of story Joshi says Bierce does not write: an ambiguous horror tale in which it is not clear whether there is anything supernatural or not.

Moving beyond the literal level, there are other puzzling questions, having to do with the significance of what has happened. Why does the panther come for the wife? What does that signify? And if the wife was really only in a coma, what point is Bierce trying to make? That Murlock was too ignorant on medical matters and should have gone for a doctor or a nurse? But then the panther would have killed her in any case.

The story raises other questions as well. For instance, why did the narrator throw stones at Murlock's ruined cabin? Also, why did Murlock board up the cabin window? Not to keep the sun out, the narrator says. Then why? His wife is dead; what more could happen? Is he afraid the panther will come for him? Is this some sort of symbolic protection against the dangerous world out there? But if it is so dangerous out there in the woods, why does he stay? He could move.

The narrator suggests that Murlock stays out of love for his wife, but is he right? Could he be staying out of guilt? Out of a feeling that he could have saved his wife by acting differently?

Perhaps the answers to some of these questions can be found by considering Murlock's reclusive nature. From the beginning of the story we are told that Murlock lived alone in the forest. Of course, before his wife died, he lived with her, but it is interesting that the main events of the plot are set in motion by Murlock's being away "gunning in a distant part of the forest" while his wife falls ill. He is perhaps too much apart, even from his wife.

He also seems to have an excessively antagonistic relationship to the natural world around him, as is indicated by his being off "gunning." And earlier, in describing Murlock's attempts at farming, the narrator makes him sound violent by talking of "the ravage wrought by [Murlock's] ax." The narrator also refers to Murlock's zeal for agriculture as a "flame," which makes him sound like a danger to the forest, although it is true that his flame is "failing" and "expiring in penitential ashes."

Murlock had arrived in the area "young, strong and full of hope" and had begun "laying sturdily about with his ax to hew out a farm" while also using his rifle to shoot wild game. After his wife's death, he lets the forest retake the land he had cleared for a farm, perhaps feeling guilty about his previous actions (hence the term "penitential" in describing what happened to his zeal for farming).

Perhaps what the story is trying to suggest in all this is that Murlock was both too much apart from other people (or civilization) and too antagonistic to nature. And what happens to his wife is then some sort of punishment, or a revenge taken by civilization and nature together. The panther is then a symbol of the world's hostility towards those who fail to interact with it normally, who push it away or attack it. Similarly, the narrator's throwing of stones at Murlock's cabin seems to represents the world's

> **Despair may thus explain his actions after his wife's death: his giving up on farming, his becoming more of a recluse, and his boarding up of the window as a symbolic form of withdrawal."**

naturally hostile response to one who has kept himself too much to himself.

If the point, though, is to suggest the dangers of being a recluse, it is a point that Murlock himself does not grasp. He continues to live by himself. He may feel guilty over what has happened, but he does not change his relationship with civilization. What does change is his relationship with nature; he gives up on the farm and lets the forest reclaim the land, out of guilt or resignation. He also ages prematurely and looks bowed down by a burden. He seems defeated by life. He has not fought well. When the panther attacked, he was at first frozen in paralysis; he fired too late and let the panther slash his wife's throat. Similarly, he was unable to protect his wife from her fever; and even in making her burial preparations he continually blundered. He had seemed so capable and strong, and yet it turns out he was not, perhaps because one man alone cannot be capable.

There remains the puzzle of the window. Why does Murlock board it up? Perhaps, like the firing of his rifle at the panther, it is simply a too tardy response to nature's attack. Perhaps it is a statement of despair, a way of withdrawing from the world that has defeated him—though why, then, does the narrator make a point of saying that Murlock likes to sun himself on his doorstep?

Still, despite his penchant for sunning himself outdoors, Murlock mostly seems to withdraw from the world, becoming an unsmiling, untalkative recluse. And despair does seem to underlie this withdrawal. The narrator suggests that his grief never leaves him; and as already mentioned, he looks prematurely aged and bowed down by a burden. Despair may thus explain his actions after his wife's death: his giving up on farming, his becoming more of a recluse, and his boarding up of the window as a symbolic form of withdrawal.

At the same time, the withdrawal, the despair, may be tinged by fear, and boarding up the window may be Murlock's attempt to ward off the dangers that have already carried off his wife.

In the end, it remains a bit of a mystery, and the mysterious effect is added to by the method of narration. The narrator has only heard the story from his grandfather; there are things he does not know. Indeed, there are things that nobody knows, for instance the name of the wife, the nature of her character, and so forth.

Even the happiness in Murlock's marriage is in doubt. The narrator assures us that the Murlocks had a happy marriage, but he does not really know that; he is deducing it from the fact that Murlock remained at the cabin after his wife's death. But in making this deduction, the narrator says that the memory of the supposedly happy marriage "chained that venturesome spirit [Murlock]" to the cabin: the use of the term "chained" does not suggest happiness, and the whole phrase reminds us how much of a venturesome spirit Murlock was, the sort of spirit who likes to be on his own and who therefore may feel chained, not happy, in a marriage.

In the end, then, this does seem to be one of Bierce's mysterious stories, part of whose point is that the world cannot be fully understood. But it is possible to say that Bierce here was exploring the dangers of reclusiveness and the revenge the world can take on those who spurn it.

Source: Sheldon Goldfarb, for *Short Stories for Students*, The Gale Group, 2000.

Liz Brent

Brent has a Ph.D. in American Culture, specializing in cinema studies, from the University of Michigan. She is a freelance writer and teaches courses in American cinema. In the following essay, Brent discusses the literary device of the "unreliable narrator" in Bierce's short story.

Ambrose Bierce's short story, "The Boarded Window" is an example of his skillful use of an *unreliable narrator* to self-consciously illustrate the workings of the *oral tradition* in the creation of *ghost stories*. The literary device of the unreliable narrator

refers to stories in which the teller of the tale is not to be trusted to tell *the truth, the whole truth, and nothing but the truth*. Rather, the device of the unreliable narrator invites the reader to read *between the lines* of the story, and to question the narrator's motives in telling it. Often, such stories communicate more about the psychology or character of the narrator himself, than an accurate depiction of the events or characters he describes. In addition, the device of the unreliable narrator often communicates to the reader more about *the nature of story telling* than about the subject of the story itself.

Bierce's narrator in "The Boarded Window" relates as fact a bizarre, unlikely story, hinting at the supernatural. The story is patched together from a variety of *unreliable* sources, such as local lore, distant memory, a grandfather's story to a little boy, gossip, rumor, conjecture and pure imagination. In this way, Bierce pays homage to the oral roots of the ghost story, which lays claim to proof positive of supernatural events. In the following essay, I will examine the various unreliable sources of the so-called "facts" of the tale, as indicated by the narrator. I will also look at the points at which the narrator betrays the questionable nature of his tale, while simultaneously presenting it as truth. In using the literary device of the unreliable narrator, Bierce thus satirizes superstitions, such as belief in ghosts and other supernatural forces, by revealing the bogus evidence upon which such superstitions are built, and the process by which such stories develop through the oral tradition.

The narrator of "The Boarded Window" tells the story of an early American settler, who lived by himself in a log cabin in the semi-tamed wilderness of the Midwest. The log cabin he built for himself is said to have a single door in front, and a single window in the wall opposite the door. While the old settler is long dead at the telling of the tale, the narrator sets out to reveal the mystery of why the man would have boarded up the only window in his home. The narrator asserts that he may be one of only a few living beings who know the "secret" of why the single window in the cabin of a long-dead homesteader had remained boarded up for as long as anyone could remember.

The narrator relates this tale based on information from a number of categories of unreliable sources: childhood memory, local tradition, conjecture, bogus logic, and pure imagination. The narrator, however, confidently claims nearly exclusive knowledge of the true reasons for the boarded window—but, again, even this claim is based on conjecture as to who else knows the true story: "I fancy there are few persons living to-day who ever knew the secret of that window, but I am one, as you shall see." Such a statement epitomizes the style of the unreliable narrator, who heartily asserts his exclusive claim to some truth, while simultaneously hinting to the reader that he is not to be trusted as a purveyor of truth.

The "secret" of the boarded window, as related by the narrator, is that Murlock's wife had become ill and died one night, upon which he prepared her body for burial the next day. Falling asleep at the table across from which the body was laid, Murlock awoke during the night to the sounds of screaming and scuffling. Grabbling his rifle, Murlock shot into the darkness. From the light of the gun's fire, he perceived the body of his wife locked in the jaws of a panther, which, frightened by the rifle shot, escaped through the window in the back of the cabin. In the light of day, Murlock found the body of his wife lying on the floor, in a pool of blood which had emanated from a throat wound imposed by the panther. Her hands were "tightly clenched," and "Between the teeth was a fragment of the animal's ear." Henceforward, Murlock's single window in his cabin was boarded up.

The narrator's earliest source of so-called knowledge of the "secret" of the boarded window is based on his own childhood memories. The primary basis of the narrator's knowledge is revealed to be, not his own acquaintance with the owner of the cabin, but his memory of a story his grandfather told him as a lad. This admission alerts the reader to the fact that this "true" story may be patched together from a series of distorted re-tellings: apparently, the narrator's grandfather had known the man "when living near by in that early day." The grandfather's original claim to knowledge of the true story of the boarded window may be assumed to be questionable in the first place, for the reader may conjecture that an old man telling his grandson a gruesome tale may engage in a distortion of facts for the sake of entertainment. Further, the narrator thus indicates that he is recalling from distant memory a story related to him as a young child, at an age when such fantastical tales are liable to be taken as indisputable fact.

The narrator further brings the story into the realm of childhood superstitions about ghosts and boyish bravado in throwing stones at supposedly haunted houses, for he recounts "the circumstance

> **The reader is thus alerted to the possibility that perhaps Murlock desired, either consciously or unconsciously, that his wife should die."**

that many years afterward, in company with an equally intrepid spirit, I penetrated to the place and ventured near enough to the ruined cabin to throw a stone against it. . . ." The narrator thus alerts the reader further to the questionable nature of his assertions that he is "well-informed" as to the true story of the boarded window, for he states that, having thrown a stone at the abandoned cabin, he "ran away to avoid the ghost which every well-informed boy thereabout knew haunted the spot." Clearly, "what every well-informed boy" knows of local superstition regarding haunted houses is hardly convincingly presented as a reliable source of evidence.

In addition to these childhood memories of his grandfather's telling of the tale and his own "well-informed" knowledge of the circumstances of this ghost story, the narrator further reveals the sources of the tale to be unreliable to the extent that they are based on a sort of collective knowledge of the community in which the story takes place; the narrator cites as sources, both of his own and his grandfather's knowledge of the story, "tradition," small-town gossip, and local lore. The condition of the boarded window in this humble log cabin is first presented to the reader by way of a local collective memory in the statement that, "nobody could remember a time when it was not" boarded up. Already, the narrator has indicated that this is a tale based on the local gossip and collective memory of a small settlement in the wilderness. Further evidence that the man's reasons for boarding up the window must be other than "the occupant's dislike of light and air," is rendered from local gossip based on the testimony of individuals who passed by the log cabin, "for on those rare occasions when a hunter had passed that lonely spot the recluse had commonly been seen sunning himself on his doorstep. . . ." Even information regarding the name of the recluse is presented on the basis of collective rumor, or local "tradition," of a small community, according to which, "his name was said to be Murlock."

The narrator goes on to relate his knowledge of Murlock's wife, and their marriage, in a manner which invites the reader to question the validity of this part of the story. In describing Murlock's wife, the narrator first asserts that "There is no known record of her name." By mentioning the concept of a "record," from which evidence may have been gathered, the narrator inadvertently highlights the discrepancy between his own unreliable sources for the story, and more legitimate sources of historical fact, such as written "records." He then explains that, "of her charms of mind and person tradition is silent." The mention of "tradition" places the burden of evidence on the unreliable source of local legend and community gossip; furthermore, that this tradition is "silent" on the matter of "her charms of mind and person" suggests to the reader that this communal silence may be born of tact. In other words, the reader is invited to speculate that perhaps Murlock's wife was not the least charming, and perhaps even an unpleasant woman. This seed of doubt is further nurtured through the narrator's statement that "the doubter is at liberty to entertain his doubt." But he immediately denies the validity of this "doubt" as to the charms of Murlock's wife, exclaiming, "But God forbid I should share it!" The overzealous statement on the part of the narrator as to his own lack of doubt has the effect of further reinforcing the reader's doubt—for the tone of the narrator's emphatic denial smacks of insincerity. But the narrator goes on to assure the reader that, "Of their affection and happiness there is abundant assurance. . . ." However, the "assurance" which follows involves a leap of logic not at all convincing.

The highly ironic tone of this passage of the story is a key to interpreting the significance of the events which lead to the death of Murlock's wife. The narrator, while assuring the reader of his own faith in the marital bliss between Murlock and his wife, simultaneously plants a seed of doubt as to the validity of this statement. In other words, the reader is invited to question Murlock's happiness with his wife. This doubt as to the quality of his marriage implies, by the end of the story, that perhaps Murlock had reason to *wish* his wife dead. The reader is thus alerted to the possibility that perhaps Murlock desired, either consciously or unconsciously, that his wife should die. This would explain his eagerness to

determine her dead, to the point where he seemed to have prepared her for burial while she was yet still alive. Taken further, this line of thinking may cause the reader to speculate as to the actual cause of his wife's death.

The narrator's tale, though based on that of his grandfather, is further liberally embellished with no more recourse to fact than his own *imagination*, as he states, "From what we know of a nature like his we may venture to sketch in some of the details of the outline picture drawn by my grandfather." The narrator thereby compares his tale to that of a drawing, in which the artist first "outlines" the details of his or his subject, and later "sketches in" the details. Bierce here makes use of his unreliable narrator to further imply to the reader that storytelling, particularly "true" ghost stories, are akin to the visual art of drawing—both are based on liberal use of the imagination in constructing a representation of "truth."

By use of an unreliable narrator, Bierce infuses "The Boarded Window" with a note of bemused irony, inviting the reader to relish the variety of unreliable sources from which ghost stories and local lore are patched together. Perhaps the closest surviving practice of such an oral tradition is the "ghost stories" children still tell each other late at night around campfires or at slumber parties, brought down through generations of "unreliable narrators."

Source: Liz Brent, for *Short Stories for Students*, The Gale Group, 2000.

Sources

Bates, H. E. *The Modern Short Story*, Boston: The Writer, Inc., 1972.

Bierce, Ambrose. "The Boarded Window," in *The Complete Short Stories of Ambrose Bierce*, edited by Ernest Jerome Hopkins, Garden City, NY: Doubleday, 1970, pp. 227-31.

Davidson, Cathy N. *The Experimental Fictions of Ambrose Bierce: Structuring the Ineffable*, Lincoln: University of Nebraska Press, 1984.

Harte, Walter Blackburne. "A Tribute to Ambrose Bierce," in *The Biblio*, July, 1924, pp. 680-81.

Joshi, S. T. *The Weird Tale*, Austin: University of Texas Press, 1990.

Lovecraft, Howard Phillips. *Supernatural Horror in Literature*, New York: Dover Publications, 1973.

Review of *In the Midst of Life*, in *The Nation*, August, 1918, p. 232.

Review of *The Collected Works, Vol. II*, in *The Athenaeum*, March 10, 1910, p. 367.

Further Reading

Bierce, Ambrose. *The Letters of Ambrose Bierce*, edited by Bertha Clark Pope, San Francisco: The Book Club of California, 1922, reprinted by Gordian Press, 1967.

A collection of some of Bierce's letters.

———. *A Sole Survivor, Bits of Autobiography*, edited by S. T. Joshi and David E. Schultz, Knoxville, TN: University of Tennessee Press, 1998.

A collection of Bierce's own writings, which reflect on his life, his adventures, and his thoughts.

Grenader, M. E. *Ambrose Bierce*, New York: Twayne Publishers, Inc., 1971.

A critical overview of Bierce's major texts.

Lovecraft, Howard Phillips. *Supernatural Horror in Literature*, New York: Dover Publications, 1973.

A thorough discussion of the supernatural horror genre and its most important writers as well as schools of writing.

Morris, Roy, Jr. *Ambrose Bierce, Alone in Bad Company*, New York: Crown Publishers, Inc., 1995.

A biography of Bierce.

A Clean, Well-Lighted Place

Ernest Hemingway

1932

Many of the 1933 short stories which make up the collection *Winner Take Nothing* were published just before the book. *"A Clean, Well-Lighted Place"* is one of these. Its publication in collected form only succeeded by months its initial publication in *Scribner's Magazine*, a magazine, not uncoincidently, belonging to the titular publisher who first printed most of Ernest Hemingway's major fiction (including this collection).

By 1933, Hemingway was an established writer and this exceptional minimalist short story was seized upon for its presentation of major authorial concerns in an unprecedentedly concentrated form. These major authorial preoccupations include good conduct and solidarity. The younger waiter must be judged for his refusal to play by (unspoken) rules that say he must be polite and courteous to the old man. The older waiter, in contrast, upholds these standards by being willing to stay as late as the old man wants him to. The exceptionality of the piece made it an obvious choice for critics. Critics used the story either to laud or condemn Hemingway on the basis of their judgment of these minimalist aesthetics and these ethical concerns.

For supporters of Hemingway's talent, the story's emotional and philosophical austerity and bleakness amounts to profound and true tragedy. For detractors of Hemingway, it is Hemingway as a parody of himself, in which a purported thematics of stoic endurance only poorly covers an underlying

self-indulgent masochism. This masochism, his detractors argue, blinds Hemingway to the variety and
complexity of life. Stories in which little happens
but extremes of simplicity interrupted by the highest
drama do not resemble life, these critics insist. In
defense of Hemingway, admirers argue that his
stories are not meant to compete with fiction that
presents life just as it is lived. The story's admirers
argue that *"A Clean, Well-Lighted Place"* is Hemingway at his most pure because he captures in both
form and content an irreducible and tragic essence of life.

Author Biography

Ernest Hemingway will always be associated with
the dynamic group of artists known as the
"modernists" whose ideas set the European continent on fire in the first decades of this century.
These artists came from many countries, and many
of them, like Hemingway, honed their art and thought
in Paris in the 1920s.

Ernest Miller Hemingway was born on July 21,
1899, in Oak Park, Illinois. By all accounts, he
enjoyed a secure and unexceptional youth. His first
taste of Europe came, at the age of eighteen (1918),
when he volunteered to drive an ambulance in Italy
during World War I (1914-1918, known as the
"Great War"). He was wounded in Italy, and once
he had recovered, he returned to the U.S.

He began his writing career as a journalist for
the *Kansas City Star*, but soon interested himself in
fiction. He befriended the writer Sherwood Anderson, who gave him letters of introduction to important writers in Paris. 1921 found him with his letters
of introduction, and his first wife, sailing for the
continent where he would socialize with, or learn
from the likes of, Gertrude Stein, F. Scott Fitzgerald, James Joyce, and Djuna Barnes. Metropolitan,
especially European, capital cities were bustling
with artists in the 1920s, and this was why Paris was
Hemingway's destination. These artists were restless war exiles (WWI) and other expatriates who
espoused dramatic new ways of thinking accompanied by dramatic new styles in representation.
Expatriates like Hemingway were self-styled inter-
nationalists in order to deplore the national borders
and colonial politics that had caused the war conflict.

Hemingway's time in Europe confirmed his
decision to be, first and foremost, a fiction writer,

even though he never gave up writing journalism
and other nonfiction. This time also confirmed his
life-long attachment to Spain, its traditions, and
peoples, and once he had returned to the states for
good, he spent much time in other Latin enclaves
(Southern Florida and Cuba). Indeed, he wrote
about Spanish and Latin American subjects throughout his career, as in the short story "A Clean, Well-
Lighted Place." And although after the 1920s he
never again lived exclusively in Europe, he traveled
around the world constantly until his death (Africa
was a favorite destination).

Hemingway was a prolific writer who schooled
himself relentlessly. He produced a large body of
short stories, much journalism and nonfiction, a few
novellas, and a series of novels. He never lost
interest in news reportage and covered many world
conflicts, including the devastating Spanish Civil
War, which began in 1936. His personal life was
adventurous and privileged. Financially comfortable thanks to his writing, his fame, or perhaps a
wealthy wife (he married four times), Hemingway
was able to cultivate his sporting passions expan-
sively (big-game hunting and deep-sea fishing).

Ernest Hemingway wrote, hunted, sailed, traveled, and drank himself through a hectically muscu-
lar life. He seems to have been a driven man, and
whatever propelled him finally led him to choose
suicide as a means to die, in 1961. Hemingway
suicided like his father before him, and one of his
daughters after him. Before this sad event, however,
he secured himself a central place in American
letters and lore. His renown and reputation was
such, in fact, that he won the Nobel Prize for
Literature in 1954.

Plot Summary

The story begins at a cafe very late at night. Two
waiters are watching their last, lingering customer,
an old man who is by now very drunk. These are the
story's three major characters. The older of the two
waiters informs the young one that the old man tried
to commit suicide the previous week. They then
watch a couple go by, a soldier and a young woman,
and comment on the soldier's chances of going
undetected after curfew.

Next, the young waiter moves into action. When
the old man indicates that he wants another drink

Ernest Hemingway

insists that special deference is due the old man because of his recent suicide attempt.

Once the cafe is tidied and locked, the two waiters part amicably enough. The reader now finishes out this very short story with the older waiter. He does not go straight home. He thinks how he completely understands the old man's desire to linger at a cafe, because the ambiance of a cafe is entirely different from that of a bar or bodega. He ends up, however, at a bar. All the cafes are, after all, closed. The old waiter looks at the bar where he stands and points out to the barman that his venue is well-lighted, but not clean: ''The light is very pleasant but the bar is unpolished.'' The barman ignores the waiter. The waiter does not stay for a second drink. Apparently, he now feels strong enough to go home to his insomnia: ''He disliked bars and bodegas. A clean, well-lighted cafe was a very different thing. Now, without thinking further, he went home to his room. He would lie in the bed and finally, with daylight, he would go to sleep. After all, he said to himself, it is probably only insomnia. Many must have it.''

served, the young waiter mutinies. He decides he wants to go home, regardless of an unspoken rule that dictates he not go until the last customer voluntarily leaves. He pretends not to know what the old man wants. The old man realizes that the younger waiter is being offensive, but ignores him and asks out loud for the drink. When the waiter brings it, he makes it spill deliberately. Moreover, knowing that the old man is deaf, as he walks away he says, ''You should have killed yourself last week.'' With these actions, the character of the young waiter is established.

The two waiters then have a number of conversations about the old man and his suicide and situation. These talks are interrupted by the younger waiter finally telling the old man to leave, which he does. We learn various facts from these interchanges. For example, the young waiter is ''all confidence,'' he is married, he has a job, he is content with life and has little pity for those who are not content. He defends his actions (being churlish and making the old man leave): a cafe is not an all-night venue; if the old man were considerate he would let the waiters go home to their beds; there are bars and bodegas for people wanting to stay out late. The older waiter resembles the old man: he is lonely and he lives alone with no wife. He is an insomniac. He

Characters

Old Man

The old man is drowning his sorrows in drink, and his sorrows grow out of loneliness, if we are to believe the old waiter (the old man lives alone, his wife now dead). However, lest this turning to drink be interpreted as weakness, the author is careful to depict the old man as being punctiliously neat and controlled in his despair. He does not, after all, spill a drop. Rather, the old man is a heroic drunk, one whose pursuit of oblivion is depicted as a reasonable, even noble course of action in a world which can be too much for certain souls to withstand. Where the younger waiter seems to feel not enough, this man seems to feel too much.

Old Waiter

The older waiter, in contrast to the selfish younger one, is a sympathetic man. He knows the old man's history and identifies with it. Like the old man, the old waiter is lonely, a little sad, and he takes pleasure in a quiet public place. The old waiter is not, however, as desperate as the old man is. He seems to endure his loneliness with a certain objectivity, realizing that although he is alone, he is not alone in suffering. The older waiter seems wise and resigned.

Young Waiter

Set against the two mild and weary older men, the younger waiter's personality seems acerbic, even cruel. We learn about an unspoken rule of service which dictates that a cafe only close when the last customer leaves voluntarily, and never because of a pre-established closing time. But it is very late and the younger waiter wishes above all else to go home to bed. Accordingly, he serves the old man in a churlish way, purposefully slopping his drinks, to make the old man feel unwelcome and unwanted. Then, as the two waiters discuss the drunk old man, the younger waiter has only nasty things to say. He is depicted as someone who does not follow the rules of good social conduct, and who considers his own wishes more significant than anybody else's.

Themes

Solidarity

One of the most touching aspects of this short story is the older waiter's expressed solidarity with the old man. While the young waiter is all "youth" and "confidence," the old waiter and the old man seem overwhelmingly lonely and tired-out by life. This communality structures the older waiter's consistent thoughts of solidarity with the old man. He understands and defends him; he too prefers a clean, well-lighted cafe to a bar or bodega; he too seeks out such a place to forestall his own despair that night. The climax of this theme of solidarity is the climax of the story itself. It comes in its final line: "He disliked bars and bodegas. A clean, well-lighted cafe was a very different thing. Now, without thinking further, he went home to his room. He would lie in the bed and finally, with daylight, he would go to sleep. After all, he said to himself, it is probably only insomnia. Many must have it." It is the "many" of the final sentence of the story with which the story is concerned. Against the singular and selfish young waiter, the coupled old men signify the group or community that hangs together out of loyalty and a sense of common cause. Hemingway's fiction around the time of "A Clean, Well-Lighted Place" frequently thematizes solidarity, undoubtedly because this principle of conduct was highly valued at the time. Much political advance was achieved in the first three decades of the century through the

methods of mass demonstrations and movements (e.g., groups of workers and women bonded together for better working conditions and the vote). Solidarity fueled these mass rights' movements and ensured their success.

Good Conduct

Hemingway is a writer obsessed by ethical conduct. The bulk of his writing is concerned with questions of good versus bad actions. In this fiction, it's not about winning or losing, it's about how you play the game. This is true, perhaps, because in Hemingway's fictional universe one rarely wins. The title of the collection from which "A Clean, Well-Lighted Place" comes suggests this complicated stance. It is called *Winner Take Nothing*. If one has won nothing as a winner, then all one has done is played the game.

The old waiter is the epitome of a someone who plays by the rules. No matter that it is a lone and drunk old man making this waiter stay up all night; the cafe offers a specific service, and is run according to certain rules from which the old waiter will not deviate. He cuts no corners in his social responsibilities.

The centrality and repetitiveness of this theme in this author's oeuvre costs him popularity in many camps. Hemingway's heroes consistently detect and perform unspoken ritual, usually in trying conditions so that their upholding of these rules seems all the more admirable. These beset characters are always male, and they are usually proving themselves while pursuing very traditional male pursuits (e.g. while big-game hunting or deep-sea fishing). This self-conscious cultivation of, and propensity for, an agonistic and all-male world is immortalized in a title of another of his short story collections. Appropriately, it is called *Men Without Women*. This highly gendered world of strenuous physical and moral contest makes Hemingway's fiction seem dated in many respects.

The Unknowable and Nothingness

"Nothing," or the Spanish equivalent "nada," is the most important word in this short story—if only by virtue of the high number of times it is repeated in a story so very brief. It is the reason why the old man kills himself, according to the older waiter: "'Last week he tried to commit suicide,' one waiter said."/"'Why?'"/"'He was in despair.'"/ "'What about'"/"'Nothing.'"/ "'How do you know it

Topics for Further Study

- Research the famous U.S. brigade of the Spanish Civil War, the Abraham Lincoln Brigade. Which U.S. artists and writers fought or raised money for the Spanish Loyalists during this conflict?

- Examine the rise of fascism in the 1930s in Europe. How do historians account for the popularity or power of Mussolini, or Hitler and/or Franco? Or, research what platforms and positions characterize fascism. Hitler's party, for example, was called the National Socialists. Why was it named this? What was ''national'' about it? What ''socialist''?

- Explore theories about the ''folk'' that were circulating amongst artists and intellectuals of the Harlem Renaissance (1919-1935). Alain Locke's 1925 essay ''The New Negro,'' a manifesto for this social and artistic movement, is a good place to begin. A seminal precursor text of the movement, also dealing with issues relating to ''folk,'' is W. E. B. Du Bois's *The Souls of Black Folk*.

- Examine Hemingway's continued cultivation of Latin connections after his experiences in France and Spain. How was southern Florida and Cuba important to his life and development as a writer once he returned to the U.S.?

---

was nothing?'''/ '''He has plenty of money.''' It is the word which obsesses the old waiter as well. After work, he leans against a bar and recites two prayers to himself substituting ''nada'' for most of the prayer's major verbs and nouns. The result is a litany of ''nadas.''

This narrative pattern suggests at least two possible explanations. The first follows from considering the character of the older waiter. The waiter is a man of few words, an elemental soul. He is face to face with humanity itself under duress, what he identifies as ''despair,'' and attributes the cause of this despair to be ''nothing.'' This paradox of believing in an emotion (despair) with no cause (''Nothing'') is unraveled if one decides that with ''nothing'' the waiter refers to intangible yearnings, as opposed to referring to bodily or material yearnings (''He has plenty of money''). In this case, he exemplifies a stance which does not presume to fathom the mysteries of life (intangible yearnings), but prefers to stand before them mute. ''Nothing'' has become his way of indicating the mystery of humanity and his own professed conceptual and verbal limitations when faced with it. Thus, this old waiter might be elemental or simple, but it is this simplicity that makes him wise. He is not afraid of admitting that the task of explaining humanity is beyond him, and his manner of speaking indicates this humble stance.

A second explanation follows from taking the old waiter's answer (''Nothing''') to mean that the old man, at least in his opinion, is in despair over the fact that his life means ''nothing.'' This can be linked, for example, to the old waiter later thinking, ''It was all a nothing and a man was nothing too.'' In this case, despair follows from a belief in the inherent meaningless or absurdity of life. If one suffers one does so for no reason; it does not matter if one lives or dies. This is why despair is over nothing if one has ''plenty of money.'' In this world view, there is no meaning beyond the bodily and material; all intangible yearnings are nothing but illusion. If the old man does not sink into nihilism because of this bleak knowledge, it is because of his ethical bylaws and his ability to revel in the physical present: ''It was all a nothing and a man was nothing too. It was only that and light was all it needed and a certain cleanness and order.'' In the view above, however, this reveling in ''light. . .[and] a certain cleanness and order'' would indicate a certain blind, dumb faith. One's environment gives one proof of some ''order'' or meaning, it is simply that this meaning will never be known, expressible, or representable by mere human beings.

Style

Minimalism

A short story as glaringly brief and simplified as this one is rightly called ''minimalist'' in its aesthetics (the word aesthetics refers to *how* the author tells his or her story). It uses the minimum building blocks necessary to accomplish the job of telling a story. Hemingway uses simple diction, usually monosyllabic words of Anglo-Saxon, as opposed to Latin, origin. Grammatically, he uses simple as opposed to complex sentences. There is little figurative language—no metaphor or simile, for example. Character and plot are minimized. These three characters do not even have names. All that happens is that the two waiters talk, the old man drinks, and then they all go home.

Repetition

It is very clear to the reader what Hemingway does *not* do in this minimalist short story, but what *does* he do? One thing he does beyond the narrative minimum is repeat, or repeat with variation. For example, the story opens with an old man ''who sat in the shadow the leaves of the tree made against the electric light.'' A bit further in the story the old man is said to sit ''in the shadow of the leaves of the tree that moved slightly in the wind.'' And a few sentences later the old man is the one who is ''sitting in the shadow. . . .'' This repetition of the same with variation is the barest gesture at the figurative delights art can offer. In repeating, Hemingway seems to acknowledge the beauty of pattern or artifice, but instead of actually providing any he simply gestures at its possibility.

Point of View

Hemingway's narration seems designed to lessen the effect of a judging presence. His omniscient narrator may see and know all, but precious little is offered for consideration. This is an effaced narrator. Setting and character are barely described. What the cafe might look like, apart from the fact that it is clean and well-lighted, the reader never knows. Neither does the reader know what the waiters look like, what they are wearing, and so forth. More important, this narrator does not describe a character's psychology, or tell the reader what should be thought about a character or event. Omniscience like this hardly deserves the name. Third person narrators are supposed to know and tell all, but this narrator strives for objectivity. The readers are to judge what the characters say and do

for themselves. Of course, the situation or plot is engineered by the author, so this sense of readerly autonomy is artificial. Nevertheless, the point of this style of narration is to cut down on authorial intervention.

Historical Context

Hemingway's Folk

Many things account for the rural or small town Spanish characters and scenery of Hemingway's ''A Clean, Well-Lighted Place.'' First, as an expatriate artist living on the continent in the 1920s, Hemingway developed a passion for Spain. He was a lifelong fan of Spanish popular traditions. He enjoyed the festivals, and he keenly appreciated the bullfight. He went to Spain often to fish in the countryside, and so he came to know its plainer people.

In addition to this familiarity with Spain's rural peoples, 'plain folk' (e.g. waiters in small towns) provide an escape from the effete, or anything resonant of ''civilization'' which Hemingway scrupulously wishes to avoid in his art. This is so because the disaster that was WWI was a founding event and trauma in Hemingway's life. His most admired novel, *The Sun Also Rises* (1926), takes place around a Spanish popular festival and is about a wounded WWI veteran who is terribly in love but who has been made impotent by war injuries. This character's situation is highly symbolic. He is the sterile scion of a disastrous past, which is like saying that civilization has progressed so far only to have progressed not at all. It is no wonder that Hemingway turns to folk. If civilization and progress has wrought such ugliness and pain, then where better to turn than to those whom progress has seemed to pass by or touched less?

Everybody's Folk

The folk, as in the peasantry or working class of European cultures, were a population of keen historical import and significance during the teens, 20s and 30s. They were so for various reasons, the most important of which, however, boils down to the reformism of the time. The first three decades of the west are characterized by reformist mass political movements. The excesses of the nineteenth-century industrial revolution were curtailed thanks to workers' demonstrations fueled by socialist and communist ideologies. This striving for more equal or fair

Compare & Contrast

- **1920s:** WWI is a notorious war. There was no clear villainous enemy, as in the fascists of WWII. It was terribly inefficient. It was considered then how the Viet Nam war is considered today, a fight that used soldiers sorely and traumatically. It ate up young men with all the efficiency of a giant thresher. The term ''shell shock'' was invented to name the hysteria and psychosis that the war induced in so many of the soldiers.

    1990s: Countries like the U.S. which have technologically sophisticated warheads are now able to conduct ''limited'' wars. In contrast to WWI, the recent U.S. and European fighting against Serbia was conducted entirely from the air. Things and not people were the primary targets.

- **1930s:** The Spain of Hemingway's story suffered a great deal during the 1930s. The country, moving to more fully democratic rule, had elected a new government around the time Hemingway was writing ''A Clean, Well-Lighted Place.'' This latest election was ignored by the armies of Francisco Franco. Funded by fellow fascists Adolf Hitler of Germany and Benito Mussolini of Italy, Franco's troops overcame the legitimate government in a bloody Civil War which lasted from 1936-39. The Spanish Civil War was a popular cause internationally. The world reacted most anxiously to the growth of fascism, and the defending Spanish Loyalist armies drew to their ranks an international group of soldier-sympathizers, many of whom were American men and women (''The Abe Lincoln Brigade''). Hemingway went to Spain to cover the war for the U.S. press (and an attachment with the woman and fellow journalist who would become his third wife was consolidated at this place and time).

    1990s: A strong memory of Franco has not yet faded from Spanish memory. His forces were not subdued, and he was a dictator of this country until 1975. Franco's death was, on the whole, exuberantly and widely welcomed, and the country became, fairly quickly, a typical continental nation. The European nations, on the whole, are prosperous in comparison to the rest of the world, despite persistent high levels of unemployment. The most pressing situation for Europe at present is the European Economic Union (EEU), in which the nations of Europe will share a single currency called the ''Euro.'' The Euro has been brought into circulation, and will become the sole currency of this group of nations on January 1, 2001.

- **1920s:** The 1920s in the U.S. are known as the Roaring Twenties. They roared because the U.S. emerged, somewhat to its own surprise even, as a new superpower after WWI. It had sold plenty of armaments to Europe, and most of war-torn Europe was in its financial debt. America was not only rich, it was also culturally vibrant. Women had just gotten the vote in England and the U.S., and the French fashion genius Coco Chanel revolutionized women's fashion. Flappers cut their hair and wore simple shifts that left them free to dance all night, and the new technology was awesome to contemplate: Phonographs, radios, planes, telephones and automobiles.

    1990s: The U.S. is still a so-called superpower, but in a much tighter global context. Technology has now delivered the computer and the internet, the latter facilitating this aforementioned global interconnectedness. And this, perhaps, is what seems really new, politically and economically, technologically and communicationally: for all of the U.S.'s wealth and power, there is the sense now that transnational financial ties are such that what happens in remote global markets can substantially affect U.S. fortunes. In effect, the need to be apprised of these wide-ranging global connections and relations is now a requirement, and the internet and other advanced communications networks are delivering this information.

treatment extended to women, who gained the vote at this time. Immediately post-WWI, New York City saw the first twentieth-century race movement, the African-American Harlem Renaissance (1919-1935). Given how rights movements entail the basic argument and principle of each person's equal worth, regardless of race, status, or gender, the ideal of equality was touted frequently. Everyone, down to the simplest or uneducated man or woman is of equal worth, the argument goes, and in order to prove and support this, fiction writers everywhere turned to the folk for material. The desire to extend democracy and correct persistent social inequalities is mirrored in the aesthetics and subject of Hemingway's story. Hemingway's prosaic little story stresses the foundational sameness and dignity of all human beings.

Europe, Theater of War

"A Clean, Well-Lighted Place" was written at the start of the 1930s, a decade, it turns out, that would be as fraught as the one that preceded it. During the 1920s, most people were trying to come to terms with two major events. First, WWI, which killed and mutilated millions of young men, wiping out an entire male European generation and, second, the first wave of what we now call technology. Telephones and automobiles, for example, were becoming widely used and available. The 1930s, after the post-War trauma of the 1920s, delivered nothing other than the second major European war of the twentieth-century, World War II. This conflict grew out of the rise of European fascism. The fascist troops of Benito Mussolini and Adolf Hitler were beaten down during WWII, but fascism triumphed in Hemingway's beloved Spain in 1939 when Francisco Franco's rebel forces overcame the government.

Critical Overview

The critical literature on Ernest Hemingway is quite massive, and it is very diverse. His style and mechanics have been thoroughly analyzed, and he and his work have been the subjects of numerous studies by critics employing historical, biographical, psychological, feminist and other paradigms. His literary reputation has been strong ever since his fiction began to be taught widely in the 1950s. He is generally considered to be a talented, prolific, and disciplined writer whose early work was seminal in

defining the sparer prose aesthetic that characterizes most twentieth-century anglophone fiction.

Any longer study of Hemingway's fiction will inevitably touch on "A Clean, Well-Lighted Place." It was considered, from the first, the best of the stories in the 1933 collection, *Winner Take Nothing*. Along with a few African stories (about big-game hunting), it is one of a handful of perennially popular stories by the writer. Hemingway is particularly well-known for stylistic minimalism, and this brief gem is considered to be a tour de force in this respect.

Hemingway's major literary successes at the time this story was published were, from the point of view of the critics, the earliest sketches and stories of the 1920s and his first two novels (*The Sun also Rises* and *A Farewell to Arms*). Less favored was the nonfiction, and the collection *Winner Take Nothing* was not especially admired by critics. As a collection, it often received the epithets "bitter" or "depressing." Critical interpretation of the significance of "A Clean, Well-Lighted Place" is quite consistent. For those who think the story too slight to be great, it is just more Hemingway "dumb ox" fiction (or so his fiction is described by his acerbic contemporary, Wyndham Lewis, in an essay entitled "The Dumb Ox: A Study of Ernest Hemingway"). By "dumb ox," Lewis means Hemingway's characters, and not Hemingway himself, no matter how confusing the title of his essay is. Lewis considers them beneath anybody's notice. Less elitist critics fault Hemingway for a "dumb ox" aesthetic by contending that simplicity of this nature could only be found in the writer's imagination, and that no one (not even a real rustic) is as simple as Hemingway's characters are. Even Frank O'Conner (a well-known writer in his own right), who finds much to admire in Hemingway, expresses this frustration. In his *The Lonely Voice: A Study of the Short Story*, a chapter concerning Hemingway presents his fiction as far too "abstract." He argues that is does not sufficiently capture the social and interpersonal complexity of life: "I. . .ask myself if this wonderful technique of Hemingway's is really a technique in search of a subject or technique that is carefully avoiding a subject, and searching anxiously all the time for a clean well-lighted place where all the difficulties of human life can be comfortably ignored."

For critics who take Hemingway seriously, the story is often aligned to notions associated with the 1950s philosophical doctrine known as existentialism. Propounded especially by two French thinkers, Jean-Paul Sartre and Simone de Beauvoir, existentialist belief stresses the need to live with stoic and ethical dignity in a meaningless or absurd world. The philosopher William Bennett discusses this short story in a book on existentialism entitled *Irrational Man*. Related to this position is Warren Bennett's in *"Character, Irony, and Resolution in 'A Clean, Well-Lighted Place'."* He states that Hemingway espouses a type of despair in the story which "is a negation, a lack . . . . [a] lack of life after death, [a] lack of a moral order governing the universe, [and a] lack of trustworthy interpersonal relations."

An interesting problem associated with a "A Clean Well-Lighted Place" is a long-standing debate about discrepancies and variations in Hemingway's original manuscript versions of the story. Debate centers around the dialogue, and which lines should be attributed to which waiter. Specifically, there is a question as to which waiter should be given the line indicating knowledge of the old man's suicide attempt. Most critics argue that giving this knowledge to the older waiter maintains the story's logical and characteriological consistency throughout. This view is generally the one which informs publishing houses, and printed versions of the story uphold this logic and dialogical sequence. Hemingway's extreme minimalism which induces him to dispense with tags like "the old waiter said" or "the younger waiter replied," opens the door to this type of confusion.

Criticism

Carol Dell'Amico

In the following essay, Dell'Amico discusses Hemingway's short story within the context of the art movement known as modernism. The story's aesthetic minimalism is presented as an integral style of this movement, and the significance of this style is examined as a historical posture.

What stands out about "A Clean, Well-Lighted Place" is its minimalism. Known for simple sentences and simple diction, Hemingway positively outdoes himself in this famous short story. In the most pared down English imaginable, three nameless and unexceptional characters rehearse a brief, nocturnal scene. Thus, this story ostentatiously extols the virtues of the simple. This minimalism is so

very dramatic, in fact, one feels that complexity or sophistication is not simply precluded, but actually *written against*. In writing such stripped-down prose and narrative, Hemingway counters the era which precedes him. Nineteenth-century prose and narrative is, by contrast, the epitome of ornateness and complexity. The extreme minimalism of a "A Clean, Well-Lighted Place" connotes a turning away from the past, from history and progress, war and technology.

In *"Modernist Studies,"* a review essay in a collection called *Redrawing the Boundaries*, Marjorie Perloff states that "modernism perceived its own mission as a call for rupture." By "rupture," Perloff means that modernists dealt with what appeared to them to be a disappointing history by searching for completely transformed ways of going about politics and life. The idea was to break with a civilization that had not yielded the positive social progress it had so believed in and so loudly proclaimed it was delivering. This bleak sense of western culture not living up to its best promise was felt already before World War I, but the shocking carnage of the Great War, in terms of the sheer number and sheer horribleness of deaths and injuries, intensified and galvanized this feeling. This war left the west, but particularly Europeans, reeling. What had been an energetic movement in the arts before the war became deadly serious after it. Some modernist artists experimented with their prose (e.g. Virginia Woolf), or their painterly techniques (e.g. Picasso's cubism), in an effort to point to and usher in the transformations in social relations they so strongly desired. Others—Hemingway is preeminent in this group—chipped away at language and action to shuck off and scrupulously avoid the no longer desired. "A Clean, Well-Lighted Place" is glaring proof of this. No "fancy" or sophisticated words or situations weighted with undesired history or civilization are of interest to him. Hemingway is after the truly enduring and noble underneath the destructive and suffocating clutter of civilization and history.

"A Clean, Well-Lighted Place" rests on the dramatic information of the old man's attempted suicide, and the difference between the two waiters. An old man sits alone, far too late into the night, drinking steadily. This is a scene of pathos. This is pathos, however, in which much is made of pathos contained, or reigned in. The man is known to be very drunk, but he is "clean," neither belligerent nor messy. By not calling attention to himself or his suffering he avoids making of it or himself an event.

What Do I Read Next?

- *The Sun Also Rises* (1926) is generally considered to be Hemingway's best and most enduring novel. The main character has been maimed in WWI, and he is desperately in love with a woman he cannot have. The story recounts his and his friends cynical and disillusioned experiences in Spain during a festival.

- *The Great War and Modern Memory* (1975) by Paul Fussel examines the literature and culture of WWI, the Great War.

- *The Great Gatsby* (1925) is a novel written by one of Hemingway's contemporaries, F. Scott Fitzgerald. It takes place in the U.S. northeast, and the wild and desperate Roaring Twenties are beautifully captured.

- *Winesburg, Ohio* (1919) is a book of inter-connected short stories by the U.S. writer who was Hemingway's first inspiration and mentor, Sherwood Anderson. The stories are interconnected, as each covers yet more terrain in small town Winesburg.

- *Ernest Hemingway: A Life Story* (1969), by Carlos Baker is a definitive and widely respected Hemingway biography.

- *Jacob's Room* (1922) is one of Virginia Woolf's WWI novels, and it is about a young man who never returns from WWI. Jacob is evoked throughout this strange and haunting work more by virtue of his absence than by his presence.

- *Death in the Afternoon* (1932) is a major nonfiction book by Ernest Hemingway about bullfighting in Spain.

This story about quietly endured pain connotes the idea that suffering is indeed so common, so mundane, no commemoration of it is necessary.

In the rather tragic universe of the cafe, there are two waiters. One of them sees a single customer sitting alone, someone who has been the last customer and has been sitting there alone for a long time. He decides he wants the person to leave so that he can close up and go home. This prosaic situation and wish is set against the older waiter's argument that they should not close up in case the man is finding solace in this ''clean, well-lighted place.'' His having tried to kill himself, and his being in the cafe drinking at all, seems to suggest this. The older waiter's argument is a plea based on the simple question of ''Wouldn't you want to be here if you were him?'' The younger waiter must grudgingly agree, finally, that it means something to drink in a clean, well-lighted place, instead of at home alone. Nevertheless, he defends his actions and so essentially revels in the unthinking and selfish power of youth that cannot see ahead to the weakness of its own old age. Against this waiter, the second waiter exemplifies solidarity with the old and with all those who suffer on this earth.

This primal expression of solidarity and suffering characterizes the mood of Hemingway's modernism. As for his modernism itself, the substance of it can be approached through an examination of the story's transformation of the Catholic prayers ''Our Father'' and ''Hail Mary.''

By the time the older waiter thinks his crazily modified versions of the prayers, the younger waiter has expelled the old man from the cafe, the waiters have closed up, and the reader has learned that the older waiter is an insomniac. He is, like the old man, ''[w]ith all those who need a light for the night.'' In fact, the older waiter intends to find himself a clean, well-lighted place of his own in order to consummate, as it were, his solidarity and pact with the old man. The older waiter has sunk into his own thoughts, and at some point in his physical transition from the cafe to the late-night bar to which he goes, he asks himself:

> What did he fear? It was not fear or dread. It was a nothing that he knew too well. It was all a nothing and

> To pray is to indicate a belief in a religion, in a system and an order for life, to indicate, in short, that one has a map to life's profundities. But the reader knows from the story's opening that this is precisely what the older waiter does not have."

a man was nothing too. It was only that and light was all it needed and certain cleanness and order. Some lived in it and never felt it but he knew it was nada y pues nada y pues nada. [the modified "Our Father" and "Hail Mary" prayers now begin:] Our nada who art in nada, nada be thy name thy kingdom nada thy will be nada in nada as it is in nada. Give us this nada our daily nada and nada us our nada as we nada our nadas and nada us not into nada but deliver us from nada; pues nada. Hail nothing full of nothing, nothing is with thee. He smiled and stood before a bar with a shining steam pressure coffee machine.

If the reader feels this short story pulls off this litany of "nadas," the reader smiles with the old waiter. Indeed, if the story had not been called what it is, "Nada" or "Nothing" would have been a good second choice as it is the single-most important word in the story. Its importance is established, indeed, at the story's start, when the older waiter is asked by the younger why the old man tried to kill himself:

"Last week he tried to commit suicide," one waiter said. "Why?" "He was in despair." "What about?" "Nothing." "How do you know it was nothing?" "He has plenty of money."

Once it is learned that the older waiter sympathizes with the old man, this "nothing" takes on major significance. How can he sympathize with someone so completely if he feels that the man killed himself for no reason? What, then, does this "nothing" really mean? We are given a clear and obvious clue. Nothing is what is left over after money is taken is care of: "'How do you know it was nothing?'"/"'He has plenty of money.'" What

that means is that all the man's physical wants must be guaranteed, so all that could be plaguing him are intangible yearnings. Or, to put this another way, what is plaguing the old man are not wishes for things he needs like food and shelter, but rather thoughts about profundities. "Nothing" is the old waiter's way of referring to the most important things in life after one's bodily wants have been satisfied. Thus, it is not surprising that the old man inserts a series of "nadas" into a prayer; a prayer, after all, is a significant event. To pray is to indicate a belief in a religion, in a system and an order for life, to indicate, in short, that one has a map to life's profundities. But the reader knows from the story's opening that this is precisely what the older waiter does not have. Profundities are precisely that for which he has no name. Thus, it comes as no surprise that what he does in his praying is utilize a "form" (a prayer) but then deny its "contents" (Catholicism). He borrows the structure of the "Our Father" and the "Hail Mary," but inserts "nada" into any place that matters. In these prayers, the values upon which the religious faith of the west are based are not so much denied, as "no thing" is put in their place. Thus, this story by Hemingway could be said to desire belief or faith, in its gesturing toward the "forms" of faith and belief, but as to what those beliefs or values might or could be, the story is overwhelmingly silent ("nada"). What Hemingway's minimalism is ultimately designed to achieve is precisely this refusal or forestalling of values or valuation. If western civilization has gone wrong, this modernism seems to convey, then it is best to hold off believing for a time in order to discover new and better beliefs and values.

The twentieth-century had dawned fully industrialized and fully armed for the bloodiest of wars. Like many of his "lost generation" (so named by the writer Gertrude Stein), Hemingway in this story exemplifies a disaffection with, and avoidance of, tradition and history. Hemingway's "A Clean, Well-Lighted Place" is a preeminent, representative example of modernist minimalist narrative. In utilizing only the bare minimum for narrative, in terms of language, character, scene, and action, Hemingway tries his best to skirt the traps and habits of the past. Modernists, thus, are as attached to notions of progress as their nineteenth-century predecessors, it is simply that they decide that the best way to get ahead is to start from scratch.

Source: Carol Dell'Amico, for *Short Stories for Students*, The Gale Group, 2000.

David Kerner

In the following essay, Kerner discusses the ambiguity of the dialogue between the two waiters and the importance of understanding who says what, and why.

Since Warren Bennett's 13,000-word defense—concluding, ''All printings of [''A Clean Well-Lighted Place''] should, therefore—in fairness . . . most of all, to Hemingway—follow the 1965 emended text''—has passed muster with Paul Smith, the earlier cries of ''Enough!'' were premature: a comprehensive demonstration of the accuracy of Hemingway's text is needed, lest we wake up one day to find the emendation enshrined in the Library of America. The need is evident too when Gerry Brenner can write: ''*must* we know which waiter answers the question 'How do you know it was nothing?' with 'He has plenty of money.'? I think not.'' One cannot take this answer away from the younger waiter without redistributing 19 other speeches; and to think that this can be done without damaging the intention in a story that so sharply differentiates the two waiters is to reveal once again that the story being read is not yet the one Hemingway wrote.

Anyone drawn to the notion that in Hemingway's text, whether by accident or design, there is an inconsistency that cannot be resolved has failed either to consider or to study the context of the crucial disputed line. No one, when first reading the story, can know which waiter is saying, as the dialogue opens, ''Last week he tried to commit suicide.'' The deliberateness of the uninformative ''one waiter said'' is undeniable, for in the second short dialogue (about the soldier), critics will never agree that it is possible to *know* which waiter is saying what. The third dialogue continues the challenge, as the younger waiter begins:

''He's drunk now,'' he said.

''He's drunk every night.''

''What did he want to kill himself for?''

By habit we assign this question and the succeeding ones to the younger waiter, so we are surprised, some lines later, to find the *older* waiter saying, ''You said she cut him down,'' for *he*, it would seem, has been answering the questions. But since this apparent inconsistency complements the riddling ''one waiter said''s, the context of controlled ambiguity assures us that when Hemingway decided to insert ''You said she cut him down,'' he knew that his assignment of this indispensable line

> '' In this way, the younger waiter's desperate flailing when he feels his identity escaping him becomes a microcosmic suggestion of the suicidal extremes that erupt in all racial, religious, ethnic, and political hostilities where persecution of a scapegoat is needed to shore up a precarious identity.''

was decisive, and consequently he knew which waiter he was giving it to. The function of this dual ambiguity is clear even before we know it is dual: once we have heard about ''nada,'' the withholding of identification throws a spotlight on the opening ''Nothing'':

''What [was he in despair] about?''

''Nothing.''

Then, after we have detected the apparent inconsistency, we realize that without the disputed insertion, we might decide that this ''Nothing'' (whose overtones Hemingway must have been aware of before he began) is the older waiter's ''nada,'' and the insertion is there to tell us we would be mistaken. But it tells us ambiguously, not immediately ending the puzzle of the ''one waiter said''s, prodding us to see *why* ''Nothing'' cannot be the older waiter's ''nada'' and must be the younger waiter's line. If the opening ''Nothing'' *were* the older waiter's line, there would be no reason for the web Hemingway took pains to weave. In pulling that web apart without studying it, the emenders, like surgeons cutting blindly, destroyed its function and lopped off an organic part of the story's meaning, for the younger waiter's ''Nothing'' opens up a kind of flanking attack that turns out to be the central location of the battle.

Bennett argues that the reply to ''Why [did the old man try to commit suicide]?''—''He was in despair''—indicates the speaker's familiarity with ''nada,'' and therefore the older waiter must be the one answering the questions. True, in the whole story this ''despair'' is the one word that can make us hesitate, but what follows it only supports our seeing the younger waiter throw up his hands mockingly as he replies, ''He was in despair''; for, coming from him, these words are a vacuous formula, forcing the questioner to repeat his question, and the mockery is confirmed when we see that the proffered answer ''Nothing'' is a set-up for a joke:

> ''How do you know it was nothing?''

> ''He has plenty of money.''

Because the older waiter could not think that anyone with ''plenty of money'' can have no reason to kill himself, Bennett is forced to construe ''Nothing'' as the later ''nada.'' But a premature, ambiguous ''Nada'' here, followed by an equally unenlightening, mocking deflection of the appeal for an explanation, would make the whole passage a pointless, as well as a misleading, anticipation, and it would also make the older waiter uncharacteristically glib and smug: it would be inconsistent with his patience as a teacher (''You do not understand. This is a clean and pleasant café''), with his feeling for the old man, and with the fact that, as he begins his interior monologue, he is not out to explain the old man's suicide attempt—he is asking, rather, why he himself has ''never had confidence,'' why does *he* ''need a light for the night,'' ''What did he fear?,'' as though he is only now, for the first time, naming his trouble. If ''Nothing'' were the older waiter's reply and meant what Bennett claims, this waiter's next reply would make sense—for example:

> ''How do you know it was [nada]?''

> ''He has a loving wife.''

That is what but ''nada'' can explain the suicide attempt when even such affection fails? The hypothetical answer helps us see the actual answer as a coarse joke; but that it *is* such a joke and stays a joke, Hemingway makes clear when the persistent questioner asks, ''What did he want to kill himself for?'' The new answer is not an explanation of ''nada'' but a callous dismissal—''How should I know''—which shows us again that behind the answer ''Nothing'' there was no idea the speaker might expand on; he now openly shrugs the question off, as though saying, ''What are you asking foolish questions for? What difference does it make? Who cares?'' Three times the older waiter has asked ''Why?'' and three times there has been no genuine

answer. This persistent rebuff of a serious question is not the way of the older waiter. Bennett is insensitive to the tone of ''How should I know'' when he hears in it the older waiter's ''existential un-certainty,'' not the crude impatience that Hemingway helpfully suggested by removing the question mark and restoring the period with which he had originally ended the line (MS 3). And since the opening ''Nothing'' was meant as a set-up for a wise-guy answer, the older waiter cannot be said, in his monologue, to be expounding already, with stunning eloquence, on the '''despair''' he had just '''learned' about from'' his insensitive colleague.

The principal argument, however, against attributing ''Nothing'' to the older waiter is in what Hemingway meant by contriving this line for the younger waiter. Bennett asserts that since the older waiter ''knows and understands the 'nothingness' behind suicidal thoughts,'' *he* ''could not 'stupidly' ask 'Why [did the old man try to commit suicide]?''' This distortion makes us think immediately of Hemingway's suicide. We are still asking ''Why?''—as Hemingway himself asked, more than once, about his father (*Winnerw; Bell*). In *Darkness Visible* William Styron concludes that clinical depression, even when it does not end in suicide, is an ''all but impenetrable mystery.'' The older waiter's persistent return to the question ''Why?''—an effort to learn what may be known—reflects the compassionate, intelligent involvement behind his pursuit of the subject— ''*How* did he do it?,'' ''*Why* did they do it [cut him down]?'' (emphasis added). But the more important mistake in Bennett's distortion here is his failure to realize that the older waiter neither says nor implies that ''nada,'' as he defines it, causes suicide. His monologue laments the loss of the traditional image of a fatherly God; what it says is what Freud says in *The Future of an Illusion* (had Hemingway read it?), though Freud, arguing, like the waiter, ''light was all it needed'' exhibits rather more confidence in the café he had opened. In this context, ''a man was nothing too'' has two meanings, which Hemingway, with grim humor, had recently explained in ''A Natural History of the Dead,'' puncturing the rhetoric of Mungo Park: our individual survival means nothing to the universe, and what happens to an untended corpse ridicules our exalting ourselves above natural law. No more than Hemingway there does the waiter here connect this atheism with suicide. Rather, he is raising the question, What *are* we (the human race), now that the God who marks the sparrow's fall is gone and we are no longer immortal? The answer, ''a man was nothing too,'' means we are only another kind of animal, so that our ''place'' now is merely a refuge, a sort of wildlife sanctuary, like the café for the old man. The symbolic meaning of this refuge is not the older waiter's—he is too modest (''it is probably only insomnia''); behind him, it is Hemingway who is suggesting that religion—and every other kind of home we carve for ourselves out of this harsh cosmos that doesn't know we are here—is no more than such a refuge.

But the story does not stop with the monologue: having shown us how different the waiters are, Hemingway has maneuvered us into going back to see what he is up to with those ''one waiter said''s—a challenge that is reinforced when, as we puzzle over it, we detect the apparent inconsistency; and now we discover that the younger waiter's role is to dramatize how ''a man was nothing too,'' in the way his behavior answers ''What are we?'' with the complementary question ''Who am I?'' His bristling when his colleague teases, ''You have no fear of going home before your usual hour?,'' implies that under the boast ''I am all confidence'' is a man who does not know himself, and who is fated, like Oedipus, to find out who he is, disastrously. This ominous ignorance is equally noticeable when he tells the deaf old man, ''You should have killed yourself last week'': such self-satisfied callousness is excessive, a gratuitous display of this waiter's assurance that he has nothing in common with the despairing old man; and the excess, like a neurotic symptom, is a measure of the strength of the anxiety the waiter is hiding from himself. Our understanding of this defensiveness is enlarged by Mr. Frazer's interior monologue at the end of ''The Gambler, the Nun, and the Radio,'' which Hemingway was finishing around the time he wrote ''A Clean, Well-Lighted Place'': life, Frazer thinks, is surgery without anesthesia—what Dr. Adams does in ''Indian Camp'' is how the universe operates—and we block the pain openly, with alcohol or other drugs, or covertly, with the protective coloration or identity we assume. Frazer's catalogue of such identities includes the macho facade—the anxiety-pacifying use of ''sexual intercourse''—that is the younger waiter's ''opium.'' Hemingway leaves it to us to figure out that the incident of the soldier hurrying with the girl is meant to give this waiter the rope to hang himself, when he says, in a display of his own sexual powers, ''What does it matter if he gets what he's after?'' We hear the choral commentary on this line when Frazer, learning that the nun wants to be a saint, tells her, ''You'll be one. Everybody gets

what they want. That's what they always tell me.'' Behind the restrained, good-humored irony of this speech is Frazer's knowledge of how we disappoint ourselves (the rodeo rider ''now, with a broken back, was going to learn to work in leather and to cane chairs''). The younger waiter needs to delude himself that he is ''of those'' who get ''what they want,'' he ''gets what he's after.''

So when the old man's ''despair'' is said to be about ''Nothing''—and we listen carefully, rereading, because the ambiguity has forced us to wonder what this means (Is it a contemptuous dismissal? Is it the older waiter's ''nada''?)—the conjunction of these alternatives, now that we have seen what thin ice the younger waiter is on, suddenly makes him the concealed subject of the inquiry when his unwitting ''Nothing'' explodes into a revelation of a second kind of ''nada'': since he is ''of those'' who ''lived in it and never felt it,'' we realize that the cause of his eventual despair, when his macho conception of himself collapses, will not be the older waiter's metaphysical, outer ''nada,'' but a psychological, inner ''nada''—the younger waiter's own nothingness that, unconsciously, he is anesthetizing with his sexual persona—which we are being asked to hear in the resonance of that spotlighted ''Nothing,'' as though Hemingway, whose symbolism looms behind the older waiter's monologue, could here be heard murmuring in the wings, like Bugs in ''The Battler,'' ''Nothing,' eh? Ah, Buster! You've 'got a lot coming to' you.'' With this, we have discovered the initial purpose of the ambiguity: we have been driven to see that the story is a tale of two ''nada''s. The conclusion ''a man was nothing too,'' which is contestable when the older waiter infers it from the silence of the cosmos, is reached unarguably from below, in the human condition the younger waiter's insubstantial identity reveals; for it is this inner ''nada'' that turns out to be fundamental, since it still takes its toll when the outer ''nada'' is vigorously denied (as in Hemingway's view of his father's suicide, for Dr. Hemingway was a lifelong devout Christian).

The initial purpose of the ambiguity is joined by a corollary purpose when we realize the relation between the two ''nada''s. The young waiter's ''bogus self-assurance,'' as Steven Hoffman has observed, is matched in ''Indian Camp'' when little Nick Adams, with ''willed ignorance,'' feels ''quite sure he would never die.'' Hoffman does not explore where this leads. In ''Three Shots,'' the discarded original opening of ''Indian Camp,'' three times we are told that "Nickie" (like Mr. Frazer) tries to avoid thinking, about either his shame or his fear. A few weeks before, the hymn "Some day the silver cord must break" had made him realize for the first time "that he himself would have to die sometime," and he had sat up all night in the hall, reading. That is no small feat for a little boy—it expresses intolerable anxiety, which returns now when he is alone in the tent, where no "silver cord" ties him to his source. "Nickie" here—can he be more than 10?—knows nothing of "the death of God"; the absence frightening him is that of his earthly father, for his fear goes away, and he falls asleep, as soon as he fires the signaling shots, since he has complete faith his father will return at once, and the firing itself identifies him with his father—which shows that the threat facing the boy was not death but separation, the inescapable demand that he be himself, with an identity of his own to protect him. So his concluding denial of how he must end expresses his unwillingness to relinquish the Nirvana of his "silver cord" beginnings.

In little Nick this childish denial is healthy; in the younger waiter it has become a sick denial that exposes his whole character structure as a defense against the reactivation of an intolerable indelible infantile threat. Hemingway's appreciation of this threat is clear in Frazer's belief that we are being operated on without anesthesia when we are stripped of the illusory identity that is all we have. And since, from the older waiter's mock prayer and "A Natural History of the Dead," we see that for Hemingway, as for Freud, the God who marks the sparrow's fall can be nothing but a projection of the infant's experience of omnipotent parental protection, then the older waiter's sense of cosmic desolation is a recapitulation of the primal psychological loss the younger waiter has unsuccessfully buried. Astonishingly, we now gather that the ambiguity, by leading us to entertain the possibility that either waiter might be saying certain significant lines, has as a corollary purpose a dreamlike blurring of the explicit difference between the waiters: though the older one says, "We are of two different kinds," we are meant to see that the younger one's overpowering need to deny the residue of his smoldering infantile helplessness makes his blustering "confidence"—his assurance that the old man's despair is "a way [*he'll*] never be"—an illusion, which may well be identified before long as the mask of the first stage of the depression that, when catastrophe strikes, may overwhelm *him* with the older waiter's insomnia, and may in the end bring him too to suicide (just

as little Nick's confidence "he would never die" presages that he too will one day suffer the Indian husband's unanesthetized anguish). This psychological relation between the waiters does not, of course, make their speeches interchangeable. The older waiter himself—with his protesting "What did he want to kill himself for?"—does not yet realize where he is heading. The three characters in the story are an allegory for the stages of our encounter with our inner "nada"—a post-theological pilgrim's progress that Hemingway's life has mapped for us.

The "clean, well-lighted place," then, insofar as it symbolizes a refuge one can achieve for oneself, is only a resting place, a holding action, as Hemingway intimates by the sly echo when Frazer attributes his climactic discovery ("Bread is the opium of the people") to "that well-lighted part of his mind that was there after two or more drinks in the evening; . . . (it was not really there of course)." In "Big Two-Hearted River" Nick Adams builds "the good place" of his own tent and camp, his "home where he had made it"—he has learned how fishing can control his anxiety, whatever its roots; but when Frazer concludes, "He was thinking well, a little too well," it is not fellow-traveling book reviewers he is afraid of, if he lets them read, in 1933, his judgment on the Russian revolution—he is afraid that in another minute he will be asking himself why he has omitted fishing and hunting from his catalogue of opiums (for the story is autobiographical), and his next question would be, Why did he omit art—his stories? Does the "clean, well-lighted place" his talent makes available certify his salvation? Hemingway does not have to identify for us the personal failings implied in "Usually [Frazer] avoided thinking all he could, except when he was writing"—such failings are universal, and Hemingway could be a merciless judge of his own, as in "Hills Like White Elephants." In "The Snows of Kilimanjaro," which too is autobiographical, Harry's dream of heavenward flight as he dies—a remorse-inspired illusion rising from his betrayal of his talent—is only one of the story's echoes of Tolstoy's "The Death of Ivan Ilych," perhaps the most devastating story ever written about inauthentic identity as a defense against the anxiety radiating from the buried soul. For though the loss of the parental God has again brought our professed identity into question, the unique willingness of the human animal to submit to judgment survives. "Fear for his soul" on the lips of the younger waiter is part of the Sophoclean irony. He does not know what danger his own soul is in, since he has not permitted himself to learn that the soul is no imaginary religious atavism—it is still, as it always was, inescapably, the self we create by our choices (insofar as we have them). That Hemingway, after his affair with Jane Mason (following his choice of Pauline Pfeiffer), could make the younger waiter a withering caricature of his own macho bristling, and then imagine for himself an inauthenticity that evoked for him ''The Death of Ivan Ilych,'' reinforces the allegory revealing the ''clean, well-lighted place'' as hardly more secure than the heaven that has dissolved like a mirage.

But we have yet to see the range of Hemingway's insight into the younger waiter's insubstantial identity as representative of the human condition. The younger waiter unwittingly betrays himself by overeagerly proclaiming that *he* is something (he is not ''nothing too''), while Hemingway, behind the older waiter, is telling us that our need to establish a ''clean, well-lighted place'' of our own is due to the failure of social institutions to live up to *their* claims that we are something (they have provided us such well-lighted mansions of meaning as the one that sustained Mungo Park in the desert); and this parallel between the younger waiter and civilization—a bristling ''confidence'' in the solidity of a shaky identity—is what gives the story its fundamental unity, climaxing the significance our attention to the ambiguity has found in the younger waiter. The range of the parallel is immense—it takes us immeasurably back and forward. For the older waiter's ''What are we *now*?'' is not new—it goes back to the emergence of the human race, when there was no question of ''the death of God'' or the ''meaninglessness'' of life: we alone among animals had to ask ourselves what we were, now that we'd been ejected from the closed programming of our animal Eden; we were already bristling, like the younger waiter, the first time a tribesman shrouded his head and trunk in an animal hide to reassure himself (and all others concerned) who his ancestors were; and the problem is permanent, as Hemingway learned from the collision of Oak Park with the twentieth century, which we see in ''Soldier's Home.'' In ''Winner Take Nothing'' Frazer's monologue is followed immediately by the first paragraph of ''Fathers and Sons,'' where ''the traffic lights'' ''would be gone next year when the payments on the system were not met.'' As an allusion to Prohibition (the story before ''The Gambler, the Nun, and the Radio'' is ''Wine of Wyoming''), this introduces a bristling theocratic eagerness to overregulate; for Dr. Adams's contribution to the sexual education of his son advises us that a system of rules telling us when to stop and when to go, permitting us to go about our business without slaughtering each other, must be inspired by a mistaken image of ourselves when it comes at a price we cannot afford (Dr. Adams will pay with his life).

In ''A Clean, Well-Lighted Place'' Hemingway faces us with such a system in the injunction against suicide, the dereliction the girl's uncovered head represents, the hurry of this couple, the curfew, and the patrolling police. As ''Fathers and Sons'' opens, a detour sign has not been removed, though ''cars had obviously gone through,'' so Nick Adams does not detour; but the soldier's graceless infraction classes him with the drunks the Fontans turn away in ''Wine of Wyoming.'' What his hurry exposes (emphasized by the contrast with the ''very old man walking unsteadily but with dignity'') is less a self than a sexual urgency that we are invited to see as an inner uniform—a biological herding that pacifies us with an illusion of identity; and this implicit metaphor explains why ''walked out to the old man's table'' in the holograph (3) was changed to ''marched'' in the typescript (2). We are not told precisely how the younger waiter's macho uniform will one day explode, but the strength his behavior leads us to attribute to the unresolved threat he has buried urges us to realize that when a man murders his estranged wife and her lover and then kills himself (a news item we've seen often), he has found that losing her robs him of his identity—without her he is *nothing* —and this is a danger that makes death preferable. In ''The Battler'' Bugs says of Ad Francis's wife, ''one day she just went off and never come back.'' ''. . . He just went crazy.'' But whether or not the crazy violence with which the punch-drunk ex-fighter hallucinates his old identity in the ring may be expected, in one form or another, from the similarly dependent younger waiter, his double, the soldier, is there so that we may ponder the possible imminent collision with the police, which adumbrates the younger waiter's problem in its broadest, tragic significance; for the state or culture, when *its* uniform—its bristling profession of a deep-rooted illusory identity (like the primitive animal hide)—is seriously threatened, knows no restraint, and lesser groups often claim such juggernaut authority. In this way, the younger waiter's desperate flailing when he feels his identity escaping him becomes a microcosmic suggestion of

the suicidal extremes that erupt in all racial, religious, ethnic, and political hostilities where persecu-
tion of a scapegoat is needed to shore up a precarious identity.

This is what Frazer is thinking in 1933 when he
sees patriotism as ''the opium of the people in Italy
and Germany'': the ''doctor,'' it would turn out (in
Scribner's Magazine the story was called ''Give Us
a Prescription, Doctor''), was prescribing, for those
people's tranquility, 50 million deaths. Every culture struggles, with its back to the wall, against the
realities threatening the identity it claims. For
Socrates, wisdom begins when we admit we do not
know; but society, denying to the end what its
professed identity will not permit it to admit, must
bristle like the younger waiter, and self-destruct.
From the older waiter's rejection of the bodega,
with its ''shining steam-pressure coffee machine,''
we gather that Hemingway foresees no salvation in
the identity technological civilization offers. Our
effort to discover what the human race is turns out to
be back-breaking Sisyphean labor—a cruel joke—
if our vaunted openness to cultural development is
an endless, savage turmoil of one self-deception
after another. But Hemingway does not believe it
endless. Whether justifiably, or only reflecting his
own depression, he gives us, in his next book, *Green
Hills of Africa*, his opinion of our ability to solve our
problem. He compares what the human race will
leave behind—after ''the systems of governments,
the richness, the poverty, the martyrdom, the sacrifice and the venality and the cruelty are all gone''—
to the five loads of garbage dumped on a good day
outside Havana, turning the Gulf Stream to ''a pale
green to a depth of four or five fathoms'': ''in ten
miles along the coast it is as clear and blue and
unimpressed as it was ever before the tug hauled out
the scow.'' There, for Hemingway—after the floating debris is gone (''the worn light bulbs of our
discoveries and the empty condoms of our great
loves'') and as long as the sun rises—is the lasting
''clean, well-lighted place.''

Source: David Kerner, ''The Ambiguity of 'A Clean Well-
lighted Place,''' in *Studies In Short Fiction*, Vol. 29, No. 4,
Fall, 1992, pp. 561-74.

Steven K. Hoffman

*In this essay Hoffman examines the three char-
acters' experiences of ''nada,'' or nothingness, in
''A Clean, Well-Lighted Place'' and shows how the
concept pervades Hemingway's work.*

One of his most frequently discussed tales, ''A
Clean, Well-Lighted Place'' is justly regarded as
one of the stylistic masterpieces of Ernest Hemingway's distinguished career in short fiction. Not only
does it represent Hemingway at his understated,
laconic best, but, according to Carlos Baker, ''It
shows once again that remarkable union of the
naturalistic and the symbolic which is possibly his
central triumph in the realm of practical aesthetics.'' In a mere five pages, almost entirely in dialogue and interior monologue, the tale renders a
complex series of interactions between three characters in a Spanish cafe just prior to and immediately after closing: a stoic old waiter, a brash young
waiter, and a wealthy but suicidal old man given to
excessive drink.

Aside from its well-documented stylistic achievement, what has drawn the most critical attention is
Hemingway's detailed consideration of the concept
of *nada*. Although the old waiter is the only one to
articulate the fact, all three figures actually confront
nothingness in the course of the tale. This is no
minor absence in their lives. Especially ''for the old
waiter,'' Carlos Baker notes, ''the word *nothing* (or
nada) contains huge actuality. The great skill in the
story is the development, through the most carefully
controlled understatement, of the young waiter's
mere *nothing* into the old waiter's Something—a
Something called Nothing which is so huge, terrible, overbearing, inevitable and omnipresent that
once experienced, it can never be forgotten.'' Because the terrifying ''Something called Nothing''
looms so very large, and since ''A Clean, Well-
Lighted Place'' appeared in a 1933 collection in
which even ''winners'' take ''nothing,'' critics have
generally come to see the piece as a nihilistic low
point in Hemingway's career, a moment of profound despair both for the characters and the author.

If this standard position does have a certain
validity, it also tends to overlook two crucial points
about the story. First is its relation to the rest of
Hemingway's highly unified short story canon. In
the same way that two of the three characters in ''A
Clean, Well-Lighted Place'' meet *nada* without
voicing the fact, all of the major short story characters also experience it in one of its multiple guises.
Thus ''A Clean, Well-Lighted Place,'' a rather late
story written in 1933, is something of a summary
statement on this recurrent theme; the tale brings to
direct expression the central crisis of those that
precede it—including the most celebrated of the
Nick Adams stories—and looks forward to its reso-

lution in the masterpieces that come later, ''The Short Happy Life of Francis Macomber'' (1936) and ''The Snows of Kilimanjaro'' (1936).

Second, because *nada* appears to dominate ''A Clean, Well-Lighted Place,'' it has been easy to miss the fact that the story is not about *nada per se* but the various available human responses to it. As a literary artist, Hemingway was generally less concerned with speculative metaphysics than with modes of practical conduct within certain *a priori* conditions. The ways in which the character triad in ''A Clean, Well-Lighted Place'' respond to *nada* summarize character responses throughout the canon. The fact that only one, the old waiter, directly voices his experience and manages to deal successfully with nothingness is also indicative of a general trend. Those few Hemingway characters who continue to function even at the razor's edge do so in the manner of this heroic figure—by establishing for themselves a clean, well-lighted place from which to withstand the enveloping darkness. For these reasons, ''A Clean, Well-Lighted Place'' must be termed the thematic as well as the stylistic climax of Hemingway's career in short fiction.

Although the difficulty of attributing certain individual statements in the tale creates some ambiguity on the subject, it is clear that the young waiter's use of the term *nada* to convey a personal lack of a definable commodity (*nothing*) is much too narrowly conceived. In his crucial meditation at the end, the old waiter makes it quite clear that *nada* is not an individual state but one with grave universal implications: ''It was a nothing that he knew too well. It was *all* a nothing and a man was nothing too'' [my italics]. According to William Barrett, the *nada*-shadowed realm of ''A Clean, Well-Lighted Place'' is no less than a microcosm of the existential universe as defined by Martin Heidegger and the existentialist philosophers who came before and after him, principally Kierkegaard and Sartre. Barrett's position finds internal support in the old waiter's celebrated parody prayer: ''Our nada who art in nada, nada be thy name thy kingdom nada thy will be nada in nada as it is in nada. Give us this nada our daily nada and nada us our nada as we nada our nadas and nada us not into nada but deliver us from nada; pues nada.'' The character's deft substitution of the word *nada* for all the key nouns (entities) and verbs (actions) in the Paternoster suggests the concept's truly metaphysical stature. Obviously, *nada* is to connote a series of significant absences: the lack of a viable transcendent source of power and

> In their dealings with the various faces of nada, then, the old waiter figures represent the highest form of heroism in the Hemingway short story canon. . . ."

authority; a correlative lack of external physical or spiritual sustenance; the total lack of moral justification for action (in the broadest perspective, the essential meaninglessness of *any* action); and finally, the impossibility of deliverance from this situation.

The impact of *nada*, however, extends beyond its theological implications. Rather, in the Heideggerian sense (''das Nicht''), it is an umbrella term that subsumes all of the irrational, unforeseeable, existential forces that tend to infringe upon the human self, to make a ''nothing.'' It is the absolute power of chance and circumstance to negate individual free will and the entropic tendency toward ontological disorder that perpetually looms over man's tenuous personal sense of order. But the most fearsome face of *nada*, and clear proof of man's radical contingency, is death—present here in the old man's wife's death and his own attempted suicide. Understandably, the old waiter's emotional response to this composite threat is mixed. It ''was not fear or dread,'' which would imply a specific object to be feared, but a pervasive uneasiness, an existential anxiety that, according to Heidegger, arises when one becomes fully aware of the precarious status of his very being.

That the shadow of *nada* looms behind much of Hemingway's fiction has not gone entirely unnoticed. Nathan Scott's conclusions on this issue serve as a useful summary of critical opinion: ''Now it is blackness beyond a clean, well-lighted place—this 'nothing full of nothing' that betrays 'confidence'; that murders sleep, that makes the having of plenty of money a fact of no consequence at all—it is this blackness, ten times black, that constitutes the basic metaphysical situation in Hemingway's fiction and that makes the human enterprise something very much like a huddling about a campfire beyond which looms the unchartable wilderness, the great

Nada.'' The problem with this position is that it tends to locate *nada* somewhere outside of the action, never directly operative within it. It is, to William Barrett, ''the presence that had circulated, *unnamed* and *unconfronted*, throughout much of [Hemingway's] earlier writing'' [my italics].

The clearest indication of *nada*'s direct presence in the short stories is to be found in the characters' frequent brushes with death, notably the characteristic modern forms of unexpected, unmerited, and very often mechanical death that both Frederick J. Hoffman and R. P. Warren consider so crucial in Hemingway. Naturally, these instances are the climactic moments in some of the best known tales: the interchapters from *In Our Time,* ''Indian Camp,'' ''The Killers,'' ''The Capital of the World,'' and ''The Snows of Kilimanjaro.'' But death or the imminent threat of death need not be literally present to signal an encounter with *nada.* What Philip Young and others have called Nick Adams's ''initiation'' to life's trials is actually his initiation to *nada.* In ''The End of Something'' and ''The Three Day Blow,'' Nick must cope with the precariousness of love in a precarious universe; in ''The Battler,'' with the world's underlying irrationality and potential for violence; in ''Cross-Country Snow,'' with the power of external circumstance to circumscribe individual initiative. In several important stories involving the period in Nick's chronology after the critical ''wound,'' *nada* as the ultimate unmanageability of life, appears as a concrete image. In ''Big Two-Hearted River,'' it is both the burnt-out countryside and the forbidding swamp; in ''Now I Lay Me,'' the night; in ''A Way You'll Never Be,'' a ''long yellow house'' (evidently the site of the wound).

Other imagistic references to *nada* appear in the non-Nick Adams tales. In ''The Undefeated,'' it is the bull, a particularly apt concrete manifestation of active malevolence in the universe, also suggested by the lion and buffalo in ''The Short Happy Life of Francis Macomber.'' These particular images, however, are potentially misleading because *nada* does not usually appear so actively and personally combative. An example to the contrary may be found in ''The Gambler, the Nun, and the Radio'' where *nada* is the distinctly impersonal and paralyzing banality of life in an isolated hospital, as well as the constant ''risk'' of a gambler's uncertain profession. Regardless of its specific incarnation, *nada* is always a dark presence which upsets individual equilibrium and threatens to overwhelm the self. And, as Jackson Benson has pointed out, ''A threat

to selfhood is the ultimate horror that the irrational forces of the world can accomplish.'' In that each story in the canon turns on the way in which particular characters respond to the inevitable confrontation with *nada,* the nature of that response is particularly important. The only effective way to approach the Void is to develop a very special mode of being, the concrete manifestation of which is the clean, well-lighted place.

Again, it is the old waiter who speaks most directly of the need for a physical bastion against the all-encompassing night: ''It is the light of course but it is necessary that the place be clean and pleasant. You do not want music. Certainly you do not want music. Nor can you stand before a bar with dignity.'' In direct contrast to the dirty, noisy *bodega* to which he repairs after closing and all the ''bad'' places that appear in Hemingway's fiction, the pleasant cafe at which the old waiter works possesses all of these essential attributes: light, cleanness, and the opportunity for some form of dignity. Perhaps the most direct antithesis of this legitimate clean, well-lighted place is not even in this particular story but in one of its companion pieces in *Winner Take Nothing,* the infernal bar in ''The Light of the World'' (1933). Here, light does little more than illuminate the absence of the other qualities, the lack of which moves one of the characters to ask pointedly, '''What the hell kind of place is this?''' Thus, in an inversion of the typical procedure in Hemingway, Nick and his companion are impelled outside where it is ''good and dark.''

Evidently, well-lighted places in Hemingway do not always meet the other requirements of the clean, well-lighted place. Moreover, since the cafe in ''A Clean, Well-Lighted Place'' must eventually close, even the legitimate haven has distinct limitations. These facts should be enough to alert us to the possibility that tangible physical location is not sufficient to combat the darkness. The clean, well-lighted place that is, is not actually a ''place'' at all; rather, it is a metaphor for an attitude toward the self and its existential context, a psychological perspective which, like the cafe itself with its fabricated conveniences and electric light, is man-made, artifical. The ''cleanliness'' of the metaphor connotes a personal sense of order, however artifical and temporary, carved out within the larger chaos of the universe, a firm hold on the self with which one can meet any contingency. By ''light'' Hemingway refers to a special kind of vision, the clear-sightedness and absolute lack of illusion necessary to look into the darkness and thereby come to grips with the *nada* which is everywhere. At the same time, vision must also be directed at the self so as to assure *its* cleanness. With cleanness and light, then, physical locale is irrelevant. Whoever manages to internalize these qualities carries the clean, well-lighted place with him, even into the very teeth of the darkness. The degree to which the Hemingway character can develop and maintain this perspective determines his success (or lack thereof) in dealing with the Void.

The man who does achieve the clean, well-lighted place is truly an existential hero, both in the Kierkegaardian and Heideggerian senses of the term. In the former, he is content to live with his *angst*, and, because there is no other choice, content to be in doubt about ultimate causes. Nevertheless, he is able to meet the varied and often threatening circumstances of day-to-day living, secure in the knowledge that he will always "become" and never "be." In the latter, he can face the unpleasant realities of his own being and the situation into which he has been "thrown," and can accept with composure the invitability of his death. In both instances, he is an "authentic" man.

Two of the main characters in "A Clean, Well-Lighted Place," as well as a host of analogous figures in other tales, fail to develop this attitude either for lack of "light" (the young waiter) or for lack of "cleanness" (the old man). As is evidenced by his inability to grasp the full impact of his partner's use of the word *nothing,* the egotistic young waiter has not even grasped the fact of *nada*—has not *seen* clearly—and therefore can hardly deal with it. "To him," comments Joseph Gabriel, "*nada* can only signify a personal physical privation. *Nothing* refers simply to the absence of those objects capable of providing material satisfaction. And by extension he applies the term to all behavior which does not grant the sufficiency of things." Unable to see that the old man's wealth is a woefully inadequate bulwark against the Void, he is, in his ignorance, contemptuous both of the man and his predicament. Perhaps as a direct outgrowth of this lack of light, the young waiter also violates the principle of cleanness by sloppily pouring his customer's desperately needed brandy over the sides of the glass. Thus, he easily loses himself in a fool's paradise of blindness and illusion. Still young, secure in his job, and, as he boasts, "'I'm not lonely. I have a wife waiting in bed for me,'" he is "all confidence": as such, a particularly patent example to the old waiter of those who "lived in it [*nada*] and never felt it."

Yet, in the course of the story, even this naif has an unsettling glimpse of the fundamental uncertainty of existence and its direct impact on his own situation. What else can account for his sharply defensive reaction to the old waiter's joke? [Old Waiter]: "'And you? You have no fear of going home before your usual hour?'" [Young Waiter]: "'Are you trying to insult me?'" [Old Waiter]: "'No, hombre, only to make a joke.'" The youth's subsequent grandiose claims to security notwithstanding, the force with which he objects to the merest possibility of marital infidelity clearly underscores the shaky foundations of his "confidence." This bogus self-assurance does not emanate from a mature awareness of himself and his world, but is based on the most transitory of conditions: youth, present employment, sexual prowess, and the assumed loyalty of his wife. The young waiter depends for his very being on factors over which he has no control, leaving him particularly vulnerable, in the case of marital uncertainty, to what Warren Bennett calls the "love wound," a common form of deprivation in Hemingway. But because he is essentially devoid of light or insight, he is not cognizant of the significance of his testy reply; his vision is so clouded by putative "confidence" that he fails to see through the ephemeral to the underlying darkness in his own life. Consequently, he cannot even begin to reconstruct his existence upon a more substantial basis.

Hemingway must have reveled in such naifs, aflame with so obviously compromised bravado, for he created many of them. Perhaps the most notable is Paco, the would-be bullfighter of "The Capital of the World" (1936), who even in the face of his own death, is "full of illusions." For many of these characters, moreover, blindness is not a natural state but a willed escape from *nada*. Conscious flight from reality is particularly prevalent in the early stages of the "education" of Nick Adams. In "Indian Camp" (1924), for instance, one of the first segments in the Adams chronology, Nick has a youthful encounter with *nada* both as the incontrovertible fact of death (the Indian husband's suicide) and as human frailty, the intrinsic vulnerability of mankind to various species of physical and psychic suffering (the Indian woman's protracted and painful labor). The pattern of avoidance set when he refuses to witness the Caesarean section climaxes in his more significant refusal to recognize the inevitability of death itself at the end. Lulled by the deceptive calm of his present circumstances—a purely fortuitous and temporary clean, well-lighted place—he maintains an internal darkness by retreating into willed ignorance:

> They were seated in the boat, Nick in the stern, his father rowing. The sun was coming up over the hills. A bass jumped, making a circle in the water. Nick trailed his hand in the water. He felt the sharp chill of the morning.
>
> In the early morning on the lake sitting in the stern of the boat with his father rowing, he felt quite sure that he would never die.

In another early story, "The Killers" (1927), the somewhat older Nick is again faced with harsh reality, but his reaction to it has not appreciably altered. Again, death (the Swede's) is the primary manifestation of the Void. But here the manner of its coming is also particularly important as a signature of *nada*. As represented by the black-clad henchmen who invade the cafe—another inadequate place of refuge— *nada* is totally impersonal; in the words of one of the killers, "'He [the Swede] never had a chance to do anything to us. He never even seen us.'" Moreover, *nada* displays its tendency to disrupt without warning any established external order, and, ironically, is visited upon its victims not without a certain macabre humor. Naturally, as Nick learns from the intended victim, its effects are totally irremediable. Thus, in spite of their suggestive black clothing, the killers do not represent forces of evil unleashed in an otherwise good world, as so many critics have claimed: rather, they stand for the wholly amoral, wholly irrational, wholly random operation of the universe, which, because it so clearly works to the detriment of the individual, is *perceived* to be malevolent and evil.

In spite of the clearly educational nature of his experience, Nick once again refuses initiation. Only now his unreasoned compulsion to escape is more pronounced than that of his younger counterpart. Deluded into thinking that this is the kind of localized danger that can be avoided by a mere change in venue, Nick vows not only physical flight ("'I'm going to get out of this town'") but psychological flight as well: "'I can't stand to think about him waiting in the room and knowing he's going to get it. It's too damned awful.'" Both versions of Nick Adams, then, are "young waiter" figures because they neither will allow themselves to look directly at the fearsome face of *nada* nor recognize its direct applicability to their own insecure lives.

That such an attitude is ultimately insupportable is exemplified by a third early tale, "Cross-Country Snow" (1925). Here, yet another Nick employs a physically demanding activity, skiing, as an escape from yet another incarnation of *nada*, entrapping circumstance. This appearance of the Void is also ironic in that the specific circumstance involved is the life-enhancing pregnancy of Nick's wife. Nevertheless, its impact on the character is much the same as before in that it serves to severely circumscribe independent initiative, even to the point of substituting an externally imposed identity—in this case, fatherhood—on the true self. Once again misled by the temporary security of the "good place," this Nick also attempts to escape the inescapable, and, at the height of his self-delusion, is moved to raise his pursuit of physical release to the level of absolute value: "'We've got to [ski again]. . . . It [life] isn't worth while if you can't.'"

The ski slope, however, offers only apparent protection from *nada*, for even in his joyous adventure, Nick encounters its own form or hidden danger: "Then a patch of soft snow, left in a hollow by the wind, spilled him and he went over and over in a clashing of skis, feeling like a shot rabbit." Unlike the others, this story ends with clarified vision, and Nick does come to terms with the inevitable external demands upon him. Finally, he is no longer able to pretend that the pleasures of the ski slopes— themselves, not always unmixed—are anything more than temporary, in no way definitive of human existence or even a long-lived accommodation to it. Thus, in response to his companion's suggested pact to repeat their present idyll, Nick must realistically counter, "'There isn't any good in promising.'"

In his relationship to *nada*, the old man of "A Clean, Well-Lighted Place" is cast as the polar opposite of the young waiter. Said to be eighty years old, virtually deaf, and recently widowed, he is "in despair" in spite of his reputed wealth, and has attempted suicide shortly before the story begins. Unlike the young waiter, he has the light of unclouded vision because he has clearly seen the destructive effects of time and circumstance on love and the self and directly witnessed *nada* in its death mask. But unlike the old waiter, he has not been able to sustain a satisfactory mode of being in the face of these discoveries. He therefore seeks escape from his knowledge either through the bottle or the total denial of life in suicide. Undoubtedly, the old man senses the importance of the clean, well-lighted place, but to him it is very literally a "place" and thereby no more helpful in combatting *nada* than Nick's ski slope. That it is inadequate is suggested imagistically at the outset; darkness has indeed invaded this character's "place," for he sits "in the shadows the leaves of the trees made against the electric light.''

What seems to offer the old man the little balance he possesses, and thus helps keep him alive, is a modicum of internal cleanness and self-possession, his dignity or style. Of course, this is an issue of great import in Hemingway in that an ordered personal style is one of the few sources of value in an otherwise meaningless universe. The old waiter draws attention to this pitiful figure's style when he rebukes the young waiter for callously characterizing the old man as '''a nasty old thing''': '''This old man is clean. He drinks without spilling. Even now, drunk.''' But even this vestige of grace has been compromised over time. While the old man leaves the cafe ''with dignity,'' he is ''walking unsteadily.''

The product of a series of encounters with *nada*, the old man's despair is mirrored in two Nick Adams stories on the period immediately following the critical war wound. In ''Now I Lay Me'' (1927), the emotional dislocation stemming from his brush with death is continued in an almost psychotic dread of the night and sleep. *Nada* is imaged both as the night itself and, as Carlos Baker has suggested, by the disturbing and seemingly ceaseless munching of silkworms, just out of sight but most assuredly not out of Nick's disturbed mind. Paradoxically, the protagonist's abject terror in the face of potential selflessness—permanent in death; temporary in sleep—has resulted in a severe dissociation of the self. Using Paul Tillich's descriptive terminology from *The Courage To Be*, one can say that he is burdened by ''pathological'' anxiety: a condition of drastically reduced self-affirmation, a flight from nonbeing that entails a corresponding flight from being itself: ''I myself did not want to sleep because I had been living for a long time with the knowledge that if I ever shut my eyes in the dark and let myself go, my soul would go out of my body. I had been that way for a long time, ever since I had been blown up at night and felt it go out of me and go off and then come back.''

Awakened to the fact of his own death, Nick experiences *angst* so strongly that he is virtually paralyzed. Unwilling to sleep in the dark and not yet able to develop an internal light and cleanness to cope with his trauma, he depends entirely on external sources of illumination: ''If I could have a light I was not afraid to sleep.'' In the absence of this light, however, he attempts to pull back from the awareness of *nada* by reliving the happier times of his youth, a period of cleanness and assured order. But

the search for a good ''place'' in the past is ultimately fruitless; his memories of favorite trout streams tend to blur in his mind and inevitably lead him to unpleasant reminiscences of his father's ruined collection of arrowheads and zoological specimens, a chaotic heap of fragments that merely mirrors his present internal maelstrom.

In ''A Way You'll Never Be'' (1933), Nick's dissociation has not been remedied and is suggested initially by the post-battle debris with which the story opens. Plagued by a recurring dream of ''a low house painted yellow with willows all around it and a low stable and there was a canal, and he had been there a thousand times and never seen it, but there it was every night as plain as the hill, only it frightened him,'' he is close to an old man's despair. He now intuits something of the significance of the vision: ''That house meant more than anything and every night he had it [the dream]. That was what he needed.'' But he is still too traumatized by the experience there to examine it more closely, and can only ramble on in self-defense about the ''American locust,'' another familiar item from his childhood. In his present condition, Nick is an oddly appropriate choice for the absurd mission on which he has been sent, to display his American uniform in order to build morale among the Italian troops. At the moment, his ''self,'' like the entire American presence in the region, is solely the uniform; the clothes are as dimly suggestive of a more substantial identity as they are of the substantial military support they are designed to promise. For the present, though, this barely adequate package for his violently disturbed inner terrain is Nick's only semblance of the clean, well-lighted place. Still insufficiently initiated into the dangerous world in which he is doomed to live, he desperately clutches at any buffer that will hold *nada* in abeyance.

The other side of Hemingway's ''old man'' figure is epitomized by Manuel Garcia, the aging bullfighter of ''The Undefeated'' (1925). After numerous brushes with death in the bullring, he too depends for his very being on style. Garcia's style has also eroded, leaving him defenseless against the bull, Harold Kaplan's ''beast of *nada*.'' Banished from the brightly lit afternoon bouts, he now performs in the shadowy nocturnals for a ''second string critic'' and with bulls that '''the veterinaries won't pass in the daytime.''' The performance itself is merely ''acceptable'' if not ''vulgar.'' Largely as a result of his diminished capabilities, he is seriously (and perhaps mortally) wounded, and, at the conclusion, is left with only his *coletta*, as is the old man his shred of dignity. With these all-important manifestations of internal cleanness sullied, the fates of both are equally uncertain: Manuel's on the operating table, and the old man's in the enveloping night.

Of all Hemingway's short story characters, however, the one who most fully recapitulates the "old man" typology is Mr. Frazer of "The Gambler, the Nun, and the Radio" (1933). Confined to a backcountry hospital as a result of a riding accident, Frazer too experiences *nada,* "the Nothingness that underlies pain, failure, and disillusionment alike," in the form of his own incapacity and that of the broken men who share his predicament. He also experiences banality, one of the less overtly disturbing but nonetheless ominous visages of *nada,* in the form of the numbing routine of this claustrophobic, but clean and well-lighted place. If Frazer has an old man's clear perspective on nothingness, he is no better able to achieve the cleanness of character necessary to cope with it. As is suggested by Hemingway's first title for the story, "Give Us a Prescription, Doctor," Frazer too seeks external anodynes for his *nada*—induced pain. His compulsion to monitor random radio broadcasts and so imaginatively transport himself from his present circumstances is analogous to the old man's drinking because each involves a flight from, rather than a confrontation with reality. His very choice of songs—"Little White Lies" and "Sing Something Simple"—serves to underscore the escapism of this pastime.

In the end, however, neither escape succeeds. The old man remains in despair, and Frazer is given to periodic fits of uncontrollable weeping. In the same way that the former cannot entirely banish the specter of loneliness and death from his consciousness, neither can Frazer, nor any man, completely cloud his view of *nada* with the various "opiums" at his disposal. The very consideration of the question of release leads Frazer through the opium haze to the terrible truth that lies beneath:

> Religion is the opium of the people. . . . Yes, and music is the opium of the people. . . . And now economics is the opium of the people; along with patriotism the opium of the people in Italy and Germany. . . . But drink was a sovereign opium of the people, oh, an excellent opium. Although some prefer the radio, another opium of the people, a cheap one he had just been using. . . . What was the real, the actual opium of the people? . . . What was it? Of course; broad was the opium of the people. . . . [Only] Revolution, Mr. Frazer thought, is no opium. Revolution is a catharsis; an ecstasy which can only be prolonged by

tyranny. The opiums are for before and for after. He was thinking well, a little too well.

The old waiter definitely stands apart from the other two characters in "A Clean, Well-Lighted Place." If the running controversy over dialogue attribution has thrown some doubt on whether he or his young partner first learns of the old man's attempted suicide, it has done nothing to contradict earlier assumptions on which of the two is more sensitive to the reasons for it. It is evident throughout that the old waiter's insight into the word *nothing* he so frequently uses is much broader. He recognizes from the first that the old man's despair is not a reaction to a material lack but to a basic metaphysical principle. Thus, he is unable to delude himself into a bogus "confidence." When he responds to the youth's boasting with "'You have everything,'" he is clearly being ironic; the latter indeed has "everything," *except* a firm hold on the "nothing" which underlies "everything." They are "of two different kinds" because the old waiter knows the ability to withstand the dark "is not only a question of youth and confidence although those things are very beautifu." In spite of their superficial beauty, both the transitory condition of youth and the illusory confidence that so often goes with it are clearly inadequate tools with which to combat the darkness.

There is a closer connection with the old man, however, initially because the news of his attempted suicide begins the old waiter's formal consideration of the reasons for it. In this sense, at the beginning of the tale, the old waiter is a representation of Earl Rovit's "tyro" and Philip Young's "Hemingway hero" (as opposed to the "tutor" and "code hero") in that he is in the process of learning about the dark underside of life. But while the old man's plight is a necessary goad for the old waiter's musings on his own situation, the latter certainly outstrips his "mentor" in the lengths to which he pushes his speculations on *nada* : "What did [the old waiter] fear? It was not fear or dread. It was a nothing that he knew too well. It was all a nothing and a man was nothing too. It was only that and light was all it needed and a certain cleanness and order. Some lived in it and never felt it but he knew it all was nada y pues nada y nada y pues nada."

Like the old man, then, the old waiter sees clearly, in fact more clearly, the fearsome nothing, but he reacts far differently to his discovery. Instead of lapsing into despair or escaping into drunkenness, this character displays true metaphysical courage in raising the concept of *nada* to a central article in his overtly existentialist creed, climaxing with his mock prayer of adoration, "Hail nothing full of nothing, nothing is with thee." Perhaps even more importantly, he refuses to limit himself to abstract speculation but willingly embraces the impact of universal nothingness on his own person. Thus, in response to the barman's question, "'What's yours?'" he demonstrates the ironic sense of humor that typifies him throughout by unflinching answering, "'Nada.'" No other statement in the tale so clearly designates the old waiter as the central figure of Hemingway's 1933 collection: he is the "winner" who truly takes "nothing" as his only possible reward.

If his stoic courage in the shadow of the Void differentiates the old waiter from the old man, so does his method for dealing with it. Again, the old waiter provides some grounds for confusing the two modes of existence when he insists upon the importance of a purely physical haven: "'I am one of those who like to stay late at the cafe. . . . With all those who do not want to go to bed. With all those who need a light for the night.'" Yet, he does more than merely accept the dubious protection of an already established "place"; he is, in fact, the keeper of the "clean, well-lighted place," the one who maintains both its cleanness and its light. To cite Cleanth Brooks on this subject, "The order and right are supplied by *him*. They do *not* reflect an inherent, though concealed, order in the universe. What little meaning there is in the world is imposed upon that world by man." Given the stark contrast between his cafe and the distinctly unclean and ill-lighted bar he frequents after work, his almost ritualistic efforts to furnish and consistently maintain these essential qualities are definitely not representative of those around him. Finally, the old waiter's clean, well-lighted place is distinctly portable—transcending "place" altogether—because it is so thoroughly internalized. He carries it in the form of equanimity and dignity to the shabby *bodega*, and he carries it home as well.

Thus, it is the old waiter, a man who can see clearly the darkness surrounding him yet so order his life that he can endure this awareness, who most fully attains the attitude symbolized by the clean, well-lighted place. In the society presented by this tale, and in the Hemingway canon as a whole, he is indeed "*otro loco mas*" when set against a standard of sanity epitomized by an egotistical partner, unfeeling barmen, lustful soldiers, and suicidal old men. Both realist and survivor, epitome of "grace under pressure," he is by the end of the tale an exceptional man and very much a representation of the highest level of heroism in Hemingway's fictional world, whether it be denoted by Young's "code hero" or Rovit's "tutor." Even his insomnia, which he regards as a common trait ("Many must have it"), is a mark of his extraordinary character: his vision is too clear, his sense of self too firm, to allow him the ease of insensate slumber. One need only compare this insomnia with Nick Adams' pathological fear of sleep in "Now I Lay Me" to appreciate the qualitative difference between the old waiter and other men.

Some of Hemingway's most important tales also contain characters who either presage an achievement of or actually attain the old waiter's clean, well-lighted place. A notable early example is the Nick Adams of "Big Two-Hearted River" (1925). Again, the confrontation with *nada,* is critical here, but the appearance of *nada* is more artfully veiled than in other tales. There are hints of the Void in the description of the burned-over countryside at the beginning, in Nick's vision of the trout "tightened facing up into the current" shortly thereafter, and in the methodical series of tasks that comprise the central action of the story. As Malcolm Cowley first suggested and Sheridan Baker has since amplified, the ritualistic series connotes a desperate attempt to hold off something "he had left behind"; in Philip Young's reading, the "something" is the memory of the traumatic war wound that so discomfits other versions of Nick in "Now I Lay Me" and "A Way You'll Never Be." But *nada* is most overtly suggested by the forbidding swamp: "Nick did not want to go in there now. . . . In the swamp the banks were bare, the big cedars came together overhead, the sun did not come through, except in patches; in the fast deep water, in the half light, the fishing would be tragic." Aside from the old waiter's prayer, this is Hemingway's most detailed characterization of *nada*: it too is dark; its depth is ungauged but considerable; and, with its swiftly moving current and bare banks, it is most assuredly inhospitable to man.

As the "patches" of sunlight suggest, though, the *nada*/swamp can be discerned and therefore analyzed by human vision. And, by the end of the story, Nick seems to have gained the light necessary to see into the Void—at the very least, to realize that he can never truly leave it behind him. Yet Nick still lacks the inner cleanness to delve further into *nada*; he is still too dependent on a distinct physical locale as a buffer zone. As he says early on, "He was there, in the good place." But the very ritualistic behavior that alerted Cowley to the possibility of a mind not right also suggests progress toward an internalized order. Like the trout's in the potentially destructive current, this discipline could hold Nick steady in the dangerous eddies of life and so enable him eventually to enter the swamp. Thus, while the tale ends with a temporary withdrawal from direct confrontation, Nick strikes a positive note when he says, "There were plenty of days coming when he could fish the swamp."

Two characters in the late short stories actually do "fish" the swamp of *nada,* the sportsman Macomber in "The Short Happy Life of Francis Macomber" (1936) and the writer Harry of "The Snows of Kilimanjaro" (1936). The two men approach the clean, well-lighted place from different directions, however: Macomber, from an old man's despair; and Harry, from a young waiter's naive faith in transitory material security. For Macomber, the master of "court games" and darling of drawing rooms, it is necessary to leave the protective enclosures of the rich to meet his *nada* in the African tall grass in the figure of the wounded lion, an epitome of pure destructive force: "All of him [the lion], pain, sickness, hatred and all of his remaining strength, was tightening into an absolute concentration for a rush." The brush with externally conceived *nada* triggers Macomber's cowardly flight, but more importantly leads him to an appreciation of his own inner emptiness, a Sartrian version of nothingness, as well as a Sartrian *nausea* at his inauthenticity. Granted, Macomber responds to the threat with fear, but it is also more than fear, "a cold slimy hollow in all the emptiness where once his confidence had been and it made him feel sick." Thus Macomber comes face to face with the fact that *nada* need not destroy the physical being to make man a "nothing"; man *is* a nothing unless and until he makes himself "something."

The black despair that follows his initiation to *nada* without and within is not Macomber's final stage. Through the ministrations of the hunter Wilson and the familiar, secure place (the jeep), he undergoes a significant and almost miraculous change at the buffalo hunt. As Wilson describes it, "Beggar had probably been afraid all his life. Don't know what started it. But over now. Hadn't had time to be afraid with the buff. That and being angry too. Motor car too. Motor cars made it familiar. Be a damn fire eater now." The jeep is indeed useful as a means for facing *nada* analogous to the old waiter's cafe and Nick Adams' peaceful campsite, but Macomber's real "place" is distinctly internal.

Again, Wilson furnishes the analysis: "Fear gone like an operation. *Something else grew in its place.* Main thing a man had. Made him into a man [italics mine]." Macomber's real achievement, then, is the creation of an ordered "something" to fill the inner void. It not only prepares him for the buffalo hunt but enables him to see clearly, as if for the first time, his inauthentic condition, not the least important facet of which has been his sacrifice of personal identity to an unfulfilling marriage and social expectation. With his "place" securely inside him, he can face with dignity and courage another brush with *nada* in the "island of bushy trees," a hostile testing ground certainly reminiscent of Nick's swamp.

In "Snows of Kilimanjaro," Harry too has multiple confrontations with *nada,* the first of which is with the ultimate manifestation of the Void, death: "It came with a rush; not as a rush of water nor of wind; but of a sudden evil-smelling emptiness." As we learn later, this appearance certainly fits Carlos Baker's oxymoronic designation for *nada* as the "nothing that is something," for "It had no shape, any more. It simply occupied space." The immediate effect of the experience is to lead Harry to an appreciation of the underlying absurdity of an existence that could be doomed by such a trivial injury— a small scratch which becomes gangrenous for lack of proper medication. With this awareness of his radical contingency, the protagonist can defuse death of its terror: "Since the gangrene started in his right leg he had no pain and with the pain the horror had gone and all he felt now was a great tiredness and anger that this was the end of it. . . . For years it had obsessed him; but now it meant nothing in itself."

Like Macomber's, Harry's brush with imminent death also awakens him to a second face of *nada,* the inner nothing caused by his failure to preserve artistic integrity, his very self, against the lures of the inconsequential: material comfort, financial security, hedonistic pleasure. Every bit as much as Macomber, this most autobiographical of Hemingway's short story characters suffers a hollowness at the very core. Therefore, the basic thrust of the tale is Harry's effort to cleanse and reorder his life through a pointed self criticism. Gradually he manages to "work the fat off his soul" by jettisoning the excess baggage of a young waiter's facile confidence in the material and replaces it with something more substantial, a pledge to take up his writing once more. Again, the process is facilitated by his being situated in a tangible clean, well-lighted place: "This was a pleasant camp under big trees against a hill, with good water, and close by, a nearly dry water hole where sand grouse flighted in the morning." But again, the important "place" is actually within. According to Gloria Dussinger, Harry's difficult rite of purification leads, as it should, to a reclamation of his own identity: "Harry is left with his naked self, the irreducible *I am* that defies chaos." Though the climactic dream flight from the plain is decidedly ambiguous, it does seem to vouchsafe Harry's success at this endeavor, for the author allows him imaginative entry into the cleanest and best lighted of all the places in the short story canon: "great, high, and unbelievably white in the sun, was the square top of Kilimanjaro. And then he knew that there was where he was going."

Although Harry and Macomber both achieve the clean, well-lighted place, their premature deaths deprive them of the opportunity to bring additional value to their lives, as the old waiter most assuredly does. Having controlled his own life through the implementation of a clean, well-lighted place, he fulfills the remaining provisions of Eliot's "Waste Land" credo by sympathizing with the plight of others and aiding them in their own pursuits of this all important attitude. In so doing, he becomes an existential hero in Martin Buber's particular sense of the term, a champion of the "I-Thou" relationship. His "style" is essentially compassion, the willingness to treat others as valid, subjective "Thous" rather than depersonalized "Its." This facet of his personality is implicit as early as his expression of sympathy for the pleasure-seeking soldier who risks curfew violation. As he himself comments on the risks involved, "'What does it matter if he gets what he's after?'" But his capacity for true compassion is made most explicit near the end, particularly in his admission, "'Each night I am reluctant to close up because there may be some one who needs the cafe.'"

The ability to extend outward to others from a firmly established self is once again in direct contrast to the narrow, selfish pride of the young waiter, who is unmoved by the needs of the old man and sees love as a matter of blind loyalty (verging on bondage) and physical gratification. This inclination is made all too clear by his insensitive comment on the old widower's plight: "'A wife would be no good to him now.'" The old waiter's attitude is also contrasted to that of the old man, who is so absorbed by his own misery that he is barely cognizant of others. This admirable figure passes beyond Rovit's "tyro" stage to that of "tutor" when he humorously, but pointedly, attempts to instruct the youth on the evanescence of "confidence" and the latter's

serious misuse of love (*e.g.,* by the joke). Moreover, he tries to provide the morose old man with some basis upon which to reconstruct his shattered life by rendering to this wretched figure the respect and sympathy he so desperately needs. Thus, in Buber's sense as in Heidegger's, Kierkegaard's, and Sartre's, the old waiter "authenticates" his life by fulfilling his responsibilities both to himself and to others.

The picador Zurito in "The Undefeated," the dignified major in "Another Country" (1927), and the guide Wilson of "The Short Happy Life of Francis Macomber" all transcend the limits of self-sufficiency by sympathizing with and proferring aid to those who most need it. But the character who most closely approximates the old waiter's multi-faceted heroism is Cayetano Ruiz, the luckless gambler of "The Gambler, the Nun, and the Radio," a story whose three main characters (Ruiz, Frazer, Sister Cecilia) form a triadic grouping analogous to the hero, victim, and nail of "A Clean, Well-Lighted Place."

That the gambler does attain the exemplary attitude is implicit in William Barrett's summary characterization of him: "Cayentano is the absurd hero who carries on his code, even if it is only the code of a cheap gambler, defiantly and gracefully against the Void." Cayetano, of course, earns his heroism in that he too encounters the death mask of *nada*. Like Harry's, his wound comes totally without warning, and, given the rather unreliable aim of his assailant, almost totally by accident. Yet even before this crisis, the perspicacious gambler with eyes "alive as a hawk's" has undoubtedly sensed its presence in the form of chance and the ever-present risk of his chosen profession. In spite of the fact that his work takes him into places that are anything but clean and well-lighted, he has so internalized the "place" that he can calmly face external hostility and internal suffering, and face them with honor and exemplary courage. Consequently, he refuses to inform on his assailant and also refuses opiates to dull the physical pain that serves as metaphor for the metaphysical pain *nada* induces.

But Ruiz is far more than Barrett's "cheap," albeit heroic, gambler because he strives to communicate his insights on life to others. Indirect proof of his compassion is to be found both in his embarrassment over the offensive odor of his peritonitis and in his considerate silence even in periods of terrible pain. Direct evidence is available in the conversations with Frazer. Here Ruiz incisively analyses the untreatable ills of the human condition—the absurd irony, the prevalence of accident and risk, and, most of all, the difficulty of maintaining a self amidst the vagaries of fortune that have driven his auditor to tears. Like the old waiter, he is quite capable of humbling himself, denigrating his own considerable courage, in order to provide comfort to one less able to withstand *nada*. Surely he consciously misstates fact when, in an attempt to assuage Frazer's shame at lapsing into tears, he declares, "'If I had a private room and a radio I would be crying and yelling all night long.'" Evidently this self-described "victim of illusions" also possesses the old waiter's ironic consciousness, for it is at the very heart of his dispassionate self-analysis, also delivered principally for Frazer's benefit: "'If I live long enough the luck will change. I have bad luck now for fifteen years. If I ever get any good luck I will be rich.'" Although he fully realizes that "bad luck" will continue to predominate, like the other residents of the *metaphoric* clean, well-lighted place, the gambler is content to "continue, slowly, and wait for luck to change." In the interim, he will continue to try to instill in others some of the light and cleanness essential to the authentication of the self.

In their dealings with the various faces of *nada*, then, the old waiter figures represent the highest form of heroism in the Hemingway short story canon, a heroism matched in the novels perhaps only by the fisherman Santiago. Those who manage to adjust to life on the edge of the abyss do so because they see clearly the darkness that surrounds them yet create a personal sense of order, an identity with which to maintain balance on this precarious perch. The failure either to see the significance of the encounter with *nada* or, if seen, to constitute an inner cleanness vitiates the lives not only of the young waiter and old man of "A Clean, Well-Lighted Place" but also of a host of similarly flawed figures throughout the canon.

Because of the frequency with which *nada* appears in the short fiction, we can only assume that the Void also played a major role in Hemingway's own life, whether as the shattering war wound or the countless subsequent experiences, both real and imagined, that threatened to make him a "nothing." Carlos Baker concluded as much in his biography: "'A Clean, Well-Lighted Place' was autobiographical . . . in the sense that it offered a brief look into the underside of Ernest's spiritual world, the nightmare of nothingness by which he was still occasion-

ally haunted." But if we are justified in seeing Hemingway's life in terms of his encounters with *nada,* are we not equally justified in following Earl Rovit's lead and thereby treating his fiction as one of the by-products of these encounters—in fact, as a primary strategy for dealing with *nada*?

Both the fiction itself and the author's comments on it seem to support us in this regard, for Hemingway's basic aesthetic suggests precisely the sort of perspective symbolized by the clean, well-lighted place. The need for clearsightedness, for instance, is the essence of the writer's celebrated remark on art in *Death in the Afternoon* (1932), a personal testament published just a year before "A Clean, Well-Lighted Place": "Let those who want to save the world if you can get to see it clear and as a whole. Then any part you make will represent the whole if it is made truly." But unclouded vision alone, not uncommon among his fictional progeny, could guarantee neither a psychological nor an aesthetic clean, well-lighted place. A careful and conscious ordering of disparate material was also required in order to fill the Void of nothing (the blank page) with an enduring something. Thus, the characteristic Hemingway style: the clean, precise, scrupulously ordered prose that so often serves to illuminate shimmering individual objects against a dark background of chaos. As for his old waiter figures, the actual places that inspired the author's descriptions pale against the deftly constructed "places" that *are* the descriptions; because the latter are no longer subject to the random, transitory world of fact but rather interiorized and subsequently transmuted into art itself, they are much more secure, and certainly more permanent, strongholds against nothingness.

In spite of the apparent disdain for utilitarian art in the passage from *Death in the Afternoon*, Hemingway also performed some of that function, albeit indirectly, by probing the sources of our well-documented modern malaise and offering at least tentative solutions to it in the form of resolute personal conduct. In this way he too displayed some of the Buberesque qualities of his short story heroes. It should come as no surprise, then, that Granville Hicks' summary of the author's artistic mission has a rather direct applicability to that of the old waiter as well. For in their potential impact on an attentive audience, Hemingway and his extraordinary character are virtually one and the same. Like the latter, "The artist makes his contribution to the salvation of the world by seeing it clearly himself and helping others to do the same."

Perhaps nothing so effectively demonstrates the difficulty of maintaining the clean, well-lighted place than Hemingway's own failure to do so in the years immediately preceding his death. Like so many of his "old man" figures, he never lost sight of *nada* but did lose the essential inner cleanness, without which the light must eventually be over-powered by darkness. With his internal defenses in disarray, Hemingway turned to an old man's despairing act. In effect, in his suicide, he opted for the release from turmoil offered by the metaphorical "opiums" of Mr. Frazer: "He would have a little spot of the giant killer and play the radio, you could play the radio so that you could hardly hear it."

Source: Steven K. Hoffman, "*Nada* and the Clean Well-Lighted Place," in *Essays In Literature*, Vol. VI, No. 1, Spring, 1979, pp. 91–110.

Annette Benert

Discussing the imagery, characterization, and theme of "A Clean, Well-Lighted Place," Benert concludes that it is not in fact a story about nothingness but "a totally affirmative story" that dramatizes "the possibility . . . of man continuing to act, to feel even for others, to think even about metaphysics, to create (with a smile), to control and thereby to humanize both himself and his environment."

"A Clean, Well-Lighted Place" has with justice been considered an archetypal Hemingway story, morally and aesthetically central to the Hemingway canon. But its crystalline structure and sparse diction have led many critics to judge the story itself a simple one, either about nothingness, "a little *nada* story," or about the author's positive values, a story "lyric rather than dramatic." I would like to suggest that it is in neither sense simple, but that the feelings and ideas which lie behind it are complex and are expressed dramatically, chiefly through the characterization of the older waiter. The latter is a man of enormous awareness continually torn between what might be called religious idealism and intellectual nihilism, a combination that surfaces in irony in several places in the story. This tension between two modes of viewing the world is developed through imagery that functions as a setting, through characterization, and, more abstractly, through a theme which I take to be the barriers against *nada*.

The most obvious source of imagery is the words of the title, the qualities of light and cleanness, to which one may add quietness. These terms admirably illustrate what Richard K. Peterson calls

"The older waiter in fact acts in various ways against Nothingness."

the "use of apparently objective words to express values"; they may be followed with profit throughout Hemingway's stories, novels, and non-fiction. But in this story each of these qualities exists also in its negative aspect, its shadow side.

Light provides the most striking image pattern. The cafe has an "electric light" that the older waiter eventually turns off. A street light is picked up by the brass number on a passing soldier's collar. The older waiter is "with all those who need a light for the night." The cafe where he works is "well lighted"; its "light is very good." In the bodega where he buys coffee "the light is very bright and pleasant." After going home he would be able to sleep "with daylight." Obviously, light is not only the antithesis of darkness but an effective barrier against it, or, rather, as Randall Stewart puts it, the light "at any rate, must be made to do."

But it is stated twice that the patron, the old man, "sat in the shadow of the leaves," and the older waiter likes the cafe not only because its light is good but because "now there are shadows of the leaves," Further, the old man particularly liked sitting in the cafe at night because "the dew settled the dust" of the day and "it was quiet and he felt the difference," though he was deaf. Here shadow clearly has a positive connotation, in the sense of shade, of protection from the glare of the light, perhaps because the light is artificial but more likely because any direct light hurts the eyes and exposes the person. In addition, the night is clean and quiet, positive values contrasted to the day's dirt and noise.

The older waiter is equally concerned that his "place" be clean. He contradicts the younger waiter's remark that "an old man is a nasty thing" with "this old man is clean. He drinks without spilling. Even now, drunk." In contrast to the younger waiter, who wipes "the edge of the table with a towel" to emphasize that the old man should leave, but earlier had poured brandy so that it "slopped over and ran down the stem into the top saucer of the pile," the older waiter emphasizes several times the necessity of cleanness. Bars and bodegas are open all night, and they have light, but one cannot ''stand before a bar with dignity, with correctness.''

Its natural occurrence, however, is at night, when ''the dew settled the dust.'' Its negative aspect is even more evident in that statement of the younger waiter that ''an old man is a nasty thing,'' which, as a generalization, the older waiter does not contradict. Since age, as opposed to youth, is specifically associated in this story with greater awareness and sensitivity, in Hemingway terms ''imagination,'' cleanness may be linked with ignorance and insensitivity.

The third positive quality of the cafe is its quietness; the old man, in addition, is deaf. There is the suggestion that another thing wrong with bars is that they may have music, but, in any case, ''you do not want music. Certainly you do not want music.'' Any form of noise, then, like darkness and dirt, is to be avoided.

In this quality is the negative side of all three most evident. The old patron not only cannot tolerate direct light and can be classified with ''nasty things,'' but also he is actually deaf so that no sound even has relevance for him. That the shadow side of quietness is its extreme, in the form of a negation of one whole sense faculty and a major art form, reminds the reader that all three qualities are in some sense negations. Light functions as an absence of darkness, cleanness as an absence of dirt, quietness as an absence of sound. Yet all three are posited as barriers against the ultimate negation, against Nothingness itself—perhaps, for once in literature, a genuine paradox, but certainly a major source of irony in this story.

Other images are less important but function in the same way. Liquor, the ''giant killer'' of other stories, is a weapon against the darkness, but it also impairs physical functioning, making the old man walk ''unsteadily,'' so that the older waiter notices with pride that he can drink ''without spilling. Even now, drunk,'' walk ''with dignity.'' The younger waiter is ''not lonely'' because he has ''a wife waiting in bed,'' but for the old man who ''had a wife once'' now ''a wife would be no good,'' making women, a relationship to a woman, a material, but very temporary and thus illusory, protection against nothingness. All Hemingway's sleepless heroes desire sleep, but the old waiter, acutely conscious of the darkness lurking behind the light, cannot allow himself to lose that consciousness

until he has light to protect him. There is a synonymity between being aware and being awake that overrides the psychologically negative connotations of insomnia. Thus, the man who can sleep is unaware and insensitive.

But in ''A Clean, Well-Lighted Place'' characterization is even more important than imagery. Though the old patron is the main topic of conversation between the two waiters, he is less important as a character than either of them. He functions more as part of the setting, a demonstration of the way things are, and as an indirect means for the characterization of the other two men. The younger waiter, also called ''the waiter who was in a hurry'' and ''the waiter with a wife,'' is not the villain he is often cast to be; he after all ''did not wish to be unjust,'' He is merely *l'homme moyen sensuel*, lacking that moral and aesthetic sensibility Hemingway calls ''imagination.'' He alone should serve as a refutation of the ''locker-room'' Hemingway, if such is still needed, but he is much less important than his co-worker, indeed serving as a kind of foil for him.

That the older waiter is also called ''the unhurried waiter'' makes evident the pun in the appellation. The younger man is ''waiting'' impatiently to go home and the older is ''waiting'' patiently or has transcended ''waiting'' altogether, has gone one step beyond Beckett's tramps, having learned that there is nothing to wait for. As Joseph Gabriel has it, he ''must bear at the same time his intense spiritual hunger and the realization of the impossibility of its fulfillment.'' His alienation is dramatized, as Robert Weeks has noted, by his being ''in the presence of others who either do not even notice him, or if they do are unaware of his ordeal and of the gallantry with which he endures it.'' But he is also something more, and something more complex, than these tragic, heroic qualities would suggest.

He first appears in that initial dialogue, which, by its lack of speech tags and the ensuing possible mis-assignment of them, has plagued so many readers. The second long dialogue makes clear that the older waiter provides the younger with information concerning the old patron's attempted suicide, and that the older man possesses the greater degree of sensitivity and awareness. This characterization is then read back into the first dialogue, making the younger waiter tell about the old man's act, so that he may be given the line ''Nothing'' to describe the old man's despair. That Hemingway, nothing if not a craftsman of the first rank, could have made such a major error is simply beyond belief. The passage surely must be read as follows:

> Older waiter: "Last week he tried to commit suicide."
>
> Younger waiter: "Why?"
>
> Older waiter: "He was in despair." [as he of all men would understand]
>
> Younger waiter: "What about?"
>
> Older waiter: "Nothing." [that is, *nada*, Nothingness]
>
> Younger waiter: "How do you know it was nothing?" [that is, nothing tangible or material]
>
> Older waiter: "He has plenty of money." [that is, his despair must have had metaphysical, rather than physical, grounds].

Ambiguity exists, not as Joseph Gabriel would have it, in that the speeches may be assigned either way, but, in addition to the above, in the possibility of the older waiter's sarcastic response to a man after all incapable of understanding either old man anyway. Perhaps he means also something like "of course, what could any man possibly despair over—he has plenty of money?" This possibility is underscored by his response later to the query, "What did he want to kill himself for?" with the abrupt "How should I know."

The older waiter manifests this kind of double vision repeatedly. He remarks that the old patron "might be better with a wife"; yet he clearly knows the transitory nature of such a comfort. He has just informed his colleague that, like the latter, the old man "had a wife once too," implying that she is dead, and later hints in jest that wives may be unfaithful. As they close up the cafe, the older waiter states that the younger has "everything," meaning "youth, confidence, and a job"; yet such attributes are temporary and at best can counteract only the young man's "nothing," not the old man's "nothingness." With some justice does the former accuse the latter of "talking nonsense" after the remark, but without sensing its latent sardonic quality.

The strongest evidence of the older waiter's double awareness is of course the long paragraph of the two parodic prayers. *It* is used eleven times with references varying from the cafe, to the merely grammatical subject of the verb *is*, to the anguish he tries to define, to the world, to nothingness itself. The fragments of the two prayers follow naturally from the catechetical dialogues at the beginning of the story and from the repetitions of *it* and *nothing*. Like the world and man himself, religious form is hollow at the core, filled with "nothing," or, rather, "nothingness," in existential terms, the abyss.

Though there is "nothing" to be gained, the older waiter does profit by thus saying his prayers. Such a vision—of lost "everything" and of realized "nothing"—does not send him into Byronic heroics. We read instead that "he smiled and stood before a bar with a shining steam pressure coffee machine". He could smile and remain upright because he knew that the world and himself, even his prayer, were "nothing," and by that act of awareness could survive with dignity, could transcend "it."

This hyper-consciousness, of course, keeps him awake at night. Thus perhaps his definitive act of self-perspective is the observation, "After all, it is probably only insomnia. Many must have it." Calling his condition "insomnia" is an act of humility eliminating the last possibility of error, of assuming himself, by his consciousness, to be more than "nothing." Even as an act of reassurance, a whistling in the dark, it forestalls the dangers of pride by an admission of uncertainty even about the existence of "*nada*." It is an act of merciless self-consistency, thus liberating him from messianic responsibilities, and enabling him to continue to smile at himself and to keep that cafe open at night. The older waiter, then, can look at the world both ways—as a man of deep religious sensibility he can see the Nothingness of existence, and as a man who "knew it all was nada" he can make jokes and, above all, smile.

Perhaps belatedly, but at least on the evidence of imagery and characterization, we may now discuss the theme of the story. Most readers take the latter to be *nada*, making "A Clean, Well-Lighted Place," despite the title, a story about Nothingness and the pessimism and despair of the human response to it. This view ignores both the definition of *nada* inferable from the story and the nature of the old waiter's response to it.

Despite Hemingway's manipulation of the pronoun *it*, the reader must not confuse Nothingness with the responses it produces, nor the response of the older waiter with that of the old man. *Nada* is depicted primarily spatially, as an objective reality, out there beyond the light; it is a final hard fact of human existence, though "some lived in it and never felt it," e.g., the younger waiter. In addition, it becomes temporal with the older waiter's repetition of "*y pues nada*" before the prayer. Though Carlos Baker, with great sensitivity, calls it "a Something called Nothing which is so huge, terrible, overbearing, inevitable, and omnipresent that, once experienced it can never be forgotten," which "bulks like a Jungian Shadow,'' its mythic qualities are perhaps not even that well defined.

More importantly, the response of the old patron—the search for oblivion through drunkenness or suicide—is not the only one, and certainly not the one of the older waiter. John Killinger observes that ''the only entity truly capable of defying the encroachments of Nothingness is the individual,'' and Cleanth Brooks that ''the order and the light are supplied by *him*,'' the old waiter, the individual. Carrying this affirmation one step further, Wayne Booth notes ''a mood of bitterness against darkness combined with a determination to fight the darkness with light—if only the clean, well-lighted place of art itself.'' But, as we have seen, all the positive imagery, including light, is ironically undercut by the presence of a shadow side, and the ''darkness'' is counteracted on more levels than that simply of ''light.''

The older waiter in fact acts in various ways against Nothingness. He expresses solidarity with the old patron, and would willingly keep the cafe open as long as anyone wants it; he is instrumental in keeping the lights on. But his acquaintance with *nada* is intimate enough to keep him awake all night, every night; yet this hyper-awareness leads him neither toward self-destruction nor toward egocentricity. He can fuse religious sensibility with existential anxiety into a parodic prayer, after which he can smile. Turning off the light in the cafe and going home to bed is a daily act of courage done silently, without complaint. His sensitivity to places which make dignity possible gives us the verbal clue that his life is one of survival with dignity.

Thematically, then, the older waiter actively demonstrates that life against *nada* is achieved by awareness, sensitivity, human solidarity, ritual (verbal and physical), humor, and courage. Together these qualities make dignity, or, to use Jamesian terms, style or form; we encounter them also in the good bullfighters in *Death in the Afternoon*, which may amplify the theme of that book as well as aesthetic relevance. Such attributes also lead to a double vision and a mode of expression which may be called irony, a potent antidote to both despair and pride. The older waiter, against the heaviest odds, is a man in control.

''A Clean, Well-Lighted Place'' is, without cheating, a totally affirmative story, one of the very few in our literature. It assumes a world without meaning, life on the edge of the abyss, but that is not what it is about. It assumes a protagonist of acute awareness and minor characters of lesser consciousness, but it is not about that difference. It is, rather, a dramatization of the possibility, given the above conditions, of man continuing to act, to feel even for others, to think even about metaphysics, to create (with a smile), to control and thereby to humanize both himself and his environment. The older waiter is neither a hero nor a saint, but, to borrow from Camus, that more ambitious being, a man.

Source: Annette Benert, ''Survival through Irony: Hemingway's 'A Clean Well-Lighted Place,''' in *Studies In Short Fiction*, Vol. XI, No. 2, Spring, 1974, pp. 181–87.

Warren Bennett

In the following essay Bennett observes the dichotomy between confidence and despair and notes the irony that works throughout the story.

Interpretation of Hemingway's short story ''A Clean, Well-Lighted Place'' has always been confronted with the illogical dialogue sequence between the two waiters. Since analysis probably became stalled on the question of which waiter knew about the old man's attempted suicide, interpretation has tended to center on either the older waiter's *nada* prayer or the problem of the illogical sequence itself. The result seems to be a partial misinterpretation of the character of the younger waiter, a failure to see the wide play of irony in the story, and the absence of any interpretation of the story's ironic resolution.

However, before these latter matters can be successfully dealt with, the story's troubled dialogue must still be preliminarily considered. Scribner's claims that the dialogue inconsistency occurred when a slug of type was evidently misplaced in the first printing of the story in *Scribner's* magazine in 1933, and since reprint plates were made from that printing and not from the original manuscript, which is no longer extant to anyone's knowledge, the error was perpetuated until 1965. At that time Scribner's issued a new edition of The Short Stories of Ernest Hemingway and made an ''editorial'' correction in the illogical sequence because the dialogue dictated it.

All texts from 1933 to 1965:

''His niece looks after him.''

''I know. You said she cut him down.''

The 1965 text and all subsequent printings:

''His niece looks after him. You said she cut him down.''

''I know.''

This solved the problem of the illogical sequence, but because it gives the knowledge of the old man's attempted suicide to the older waiter instead of the younger waiter, it is contrary to some critical opinion and compatible with others. The correction, therefore, traded one kind of question for another kind: since Hemingway did not correct his own story during his lifetime, does that make the old text Hemingway's story and the new text his publisher's story? Should the critic use the old text or the new text?

In order to put my own interpretation on a firm footing, I hope to demonstrate, first of all, that even though no corrections were made in the story, it is still possible to determine that the older waiter is the one who knows about the old man's attempted suicide.

The structure of the story is based on a consistent polarity: "despair," characterized by depth of feeling and insight into the human condition, in opposition to "confidence," characterized by a lack of feeling and, therefore, a lack of insight. Each pole is seen as an attitude, or stance, in relation to Hemingway's *donnee*, which is a nihilistic concept of life: nothingness or *nada*. The spark which ignites the conflict of stances is the deaf old man who has tried to commit suicide and needs a clean, well-lighted cafe in which to stay late. The denouement is an irony of fate, presented by image and understatement, which will shatter "confidence" against the hard truth that "it [is] all a nothing and a man [is] nothing too."

The tension of the conflict is rendered almost exclusively through the dialogue of the two waiters, who are said to be of "two different kinds," and we can identify one waiter by tracing the use of the word "kill." When the younger waiter returns from taking the old man's brandy order, he says to the older waiter, "'I'm sleepy. I never get into bed before three o'clock. He should have *killed himself* last week'" (italics mine). Then when the younger waiter takes the brandy out to the old man, he says to him, "'You should have *killed yourself* last week'" (italics mine). Since there is no textual basis for transferring the younger waiter's mode of expression to the older waiter, the text clearly establishes that it is the younger waiter who asks for further information: "'What did he want to *kill himself* for?'" (italics mine). Consequently, it is the older waiter who knows the history of the old man and speaks the first line of dialogue in the story: "'Last week he tried to commit suicide.'"

> The scene--a prostitute and a soldier--is the epitome of a meaningless and chaotic world full of loopholes: an interwoven fabric of ironies punctured by nothingness."

This is supported by a structural pattern, utilizing verbal irony, which is repeated in three separate scenes—two formerly in question and one not in question. For the pattern to emerge clearly, it is necessary to look at the scenes in reverse order, beginning with the scene where the lines are not in question. The scene is the bodega where the older waiter stops for a drink.

"What's yours?" asked the barman. [Serious question.]

"Nada." [Verbal irony: the older waiter.]

"Otro loco mas," said the barman and turned away. [Dropping the subject.]

"A little cup," said the waiter. [Serious reply.]

The bodega barman, of course, must be equated with the younger waiter because he has an "unpolished" bar, equivalent to the younger waiter pouring into the old man's brandy glass until it "slopped over and ran down the stem." Also, the barman calls the older waiter "another crazy one," as the younger waiter has accused the older waiter of "talking nonsense." But for our purposes, the important aspect is the pattern: serious question, verbal irony by the older waiter, a dropping of the subject, and then a serious reply. The significant factor in the pattern is the older waiter's use of verbal irony in response to a serious question.

The complete pattern appears earlier in the story, in that exchange concerned with why they cut the old man down.

"Why did they do it?" [Serious question.]

"Fear for his soul." [Verbal irony: the older waiter.]

"How much money has he got?" [Dropping the subject; serious question.]

"He's got plenty." [Serious reply.]

The third scene is the first exchange between the two waiters, near the beginning of the story. The pattern here is abbreviated, repeating only the older waiter's use of verbal irony in response to a serious question. One waiter says the old man was in despair, and the other waiter asks,

"What about?" [Serious question.]

"Nothing." [Verbal irony: the older waiter.]

"How do you know it was nothing?" [Serious question.]

"He has plenty of money." [Verbal irony: the older waiter.]

In this last scene, the reply, "nothing," and the reply, "he has plenty of money," both carry an undertone of irony, regardless of which waiter speaks the lines. The irony is inherent in them as answers to the serious questions asked. For example, if the younger waiter answered that the old man was in despair about "nothing," the reply still carries the charge of double meaning, i.e., a serious meaning: there was, in fact, no apparent reason; *and* a malicious meaning: the reason seems ridiculous and unimportant to me: he was only feeling sorry for himself.

Since verbal irony is employed, we must look to the text for hard evidence of which waiter employs it as a mode of speaking, and that evidence is in the scene with the bodega barman. It is the *older* waiter who uses verbal irony; he even thinks ironically: "After all, he said to himself, it is probably only insomnia. Many must have it." There is no definite evidence, anywhere in the story, that the younger waiter has mastered such a manner of speaking, or thinking. On the contrary, the younger waiter is consistently serious and changes his form of address only once, "speaking with that omission of syntax stupid people employ when talking to drunken people or foreigners."

Once it has been established that the older waiter is the one who knows about the old man, it is then possible to see the characters of the two waiters in correct perspective.

Essentially, the younger waiter is not a "materialist," as critics, explicitly or implicitly, have tried to make him. Expressing interest in money and sex does not automatically relegate one to the pigeonhole labeled "materialist," which critics like to use in a pejorative sense, although it should not be so used. Materialism denotes a complex set of ideas, and to the extent that the story is held to have philosophical import, the philosophical senses of "materialism" must be recognized.

Briefly, a materialist is one who affirms matter as the only reality, or one who gives it an effective

priority. Looking at the two waiters in this light, it is the older waiter who holds the view which is most compatible with philosophic materialism, not the younger waiter.

It is better, undoubtedly, to avoid classifying the youngest waiter at all, than to misclassify him. The most we can do with the younger waiter is describe him, an effort which results in showing him to be something of a "type," the average individual, "in a hurry." He is self-interested and indulges himself with believing an hour is "'more to me than to him [the old man].'" He does not especially like work, and accuses the old man of having "'no regard for those who must work'"; nevertheless, he seems to accept it as economically necessary and is quite an efficient waiter, making sure the shutters are closed before he leaves. He is satisfied with his marriage and is eager to get home to his wife "waiting in bed" for him. He is a legalist in his attitude toward the soldier, although even when refusing to serve the old man, he does not "wish to be unjust. He was only in a hurry." He is no Christian zealot but accepts the church with its transcendent values, illustrated by his changing the subject to money when told the niece cut the old man down because of "fear for his soul." In short, he is one of those who have "confidence," or faith, in the established system in which they live. He has "'youth, confidence, and a job . . . everything.'" His job gives him a sense of economic success within the community. The institution of marriage has provided him with a "waiting" wife who satisfies the biological drive and gives him a sense of male effectiveness. His youth gives him a sense of life as infinite continuum, and the institution of the church confirms such immortality for him. "'I have confidence,'" he says, "'I'm all confidence,'" and as long as he has this confident faith in the value and permanence of these cultural structures, he has "everything."

The older waiter, on the other hand, is unable to muster such faith or confidence. He *is* a materialist and beyond the material there is "nothing." "Some lived in it and never felt it but he knew it all was nada y pues nada y nada y pues nada." The individual "cannot find anything to depend upon either within or outside himself." There is no a priori order or value system, either providential, natural, or social, on which man may intelligently depend and predict a future. "'No. I have never had confidence and I am not young.'" The material world, which includes the mental processes, is the only reality and has priority, but it is found lacking: life is a net of illusions. "'And what do you lack?'" asks the younger waiter. "'Everything but work,'" replies the older waiter. And even the ability to "work" has been taken from the old man, as it evidently was from Hemingway by July 2, 1961.

This profound, but masked "difference" between the two waiters is imbedded in the casual-appearing conversation about the old man. When the younger waiter asks, "'How do you know [the old man's despair was about] nothing,'" the reply, "'He has plenty of money,'" is more philosophically precise than an entire chapter of discursive contortions. *Nada* can be described only in terms of an opposite because to make some-thing out of nothing is not only incomprehensible but impossible. And "plenty of money" provides the most nearly perfect polar opposite to "nothing." The holes in a fish net are perceptible because of the net. When a man has the power of money and the plenty which it makes possible, it also makes the "lack," *nada*, that much more apparent and unbearable. "Plenty" intensifies what is lacking to the psychological breaking point. The old man's severe despair, and the serious despair of the older waiter, are not caused by some-thing, and are not *about* anything. Despair is a negation, a lack. The lack of life after death, the lack of a moral order governing the universe, the lack of trustworthy interpersonal relations, the lack of an ordering principle in the individual consciousness, the lack of the ability to work, and the lack, therefore, of even self-respect and dignity. The old man lacks any-thing to live *for*. "'It was a nothing he [the older waiter] knew too well.'"

However, to quit the story on the philosophical level is to leave the primary question of "confidence" or "despair" artistically unanswered. The younger waiter would go confidently home to his "waiting wife" and live happily ever after: a winner who takes everything. The older waiter's *nada* is "probably only insomnia" and will pass with daylight, which, if not a happy ending, is at least a very tolerable ending. This is essentially an uncommitted balance, which is where interpretation to date has left it.

But this is to understand only the "literal" ending of the story; that is, what happens to the older waiter after *he* leaves the cafe. It does not reveal what happens when the younger waiter arrives home. For this insight, which Hemingway refers to as the "real end," which may be "omitted" on the basis of his "new theory," it is necessary to go back into the story.

In the silence that takes place immediately following the older waiter's ironic "'He has plenty of money,'" A girl and a soldier went by in the street. The street light shone on the brass number on his collar. The girl wore no head covering and hurried beside him.

> Y.W. "The guard will pick him up," one waiter said.
>
> O.W. "What does it matter if he gets what he's after?"
>
> Y.W. "He had better get off the street now. The guard will get him. They went by five minutes ago."

The younger waiter emphasizes the military guards because to him they represent guardians of a culture in which one may be confident of success. He is not concerned about the soldier. Individual needs, whether they are the need of a girl or the need of a drink for a lonely old man, must be sacrificed to the punctualities of the job, the ignorant securities of rule and routine. The younger waiter wants everyone off the street, as he wants the old man out of the cafe. He wants to be off the streets himself, and is, in fact, also a kind of guard. "'No more tonight. Close now,'" he says to the old man and begins "pulling down the metal shutters."

But the older waiter does understand that agonizing lack in an individual: "'What does it matter if he gets what he's after?'" Company punishment will be minor compared to the anguish of being alone. Everything is a temporary stay against despair: a light for the night, another drink, relations with a girl. "'You can't tell,'" even the old man "'might be better with a wife.'"

The soldier's kinship with the older waiter and the old man is illustrated by the metaphor of light and something clean or polished. "The street light shone on the brass number on his collar." They are all of a "kind," the soldier as disillusioned with the military machine as the older waiter and the old man are disillusioned with the machine of the world. The soldier is not concerned about curfew as the older waiter is not concerned about closing the cafe on time, and the old man is not concerned about letting the cafe close. The soldier needs the sexual intoxication of this girl as the older waiter and the old man need a drink. The soldier is no more concerned about military regulations than the old man is concerned about financial regulations, and "would leave without paying" if he became too drunk. "As Hemingway once put it, 'There is honor among pickpockets and honor among whores. It is simply that the standards differ.'"

The scene—a prostitute and a soldier—is the epitome of a meaningless and chaotic world full of loopholes: an interwoven fabric of ironies punctured by nothingness. Everything is possible through love or aggression, but paradoxically nothing is permanent. There is a constant, desperate struggle against the coefficients of adversity. Living becomes a deadly affair, or conflict, essentially devoid of humor because everything is ultimately a ''dirty trick.''

This is the basis for the older waiter's not so funny ''joke'' later in the story. The younger waiter has just suggested that the old man could buy a bottle and drink at home, to which the older waiter replies, '''It's not the same.'''

> ''No, it is not,'' agreed the waiter with a wife.
>
> He did not wish to be unjust. He was only in a hurry.
>
> ''And you? You have no fear of going home before your usual hour?''
>
> ''Are you trying to insult me?''
>
> ''No, hombre, only to make a joke.''
>
> ''No,'' the waiter who was in a hurry said . . .
>
> ''I have confidence. I am all confidence.''

The joke is crucial and hinges directly on the scene with the girl and the soldier. Structurally and texturally they establish the love wound motif which is so dominant in Hemingway that it becomes the other side of the same psychic coin as the war wound. Through either the death of one of the partners or the inability of one partner to fulfill the promise of love—satisfy the other's needs—an individual is isolated and pushed to despair by the failure of the love alliance.

The complete working out of this motif is the ''real end'' which Hemingway omitted, and the phrase ''waiter with a wife'' preceding the joke, functions as a lens to bring into focus the catastrophe which the younger waiter will face. When the younger waiter goes home before his ''usual time,'' his wife will be gone, or perhaps, though at home in bed, engaged in another desperate relationship. The girl and the soldier appear again like ghosts, only this time the girl without a ''head covering,'' ironically ''hurrying,'' is suggestive of the younger waiter's wife.

The story now becomes superbly charged with dramatic as well as verbal irony. The younger waiter's confidence dissolves into tragic hubris, and his statements, such as '''I'm not lonely,''' are imbued with an impending doom that is near classic. Situations become ironically transferred. The old man's despair and loneliness without a wife, the older waiter's insomnia and need of light, the soldier's risk for temporary sexual meaning—all are now the younger waiter's future. At the very moment that he is playing the heartless and uncompromising judge, he is also reality's dupe and victim. Whatever he has said about the others may soon be said about him. And with equal irony, he has ''hurried'' to his own undoing. His all-confident intentions will be reversed. His recognition of another truth is imminent. The radical contingencies of life will have taught him the absurdity of the human condition, and the twist of events will topple him from his pinnacle of confidence into the phantasmagoria where the older waiter and the old man cling despairingly to their clean, well-lighted place. The younger waiter will become a new member of Hemingway's collection: *Winner Take Nothing*.

Source: Warren Bennett, ''Character, Irony, and Resolution in 'A Clean Well-Lighted Place,''' in *American Literature*, Vol. XLII, No. 1, March, 1970, pp. 70-79.

Sources

Bennett, Warren. ''Character, Irony, and Resolution in 'A Clean, Well-Lighted Place,''' in *America Literature*, Vol. XLII, March, 1970, pp. 70-79.

Lewis, Wyndham. ''The Dumb Ox: A Study of Ernest Hemingway,'' in *The American Review*, Vol. III, June, 1934, pp. 302, 312.

Perloff, Marjorie. ''Modernist Studies,'' in *Redrawing the Boundaries: The Transformation of English and American Studies*, edited by Stephen Greenblatt and Giles Gunn, New York: The Modern Language Association, 1992, pp. 154-178.

O'Connor, Frank. *The Lonely Voice: A Study of the Short Story*, Cleveland: World, 1963, pp. 156-69.

Further Reading

Fiedler, Leslie A. *Love and Death in the American Novel*, New York: Criterion Books, Inc., 1959.
   This is a classic in American literary criticism, and it contains a well-known chapter on gender and sexuality in Hemingway.

Hemingway, Ernest. ''The Nobel Prize Speech,'' in *Mark Twain Journal*, Vol. 11, Summer, 1962, p.10.
   Hemingway's acceptance speech.

Ross, Lillian. "How Do You Like It Now, Gentlemen?" in *The New Yorker*, May 13, 1950.

A bravura period piece written at the height of Hemingway's popularity.

Stanton, Edward F. *Hemingway and Spain: A Pursuit*, Seattle and London: University of Washington Press, 1989.

An examination of Hemingway's Spanish connection.

Wagner-Martin, Linda W. *Hemingway: A Collection of Critical Essays*, Cambridge: Cambridge University Press, 1987.

This is a recent reference work (bibliography) which provides a welcome overview of Hemingway criti-cism. By flipping to the 1980s and 1990s, students can easily review the latest trends in Hemingway criticism.

Weeks, Robert P. , ed. *Hemingway: A Collection of Critical Essays*, Englewood Cliffs: Prentice Hall, Inc., 1962.

A student of Hemingway will do well to look at this volume of early essay in order to get a sense of the history of Hemingway criticism.

Young, Philip. *Ernest Hemingway: A Reconsideration*, University Park: Pennsylvania State University Press, 1966.

An influential and innovative biographical study of Hemingway.

Death in Venice

Thomas Mann

1912

Death in Venice was first published in German as *Der Tod in Venedig* in the October and November 1912 issues of a literary magazine called *Rundschau* and in book form the following year. It was the most popular writing of Mann's early career and 18,000 copies were printed by the year's end. Immediate critical reception of the story centered on its sexual themes and dense, meticulously crafted prose. Some condemned the homosexual theme of the story but saw the ending as a moral judgment against the main character. Others condemned Mann's ending for treating homosexuality as in itself wrong and associating it with the disease of cholera.

The story was regarded as an extension of Mann's earlier work about the life and struggle of artists. While some thought the dense style was an echo of Flaubert's psychological mastery, others argued that the text lacked life or what D. H. Lawrence called organic energy and dynamism. In the decade after World War I, younger critics looked to *Death in Venice* as an epitome of German classical form and tended to avoid discussing its sexual themes. In 1930, the Knopf publishing house released the first English translation of the story in H. T. Lowe-Porter's *Stories of Three Decades*. When portions of Thomas Mann's private journals were first published in the late nineteen seventies, Mann's private writing about his homosexual feelings became public knowledge. Critics revisited the story, realizing the importance of the protagonist's sexual

conflict to the general themes of the story. Mann's story has not only immensely influenced German and Austrian writers (Herman Hesse, Gunter Grass, Thomas Bernhard) but many other world-renowned authors of the twentieth century including James Joyce and Doris Lessing.

Author Biography

Born on June 6, 1875, in Lubeck, Germany, Paul Thomas Mann became one of the twentieth century's greatest German novelists. His father was a successful businessman and senator who died when Thomas was sixteen. After his father's death, Mann inherited money on which he could rely as he began writing. At nineteen he published his first story (''Fallen'') while working as a clerk in an insurance company. Soon after this first writing success, he quit this job and enrolled in the University of Munich. Mann's early productivity is remarkable. By age twenty-eight (1903), he had published a major, critically acclaimed novel in *Buddenbrooks* and two volumes of short stories.

After pushing himself to the point of exhaustion while working on his next novel, *Royal Highness,* Mann took a break and traveled to Venice in 1907. After finishing up *Royal Highness* and starting yet another major novel in *Felix Krull,* Mann had to stop again after feeling very frustrated with its progress. While taking a break in 1911, Mann returned to Venice with his wife and wrote the short novella *Death in Venice,* published in 1912. *Felix Krull* (1954) would not be finished until shortly before his death.

When World War I broke out in 1914, Mann supported the royal government of William II, writing an essay defending Germany. However, the war disillusioned Mann to the idea of a mythic German past and he advocated establishing a republic and moved increasingly toward endorsing social democracy. Mann continued his writing career, publishing *The Magic Mountain* in 1924 and receiving the Nobel Prize for literature in 1929.

With the rise of Hitler to power in the early thirties, Mann was forced to leave Germany, living in Switzerland until he moved to the United States

and served as a professor at Princeton University in 1938. During the war, Mann continued to work on his tetralogy *Joseph and His Brothers.* While exiled, he lectured and wrote vehement condemnations of Hitler's National Socialist Party and remained politically engaged throughout the war. In 1936, Germany stripped Mann of his citizenship and he requested and was granted Czech citizenship. In 1940, Mann moved to California and worked for the Library of Congress. He also made anti-Nazi radio speeches for the England's BBC. In 1944, Mann took United States citizenship.

In 1952 after becoming increasingly concerned with McCarthyist paranoia, Mann returned to Europe and lived in Switzerland where he died in 1955. After leaving Germany before the war, he never returned to live there permanently. Mann intermittently worked on his last novel *Confessions of the Confidence Trickster Felix Krull* for over forty years before it was published in 1954.

Plot Summary

The story begins as Gustav von Aschenbach, an internationally renowned writer, leaves his house in Munich for a long walk on a spring day in early May. Gustav is ill at ease, having spent the morning frustrated with the difficult task of careful revision. Gustav finds himself staring into the cemetery while he waits for his train home. He sees at the door of the cemetery chapel a tall, thin man with a straw hat and red hair who seems to be traveling. Staring at the man, he is embarrassed when his gaze is directly returned. Curiosity and embarrassment spur Gustav to reflect suddenly on his life. His struggle as a writer has depended on strict discipline and embrace of his efforts as a sacred duty. While he has produced some nationally acclaimed writing, he remains faintly dissatisfied with his career. He decides that travel of his own might cure his restlessness and reinvigorate his writing. In the past, Gustav had thought of travel as a prescription for his chronic health problems. Planning this trip he eschews practical reasons in search for something ''strange and random'' and imagines an exotic, tropical climate as his destination.

After making arrangements to lease his summer house, Gustav first goes to a small Adriatic

Thomas Mann

island that he has heard talked about. The rain, lack of a sandy beach and provincial Austrian clientele at his hotel all conspire to drive him away, "haunted by an inner impulse" to find "somewhere incomparable," "a fantastic mutation of normal reality." His next stop is Venice.

The ferry ride from the island to Venice continues to deepen the anti-climax of Gustav's journey. He purchases a first-class ticket which isolates him from the jovial group of vacationing second-class passengers. Observing this group of vacationers, Gustav notices an old man who is pretending to be young by dying his mustache, wearing colorful

clothes, drinking and joking loudly with the younger revelers. This man's false youth, punctuated by his inebriated drooling and dislodged dentures, horrifies Gustav. When Gustav leaves the boat, disembarking with his ridiculously big trunk, Gustav directly faces the messily drunk, "dandified" old man who heckles him rudely.

Gustav's entrance to Venice is disappointing. He manages to reflect on select lines of poetry that should inspire him, but with minimal success. Not only is the weather gray but the gondolier whom he hires to take him to his hotel rudely ignores Gustav's instructions. The Venice of his youth seems to outshine pitilessly the impressions of his return. And, the shiny black of his gondola seems to remind him of a coffin. When he is dropped off at his destination he returns to pay his gondolier after getting change only to find that he has left. Gustav is told that the gondolier had no license and sneaked off in an attempt to avoid the police.

Gustav's hotel is Hotel des Bains on the small Venice island of Lido, where he is received with "obsequious obligingness." Although he is still disconcerted by his thoughts of the made-up old man and his renegade gondolier, his room is comfortable, he has a nice view of the beach and he begins to settle in. At dinner he enjoys observing the hotel clientele, seeing them in evening dress and listening to "the sounds of the major world languages mingled."

He suddenly notices a young Polish boy of about fourteen sitting with a governess and three young girls. The boy, whom Gustav overhears called Tadzio, strikes him as extraordinarily beautiful. Tadzio's hair, skin, nose and mouth combine in a picture of beauty that reminds Gustav of a "Greek sculpture" from "the noblest period." Gustav has never seen anything "in nature or in art" so "consummately beautiful." Gustav becomes obsessed with Tadzio, watching him and following him through the rest of the story. Despite the terrible Venetian weather, Gustav remains in Venice because of Tadzio.

While watching and remaining continuously if subtly aware of Tadzio's activities and wardrobe, Gustav attends to his mail, reads on the beach, ruminates on the worth of his life and reminisces about his previous visits to Venice. Foreshadowing the story's ending, Gustav remembers one visit when the "pallid overcast sky" drove him out of Venice in fear for his health.

His passionate observation of Tadzio on the beach, in the dining room or walking with his family in Venice, serve to highlight the melancholy confusion of Gustav's solitary reflection. Gustav seems to have reached a point when his aesthetic discipline threatens to erase him from life. Looking into the sea, he appreciates its sublime immensity as both negating the individual and as a statement of perfection in "nothingness." Tadzio becomes a focal point of Gustav's melancholy conflict. Tadzio's youth and his gender disconcert Gustav; however, through a language of classical Greek art Gustav struggles to understand, to control and to enjoy his adoration.

Venice itself continues to disappoint. At one point, after walking through throngs of people, avoiding beggars, enduring the stench of stale water and feeling feverish, he decides to leave for another location not far from Trieste. The next morning, he gets as far as the ferry station before grief over saying a final good-bye to Venice overcomes him. Through an oversight in his luggage, he is afforded an excuse to cancel his ticket from Venice and to return to his hotel. After his return, the weather improves and Gustav settles in for good, devoting "hours at a time to the contemplation and study of this exquisite phenomenon," Tadzio. Tadzio becomes Gustav's muse, igniting an erotic flame of prose with which Gustav attempts to "follow the lineaments of this [Tadzio's] body."

During his fourth week at Lido, the height of tourist season, Gustav notices that the hotel guests seem to be uncharacteristically diminishing instead of increasing. The hotel barber inadvertently alerts him that something is wrong by asking him if is not afraid of the sickness. When following Tadzio through the city, he notices euphemistic warnings to the local population about the weather causing gastric trouble. A shopkeeper tells him not to worry. Back at the hotel, German newspapers have articles warning of epidemic while the local newspapers and the hotel manager seem to be covering up the threat.

In the face of this threat, Gustav only worries that Tadzio will leave. The danger of illness even seems to increase his passion for Tadzio as he continues to stalk his movements, watching from afar and yearning to catch his eye. Although he keeps abreast of the severity of the problem and suspects a cover-up, he never tells Tadzio's family of the danger.

One night a group of street singers performs in the hotel garden. Throughout their acts Gustav furtively watches Tadzio. One singer is a particularly lean man with red hair and vaguely offends Gustav with his lascivious performance. Afterwards, as the performer passes his hat soliciting money, Gustav questions him about the sickness but the singer falsely reassures him. In the final song, the man's hysterical laughter disturbs Gustav.

The next day, Gustav learns the truth from an English clerk in a British travel agency. The deadly Asiatic cholera has infected Venice and there are increasing casualties being covered up daily. The city officials conceal and deny the epidemic in order to prevent loss of tourist revenue; but, a quarantine is imminent. After this direct revelation, Gustav commits himself to keeping quiet and not warning Tadzio's family. Instead, Gustav dreams of the ''stranger-god's'' arrival and an ensuing chaos that profoundly loosens social inhibitions. He dreams of men and women dressed in animal pelts, writhing, shrieking and moaning in a fiery glow. They cry out Tadzio's name. Gustav tries to assert a composed and dignified intellect but the orgiastic howling, lewd gestures and licentious hands prevail. In the shadow of ''the obscene symbol,'' Gustav surrenders in his dreams to ''the lascivious delirium of annihilation.''

In his waking state, Gustav's last gesture is to mask his aging body. He dyes his hair and puts on make-up to freshen his complexion. His last day of following Tadzio leaves him eating over-ripe strawberries and nodding off in feverish sleep as he sits in a public square waiting for Tadzio and his family to finish their sight-seeing appointment. He thinks his social position and artistic duty ludicrous as he concludes that artists are fated for the abyss of desire, capable only of ''self-debauchery.''

A few days later, Gustav learns that Tadzio's family is leaving. He goes to the beach to watch Tadzio for the last time. His last glimpse before he dies is of Tadzio. The world is respectably shocked to hear of Gustav's death.

Characters

Captain of Italian Boat

The unnamed captain of a ferry boat takes Gustav from the small island in the Adriatic Sea to Venice. He wears his cap askew, has a goat-beard and a slick business manner as he issues Gustav a ticket. He also seems anxious to take Gustav's money and speaks loudly and approvingly of Gustav's destination as if trying to prevent him from changing his mind.

English Travel Clerk

Young, with blue eyes, the clerk tells Gustav the story beneath the official denial—it is feared that the deadly Asiatic cholera has infected Venice.

Gondolier without a License

Going from the ferry dock to his hotel on Lido, Gustav employs a gondolier who talks to himself and refuses to follow Gustav's instructions. After

dropping Gustav off at his hotel, this gondolier leaves before being paid because he wants to avoid police who would fine him for not having a license.

Hotel Barber

A minor character who first mentions the epidemic to Gustav. Near the end of the story he also makes Gustav appear younger by dying his hair and making him up.

Hotel Manager at Lido

A soft-spoken, obsequious if courteous man with a black mustache. He is accustomed to placating his guests. When rumors of the Venetian epidemic and quarantine begin to circulate, he does not advertise the situation to his guests and even falsely reassures them.

Narrator

The story is told through an anonymous but nearly omniscient narrator.

Old Man Pretending To Be Young

On the ferry to Venice, Gustav notices an old man wearing a light yellow summer suit. The man is drinking and joking with a group of young vacationers. Gustav reviles him for his ludicrous attempt to appear young by using make-up and for his crude behavior after he is drunk.

Street Singer with Guitar

One night a group of street performers entertain in the hotel garden. One of these men is red-haired, lean and ''cadaverous in the face'' with a guitar, shoddy felt hat and a ''buffo-bartone character.'' He performs brazenly, lasciviously licking the corner of his mouth, and vaguely offends Gustav. Gustav questions him under his breath about the epidemic rumors and the singer reassures him.

Tadzio

A young Polish boy of fourteen traveling with his mother, governess and three sisters. Gustav sees him while staying in his Venetian hotel on Lido and becomes enraptured with his beauty. The boy wears his ''honey-colored'' hair in long ringlets, possesses a pale and graceful reserve as well as a perfect nose and mouth. As the story progresses, Tadzio seems to notice Gustav's ubiquitous presence, meeting his gaze at various times in the story. Tadzio, like Gustav, suffers from a weak constitution and

Gustav thinks that he will probably die young from exposure to the Venetian epidemic.

Traveling Man in the Graveyard

Briefly appearing at the very beginning of the story, he is a tall, thin, clean-shaven man with red hair who wears a straw hat. Gustav notices him standing at the door of a chapel in a graveyard across from which Gustav waits for his homeward train. Gustav realizes his great desire to travel after staring at this man who himself appears to be traveling.

Venice Shop Keeper

An incidental character who notices Gustav scanning euphemistic announcements about illness and reassures him, falsely, that it is all an exaggerated precaution and that Venice is safe.

Gustav von Aschenbach

Gustav is a famous writer who lives in Munich. His literary accomplishment earned him on his fiftieth birthday the stamp of royal German approval, a title of honorable nobleman. Born the son of a civil servant, he exercised incredible self-discipline to write himself into high national standing. In his mature works, Gustav appealed to a range of readers without sacrificing his reputation for rigorous artistic and intellectual standard. His famous works include an epic about the Prussian king Frederic the Great and a story appealing to the younger generation entitled ''A Man of Misery.'' Despite his critical and popular acclaim, Gustav is vaguely unsatisfied with his career.

Although both a talented and committed writer, Gustav lacks physical strength. This weakness made it necessary for him to be schooled at home as a boy and later in life for him to think of travel as an antidote to health difficulties. In the story, he makes an uncharacteristic decision to escape his writerly duty and seek a traveling experience that is ''strange and random.''

Gustav has a daughter who is married and whom he rarely sees. He had married young although his wife passed away after a ''short period of happiness.'' In general, Gustav seems a lonely man resigned to accepting the consequences of solitary artistic struggle.

In Venice, Gustav's feelings of self-doubt and loneliness culminate in his unexpected obsession

Media Adaptations

- *Death in Venice* was adapted into a movie by the Luchino Visconti in 1971 and released by Warner Brothers.

- The story was also was also turned into the opera *Death in Venice* by Benjamin Britten and Myfanwy Piper in 1973.

with a young boy named Tadzio. In trying to account for his feelings, Gustav wrestles with the consciousness of his own inevitable death and of the worth of art in the modern world.

Themes

Death

The title reflects the importance of death to this novella. On a literal level, Gustav dies. There are simultaneous levels of symbolic meaning that are important. First, before Gustav actually dies, he sees death around him, in Venice's dreary weather, in the black-coffin gondola he takes to Lido, in the ''lean,'' cadaverous body of the brazen singer and in the newspapers that report the cholera's spread. His motivation to travel is a recognition of his own flagging energy and a sense of mortality. Throughout, Gustav rationalizes his own literal death by considering the immortality of his artistic production.

Gustav's personal attempts to come to terms with death reflects a broader commentary on the state of the world and of German culture. As Gustav approaches his death, his art means very little to him. Instead, he feels himself surrendering to the temporary pleasure of following a young boy after whom he is lusting. Gustav's ultimate inability to warn Tadzio and his family is not only selfish but despicable, showing no regard for Tadzio as a living human being. What good is art in the face of death? Is art a mask that inevitably fails to disguise one's mortality?

Topics for Further Study

- Why is the cholera given such a specific and dramatic history in the story? Consider how the story uses disease as a metaphor. In what ways does the story personify cholera and why? Are there other examples of diseases that have taken on meaning beyond their actual existence?

- Do you think that Gustav knows he is about to die? Do you think he suspects that he might be sick? Is Gustav's judgment impeded by his state of health? Retrace Gustav's steps and decide what impact, if any, his state of health has on his behavior in Venice.

- How many conversations does Gustav have in the course of the story? What is the nature of his interaction with people? When Gustav sees the traveling stranger at the beginning, why does he not say hello instead of turning away and being embarrassed? Who is the person Gustav trusts most in the story and why?

- What kind of impression does Gustav make on people? What traits would stand out to people as he sits on the beach? What is running through the hotel manager's head as he speaks to Gustav? What does Tadzio think about Gustav?

- What is Gustav's definition of art? Does he believe that art is a democratic institution in which anyone can participate? In his estimation, who becomes an artist?

Death in Venice appeared in the shadow of the Great War when trench warfare raised death to a horrifying scale. Art, politics and religion all failed to stop this crisis. Gustav's personal death as an artist might reach to foreshadow the failure of art to prevent the carnage of war.

But although death is a profoundly sad even if inevitable experience, the novel also insists that life depends on death. Gustav's artistic energy depends on his rumination and contemplation of death. A sense of mortality enables youth to be beautiful and meaning seems to depend on contemplating the mixture of extremes rather than life or death in isolation.

Guilt or Innocence

Gustav makes a series of decisions that make him seem increasingly corrupt as a moral agent. His admiration and love of Tadzio is potentially a good thing; however, Gustav's behavior proves him callously selfish. His initial notice of Tadzio is harmless and even his strangely pleasurable observation that Tadzio looks sickly may be an embarrassment but does not involve him in the boy's well-being. However, his perpetual watch and stalking of Tadzio make his interest potentially annoying and threaten-

ing. Gustav sees Tadzio as a perfect model or pristine statue and is unable to acknowledge him as a human being. When he deliberately withholds information from Tadzio's family, Gustav knows he could be endangering the boy's life. In the end, Gustav cares more about his own infatuation with the boy than he cares about the boy as a human being.

The novel moves from posing questions regarding Gustav's responsibility as an adult who is infatuated with a boy to illustrating Gustav's irresponsible and even despicable behavior. While life in Gustav's world seems to be about the struggle between opposing extremes—old and young, nature and beauty, waste and productivity, life and art, lust and self control—Gustav loses his sense of balance and opts for a pitifully selfish extreme.

Sex

Gustav's infatuation with Tadzio is an important but complex theme of the story. On one level, Mann questions the boundaries of sexual feelings. As a great artist with the wisdom of many years, Gustav challenges the ideas that desire only operates heterosexually. His reflections on classic Greek art and on artists who wrote about homosexual or gay desire creates a literary history that acknowledged men loved other men and not just women. Mann's character makes particular sense given the historical period in which he was writing (see Historical Context below).

Although part of Gustav's wisdom may be his ability to see a bigger picture regarding sexual identity, on another level Gustav's sexual desire is expressed in a very disturbing fashion. Gustav seems to be a deeply frustrated person, incapable of intimacy with anyone, male or female. Especially disturbing is Tadzio's youth and Gustav's inability to communicate with anyone around him. His desire for Tadzio turns deplorable as he stalks the boy through the city and preys on him by not warning his mother of the epidemic. Perhaps Gustav has internalized the prejudices of the time—religious mandates that called homosexually sinful and medical pronouncements that declared it sick. While he is intellectually capable of imagining same-sex desire he is emotionally incapable of responding in a responsible and adult fashion. Gustav's art may allow him to idealize his feelings but by not considering Tadzio as a separate human being, Gustav does harm.

Alienation and Loneliness

There are reasons that so few characters have names in this story. Following a life of disciplined ritual that promotes his writing, Gustav seems to have isolated himself from people around him. His wife is dead, he has no friends, only those who work for him, and his married daughter is not close to him. Even in his own town he walks solitary. As a tourist in Venice, he knows no one and no one knows him.

He makes little effort to socialize with people, speaking only to extract information or to make arrangements for his care. Tadzio's last name is never even mentioned. Gustav is unable to bring himself to speak with Tadzio or Tadzio's mother, even to warn them about the epidemic. The strength of his passionate infatuation with Tadzio might be a gauge of his profound loneliness. Further, it seems inconceivable for Gustav to discuss his feelings with anyone in an attempt to understand them. Instead, Gustav bottles up his desire in private reflection.

Artists and Society

A central tension in the novel is the importance of Gustav's art to the world. While he has been

honored by the German nation for his important works, he remains dissatisfied with his life. Before he dies, Gustav seems to dismiss his entire life of disciplined living and artistic productivity in favor of his lustful pursuit of Tadzio's image. Despite this dismissal, Gustav experiences his personal life through a filter of aesthetic reference and imagery. Are artists trapped in their own world? Can artists claim a political significance to their work? Has Gustav sacrificed a fulfilling life experience for a world of art? Is the problem art itself or the attitudes with which people create and experience it?

Style

Narrator

The story is told by a third person narrator with limited omniscience. The narrator tells the reader nearly everything in Gustav's head but the perspective is limited to Gustav as the center of perspective and intelligence. Mann utilizes free indirect discourse to not only tell the reader what the protagonist thinks but to show the reader his view of the world as well as his impressions and emotions. The narrator's discourse is free because there is not explicit reference to a narrator as the communicating agent; the narrator's discourse is indirect in coloring the facts and things of the world with Gustav's mood and opinion. Finally, the narrator ties Gustav's consciousness into broader considerations of the historical time period.

Setting

The story takes place in 1911 as tensions between Germany and France foreshadowed the coming world war. Gustav's initial decision to travel occurs to him as he walks in his home city of Munich. From Munich the story briefly shifts to a small island in the Adriatic, to a ferry boat and finally to Venice where most of it takes place and where it ends. Gustav is a man past his prime in life and contemplating his end. He reminisces about his life and feels faintly unsatisfied and lonely. His most personal doubts about his life use artistic metaphors, figures and characters as a point of reference.

Structure

Like a typical Greek tragedy, the story is divided into five parts. While the Greek tragedy is a performed as a play, allowing the audience to see the rise and fall of the dramatic hero, Mann presents his hero in a novel. The audience may be a reader, but Gustav's fall is a familiar tragic pattern. In the final, fifth act of a tragedy, the events plunge the hero quickly and dramatically to destruction. The hero recognizes his misperception and shares with his audience a sense of his real predicament. The tragedy's final act simultaneously sacrifices the hero and allows that hero to see and even understand his destruction. The audience witnesses both a downfall and the doomed hero's supreme knowledge of the meaning of this downfall. Mann was heavily influenced by the thinking of Friedrich Nietzsche who wrote *The Birth of Tragedy* (1872 and 1886), arguing that individual and social existence depended on struggle between opposing extremes, between order and chaos. In the end, chaos always overwhelmed the individual ability to enforce order; however, the individual's true strength came in laughing at inevitable defeat and in facing directly the inevitability of tragedy.

Symbol, Images

While images of death are prevalent, Mann most thoroughly deploys references to classical Greek and European art. These references are symbols of at least two simultaneous meanings. First, references to classical art demonstrate the idea of art's immortality. By reaching back thousands of years to Plato, Gustav elevates his personal reflections and his artistic production to space of meaning that transcends time, place and people. The immortality of art clashes with Gustav's realization of his ebbing mortality.

Second, Mann's references to Greek art develop a theme of homosexual love and sexual desire. In addition to Greek art, Mann invokes images that were famous for displaying men's bodies in erotic fashion, such as the naked and arrow-pierced body of St. Sebastien. By simultaneously referencing the immortality of art and the socially transgressive power of homosexuality, Mann depicts Gustav and by extension European culture as mired in contradiction, paying homage to empty ideals that have lost their original meaning.

Historical Context

Prelude to World War I

Germany's Second Reich existed from 1871 to 1914 as an empire led by William I and, after the resignation of Bismarck in 1890, William II. The Second Reich was composed of many smaller regions. In the new Germany, William II frustrated attempts to establish a parliament. Working class movements that promoted unions or socialism were crushed by the force of a king's authority backed by the military's force. Through William II, the military, wealthy aristocrats and industrialists were served best. Non-Germans—including the Polish, Slavs, and French—were seen as inferior and as not belonging in the German nation. Germany increased their army to its largest to that point in history, 870,000. Industrial production skyrocketed. Germany began to look to extend its power beyond continental Europe.

Germany's rise in power was regarded as a threat by other countries, especially England and France; the 1800s had been filled with mean wars of empire and conquest. When Mann wrote his story, Europe was divided into two camps, the Triple Alliance (Austria-Hungary, Germany, Italy) and Triple Entente (England, France, Russia), and relations between these countries were very tense. There were a few crises that threatened to begin small and to proliferate antagonism, dragging the two sides into continental and eventual world war.

Moroccan Crises of 1905 and 1911

The first line of the story most likely refers to the Moroccan Crisis of 1911 between Germany and France. Gustav goes for a walk on a spring afternoon in "19_" when "so grave a threat seemed to hang over the peace of Europe." The North African country of Morocco was strategically important to European imperial interests because it sits on the edge of the Atlantic Ocean and Mediterranean Sea. In 1905, France and England agreed to give Morocco to France; Germany strenuously objected and declared Morocco to be a free state. After an international meeting, France was allowed to control the Moroccan police force and bank. In 1911, France tried to send troops into Morocco to quell an uprising. Germany objected and brought in a gunship, the *Panther*. After much tension and threat of war, France bought Germany off by giving them part of the French Congo.

Balkan Wars, 1912-13

Serbia, Bulgaria, Greece and Montenegro declared war on Turkey. Russia backed the Serbian efforts to expand, hoping that Serbia would gain a seaport to the Adriatic Sea (coincidentally, an "Adriatic island" is the site of Gustav's first hotel resi-

Compare & Contrast

- **1912-13:** Serbia, Bulgaria, Greece and Montenegro declare war on Turkey. Russia supports the Serbian efforts to expand. Austria-Hungary counter Serbian aggression. Albania is created in partial satisfaction of Serbian demands. Serbia, Greece, Rumania, Montenegro and Turkey then move on Bulgaria.

1999: United States-led NATO (North Atlantic Treaty Organization) forces begin Operation Allied Force, bombing the Balkan republic of Serbia in attempt to prevent Serbia's killing of ethnic Albanians in the Serbian province of Kossovo. Italy, a NATO country, is the staging ground for U. S. air forces.

- **1910:** By early in the century, six waves of epidemic Cholera (*Vibrio Cholerae*) had broken out in the world. Cholera is a micro-organism that destroys the intestinal tract, causing severe diarrhea and death by dehydration. Death can occur within twenty-four hours of initial symptoms. There was no effective treatment for cholera.

1999: The most recent Cholera epidemics broke out in Central and South America (1991, 1992, 1993) after a 100-year hiatus, and in Bangladesh (1992). Thousands died in each wave of cholera infection. In the United States there are very few cases of cholera. Treatments today include tetracycline, which can help the body retain fluid. There is also a temporary vaccine that lasts for six months but it is not 100% effective. There remains no cure for cholera.

---

dence). Austria-Hungary opposed this Serbian aggression. To stem the conflict, Albania was created and other Serbian demands satisfied. Soon after, Serbia, Greece, Rumania, Montenegro and Turkey moved on Bulgaria. In these conflicts, peace was maintained by Germany curbing the Austrians and Great Britain the Russians.

However, that peace did not last for long. In 1914, the Austrian Archduke Franz Ferdinand was assassinated in Sarajevo, Bosnia-Herzegovina. Although aware of it, the Bosnian government had not stopped the plot. Austria, backed by Germany, partially mobilized against Bosnia. Russia responded and the Triple Entente and Triple Alliance faced off in world war.

Medicalization of Sexuality

Much of Mann's novel refers to an historical time of classical Greek culture when sexuality was thought of very differently. In Greece, a person was not as strictly categorized according to whom they found sexually attractive. The Greek god Zeus lusted after his wine-pourer Ganymede who was an adolescent boy. Alexander the Great preferred men to women. Plato, like most of Greece, considered the relationship between an older man and a younger boy to be a motivation to truth and beauty. Despite an acceptance of sexual interest between males, no one was considered ''a homosexual'' or ''a heterosexual.'' Sexual desire was considered a changing aspect of one's life instead of an inherent and static characteristic.

In the Middle Ages, as Christianity spread across Europe, Christian scholars like St. Augustine and Thomas Aquinas targeted earthly concerns—money, social status and sexual pleasure for example—as not only a distraction to the spiritual world but sinful. While sex was recognized as necessary in having children, gaining pleasure from sex was frowned upon. Sexual activity that could not produce children was labeled ''sodomy'' and considered a sin of the flesh which offended God. But, even in the middle ages, sexual behavior did not make someone into a type of person.

The word ''homosexual'' was coined in Germany in the last third of the nineteenth century and named a category of person based on the specific kind of sexual behavior they practiced. The Oxford English Dictionary lists its first usage in 1892 when C. B. Chaddock translated from German Krafft-Ebing's book *Psychopathia Sexualis*. Krafft-Ebing used science to study people's sexual behavior. As a result, he hoped to recognize types of people. The same type of science hoped to recognize criminals by examining their facial types. Although much of the science that attempted to define types of people has been discredited, many gay men and women paid heavy prices in courts of law and public opinion. In 1895, Oscar Wilde's imprisonment was perhaps the best symbol of the legal vulnerability involved in male-to-male relations.

Today, we have inherited terms that continue to categorize people by their sexual behavior (homosexual, heterosexual, gay, lesbian). Even though these terms are prevalent, it is difficult to understand people's lives based on such clear-cut categories. Gustav seems to have an appreciation for the classical Greek history when love between men was celebrated. He also seems to have a sense of religious principle that demands he work and shun earthly enjoyment. Further, Gustav was married and had a family when a younger man. Mann's story is not about a "homosexual" but about the complex and passionate blend of an artist's private feelings, of love for art, of loneliness, of realization of death, and the physical and intellectual dimensions of sexual desire.

Influence of German philosophers Arthur Schopenhauer and Friederich Nietzsche

The philosophic writings of the nineteenth and early twentieth century matched the social turmoil and desperation. Arthur Shopenhauer (1788-1860) and Friedrich Nietzsche (1844-1900) were German philosophers whose ideas suffuse Mann's story. Schopenhauer's most famous work was entitled *The World as Will and Idea*, a pessimistic view on life that characterized life as a battle between the will and the world. Schopenhauer argued that individuals' wills ultimately failed; this caused him to advocate a necessary renunciation of the world. Nietzsche's book *The Birth of Tragedy* (1872) influenced Mann. Of particular interest was Nietzsche's idea that both individual life and civilization in general relied on the crucial tension between the disciplined structure of one's moral and intellectual architecture (masculine Apollonian will) and the

irrational chaos of unregulateable urges (feminine Dionysian desire).

Artistic Movements: from the Nineteenth to the Twentieth Century

The social turmoil from the later half of the nineteenth to the turn of the twentieth century generated many artistic movements that attempted to understand the world. Some of these movements contradicted each other. Some thought art should be a statement of "realism," documenting the social context of individual experience, focusing on the psychological dimension of people's lives, and presenting the not-so-pretty struggles of existing in a quickly changing economy of industrial production. Others rejected reality, using art as a space in which to aspire toward a perfection that left the contaminating world behind. By cutting art from "real" life, artists protested the pressure of economic conditions on artistic expression. Movements like "art for art's sake" or the "decadent" movement were controversial even if they eschewed association with real-world politics and industrial systems.

Critical Overview

The first English version of the story was published in 1930, translated by H. T. Lowe-Porter. In 1970 Kenneth Burke published another translation and in 1988 David Luke a third. The most recent translation (1994) is Clayton Koelb's for the Norton Critical Edition of the story which "[offers] North American students a text that strives to say as close to Mann's German as one can without straining the norms of American English." There is not clear consensus on which translation is best.

Critical treatment of Mann's novella is extensive, written in German, English, French, Russian and many other languages. In 1992, the Modern Language Association (MLA) published results from a survey of approximately ninety university professors who teach the text. *Approaches to Teaching Mann's "Death in Venice" and Other Short Fiction* (edited by Jeffrey B. Berlin) outlines various teaching strategies and critical materials, targeting an advanced audience who perhaps are reading German texts in addition to the English translation. Berlin's book provides a wealth of critical recommendations, an overview of important critical trends and a selection of critical essays that speak to historical perspective; influences on Mann (Nietzsche, Wagner, Schopenhauer); the development of a Modernist literary tradition and the decline of the Decadent literary movement; the advent of psychoanalysis as well as conflicts of gender and sexual identity. The 1994 Norton Critical Edition offers a new translation as well as both representative and accessible selections from essays and Mann's source material. Finally, T. J. Reed's *Death in Venice: Making and Unmaking a Master* (1994) for Twayne's Masterworks Series provides a basic and clear overview of the text, outlining the historical context, suggesting readings of the story and excerpting Mann's source material. Reed is himself an internationally acclaimed scholar on Mann and his book is a good beginning point that succinctly and directly provides important context. These are all excellent places to begin a consideration of the story's critical history.

The most important critical treatments of the story would have to include T. J. Reed's *Thomas Mann: The Uses of Tradition* (1974) which studies Mann's work in relation to German literary and political history. Although it does not focus only on *Death in Venice*, Reed gives the reader a clear picture of how to fit Mann and the story into the historical, artistic, and intellectual movements of the late-nineteenth and early-twentieth centuries. Esther H. Leser's *Thomas Mann's Short Fiction: An Intellectual Biography* (1988) provides similarly clear discussion of the intellectual and historical contexts of Mann's stories. For a theoretically complex analysis of Mann's style that uses contemporary literary theory see Geoffrey Harpham's ''Metaphor, Marginality, and Parody in *Death in Venice*,'' in his *On the Grotesque: Strategies of Contradiction in Art and Literature*, Princeton: Princeton University Press, 1982, p. 122-45.

The story's initial reception registered Mann as an important writer even if criticizing the novella for being too convoluted or for its sexual theme. In 1913, the English writer D. H. Lawrence derided the story for being so carefully designed that it lacked a feel for real life. In Germany, one contemporary poet complained that Mann had rendered an unjustifiably ugly picture of Greek art and Greek love. After World War I, younger artists in Germany admired the classical tone and references of the novella. In a world of artistic experiment, Mann's novel provided both an example and self-conscious critique of a German literary tradition. As Mann

Gondolas near Bridge of Sighs in Venice.

achieved international acclaim for the novella, critics commented on his virtuosity while minimizing the importance of sexual themes.

Since its publication, Mann's story has been reinvented by critics. This reinvention has continued in other mediums than print as Luchino Visconti's movie (1971), and Behnamin Britten and Myfanwy Piper's opera version (1973) demonstrate. While homosexuality or gay desire had been written about from the story's first appearance, the publication of Mann's private journals in the late seventies and Visconti's film contributed to motivating reassessments of sexuality to the novella's message. See "Why is Tadzio a Boy? Perspectives on Homoeroticism in *Death in Venice*," in *Death in Venice*, Norton Critical Edition, pp. 207-232; Ignace Feuerlicht's "Thomas Mann and Homoeroticism," in *Germanic Review*, Vol. 57, 1982, pp. 89-97; and, sections in Reed's 1994 overview of the story, specifically "Homosexuality: Greece versus Wilhelmine Germany," pp. 80-90.

The relationship of the story to developments of psychology and to Freudian pschyoanalysis is complex. For a basic overview see Jeffrey Berlin's "Psychoanalysis, Freud, and Thomas Mann" (in the MLA series, 1992). Earlier, overviews such Frederick J. Beharriell's "Psychology in the Early Works of Thomas Mann," *PMLA*, Vol. 77, 1962, pp. 148-55, and Andre von Gronicka's "'Myth plus Psychology': A Style Analysis of *Death in Venice*," in *Germanic Review*, Vol. 31, 1956, pp. 191-205 offer an instructive comparison to more recent accounts such as Dorrit Cohn's "The Second Author of *Der Tod in Venedig*," in *Critical Essays on Thomas Mann*, edited by Inta M. Ezergailis, Boston: G. K. Hall, 1988, pp. 124-43 and in the Norton Critical Edition. In general, the later accounts of Mann's relationship to Freud and psychology are more circumspect, emphasizing the ways in which Mann struggled against a merely psychological explanation through his development of artistic form. In addition to Freud, there is work on the connection between Mann and the psychology of Jung (Hunter G. Hannum, "Archetypal Echoes in Mann's *Death in Venice*," in *Psychological Perspectives: A Jungian Review*, Vol. 5, 1974, pp. 48-59. In addition to psychology, there is a book-length study on Mann's relationship to the sociological thought of his contemporary Max Weber; see Harvey Goldman's *Max Weber and Thomas Mann: Calling and the Shaping of the Self*, Berkeley: University of California Press, 1988.

On the influence of Nietzsche on Mann see R. A. Nichol's *Nietzsche in the Early Works of Thomas Mann*, Los Angeles and Berkeley, 1955. The Norton Critical Edition includes a translation of part of Manfred Dierks' *Studien zu Mythos und Psychologie bei Thomas Mann* (1972). The excerpt "Nietzsche' *Birth of Tragedy* and Mann's *Death in Venice* offers a clear application of Nietzsche's ideas of the Appollonian and Dionysian pressures on the story's concept of art.

Initially, the story was read in context of the economic climate of Germany before and after World War I. Consequently, his reading public in Germany emphasized Mann's relationship to a noble German social tradition and revival of a classical aesthetic tradition. After the war, the story was seen as a foundation for a new classical German literature. As Europe rebuilt itself after World War II and a refurbished capitalism made Europe wealthy again, literary critics began to scrutinize Gustav's relation to business and the market place. Is art a separate sphere if it relies on the overall economic well-being of a nation? See Dominick La Capra's "Mann's *Death in Venice*: An Allegory of Reading," in *History, Politics and the Novel*, Ithaca: Cornell University Press, 1987, pp. 111-28; and, Tom Hayes and Lee Quinby's "The Aporia of Bourgeois Art: Desire in Thomas Mann's *Death in Venice*," in *Criticism*, Vol. 31, 1990, pp. 159-77.

Criticism

Kendall Johnson

Johnson teaches American literature at the University of Pennsylvania, where he recently received his Ph.D. Johnson discusses the "intersections of social attitudes regarding work, sexuality and cultural identity."

"The Protestant Ethic and the Spirit of Sexuality: Artistic Nationalism in Thomas Mann's Death in Venice*"*

Gustav von Aschenbach's lonely demise in Venice is a key element in the story's broader consideration of German culture and Western civilization as it existed in 1912, on the brink of world war. By analyzing Gustav's personal fall from the status of a great author, one notices more general intersections of social attitudes regarding work, sexuality and cultural identity. The full force of the novel's message depends on recognizing these intersections, examining why Gustav's sense of authorial mission erodes in Venice as he trips after a young Polish boy, brooding over the oppressive sirocco and finally fearing the Asiatic cholera that waits for him as if a tiger crouching in a bamboo thicket.

Thomas Mann's story was published just seven years after the German sociologist Max Weber's *The Protestant Ethic and the Spirit of Capitalism* (1905). Both Mann and Weber share observations about society that regard the most spiritually fulfilling life as a *Beruf*, a vocation through which one

What Do I Read Next?

- *The Magic Mountain* (1924) is one of Mann's most well-known and popular novels.

- Robert Musil's *The Man Without Qualities* (1930) is set in Vienna, Austria, in the days before World War I. Ulrich watches helplessly as the Austro-Hungarian Empire speeds toward war.

- *Jacob's Room* by Virginia Woolf was written in 1922 but remembers the time in England before the war's outbreak. It follows the life of young Jacob Flanders as he goes to Cambridge and then to war. In the end, who is Jacob Flanders?

- *The Good Soldier* (1915) by Ford Maddox Ford is the story of an American, John Dowell. Dowell travels Europe with his sick wife and a British couple whose public facade of a happy marriage hides the anguish of infidelity. Dowell is the story's narrator, pathetically remembering bits and pieces of his life, trying to understand what has happened to him. The personal tensions parallel a deep rift in Europe that began in the 1500s with the Protestant reformation in Germany.

- *The Birth of Tragedy* (1872, 1886) by Friederich Nietzsche is not only an inspiration to Mann but an exciting and very readable analysis of history. Nietzsche targets the seemingly placid works of Greek art and myth and turns them inside out, revealing a dynamic human struggle between chaos and order—a struggle that motivates not only art but religion and history.

---

participates in society by responding to a spiritual calling. A vocation is very different than a job or even a career. One "does" a job for a paycheck. A career is a supposedly more respectable endeavor in which one's personal talent and efforts are involved in the performance of a skill or knowledge. When a job turns into a career it implies more than monetary exchange but a life course, weaving together social prestige, money and professional accomplishment. A vocation or calling implies yet another dimension; a vocation is a career raised to the spiritual level, pursued in response to a moral duty that transcends considerations of money and even social prestige. Through a *Beruf* an individual finds spiritual completion in her or his community.

Literary art is Gustav's vocation. Reading and writing is not merely something to be enjoyed either as entertainment or as an element of instruction but is a living principle and priceless ideal. Gustav's idea of art carries a power that may be best understood only through a comparison with religion; his art not only carries a message but prescribes a regiment of life; it is not only a vehicle of communication or self-expression but also molds the self in a belief system and world view. Gustav spends his years in service of this ideal. His life is a series of days regimented by Spartan efficiency, begun early "by dashing cold water over his chest and back." Writing is a ritual, complete with candles lit at the head of his manuscript.

Although he "offers up" "the strength he had gathered during sleep," it is important to realize that this is not a religious moment. Weber best describes the work ethic Gustav brings to his writing. He argues that religious Protestantism in Germany, beginning with Luther in the 1500s and spreading throughout Europe, reorganized the way in which people thought of themselves. In basic terms, Protestantism argued against the Catholic system in which individuals related to God through the intercession of a priest; instead, Protestants felt that the best relationship to God was personal: corrupt priests and ornate churches were merely distractions to individual salvation. Weber noticed that as Protestantism chipped away at a Catholic social system, modern patterns of work in a capitalistic economic system emerged. People thought of themselves as individuals and were employed as

> **" Gustav's art negotiates a blend of what Mann encodes as a fundamentally biological ethnic conflict between disciplined will and 'fiery' impulse."**

such. These individuals were paid flexible currency (money) for daily work on an hourly basis. Using Benjamin Franklin as his model, Weber pointed out that Franklin's success in the world depended on a remarkable emphasis on individuality. Franklin became rich by converting religious principles of sacrifice into tactics of personal efficiency with which he accumulated worldly wealth: and an individual's time became equal to money. By deflecting spirituality into one's daily efforts in the marketplace, work becomes a goal in itself. Work can be regarded, then, as not just a job or a self-serving career but a vocation—a duty that is self-fulfilling in a spiritual way. Franklin's secularization of religious piety is something Gustav shares; however, instead of banking money, Gustav borrows a religious aura from art, specifically from the Greeks. In Greece, however, the morality and attitudes toward work, toward the spirit, toward the body and toward sexuality are all very different and in conflict with a system based on Christian morality.

In *The Birth of Tragedy out of the Spirit of Music* (1872), a book that Thomas Mann admired, Friedrich Nietzsche writes about Greek tragedy to destabilize the idea of a static classical form. Behind the pristine and inherited forms of classical art—specifically the dramatic form of tragedy—Nietzsche locates a seething conflict between the Apollonian will and Dionysion chaos. Apollo is the god of sculpture, representing ''the calm repose of the man wrapped up in'' secure individuality, who is able to sit quietly in the midst of the world's torment and to perceive beauty. The opposing Dionysius is the god of music, representing an intoxicating energy that destroys individual sense of self. According to Nietzsche, the Greek conflict between Apollo and Dionysius was radically altered when Christianity defined the physical world as a fallen state, forever separate from divine spirituality, forever

secular and sinful. Like Gustav, Nietzsche's artist produces art by mediating between these conflicting energies; but, unlike Gustav, the Greek artist had not internalized a Christian religious system that regarded non- procreative sexuality and homosexuality as spiritually depraved and sinful.

In the 1886 preface to *The Birth of Tragedy*, Nietzsche explains that his reflection on Greece was motivated by the tumult of the Franco-Prussian War of 1870-1. The focus of Nietzsche's text is remarkably broad, speaking about developments in human history that span over two thousands years. By infusing his story with Nietzschean allusions, Mann implicitly raises Germany to the classical status of Greece; however, Gustav lends particular insight on the ways in which German culture is very different than that of the Greek of antiquity. While Gustav reaches to retain the sublime conflicts outlined by Nietzsche, he lives in a time that has been saturated by the work ethics of Christian piety that Nietzsche makes it his point to lampoon.

The most striking element of the story may be Gustav's obsession with Tadzio, a Polish boy who is too young to understand adult sexuality. Gustav's personal confusion over falling in love with Tadzio ruptures his Spartan artistic ritual and signals a failure of his will to dominate his body's desire. His helpless surrender to emotion overwhelms years of dutiful pursuance of art. But as the themes of the story develop, Gustav's personal decline implies a broader critique about the state of German culture.

Gustav's rigorous repression of his earthly desire in favor of art may seem powerful and good; after all the idea of one's country, culture and people is often regarded as positive value. Clearly, the ennobled Gustav finds a fair amount of pride in having become an exemplary German artist of classical heritage. His work on Frederic the Great (King Frederic II, 1712-1786) reflects his grand achievement and connects his contemporary Germany to a proud history. While Frederic made Prussia a dominant European empire in the 1700s, Gustav's king defeated France in the Franco-Prussian War and established the Second Reich of German Empire. Gustav's art relishes this Prussian and German national heritage that is substantiated by a noble aristocracy. However, in 1912 this endorsement of cultural heritage sits on the precipice of a world war in which millions of lives were sacrificed to conflicting imperial pride. Mann's story demonstrates how Gustav's national German pride depends not only on solitary ritual but a war-enabling social system of ethnic prejudice and stereotype.

For Gustav, being a good writer, a good artist, and a good German depend on clench-fisted discipline. In foreign parts this Germanic structure is invigorated by contrast to people who Gustav regards as dissolute and inferior "others" whose lifestyle threatens to overwhelm his discipline. The story implies a biological foundation to conflicts between the disciplined, Appollian German culture and the Dionysian other cultures (Bohemia, Poland, Italy, Africa, Asia). Gustav's parents are themselves ethnically mixed. On the one hand, his father's side is composed of "military officers, judges. . . men who had spent their disciplined, decently austere life in the service of the king and state"; on the other hand, his mother offers "a strain of livelier, more sensuous blood" from "Bohemia" which gives Gustav "certain exotic racial characteristics in his external appearance." Gustav's art negotiates a blend of what Mann encodes as a fundamentally biological ethnic conflict between disciplined will and "fiery" impulse.

The theme of travel activates the cultural and racial politics undergirding Gustav's vocational valorization of German culture. Throughout his life Gustav regarded travel as no more than a therapeutic component in a strategy maximizing artistic efficiency. Previous trips had been "nothing more than a health precaution, to be taken from time to time however disinclined to it one might be." As the story begins, he has an unprecedented urge to travel and to "escape, to run away from his writing, away from the humdrum scene of his cold, inflexible, passionate duty." While looking at the red-haired traveler in the graveyard, Gustav feels an undeniable wanderlust. The hyperbole of his imagined destination is striking as he envisions "a tropical swampland under a cloud-swollen sky, moist and lush and monstrous, a kind of primeval wilderness of islands, morasses and muddy alluvian channels"; he continues seeing, "hairy palm-trunks thrusting upward from rank jungles of fern, from among thick fleshy plants in exuberant flower." The language composing this image is emphatic of a Dionysian dissolve, inimical to the fist-clenched, rigidly-structured individual. While the image stresses the dissolve of boundaries, there is also a seemingly sexual clarity to the scene (the "cloud-swollen sky" and "hair palm-trunks thrusting upward") as if sensuousness and sexuality are themselves threatening to Gustav's self-consciousness.

It is significant that this fantasy's landscape is "tropical," literally to the south from Germany. In the story, Gustav's unconscious understanding of geographical place echoes the cultural duty of his vocational commitment. The connotations of "North" and "South" reflect cultural and racial stereotypes that enable his Germanic integrity. In moving first South to an island in the Adriatic, Gustav tries to escape not only his daily pattern or the weather in Munich but his vocational duty as a German writer. In Venice, Gustav's demise plays out in a network of cultural signifiers. Tadzio is pointedly not German, but exotically Polish, echoing Gustav's exotic mother who is associated with music rather than the magisterial discipline of his father's family. The Venetians are described according to physical attributes that emphasize their "darkness" as if tacitly signaling to the reader a predisposition to dishonesty that is at the root of the epidemic's cover-up. The "truth" about the epidemic is relayed to Gustav by a blonde, blue-eyed Englishman who like Gustav is from the North.

The "Asiatic cholera" is nearly a character in the story, pushing the exoticism beyond Gustav's aesthetic power to negotiate extremes. It comes from Asia, "originating in the sultry morasses of the Ganges delta [a river in northern India and Pakistan], rising with the mephitic exhalations of that wilderness of rank useless luxuriance, that primitive island jungle shunned by man, where tigers crouch in the bamboo thickets." The cholera makes its way across continents in a progression that is distinctively noted by the English travel agent—"it had struck eastward into China, westward into Afghanistan and Persia, and following main caravan routes, it had borne its terrors to Astrakhan and even to Moscow." The vision of choleric rampage echoes Gustav's early vision in Munich of a tropical dissolve. The difference between the early and later vision is that the cholera of the later vision does not only figuratively dissolve Gustav's self-discipline but threatens literally to tear his body apart. Even the "sirocco" wind persistently blowing warmer, threateningly humid air into Venice throughout the story originates from North Africa (according to the Oxford English Dictionary), a place further south than Venice where the Moroccan crisis of 1911 was unfolding.

As an artist, Gustav is continually watching and negotiating extremes that are both individual and social—extremes that reflect the cultural and racial politics preceding the Great War. He watches the reveling second-class passengers; he watches the "spectacle of civilization" on the beach; and, he watches the social interactions of his fellow hotel lodgers at dinner. It is perhaps important to realize that without speaking to or conversing with others, Gustav can only rely on stereotype to know and understand the scene around him. Gustav's aesthetic rhetoric of depth depends on a mere superficial knowledge of Tadzio. The narrative is quite direct on this point, "Nothing is stranger, more delicate than the relationship between people who know each other only by sight. . . ." In Gustav's world, distance paradoxically allows the illusion of intimacy, "For man loves and respects his fellow man for as long as he is not yet in a position to evaluate him, and desire is born of defective knowledge." Even though Gustav is attempting to break out of his rigid formula of artistic production, he has been conditioned into a habit of engaging the world which make real escape impossible. Tadzio is beautiful but inaccessible as a human being, able merely to stand apart as a "statuesque masterpiece of nature."

In the end, Gustav can not relate to others as more than servants who tote his trunk; extending art into an interaction with other people seems impossible. His ingrained repression of sexual desire strands him in contemplation of classical Greek culture yielding sterile vocabulary that he is unable to translate into lived experience. While Gustav's vocational determination to intensify life through art promises a spiritual completion, it isolates him in morbid contemplation, turning Tadzio into a beautiful object with whom he is never able to speak. Art is supposed to transcend mere communication, but in relying too much on a transcendent cultural heritage, art falls dreadfully short of promoting spiritual completion. Instead, Gustav's art invigorates national exclusivity and individual self-righteousness in the face of impending international crisis. As the twentieth century closes amidst ethnic conflict and Western systems of economic exploitation, Mann's story continues to resonate with poignancy.

Source: Kendall Johnson, for *Short Stories for Students*, The Gale Group, 2000.

Richard White

In this essay, White examines Death in Venice *in light of Plato's philosophy, concluding that because Mann's "account of Aschenbach's obsession is both convincing and compelling it can serve as the disproof of Plato's idealization of art and beauty."*

Thomas Mann's novella *Death in Venice* is a sustained and very powerful meditation upon the proper relations of art and beauty, eros and death. In particular, even though the story is set in what was then contemporary Venice, Mann emphasizes the perennial nature of the themes and issues that he considers by using imagery and allusion to evoke the mythical atmosphere of ancient Greece and by dwelling upon the classical parallels to Aschenbach's own obsession. Thus it is clearly the Socratic ideal of the older male lover and his younger male beloved which orients Aschenbach's own perception of his relationship to Tadzio, while this also forms the most obvious framework in terms of which we as readers are meant to understand and even to judge him. Again, at two crucial points in the text Mann inserts his own version of a conversation between Socrates and Phaedrus, in which Socrates' position in Plato's original dialogue is first affirmed and then emphatically rejected. In this respect, the final resolution of the story, with Aschenbach's moral degeneration and death, really seems to call into question the Platonic conception of beauty as a means to the higher end of the Good.

From the first discussion of Aschenbach's own artistry to the final verdict upon the power of art, *Death in Venice* may therefore be viewed as a paradigm case of a work of literature which comments effectively upon a philosophical position. In the present essay, I will argue that *Death in Venice* represents a powerful response to Plato and every other philosopher who has argued in favor of the redemptive power of art. Clearly, though, this discussion requires us to consider in what respect "literary" conclusions *can* have philosophical validity. For even if Mann's story is entirely compelling, it is not clear how it could serve as the critique of a particular philosophical position, which presumably stands or falls with *argument*. In effect, this analysis of *Death in Venice* can illuminate the interplay of philosophy and literature, and may force us, in the end, to question the absolute distinction between them.

I

The "story" of *Death in Venice* is quite straightforward and may be briefly told: Von Aschenbach, a distinguished German writer, is seized one day with a profound longing for travel. He decides to go to Venice, and after a couple of curious incidents with an "old-young man" on the ferry, and a mysterious gondolier, he arrives at his hotel. Here, Aschenbach soon notices an exceptionally beautiful

Polish boy. After a futile attempt to leave, he gradually becomes obsessed with Tadzio, and he even follows his family on their excursions to Venice. Meanwhile, it is rumored that Venice is in the grip of a plague. Aschenbach eventually discovers the full extent of the sickness, but rather than leave he continues to follow Tadzio. On the same day that he finds out that the boy's family is leaving, he dies as he watches Tadzio on the beach.

Now although the actual events of *Death in Venice* are clear, the overall intention or "message" of the story remains profoundly ambiguous. It is fairly obvious, for example, that we are meant to associate the progress of Aschenbach's obsession with Tadzio with the progress of the plague. In the text, almost as soon as he admits his obsession (when he whispers the "hackneyed . . .; I love you"), he discovers the full extent of the sickness in Venice. Regardless of our own moral ideas, it is apparent that Mann wants us to regard Aschenbach's obsession as a moral degeneration which is the inward parallel of the plague itself. There must be some kind of a lesson here, but what is it that the story is warning us against? At this point, the indeterminacy of literature, the apparent impossibility of a final univocal meaning, stands as an obstacle to the philosophical appropriation of the text. Could it be that Aschenbach's insistence upon self-discipline is morally correct and that he fails only because in Venice he foolishly surrenders his guard? Or is this strict self-discipline the cause of his downfall, so that the emotional life that he has denied himself finally irrupts and destroys him? Perhaps a third interpretation is that art itself is an evil, and since any service to aesthetic form is oblivious to *moral* considerations, it is bound to result in moral degeneracy. There are clues in the text which can be used to support each one of these readings. As we will see, there are also resonances, and even direct references to Plato's theory of beauty and to other theories of art. More obviously than most literary works, *Death in Venice* defines itself in terms of "the problem of art" and the various positions which have been taken in the history of aesthetics. We must now ask whether it is possible to specify any further the nature of the work's overall claim, or whether its literary form must forever prevent this.

Let us begin by looking at the second section of *Death in Venice*, where Mann offers a detailed picture of Aschenbach's artistry. In a manner reminiscent of Nietzsche's account in *Ecce Homo*, he tells us that Aschenbach's forebears on his father's

> More explicitly, because his account of Aschenbach's obsession is both convincing and compelling it can serve as the disproof of Plato's idealization of art and beauty."

side were all official functionaries while his mother was the daughter of a composer. This union of "dry, conscientious officialdom and ardent, obscure impulse" is supposed to determine Aschenbach as a writer distinguished not so much by innate "genius" as by an incredible scrupulosity and capacity for hard work. He has the self-discipline required to sit at his desk day after day, so that eventually he produces an astonishingly well-crafted work from scores of individual inspirations. We are also told about his daily regimen: "He began his day with a cold shower over chest and back; then setting a pair of tall wax candles in silver holders at the head of his manuscript, he sacrificed to art in two or three hours of almost religious fervor, the powers he had assembled in sleep." Mann emphasizes that Aschenbach's power of self-control and self-denial is essential to his particular artistic nature. Not only does he modify his own existence in his service to art, living as a solitary and apparently without any emotional attachments, but his works themselves also testify to the validity of such a life of endurance. Aschenbach's heroes are those who struggle against all odds, who "hold fast" in the face of every danger both from within and from without, and continue in spite of everything. In this respect, Aschenbach is the champion of "the heroism born of weakness," and he is aptly described as "the poet-spokesman of all those who labor at the edge of exhaustion."

Mann suggests that the mature Aschenbach is successful because his work captures the spirit of his times. In fact, Aschenbach is the consummate "bourgeois" artist, who valorizes the bourgeois ideals of hard work and accomplishment, and who rejects any kind of moral ambivalence as decadent and corrupt. While the young Aschenbach had "overworked the soil of knowledge" and raised questions about the place of art, the mature writer is the champion of bourgeois decency who deliberately turns his back on the realm of knowledge lest it paralyze his actions. He is preoccupied with form. His refined style is regarded as exemplary, and his work is excerpted in school textbooks. Soon the bourgeois apologist becomes a bourgeois institution; and when nobility is conferred upon him he gladly accepts, for as Mann indicates, the self-regarding pursuit of recognition and fame is one of the chief spurs to his existence.

After establishing Aschenbach's severe self-mastery at the beginning, the rest of *Death in Venice* records the gradual undermining of his resolve. Thus, almost as soon as he arrives in Venice, Aschenbach begins to experience the pull of an alien force which gradually overcomes his will and destroys his self-mastery; and he quickly abandons himself to his obsession for Tadzio. When the mysterious gondolier rows him to the Lido against his wishes, the normally self-possessed Aschenbach finds it impossible to resist: "A spell of indolence was upon him. . . .; The thought passed dreamily through Aschenbach's brain that perhaps he had fallen into the clutches of a criminal; it had not power to rouse him to action." Likewise, when he discovers that his trunk has been misdirected, he does not experience annoyance so much as a "reckless joy" that seems to be bound up with the oblivion of personal responsibility and the happiness of self-dispossession. Later we are told that Venice alone "had power to beguile him, to relax his resolution, to make him glad." Indeed, the city itself seems to lure Aschenbach into self-abandon, as he begins to live only for Tadzio, following the family all over Venice, and even resting his head, one evening, on the boy's bedroom door: "It came at last to this—that his frenzy left him capacity for nothing else but to pursue his flame; to dream of him absent, to lavish, loverlike, endearing terms on his mere shadow." By the close of *Death in Venice*, Aschenbach is quite overwhelmed by all of those *unreasonable* forces and aspects of himself that he had previously sought to suppress: his spiritual destruction is therefore complete.

Towards the end, Aschenbach has a dream which seems to measure exactly how far he has fallen:

> He trembled, he shrank, his will was steadfast to preserve and uphold his own god against this stranger who was sworn enemy to dignity and self-control. But the mountain wall took up the noise and howling and gave it back manifold; it rose high, swelled to a

madness that carried him away. His senses reeled in the steam of panting bodies. . . .; His heart throbbed to the drums, his brain reeled, a blind rage seized him, a whirling lust, he craved with all his soul to join the ring that formed about the obscene symbol of the godhead, which they were unveiling and elevating, monstrous and wooden, while from full throats they yelled their rallying-cry.

This is clearly a description of a Dionysian orgy, and it is based on Euripides' original depiction of this in *The Bacchae*. In Euripides' play, the ruler Pentheus is the champion of decency and self-control, who attacks Dionysus and will not recognize him as a god. In revenge, Dionysus makes him mad; by appealing to his curiosity, he tricks Pentheus into visiting the scene of the Dionysian orgy, where he is torn to pieces by Dionysus' followers. Just before he leaves, however, there is a very important scene in which Pentheus, now completely under Dionysus' spell, is persuaded to dress in women's clothing in order to visit the Bacchae undetected. This scene really represents Pentheus' final humiliation, since it was precisely his contempt and hatred for Dionysus as the effeminate "man-woman" that led him to see the latter as a threat to public decency in the first place. Significantly enough, there is a similar dressing scene in *Death in Venice* when Aschenbach goes to the hotel barber, having his hair dyed and his face rouged in order to look as young as possible for Tadzio. We are bound to recall the earlier incident on the ferry, when Aschenbach was totally repulsed by the appearance of the "old-young man" and the contemptible desire to pretend that one is much younger than one actually is. If Aschenbach now succumbs to the same temptation, we must regard it as his final degradation and humiliation, to be doing that which should disgust him more than anything else. But in this way, Dionysus the stranger-god punishes all those who deny him.

There is obviously a close parallel between Euripides' play and the progress of *Death in Venice*. Both works warn us of the dangers of rigid self-control and the refusal of the irrational part of our nature. And in this respect, it could be argued that both works offer a response to Plato's famous attack on poetry in the *Republic*. Here, in Book X of the *Republic* especially, Plato puts forward an ideal of rational self-constraint which allows him to condemn most poetry as a dangerous appeal to the unreasonable part of the soul. He only exempts "the unmixed imitation of the decent" as an acceptable way of promoting worthy ideals. In *Death in Venice*, Aschenbach serves as the representative of this "approved" kind of poetry insofar as his work confirms existing moral ideals and seems to threaten nothing. Nevertheless, such a stance leads to the disastrous explosion of his passionate nature. And from this it may be inferred that *Death in Venice* raises a profoundly anti-Platonic perspective. Having mapped out some basic themes, I shall now focus upon *Death in Venice* as an implicit critique of Plato.

II

Plato's discussion of beauty in the *Phaedrus* or *Symposium* has often been used to offset his extreme strictures against art in the last book of the *Republic*. For if it is true that the beautiful form can draw us towards the Absolute, then it follows that artistic beauty must also be charged with such power. This calls into question any literal reading of the argument of Book X, and forces us to reconstrue Plato's attack on poetry as at least rhetorical in part. In *Death in Venice* Thomas Mann rejects Plato's position in the *Republic*. A more interesting question now is to consider whether Plato's *other* account of beauty is espoused or rejected, since it is the latter which clearly informs the dramatic progress of *Death in Venice*.

At the beginning of the *Phaedrus*, Socrates persuades Phaedrus to read him Lysias' speech, according to which it would be wiser for a boy to yield to someone who does *not* love him as opposed to someone who does. Challenged to produce a better speech on the same theme, Socrates argues, like Lysias, that the lover is a madman whose desire for total possession of his beloved can only lead to the spiritual detriment of the latter. Socrates reminds Phaedrus, however, that love is a god: hence, love cannot be evil, and he is bound to make a further speech, a "palinode," to atone for what he has just said. In the palinode Socrates introduces his mythical description of the human soul, comparing it to a winged charioteer who drives a team of winged horses, one of which is good while the other is bad. As the charioteer struggles to follow the procession of the gods and contemplate the sights of pure Being beyond the heavens, the bad horse drags the chariot down to earth. As a result, the soul loses its wings, and it has to wait 10,000 years for its next celestial journey.

By elaborating this crucial image of the charioteer, Socrates is able to justify the lover's *divine* madness, and distinguish it from the ordinary carnal appetite which only aims at self-indulgence. He argues that when the soul approaches the image of

beauty, as in the appearance of the beloved, it is reminded of the pure form of Beauty which it first encountered in the celestial procession: "Such a one, as soon as he beholds the beauty of this world, is reminded of true beauty, and his wings begin to grow." And while the evil horse will drag the chariot towards the beloved in expectation of erotic fulfillment, if the charioteer pulls in the reins by not yielding to his physical desire, his wings will grow back and he will finally recover the divine vision of the eternal forms of Being. Plato develops a similar claim in the *Symposium*, where, according to Socrates' recollection of the mysteries, there is a direct connection between the love of a beautiful individual, love of all physical beauty, the love of moral and intellectual beauty, and finally love of the Good itself. In each case, an intense passion is mastered and controlled so that the individual is empowered to reach a higher level of knowledge and Being. From this perspective, beauty and the pursuit of the Good are inextricably linked.

Plato's account of love and beauty is given dramatic expression in several Socratic dialogues. In the *Phaedrus* it is clearly Phaedrus' enthusiasm and beauty which inspire Socrates to reach philosophical heights. Likewise, in the *Charmides*, Socrates is completely overawed by the beauty of the young boy—so much so that at one point he admits that he has "taken the flame," and wonders whether he can maintain his self-control. In line with Plato's theoretical position, however, the passion that is generated by the beauty of Charmides leads eventually to a philosophical discussion of temperance. There is no formal resolution to this dialogue since no final definition of temperance is reached; but there is a dramatic resolution insofar as Socrates *achieves* temperance by the end of the dialogue. Once again, erotic passion is mastered, and the energy that is thereby released allows Socrates to penetrate further into the realm of Forms and attain the transcendence of philosophy.

All of the essential Socratic elements are also present in *Death in Venice*: the beautiful youth, the older enthusiast of beauty and morality, and the erotic atmosphere of Venice itself. Initially, of course, Aschenbach affects to respond to the boy's beauty as if he were a completely detached observer: "'Good, oh, very good indeed!' thought Aschenbach, assuming the patronizing air of the connoisseur to hide, as artists will, their ravishment over a masterpiece." Soon after he returns from his abortive departure, however, it becomes clear to him that he cannot endure to be away from Tadzio. And after a long passage in which he reflects upon the boy's beauty as a godlike work of art, Aschenbach repeats the Socratic claim that it is the function of corporeal beauty to remind us of the spiritual realm by pulling us out of our attachment to the world and its ordinary pleasures: "the god," he muses, "in order to make visible the spirit, avails himself of the forms and colours of human youth, gilding it with all imaginable beauty that it may serve memory as a tool, the very sight of which then sets us afire with pain and longing." In the next paragraph, Aschenbach recalls the atmosphere of ancient Greece and the sacred grove where Socrates' conversation with Phaedrus took place. But after repeating some of the basic points of Socrates' original argument, he gives the following warning, that "beauty . . .; is the beauty-lover's way to the spirit—but only the way, only the means, my little Phaedrus." This is interesting because although it may be construed as "correct" Platonic doctrine, it is not a point that is emphasized or even made explicit in the *Phaedrus* itself. Hence the warning draws attention to itself; and the very denial forces us to consider whether Aschenbach might already be guilty of what he fears: that in spite of the Socratic justification, the pursuit of Tadzio *has* become an obsession and an end in itself.

Aschenbach decides that he will compose in the presence of Tadzio, using the boy's beauty as the catalyst for his own artistic powers. Once again, Aschenbach views his relationship to Tadzio in Socratic terms; for him, as for Socrates, beauty confronted and withstood is supposed to lead to an achievement of the spirit. As Mann tells us, he "fashioned his little essay after the model Tadzio's beauty set: that page and a half of choicest prose, so chaste, so lofty, so poignant with feeling, which would shortly be the wonder and admiration of the multitude." Having said this, however, Mann deliberately forces us to question the analogy that Aschenbach has established by telling us at the end of the passage that, "When Aschenbach put aside his work and left the beach he felt exhausted, he felt broken—conscience reproached him, as it were after a debauch." Later it becomes clear that Aschenbach's obsession will not lead to any kind of spiritual achievement or self-empowerment. And as he follows the boy and his family all over Venice it becomes evident that Aschenbach is to be associated with the "bad" kind of lover who cannot control himself.

What are we to make of all this? It might be suggested that Aschenbach is simply a moral fail-ure, who manages to deceive himself about the purity of his concern for Tadzio, when in fact he is not really interested in the boy's welfare at all, only his own delight in being near him. We are told, for example, that the thought of Tadzio dying young gives Aschenbach an unaccountable feeling of pleasure. Likewise he will not do what he knows he ought to do, and tell Tadzio's mother about the plague, because he fantasizes about surviving alone with Tadzio. Even so, the argument of *Death in Venice* goes deeper than this. It may be true that Aschenbach fails to measure up to the Platonic ideal and that he is not a good kind of lover. But given the story's final judgments on art and form, and the *later* conversation between Socrates and Phaedrus which ends with Socrates' admission of guilt, *Death in Venice* may be viewed as a challenge to every idealizing impulse, including that of Plato, which seeks to justify the erotic impulse or the pursuit of beauty for the sake of something higher.

Let us consider this point: in Plato's dialogues there is a nice mythology, an ideology of the lover and his beloved which is theoretically appealing and dramatically effective. For the most part this "myth" is accepted, both by Aschenbach and by ourselves, as the ultimate truth about the role of beauty in the achievement of a higher order of Being. But what if all of this is *only* a myth?—a false attempt at a justification for something which is basically oblivious to moral concerns? I would suggest that this is the point of Mann's encounter with Plato: Aschenbach is one who has simply accepted Plato's classical account of beauty as a force of redemption. In this way he justifies his obsession to himself. Nevertheless, as Mann had earlier suggested, the artist's devotion to beautiful form has two contradictory aspects: "Is it not moral and immoral at once: moral in so far as it is the expression and result of discipline, immoral—yes, actually hostile to morality—in that of its very essence it is indifferent to good and evil, and deliberately concerned to make the moral world stoop beneath its proud and undivided sceptre?" In opposition to Plato, *Death in Venice* shows accordingly how the concern for beauty can ultimately lead to moral dissolution and death.

The final verdict of *Death in Venice* actually appears close to the end of the work in Socrates' second speech to Phaedrus. Aschenbach the great artist, and the representative of moral certainty, sits dazed and confused in the square; and at this point, Socrates makes his reappearance in order to condemn the activity of the artist, and the pursuit of beauty, as a "path of perilous sweetness" and way of transgression: "We may be heroic after our fashion, disciplined warriors of our craft, yet are we all like women, for we exult in passion, and love is still our desire—our craving and our shame. And from this you will perceive that we poets can be neither wise nor worthy citizens." And he adds, "We must needs be wanton, must needs rove at large in the realm of feeling. Our magisterial style is all folly and pretense, our honorable repute a farce, the crowd's belief in us is merely laughable. And to teach youth, or the populace, by means of art is a dangerous practice and ought to be forbidden." Although this judgment comes from Aschenbach's disordered brain, it represents a final moment of self-understanding in which Aschenbach rejects the myth of art that he had previously lived by. Here, Mann seems to be telling us the pure concern with form is by definition immoral, and it is a lie which says that art or beauty necessarily produces transcendence. Art may be used in the service of the good, but the essential thing about art is its independence and power of attraction. It would be false to say that art is of itself a force of redemption. In fact, the opposite appears to be true: that in standing outside of all moral considerations, beauty is the danger that leads us to death. In the final analysis, the power of art and beauty is to be celebrated and condemned.

All of this must lead us to appreciate the essentially complex nature of Mann's argument. On the one hand, as we have seen, Mann is no puritan. *Death in Venice* attacks Plato's strictures against art in Book X of the *Republic* by showing us what happens to someone who tries to exercise such a sovereign self-control and denial of the passions. *Death in Venice* is so lavishly written and so finely styled that we could never regard this work as *simply* a moral lesson against the excesses of feeling and form. On the other hand, while Mann obviously does value art and beauty as both delightful and necessary, he is under no illusion about the deadliness of these forces. In effect, his story argues powerfully against the romantic valorization of art as a redemptive power; and in this respect he obliges us to re-read Plato with suspicion.

III

I have argued that *Death in Venice* may be regarded as Thomas Mann's sustained response to Plato, insofar as it calls into question Plato's elevation of beauty as a means of achieving a higher realm of truth. In fact, it may be added that *Death in*

Venice expresses the rejection of any philosophical theory which supports the redemptive power of art. Schopenhauer's philosophy, for example, is clearly suggested by the description and title of Aschenbach's book, *Maia*; for according to Schopenhauer "the *veil* of Maya" is supposed to hide relentless striving of the one primordial Will, and allows us to believe in our illusory individuation. Schopenhauer argues that art is a redemptive force since concentration upon the pure forms of beauty allows us to withdraw from our everyday concerns to achieve a disinterested repose, as pure will-less subjects of knowledge. In *Death in Venice*, however, this account is rejected, as Aschenbach's objective appreciation of Tadzio's beauty ("'Good, oh, very good indeed!;' thought Aschenbach, assuming the patronizing air of the connoisseur . . .;'") cannot be maintained. Here, Aschenbach's refined aesthetic sense does not save him but actually drags him deeper into the madness of the Will.

The two Nietzschean elements of the Apollonian and the Dionysian are also clearly present throughout *Death in Venice*. Aschenbach's strict self-control and his preoccupation with artistic form confirm him as the Apollonian artist *par excellence*. Mann's story describes the release of Dionysian powers through Aschenbach's obsession for Tadzio and the seductive charm of Venice; and this culminates with Aschenbach's dream of Dionysian orgy and excess. But while in Nietzsche's *Birth of Tragedy*, the *unity* of Apollonian and Dionysian forces represents the empowering goal of art, in *Death in Venice* there is no possibility of a union between these extremes: either the rigid self-control of the artist or scholar *or* the self-abandonment of the lover. There is no chance of a mediation between these positions, and Nietzsche's ideal synthesis is accordingly a sham.

This brings us, then, to the nature of the relationship between literature and philosophy. A work of literature, such as *Death in Venice*, can be shown to serve as a useful commentary upon a particular philosophical position. But how is it possible for such a commentary to be effective and appropriate, given the essential ambiguity of literary texts, and the contrary ideal of a univocal philosophical meaning? Clearly, *Death in Venice* is not a didactic work. It is not a moral fable whose meaning is patently obvious for everyone to see. On the other hand, I have suggested that the text as a whole does have an overall intention which directs the reader towards a particular perspective on art and its philosophical relevance. In *Death in Venice*, Mann effectively challenges a philosophical position on the nature of art by giving us a convincing counter-example that calls the original philosophical model into question. More explicitly, because his account of Aschenbach's obsession is both convincing and compelling it can serve as the disproof of Plato's idealization of art and beauty.

Now it may be objected that whether or not a work of literature is dramatically convincing is really quite irrelevant to the question of its final validity or truth. This is undeniably correct. As Socrates knew, the most rhetorically effective speech is not necessarily the most veracious. Nevertheless, if a story *is* psychologically compelling, then this gives at least *prima facie* support for the vision of human nature that is embodied in the text. To argue that a work like *Death in Venice* is only dramatically effective without being philosophically interesting is to insist upon a distinction which is difficult if not impossible to maintain. Our analysis of *Death in Venice* forces us to make a closer scrutiny of works like Plato's *Phaedrus*, for it is plain that the philosophical claims of the latter *also* rely upon the evocation of an idyllic scene, where, in an erotically charged encounter with the beautiful youth, the ordinary restrictions on passionate discourse need not apply. The mythical context that is thereby established supports and gives credence to Socrates' visionary *assertions* on the nature of beauty and the soul. In Plato, as in Thomas Mann, the philosophical argument is therefore inseparable from the dramatic situation of the text, so that any fixed separation of ''literary'' as opposed to ''philosophical'' concerns must accordingly be challenged.

Source: Richard White, ''Love, Beauty, and *Death in Venice*,'' in *Philosophy and Literature*, Vol. 14, No. 1, April, 1990, pp. 53-64.

Harry Slochower

In the essay below, Slochower explores the interrelationship between Mann's life and works as well as the influence Nietzsche and Schopenhauer had on him.

Thomas Mann would have it that his literary work is mainly autobiographical in nature. Yet, he gives us only bare hints of the personal experiences which mobilized the depths of his visions. It is as though Thomas Mann would keep the sources of his creativity a secret from us, and perhaps from himself as well.

In *A Sketch of My Life*, Mann writes that he had a happy childhood and that, on the whole, he led a serene, ordered life. But he also speaks of his isolation, of being apart and that he addressed very few people with the familiar *du*. He mentions periods of depression and of occasional suicidal impulses.

Mann hints at a strong attraction he felt for a boy during his school years. This homosexual motif recurs in Mann's work: Tonio Kroeger's feeling for Hans Hansen, Aschenbach's infatuation with Tadzio, Hans Castorp's ''confusion'' between Madame Chauchat and the schoolmate Hippe, the relation between Adrian and Rudi in *Doctor Faustus* and, by implication, in the incest themes of *Blood of the Waelsungs* and *The Holy Sinner*.

Repeatedly, Mann assures us that he was a happily married man, wedded to a woman who watched over him with intelligence, patience and consideration. Yet, one is struck by the fact that generally Mann refers to his wife as his ''companion,'' and that he never alludes to any of the personal complications in the family relationships which appear in the homoerotic and incest themes of his work.

That there was a deep insufficiency in Mann's personal life may be adduced from his nearly compulsive need to recast his life experiences in symbolic and critical forms. Thomas Mann wrote at an almost uninterrupted pace. Aside from his many stories and novels, he hints at having written poetry, composed a drama, *Fiorenza*, wrote numerous essays on figures in literature and art, published political tracts and carried on a voluminous correspondence.

In *A Sketch of My Life,* Mann writes of two momentous cultural experiences of his early youth: Nietzsche—whom he read first—and Schopenhauer. What impressed him most in Nietzsche, Mann states, was the philosopher's *self*-criticism. It made him ''proof against the baleful romantic attraction which can—and today so often does—proceed from an un-human valuation of the relation between life and mind.'' Elsewhere, he pays greater homage to Nietzsche's insight ''that there is no deeper knowledge without experience of disease, and that all heightened healthiness must be achieved by the route of illness.'' In the story *Weary Hour* (1905), art and disease go hand in hand, and in the novel *Royal Highness*, Martini says that his talent is ''inseparably connected with my bodily infirmity.''

In his essay on ''Schopenhauer,'' Mann writes that ''the essence of the creative artist is nothing else . . . than sensuality spiritualized, than spirit informed and made creative by sex." If the Nie-tzsche experience was primarily artistic and intellectual, Mann's reading of Schopenhauer in his twentieth year was "closely related to a late and violent outbreak of sexuality" (*A Sketch of My Life*). Mann read him day and night "as perhaps one reads only once in his life." What affected him most was "the element of eroticism and mystic unity in this philosophy." At that time, Mann was emotionally close to suicide, but was able to transform these feelings into his novel *Buddenbrooks* in which Thomas Buddenbrook's reading of Schopenhauer's thoughts on immortality prepares him to accept the decline of his family and his own death.

In Mann's work, fulfillment of sex is both a passionate longing and a constant threat. And this threat is extrapolated into a fear of success. Was this an expression of Mann's personal fear of assuming the dominant position of his father? In the drama *Fiorenza*, we read that "yearning is giant power, possession unmans."

In his essay "Freud and the Future," Mann says that "we are actually ourselves bringing about what seems to be happening to us." Freud's impact on Mann came late. However, he was prepared for it by his reading of Nietzsche and Schopenhauer. Mann sees a close kinship between his own attempt to weld music, myth and depth psychology with, what he calls, Freud's depth-science. He regards his interest in mythology, "in the primitive and pre-cultural aspects of humanity" as being "in the closest manner bound to his (Freud's) psychological interest."

Art, for Mann, consists of "the forbidden, the adventurous, scrutiny and self-abandonment." But, in the spirit of Freud, he opposes the Romanticists who would return to the "prehistorical mother-womb." In his essay on "Freud and the Future," and with a view of the Nazi Night Riders, Mann warns of the moral devastation made possible "by worship of the unconscious, the glorification of its dynamics as the only life-promoting force, the systematic glorification of the primitive and the irrational." He pays tribute to Freud for his *analysis* of the unconscious and of the myth, thus offering a promise of "a wiser and freer humanity." Freud's humanism, he concludes, is one of the future and stands "in a different relation to the powers of the lower world, the unconscious, the Id: a relation bolder . . . freer, blither, productive of a riper art than any possible in our neurotic, fear-ridden, hate-ridden world." Thomas Mann's monumental epic

> **Like Goethe's Faust,**
> **Thomas Mann's work warns**
> **against the two major**
> **temptations of the demon: The**
> **bed of sloth and the ravages**
> **of vagabondage, with the one**
> **calling forth the other."**

of Jacob and his sons is a high expression of this view.

The event which had the most direct bearing on the ErosThanatos theme in *Death in Venice* was the suicide of Mann's second sister Carla, which occurred in 1910, one year before the story was written. In *A Sketch of My Life*, Mann writes with an openness, unusual in his autobiographical account, of the effect which her suicide had on him. The event, he writes.

> shook me to my depths." (It) "seemed somehow like a betrayal of our brother-and-sisterly bond, a bond of destiny . . . which I—it is hard to put into words—had ultimately regarded as objectively superior to the realities of life.

Thirty years later (1947), her suicide still haunted him. Carla aspired to become an actress, led a "bohemian" life, and Mann hints that it was such formless life pattern which led to her suicide.

Here, we meet one of Mann's leading motifs: the relation between discipline and dissolution, the bourgeois and the romantic. These were, indeed, the two strains in Mann's family background: his father, the businessman and senator; his mother who was of Portugese-Creole blood and who loved music. Mann himself felt the conflict and tension between these two powers. They appear in his art, as well as in his essays on Platen, Tolstoy, Dostoyevsky, and especially in his agonizing evaluations of Richard Wagner.

Seventeen years later, Mann's sister Julia also committed suicide. Mann calls her his "mother's daughter," and writes that with her fate "I am reluctant to deal here. Her grave is too new; I will leave the story to a later narrative in a larger frame" (*A Sketch of My Life*). Possibly, Julia was the more hidden incest object in Mann's life; it is her suicide which is symbolically depicted in *Doctor Faustus*.

Attention has been called to the recurrence of the themes of disease, death and suicide in Thomas Mann's work. Yet Mann would convert such tendencies into a value. Indeed, unrest, fear and anguish, as depicted in Jacob and the young Joseph, make them the carriers of a creative future. And, it is because Judah retains this "Geist" that Jacob bestows the blessing on him, taking it from Joseph who had become a satisfied Egyptian. In the Joseph story, Thomas Mann confesses that he shares Abraham's "restless unease":

> To me too has not unrest been ordained, have not I too been endowed with a heart which knoweth no repose? The story-teller's star—is it not the moon, lord of the road, the wanderer. . . . For the story-teller . . . feels his heart beating high, partly with desire, partly too from fear and anguish . . . as a sign that he must take the road . . . according to the restless spirit's will.

It is in such unease that Thomas Mann sees a necessary condition for creativity.

But Mann has ever been aware that a further requirement for creativity is the existence of a favorable social soil. In *The Magic Mountain*, Mann tells us that the individual does not only live his personal life, but also that of his epoch. And, if the social life about him does not answer the questions which he asks, consciously or unconsciously, then a certain laming of the personality is apt to take place. In 1911, when *Death in Venice* was written, the Western world was preparing for the First World War. The Venetian state is shown as harboring its disintegration. It is concerned with hushing up knowledge of the epidemic, concerned with business as usual. Aschenbach welcomes this disease for it reveals a disorder "in the bourgeois structure." The secret disease of the city merges with his own innermost disease.

I. Death in Venice

> "The truth is that life could never in all its life get on without the morbid; and anything more stupid would be hard to find than the saying that from disease only disease can come. Life is not fastidious: one may truthfully say creative genius, genius-purveying disease, taking its obstacles on high horse, leaping exultant from crag to crag, is a thousand times dearer to it than healthiness trudging afoot. Life . . . clutches the dating products of disease, consumes and digests them, and what it does with them makes them health."

I propose to examine Thomas Mann's *Death In Venice* as revealing, in art-form, a psychoanalytic process on two interconnected levels:

1. Aschenbach's development from an apparent integrated personality to the return of long-repressed forces within him. At this stage, id-derivatives emerge and Aschenbach succumbs to a dream-like state in the course of which he "falls in love" with a young boy, and emotionally surrenders to the waves of his homoerotic impulses. At the end, Aschenbach is confronted by "reality." But, at this point, Eros merges with Thanatos and Aschenbach dies.

2. The function of Thomas Mann as the "interpreter" of Aschenbach's "dream." Here, ego and superego powers make themselves felt in the author's interpolations and, more crucially, through his technique which molds Aschenbach's visions into an art-form, creating a work that is perhaps the greatest short novel in world literature.

The implication of my approach is that an artist is not a living patient and that his creation is not a clinical case history. The artist goes beyond "sublimation" of pathological pressures, finds more than "substitute gratification," and gains a measure of secondary autonomy.

Traditionally, examination of imagery in art has not been considered as the proper province of psychoanalysis and works of art have been treated as essays, tracts or "cases." In this approach, the organic concatenation between "the what" and "the how" has been ignored. However, such examination is essential. Indeed, the psychoanalytic critic needs to approximate the artist's own pace and rhythm in his analysis of the art product.

A. The Art of Death In Venice

In *A Sketch of My Life*, Mann tells us that "nothing is invented" in the story. Yet, he adds that, in the process of writing it, he had "at moments the clearest feeling of transcendence, a sovereign sense of being borne up, such as I have never before known." The reader too experiences a feeling of transcendence and is held in a kind of magic spell. At the same time, he is kept from being lulled into a dreamy surrender by Mann's strategy which introduces concrete, realistic detail that gives the unreal a measure of reality. The author's careful thematic and symbolic elaborations at once give us the fantasy and keep it within limits. The story is a delicate and dynamic interweaving of dream and analysis, of the latent and the manifest, the preconscious and the conscious. In this way, the artist, like Plato's Eros, becomes the mediator between the phenomenon and the idea.

The style of the opening sections—up to Aschenbach's first view of Tadzio—is severe, formal, and factual. Later, it becomes soft, flowing and sensuous, combining plastic imagery and musical rhythms. (Mann uses a similar structural sequence in *The Magic Mountain* and *Doctor Faustus.*) The whole produces a mesmerizing effect, similar to that of "Walpurgis-Night" and "Snow" in *The Magic Mountain* and in the scene where Potiphar's wife, Mut, attempts to seduce Joseph in Mann's epic. We are enveloped by primitive affects which are natively familiar and seem to have been experienced in the long ago.

Each section sounds a motif, followed by another which dialectically "takes in" the first, enriches it, and prepares us for the next. The reader, for example, is initially startled to recognize characteristics of the first apparition in the figures who appear later. But only initially; for he has been prepared for this by the author's use of similar imagery. Mann employs an analogous strategy in the development of his mythic motifs. Vernon Venable points out that, at the beginning, the symbols are relatively unambiguous: The stranger whom Aschenbach sees at the Funeral Hall embodies the appetite for life, with the death theme of the cemetery relegated to the background. Later, these central motifs interpenetrate and, in Aschenbach's nightmare at the close of the story, we have a dance of death which is also a "fertility" dance. This dialectic technique pervades each scene and the mood of the story as a whole.

B. The "Crouching Tiger" and "Redness"

The "crouching tiger" and "redness" are two of the leading motifs of the story. In Aschenbach's day-dream at the beginning of the *Novelle*, the metaphor of the crouching tiger sounds the overture to the theme of the desired and feared sexual assault by the several tempters. It is foreshadowed by the Wanderer at the cemetery with his bold, savage bearing which compels Aschenbach "to capitulate." At the end, it reappears in Aschenbach's nightmare and in Jaschu's savage assault on Tadzio forcing him to capitulate. In his day-dream, Aschenbach sees a swampland in a rank lecherous thicket and the sight of the crouching tiger makes his heart knock with fear and puzzling desires. In the nightmare, Aschenbach experiences the ragings of a mob which are "interspersed and dominated by the deep cooing of wickedly persistent flutes which charmed the bowels in a shamelessly persistent manner."

The color red also runs through the narrative, and is characteristic of all the tempters: the red hair of the first apparition, the red necktie of the old dandy on the boat, the reddish brow of the gondolier, the red hair of the guitar player. The color also points to sexual temptation, climaxed in Aschenbach's desire for Tadzio. The boy too wears a red necktie on his breast, and at the end, Aschenbach puts on a red necktie and his skin, rejuvenated by the barber, is tinted with a crimson color and his lips become "red as raspberries." The color, like "the red-one," has an ambivalent function, manifested in the strawberries which Aschenbach eats—the large ones on which he breakfasts earlier in the story and the soft, overly ripe strawberries—presumably infected—which he eats at the end.

Another leading imagery of the story is *looking* and *watching*. Aschenbach engages in a kind of voyeurism with Tadzio as the object. What he sees may be characterized as mirror-images, and his "creativity" may be said to be an esthetic onanism, and the famous author ceases to write in Venice. Our pleasure tends to turn into sadness as we become aware of Aschenbach's central self-deception, namely, that Tadzio can be an object of his love. In essence, *the boy is Aschenbach's "double."* In his yearning for Tadzio, Aschenbach is reaching out for that which lies beyond his grasp. We realize that Tadzio has no independent existence, that Aschenbach is creating the boy and his beauty out of his phantasy. This gives the story a mythico-tragic character.

C. Anamnesis

As in *The Magic Mountain* and *Doctor Faustus*, following "the presenting symptoms," Mann sketches the biographical background of the main character.

Aschenbach's father was a higher law official and, like his forbears, had led a "severe, steady" life, serving the state. In contrast, the mother, the daughter of a Bohemian band-master, had "impulses of a darker, more fiery nature."

Aschenbach himself was pledged to disciplined and steady efforts, but "was not really born to them." At thirty-five, he was taken ill—we are led to suspect that it was partly due to the tension between the father-and-mother elements within him. Aschenbach had grown up alone, without siblings or friends. At the age of fifty, he was raised to knighthood by a German prince and moved from northern Silesia to Bavaria in the South. His wife died, leaving him with a married daughter. He had never had a son.

Aschenbach's life and work followed the pattern set by his parents. He led an ascetic, rigid existence "which demanded a maximum of wariness, prudence, penetration, and rigor of the will." Similarly, his writings were attuned to the demands of the times. One of his works was a tribute to "Frederick of Prussia," (!) and he was accorded official recognition. In the imagery used by one observer, Aschenbach had always lived in the posture of a closed fist—in imitation of his father. But, he also followed the model of his mother, and wrote stories, such as "Maya."

Aschenbach's favorite figure was Sebastian, which combined the father-mother realms in a taut equilibrium. For Aschenbach, Sebastian represents "an intellectual and youthful masculinity" which stands motionless, in proud shame ("stolzer Scham"), while swords and spear-points beset the body. Here, we have at once the challenging and passive posture. Behind Sebastian's elegant self-mastery there lies a crude, vicious sensuality. The passive homosexuality in the figure of Sebastian (historically, St. Sebastian was the unwitting erotic charmer of the homosexual emperor Diocletian) also appears in Aschenbach's story "The Wretch" in which the character guides his wife into the arms of an adolescent, doing this "from powerlessness, from lasciviousness, from ethical frailty."

When we first meet Aschenbach, he is still successfully defending himself against his libidinal urges by carrying out a compulsive pattern of disciplined life and work, characteristic of his father. But, it is apparent that the dual forces within him are in a precarious balance. At this point—Aschenbach is around fifty—the defense of masculinity is upset by an apparently chance encounter with a stranger. Now, the enslaved emotions begin to take vengeance on him, and we see the gradual emergence of the repressed, with the feminine model pressing into the foreground. Attention to the object gives way to narcistic wishing, disciplined routine to a sickled sensualism. Aschenbach now tries to live the life of his mother. The closed fist gives way to the open hand. The imagery swerves between Olympian heights and Chthonic depths. In the end, Aschenbach is engulfed by oceanic feelings and dim with the vision of his beloved beauty outlined against the sea. His journey may be said to consist of stages of death, stages in reunion with the mother. Yet, throughout, Mann's principle of "irony" is maintained. His art at once celebrates this surrender and warns against the submission to Eros-Narcissus.

II. Phases in the Pact with "The Red-One"

The Novelle opens on a note of foreboding: It is a time when the situation in Europe had been menacing. Although it is the beginning of May, the English Gardens of Munich were "as pungent as in August."

A. Overture: The Primal Tempter

While taking a walk, Aschenbach is struck by the sudden apparition of a man. He is red-haired, has a protruding Adam's apple, long, white teeth. His posture—left arm resting on his thigh, feet crossed, leaning hip—suggests Grecian sculpture from the Hellenic period. But this "Apollonianism" is crossed by "Dionysian" features: In the background is a Funeral Hall of Byzantine architecture—foreshadowing Venice—and the man's bearing is bold, "even savage." His commanding bearing was "compelling him to capitulate." The man, with his knapsack, appears like a "Wanderer." He rouses in Aschenbach an "appetite for freedom, for unburdening, for forgetfulness," stirs his long-repressed desire to "travel" and escape the pressures of "a coldly passionate service." Aschenbach looks about for the man, but he is nowhere to be seen. He has become part of Aschenbach.

This is "the day-residue" which mobilizes the frightening day-dream of the crouching tiger which follows:

> He saw a landscape, a tropical swampland under a heavy, murky sky, damp luxuriant and enormous, a kind of prehistoric wilderness, . . . sluggish with mud; he saw, near him and in the distance, the hairy shafts of palms rising out of a rank lecherous thicket . . . he saw the glint from the eyes of a crouching tiger—and he felt his heart knocking with fear and with puzzling desires.

Aschenbach's fantasy hints at the internalization of his "tigerish" sexuality and foreshadows the mob-assault in his nightmare at the end and his Eros-Thanatos destination.

B. Entry Into The Underworld

Aschenbach experiences the next metamorphosis of the devil's temptation while on the boat which is taking him south. He sees an old man who had painted his cheeks and wore a wig, playing as though he were youthful. Aschenbach is at once fascinated and horrified by this spectacle, and feels ''as though some dream-like estrangement, some peculiar distortion of the world, were beginning to take possession of him.'' It foreshadows the end when Aschenbach himself will paint his face and tint his hair.

It has been noted that Aschenbach's journey to Venice contains allusions to Dante's *Inferno*: The canal-crossing evokes the imagery of Dante's journey, led by Charon. It suggests ''criminal adventures'' and a dream-journey into the land of the dead, with the barque offering ''the softest . . . most lulling seat in the world.'' It is also a journey into Purgatory. As he crosses the waters, he forgets his earlier life, and like Dante's sinners, Aschenbach exposes himself to temptations. And, like them, he does not yield, but only relives them symbolically.

The gondolier resembles the Wanderer (turned-up nose, white teeth, reddish brow), but he also has characteristics of the old dandy on the boat. The first tempter in Munich was not a Bavarian; the Venetian gondolier is not an Italian. He, like the Wanderer, is powerful, insolent, imperious, with gestures of ''uncanny decisiveness.'' And, like the dandy, he is a cheat—it turns out that he was the only gondolier who did not have a license.

Aschenbach's journey to the South reverses that of the man in Plato's *Republic*. It reverses the classical Apollonian quest of Goethe's Mignon, Iphigenia and Faust, of Gluck's ''Iphigenia in Aulis,'' the ideal of ''noble simplicity and quiet grandeur'' (''edle Einfalt und stille Grösse''), as Winckelmann called it.

The journey to Venice constitutes the second act of Aschenbach's mythic journey. He leaves the false Eden of an illusory security, rejects the discipline which was the ''direct inheritance from his father's side'' and begins the regressive dreamjourney towards the Dionysian swamp, the land of the tiger and of the homoerotic object. At the same time, it is a journey by water—a rite of passage—and a promise of rebirth. Its destination is the City and the Sea, that is, the Mother.

C. Major Temptation: The Heavenly Child

In *Moby Dick*, Melville prepares us for the awesome entry of Ahab and of the White Whale by building up a tense expectation of their appearance. It is characteristic of Mann's art that the reader is led only gradually to the apocalyptic vision of Tadzio. This again is a defense against being overpowered. And again, Mann uses the technique of ''relief,'' diverting attention by detailed description of physical objects and neutral events. This also illustrates Mann's technique of ''working through'' in aesthetic idiom,

Upon seeing the ''long-haired boy about fourteen years old,'' (Mann was fifteen when his father died), Aschenbach notes with astonishment that the boy was ''absolutely beautiful.'' Except for the red in his attire, Tadzio looks like the reverse of the earlier tempters: His face is ''pale and reserved, framed with honey-colored hair, the straight sloping nose, the lovely mouth, the expression of sweet and godlike seriousness.'' His complete purity of form recalls to Aschenbach ''Greek sculpture of the noblest period.'' His head is poised ''with an incomparable seductiveness—the head of an Eros.'' His figure is also surrounded by musical rhythms, Aschenbach hearing his name as ''two melodic syllables like 'Adgio,' or still more frequently 'Adgiu,'; with a ringing *u*-sound prolonged at the end.'' This is how Aschenbach sees and hears the boy. And, as noted, we never see Tadzio apart from the view which Aschenbach has of him. Tadzio becomes Aschenbach's idealized and eroticized self-image.

Tadzio is surrounded by women, his mother and three sisters, who are drawn in contrast to him. The mother appears detached, standing apart at a dignified and respectful distance. The sisters dress with cloister—like chasteness which borders on disfigurement. (Is Mann overcompensating here for the seductive sensuousness of his own mother and sisters?)

Sensing that he was about to be overwhelmed by the godlike beauty of the boy, Aschenbach is seized by the impulse to run away. But he is held by Tadzio, by archaic powers symbolized by the ocean which frames Tadzio's figure:

> He loved the ocean for deep-seated reasons: because of that yearning for rest, when the hard-pressed artist hungers to shut out the exacting multiplicities of experience and hide himself on the breast of the simple, the vast; and became of a forbidden hankering—seductive, by virtue of its being directly opposed to his obligations—after the incommunicable, the incommensurate, the eternal, the nonexistent. To be at rest in the face of perfection is the hunger of every one who is aiming at excellence; and what is the non-existent but a form of perfection?

Here, we have allusions to the mother-figure, hidden in Tadzio—sought but never reached. And, as Aschenbach watches Tadzio in the water, he is reminded of a frail god, suggestive of Aphrodite, who comes up "out of the depths of sky and sea." He is therefore almost overjoyed when he learns that his trunk was sent in "a completely wrong direction," and thus has an external motive for staying on in Venice.

From now on, Aschenbach's defenses become weaker and weaker and he gives in more and more to the enchantment. He becomes the ever-alert observer, watching for Tadzio "everywhere." Aschenbach makes a half-hearted attempt to write, but manages only about a page and a half of an essay. The creative impulse has been resexualized. He is more successful in invoking mythic paralells to his infatuation. Aschenbach muses over Socrates' attraction for the beautiful, incorporated in Phaedrus and his diversion of this attraction toward philosophic-esthetic ruminations. And Mann himself resorts to transposing the object of his forbidden desires to the mythic.

The leading affect in *Death In Venice* is the sensual, not the sexual. Here, as in the relation between Castorp and Claydia in *The Magic Mountain*, tension is rarely reduced and there is no release. For all his obsessive yearning for Tadzio, Aschenbach never touches him. Even when, towards the end, he openly stalks his beloved in alleys and vestibules, he does so at a safe distance.

Once, it does happen that a "meeting" takes place—when Tadzio smiles at Aschenbach.

Mann carefully prepares us for this meeting with some of the most beautiful imagery in literature with accompanying mythico-sexual allusions. As the sun rises, the motif of "redness" reappears. And, as the "godlike power" of the sun breaks out into "an intense flame of licking tongues," Aschenbach experiences in aesthetic imagery "the sentiency" of his creation by his mother and father, symbolized by the various elements, with suggestions of the primal scene here being "announced":

> Sky, earth and sea still lay in glassy, ghostlike twilight; a dying star still floated in the emptiness of space. But a breeze started up, a winged message from habitations beyond reach, telling that Eos was rising from beside her husband. And that first sweet reddening in the furthest reaches of sky and sea took place by which the sentiency of creation is announced. The goddess was approaching, the seductress of youth who stole Cleitus and Cephalus, and despite the envy of all the Olympians enjoyed the love of handsome, Orion.

As the sun rises,

> Golden spears shot up into the sky from behind. The splendor caught fire, silently; with godlike power an intense flame of licking tongues broke out.

Aschenbach closes his eyes and lets himself drift back towards "precious early afflictions and yearnings which had been stifled by his rigorous program of living . . ." Aschenbach recognizes them with "an embarrassed, astonished smile," and as he does so, his lips slowly form Tadzio's name. Smiling, he falls asleep in his chair.

The Olympian-Apollonian mood of the morning is followed by "a strange mythical transformation." (The primal father is not dispelled by art and dream.) Threatening winds arise, fore-shadowing the Dionysian tempest which is to follow:

> A stronger wind arose, and the steeds of Poseidon came prancing up, and along with them the steers which belonged to the blue-locked god, bellowing and lowering their horns as they ran.

We have here suggestions of the terrors evoked by the "Urazene"—not consummated, but transfigured by art and narcissistic identification. Aschenbach lets himself be "caught in the enchantment of a sacredly distorted world full of Panic life—and he dreamed delicate legends." As he observes Tadzio, "it was Hyacinth that he seemed to be watching. Hyacinth who was to die because two gods loved him." In the myth, Narcissus resists the love of the Great Mother, as well as homosexual advances. He is punished by being made to surrender to her or by turning towards himself as an object of love which proves fatal to him.

Aschenbach's fatal meeting and the fatal smile transpire when he comes upon Tadzio "unprepared." One day, the boy's schedule—which Aschenbach had followed scrupulously—was disrupted. And, suddenly, Tadzio appears:

> He had not been prepared for this rich spectacle; it came unhoped for. He had no time to entrench himself behind an expression of repose and dignity. Pleasure, surprise, admiration must have shown on his face as his eyes met those of the boy—and at this moment it happened that Tadzio smiled, smiled to him, eloquently, familiarly, charmingly, without concealment; and during the smile his lips slowly opened. It was the smile of Narcissus bent over the reflecting waters, that deep, fascinated, magnetic smile with which he stretches out his arms to the image of his own beauty—a smile distorted ever so little, distorted at the hopelessness of his efforts to kiss the pure lips of the shadow. It was coquettish, inquisitive, and slightly tortured. It was infatuated and infatuating.

> He had received this smile, and he hurried away as though he bore a fatal gift . . . Strangely indignant and tender admonitions wrung themselves out of him:

'You dare not smile like that! Listen, no one dare smile like that to another!' He threw himself down on a bench; in a frenzy he breathed the night smell of the vegetation. And leaning back, his arms loose, overwhelmed, with frequent shivers running through him, he whispered the fixed formula of desire—impossible in this case, absurd, abject, ridiculous, and yet holy, even in this case venerable: 'I love you!'

Aschenbach's meeting with Tadzio is a symbolic reliving of the meeting between the parents prior to their union.

D. The Last Sexual Temptation and the Dream of Eruption

Aschenbach is watching a performance in the garden of his hotel given by a band of strolling singers. In the center is a guitar player who acts the part of a "brutal and audacious" clown. With his red hair, snub nose, and large Adam's apple, he represents the final metamorphosis of "the red-one" and the hidden sexual temptation. Where Aschenbach had maintained a psychic distance between himself and the other figures, this time the feeling is that the clown, surrounded by a strong carbolic smell and Aschenbach are one and the same. He now recalls the wanderer who had stirred in him the desire for "life." But Aschenbach rejects the thought of "return": "What were art and virtue worth to him over against the advantages of chaos?" It occurs to him to warn the Polish family about the cholera. But the death wish is stronger, and Aschenbach keeps silent.

In Euripides' *The Bacchae*, the frenzied passion of Dionysus invades the realm of Pentheus whose Apollonianism had become formal, brittle, and unproductive. So it happens with Castorp, following his seven years on the Apollonian mountain and with Potiphar's wife Mut who had long lived in abstinence and ritual order. In *Joseph In Egypt*, Thomas Mann comments on this phenomenon:

It is the idea of affliction, the sudden invasion of wanton, destructive, annihilating forces into the ordered scheme of a life that is composed, and sworn to discipline and composure—a life bent upon honor, dignity, and happiness in restraint . . . (it is) the story of mastery overmastered, and of the coming of a stranger god—all this was here in the beginning, just as it was in the mid-course of our life.

The night after Aschenbach had watched the clown's performance, he has a nightmare whose latent content nearly becomes conscious.

Aschenbach is witness to an orgy, reigned over by "The strange god" in which whirling figures of men and women engage in chaotic and indiscriminate sexual activity. Through it all, the bacchantes wail a *u*-sound, associated with Tadzio's name:

Clanking, blaring, and dull thunder, with shrill sounds and a definite whine in a long-drawn-out *u*-sound— all this was sweetly, ominously interspersed and domin the deep cooing of wickedly persistent flutes which charmed the bowels in a shamelessly penetrative manner.

It coaxes Aschenbach to participate in these excesses. He was set on defending himself and at first, he is only a spectator. But as he watches with anguish and desire, with a terrifying "curiosity" (suggestive, as Kohut observes, of a primal scene experience), he is irresistably drawn to become one with them:

At the beating of the drum his heart fluttered, his head was spinning, he was caught in a frenzy, in a blinding deafening lewdness—and he yearned to join the ranks of the god . . . the dreamer now was with them, in them, and he belonged to the foreign god. Yes, he and they were one, as they hurled themselves biting and tearing upon the animals, got entangled in steaming rags, and fell in promiscuous union on the torn moss, in sacrifice to their god And his soul tasted the unchastity and fury of decay.

E. Return to Reality: Jaschu

Aschenbach's words "I love you" in the climactic meeting in which he receives Tadzio's smile, are addressed to himself—Tadzio is not there to hear them. Here, Aschenbach has come to the furthest recesses of his narcissism—similar to Don Quixote's in *"The Cave of Montesino"* and Hans Castorp's in *"Walpurgis-Night."* And now, Aschenbach,—like the Don and Castorp—begins to evince a readiness to confront reality. He becomes aware of the Indian cholera, becomes aware of the social sickness of the city which would keep the fact of the pestilence quiet, so as not to lose the tourist trade.

Death in Venice ends with an episode—which I consider the peripety of the story—whose pivotal significance has been passed over by critics. The scene exhibits the last "tigerish" assault, a "masculine" conquest of "the beauty." It is also a scene in which Aschenbach, for the first time, sees something which is not his projection, a scene in which another character, Jaschu, determines what is to happen with Tadzio.

Earlier, Aschenbach had noticed this stocky Polish boy who seemed to be Tadzio's "closest vassal and friend." Now, Aschenbach is watching a game in the course of which Jaschu becomes angered by sand having been flung in his face:

He forced Tadzio into a wrestling match which quickly ended in the fall of the beauty, who was weaker. But, as though, in the hour of parting, the servile feelings of the inferior had turned to merciless brutality and were trying to get vengeance for a long period of slavery, the victor did not let go of the boy underneath, but knelt on his back and pressed his face so persistently into the sand that Tadzio, already breathless from the struggle, was in danger of strangling.

As Aschenbach is witness to Tadzio's face being rubbed in the ground, with Jaschu pressing down on him, he "sees" at last that—as Mephistopheles puts it in Goethe's *Faust*—man must learn to eat dust ("Staub soll er fressen"). With this, he is released from his phantasy. Here, Aschenbach "loses" Tadzio, that is, can no longer mold him in accordance with his wishes. And, I submit, that this constitutes one of the affirmative elements of the story.

Still, Aschenbach cannot return to the bourgeois world, chooses to say where Tadzio can still be seen, chooses to stay and die in Venice. With Tadzio in the distance, moving away from him, Aschenbach has his final Thanatos dream:

> The watcher sat there . . . His head, against the back of his chair, had slowly followed the movements of the boy walking yonder. Now, as if to meet that glance it rose and sank on his breast, so that his eyes looked out from underneath, while his face took on the loose, inwardly relaxed expression of deep sleep. But it seemed to him as though the pale and lovely lure out there were smiling to him, beckoning to him; as though, removing his hand from his hip, he were calling him to cross over, vaguely guiding him towards prodigious promises. And, as often before, he rose to follow.

Death In Venice is a salute to both Richard Wagner and Gustav Mahler. Wagner died in Venice and Mann gives Aschenbach Mahler's first name. The story invokes Wagner's "Liebestod" and the Jaschu episode points toward Mahler's "Lied von der Erde." (The name "Aschen-bach" contains the complex of "ashes" and "brook").

F. Androgeny and The Climacteric

Earlier, Aschenbach had attempted to support his masculinity by literary exposition of powerful figures, such as Frederick the Great to offset the feminine identification in his other work, such as "Maya." In Venice, he would be father to Tadzio and as the artist-dreamer, would also be his mother—give birth to him. Tadzio, his esthetic issue, also partakes of the feminine in his role of Eros. In this androgynous guise, Aschenbach begets the

virile strangers, the strong boy Jaschu, as well as the womanish dandy.

Indeed, the story deals with border-line situations and with characters who are in a transition stage of their life. At fourteen, Tadzio is between boyhood and youth, and we meet Aschenbach at the stage when he would reverse the pattern of his previous life. As Goethe's Faust would be rejuvenated by a magical potion, Ibsen's Solness by attachment to a young girl and Tolstoy's Anna Karenina by taking a young lover, so Aschenbach would experience a regeneration by falling in love with a young boy.

G. Heinz Kohut's Analysis of "Death In Venice."

Kohut's essay interprets the story as a "sublimation" of Mann's emerging profound conflicts. It traces them to Carla's suicide, to the illness of Mann's wife who was at the sanatorium when Mann was completing the story in Tölz. Kohut argues that Mann's successful sublimation of passive attitudes into artistic creativity "must have called forth the guilt of masculine achievement." This guilt is expiated in the portrayal of an artist—Aschenbach—in whom sublimation breaks down. Applying this syndrome to Aschenbach, Kohut sees the decisive threat to his defensive system in the breakdown of sublimated homosexual tenderness and the onrush of unsublimated homosexual desire. These are expressed in Aschenbach's last dream which points to a partial desire for identification with the mother so as to get the sexual love of the father.

Kohut focuses on the role of the father figures, symbolized by the four apparitions. He views them as

> the ego's projected recognition of the breakthrough of ancient guilt and fear, magically perceived as the threatening father figure returning from the grave . . . The varying combinations of fear and contempt which are experienced by Aschenbach in these encounters express the original hostile and loathing attitude toward a father figure with the secondary fear of retaliation from the stronger man . . .

Following a characteristic compulsive mechanism, the father is split into the revered and despised figure: The good father is Aschenbach who loves only the son, Tadzio, and foregoes heterosexual love. However, Aschenbach's ferocious hatred is primary and is revealed in his nightmare where the totem animal is killed and devoured. But, "the law of talion, which is the immutable authority for the archaic ego of the compulsive, death must be punished by death and Aschenbach has to die."

Kohut's perceptive analysis, it seems to me, does not do sufficient justice to the ambivalent ("ironic") element in Mann's approach, through which each element contains its dialectic other pole. Kohut writes of Aschenbach's identification with the mother so as to get the sexual love of the father. This needs to be supplemented by noting that the various father-figures in turn *arouse* and *lure* Aschenbach towards the sexual "tiger" in the swamp.

Kohut considers all the four tempters as leading Aschenbach to his death. This holds for the last three, but not for the wanderer whom I have termed the Primal Tempter. His crucial function is that of stirring Aschenbach to "life," to break with a pattern which left him inwardly sterile, even as the form of life which Aschenback seeks leads to his death. In this connection, it should be noted that whereas the others exhibit a fake strength and a caricature of potency, the first apparition with his white and long teeth, Adam's apple, his commanding bearing, is the sole strong figure who makes Aschenbach sense that the threat to him lies in continuing his former rigid existence.

Kohut draws a symbolic connection between Tadzio and the sea-death-mother motifs. However, sea and the mother also connote the womb and life. And, as indicated elsewhere, for Mann, death can be a rite of passage towards a higher life.

Summing up his hypothesis, Kohut observes that it is "particularly compatible with certain qualities of Mann's art, his detachment and irony." He writes:

> Primal scene experiences, creating overstimulation, dangerous defensive passive wishes, and castration anxiety, may lead to the attempt to return to the emotional equilibrium at the beginning of the experience and prepare the emotional soil for the development of the artistic attitude as an observer and describer. This hypothesis seems particularly compatible with certain qualities of Mann's art, his detachment and irony.

This perceptive psychoanalytical exposition fits that element of Mann's art which is used as *a defense*. As I have had occasion to point out, Mann has recourse to neutral descriptions and detached philosophic-mythic ruminations; but he does so to keep the charged emotions within communicable bounds. The aesthetic heart of the story is not "detachment," but a tension which at times is nearly explosive, even as some of the tension is projected on to Aschenbach.

The point has bearing on Kohut's central thesis that in creating this masterpiece, Mann "sublimated" his personal conflicts. But sublimation alone does not account for the magic of the work, for the affirmative and bouyant affect wrought by its art. My analysis has attempted to examine the technique by which this magic is produced. It is a technique—to put it formally—which allows for a shift of levels in psychic functioning and is the decisive factor in Mann's creative process.

Schopenhauer calls death "the principle of genius," and in *The Magic Mountain*, we read that the path of genius ("der geniale Weg") leads through death. Referring to *Death In Venice*, Thomas Mann quotes the lines (inspired by Venice) of the homoerotic poet Platen:

> "Wer die Schönheit angeschaut mit Augen Ist dem Tode schon anheimgegeben." (Whoever has looked on Beauty fully Has already surrendered to Death)

His art, Mann states (*Demands of the Hour*) is "sympathetic to life." But to achieve the new, he tells us in *A Sketch of My Life* calls for "deliberate abandonment . . . the leap in the dark." This thought is close to that expressed in Goethe's celebrated poem "Sehnsucht":

> Und wenn du das nicht hast, Dieses: Stirb und werde!
> Bist du nur ein trüber Gast Auf der dunklen Erde.
> (And if you do not have This: Die and transcend! You are but a dreary guest On the sombre earth.)

Hans Castorp experiences such transcendence following his death-like sleep in the snows, as does young Joseph after he is thrown into the pit by his brokers; and in *Doctor Faustus*, hope emerges from "hopelessness," from Leverkühn's descent into the lowest depths.

Such rebirth is but a prayer in *Death In Venice*, for Aschenbach is too old, Tadzio too young. The prayer continues in *The Magic Mountain* and is revitalized in the first three volumes of the Joseph story. It is dimmed in *Joseph The Provider* and tinged with despair in *Doctor Faustus*. In *Felix Krull,* which Mann worked on before his death, it assumes a comic form.

Like Goethe's *Faust*, Thomas Mann's work warns against the two major temptations of the demon: The bed of sloth and the ravages of vagabondage, with the one calling forth the other. Now, rebellion can take form in different attitudes. In the German tradition, its most characteristic shape has been an aesthetic romanticism. In *Death In Venice*, it takes the form of an aesthetic homoeroticism. This is shown to be "useless," for there can come no living issue from it. Still, Mann is saying here that in a world preparing for World Wars, it is nobler to dream a beautiful dream. Indeed, as a whole, Mann's art pictures the dissolution of the bourgeois order. In the *Buddenbrooks*, it appears in a family framework, set in a town; in *Death In Venice*, it is broadened to a city: in *The Magic Mountain* to the European continent and in *Doctor Faustus* to the Western world as a whole. The disintegration also appears "somatically": Thomas Buddenbrook's decaying tooth and Hanno's typhus, the cholera in Venice, tuberculosis on the Berghof mountain, and Leverkühn's syphilitic infection.

However, Mann's story of Jacob and Joseph presents a possible wholesome alternative. Here, he takes both West and East for his landscape. In the manner of Theodor Reik's later work, Mann's epic would unite the historic with explorations of the depths, the coulisses of pre-history. Written under the demonic shadows of Nazism, it is Mann's most valiant attempt to indicate the possibility of creativity emerging from the dark ground of chaos. In nearly all of Mann's works, hope is seen in the involvement of the individual with the creative ground of "the folk."

Source: Harry Slochower, "Thomas Mann's *Death in Venice*," in *American Imago*, Vol. 26, No. 2, Summer, 1969, pp. 99-122.

Isadore Traschen

In the following essay, Traschen asserts that Death in Venice *is the first literary work "to use the mythic method as a way of giving shape and significance to contemporary history by manipulating a continuous parallel between contemporaneity and antiquity."*

In reviewing Joyce's *Ulysses* in 1923 T. S. Eliot observed that "In using the myth [of the *Odyssey*], in manipulating a continuous parallel between contemporaneity and antiquity, Mr. Joyce is pursuing a method which others must pursue after him. . . . It is simply a way of controlling, of ordering, of giving shape and a significance to the immense panorama of futility and anarchy which is contemporary history. It is a method already adumbrated by Mr. Yeats, and of the need for which I believe Mr. Yeats to have been the first contemporary to be conscious. . . . Instead of the narrative method, we may now use the mythical method." Eliot was, of course, affirming his own practice as well, his recreation the year before of the "long narrative

poem" in *The Wasteland*. Yet, as we know, back in 1911 Thomas Mann had already employed the mythical method in giving shape to *Death in Venice* by drawing upon Nietzsche's concept of the Apollonian-Dionysian mythology in *The Birth of Tragedy*. But Mann anticipated Joyce and Eliot by drawing upon still another area of myth, one apparently disguised so well that it has gone unnoticed. This area of myth has been established by Joseph Campbell in his exhaustive and brilliant study, *The Hero with a Thousand Faces*. This study reveals that the heroes of mythology undergo a common pattern of experience; Campbell calls this pattern the monomyth. The monomythic pattern is that of the Adventure of the Hero, divided into the phases of Departure, Initiation, and Return. Gustave von Aschenbach, Mann's hero, does not return. Thus the last phase of the monomyth points to the difference between the divine comedy—the reunion with the Deity—which actually or figuratively shapes the old myths, and the tragedy which shapes *Death in Venice*. The mythic hero's adventure takes place in a world which, even if haunted by unfriendly spirits, is nonetheless made for him; Aschenbach's adventure takes place in a world he does not belong to, a formless, polyglot, perverse, cosmopolitan society. This difference in the last phase suggests that Mann will use the mythic pattern ironically, parodistically, again anticipating Joyce and Eliot.

Death in Venice, then, embodies two primary myths, the Apollonian-Dionysian and the monomyth. But what I have said about the corresponding patterns of Mann's tale and the monomyth is hardly sufficient evidence that Mann was drawing upon this mythic type; *bildungsroman* and picaresque novels can be shown to have the same pattern, with a "happy" ending. That Mann would have turned to myth is likely from his own earlier work, stimulated as it was by the strong disposition toward myth in the nineteenth century, particularly in Germany. Further, that myths had common patterns was a familiar notion by 1911—*The Golden Bough* had already been an influence for some twenty years. But that *Death in Venice* is the first to use the mythic method as a way of giving shape and significance to contemporary history by manipulating a continuous parallel between contemporaneity and antiquity still needs to be demonstrated. This I will now do, and at the same time show how Mann integrated the monomyth into the Apollonian-Dionysian mythology.

In the first phase, that of departure, the monomythic hero is one who is exceptionally gifted and frequently honored by society; so with Aschenbach, the master of official, Apollonian art, and so officially von Aschenbach since his fiftieth birthday. But Mann is at once ambiguous about his hero, for the name means both life and death. *Bach* is a brook or stream, a life symbol; but also the root of Bacchus, or Dionysus, a death symbol here, as is *Asch*, ashes. The condition in myth which gives rise to the adventure is an underlying uneasiness in the hero and society. In our story the social uneasiness is owing to the plague which has been menacing Europe for some months, the personal uneasiness *apparently* to overwork. In myths this condition is presented openly as disastrous: "In apocalyptic vision the physical and spiritual life of the whole earth can be represented as fallen or on the point of falling into ruin." Mann, though, beguiles the reader through understatement: with Europe and Aschenbach menaced, his hero responds with a short stroll. We are beguiled further by the casual account of the chance meeting, as often in myths, with a stranger, here standing in the portico of the mortuary chapel. But Mann is pointing to an apocalyptic moment, for the stranger is standing above "two apocalyptic beasts"—plague and death in our story. Now Mann unleashes the full apocalyptic vision; stimulated by something unpleasant in the stranger, Aschenbach suddenly feels a "widening of inward barriers," and this brings on "a seizure, almost an hallucination." "Desire projected itself visually," and it takes the form of a tropical marshland, a jungle rampant with male and female symbols of sexuality. The jungle is the source of the plague; and it is in India, where the cult of Dionysus presumably originated; thus the plague symbolizes the apocalyptic, destructive force of Dionysus. Now with the mythic hero, an apocalyptic event signalizes the beginning of a moral rebirth; the summons of a stranger usually marks "the dawn of religious illumination and 'the awakening of the self,'" followed by the "mystery of transfiguration." In *Death in Venice* all this is realized with tragic irony in Aschenbach's religious debauch, the awakening of his self to sensual lawlessness, and his mock transfiguration.

The hallucination points to a modern refinement of the mythic material. Mann said he came late to Freud, yet the phrase, "Desire projected itself visually," and the "Freudian" symbols throughout suggest a familiarity with Freud's work; *The Interpretation of Dreams* had come out some twelve years before *Death in Venice*. Thus the landscape of the monomyth, filled with sinister figures, is in this

> Mann was among those who pointed to the absence of a vital myth as a fatal quality of modern existence."

sense the naive, external equivalent of the terrain of Aschenbach's inner self. He journeys to the darkest recesses of the self, to the unconscious. From this point of view the action of the story is the gradual unveiling of Aschenbach's unconscious, fully revealed in the Dionysian orgy through the appropriately Freudian dream mechanism.

Who is the stranger? He is "the herald" of the myth who summons the hero to the adventure, the "carrier of the power of destiny," often loathsome and underestimated; he calls up feared, unconscious forces. So Aschenbach feels an unpleasant twinge, but in a minute forgets the stranger, pushing him out of his consciousness. But Aschenbach's unconscious has been sounded, and the hallucination follows. In the myths, as Campbell observes, "The regions of the unknown (desert, jungle, deep sea, alien land, etc.) are free fields for the projection of unconscious content." Jungle, sea and alien land all figure crucially in "Death in Venice," and if we stretch a point about the sandy beach, the desert too. Now why does the stranger resemble the others Aschenbach meets, all of whom share many features with Aschenbach and, to a lesser extent, Tadzio? Vernon Venable has pointed out that "as morbid caricatures of the heroes of his [Aschenbach's] own novels [they] are really images of himself and his loved-one Tadzio. . . ."; in other words, projections of Aschenbach's unconscious. The stranger's features make it clear that the latent forces are an ambiguous mixture of refinement and coarseness, which will be manifest later in Aschenbach as homosexuality and bestiality. The ambiguities in his appearance reflect the Apollonian-Dionysian polarity. The man is beardless, with milky freckled skin; this suggests youthful innocence, yet with homosexual implications—all pointing to Tadzio. His red hair, though, indicates sensuality, as does his snub-nose, a notable aspect of the mask of the satyrs in Greek tragedy. The snub-nose also suggests the human skull, or death, the consequence of sensuality in our story; the stranger resembles Dürer's

''Death.'' Mann's use of the snub-nose as a Dionysian symbol becomes positively brilliant when we remember it was a feature of Socrates, at first Aschenbach's rationalizing Apollonian spokesman. In the *Symposium* Socrates is further described as having a face ''like that of a satyr''; and he is also called a ''bully,'' the term Mann uses for the Dionysian guitarist at the hotel—Dionysus had an epiphany in the form of a bull. All this points to the Dionysian underlife in what this supreme rationalist says to Phaedrus-Tadzio. Further ambiguities in the stranger are indicated by his indigenous rucksack and yellowish woolen suit which are oddly coupled with a straw hat suggesting the South. The stranger is also bold, domineering, ruthless, and possibly deformed, all Dionysian elements. Like many of the others, he has long, white, glistening teeth, suggesting the threatening Dionysian animal; the threat is brought to the surface in the unhealthy teeth of Tadzio which carry out the motif of the Dionysian plague.

These exotic qualities, aspects of the theme of dislocation, stimulate a longing for travel in Aschenbach which leads to a loss of control, a farewell to disciplined work. So in the adventure of the monomythic hero that which is ''somehow profoundly familiar to the unconscious—though unknown, surprising, and even frightening to the conscious personality—makes itself known.'' And the consequence is that ''what formerly was meaningful may become strangely emptied of value.'' For Aschenbach, too, the old occupations are no longer attractive, and though terrified, he feels an inexplicable longing for the new. ''The familiar life horizon has been outgrown; the old concepts, ideals, and emotional patterns no longer fit; the time for the passing of the threshold is at hand.'' He whimsically decides he will go on a journey, but not—and here the whimsy is overtaken by his unconscious—all the way to the Dionysian tigers of his hallucination. A night in a *wagon-lit*—a phrase which sounds the motifs of the Dionysian night, sleep, and death; three or four weeks of lotus eating—the familiar Apollonian temptation of Odysseus, with an undertone of the ''lethargic element'' of the Dionysian—this beguiles Aschenbach, all he believes he will allow himself.

As the monomythic hero sets out on his journey he sometimes has a guide; so Aschenbach parodistically studies ''railway guides.'' Supernatural aids are frequent. ''The first encounter of the hero-journey is with a protective figure (often a little old crone or old man) who provides the adventurer with amulets against the dragon forces he is about to pass''; and ''ageless guardians will appear.'' The figure is parodied in the ageless young-old man encountered on the boat. And though repellent, he suggests to Aschenbach the ''amulets'' he will eventually use in his pursuit of Tadzio: carmine cheeks, strawberry lips, etc. In the more sophisticated myths supernatural guides often take the form of ''the ferryman, the conductor of souls to the afterworld.'' This is parodied in the gondolier Charon with his incoherent muttering which foreshadows Tadzio's blurry tongue—the inarticulate, the bestial which overcomes Aschenbach. The gondolier forces Aschenbach to submit to his will, even if, as Aschenbach says in his first overt surrender, this means sending him ''down to the kingdom of Hades,'' that is, the unconscious, the demonic. The sinister aspect of the man is further indicated by the casually realistic fact that he has no license to ferry people, so that he cannot stay for Charon's usual fee. The passage of the hero is often made in the belly of a whale, which functions as the womb in which he is reborn. In parodistic contrast the coffin-gondola is the tomb foreshadowing the death of Aschenbach; in both cases the passage is over water, here the ambiguous symbol of life and death.

In crossing the first threshold the hero feels a strong urge to venture beyond the protection of his own society; so Aschenbach is dissatisfied with the island off the Adriatic because the people are mostly Germanic, Austrian; also because the cliff formations do not provide easy access to the sea, the death-wish object. He rejoices in cosmopolitan Venice—in strange places the unconscious is freed. Campbell points out that ''incestuous *libido* and patricidal *destrudo* are thence reflected back against the individual and his society in forms suggesting threats of violence and fancied dangerous delight. . . . There is incest in the implied son-father relationship of Tadzio and Aschenbach, who never had a son and so was presumably untutored in his potential homosexuality. The implication of incest is reinforced by the fact that it is the leitmotif in the Greek mysteries of the initiatory second birth. Thus in the *Bacchae* Zeus' cry to his son Dionysus is what Aschenbach is really saying to Tadzio: ''Dithyrambus, come/Enter my male womb.'' Aschenbach's surrender to his homosexual and incestuous feelings is a blow at his respectable father, his fatherland, and the entire bourgeois structure—passion is like crime, Mann points out.

The monomythic hero encounters threatening as well as protective figures. Some are ''adroit shapeshifters.'' They try to seduce him by appearing as attractive young men. Aschenbach meets the same person, not merely in different shapes, but in different stages of youth—parodied in the case of the young-old man. These figures are the shifting shapes of his unconscious. Again, the hero often meets wild women; these would be the maenads in the Dionysian dream. But where the hero overcomes the dangers, in Mann's ironic treatment Aschenbach surrenders to their degenerate sexuality. The most familiar of these figures is the disarming Pan, who appears in a passage of unusual symbolic density. Its tempo, gentle then increasingly violent, is analogous to that of the entire story. It opens in Apollonian innocence: ''At the world's edge began a strewing of roses [Homer's ''rosy-fingered dawn''], a shining and a blooming ineffably pure; baby cloudlets hung illumined, like attendant amoretti, in the blue and blushful haze.'' This is love without sex, the ''pure'' thing. But after this disarming correspondence between nature and Aschenbach's first sense of his feelings for Tadzio, Mann works in overt male and female sex symbols which fuse with images of a pronounced Dionysian kind: ''purple effulgence fell upon the sea, that seemed to heave it forward on its welling waves; from horizon to zenith went great quivering thrusts like golden lances, the gleam became a glare; . . . with godlike violence . . . the steeds of the sun-god mounted the sky . . . like prancing goats the waves on the farther strand leaped among the craggy rocks. It was a world *possessed*, peopled by Pan, that closed round the spellbound man . . . [my italics].'' The movement from innocence to sensuality illustrates the bondage of the Apollonian to the Dionysian. In the passage quoted even the innocent opening is implicit with depravity when we consider another aspect of Mann's technique that Venable has pointed out, the poetic structure of associated images. For example, the innocent red of the roses and the ''blushful'' haze are linked to the sensual red of the hair and lashes of the strangers, the cheeks and lips of the young-old man and the later Aschenbach, the ripe and dead-ripe strawberries, etc.; the ''blushful'' haze itself contains a first awareness of sex. The innocent blue is linked with Tadzio's bluish teeth (physical decay), the bluish sand (decay and sterility) of the ticket seller, the various sailor blouses (homosexuality), the ocean (formlessness), etc. The purple suggests the Dionysian wine, and the gold reminds us of Dionysus-Tadzio's curls. Similarly, the four golden steeds of Apollo are also the four horses of the Christian-Dionysian apocalypse. Perhaps the finest irony in the paragraph is the first of

several parodies of the transformation and rebirth of the monomythic hero. As Aschenbach is assaulted by this Apollonian-Dionysian vision, he feels ''strangely [suggesting the strangers and the stranger god] metamorphosed'' by ''forgotten feelings, precious pangs of his youth, quenched long since by the stern service that had been his life and now returned.'' This feeling of rebirth is of course illusory, one of the many forms his temptations take.

Among the dangers encountered in crossing the threshold to the unknown are ''the clashing rocks (Symplegades) that crush the traveler, but between which the old heroes always pass,'' for example, Jason and his Argonauts, and Odysseus. The rocks stand for ''pairs of opposites (being and not being, life and death, beauty and ugliness, good and evil, and all the other polarities that bind the faculties to hope and fear . . .).'' But where the heroes of myth succeeded in passing through, Aschenbach is crushed by them, the face of innocence turning out to be evil. For a while, though, there is the possibility that he may escape. The faintly rotten scent of swamp and sea which he breathes in ambiguously ''deep, tender, almost painful draughts'' forces him to flee for his life. His escape, his salvation, is a passage through the very valley of regrets, a parodistic reversal of values. But his luggage has been shipped in the wrong direction, and this provides Aschenbach with an excuse to return to his hotel. On the return trip a wind comes up from the sea and the waves are now ''crisping,'' that is, curling (in the original, *gekrauselten*, with the same meaning)—Aschenbach is being driven by the ambiguously lively sea to his death, to curly-haired Tadzio-Dionysus, who, it should be noted, resembles the god. The death symbolism in the apparently life-giving ''crisping'' is made clear at the end: as Aschenbach sits on the beach for the last time, ''little crisping [*krauselnde*] shivers'' run across the wide stretch of shallow water. The idea of death is reinforced by the cold and shallow water, the deserted beach, and the out-of-season (another frequent kind of dislocation) autumnal look; but most interestingly by a camera on a tripod, at the edge of the water, apparently abandoned, its black cloth snapping in the freshening wind. The tripod, a prize in the funeral games for Patroclus, carries with it overtones of the Apollonian Homer; it is also the seat of the priestess of Apollo at Delphi, secured when Apollo slew the python. Linked with the black cloth and the camera, it suggests the death of plastic, Apollonian art, and the birth of the pseudo-Apollonian, mechanical art of the camera. The death symbolism in this scene is consummated in the figure of Tadzio as the youthful Hermes Psychopompos (translated as Summoner), conductor of souls to the dead, fused with the sea. Yet the sea, the ''misty inane,'' is still for Aschenbach ''an immensity of richest expectation'' just as Tadzio is still ''pale and lovely.''

The figure of Hermes concludes the sequence of mythological persons who make up one kind of temptation on the Road of Trials. They are all attractive, and they all remind us of Tadzio. They appear innocent at first, as with Apollo and Amor; become somewhat suspect, as with Narcissus; then openly fatal like Dionysus. Along the way we meet others too; pairs like Apollo and Hyacinth, and Zeus and Ganymede, suggesting homosexuality. These two pairs, incidentally, may be seen together with Narcissus in a room in the Bargello Palace in Florence; they are the creations of the unmarried Cellini.

The second phase of the adventure of the monomythic hero is that of Initiation, and it begins with the Road of Trials we have just noted. ''Once having traversed the threshold, the hero moves in a dream landscape of curiously fluid, ambiguous forms, where he must survive a succession of trials.'' Aschenbach's trials develop on the boat to Venice. The trip is a kind of dream-passage. His ''time-sense falters and grows dim'' under the impact of the vast sea; and in his dreams the ''strange, shadowy figures'' of the elderly coxcomb and the goat-bearded man pass and repass through his mind. In the gondola a ''spell [Dionysian term] of indolence [lotus motif]'' overtakes him; the ''thought passed dreamily'' through him that he had fallen into the clutches of a criminal. He fails this trial, too, for the thought ''had not power to rouse him to action.'' The voyage to the underworld is another typical trial, as with Odysseus, Theseus, and Hercules, but where the mythical hero wills it, Aschenbach surrenders to it; he allows Charon to impose his will on him, and accepts Hades as his destiny; that is, he surrenders to the forces of his unconscious.

Symbolically, the Road of Trials is the hero's descent into ''the crooked lanes of his own spiritual labyrinth,'' a precise formulation of Aschenbach's adventure. Now the image of Venice as a labyrinth—an exact translation—is used twice, both times when Aschenbach is pursuing Tadzio. This should not be taken as a conventional, dead metaphor, for its mythic content bears directly on our analysis. There is, first, an ironic analogy to Theseus

as Aschenbach loses his bearings in the labyrinth—not merely geographically, but also morally and spiritually. The primary significance of the image lies elsewhere, though; according to Robert Graves, the labyrinth served in Crete and Egypt as ''a maze pattern used to guide performers of an erotic spring dance.'' Thus Aschenbach's sterile pursuit of Tadzio parodies the fertility rite of the earlier cultures.

In the initiation phase the ''ultimate adventure, when all the barriers and ogres have been overcome, is commonly represented as a mystical marriage . . . of the triumphant hero-soul with the Queen Goddess of the World. This is the crisis at the nadir, the zenith, or . . . within the darkness of the deepest chamber of the heart.'' This triumphant marriage is presented with savage irony in the first climax, the dream of the Dionysian rites. In the myth, the soul marries the Queen Goddess; in the dream, body copulates with body. This apocalyptic fall is the ironic counterpart of the heroic apotheosis in the monomyth. The apocalyptic climax, further, is set in the center of Greek irrationalism, showing its destructiveness; the second, philosophic climax—between Socrates-Aschenbach and Phaedrus-Tadzio—is set in the center of Greek rationalism, showing its inadequacy. Aschenbach's fall is in tragic contrast to the salvation of the mythic hero who, after his trials, can now concentrate ''upon trancendental things''; the lesson of the second address to Phaedrus is that man can not endure transcendence, that poets in particular ''can not walk the way of beauty without Eros as our companion and guide.'' We should note Mann's pacing, from the violent tempo of the apocalyptic vision to the calm, yet moving detachment of the philosophic discourse.

After the trials the monomythic hero is reborn or undergoes a metamorphosis. Mann presents a parody of both possibilities in the interlude between the two climaxes, the scene with the hotel barber. He is clearly no ordinary one. His garrulousness is a realistic echo of actual barbers, but his verbal flourishes—as elegant as his manual—indicate that this ''oily one'' is a parody of the magician or shaman performing the fertility rites of death and rebirth. He ''restores'' Aschenbach by washing his hair ''in two waters,'' ambiguously clear and dark; ''and lo,'' magically, Aschenbach's hair is black—he is young again, reborn. This parody of the fertility ritual is pursued further. The ''delicate carmine'' on Aschenbach's cheeks corresponds to the red dye, extracted from the Dionysian ivy, used to color the faces of male fertility images; and his lips are the color of the ironically ripe strawberries (*Erdbeere*), hence a mock-fertility symbol. Aschenbach is both ''transformed'' and ''reborn.'' ''Young again,'' he goes off ''in a dream'' to ''fall in love as soon as he likes''—a shattering line. Aschenbach is in effect wearing the mask of Dionysus, like the young-old man he was repelled by earlier. In the *Symposium* Socrates' ''outer mask is the carved head of the Silenus; but . . . what temperance there is residing within!'' With Aschenbach there is no Socratic transcendence of sensuality; the outer mask reflects his inner self. And with our modern sense of the perpetual tensions of the inner life, we can either marvel at Socrates' equilibrium, or we can question the Platonic psychology. Mann questioned it in the entire story, and specifically in the second Platonic discourse by showing that spiritual heights and sensual abyss are the same. Plato himself seems to be aware of this elsewhere when he has the drunken Alcibiades charge that Socrates ''clothes himself in language [Platonic] that is like the skin of the wanton satyr.''

Aschenbach is ''metamorphosed into the satyr,'' a parody of Nietzsche's glorification of this creature as ''truth and nature in their most potent form.'' As with the hero in myth, he ''assimilates his opposite (his own unsuspected self) . . . .'' But for the hero this action means that he must put aside his ''pride, his virtue, beauty, and life, and bow or submit to the absolutely intolerable.''; Aschenbach puts aside his pride and virtue, and he does submit, but out of depravity, not humility.

The last phase of the adventure is The Return of the Hero—but Aschenbach does not return. It is true that in the myths the hero occasionally refused to return, taking up ''residence forever in the blessed isle of the unaging Goddess of Immortal Being.'' Odysseus' seven years with Calypso may be an echo of this. Midway in his adventure, in his Apollonian phase, Aschenbach does feel ''transported to Elysium . . . to a spot most carefree for the sons of men . . . entirely dedicate to the sun and the feasts of the sun.'' But the sun-Apollo-Tadzio is destructive Dionysus. Aschenbach makes one effort to leave, then surrenders to his blissful fall. His death is his ultimate refusal of society. When the mythic hero does will to return, he brings a transcendental message, one which will put an end to passing joys, sorrows, and passions. This transcendentalism is parodied in Achenbach's ravaging sensuality. At the end the hero of myth achieves a ''world-historical triumph''; Aschenbach's tragedy symbolizes the decline of European civilization.

From this demonstration of Mann's use of myth it is fair to conclude that *Death in Venice* is the first novel of our time to apply the symbolic mode with all the complexity and multiplicity of theme of *Ulysses* or *The Wasteland*, and the first to use myth to control and order what Eliot called the futility and anarchy of the modern world. Why then did Mann's innovation go unremarked? In part, no doubt, because of the way he disguised his use of myth; in part, too, because of the fact that he subdued his material to the conventional narrative form. Mann never abandoned the old form, though he took more and more liberties with it. Since the novel is a bourgeois form, the strain Mann put on it while leaving it apparently intact constituted a formal analogy of the substantive strain he put on bourgeois values and mores. In *Death in Venice* and elsewhere the orderly, bourgeois surface worked as a formal understatement of and an ironic container for Mann's radical themes. It beguiled the bourgeois reader with its apparent conventionality while at the same time disturbing him with anti-bourgeois matter in the anti-bourgeois symbolic mode. And one principal matter was myth; more precisely, modern man's relation to it.

We can explore Mann's views on this subject further by inquiring into the connection between the two areas of myth that Mann used. How do they work together? From the modern point of view we can say that the ancient sense of life as realized in the monomyth was both ''naive'' and profound. It was profound in its images of the underlife; it was ''naive'' in its confidence in an orderly resolution, usually through the union of the human and divine. But Mann saw that our modern sense has been even more naive, as in our Apollonian, dream-like illusion of a rational, myth-denying civilization; or our cult of art as a substitute religion, with the esthetic attitude superseding the ethical. Mann saw the analogy between the monomyth and the modern experience; but he also saw that where the ''naive'' past took cognizance of the underlife, we did not. And so he set his Apollonian hero on a modern road of trials, a journey not through but *into* life, into the deep well of the unconscious where the Dionysian passions thrive. *Death in Venice* is a warning that art is not life nor a substitute for it; and a prophecy—fulfilled all too well—of the fate of our naive, European civilization, its fall into barbarism.

Nor did Mann naively embrace Nietzsche's clamor for myth. In the closing pages of *The Birth of Tragedy* Nietzsche declares, ''Without myth every culture loses its healthy creative natural power: it is only a horizon encompassed with myths that rounds off to unity a social movement. It is only myth that frees all the powers of the imagination and of the Apollonian dream from their aimless wanderings . . . the mythless man remains eternally hungering amid the past, and digs for grubs and roots . . . .'' Yeats and Lawrence responded passionately and naively to this kind of call; and Eliot only somewhat less so—the metaphor of ''roots'' as well as others suggests he was conscious of Nietzsche at the time of *The Wasteland*. Mann did not respond so simply, and I would guess that it was just that humanism which Eliot and others deplored which made him more critical. Consider Mann's use of Nietzsche's conception of the Apollonian-Dionysian polarity. At times, certainly, *Death in Venice* seems to be a direct, though creative transcription of Nietzsche's work. For example, Tadzio as ''the noblest moment of Greek sculpture'' symbolizes Nietzsche's idea of the highest reaches of Apollonian art; or Nietzsche's observations that ''the dithyrambic chorus is a chorus of transformed beings, whose civic past and social position are totally forgotten'' is undoubtedly the inspiration of Aschenbach possessed by the satyrs and the stranger god in the dream orgy; and Mann's imaginary Platonic discourses seem to be a re-creation of Nietzsche's attack on Socratic rationalism. But Mann was too sane to go all the way to the tiger, to champion Nietzsche's romantic Blakean doctrine that ''excess revealed itself as truth''— wisdom for Blake. What Mann did was to take the concept of the union of the Apollonian and the Dionysian, show their coexistence within the individual and the tragic consequences which might follow. But he went further. Steadfast in his conviction of the ambiguity in all ideas, he proceeded to parody Nietzsche's as he had the modern myths of civilization and art. For example, Nietzsche approvingly cites Lucretius as saying that in dreams ''the glorious divine figures first appeared to the souls of men; in dreams the great shaper beheld the splendid corporeal structure of superhuman beings''; this is parodied in the animal-like men in the dream orgy. And Aschenbach's frequent dream state, we remember, is filled with sinister rather than glorious figures—perhaps a Freudian parody, further, of Nietzsche's notion of dream as a metaphor of Apollonian art. Again, Nietzsche is lyrical about the prospect that ''under the charm of the Dionysian . . . the union between man and man [is] reaffirmed''; this is mocked everywhere, in all the suggestions of homosexual degeneracy and in the last dream. Indeed, the dominant homosexuality undoubtedly paro-

dies Nietzsche's often-repeated phrase that the genius of Greek tragedy lies in the ''fraternal union'' of the Apollonian and Dionysian. Again, Nietzsche says that the Dionysian drunken reality ''seeks to destroy the individual and redeem him by a mystic feeling of Oneness,'' a phrase parodied in Aschenbach's fallen state of oneness with the stranger god. Further, for Nietzsche individuation is ''the prime cause of evil''; but Aschenbach's surrender to the Dionysian mass is evil, a consequence of his loss of individuality. For Nietzsche the Dionysian orgies signify ''festivals of world-redemption and days of transfiguration''; in *Death in Venice* they signify world decline and disfiguration. A sketch of the evolution of the story in terms of the Nietzschean mythology rather than the monomyth is the clearest indication of Mann's ironic use of *The Birth of Tragedy*. From this point of view—and with the reservation that the Apollonian and the Dionysian are ambiguously present from the beginning—the story may be divided into three esthetic phases: (1) Christian, as symbolized by Aschenbach's fictional hero, St. Sebastian; (2) pagan-Apollonian, as in the sun motif and the sculptural metaphors of Tadzio; and (3) pagan-Dionysian, as symbolized by the plague, which now comes to the foreground, and the dream orgy. But the third phase also marks the ascent of vulgar art, that of the guitarist, the barber, and the camera. Hence it is the *un*esthetic phase— another way of marking Aschenbach's decline.

Mann made full use of the insights of the Apollonian-Dionysian polarity, expanding it beyond the fatal passion of an old man for a young boy into a symbolic tale about—among other things— the relation between art and life, the artist and society, the aristocratic past and the bourgeois present, the North and South, Platonic idealism and bodily eroticism, the conscious and the unconscious . . . about, we might say, civilization and its discontents. But Mann was not swept up by Nietzsche's romantic glorification of the polarity. In fact, just as Mann's ironic treatment of the monomyth points up the rootless existence of modern man, so his parodistic treatment of *The Birth of Tragedy* points to a disagreement with Nietzsche's optimistic prophecy of a rebirth of tragedy, with its traditional regenerative function. Nietzsche's view is reflected in a summary observation of the significance of the Apollonian-Dionysian polarity. He says that the Apollonian illusion is ''the assiduous veiling during the performance of the tragedy of the intrinsically Dionysian effect: which, however, is so powerful, that it ends by forcing the Apollonian drama itself into a sphere where it begins to talk with Dionysian wisdom, and even denies itself and its Apollonian conspicuousness.'' What we have in this passage is an elegant phrasing of the familiar archetypal pattern of death (the denial of the Apollonian self) and transcendence-rebirth (the discovery of Dionysian wisdom). And exactly here is where Mann is most critical in his parody. Is transcendence possible for a modern tragic hero? It is in the bleakest Greek and Shakespearean tragedies where the hero believes that the cosmos, no matter how irrational and unjust, is significant for him. But with the breakdown of this belief in the last century or so, any final affirmation now is more like an empty gesture, made in an empty theatre, with no gods on the stage or in the audience. It is this which shapes our conception of the modern tragic hero. Where once his recognition of himself as a poor, naked, forked animal led to his eventual transcendence of that fact, in *Death in Venice* each recognition by Aschenbach of his capture by Tadzio-Dionysus leads only to the acceptance of his further spiritual decline. His collapse symbolizes the breakdown of the European will, of European civilization confronted by the forces of darkness. And yet, we must add, this is not Mann's last word. Some thirty-five years later in *Doctor Faustus,* in the context of the barbarous underworld of Nazism, Adrian Leverkuhn confronts the diabolic in himself and realizes the ''transcendence of despair . . . in which the voice of mourning . . . changes its meaning; it abides as a light in the night.'' Leverkuhn convinces us of his transcendence by his unceasing creativity, realized by selling his soul to the devil; transcendence is possible only through despair, through the diseased ''hellish yelling'' in his masterwork, ''The Lamentation of Dr. Faustus.'' But surrender to disease destroys Aschenbach's creativity; he abdicates his creative powers. Thus Kenneth Burke is surely wrong in reading the Socratic doctrine of transcendence whereby corruption is transformed into a saving of souls as applicable to Aschenbach. It is precisely Socrates' idea of transcendence which Mann repudiates in the second imaginary conversation with Phaedrus-Tadzio.

But if Mann has in good measure parodied Nietzsche in *Death in Venice,* the fate of the mythless and rootless Aschenbach would nonetheless indicate a sympathy with Nietzsche's views on the necessity of myth, both psychologically and as a mode of knowledge. If modern rationalistic man denies myth as folk nonsense, the primal forces which myths embody will take their revenge on

him. And yet, how perilous a literary, fashionable turn to myth might be is fully indicated in *Doctor Faustus* in the figures of the proto-Nazi intellectuals. Campbell summarizes the adventure of the monomythic hero with the observation that it is fundamentally inward—''into depths where obscure resistances are overcome, and long lost, forgotten powers are revivified, to be made available for the transfiguration of the world.'' Mann's point is that the revivification of these powers is not necessarily an occasion for celebration, and indeed may well be a death spasm, as with Germany under the Nazis. Once or twice Nietzsche seems to be aware of the destructive alternative to the glorious fusion and interdependence of the Apollonian and Dionysian. ''Indeed, it seems as if the myth [of Oedipus] were trying to whisper into our ears the fact that wisdom, especially Dionysian wisdom, is an unnatural abomination; that whoever, through his own knowledge, plunges nature into an abyss of annihilation, must also expect to experience the dissolution of nature in himself.'' But this is rare, and it hardly qualifies his rapture. It may be that such a passage, with its ambiguous regard of the Apollonian-Dionysian polarity, was the final touch to Mann's inspiration. For inspiration is generated in Mann by the ambiguity which paralyzes most of us.

Mann was among those who pointed to the absence of a vital myth as a fatal quality of modern existence. In doing so he gave us a marvellously complex expression of what is probably the central concern of our time—or was before the thermonuclear bomb made all questions but that of survival irrelevant—the problem of realizing our irrational drives within the framework of a rational society. In the modern polar view of existence developed by the romantics, reason, common sense, and civilization dry us up and emotion, unreason, and nature revitalize us. This polarity takes on varied expression: abstract-concrete, essence-existence, science-art, objective-subjective, thought-feeling, mind-body, reason-passion, classicism-romanticism, society-individual, conventional-authentic, bourgeois-artist, god-devil. We may be sympathetic with this romantic existentialist revolt, with its attempt to return men to themselves; still, *Death in Venice* foreshadowing *Doctor Faustus*—is a reminder that one-sided excess may bring not only Dionysian wisdom but destruction as well, that if the virtues of science, reason, and civilization are of ambiguous value, so are those of myth, passion, and the so-called natural life. It is a reminder, too, that those of us who have only an external, literary relation to myth are peculiarly ripe for debauchery—intellectual as well as sensual.

Source: Isadore Traschen, ''The Uses of Myth in 'Death in Venice,''' in *Modern Fiction Studies*, Vol. XI, No. 2, Summer, 1965, pp. 165-79.

Sources

Berlin, Jeffrey B. *Approaches to Teaching Mann's ''Death in Venice'' and Other Short Fiction*, New York: MLA, 1992.

Goldman, Harvey. *Max Weber and Thomas Mann: Calling and the Shaping of the Self*, Berkeley: University of California Press, 1988.

Nietzsche, Friedrich. *''The Birth of Tragedy'' and ''The Case of Wagner,''*, translated by Walter Kaufmann, New York: Vintage Books-Random House, 1967.

Reed, T. J. *Death in Venice: Making and Unmaking a Master*, New York: Twayne Publishers, 1994.

Tobin, Robert. ''Why is Tadzio a Boy? Perspectives on Homoeroticism in 'Death in Venice,''' in *Death in Venice*, translated and edited by Clayton Koelb, Norton Critical Edition, New York: W. W. Norton & Co., 1994, pp. 207-232.

Weber, Max. *The Protestant Ethic and the Spirit of Capitalism*, translated by Talcott Parsons, 1930, reprinted, London and New York: Routledge, 1992. First published in article form 1904-5.

Further Reading

Prater, Donald. *Thomas Mann: A Life*, Oxford: Oxford University Press, 1995.
   A clear and engaging treatment of Thomas Mann's life including a section considering *Death in Venice* and considerations of Mann's war-time exile in the United States.

Reed, T. J. *Death in Venice: Making and Unmaking the Master*, New York: Twayne Publishers, 1994.
   An excellent overview of critical consideration of the novel. Reed is cogent in introducing several approaches to understanding Mann's novella.

Tobin, Robert. ''Why Is Tadzio a Boy?'' in *Death in Venice*, translated and edited by Clayton Koelb, Norton critical Edition, New York: W. W. Norton & Co, 1994, pp. 207-232.
   The clearest treatment of the novella's sexual themes.

The Difference

Ellen Glasgow
1923

Although Ellen Glasgow's literary reputation rests on the strengths and popularity of her numerous novels, it was in her short stories that the author first began to explore one of her important themes—the female consciousness. Her interest in issues such as women's problems carrying on a career or in not marrying—issues that Glasgow faced—has since led many critics to call her an early supporter of women's rights, long before it became a national issue.

In "The Difference," published in 1923 in both *Harpers Magazine* and the short story collection *The Shadowy Third and Other Stories,* Glasgow effectively grapples with the role of women in turn-of-the-century society. In it she portrays a Victorian woman's discovery of her husband's infidelity and examines the heroine's difficulty in adjusting her romantic ideals to those of the modern world. With this story, Glasgow's story also indirectly points out the restrictive nature of women's role in early-twentieth-century society. Glasgow, whose writings were largely concerned with chronicling the South's history and changing cultural conditions, shows herself to be equally skillful at depicting the more interior woman's world.

The story, however, generated little attention at the time of its publication. Such disregard is a reflection, not of the story's quality, but of Glasgow's distinguished and productive career as a novelist, which lessened interest in the author's

short fiction. Although most reviewers in the early 1920s commented favorably on the story, as do contemporary critics, it remains until present-day as a sidenote in most discussions of Glasgow's writings. Yet, of the relatively few short stories Glasgow published, "The Difference" is generally considered one of her best. In it, Glasgow clearly demonstrates her ability both to produce a well-crafted story as well as create a realistic and universal heroine.

Author Biography

Ellen Glasgow was born in 1873 to a well-established Richmond, Virginia, family. A frail child, Glasgow led a secluded life and even was primarily educated at home. At the age of 16, she began to lose her hearing. This debility only increased her desire for solitude.

Glasgow began writing at a young age. By 1890, she had completed some 400 pages of a novel, *Sharp Realities*, but she destroyed it the following year after an unfavorable meeting with a publisher's agent in New York. Despite this failure, she began writing *The Descendant* that same year. The writing of fiction, however, was not deemed an appropriate behavior for a young southern woman. The novel was published in 1897, under the author "Anonymous." *The Descendant* drew immediate critical attention and was widely perceived to be work of the popular author Harold Frederick; Glasgow took being mistaken for a male writer as a compliment. Although most of her family and friends did not read Glasgow's first published work, it was personally relevant for Glasgow, as she believed it to contain "the germ" of all her future writings.

Because of her loss of hearing and frailty, and the depression brought on by her mother's death in 1893, Glasgow primarily resided in the family home in Richmond. She never married, but her travels to New York, the East Coast, and Europe, through which she met fellow writers, made her feel less isolated as she immersed herself in her career and in developing her talents.

Glasgow continued to write steadily, publishing about a dozen novels in little more than a decade. Many of these earlier works were bestsellers. By the 1920s, however, she had begun to win recognition as an important southern novelist as well as a popular one. Many critics felt that her work detailed the changing southern history of the past century.

Glasgow also dealt with issues important to women such as marriage, career, and independence. Her autobiography, *The Woman Within*, published posthumously in 1954, suggests that she faced the same dilemmas that she raised in her novels.

Throughout Glasgow's formidable and lengthy career, her reputation and popularity grew. In addition to publishing 19 bestselling novels, Glasgow also wrote poems, essays, short stories, and the aforementioned biography. While Glasgow's contemporaries widely regarded her as a commercial success—her books were purchased by book clubs such as the Book-of-the-Month Club and the Literary Guild—they also honored her with numerous awards as well as honorary degrees. She was only the sixth woman elected to membership in the American Academy of Arts and Letters, in 1938, and in 1940, that same organization awarded her the Howells Medal. She received the *Saturday Review of Literature* award for Distinguished Service to American Literature in 1941, and later that year her novel *In This Our Life* won the Pulitzer Prize for Fiction. While today Glasgow is not as well-remembered as such contemporaries as Edith Wharton and Willa Cather, she was one of America's first realist writers. Ellen Glasgow died in 1945.

Plot Summary

As the story opens, Margaret Fleming stands at the window of her home, watching the leaves fall in an autumn wind. Margaret has just received a letter from a woman named Rose Morrison, a woman who claims to be in love with and loved by Margaret's husband of 20 years, George. As Margaret contemplates the destruction of her happiness, George enters the room. The couple talk of household matters, demonstrating the ease with which Margaret cares for George's personal and professional needs. Then he departs again, leaving Margaret alone with her complete terror at the unexpected turn this most important relationship has taken.

As Margaret vows to fight for George, the butler announces the arrival of Margaret's friend Dorothy. This lifelong friend uncannily brings up a pertinent topic: the refusal of a mutual friend to give her philandering husband a divorce and his subsequent return to their home. Margaret declares her incomprehension at the friend's actions, wondering why she would want to stay with her husband when he does not love her. Thus the two friends embark on a short debate on love. Dorothy points out that Margaret sees love as "a kind of abstract power," but for the friend's husband, as with most men, love is simply a way of feeling. Margaret believes that a man cannot love two women at the same time. Dorothy finds Margaret desperately naive, pointing out that a marriage provides a man and a woman with more than merely love. Then Dorothy asks Margaret what turns out to be a crucial question: "Would you [give up your husband], if it were George?" Margaret's answer, which comes slowly, shows a complete turnaround from her previous way of thinking; she declares that indeed she would give up George.

After Dorothy's departure, Margaret resolves to stick to her decision. She takes care of her household chores for what she believes to be the last time, and heads out the door to visit Rose Morrison. During the long street car ride, Margaret reflects on her marriage to George.

Rose Morrison turns out to be a lovely, flamboyant woman, clearly an artist and a member of the younger, Bohemian generation. Margaret declares her intention of discussing the situation. Rose apologizes for how the letter must have hurt Margaret but felt that the women should spare George in resolving the problem. Margaret and Rose civilly discuss the latter's feelings for George. Although Rose says that George would rather suffer his love for her in silence than hurt Margaret, she finds this situation unfair to George, for she believes that the subterfuge is spoiling his life. While Rose does not tell Margaret what to do, she makes it clear that if Margaret does not give him his freedom, she is halting his "self-development." George, she claims, needs to be around modern ideas and modern people.

Margaret again settles on sacrificing herself to George's happiness, believing he must truly love Rose in order to hurt her so deeply. She declares her intention of giving up George. Then she leaves her rival and goes home. On the long street car ride, she reflects on how George must love Rose and how the younger generation differs morally from hers.

George has been anxiously awaiting Margaret's return, and she instantly tells him she has been to see Rose Morrison. As the name leaves her lips,

Ellen Glasgow

she sees in her husband's face, not humiliation, but emptiness. She explains that Rose wrote to her of his love and asked her to give him up. George, who for most of the conversation has been merely repeating Margaret's words, does not understand why Margaret has gotten involved in the situation. Further he declares that he does not love Rose at all and that he will not see her anymore. He notes that Margaret seems angry that he does not love Rose, and at a query from Margaret, declares he has no intention of leaving her for the younger woman. When Margaret reminds him that Rose believes he is in love with her, he says that he has been foolish but that Margaret is making too much of the situation.

Margaret realizes the truth of his words and that, in fact, she has overdramatized her approach to life in her high ideals of nobility and self-sacrifice. As George stammers out excuses and calls Rose "a recreation," she briefly feels united with Rose as she understands the disillusionment with love that she feels and that Rose soon will feel. Margaret was willing to sacrifice her own happiness for her husband's, but the fact that he would hurt her for anything less than great love has taken away her very belief in life. George sees nothing of the immense anguish that his wife is experiencing, instead urging her to eat a good dinner.

Characters

Dorothy Chambers

Margaret's good friend Dorothy comes to visit on the fateful day that the story plays out. The short visit provides Glasgow with the chance for Margaret to share her most important ideals about love: that all people should be with those they love, even if it means giving up a spouse. When Margaret wonders why a woman would want to be with a man who clearly prefers another, Dorothy points out that couples stay together for other reasons, such as comfort and material gain. Dorothy's crucial question—''Would you [give your husband up], if it were George''—makes Margaret decide to give up her life with George so that he can be with Rose.

Dorothy also serves as a bridge between the generations. Unlike Margaret and like Rose, she smokes cigarettes. The knowing manner in which she speaks of a husband's affair implies its commonness in the lifestyle of she and her circle.

George Fleming

George Fleming appears to be a ''typical'' husband of his time—he relies on his wife to take care of all his creature comforts and depends on the strength of her love while doing little to demonstrate his own. A lawyer, George appears to be driven less by passion than by convenience; even his affair with Rose began less out of desire for the younger woman and more out of convenience as Margaret was incapacitated at the time. When faced with the affair, instead of apologizing to his wife, George forms lawyerly, logical arguments. He believes that the affair should not bother Margaret because he never loved Rose. In doing so, he irrefutably proves that he neither understands his wife nor is willing to make any effort to do so.

Margaret Fleming

Margaret Fleming, the story's protagonist, has been happily married to George for 20 years when she learns his alarming secret: that he is having an affair with a woman named Rose Morrison. Margaret has centered her life around that of her husband, taking care of his personal needs as well as assisting him professionally. She has sacrificed any independent life and suppressed her own desires. Now she feels that her whole life is an illusion and that her perfect world is destroyed.

Margaret's beliefs that all people should be with those they love lead to her decision to sacrifice her own happiness and give up George. She reasons that George must love Rose, or else he would not betray her, Margaret. She also embraces her own martyrdom to elevate the pedestrian situation. Not until George rejects her offer to set him free, telling her the affair with Rose was merely a dalliance, does Margaret realize the futility of her gesture. She has lost her former happiness as well as the opportunity to be selfless—both the fundamentals of her life with George. By the end, Margaret has lost her idealistic view of love, her own marriage, and life itself.

Rose Morrison

Rose Morrison, a woman in her twenties, is a Bohemian artist type. She dresses in strange modern clothes, reads the latest books, and has a studio in Greenwich Village in New York City. At first she appears to the reader and to Margaret as the antithesis of her rival: wild, artsy, impassioned, and careless. However, her feelings for George prove that when it comes to matters of the heart, she is not so unlike Margaret, whom she calls a ''Victorian woman''; like the older woman, she believes that George's happiness is more important than anything else.

Rose acted without George's knowledge when she wrote of the affair to Margaret, and thus the feelings that she shares with the older woman reflect only her views, not George's as well. Rose believes that the passion she and George share is indeed love, yet, unlike Margaret, she does not believe in the finality of love. In this way, her more Bohemian nature does assert itself.

Themes

The Generation Gap

The generation gap that so often exists between older and younger members of society is an important theme in the story. In Rose's eyes, Margaret is a ''Victorian woman,'' meaning she is hopelessly old-fashioned and behind the times; in Margaret's eyes, Rose is clearly a ''Bohemian,'' someone who embraces new thoughts and ideas and rebels against the old order. Because the story is told strictly from Margaret's point of view, readers only understand her criticism of the younger generation: Rose's talk of ''self-development'' as simply the ''catchwords'' of the "new freedom"; Rose's generation's lack of understanding the compromises that make a good relationship. Readers do not internally experience Rose's impression of Margaret's Victorianism, but Rose's feelings are neatly summed up in the phrase, "Oh, I wonder what you Victorian women did for a solace when you weren't allowed even a cigarette!" Rose also demonstrates her generation's liberal attitude toward love and partnerships when she declares that should she come to love another, George will give her up.

Margaret further equates Rose's generation with a more general breakdown of society. Rose's generation, according to Margaret, has bypassed all the traditions that make society stable. She sees this not only in Rose's usurpation of her husband but in the very circumstances with which she surrounds herself—the neglected villa, the leaves left to rot in the yard, the run in Rose's stocking. Margaret believes that her own adherence to what is proper and moral shows her generation's superiority. To Margaret, Rose epitomizes a younger, selfish breed of Americans, willing to sacrifice anything or anyone to meet their own needs.

Other elements of the story, however, show that the generation gap is not the primary reason for the conflict between Margaret and Rose, nor does it have to separate women of different age groups. Similarities between Margaret and Rose do exist, particularly in their mutual belief that George's having an affair with the younger woman proves that he loves her. Dorothy Chambers also represents a character conscious of her generation's ideals, yet open to a changing moral landscape. Dorothy seems more responsive to modern influences; not only does she smoke, but, unlike Margaret, she does not believe that an affair means the end of a marriage.

Love and Adultery

The different ways of looking at love and adultery cause the plot conflict in the story. Margaret believes that the only reason that her husband would betray her is for love, while George believes that an adulterous relationship can be embarked upon merely as "recreation." He never denies his love for his wife nor does he claim to love Rose. Instead, as justification for the affair, George subtlety presents quite stereotypical reasons for his involvement with Rose, that she was young, amorously adventurous, and available. George never fathoms that his attachment could have any bearing on his affection for his wife.

Topics for Further Study

- Conduct research to find out more about women's roles in the early-20th century. Use this information to more thoroughly compare and contrast Margaret Fleming and Rose Morrison.

- Choose one of the artistic movements of early-20th century America, such as realism in literature or cubism in the visual arts, to investigate. Then imagine you are a journalist, and write an article about this movement.

- Read one of Ellen Glasgow's novels. How do the characters, situations, and gender roles compare to those in "The Difference"?

- Find out more about the Bohemians in Greenwich Village. Do you think Rose Morrison accurately reflects their sensibility?

- Imagine that you are a psychologist. How would you analyze Margaret Fleming's actions and motivations in the story? (Conduct research as necessary.)

To Margaret, however, George's actions come to symbolize his lack of love for her. Only a man who holds her in such little regard, she reasons, could hurt her so much for no good reason (fun is not good enough reason, but love is). Margaret's anguish truly revolves around the question of what is love and what it means. For Margaret it is an abstract, powerful bond between two people, but for George it more of a basic part of daily living. As Dorothy puts it, "women love with their imagination and men with their senses."

While the story questions what love means to different people, it does not question why people stray in their relationships. Because the story is so defined by Margaret's vision and thoughts, and because she cannot conceive of adultery without love, the story never explores the meaning of adultery in a similar way to its treatment of love. This may also be a reflection of the morals of the period in which the story was written and published.

Sex Roles

Margaret clearly plays out the role of many women of her generation; she is the thoughtful helpmate of her husband, taking care of all household chores and problems while at the same time assisting George as needed in his professional duties. She revels in this role, never questioning the importance of her life's duties though they are constrained by her sex, until she learns of George's unfaithfulness. When she receives Rose's letter, her whole world is shattered. For while Margaret was never a "partner" in any late-20th century sense of the word, she always believed that her role in George's life made her irreplaceable. She also admits to her willing subordination of her own desires to his, though she does not admit to any hidden desires until her world has been turned upside down.

George makes clear to Margaret his need for her to continue this role, while asserting that he never loved Rose. In so doing, he distinctly separates the roles of "wife" and "mistress"; he also demonstrates that women of that time period had more than one role to play, but that in all probability, neither of these options—helpmate or lover—could entirely fulfill a man.

George's obtuseness to his wife's pain and disillusionment can be attributed to a gender gap. As Dorothy succinctly puts it: "When a man and a woman talk of love they speak two different languages. They can never understand each other." This truth plays out in the Fleming's marriage. Margaret believes that all she does to help George irreparably ties him to her with bonds of love, not necessity, while George seeks out Rose simply because he enjoys her company. For George, Rose is of the moment, but this does not detract from his desire to spend his life with Margaret.

Style

Point of View

The story is told from a third-person, limited point of view. This means that readers see and hear only what one character sees and hears, and that readers are also privy to that character's thoughts. In "The Difference," all events are filtered through Margaret. Glasgow typically chooses one protagonist through which to view the action. This tech-

nique is particularly important to the development of the story—the reader can follow the transformation of Margaret's thought processes, leading to a better understanding of why she acts as she acts, and thus more deeply feel what she is going through. The reader is with Margaret as she feels the terror at the idea of losing her husband, grapples with her ideals about love, comes to re-evaluate Rose's relationship with George, makes the crucial decision to give her husband up, and finally faces failure even in that aspect—a failure that points up the failure of her worldview. This point of view—almost complete immersion in one character—is well-suited to Glasgow's investigations of the female consciousness.

Mood

Mood is closely associated with point of view in the story, for the prevailing mood of the story—which is closely tied to Margaret's observations and thoughts—is melancholic, overdramatic, and at times, sentimental. The language of the narrator further emphasizes the moods, reiterating Margaret's feelings. Phrases such as "rain-soaked world," "the odour of melancholy," and "grave-like mounds of leaves," to only cull out a few, clearly set the scene upon which this mild drama plays out. The world in which Margaret now finds herself is dreary, fading, and disturbingly foreign. Margaret imbues herself with all the characteristics of a great tragic heroine because she has loved and lost. She consciously makes the decision to renounce her own happiness, thinking in terms of "sacrifice" and "self-surrender." While Margaret certainly may feel that she is giving George the "supreme gift of her happiness," there is no doubt that she chooses to do so under a somewhat theatrical guise. Unfortunately for Margaret, she comes to realize that the mood she has set for herself is not one shared by the other players. She recognizes her dramatization of the day's events—she realizes that "she had overplayed life."

Satire

Satire is the use of humor, wit, or ridicule to criticize human nature and societal institutions, and indirect satire, as found in "The Difference" relies upon the ridiculous behavior of characters to make its point. Indeed, the satire in the story can be seen as so subtle and indirect that noted scholars have disagreed as to whether it actually exists. Applying the simple definition of *satire*, however, to George's behavior at the end of the story makes a clear point for its presence. While at first George responds in a stereotypical manner-making excuses for the affair, tacitly blaming his wife, denying any emotional attachment to his mistress—he finds that his justification is making little headway with Margaret. Then his actions turn to the ridiculous, as foreshadowed by the narrative voice which remarks that "his face cleared [of gloomy severity] as if by magic." Suddenly, George has come to the epiphany that Margaret is upset because she is tired and hungry. "You must try to eat a good dinner," he says, and then lifts her in his arms to take her to the dining room. The implication is clearly that once Margaret has a full belly, her head will clear of all this nonsense. The final scene strikes a true note of humor, as the reader envisions Margaret lying deathlike in the arms of her husband, listlessly gazing out the window at the falling leaves.

Symbolism and Imagery

A number of symbols and images reinforce Margaret's feelings throughout the story. The ever-present leaves and the color red are the most powerful symbols. The leaves primarily represent the passage of Margaret's life as well as its continuity—she has stood at the same window autumn after autumn, watching the leaves fall from the trees. Even by the story's close, when Margaret has undergone a life-altering transformation, the leaves continue to fall. However, this season the autumn leaves also represent something more sinister; the leaves outside of Rose's villa are wet and remind Margaret of graves—they symbolize for Margaret the death of her marriage, her ideals, and her dreams. Further, as Margaret leaves Rose's villa, the untidy leaves cluttering up the path and the yard also symbolize for her a sense of moral superiority, her adherence to the proper traditions and the proper standards—proper, of course, as defined by her peers.

The red flowers serve as a reminder to Margaret of the flamboyance of Rose, particularly in comparison to her own restrained personality. She interprets George's approval of the red lilies in the library—"Nice colour," he says—as his disapproval of her and his predisposition for a woman like Rose. "You always liked red," she replies, and then reminds him of how pale she always was. Unknown to George, she is drawing a comparison between two types of women as represented by Rose and herself. Upon meeting Rose, the younger woman supports Margaret's expectations with her red hair and the "flame" in her face. Rose is equated with the color red, the color of passion.

Historical Context

Bohemians in Greenwich Village

Shortly after 1900, artists, writers, actors, and political thinkers from all over the United States began to flock to Greenwich Village at the lower end of Manhattan in New York City. These Bohemians—people who live an unconventional, carefree existence and react against accepted societal morality—were attracted both by inexpensive lodgings and by New York's numerous cultural opportunities, such as attending museums. After the war, however, writers and artists came to predominate in the Village. Writers were close to all the major American publishing houses, and artists could display their work in galleries, even if they were small and obscure. Greenwich Village also boasted experimental theater groups, such as the Province-town Players, which was co-founded by writer Susan Glaspell in 1915 and which was controlled by artists, not businesspeople. In its 14-year-history, the players produced some 90 plays by new writers such as Eugene O'Neill. "Little magazines," or journals, devoted to new ways of thinking also emerged out of Village culture. *The Masses*, for instance, founded in Greenwich Village in 1911, was dedicated to art, literature, and socialism, which featured works by America's most radical writers and artists. Greenwich Village was also home to a group of intellectuals, including communists, socialists, and other revolutionary thinkers. Such Bohemians came to define the region, which was considered to be artsy and alternative as well as a haven for artists.

The Modern Art Scene

By the early 1920s, the American public had been introduced to new trends in art, such as cubism, which emphasized geometric forms, shapes, and designs; dadaism, which denounced all conventional standards; and surrealism, which attempted to symbolize the unconscious and the world of dreams. The 1913 Armory exhibition in New York shocked the public with Marcel Duchamp's painting, *Nude Descending a Staircase No. 2*. New York's Metropolitan Museum of Art did not want to display these radical new styles of art, a feeling shared by other institutions that held yearly exhibitions. As a direct response, several wealthy art patrons established New York's Museum of Modern Art in 1929, a museum dedicated to the display of new art. MOMA proved that modern art had finally achieved respectability.

Compare
&
Contrast

- **1920s:** In 1925, 175,000 divorces take place—1.5 per 1,000 total population. Obtaining a divorce when both parties do not agree to it is usually a difficult proposition. Most state courts only grant a divorce under fault grounds, such as adultery, alcoholism, desertion, or mental or physical cruelty. A person seeking a divorce on a fault ground must prove that the spouse committed the fault. A spouse also may contest the divorce. Thus, if a man wants a divorce in order to marry another women, firstly, he might have no grounds under which to get the divorce, and secondly, his wife might contest it.

  1990s: In 1990 there were 1,182,000 divorces among the American population—4.7 per 1,000 total population. If this trend continues, younger Americans marrying for the first time have a 40 to 50 percent chance of divorcing in their lifetime. By the mid-1990s, around 18 million Americans have experienced a divorce. Despite these disheartening statistics, Americans continue to wholeheartedly support the idea of marriage and ''until death do us part.'' Ninety-six percent of Americans express a personal desire to marry, and only 8 percent of American women would prefer to remain single rather than marry. Additionally, almost three-quarters of Americans believe marriage is a lifelong commitment, one that should be broken only under extreme circumstances.

- **1920s:** Cubism, dadaism, and surrealism are all new artistic movements that develop among European artists. Cubist painters, such as Pablo Picasso, create pictures out of geometric forms, shapes, and designs. Dadaism denounces all conventional standards, as epitomized by Marcel Duchamp's painting of the Mona Lisa wearing a mustache. Surrealist painters, such as Salvador Dali, attempt to capture the unconscious and the world of dreams. A school of American painters focus on depicting the urban landscape in an exploration of how the machine age has influenced society. For instance, Edward Hopper's paintings of New York City convey a sense of loneliness.

  1990s: The field of visual arts offers many formats. Some artists implement modern technologies; video artists flash words and pictures across television screens. Artists mount large-scale installations, sometimes recreating entire rooms or scenes, often using multiple media. Other pieces mounted throughout the decade are interactive, inviting the viewer to become a piece of the artwork.

- **1920s:** Twenty-three percent of all American women aged 14 and older are employed outside of the home. In 1920, women make up 20 percent of the workforce, but few hold professional jobs; instead, women tend to employed as domestics and servants. Married women suffer from discrimination, earning as much as 30 percent less than their single counterparts and sometimes being forbidden from entering certain professions, such as schoolteaching.

  1990s: By the beginning of the decade, around 48 million women, aged 16 and over, are employed. These women make up about 44 percent of the American workforce. Women continue to be treated unequally, however. They generally earn less money than men.

- **1920s:** As they witness what they believe to the breakdown of moral standards, community, religious, and government groups begin a program of censorship to prevent the exposure of media featuring coarse language, radical political ideas, and discussions of sex. ''Obscene'' books, such as James Joyce's novel *Ulysses* are banned from U.S. publication, and Hollywood sets up a review board to screen movie content.

  1990s: The National Endowment for the Arts continues to be attacked by conservatives for funding artists whose work some consider to be obscene. The Recording Industry Association of America places warning labels on records that contain graphic sexual or violent lyrics. Some school and town libraries pull books from the shelves due to perceived improprieties.

Some American artists chose to chronicle aspects of the contemporary landscape, particularly the effects of the machine age on society. Many painters depicted urban, industrial settings. They often focused on such elements as factories, technology, workers, and tenements.

The Modern American Woman

Long before the start of the 20th century, "the cult of true womanhood" or "the cult of domesticity," which called for a woman to devote herself to her family and the homelife, had become firmly entrenched in American gender ideals. Women had little external personal identity. Their positions were primarily determined by the achievements and social status of their husbands. Women, however, were not seen as inferior to men; instead, they were considered to be morally superior.

By the 1920s, such notions had gone out of fashion. Throughout the decade, restrictions upon what women could and could not do significantly loosened. Not only were American women voting for the first time, they also began exhibiting greater independence in other fashions, such as wearing short dresses, cutting their hair, wearing makeup, and smoking cigarettes. With their new appearances and with their daring actions, these young flappers struck at the roots of American tradition and morality. More and more young women modeled their behavior after freethinking artists, such as the writer Dorothy Parker and the dancer Isadora Duncan. They also talked with increasing knowledge about sex, parroting the theories of Sigmund Freud. Many women began seeking jobs outside of the home, which give them greater economic and social independence. A married woman, however, did not share in these freedoms. She was still expected to function solely in her role as homemaker, which remained the ideal of American womanhood.

Critical Overview

"The Difference" was published twice in 1923, first in June in *Harper's Magazine* and then only a few months later as one of seven stories included in Glasgow's collection *The Shadowy Third*. The volume was primarily comprised of ghost stories and tales of the supernatural with "The Difference" one of the notable exceptions. While the collection was reviewed by most well-known newspapers, Glasgow was primarily a novelist. As such, *The Shadowy Third* received little attention, though most reviewers did comment favorably on Glasgow's latest effort. The *New York Times* reviewer particularly enjoyed the ghost stories, while the *Literary Review* commended Glasgow's "extraordinarily fine" construction and craftsmanship of stories. Reviewer Rebecca Lowrie went on to praise *The Shadowy Third*, finding it "without waste of words, carelessness of phrase, or ill-considered characterization."

Critical attention paid to the story did not greatly increase over the decades. Only as scholars devoted entire volumes to the writings of Glasgow could discussion and analysis of "The Difference" be found, and even then, such commentary was fleeting. This may come as little surprise since Glasgow only preserved 13 short stories over the course of her lengthy career. Glasgow is also remembered as a chronicler of changing times in the South, and "The Difference" does little to add to such a body of work (though it is set in Richmond, Virginia, the location does little to inform the work).

Several Glasgow scholars, however, have made a study of Glasgow's short stories and commented on the place of "The Difference" in the author's body of work. J.R. Raper contends that the stories she wrote during the early 1920s show her development as an artist more so than do the novels of this same period. They also show her interest in examining psychological structure and issues. Other critics have noted Glasgow's increasing understanding of the female consciousness as exemplified in stories from *The Shadowy Third*. Such an understanding of psychological shifting is "adroitly demonstrated" in "The Difference," writes Frederick P. McDowell in the *Dictionary of Literary Biography* as "the heroine develops a kinship with her rival, her husband's mistress, as well as jealousy."

Louis Auchincloss, in a general discussion of Glasgow's fiction, contends that the writer "will be remembered for her women, not her men." Indeed, critics have noted that many of the stories in the collection are similar in their portrayal of independent female characters or female characters who must become strong juxtaposed against male characters who are insensitive, stupid, cowardly, and traitorous. While some critics have objected to such fictitious portrayals of men, a practice which Glasgow also employs in her novels, others maintain that that George's actions clearly show him to be inferior to the wife he has betrayed.

One similarity shared by the majority of contemporary critics, however, is their singling out ''The Difference'' as one of Glasgow's best of the collection. Edgar MacDonald, in his discussion of Glasgow's short stories in a special issue of *The Mississippi Quarterly* devoted entirely to the author, calls ''The Difference'' ''perfectly plotted, a series of scenes in which the central character learns something about herself, a novel in miniature.''

Critics have disagreed in their analysis of the story and the literary devices it employs. For instance, Raper, writing in *From a Sunken Garden*, declares that the story lacks the ironic perspective and comic vision of other of Glasgow's short stories; ''its tone is chiefly pathetic, if vaguely amusing; its perspective, that of flat realism.'' MacDonald, however, directly refutes Raper's argument: ''Glasgow handles superbly George's bewilderment over Margaret's taking his little fling so seriously. Raper misses the happily ironic tone. . . but nothing could be more delicious than Margaret swept up in George's protective arms and his telling her she's upset because she's hungry.'' MacDonald ends his discussion of ''The Difference'' by calling it a ''serio-comic curtain-raiser.'' Marion K. Richards in *Ellen Glasgow's Development as a Novelist* would likely agree with MacDonald's analysis, finding George's behavior demonstrative of ''the satire where she [Glasgow] excels.'' Unlike these critics, Linda W. Wagner, writing for the *Dictionary of Literary Biography* finds the content more interesting than the form, bluntly calling the story ''bitter.'' She further notes in her book *Ellen Glasgow, Beyond Convention* that Glasgow makes her important statement of the different ways in which men and women think about and speak about love.

Criticism

Rena Korb

Korb has a master's degree in English literature and creative writing and has written for a wide variety of educational publishers. In the following essay, she discusses how people are not what they seem in ''The Difference.''

In the *Dictionary of Literary Biography* noted Glasgow scholar Frederick P. McDowell called Ellen Glasgow ''the first truly modern writer in the South.'' Not only did Glasgow break with tradition when she embraced what was then considered to be an entirely inappropriate activity for a young southern woman—writing—she also used her writing to rebel against traditional values, both in the South and in literature itself. As such, Glasgow was truly a woman ahead of her time. At the beginning of the 20th century, woman's accepted role in society was that of wife and mother, and women were expected to subordinated their interests to those of their husband. As a successful woman writer who never married, Glasgow broke away from this restrictive mode. Although she was raised in a typical southern fashion, and received virtual no encouragement to pursue writing, Glasgow developed into a woman very different from what society would preordain for her.

In her numerous novels as well as in some of her short stories, Glasgow explores many of the problems women and women artists of her time faced. Her autobiography points out the similarities between many of Glasgow's characters and the writer herself. Early in her career, as in her 1913 novel *Virginia*, Glasgow clearly had a hard time imagining, and thus creating, a female character who broke away from her accepted societal role. By mid-life, however, Glasgow had made the choice to live independently and pursue her career instead of marriage and family. As her career and life experiences progressed, Glasgow began a deft exploration of the consciousnesses of women who made similar choices or who were coming to understand the inequality under which they had been living.

Margaret Fleming, the protagonist in Glasgow's 1923 short story ''The Difference'' is one of those woman in the process of undergoing a life-altering transformation as she comes to realize that her lifelong subordination to her husband has brought her, not happiness, but a life built upon deceit and unappreciated self-sacrifice. While the story was little noted at the time of its publication (Glasgow was primarily a novelist, penning 19 novels in her almost five-decade-long career) and has received little critical attention in the intervening decades, several scholars have noted the important place it holds in the body of Glasgow's work devoted to examining the female psyche.

As the story opens, Margaret Fleming is beginning to feel the end of the world as she knows it: she has just discovered, via letter, that her husband George has been having an affair with a woman named Rose Morrison. After her initial fear at losing her husband, Margaret decides to sacrifice her own happiness to George's; she visits Rose to

What Do I Read Next?

- Glasgow's autobiography, *The Woman Within*, published in 1954, presents an intimate portrait of the writer and recounts the difficulties of being a woman writer.

- *A Certain Measure* (1943) collects Glasgow's meditations on the art of fiction.

- Glasgow's novel *Virginia* (1913) demonstrates what happens when a woman believes that marriage requires self-sacrifice.

- Like ''The Difference,'' Edith Wharton's short story ''Roman Fever'' (1934) challenges Victorian morality and ideals, while exploring a pivotal moment in a woman's life.

- Willa Cather's 1915 novel, *The Song of the Lark* depicts an opera singer forced to chose between her career and her friends and family. Members of her community, who do not believe that women should be artists, alienate the heroine as she pursues her career.

- F. Scott Fitzgerald's *This Side of Paradise* (1920) and *The Great Gatsby* (1925) both explore the Jazz Age generation that emerged in the 1920s. These novels reveal the new morals and cynical attitude of younger Americans.

- *The Group* (1963) by Mary McCarthy follows the lives of several women who have just graduated from college in the early 1930s. Their stories fascinatingly detail the changing morality as well as the roles that women of that decade took on.

---

announce her intention of giving him up, but when she shares the news with her husband he is shocked and appalled. For George does not love Rose, in fact, he had merely viewed the affair as ''recreation.'' With George's revelation, Margaret realizes she has nothing left in life, not her belief in the eternal bond of love, not happiness in the life she has led, nor even the sense of moral superiority that would come with giving up what she loves most— George. Margaret's epiphany at the end of ''The Difference'' understates one of the themes of the story: that people and situations are not always what they seem.

Margaret's saga epitomizes the plight of women in a society where they are allowed little functionality other than being wives and mother. Up until receiving Rose's letter, Margaret has considered herself to lead a contented and fulfilling life. She had always reveled in her ability to make his life comfortable; the very room in which the opening action takes place, the upstairs library, Margaret called ''George's room'' because everything in it ''had been chosen to please him.'' Margaret also has taken pride in her assistance to George in his work writing a book on the history of law, a book ''that could not have been written without her.'' Until she learns about Rose Morrison, nothing in Margaret's life could make her question her role and importance to George and the choices she has made in her life. Once she does learn of George's betrayal, however, an interesting transformation happens: Margaret immediately acknowledges that her life has not brought her great personal satisfaction. The emergence of the truth about George causes Margaret to face an even greater truth about herself.

While historical studies and Glasgow's own life show the difficulties that turn-of-the-century women had in forging independent lives and careers, ''The Difference'' focuses on the difficulties that one woman has in recognizing her own true desires and separating them from those of her husband. Margaret's name means ''pearl,'' and her reflections show that she is just that: a small treasure hidden away under a hard, almost indestructible shell. Only upon learning of her husband's treachery does she acknowledge that ''the real Margaret, the vital part of her, was hidden far away... She knew that there were secrets within herself which

---

> With George's revelation, Margaret realizes she has nothing left in life, not her belief in the eternal bond of love, not happiness in the life she has led, nor even the sense of moral superiority that would come with giving up what she loves most—George."

she had never acknowledged in her own thoughts; that there were unexpressed longings which had never taken shape even in her own imagination." With these words, Margaret reveals that she has been less than honest with herself and George, and even more importantly, that she finds her life to be significantly lacking. As with many people, only experiencing such personal devastation brings Margaret to this point of brutal self-reflection.

Margaret's confession emphasizes that the role of looking after a husband is not enough to fulfill a woman. Margaret had always equated her caretaking of George with her love for him, and she had previously believed that his acceptance of it—indeed, his need for it—showed his own deep love for her. Learning of his affair makes Margaret realize that he does not love her as she loves him. Further, George's taking a mistress merely for fun instead of for love seems clear evidence to her that he does not recognize her feelings for him as true love, for if he did, she reasons, he would never choose to hurt her so deeply.

Margaret, like many women in her situation, primarily sees George's affair as a betrayal, but not merely one based on sexual infidelity and alienation of affection, but one based on his inability to see beyond the surface Margaret that she presents to the world. During her confrontation with George, she "longed with all her heart to say: 'There were possibilities in me that you never suspected. I also am capable of a great love. In my heart I also am a creature of romance, of adventure. If you had only

known it, you might have found in marriage all you have sought elsewhere. . . .'" But she cannot give voice to these words. To do so would demonstrate to George her newly discovered dissatisfaction with her life. Further, it would make her own disillusioned feelings permanent. For his part, George has made it clear that he follows that dichotomy men often apply to women: the woman they love versus the woman they can have fun with. Margaret had made the critical mistake of believing because she loved George and because he relied upon her, that he loved her in the same way that she loved him.

Dorothy Chambers, Margaret's friend, is the only character in the story who understands that "When a man and a woman talk of love they speak two different languages"; for Margaret love is "a kind of abstract power like religion" but to a man "it is simply the way he feels." Margaret takes on the rather naive tack that if a man "love the other woman, he doesn't love" her. For Margaret, the only kind of love that exists in the one she has practiced throughout her 20 years of marriage to George: a self-sacrificing love. To remain true to "the ideal of self-surrender, which she had learned in the past," Margaret is willing to give up "her greatest happiness" and give George his freedom to be with Rose, for she believes that this and this alone will bring George his greatest happiness. Even at her lowest moment, Margaret can only put the desires of George ahead of her own. In remaining true to herself, Margaret can at least derive some personal satisfaction and "the opportunity to be generous."

For her part, Rose would seem to be the antithesis to Margaret: she is a young Bohemian artist, prone to slovenliness, up-front behavior, and a willingness to speak her mind to get what she wants. However, the reader's first introduction to Rose demonstrates that Rose is not as free as she appears. In Rose's living room Margaret sees "a canary in a gilded cage [that] broke into song as she entered." Clearly, Rose, who "waited alone [in George's villa] for happiness" is like the colorful but caged canary. This parallelism is further emphasized by Rose's clothes which are "dyed in brilliant hues" and by her voice, which is "like the song of a bird." It should come as little surprise, then, to find that Rose and Margaret do share one important similarity: a romantic view of love. Both women believe that because George is having an affair with Rose he truly loves her. By the end of the story, Margaret openly acknowledges this similarity; it seemed to her "that she and this strange girl were united by some secret bond which George could not share—by the bond of woman's immemorial disillusionment.

Of the female characters, only Dorothy appears to have the talent to see people and their actions for what they are. Her ability to straddle the Victorian world and the modern world is demonstrated in her brief appearance, as she speaks of mundane, upper-class matters (charity bridge parties and committee luncheons) but still smokes cigarettes. She also understands the difference with which women and men view love and dispenses practical advice for the forsaken wife ("'For when George ceases to be desirable for sentimental reasons, he will still have his value as a good provider.'"). In a sense, Dorothy is more modern than even Rose as she sees things for what they are, refusing to dress them up in pretty, more acceptable terms. Even Margaret recognizes Rose's talk of George's need for "self-development" as one of the "catchwords of the new freedom."

By the end of the story, although Margaret still has George, "She had lost more than love, more than happiness, she had lost her belief in life." Her pleasant world has been turned upside down, her husband has brought into her life a "cheap and tawdry" reality, and she retains none of the dignity which she had previously brought to her existence. Instead, she realizes she had "overplayed life" by endowing serious, deep traits in a man who believes that all she requires to feel better on this fateful day is a "good dinner." Margaret has paid the price for subordinating herself to a husband who is unworthy of her ideals and morality. As Louis Auchincloss stated, "Miss Glasgow's heroines . . . are devastated by her worthless men."

Source: Rena Korb, for *Short Stories for Students*, The Gale Group, 2000.

Elisabeth Piedmont-Marton

Elisabeth Piedmont-Marton teaches literature and writing classes at Southwestern University. She writes frequently about the short story. In this essay she suggests that Margaret's evasive idealism is at fault for her inability to understand herself and others.

Since Ellen Glasgow used her short stories as a way of practicing new techniques and developing themes, the best of the stories possess the density and richness of her fully-formed novels, and they measure up to the work of her better known contemporaries such as Henry James. Critics generally agree that "The Difference" is one of Glasgow's best and that

its drawing-room setting is reminiscent of James's "The Beast in the Jungle." One of the themes that "The Difference" articulates, according to many readers, is woman's moral superiority to man's. But to read the story as a tale of moral superiority—as if that is the main difference between men and women—is to miss Glasgow's subtle social critique and her nuanced understanding to gender relations. "The Difference" is about more than the disparity between women's and men's moral sensibility; it's also about the difference between the Victorian and modern ages, between beauty and substance, and between belief and truth.

Glasgow's characterizations of the differences between George's and Margaret's moral constitutions and attitudes toward love and marriage is more complex than some of her critics give her credit for. Readers of "The Difference" will be tempted to interpret Glasgow's point of view—the entire story is seen through Margaret's eyes—as evidence of her sympathy for the wife. But evidence in the story and in her novel *The Sheltered Life* which contains more fully developed characters based on George and Margaret, reveals Glasgow's more richly textured views of gender differences and the institution of marriage.

One of the hallmarks of Glasgow's fiction is her choice of interior monologue over dialogue, and one of the effects of this stylistic device is that it highlights the difference between the character's perceptions of events on the one hand, and the objective reality and other characters' perceptions on the other hand. In the first scene of "The Difference," for example, Margaret has just received the letter from Rose Morrison informing her that she is in love with George, and is convinced that her twenty-year marriage is over. She engages in domestic small talk with her wayward husband while the "letter in her bosom scorched her as if it were fire." But she's so practiced at managing appearances that she knows "on the surface of her life nothing had changed." She's able to maintain appearances under such emotional strain because that's what she has been trained to do. While she chats with her husband about trivial things, she is aware that "the real Margaret, the vital part of her, was hidden far away in that deep place where the seeds of mysterious impulses and formless desires lie buried."

Margaret practices what Glasgow calls "evasive idealism." That is, she has been trained as a southern woman of the upper class to maintain at all

"Margaret's commitment to the doctrine of evasive idealism has never wavered. Though she faces serious challenges to her worldview when she must confront several instances of difference, she cannot or will not seize the opportunity."

costs the illusion that all is well. Describing the faded beauty Eva, who is modeled after Margaret, another character in *The Sheltered Life* says: "Even the sanguine brightness of her smile, which seemed to him as transparent as glass, was the mirror, he told himself, of persevering hypocrisy. A living triumph of self-discipline, of inward poise, of the confirmed habit of not wanting to be herself, she had found her reward in that quiet command over circumstances." What motivates Margaret, from the moment she receives the letter then, is not so much a desire to save her marriage as a compulsion to maintain appearances and protect her pride and her husband's reputation.

When Margaret undertakes the journey to call upon Rose Morrison, she crosses entirely from one world to another, from the predictable and safe home of the Victorian woman to the unknown and volatile domain of the modern woman. But despite her inner turmoil, Margaret's commitment to the doctrine of evasive idealism ensures that nothing on the surface of her life appear different. Having fulfilled all George's requests—ordering flowers for a funeral, mending and laying out his clothes—Margaret then turns her attention to her troubles. She assures herself that "now that she had attended to the details of existence, she would have time for the problem of living." When she leaves her comfortable and fashionable house, Margaret believes that "the door closed sharply on her life of happiness." She doesn't believe she can change the facts of the relationship between George and Rose; her only ambition is to preserve dignity and maintain appearances. She is thwarted in even this modest

goal, however, when she discovers that Rose does not share the same values, that she is different.

Margaret can tell immediately that Rose is a new woman because she greets her "with the clear and competent eyes of youth," and "an infallible self-esteem." Margaret finds her "vulgar" and "a picture of barbaric beauty." But the object that seems to embody all the differences between the two women is the "queer piece of rope" that holds Rose's kimono-like dress closed. This piece of cording represents to Margaret everything she isn't and everything she fears. On one level she realizes that the tied belt is a casual, contingent closure that signals sexual liberation and availability. But it also signifies an entire set of beliefs and attitudes that threaten not only Margaret's marriage to George, but her entire worldview as well. Rose's appearance indicates that she has betrayed the code of womanhood to which Margaret has dedicated her life. It's not just that "her fingernails needed attention; and beneath the kimonolike garment, a frayed place showed at the back of her stocking," it's that she has refused to commit herself to the maintenance of appearances that Margaret believes is every woman's duty, and to which she believes George also subscribes. As Margaret puts it, "the girl was careless about those feminine details by which George declared so often that he judged a woman." Suspecting that "this physical negligence extended to the girl's habit of thought," Margaret soon discovers that the George of Rose's imagination doesn't even resemble the reserved Victorian to whom she has been married for more than twenty years.

Reeling from the dissonance between Rose and herself, Margaret must then wrestle with yet another fundamental difference. Rose claims to have discovered or liberated the "real" George. She accuses Margaret of misjudging her husband and insists that "he is so big, so strong and silent, that it would take an artist to understand him." Margaret begins to think that her privileging of surface over substance may have led her to misjudge her own husband. Interested only in the outer surface of her own subjectivity, Margaret has come to believe that she need only attend to her husband's surfaces as well. The encounter with Rose makes her wonder for a moment if George possesses "profounder depths of feeling that she had ever reached" or cultivated "some secret garden of romance where she had never entered." Glasgow pulls back on Margaret's opportunity for genuine self-reflection, however, and Margaret fails to seize the chance for epiphany and real change. Preparing to confront her husband with Rose's claims that he is in love with her and willing to sacrifice herself for his happiness, Margaret "slipped into her prettiest tea gown" and "reflected that even renunciation was easier when one looked desirable." In other words, her only defense against and preparation for this decisive moment is to look pretty.

Margaret's commitment to the doctrine of evasive idealism has never wavered. Though she faces serious challenges to her worldview when she must confront several instances of difference, she cannot or will not seize the opportunity. Readers and critics who see this stance as noble misread Glasgow's attitude toward her character. Glasgow is less interested in dramatizing Margaret's stoic martyrdom or in proving that George is a cad (he is), than she is in critiquing Margaret's adherence to an oppressive and retrograde code. When Margaret finds out that George's affair with Rose is only casual and cannot be recast into a beautiful and noble drama, she is devastated: "So it was all wasted! Nothing that she could do could lift the situation above the level of the commonplace, the merely vulgar. She was defrauded not only of happiness, but even of the opportunity to be generous." The story ends in the drawing room where it started and George and Margaret's life together is no different. George appeals to her desire to make-believe all is well and suggests that the only problem is that she's nervous and hungry. Margaret succumbs both to his embrace and to his outrageous lie that nothing has happened.

Source: Elisabeth Piedmont-Marton, for *Short Stories for Students*, The Gale Group, 2000.

Liz Brent

Brent has a Ph.D. in American culture, specializing in cinema studies, from the University of Michigan. She is a freelance writer and teaches courses in American cinema. In the following essay, Brent discusses the theme of the "difference" in the protagonist's perception of her exterior social manners and her interior emotional life.

Ellen Glasgow's short story "The Difference" opens shortly after Margaret Fleming, a woman of middle age, has read a letter from one Rose Morrison, informing her of an ongoing affair with George, Margaret's husband of twenty years. The story's title focuses on the theme of the "difference" in Margaret's perception of her husband, her marriage, the world around her and even herself, as a result of receiving this shocking information. The "differ-

ence" also refers to the difference in the significance of the extra-marital affair to George and to Margaret, as well as the general "difference" in women's versus men's perceptions of marriage, romance and infidelity. While Margaret's perceptions of her entire life are reorganized as a result of this sudden revelation, she also develops a sense of the "difference" between her external behavior toward others and her internal thoughts, feelings and urges.

Ellen Glasgow's writing has been noted as a fiction of "manners," which critiques the hollow social niceties of upper middle class Southern Victorian society. Stephanie Bronson has noted that "Glasgow satirized the conventions of her society, especially as they effected women, but always with a degree of self-reflection." In this story, the main character becomes aware, perhaps for the first time, of her surface level social gestures and behaviors which belie a more complex internal psychology. Thus, while her illusions about her marriage are punctured, and she begins to see around her a different world from that in which she had imagined she'd been living for the past twenty years (for "never until this afternoon had she felt that the wind was sweeping away the illusion of happiness by which she lived"), she becomes all the more aware of her own disingenuousness in her interactions with others. In the following essay, I will examine the moments of Margaret's afternoon after her discovery of her husband's affair in which she becomes painfully aware of the "difference" between her behavior toward others and her inner self.

"On the surface of her life nothing had changed." Yet, in discovering her husband's ongoing secret life in an affair with a younger woman, Margaret discovers that she, too, leads a secret internal life she was not even aware of:

> But the real Margaret, the vital part of her, was hidden far away in that deep place where the seeds of mysterious impulses and formless desires lie buried. She knew that there were secrets within herself which she had never acknowledged in her own thoughts; that there were unexpressed longings which had never taken shape even in her imagination.

In learning of his secret affair, Margaret begins to wonder if her husband, too, hides beneath his supreme civility toward her secret depths of passion and emotion equal to her own: "Was there in George, she asked now, profounder depths of feeling than she had ever reached; was there some secret garden of romance where she had never entered? Was George larger, wilder, more adventurous in

> In other words, she now
> sees her own part in her
> marriage as an 'act' which she
> has 'overplayed,' or endowed
> with romance and
> melodramatic emotion, but
> which is really the 'comic'
> part of the wife who has made
> a fool of herself by believing
> in the 'illusion' of her
> husband's love for her."

imagination, than she had dreamed? Had the perfect lover lain hidden in his nature, awaiting only the call of youth?'' It is the realization that her husband harbors a hidden passion, as evidenced by his affair with the beautiful artist, that leads Margaret to the realization that she, too, harbors secret, primitive, ''savage'' passions within her, for ''Somewhere beneath the civilization of the ages there was the skeleton of the savage.''

With this knowledge of her own hidden desires, as well as the depths of pain she hides at the discovery of her husband's affair, Margaret becomes increasingly aware of the ''superficial'' nature of her interactions with him, as well as with others around her. When George comes home, and before she admits to him her knowledge of his affair, their interactions are no different from their daily interactions of the past twenty years, yet, as she speaks to him, she ''knew it was only the superficial self that was speaking.'' And, when she smiles up at him in what appears to be perfect sincerity, ''it was a smile that hurt her with its irony.'' Her face indeed becomes a mask of insincere civility, over which she barely has control: ''The expression on her face felt as stiff as a wax mask, and though she struggled to relax her muscles, they persisted in that smile of inane cheerfulness.'' Even a visit from Dorothy, her dearest friend, becomes an exercise in insincere expressions of warmth, for ''her welcome was hollow, and at the very instant when she returned her friend's

kiss she was wishing that she could send her away. That was one of the worst things about suffering; it made one indifferent and insincere.'' Throughout their visit, Margaret's face continues to compulsively mask her emotions, so that, ''she asked herself if Dorothy could look into her face and not see the difference?''

As Margaret dresses to go out and confront her husband's mistress, she makes a metaphor of the ''veil'' she wears, as ''she reflected, with bitter mirth, that only in novels could one hide one's identity behind a veil.'' And yet, Margaret continues to hide her inner identity behind the veil of her well-bred manners and mask-like facial expressions. Even when she confronts Rose face to face, she compulsively hides her true emotions behind her gracious manners: ''and though she tried to make her voice insolent, the deep instinct of good manners was greater than her effort.'' Furthermore, Rose Morrison's ''candidness'' and ''sincerity'' make Margaret all the more aware of her own insincerity and hidden emotion. The younger woman's ''barbaric simplicity of emotion'' in contrast to Margaret's repressed formality ''repels'' her. Rose further emphasizes her motivation in writing Margaret the letter in the name of ''sincerity''; she tells Margaret that, ''I felt we owed you the truth.'' Rose Morrison's unguarded expression of her feelings for Margaret's husband becomes an implicit critique of the older woman's inability to match outward expression to inner feeling. ''I know that subterfuge and lies and dishonesty cannot bring happiness,'' Rose declares. Yet Margaret continues to contort her face in the service of hiding her emotions; as she speaks to Rose, ''Her lips felt cracked with the effort she made to keep them from trembling.''

In preparing to confront her husband the evening after meeting Rose Morrison, Margaret, impelled by a desire to evoke his hidden passion for her own sake, ''slipped into her prettiest tea gown,'' and ''touched her pale lips with color.'' But even this late attempt at donning the accoutrements of passion and romance becomes only another false attempt to bring life to a dead marriage, for, even as she does so, she thinks defeatedly that, '''. . . it is like painting the cheeks of the dead.''' In her vain and abortive attempt to kindle a long-repressed passion with her husband, when she confronts him that evening with her knowledge of the affair, Margaret envisions herself as an actress, or a simple doll, a ''marionnette,'' playing a ''scene,'' rather than a sincere woman in an emotionally intimate encounter with the man she loves.

While she sat there she realized that she had no part or place in the scene before her. Never could she speak the words that she longed to utter. Never could she make him understand the real self behind the marionette at which he was looking. She longed with all her heart to say: "There were possibilities in me that you never suspected. I also am capable of a great love. In my heart I also am a creature of romance, of adventure. If you had only known it, you might have found in marriage all that you have sought elsewhere..." This was what she longed to cry out...

Despite these longings, however, Margaret is unable to express such sentiments to her husband. Again, it seems that she is incapable of the sincerity which would allow her face to express, and mouth to utter, her true feelings: "Her heart was filled with noble words, with beautiful sentiments, but she could not make her lips pronounce them in spite of all the efforts she made."

While discovering her husband's secret affair has made Margaret supremely aware of both her own hidden depths of passion and her surface level insincerity—the tragedy for her becomes, not the jealousy aroused by her knowledge of the affair, but the disillusionment of finding that the affair is not evidence of a repressed romantic in George, but merely of an unimaginative man who compares an extra-marital dalliance to a game of golf.

During their exchange in which she confronts him about his affair, Margaret, already hyper-aware of her own mask of civility, becomes painfully aware of the artificiality of her husband's surface level responses to her. When she greets George that evening, even the light by which she now sees him is described as "artificial." Margaret notes in George's initial response to her admission of knowledge of the affair that his face expresses, not any strong emotional response, but simply "emptiness." He looks at her with an expression which holds "nothing" but "the blankness of complete surprise." As their conversation about the affair continues, Margaret notices a variety of gestures and facial expressions on her husband which communicate nothing more than a façade of civility designed to "hide" any true emotion. At one point in the conversation, "he coughed abruptly as if he were trying to hide his embarrassment." When he responds to one of her statements by repeating it as a question, she again describes him as "trying to hide behind that hollow echo." His facial expressions become to her merely "mechanical" gestures, made in effort to hide a "vacant" heart; watching his response, at one point, "it seemed to her that only mechanical force could jerk his jaw back into place

> **Like most males he may have romantic fantasies about other women, but he is realistic enough to admit that he is only one of a series for the Roses of the world and that his basic comforts lie at home with Margaret."**

and close the eyelids over his vacant blue eyes." Finally, when George closes the discussion by suggesting they go eat their dinner, "his face cleared as if by magic." Again, Margaret perceives the trick of illusion, described as "magic," by which her husband responds to her.

Margaret's sense of herself as an actress merely playing the part of the scorned wife becomes an awareness that she has completely misinterpreted the play in which she is acting. "She felt like an actress who has endowed a comic part with the gesture of high tragedy. It was not, she saw clearly now, that she had misunderstood George, but that she has overplayed life." In other words, she now sees her own part in her marriage as an "act" which she has "overplayed," or endowed with romance and melodramatic emotion, but which is really the "comic" part of the wife who has made a fool of herself by believing in the "illusion" of her husband's love for her. Thus, while Margaret discovers that her "act," her façade of good manners, hides a deeper sense of self, the realization that her husband's "act" hides nothing but "emptiness" beneath his façade of good manners is what ultimately leaves Margaret having "lost her belief in life."

Source: Liz Brent, for *Short Stories for Students*, The Gale Group, 2000.

Edgar MacDonald

Recognizing the characters in "The Difference" as types drawn from an earlier story, MacDonald discusses the way Glasgow uses them in the later story to illustrate how "the doubleness of male adultery is the counterpart of female ambivalence."

Henry Anderson is nowhere apparent in ''Whispering Leaves,'' but he is very much present in ''The Difference,'' which appeared in the June issue of Harper's. Six years after writing the happy ''Thinking Makes it So,'' Glasgow saw there was a better story to be extracted from the materials of the earlier effort. Vardah and Harold had really been a companionable study team, a ''marriage of true minds,'' rather than a dalliance in the garden. ''The Difference'' is perfectly plotted, a series of scenes in which the central character learns something about herself, a novel in miniature. A cataloging of external details is limited to a few poetic images carrying psychological significance. The central intelligence is again named Margaret. ''But the real Margaret, the vital part of her, was hidden far away in that deep place where the seeds of mysterious impulses and formless desires lie buried.'' In this study of the ''Margaret'' psyche, Glasgow separates the external rose alter-ego of ''Thinking'' into a separate entity named Rose. George, described in Henry Anderson terms, is a faithful-faithless husband, loving Margaret but dallying with Rose, an early sketch for George Birdsong in *The Sheltered Life*. Meeker sees Glasgow returning to ''man's moral inferiority to woman.'' but surely the story illustrates a more telling truth: the doubleness of male adultery is the counterpart of female ambivalence, the Margaret-Rose syndrome. As one of the secondary characters observes, ''When a man and a woman talk of love they speak two different languages. They can never understand each other because women love with their imaginations and men with their senses.''

The dramatic structure suggests drawing-room comedy, similar in feeling to James's ''The Beast in the Jungle.'' The series of carefully set scenes is the ''outside'' of the interior drama, the discovery of multiple selves. ''Outside, in the autumn rain, the leaves were falling,'' doubtless revealing outlines of bare trees. As a tragi-comedy, such as several of her later works will be, living is a series of improvisations. A letter from the other woman arrives. George enters briefly with domestic requests while the letter burns in Margaret's bosom. A visitor intrudes, chatting about a domestic crisis in another household, a parallel that makes Margaret determine to confront the other woman. She leaves the ordered comfort of her in-city home to venture by streetcar to an unfashionable suburban villa. Here Miss Glasgow describes accurately a trip from central Richmond, through the Northern suburbs, to Lakeside, but it is also a symbolic trip, from past security to contemporary transience. Modern, red-haired Rose Morrison is an artist. ''Only an artist,'' Margaret decides, ''could be at once so arrogant with destiny and so ignorant of life.'' Margaret, as a beautiful Victorian, will give up her husband. She clings to ''the law of sacrifice, the ideal of self-surrender''. On the ride home in the lurching streetcar, she charitably envisions a ''remorseful'' George. ''What agony of mind he must have endured in these past months, these months they had worked so quietly side by side on his book.'' Returned home, Margaret is met by a concerned husband. Glasgow handles superbly George's bewilderment over Margaret's taking his little fling so seriously. Raper misses the happily ironic tone of ''Thinking Makes it So'' in ''The Difference'' but nothing could be more delicious than Margaret swept up in George's protective arms and his telling her she's upset because she's hungry. As Edmonia would shortly make clear in *The Romantic Comedians*, a good appetite is the best remedy for disillusionment; living on duty upsets the digestion. Glasgow is accused of being unfair to males, but her treatment of George, while comic, is not devoid of amused comprehension. Like most males he may have romantic fantasies about other women, but he is realistic enough to admit that he is only one of a series for the Roses of the world and that his basic comforts lie at home with Margaret. As a type George will reappear like a popular film star in later comedies. In this serio-comic curtain-raiser, brief images of leaves, fires, rain, flowers, mirrors are used tellingly, suggesting the four elements and the humors they engender. . . .

Source: Edgar MacDonald, ''From Jordan's End to Frenchman's Bend: Ellen Glasgow's Short Stories,'' in *Mississippi Quarterly*, Vol. 49, No. 2, Spring, 1996, pp. 319ff.

Sources

Auchincloss, Louis. *Pioneers and Caretakers, A Study of Nine American Women Novelists*, Minneapolis: University of Minnesota Press, 1961, pp. 56-91.

Lowrie, Rebecca. A review of *The Shadowy Third and Other Stories*, in the *Literary Review*, November 17, 1923, p. 256.

MacDonald, Edgar. ''From Jordan's End to Frenchman's Bend: Ellen Glasgow's Short Stories,'' in *The Mississippi Quarterly*, Vol. 49, No. 2, 1996, pp. 319-332.

McDowell, Frederick P.W. ''Ellen Glasgow,'' in *Dictionary of Literary Biography*, Vol. 9, Part II, Gale, 1981, pp. 44-65.

Raper, Julius Rowan. *From the Sunken Garden, The Fiction of Ellen Glasgow, 1916-1945*, Baton Rouge, LA: Louisiana State University Press, 1980.

Richards, Marion K. *Ellen Glasgow's Development as a Novelist*, The Hague, Netherlands: Mouton, 1971.

Wagner, Linda W. "Ellen Glasgow," in *Dictionary of Literary Biography*, Vol. 12, Gale, 1982, pp. 213-226.

Wagner, Linda W. *Ellen Glasgow, Beyond Convention*, Austin: University of Texas Press, 1982.

Further Reading

Auchincloss, Louis. *Pioneers and Caretakers, A Study of Nine American Women Novelists.*, Minneapolis: University of Minnesota Press, 1961.
    A series of essays discussing important women writers of the late-19th through mid-20th centuries.

Auchincloss examines the roles these writers play in preserving American tradition while expanding literary boundaries.

Godbold, E. Stanly, Jr. *Ellen Glasgow and the Woman Within*, Baton Rouge, LA: Louisiana State University Press, 1972.
    A complete biography of Ellen Glasgow that discusses her life and her work. Includes photographs.

Holman, C. Hugh. *Three Modes of Southern Fiction, Ellen Glasgow, William Faulkner, Thomas Wolfe*, Athens, GA: University of Georgia Press, 1966.
    A discussion of how the works of Glasgow, Faulkner, and Wolfe present various aspects of life in the South and southern history, and conversely, how the southern culture affected the development of these novelists.

Inge, Thomas M., ed. *Ellen Glasgow, Centennial Essays*, Charlottesville, VA: University Press of Virginia, 1976.
    A collection of critical essays on Glasgow's writings, including discussion of Glasgow's novels and philosophical ideals.

The Garden of Forking Paths

Jorge Luis Borges

1941

First published in 1941, "The Garden of Forking Paths" ("El jardin de senderos que se bifurcan") marked a turning point in the literary career of Jorge Luis Borges. In fact, the story helped to establish his reputation as a fiction writer.

His fiction received immediate critical acclaim in Argentina, even though he failed to win an important prize the year of the book's release. Outraged, other Argentinean writers and critics devoted an entire issue of the prominent literary journal, *Sur*, to Borges and his work.

As in his other stories, Borges uses fiction as a vehicle to explore philosophical and literary issues. Consequently, the characters in his stories seem less developed. In "The Garden of Forking Paths," he uses the genre of the detective story—a genre that requires clue-gathering and puzzle-solving—in order to explore the way time branches into an infinite number of futures.

Widely anthologized, "The Garden of Forking Paths" continues to generate interest among scholars and students. Its clever plot and sophisticated philosophical exploration of the nature of time inspires much critical commentary.

Author Biography

Jorge Luis Borges was one of the most important and influential writers of the twentieth century.

Born on August 24, 1899, in Buenos Aires, Argentina, Borges was a poet, an essayist, and a short story writer, and his career spanned six decades.

Borges was born into an old, wealthy Argentinean family. He learned both English and Spanish as a child and later studied French, German, Latin, and Old English. His early fascination with language and words became a defining characteristic of his later work. His family traveled extensively when he was a boy.

The Borges family lived in Geneva, Switzerland, during World War I. During this time, Jorge attended college in Geneva and earned his degree in 1918. When the war ended, the Borges family resumed their tour of Europe, spending the next three years in Spain. It was during this period that Borges began to write poetry and became acquainted with a group of young avant-garde Spanish poets known as the ''Ultraistas.''

In 1921 the Borges family returned to Buenos Aires. Jorge published his first book, *Fervor de Buenos Aires,* in 1923. This first publication was followed by two more books of poetry. In addition, he also published three books of essays between 1925 and 1927. These works served to establish him as a leading literary voice of Argentina.

In 1938 the death of his father and subsequent financial difficulties forced Borges into accepting a position as a municipal librarian. In the same year, he suffered a serious head injury. Some biographers suggest a link between the fall and his turn toward prose fiction in the following years. Between 1938 and 1954 he wrote several stories that elevated him to the pinnacle of Argentinean literary life. Moreover, as his stories were translated into other languages he became a writer of international reputation.

Borges' first major collection of short stories, *El jardin de senderos que se bifurcan* (*The Garden of Forking Paths*) was published in 1941 and included the title story, ''The Garden of Forking Paths.'' These stories were later collected in *Ficciones (1935-1944),* published in 1944. This volume was translated into English in 1962.

Although Borges' stories garnered critical acclaim, the jury charged with selecting the 1941 National Literary Prize did not choose *The Garden of Forking Paths* as the recipient of the award. Many Argentinean writers and critics were outraged, and they subsequently dedicated an entire issue of *Sur,* an important literary magazine, to a consideration of his work.

Borges continued to write poetry, short stories, and essays despite the blindness that plagued him during his final twenty-five years. Although Borges published little new work after 1977, he remained actively involved in literary life until his death in Geneva, Switzerland, in 1986.

Plot Summary

The story opens with a brief passage from a history of World War I, presented by an unnamed narrator. The narrator refers to a statement by a character, Dr. Yu Tsun, made during World War I. The narrator suggests the first passage is connected to Yu Tsun's statement.

Dr. Yu Tsun, a Chinese national and a former professor of English, reveals in his statement that he is a German spy. He recounts the events leading to his arrest, beginning with when he discovers that his contact has been killed. He knows he must devise a way to get an important message to the Germans. He looks in a telephone book and finds the name of a man, Stephen Albert. Yu Tsun thinks Albert will be able to help, although he does not reveal how he knows this.

Yu Tsun then recounts how he travels to Dr. Albert's house, pursued by Captain Richard Madden, an Irishman in service to the English. When Yu Tsun arrives, Dr. Albert mistakes him for a Chinese consul that he knows; Dr. Albert assumes that the Chinese man is there to view his garden. Yu Tsun discovers that Dr. Albert is a sinologist, which is a scholar who studies Chinese culture.

By a strange coincidence, Dr. Albert has created a garden identical to one created by Yu Tsun's ancestor, Ts'ui Pen, a writer who worked for thirteen years on a novel called *The Garden of Forking Paths*; he also was working on a labyrinth before being murdered by a stranger. In addition to recreating Ts'ui Pen's garden, Dr. Albert further reveals that he has been studying the novel. Dr. Albert tells Yu Tsun that he has solved the riddle of the lost labyrinth, arguing that the novel itself is the labyrinth.

Furthermore, Dr. Albert tells Yu Tsun that the *The Garden of Forking Paths* is ''an enormous riddle, or parable, whose theme is time.'' Albert explains that the novel reveals that time is not

Jorge Luis Borges

singular, but rather a "dizzying net of divergent, convergent, and parallel times." Like the labyrinth, each turn leads to different possible futures. Dr. Albert shows Yu Tsun a letter written by his ancestor that says, "I leave to the various futures (not to all) my garden of forking paths." This letter has provided the key Dr. Albert needs to make sense of both the novel and the missing labyrinth, that the "forking" referred to by Ts'ui Pen is not a forking of space, but a forking of time.

Yu Tsun experiences for a moment a sense of himself and Albert in many other times. Suddenly, he sees Madden approaching. Yu Tsun asks Albert to let him see once again the letter written by his ancestor. When Albert's back is turned, Yu Tsun shoots and kills him.

In the last paragraph of his statement (and the story), Yu Tsun is awaiting his death on the gallows as punishment for his crime. He reveals that he has shot Albert in order to send a message to the Germans. The name of the town the Germans needed to bomb was Albert. By shooting a man of the same name without apparent motive, Yu Tsun was sure that the information would appear in newspapers the Germans would read. Because the city was bombed the day before Yu Tsun makes his statement, he knows that his message had been received.

Characters

Stephen Albert

Dr. Stephen Albert is a noted sinologist, or student of Chinese language and culture. A former missionary in China, he is a student of the works of Yu Tsun's ancestor. Indeed, he has solved the mystery of the missing labyrinth, revealing that the novel of Ts'ui Pen is the labyrinth itself.

Through Albert, Borges offers a philosophical discussion of the nature of time. Albert's role in the story is to explain Ts'ui Pen to his great grandson—and to be murdered, simply by the coincidence that his name is identical to the name of a town in Belgium.

Richard Madden

Captain Richard Madden is an Irishman who works for English intelligence. After he kills Yu Tsun's contact, Viktor Runeberg, he stalks Yu Tsun to prevent him from passing along the information. Yu Tsun characterizes Madden as "a man accused of laxity and perhaps of treason." Madden tracks Yu Tsun to Albert's house, and arrests him for the murder.

Narrator

The narrator's words open the story, directing the reader to a particular page in a history of World War I. The narrator then introduces the statement made by a Dr. Yu Tsun.

Yu Tsun

Dr. Yu Tsun is a Chinese professor living in England during World War I. He is also a German spy. Yu Tsun takes on the role of narrator of the story as the original narrator provides Yu Tsun's statement to the reader.

The document is a statement made by Yu Tsun after his murder of Dr. Stephen Albert. Yu Tsun, in order to get vital information to the Germans after his contact is killed, describes how he devises a plan to relay the site of the British artillery park in Belgium.

Yu Tsun is a contradictory character; although he is Chinese, he teaches English. Although he does not like the Germans, he works for them as a spy. Yu Tsun is also the great-grandson of a Chinese writer, Ts'ui Pen, whose goal it was to write a huge novel and a build a great labyrinth. Yu Tsun visits Dr. Stephen Albert for the sole purpose of murdering him so that his name will appear in the newspaper and reveal to the Germans the name of the city Albert.

He discovers that Dr. Albert has studied the work of Ts'ui Pen and understands it. Nevertheless, he carries through with his plan to murder Dr. Albert, thus revealing to the Germans the information they need to bomb the English artillery.

Themes

Time

Dr. Stephen Albert tells Yu Tsun, "*The Garden of Forking Paths* is an enormous riddle, or parable, whose theme is time. . . ." Likewise, Borges seems to be implying that the major theme of the short story "The Garden of Forking Paths" is also time. Yu Tsun reflects early in the story, "everything happens to a man precisely *now*. Centuries of centuries and only in the present do things happen. . . ."

With this, Yu Tsun describes time in a linear manner. That is, humans experience time as a series of present moments, one following the other. As soon as the moment is experienced, however, it no longer exists. On account of this, the past is no more real than the future. Both exist nowhere but in the human mind: the past belongs to the realm of memory, while the future belongs to the realm of imagination.

When Yu Tsun arrives at the home of Albert, however, the notion of time as linear is challenged. Albert argues Yu Tsun's ancestor "did not believe in a uniform, absolute time. He believed in an infinite series of times, in a growing, dizzying net of divergent, convergent, and parallel times." In this construction of time, all presents, pasts, and futures exist simultaneously. Further, each decision a person makes leads to different future. The branching, or forking, of all these decisions suggests that time is not a line, but rather is a web or a network of possibilities. The image of the labyrinth, thought of as a forking of time, rather than space, is the clue that Albert needs to rethink the concept of time.

For a moment, Yu Tsun experiences time as Albert describes it: "It seemed to me that the humid garden that surrounded the house was infinitely saturated with invisible persons. Those persons were Albert and I, secret, busy, and multiform in other dimensions of time." The appearance of Madden, however, pulls Yu Tsun into the future he

Media Adaptations

- "The Garden of Forking Paths" was recorded on an audiocassette collection of Borges' stories titled *Selected Fictions*. The recording was made in 1998 by Penguin Audio Books, and is six hours long on four cassettes. Andrew Hurley and George Guidall read the stories.

chose when he got on the train. In this moment, in *this* present, Yu Tsun murders Dr. Albert.

Order and Disorder

In addition to the consideration of time in "The Garden of Forking Paths," Borges also seems to be exploring the concepts of order and disorder. Indeed, Thomas P. Weissert argues that the subject of the story is "chaos and order." Within the short story there exists a novel by Yu Tsun's ancestor. The novel is described variously as "incoherent," "chaotic," "an indeterminate heap of contradictory drafts," and "confused." In short, the novel appears to represent the very essence of disorder.

However, Albert believes that he has solved the mystery of the lost labyrinth and the chaotic novel. He argues that if one assumes that the novel itself is the labyrinth, and is the author's attempt to represent the webbing nature of time, the novel is not an example of chaos, but of order. Furthermore, Albert works to create order out of the disorder of the novel. He says, "I have compared hundreds of manuscripts, I have corrected the errors that the negligence of the copyists has introduced, I have guessed the plan of this chaos, I have re-established . . . the primordial organization."

In other words, Albert acts as an ideal reader of this text, imposing form and structure to what might otherwise be seen as nonsense. Like a labyrinth, which only *seems* chaotic to someone who does not hold the key to its solution, the novel itself becomes, in Weissert's words, "an ordered maze" once Albert discovers the key to the novel.

Topics for Further Study

- Investigate the political situation in Argentina during the years 1940-1960. Who was in power during that time? How did government policies affect Argentinean writers and artists? In particular, how was Borges affected?

- Stephen Albert cites Newton and Schopenhauer as he explains Ts'ui Pen's concept of time. Who are Newton and Schopenhauer? What do they have to say about the idea of time?

- Chaos theory is a concept that has gained popularity in the scientific community. What is chaos theory? What is bifurcation theory? How do these ideas relate to ''The Garden of Forking Paths'' ?

- Literary allusions are references within a story to other historical or literary figures, events, or objects. Try to identify at least five allusions in ''The Garden of Forking Paths''. Look up the allusions in a dictionary and/or encyclopedia. How does your understanding of the story change with your understanding of these allusions?

Borges seems to be implying that while the universe may appear to be chaotic and disordered, the chaos itself may represent an order-as-yet-not-understood. Certainly, the tension between Yu Tsun's reading of his ancestor's text as incoherent and Albert's reading of the same text as ordered parallels the human experience of trying to render meaningful the apparently random events of life.

Style

Narrator and Narration

One of the most interesting tricks Borges plays in ''The Garden of Forking Paths'' is his narrative technique. As the story opens, an unknown narrator speaks directly to the reader: ''On page 22 of Liddell Hart's *History of World War I* you will read. . . .'' The narrator summarizes Hart's position that rain delayed a British attack.

In the second paragraph, the narrator suggests that rain may not have been the reason for the delay. He offers as evidence a statement from a Dr. Yu Tsun, but the first two pages of the document are missing. Consequently, the narrator throws the reader into the statement mid-sentence. The effect of this is to disconcert readers momentarily as they try to piece together the missing portion of the text and to absorb the sudden introduction of a new narrator. Interestingly, although it appears that the original narrator drops completely out of the story after introducing the statement, there is one further intrusion by the original narrator in the form of a footnote.

The footnote serves several purposes in the narration. In the first place, footnotes are generally found only in scholarly works, not short fictions. Consequently, the appearance of the footnote seems to suggest that Borges wants to place the story within a certain genre of work—a nonfiction report. In the second place, the inclusion of the footnote suggests that Yu Tsun's account of his murder of Dr. Albert may not be entirely trustworthy.

Although Yu Tsun says that Viktor Runeberg has been murdered by Richard Madden, the narrator in the footnote calls this ''an hypothesis both hateful and odd.'' The narrator offers another point of view: Richard Madden acted in self-defense. This defense of Madden causes readers to wonder if the narrator and Madden might not be one and the same. At the very least, it casts serious doubt in the minds of readers over the missing two pages of the document. What else has the narrator chosen to hide from readers?

Although superficially the footnote helps to preserve the fiction that this is a factual report, its presence offers yet another troubling detail for the reader to absorb: throughout Yu Tsun's long statement, there is a narrator standing behind him, ready to edit or excise or add bits of text. Furthermore, by calling attention to the narrator that stands outside the margin of the story, Borges also calls attention to himself as the writer. The writer stands behind the narrator, manipulating and formulating plot, character, and setting. Thus, through the use of the narration inside the narration and the footnote inside the inner narration, Borges confuses the fiction of his story. He makes it simultaneously more and less ''real'' by his inclusion of the footnote.

Detective Story

Critics often refer to "The Garden of Forking Paths" as a detective story. The genre was invented by Edgar Allan Poe in the 1840s. In detective stories, details are very important. A writer of a detective story is obligated to follow certain rules and conventions, including the inclusion of clues and details that will allow the reader to solve the mystery at just the same moment the detective does. Sometimes, the resolution of a detective story requires some small bit of information that the writer withholds from the reader until the very last moment.

Certainly Borges follows the conventions. His protagonist, Yu Tsun, is a spy. He has a secret he must transmit. He has limited time. He offers clues to the reader without revealing the final secret. Borges even places another mystery within the framework of Yu Tsun's mystery. That is, he offers readers the mystery of Yu Tsun's ancestor and his labyrinth, a mystery that Dr. Albert solves.

However, although "The Garden of Forking Paths" fills the conventions of the detective story, it only resembles a detective story in structure. In reality, the story is more of a philosophical treatise, masquerading as a detective story. Yet even here, Borges plays games with his reader. Because the story is not only about time and mystery, but also about the making of fiction, it seems as if Borges is questioning the rules of fiction.

Consequently, the reader is left wondering: is this a detective story that appears to be about philosophy, or is this a philosophical treatise that resembles a detective story?

Historical Context

Argentina and Europe

In 1816 Argentina gained independence from Spanish colonial rule. Argentina was becoming a wealthy country, most notably for its beef, wheat, and wool. In spite of their growing wealth, many of the old families of Argentina, including the Borges family, looked to Europe for culture and education.

Consequently, the Borges family left for an extended vacation in Europe in 1916. After World War I broke out, the Borges family chose to stay in Geneva, Switzerland, for the next four years. Consequently, the historical and cultural milieu that shaped Borges during this period was not Argentinean at all, but continental.

While in Switzerland, Borges discovered a number of influential writers: Chesterton, Schopenhauer, Nietzsche, and Kafka. Although the war raged across Europe during this time, it seems to have had little effect on Borges or his work.

With World War I new forms of literature and art emerged throughout Europe. T. S. Eliot, Ezra Pound, Miguel de Unamuno, James Joyce, and Luigi Pirandello, among many others, published a new kind of literature that was classified as modern literature. Experimental art also flourished in the form of dada and surrealism. As Borges continued his travels across Europe in the years after the war, he found himself surrounded by new thinking and new ideas.

The Borges family returned to Argentina in 1921. During the 1920s, Argentina flourished; both mining and oil exploration were well under way, and Buenos Aires even had subway system for the city. At the same time that Argentineans embraced all things modern, they also rediscovered the traditional Argentine dance form of the tango.

While the economy was healthy, the Radical party government of Hipólito Irigoyen maintained power through the 1920s. However, the economy crashed in 1930 and Argentina slumped into depression. A military-Conservative coalition came to power and continued to rule throughout the period.

Borges continued to publish short stories throughout the 1940s. Politically, a new power began to take shape in Argentina. Juan Perón was elected president, and effectively became dictator of Argentina. Just before Perón was elected, Borges had signed a petition protesting fascism and military rule. Consequently, Perón fired him as a city librarian. He also offered Borges a post as a poultry inspector in order to embarrass him. Borges, in an uncharacteristically political gesture, denounced dictatorships at a banquet given in his honor. The Perón years were difficult ones for Borges as well as for Argentina.

Some critics have suggested that the fantastic and imaginative prose that Borges produced during the years of World War II and the Perón years was in response to the grim realities and horrors of daily life. Still others believe that he was a man ahead of his time, prefiguring many of the concerns of postmodernism some thirty years early. Whether he

Compare & Contrast

- **1940s:** World War II rages all over Europe as England, France and the Allied Powers fight Hitler's Nazi regime. When Japan bombs Pearl Harbor on December 7, 1941, the United States enters the war on the side of the Allies.

  Today: Although the decade is free of large-scale war, several regional conflicts pose threats to world peace. Problems in the Middle East, in Africa, and in the Balkans force the United Nations to send troops around the world.

- **1940s:** In Argentina, Juan Perón is elected to the presidency, but quickly becomes a dictator with the support of the military.

  Today: After decades of repression—particularly of the press and intellectuals—Argentina moves toward a more open government with the return of a civilian government in the 1980s. The government puts forth a concerted effort to find the bodies of people who "disappeared" during the 1970s.

- **1940s:** Building on the work of Albert Einstein and others, scientists build a cyclotron, which leads to the creation of the atomic bomb. Einstein's theory of relativity continues to be hotly debated, and Newtonian physics is displaced by quantum mechanics.

  Today: Unified field theories, chaos theories, and nonlinear dynamics occupy mathematicians and physicists attempting to explain the nature of the universe.

- **1940s:** Science fiction and fantasy literature become popular genres, particularly in North America. Pulp magazines such as John W. Campbell's *Astounding Science Fiction* flourish.

  Today: Science fiction and fantasy continue to generate wide readership. In addition, films such as the *Star Wars* and *Star Trek* series attract large audiences.

- **1940s:** Philosophical existentialism, developed in the works of writers like Jean-Paul Sartre, Albert Camus, and Franz Kafka, becomes an important movement. Existentialists believe that existence is of the greatest importance; however, an individual's understanding of him or herself as alone in the universe results in a sense of meaninglessness, alienation, and anxiety.

  1990s: Postmodern philosophers such as Jacques Derrida and Michel Foucault move away from the consideration of the individual human being. Derrida "deconstructs" language, demonstrating that the meaning of words and texts is not stable. Foucault examines texts as cultural artifacts; that is, as products of a given culture at a given time.

---

was a man of his times, or a man ahead of his time, Borges is considered an innovative and evocative author.

Critical Overview

When Borges' collection of short stories, *The Garden of Forking Paths*, initially appeared in Argentina in 1941, reviewers were quick to recognize something new. Most critical commentary had concentrated on his poetry, although in 1933 a special issue of the magazine *Megafono* devoted to a discussion of him reveals that critics had begun to treat him as a writer of prose as well as poetry.

The rejection of *The Garden of Forking Paths* for the 1941 National Literary Prize did much to solidify support for his work among the literary intelligentsia of Argentina who were outraged at the oversight. Nevertheless, even among those critics who felt he should have received the award, there was some reservation. Most commonly, these reservations focused on his cerebral style and his esoteric subject matter.

Other critics, however, found Borges' work to be important and original. In his book, *Jorge Luis Borges*, Martin Stabb cites, for instance, Pedro Henriquez Urena's famous comment: ''There may be those who think that Borges is original because he proposes to be. I think quite the contrary: Borges would be original even when he might propose not to be.''

In the early 1940s the translation of his work into English began in literary magazines, although it was not until the early 1960s that whole collections were translated and published. However, the work made an immediate impact. John Updike presented an important survey of his work in the *New Yorker* in 1965, a review in which he noted his fascination with calling attention to a work of literature *as* a work of literature.

Another seminal article on Borges by the novelist John Barth appeared in the *Atlantic Monthly* in 1967. In the article, Barth discussed the literature of the 1960s, placing Borges at the center of such literature. In addition, Barth paid careful attention to his use of the labyrinth as image in his work.

In the years since its initial publication and subsequent translation into English, Borges' work in general and ''The Garden of Forking Paths'' in particular have continued to inspire critical attention. Many commentators point to the influence he has had on a whole generation of South and North American writers, including Gabriel Garcia-Marquez and John Barth, among others. Moreover, as Roberto Gonzalez-Echevarria points out in the essay ''Borges and Derrida,'' Borges has exerted considerable influence on the post-modernist philosophers Jacques Derrida, Michel Foucault, and Roland Barthes.

Other critics attempt to trace the influences on Borges' work. Andre Maurois, in a preface to Donald A. Yates and James E. Irby's edition of *Labyrinths* directly addresses his sources. He cites H. G. Wells, Edgar Allan Poe, G. K. Chesterton, and Franz Kafka as important influences on Borges' writing. Borges himself noted in several places the debt he owed to Chesterton, Robert Louis Stevenson, and Rudyard Kipling.

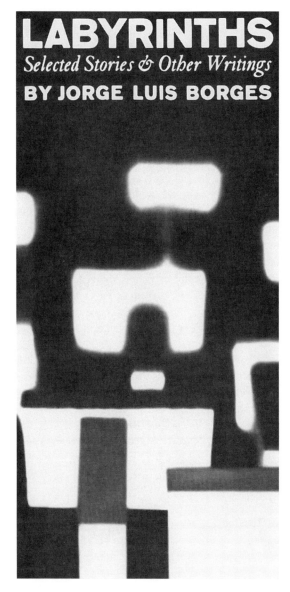

Cover illustration by Gilda Kuhlman from ''Labyrinths: Selected Stories and Other Writings'' by Jorge Luis Borges.

As James Woodall indicates in *The Man in the Mirror of the Book*, ''Chesterton's compact, witty short-story style was to have a lasting influence on the way Borges structured his stories over twenty years later.'' Kafka's influence seems also clear to many critics; Borges was largely responsible for introducing Kafka into Argentina through his translations of the Czech writer. Indeed, the image of the labyrinth is important both in Kafka as well as Borges.

Borges' choice of detective fiction as his favorite genre recalls both the stories of Poe and Chesterton's Father Brown mysteries. A number of critics have concentrated on this connection. John Irwin, for example, examines his construction of an analytic detective story in his article, "A Clew to a Clue: Locked Rooms and Labyrinths in Poe and Borges." In so doing, he also suggests that Borges associates the word "clue" with the word "thread," and in so doing, makes an allusion to the story of Theseus and the Minotaur in the labyrinth.

In other critical essays, scholars contend that Borges' early prose is essentially nihilistic. In other words, he denies any ground of objective truth in his stories. John Fraser examines the stories of *Ficciones*, including "The Garden of Forking Paths," maintaining that Borges both creates the threat of nihilism in the character of Pierre Menard in an early story, "Pierre Menard, Author of *Don Quixote*" and overcomes it through "his concern to connect rather than disjoin values, fictions, and action. . . ."

A number of commentators have explored the metafictional nature of the story. That is, they interpret "The Garden of Forking Paths" to be a story about stories, a fiction about the writing of fiction. In her *Jorge Luis Borges: A Study of the Short Fiction*, Naomi Lindstrom, for example, argues that the "spy plot is tangled with a second narrative concerning the reading and appreciation of literature."

Didier T. Jaen offers a book-length study of metafiction in Borges, *Borges' Esoteric Library: Metaphysics to Metafiction*. In this book, Jaen asserts that using a "first-person impersonal narrator is one of the most characteristic metafictional devices used by Borges."

Finally, several recent critics view Borges as a writer who, years before the postmodernist era, prefigures both postmodernism and chaos theory. Thomas P. Weissert, for example, in *Chaos and Disorder: Complex Dynamics in Literature and Science*, argues that "Jorge Luis Borges discovered the essence of bifurcation theory thirty years before chaos scientists mathematically formalized it."

Because Borges created a large body of highly esoteric, allusive prose, as well as poetry, it is likely that critical attention will continue to focus on his work. Although it is sometimes difficult for readers to grasp, his fiction, essays, and poetry offers great rewards for interested scholars and readers.

Criticism

Diane Andrews Henningfeld

Henningfeld is an associate professor at Adrian College who writes widely on literature for educational publishers. In the following essay, she discusses Borges's use of metafiction in "The Garden of Forking Paths."

Before the publication of his first collection of short stories, *El jardin de senderos que se bifurcan* [*The Garden of Forking Paths*] in 1941, Argentine readers knew Jorge Luis Borges as a writer of poetry and essays.

The publication of his first short stories, however, marked a shift in his reputation. Soon, Borges would achieve an international reputation because of his short stories. By the late twentieth century, critics and scholars listed Borges as one of the most important writers of the century.

Although Borges is widely considered an important writer, not all critics appreciate his work—particularly his short stories. There are those who find his work overly cerebral and erudite, too filled with esoteric allusions and philosophical argument to qualify as literature at all. On the other hand, there are those such as Martin Staab who admire his "literary gamesmanship . . . playful philosophizing,. . . linguistic dabbling and . . . urbane humour." It seems that with Borges, readers feel strongly one way or another.

"The Garden of Forking Paths", first published in 1941 in the collection of the same name, is a typically Borgesian story if there is such a thing. James Woodall, in his book, *The Man in the Mirror of the Book: A Life of Jorge Luis Borges*, maintains that the story "is the densest, and perhaps philosophically most nihilistic, story Borges ever wrote."

Moreover, he contends that Borges constructs an elaborate discussion of time, using "[s]inology, the philosophy of labyrinths and gardens, espionage and premonition" to demonstrate the "essentially fictitious and yet . . . inescapable" nature of time.

Readers of Borges, therefore, are left with many questions when reading this story. Is it a detective story? A philosophical treatise? Is it about time? About future(s) in potential? To these questions, it is possible to add one more: can "The Garden of Forking Paths" be read as an example of metafiction, fiction that takes as its subject the creation of fiction itself?

What Do I Read Next?

- *Detective Fiction*, (1996) edited by James Robert Smith, offers a collection of classic detective stories, including Edgar Allan Poe's ''The Murders at the Rue Morgue'' and ''The Purloined Letter.'' The collection offers students a good opportunity to examine the genre closely.

- Edited by Raymond Tostevin Bond, *The Man Who Was Chesteron: The Best Essays, Stories, Poems, and Other Writings of G.K. Chesterton* (1945) provides a glimpse into the man who influenced Borges.

- *Borges: A Life* (1998), written by James Woodall, has been called by the *The New York Times Book* *Review* the best general biography of Borges available today. The writing is accessible and well-researched.

- David Van Leer's edition of Edgar Allan Poe's *Selected Tales* (1998) also provides a good selection of mysteries from the master, including his famous detective stories.

- Borges' *Labyrinths* (1962), edited by Donald A. Yates and James E. Irby, is an excellent translation of a collection of Borges' work. For the student interested in reading more of Borges' fantastic fictions, this is a good choice.

Metafiction is an important term in postmodern literature; yet Borges' story appeared some thirty years before the self-consciously metafictional texts of the postmodern era. Thomas Weissert identifies Borges as ''a transitional figure between modern and postmodern literature,'' and it is through his use of metafiction that this seems most clear.

Indeed, writers such as Didier Jaén, Weissert, and others explore Borges' use of metafiction. The concept of metafiction may seem at first strange to readers used to reading realistic or mimetic texts, that is, texts that are constructed to reflect or mimic reality. However, by examining first, the characteristics of metafiction, and second, how ''The Garden of Forking Paths'' illustrates those characteristics, readers can grow in their understanding of both the concept of metafiction and the story itself.

A metafictional text, according to Patricia Waugh in her book *Metafiction: The Theory and the Practice of Self-Conscious Fiction*, is one that ''self-consciously and systematically draws attention to itself as an artifact in order to pose questions about the relationship between fiction and reality.'' ''The Garden of Forking Paths'' does this in a number of ways.

In the first place, the story opens with a reference to a historical event and a historical text, followed by the statement by Yu Tsun. This clearly calls into question the ''relationship between fiction and reality.'' By suggesting that the statement to follow offers yet another historical explanation for the event referred to in the historical text, Borges undermines the truth of the historical text itself.

In addition, the impersonal narrator mentions that the first two pages of the document are missing. The information serves to remind the reader that what is to follow is a description of a series of events constructed after the fact. That the two pages are missing also serves to remind the reader that the editor of the statement can change and manipulate the material in the statement.

The fact is further emphasized by the inclusion of a footnote early in the story. The unnamed narrator corrects a statement made by Yu Tsun that Richard Madden murdered Viktor Runeberg. The narrator tells the reader that even the name used by Yu Tsun for Viktor Runeberg is incorrect. As a result, the reader does not know which narrator to trust: the unnamed opening narrator or Yu Tsun.

Indeed, the inclusion of the footnote forces the reader to question the reality of the narrator, a

> " The characters that exist in the pages of the text--no matter how real they seem--are no more than ink on paper. They have no existence before the beginning of the text, and they have no future at the end of the text. They are, pure and simple, creations of language and narration."

violation of the unspoken agreement that readers enter into with writers of realistic texts. Narrators have to at least *seem* real or they cannot function as narrators.

As this further illustrates, metafictional texts often function at several narrative levels. In other words, there are stories within stories within stories in this text. At the first level, there is the unnamed narrator who instructs the reader to connect Yu Tsun's statement with a passage from a history text.

At the second level is Yu Tsun's statement describing his journey and conversation with Dr. Stephen Albert. Within this level is the story of Yu Tsun's ancestor who withdraws from the world to write a book and build a labyrinth. At the innermost level is the novel itself, "an indeterminate heap of contradictory drafts," according to Yu Tsun, or according to Dr. Albert, a brilliant novel that reveals the labyrinthine nature of time.

By naming the novel at the innermost narrative level *The Garden of Forking Paths*, Borges calls attention to the fact that there is yet another narrative level above the unnamed primary narrator. That is, the story itself, "The Garden of Forking Paths" contains the first narrator and all of the narrative levels below it.

Therefore, if the novel at the center of the story is a fictional creation of the fictional Ts'ui Pen, then the story "The Garden of Forking Paths" is also a fictional creation. What, then, does this imply about

Borges himself? Is he suggesting that the author is a fictional creation, someone constructed by the language and the reader?

Borges violates another unspoken agreement between writer and reader that the text will follow in a linear fashion from start to finish. Storytelling works because of the linear arrangement of the text. Borges, however, introduces the possibility that texts may not be linear.

He does this by revealing the nature of the fictitious novel at the center of the story. The novel, according to Albert, puts forward an infinite number of futures—many of them contradictory. According to Albert, "In the work of Ts'ui Pen, all possible outcomes occur; each one is the point of departure for other forkings."

Likewise, metafictional texts, because they are texts about texts, introduce the possibility of multiple meanings. As Peter Stoicheff argues, "This is one way of saying that within the finite space of any text are an infinite number of possible meanings, whose hierarchy metafiction refuses to arbitrate."

In other words, in the world of fiction no one meaning has any more connection to reality than any other meaning. Therefore, all meanings and no meanings are simultaneously possible, just as all of the futures in "The Garden of Forking Paths" are possible within the fictional world. However, since it is a fictional world, none of the futures exist in reality.

Furthermore, metafictional texts differ from realistic texts in that they often contain both contradictions and coincidences that force readers to question the "reality" of the universe created by the writer. In a realistic text, there is an agreement between the writer and the reader that the reader will believe the world the writer has created as long as the writer stays within the conventions of that fictional world. In a realistic text, natural law must be obeyed and characters must act as if they were real people.

However, in a metafictional text like "The Garden of Forking Paths," the coincidental nature of many of the events forces the reader to accept that the story has no connection to reality. For example, Yu Tsun picks a name out of a phone book. The person who has the name is a noted sinologist who has spent years studying a novel written by Yu Tsun's ancestor. Such coincidence calls attention to the fact that in the world of fiction, anything can happen. The writer controls the story because it is a story, not reality.

What a story like "The Garden of Forking Paths" reveals, then, is that all fiction, whether realistic or fantastic, is a product of language. The characters that exist in the pages of the text—no matter how real they seem—are no more than ink on paper. They have no existence before the beginning of the text, and they have no future at the end of the text. They are, pure and simple, creations of language and narration.

Consequently, the implications that a metafictional text like "The Garden of Forking Paths" finally introduce are profoundly disturbing. As the character Yu Tsun tells the reader early in the story, "everything happens to a man precisely, precisely *now*." Once an event is past, it exists nowhere but in memory and narration.

Likewise, the future exists nowhere but in the imagination and in narration. By calling attention to itself as fiction, the metafictional text also calls attention to the nature of reality itself, at least suggesting that the lines between fiction and the narration of lived experience are perhaps fuzzier than anyone wants to admit.

Source: Diane Andrews Henningfeld, for *Short Stories for Students*, The Gale Group, 2000.

Ralph Yarrow

In the essay below, Yarrow examines the ways Borges forces his reader to notice the act of reading and inspire in the reader an appreciation for the aesthetic experience.

> "We must never forget that [Borges's] intelligence . . . is at the service of games rather than convictions. . . .The purpose of the game is not to discover incognizable reality; it has an aesthetic aim."

The "aesthetic aim" Jurado refers to suggests that Jorge Luis Borges is concerned with the effect of his work, and that this effect may have something to do with the mental processes that give shape to what is then called reality. To suggest that Borges is concerned with stimulating the creative faculties of his audience appears legitimate; he says his work is a means of "fusing the world of the reader and the world of the book."

This possibility implies an intention similar to Robbe-Grillet's demand for the active participation

" Each central symbol, theme, or idea is assimilated into a successively more extensive context, which displaces it from central to relative importance. In this way the reader is gradually pushed into a state in which he or she doesn't totally accept or reject anything."

of the reader in the creation of the work. More than that, it is—as with Robbe-Grillet, or Proust or Coleridge before him—a recognition that "imagination" is precisely that process of constructing significance for oneself. Borges's "games" are designed to extend the "field of play" as far as possible and to make the reader aware that he or she is playing. Borges is aware, too, that the way in which this happens is through the physical changes induced in the brain by the demands made by his text: he states that "what is essential is the aesthetic factor, the thrill, the physical effect brought about by reading."

Looking at what happens when reading a story by Borges, one sees that the work necessarily and openly accepts the commitment made by the reader in entering the fictional sphere. Although the story may ultimately wish to correct the reader's notions about the relationship of fiction and reality, it first of all welcomes the assumption that these spheres are different and similar in the ways in which the reader has conventionally come to believe. The writer welcomes even more the reader's desire to gain something from the reading. This drive may be blocked, deflected, or turned upon itself, but it remains a necessity for reader and writer. The desire rests on assumptions much profounder, perhaps, than even a belief in the ability of language to signify—to say something meaningful about the world. It may reflect the sense that actions move towards some kind of completion, that there is some kind of shape to a succession of lived and willed events. That is, fundamentally, an intuition of order which is aesthetic in nature rather than merely intellectual. Thus the satisfaction gained from reading a book in its entirety has as much, if not more, to do with a grasping of pattern and plan, as with the simple knowledge of ''what happens in the end.''

A book draws, then, on two kinds of rather crucial awareness—about the nature of reality, and about the way in which relating to it is a matter of perceiving a growth of plan and order. These concerns have perhaps become oversimplified and reduced to superficiality by conventional ideas about reading (both the mental and the physical operations involved) and by the large amount of easily ''consumable'' reading material available. So, in fact, Borges and others may not be making totally new demands, but rather attempting to reestablish the fundamental issues of reading; a ''revolution'' in the sense of returning to something. That which has been forgotten must be reestablished, and in order for this to happen, the forgotten must be highlighted. The text will, therefore, at first appear extraordinary; indeed it *has* to appear extraordinary, so that people can see the process of reading as something ''new'' and worth investigation. Shock tactics may be in order at this stage in the process. Just as Rilke said that poetry needed to respond to the earth's wish to become ''invisible,'' so reading must become a new and strange experience in order for it to register. Readers must be made aware of the fact that they are reading, otherwise they will never perceive the extraordinary richness and importance of this old and familiar process. So Borges's work, like that of Robbe-Grillet and Gombrowicz, hovers incessantly around the borders of the ''normal'' and the ''abnormal,'' constantly interrelating and juxtaposing the two.

The text needs, therefore, to be doing at least two things at once: inviting and stimulating the sense that something is to be discovered, some ''point'' to the reading; and subverting or distorting the over-hasty assumptions that tend to be made about how that point is reached. A title may do the job quite well. Take, for instance, the well-known Borges story, ''The Garden of Forking Paths.''

The title both seduces and subverts. Like other Borges stories, it offers a prospect of mystery but also suggests the opposite of a closed or simple solution. The garden and the labyrinthine implications have vaguely esoteric, Eastern, or exotic con-

notations. The detective format of the story (like ''Death and the Compass'') is similar not only to G. K. Chesterton, whom Borges certainly liked, but also to Robbe-Grillet (detectives in *Les Gommes, La Maison de Rendez-Vous*, labyrinths in *Dans le Labyrinthe, Topologie d'une Cite Fontome*). Butor (*Passage de Milan*) and Beckett (*Molloy*) also have something of the detective formula. Detective stories traditionally play a kind of game with the reader; they also traditionally offer a number of blind alleys, red herrings, spurious ''clues,'' and so on. Whatever the ''truth'' may be, it will not be reached easily. In addition, the *nouveau roman* and other post-modernist writing (e.g., new American fiction in works like Pynchon's *The Crying of Lot 49*) often reverses the implicit assumption encoded into the structure of detective fiction and deliberately refuses any single or definitive solution that will ultimately be ''revealed'' to the reader. All of these possibilities float about in Borges's title, promising in addition a kind of intimate and bizarre pleasure. Getting caught up in the forking paths is a kind of Baudelairean *invitation au voyage*, leading readers to engage both narrative and mental processes, and the ways in which they may interact.

The story advertises its dubious wares clearly enough; it lays them out more fully in the combination of seductive and suggestive settings, themes, and appellations which follow. A summarization of the narrative in linear fashion is unnecessary, but the ingredients are clearly chosen for their effect: a Chinese spy for the Germans; a sinologist holding the key to the labyrinthine work of the spy's ancestor; a plot involving murder, attempted killing, and a message that will result in many deaths; the conjunction of modern (1916) war and Chinese culture; the sending of a secret message. The structure of the narrative is a typical (for Borges, as for Robbe-Grillet) ''Chinese-box'' affair, moving from the apparent neutrality of the opening paragraph [''On page 22 of Liddell Hart's History of *World War I* you will read . . .'' (*Labyrinths*)] to a statement by the Chinese spy-cum-professor, to the English sinologist Albert's outline of Ts'ui Pen's work, to direct quotation from and involvement in that work. Version is enclosed within version, each narrative with its own range of reference and association, its own standards and horizons of ''truth.'' Borges's fictional composition includes and comments upon the confessions of a spy, the philosophical exegesis of an academic, the traditionally inscrutable joke of a complex mind. The interference of the narratives incites reference back and forth, setting up analogies between contemporary historical events and cultural reflections, betwen the various levels of personal existence of Dr. Yu Tsun, between nationalities, beliefs, and codes.

This interaction is deliberately sought after in the structure and detail of the narratives. It is apparent even at the simple level of names and nationalities, with a Chinese-German spy, an English-Chinese expert, and an Irish-English secret service agent (who speaks German at the outset). The Chinese spy was formerly ''professor of English at the *Hochschule* in Tsingtao'' (*Labyrinths*). The result of his actions in Staffordshire will be understood in Berlin and translated into action in France. This confusion of nationality and identity can suggest various aspects: the complexity of political interaction and its implications for national identity; the increasing difficulty of simplistic notions about culture and genealogy; twentieth-century doubts about the singleness and stability of personality; the issue of how much our behavior is affected by the language we speak.

What happens, in general terms, is that each notation (here and in other Borges stories) works less as an attempt to ''clarify'' someone's identity and role than as a kind of magnetic field for associations. The stories are so short, and the details so few, that ''realistic'' character-portrayal is clearly not intended. (The same is true for Robbe-Grillet's longer fictions: ''characters'' frequently change names, and in *La Maison de Rendez-Vous* many of the names they adopt are aliases or have theatrical connotations, e.g. ''L'Americain,'' ''Lady Ava.'') Names (and other details), become a kind of vibratory charge—not so much a definite symbol as a means of calling up associative possibilities (Chineseness, distinguished professorship) which themselves are usually deliberately vague. In this respect, the brevity of Borges' stories produces a highly-charged symbolism of doubt and possibility, which is intensified by many other techniques including the switch between narrative levels—realism and fantasy, for instance, or the confessional and the exegetic. Or the shifting or playing between psychological exploration and fantastic inventiveness; or the typical Borges mixture of genuine quotation and ''spurious'' scholarship. Uncertainty is produced whichever way you ''read'' the story, and principally if one manages to read it all ways at once—which is what the labyrinth at the center of the story suggests. It is ''a labyrinth of symbols'' (*Labyrinths*). These symbols point, however, not to some definitive grand interpretative scheme, but to the conjunction of apparently antagonistic possibilities: all four alternative endings, Albert explains, are possible for Ts'ui Pen's work.

Yu Tsun, however, chooses one of the endings and shoots Albert, in order to convey his secret message (the name Albert, as reported in the press, will also indicate the town in France that the Germans must attack). He, by a combination of historical necessity and psychological condition, opts for a single solution, which will inevitably result in his death as a murderer. In Robbe-Grillet and Gombrowicz, as here, and elsewhere in Borges, killing as closure is always suspicious—it is usually heavily ironized, and virtually never achieves the kind of solution it promises.

Murder, then, or sudden death, is a means of presenting one of the two poles between which the story oscillates. Mentioned also is that Yu Tsun's ancestor was murdered, and Albert refers to excerpts from his book concerned with a battle and with the various possible outcomes of a meeting between a man with a secret and a stranger. Albert claims that Ts'ui Pen meant the reader to choose not one alternative outcome, but all of them: the book is intended as a demonstration of what Valery called *noeuds* and contemporary critical theory describes as *generateurs* . That is to say, there are points in a text (any point, by implication) where the reader, like the writer, may seize not only upon the self-perpetuating inventiveness of narrative and decide to draw on any prticular association or link to give the text a new twist, but the reader or writer is also aware at that moment of holding within his grasp (in his imaginative or magical power) the secret or possibility of all future developments of that text. He is at the point where the paths fork. Any path is a potential murder/death because it can lead to closure; but the dominating single-mindedness (obsession or terrorism, for Robbe-Grillet) of each textual departure can always be arrested, and hauled back to any point from which the plurality of possibility becomes available again.

Yu Tsun has a secret (Albert's name) that he must encode and transmit. Albert has a secret (the nature of Ts'ui Pen's book and of his labyrinth). The garden is a ''secret'' kind of location (with medieval, Chinese, mystical, erotic, biblical-genetic connotations). Borges's story teases us with its secretive atmosphere and offers a few clues (some helpful but hidden, others unhelpful and overt) as the reader is put in the position of trying to figure out what Yu Tsun is trying to do. In all cases, the real nature of the secret is generative rather than unitary. (A brief aside to The Sect of the Phoenix, whose aura of arcane profundity and talk of the Secret is a joke on the phoenix's propensities for sex.) Even Yu Tsun's message, when transmitted, has more than one possible outcome, and is important to him in more than one way. As an Oriental, he despises the Western conflict in which he finds himself caught up, but he needs to complete his mission to justify himself (and by implication his family and his race) in the eyes of his narrow-minded German boss (described as a ''sick and hateful man—in his arid office''— *Labyrinths*). The import of the secrets is that in messages, in wisdom, and in all encoded texts (as shown by the successive frames of the story) reside not closed ''answers'' but structures of possibility.

That kind of structure is represented by Albert's proposition (fascinating to Yu Tsun and frequent in Borges) stating Ts'ui Pen's work reveals a conjunction of all time and identity. That is to say, when you actually stand at the point where paths fork, you hold sequence and causality in your power. This bifurcation is the ''now'' point of reading in contemporary critical theory, the point where reader and text converge. (Do battle, as in Simon's *La Bataille de Pharsale* (= *la phrase*) or Ricardou's *La Prise* (= *la prose*) *de Constantinople*: hence the battle quoted from Ts'ui Pen, of which two versions are given, and the battle Yu Tsun's act will influence.) It is the location of moral choice, in existentialist theory: the place from which the self is constructed, or—consistent with phenomenology—consciousness wills or intends a new perception and construction of reality.

Borges's games are not trivial, because as L. A. Murillo contends, ''The conjecture is about radical questions of human existence, time, personal will, consciousness, and destiny.'' Such questions are pertinent to the protagonist (Yu Tsun) of ''The Garden of Forking Paths,'' and are mediated through him, and through the structure of interlocking narratives Borges builds around him, to the reader. Thus ''The Garden'' is a ''representation of the very process by which . . . events acquire their symbolical significance in the consciousness of the protagonist and . . . reader.'' The games, then, are centrally ''about'' the exploration by the reader (where else can the story ''take place''?) of certain states and procedures in consciousness: those states and procedures that concern the way in which we invest our experience with understanding or significance, by which we arrive at our ability to interact creatively and purposively with our environment. The elements of game play that Borges uses here are for the purpose of propelling the reader towards this exploration.

Murillo, in *The Cyclical Night*, suggests that Yu Tsun is presented as being in an ethical vacuum: existentially aware of his responsibility in a world whose political, social, and psychological upheaval has negated a priori values, and conscious of his need to locate himself and make a choice that endows being and acting with meaning. Again one sees the confusing intersection of personal, cultural, and historical identities in the story. The ''vacuum,'' also presented to the reader through the mystery, paradox, and symbolic condensation of the narrative, demands to be grasped and developed as text, as another way of pinpointing the source of moral choice.

Yu Tsun takes, perhaps, the easy way out. He opts for the single, deadly solution, though knowing, as his wry admission at the end makes clear, that it is not really so simple. (''He does not know . . . my innumerable contrition and weariness.''— *Labyrinths*). The odd adjective indicates Yu Tsun's acknowledgment of the chance of plurality, a chance he passes over.) Yu Tsun tries, by recalling his murder of Albert, to construct around the event a narrative that gives it the status of irrevocability (all incidents seem restrospectively compelling and essential). His ''confession'' is thus fundamentally spurious. Its format proposes an acquiescence that, in fact, is quite the reverse of the confession's purpose. His narrated version, like his act of murder, seeks to impose a unique and dominant reading.

That uniqueness and dominance is, however, undermined by the multiplicity of narratives within which Borges frames the story. It is, moreover, further placed in perspective by the contrast between Yu Tsun (actually Chinese but betraying his culture and his identity) and Albert (a Westerner who is far more an incarnation of traditional Chinese wisdom). Yu Tsun disregards or distorts Albert's possibilities; he uses him only as a cipher in a code of language and action. Yu Tsun tries uneasily to justify his action as inevitable in terms of historical necessity. Albert is, however, also the sign of many other possibilities, more inclusive than the use to which his name is put as indicating a place to be destroyed. In addition to his grasp of the fluid dynamism of the labyrinth, he seems to Yu Tsun a person of Goethean stature, endowed with wisdom and easy grace. Living within the procreative garden, or labyrinth, Albert is at the junction of East and West, uniting the contemplative and the active, the English and the German, in a harmonious and lively balance, like that of nature and the "sparkling music" through which he is approached. He is the kind of multiple possibility that Yu Tsun ignores.

Murillo describes the labyrinthine structure by which consciousness is represented as a "metaphysical ground" (*The Cyclical Night*). The "hesitation" (Todorov's term)—characteristic of postmodernist texts and here instilled by the confusions and paradoxes, the ironic juxtaposition of versions, and so on—produced in protagonist and reader is the moment of absence (of choice, significance) that impels selection of world and action. The existentialist reading suggests that the motive force is an *angst*, a desperate need to fill the vacuum by projecting anything. That is certainly one factor, and it may be the principal one in Yu Tsun's case. But the contradictions, blocks, and ironic perspectives of the story's structure, together with its repeated indications about the plural significance of secrets, and the balance of forces harmonized in Albert, offer an alternative mode of response.

Such a response is also offered to Yu Tsun. As he moves towards Albert's house, he experiences a kind of detachment combined with a liveliness of perception. The "slope of the road . . . eliminated any possibility of weariness," and he feels himself to be "an abstract perceiver of the world" (*Labyrinths*). At this point he becomes aware of the "living countryside" and of an "almost syllabic music," which he later realizes is Chinese. Here, as always in Borges, the topology is not realistic scene-setting but directions to a mental state. Robbe-Grillet clearly works in a similar fashion in *Topologie d'une Cite Fantome*, but the parallel is not quite exact. Robbe-Grillet maps out with ironic geometrical precision the moves of an imagination confined by its own obsessions and by a passion for linguistic symmetry. Borges's landscapes have perhaps more in common with the *terrains vagues* of Beckett:

they present not so much a process as a condition in which a process may take place. Beckett's world, for example, in *Molloy*, is one in which objects are cherished precisely because they are "*en voie de disparition*": the protagonists are in the process of ridding themselves of inherited assumptions about reality and its relationship with language. What we have is a curious kind of precise vagueness, a very persistent and subtle attempt to render a state in which "meaning" is loosening its hold, dissolving the links between word and experience. (Everything dissolves or disintegrates in Beckett: bicycles, limbs, relationships—the onions in Moran's Irish stew in *Molloy*: "*On n'est pas lie*?" is what the tramps in *Godot* ask each other.) Borge's descriptions, though they are in a way more detailed, frequently operate with a similar combination of the vague and the precise. That is to say, they are attempting to pinpoint a condition of increasing "vagueness," or distance from the restrictions of conventional levels of thinking and perceiving.

What increasing vagueness leads towards is exactly that moment when no single interpretation is dominant and possibility has re-established itself. Yu Tsun is in a kind of suspended animation in which the possibilities of harmony present themselves most fully to him. His state of physical ease matches the time of day (late afternoon) and the surroundings: "the afternoon was intimate, infinite" (*Labyrinths*); his consciousness is freed from its preoccupation with limited ends—he feels that it is not possible to be the enemy of a country, in the sense that he is now experiencing it. He is integrated with his surroundings, acting spontaneously, and feeling at home (he instinctively accepts the music and does not remember whether he knocks at Albert's gate or rings a bell). He is, in short, in a condition of very lively and expanded awareness in which his doubts about identity are replaced by a kind of oneness with nature as the source of order and mobility—"fireflies, words, gardens, streams of water, sunsets." Yu Tsun's state is what brings him to the center of the labyrinth, and Albert comes to open the gate, holding a symbolic lantern.

Yu Tsun is in fact blinded by the light, and cannot make out Albert's face. That is to say, in this situation where he becomes aware of himself as a center of possibility, an organizing potential, a consciousness which can shape and form, he is not able to pin Albert down as a limited and thus expendable identity. This "awareness of awareness'' is both positive and negative, a sense of hesitation in which simplistic single interpretations are found inadequate, and the pluralistic is on the verge of presenting itself.

Thus the two versions of the battle in Ts'ui Pen's book offer as reasons for victory apparently contrary states of mind: the warriors experience situations that make them feel either existential angst or joy. On the one hand, individual identity is felt to be insignificant; on the other it is merged in a communal celebration. In both cases an apparent negation of individual significance leads to a ''victory'' or fruitful outcome. In a similar way, the postmodernist ''negative aesthetic'' is a way of continually emphasizing the apparently negative in order to reveal hidden possibilities. Whatever is said also provides a way of *not* saying everything else: it puts off, conceals, and defers (differer, pace Derrida) all the other possibilities of language. So what is said is frequently contradicted or revealed to be inadequate, in order that it may be seen to have those other possibilities lurking behind or within it, as linguistic history for example, or as association, or as alternative readings.

In the one ''direct quote,'' Borges gives us from Ts'ui Pen's text, the warriors are referred to as ''heroes, tranquil their admirable hearts, violent their swords, resigned to kill and to die'' (*Labyrinths*). The line might have come out of the *Bhagavad Gita*, an epic much concerned with the problems of fighting in the proper way. (Although Borges may not have actually taken it from there, he did use the *Gita* as one source among many for esoteric references.) Taking a leaf out of Maharishi Mahesh Yogi's commentary on the *Gita*, Borges would probably interpret the quotation something like this: ''swords'' refer to the ''outer'' organs of action, ''hearts'' to the inner state of mind. An apparently contradictory condition here renders the mind still and the body violently active. This condition actually allows the warriors to perform action without attachment to the result (however drastic that may seem), and because of that the action is in fact most successful and the warriors can be classified as heroes. Taking the gloss further, one can see that this kind of neutrality is the mark of being in the state where the possibilities are held in play. ''Negative'' or ''positive'' outcomes (apparent surrender or destruction of one ''side'') are balanced, or perhaps perceived to be equally false. At this point one is the master of the opposites (as Thomas Mann puts it in *The Magic*

Mountain), as is the figure of Stephen Albert and his interpretation of Ts'ui Pen's narrative, and as is Borges with his construction of interlocking versions, and as the reader may be.

This interpretation is not inconsistent with Borgesian practice, but it does suggest a further point: ''suspended animation'' may be a more exact term than we suspected. It may be necessary to look further at this condition, since it does seem to be represented both by Yu Tsun and by the warriors. Useful parallels may be drawn between what occurs in reading and in certain states of consciousness closely analyzed in psycho-physiological terms by Maharishi Mahesh Yogi. His theory, together with experimental evidence derived from scientific investigation, can provide some interesting angles on the nature of aesthetic experience. One of the most crucial conditions for the experience is precisely the one in which stillness and activity appear to be present simultaneously.

What appears to happen is that a kind of neutral expectancy may be produced, as a background against which a variety of possibilities may be generated. I think this happens in ''The Garden of Forking Paths'' and in other Borges texts as a result of what Murillo calls ''displacement.'' In a phenomenological reading of the story, the narrator is realized via the narrative as a process; that is, as a succession of different vantage points, perceptions, or versions: the various styles and readings are a record of successive states of consciousness. (They move from the ''outer'' historical account of the war, through the deceptively confessional spy story, to Yu Tsun's more intimate sensations on approaching Albert's house, to Albert's gloss of Ts'ui Pen's work, and finally to the ''direct quotation'' given above: a graded progression towards the condition described and which Yu Tsun then reluctantly rejects.) The narrator presents this succession as a record of successive locations of his being-in-the-world, much as, for instance, Sartre's Roquentin in *La Nausee* tries out a variety of styles in an attempt to express the shifts and variations of identity. But just as from the mock-detective perspective, none of the versions offers the whole truth, so too each style is relativized by the next frame that the narrative adopts. Each central symbol, theme, or idea is assimilated into a successively more extensive context, which displaces it from central to relative importance. In this way the reader is gradually pushed into a state in which he or she doesn't totally accept or reject anything. The movement of the narrative into new frameworks takes the reader along, and at the same time serves as a block to any once-and-for-all opting for the previous perspective. One has to take part in the process by which meanings are created, but one is prevented from attributing finality to any one interpretation. The movement is something like closing and opening a pair of nutcrackers, as each possibility is grasped, then released as its kernel is found to be generative rather than final. Murillo neatly explains Borges' semi-invented locality for the 1916 battle in this vein: *Serre-Montauban* suggests a tension between ''compulsion'' and ''freedom''—which is both that of Yu Tsun's moral dilemma and of the reader's progress through the text. Interestingly, Ludovic Janvier describes Robbe-Grillet's narrative as built around the ''*couple fascination-liberte.*'' This ''disengaging compulsion toward ironical displacement'' allows the reader both to experience and to judge the progress of the protagonist/narrator. It further allows the reader to locate the source of creative and moral action, but forces him or her to return again and again to its nature as potential, and not to get carried away into one-sided choice.

The key to the production of this state is repetition. One reads on and on, and keeps getting blocked. Readers are somewhere between remembering and not remembering, between believing and not believing. They are in one sense getting lost in a labyrinth, and in another discovering that the secret of a labyrinth can be found only in that way. The reader becomes both active—in that she or he continues to read and to weigh up further possible additions and outcomes—and nonactive, in that everything is somehow held in abeyance, given a kind of nonfinite status, its seeming definitiveness undermined in advance by the ''let's wait and see'' mood established at the center of our consciousness. As a parallel to Yu Tsun's exposition of his state, with its moral and psychological implications, the text operates its own aesthetic procedure upon us. The state which Yu Tsun enters, in the labyrinthine center of Albert's enclave, but never fully explores, is offered as the means by which the thematic and structural development of Borges's tale can be most completely judged.

Irony gives more of a perspective so that more of the game can be judged. And yet one can only judge by being involved as well as detached. ''Critical distance,'' so often held up as the aim of literary

study, does not mean a kind of owlish glare that reduces a text to the status of a dead mouse. It does not mean the cultivation of a spurious and self-delusive ''objectivity'' swathed in biographical detail or critical jargon. It means, and it requires, precisely the kind of participation in the reading of a text on all levels which Borges is here working to produce. The reader must ''get lost'' in the text. Ts'ui Pen ''renounced worldly power in order . . . to construct a labyrinth in which all men would become lost'' (*Labyrinths*). The labyrinth is *the* text, in the sense of the network of meanings through which people make the world known to themselves. If we go on using this text unthinkingly, we never really own the world at all, and perhaps never really experience it either. We have to make it *our* text, which means first of all forgetting the one convention dictates, and secondly becoming aware of our own propensity for memory and organization. Yu Tsun discovers his own past where he least expects it. Borges's narratives weave their spell of mystery, symbolic density, suggestiveness, and disruption in order to propel the reader into the area, the kind of mental activity, where dream and memory and imagination operate. But more than this, the narratives offer the chance to be and to perceive that operation in process. The reader must learn to manipulate symbol, metaphor, strange registers, and rhythms; to familiarize himself or herself with the most powerful properties, the generative structures of language.

Reading this story can show us our own linguistic and moral capacity. So ''dreaming'' is not evasion, but rather (as Borges suggests with inevitable irony in ''The Circular Ruins'') a very precise kind of work. Playing this sort of game—especially if engaged in repeatedly—could very well serve as useful training for everyday activity, even if authors—and critics—tend to overplay the game for its own sake and forget the application.

Source: Ralph Yarrow, ''Irony Grows in My Garden: Generative Processes in Borges's 'The Garden of Forking Paths,''' in *The Fantastic in World Literature and the Arts*, edited by Donald E. Morse, Greenwood Press, 1987, pp. 73-86.

Stephen Rudy

In the essay below, Rudy addresses Borges's use of two different plots in ''Garden of Forking Paths'' and argues that this use is ''motivated by Borges' desire to upset any notion of plot under-

Example of the effects of bombing in the city of Rotterdam during World War II.

stood as simple chronological causality, as well as the conception of reality which underlies such a notion.''

"Ah, bear in mind this garden was enchanted.'' — E. A. Poe

". . . Magic is not the contradiction of the law of cause and effect but its crown, or nightmare.'' — Borges

Michel Foucault in his magnificent preface to *The Order of Things* quotes a text by Borges, a taxonomy of animals, which is attributed by Borges

to a certain Dr. Franz Kuhn, who in turn attributes it to "a certain Chinese encyclopedia entitled *Celestial Emporium of Benevolent Knowledge*.'' The text reads:

Animals are divided into: (a) belonging to the Emperor, (b) embalmed, (c) tame, (d) suckling pigs, (e) sirens, (f) fabulous, (g) stray dogs, (h) included in the above classification, (i) frenzied, (j) innumerable, (k) drawn with a very fine camelhair brush, (l) et cetera, (m) having just broken the water pitcher, (n) that from a long way off look like flies.

Foucault's exegesis of this passage leads him to conclude that Borges is here creating a "heterotopia," a place that is an impossible and frightening non-place, a place of language and of mind which manages to contain words "in sites so very different from one another that it is impossible to find a place of residence for them, to define a common locus." This procedure, according to Foucault, "destroys ... that less apparent syntax which causes words and things (next to and also opposite one another) to 'hold together.'" I think it could be argued that what Foucault finds Borges doing with words in general, we find the same writer doing with *plots* in "The Garden of Forking Paths," a story from the celebrated collection *Ficciones*. Plot emerges in this story in typically Borgesian fashion as a central symbolic element which embodies the author's subversive metaphysics as much as do the elements of theme or imagery more often discussed in the critical literature on this most sophisticated of contemporary writers.

I. The Frame

The first paragraph of "The Garden of Forking Paths" acts as a frame to the body of the text, a first-person confessional "document" written by Yu Tsun, a Chinese spy for the German Empire operating in England during the First World War. Ostensibly this framing paragraph serves to ground the confessional narrative in historical fact and provides the question to which Yu Tsun's "deposition" is supposedly an answer. The historical fact is the delay of a few days suffered in the British offensive on the Somme River in July, 1916. Borges (or more exactly, the "editor") cities Captain Liddell Hart's *A History of the World War* to the effect that "torrential rain caused this delay—which lacked any special significance." The reader assumes that Yu Tsun's "deposition" will prove (a) that "torrential rains" were not the decisive factor in the delay and—perhaps—(b) that the delay did have significance. This seems innocent enough if the reader is unaware, as no doubt he is, that the action on the Somme took place a month earlier than Borges quotes Liddell Hart, falsely, as having stated. He will be all the more surprised to discover that an obscure Chinese spy caused this delay by murdering a man who is, it seems, a reincarnation of his ancient ancestor Ts'ui Pen and that the delay thus had a significance of a most unsettling sort, indirectly and on another plane of "reality."

Yet Borges' intention in introducing us to the story via history is not simply to give his fiction an innocent motivation, that of answering the "official" account of a historical event, of attempting, on

> In returning to 'The Garden . . . ,' one can see clearly how essential a role details play in cementing the two plots together in line with Borges' aesthetics of 'anticipation' and 'prefiguration.'"

the basis of later "documentation," to assert historical "truth," whatever that may be. Rather, this frame is there for the purpose of exploding on itself: it is subversive. History, chronological time, has no place in Borges' universe, and since his universe so often appears as the "Book" or model of our universe, ours is left on shaky ground when he has completed his supposedly innocent operation of ascertaining the "truth." The historical work to which Borges refers is itself a "Borgesian" work: it is a startling narrative of "real" events which seem more fantastic than any fiction an author could invent. Borges understandbly likes Conrad's thought "that when one wrote, even in a realistic way about the world, one was writing a fantastic story because the world itself is fantastic and unfathomable and mysterious.") The historian Liddell Hart, who is of a positivistic bent to say the least, admits of his enterprise that "it is difficult to pick out salient features where there are either none, or else so many that they tend to merge into a formless mass." Nevertheless, he plods along, sorting out causes and effects, making judgments, interpolating the various "factors" of chance involved in a given battle (with the thoroughness of an Avalon-Hill war game)—and ends up with a fantastic narrative. Borges takes the model of this fantastic but literal narration of "real events" as his starting point: he will correct Liddell Hart (ostensibly in the interests of historical truth), outdoing the very concept of cause and effect to the point that it turns on itself, and all notions of history, causal time, and truth are overthrown by the "unfathomable."

Such a strategy is quite typical of Borges. As Ronald Christ, in his excellent book *The Narrow*

Act, states: "On the one hand Borges taints the reality which his sources describe; on the other he corrupts the authenticity of those sources themselves; in both cases the motive is to penetrate the metaphysical world which lies beyond fact and substance. . . ." In view of this critic's fine understanding of the meaningful distortion which even the simplest quoted text undergoes in Borges' hands, it is surprising that he completely misses the point of the reference to Liddell Hart in "The Garden. . . ," the opening of which, in his view, "shows Borges operating out of an historical background, grafting his fiction, once again, *on the stock of fact*" (italics mine). The mechanism of quotation, particularly quotation from an authoritative, non-fictional source, may be used as a device to mark the "factual," as opposed to "fictional," nature of a narrative. This is certainly the *overt* purpose of the opening paragraph of "The Garden. . . ." (This purpose is further served by the presentation of Yu Tsun's narrative as a "deposition," i.e., a genuine, if personal, account of an actual event, by its naturalistic fragmentation ["the first two pages are missing"], and by the "editor's note," which cantankerously corrects a supposedly slanderous accusation voiced in the deposition.) But the *covert* purpose of the opening, which, as we shall see, is more important for the story's total effect, is clearly to lull the reader into a type of false security as regards the status of "real" events, a security he will be forced to give up—if nothing else, in befuddlement. For the expectation of a "factual" type of narrative which the frame sets up is destroyed by Borges' play with two parallel yet incompatible plots, one of a detective, the other of a metaphysical, nature.

II. The Detective Plot

Into the frame of a historical plot, an effort to sort out the cause and effect of a historical event, Borges inserts a detective plot, a more modest (or usually so) effort to find the hidden order underlying a crime. Borges himself has characterized "The Garden of Forking Paths" as a "detective story": "its readers will assist at the execution, and all the preliminaries of a crime, a crime whose purpose will not be unknown to them, but which they will not understand—it seems to me—until the last paragraph" (*Ficciones*). The reader learns early in the story that Yu Tsun has a secret—the site of a new British artillery park on the Ancre—to communicate to his Chief, a "sick and hateful man . . . sitting in his arid Berlin office," and that his message will result in the bombing of the site by the

Germans and a consequent delay in the British offensive. The reader also learns that Yu Tsun is being pursued by his arch-enemy, the British secret-service agent Madden, and is desperate, and that he is contemplating, and then has planned, a crime—viz., the emphasis on the "revolver with a single bullet" and his various meditations of the sort, *"Whoever would undertake some atrocious enterprise. . . ."* Furthermore, this planned crime is somehow connected with his communicating the necessary information to his Chief, but all we learn relative to the *means* of the communication is that "the telephone directory gave [Yu Tsun] the name of the one person capable of passing on the information." Only in the last paragraph of the story do we learn that the crime is the murder of a man named Albert, whose elimination will signal to the Chief the necessity of eliminating the depot at Albert on the Ancre River. (This is, incidentally, a typical "fantastic" replacement of the inanimate [the name, a sign] by the animate [the unfortunate person who happens to bear the name].) Thus the name, not the man, is to communicate the spy's secret; the murder is a coded message, the solution of which hinges on a semantic notion, that of elimination, and a key word, the name, to express location.

III. The Metaphysical Mystery Plot

The second plot develops out of a coincidence, namely that the man named Albert, chosen by Yu Tsun as his victim-message, is a Sinologist who has solved the metaphysical mystery of the novel-labyrinth left by Yu Tsun's illustrious ancestor, Ts'ui Pen. The second plot is also a detective plot, though of a literary-critical nature, whose solution is also based on the decoding of a message. This message is Ts'ui Pen's will (just as the newspaper article on Albert's murder is in some sense Yu Tsun's will), which is decoded on the basis of the key word *time*, which Ts'ui Pen eliminated from his novel (just as the key word *Albert* was "eliminated" by proxy to insure the success of Yu Tsun's plan). The unique novel left by Ts'ui Pen, considered by posterity to be "a shapeless mass of contradictory drafts" and decoded by the ingenious Albert, is actually a symbolic labyrinth of time in which the various possible futures of the characters are depicted simultaneously. As Albert puts it:

> "In all fiction, when a man is faced with alternatives he chooses one at the expense of the others. In the almost unfathomable Ts'ui Pen, he chooses—simultaneously—all of them. He thus *creates* various futures, various times which start others that will in their turn

branch out and bifurcate in other times. This is the cause of the contradictions in the novel.

> "Fang, let us say, has a secret. A stranger knocks at his door. Fang makes up his mind to kill him. Natural- ly, there are various possible outcomes. Fang can kill the intruder, the intruder can kill Fang, both can be saved, both can die and so on and so on. In Ts'ui Pen's work all the possible solutions occur, each one being the point of departure for other bifurcations. Some- times the pathways of the labyrinth converge. . . ."

This novel conception of narrative echoes Borges' own view of time, presented throughout his stories and essays, a view which stresses the cyclic- al nature of history and the concept of the Eternal Return, resulting in a negation of the concept of "individuality" and, on the literary side, the radical assumption that all authors are ultimately one, all texts forming the collective text of a universal and eternal Author. Borges' theories of time have been admirably discussed by various critics and need not detain us here, though one could note in passing that certain pronouncements of Yu Tsun are rephrasings of Borges' own statement on the subject. In terms of plot, however, it should be stressed that the meta- physical plot parallels the murder plot in abstract form: both involve messages to be decoded on the basis of the elimination of a key term. The fact that one message relates to a man's life and the other to a literary work immediately suggests a disturbing parallelism between the universe (the "real" plane) and the book (the "fictional" plane).

IV. The Crossing of the Plots

Coincidence brings the two plots together, and the second is contained in the first just as the first is framed historically. The reader expects the second plot to illuminate the first (or at least have some direct bearing upon it) just as the first supposedly illuminates the historical event referred to in the framing paragraph of the opening. Actually, it does so only indirectly, on a different level, and thus again subversively. Before exploring the devices by which the first and second plot are linked, let us turn briefly to one of Borges' most famous theoretical statements on narrative, which is of relevance for an understanding of the overall structure of "The Garden. . . ."

In an essay on "Narrative Art and Magic," first published in Spanish in 1932 (i.e., before Borges began writing the stories in *Ficciones*) and only recently translated into English, Borges outlines a primitive typology of narrative alternatives. His statements refer primarily to the genre of the novel, but are actually of little critical use in approaching that domain; they read more like a manifesto for the future poetics of the short stories in *Ficciones*. The main problem of the novel for Borges is that of cause and effect, or the motivation of fictional events. He sees two possible approaches. The first, which typifies fiction of "the slow-moving psycho- logical variety," is grounded in character and de- pends for its success on a chain of cause and effect which may be termed "naturalistic": it is "the incessant result of endless, uncontrollable [psycho- logical] processes." This approach Borges finds wholly unacceptable: as he puts it, citing Mallarme in his support, "the pleasure of reading is in antici- pation, and the ideal lies in suggestion." The psy- chological novel succeeds through a consistency of motivation which, for Borges, is as tiresome as it is predictable. The second approach he discusses is based on "magic," and in it, "—clear and de- fined—every detail is an omen and a cause." In defining magic, "that craft, or ambition, of early man," Borges quotes the general principle formu- lated by Sir James Frazer, "the Law of Sympathy, which assumes that 'things act on each other at a distance through a secret sympathy,' either because their form is similar (imitative, or homeopathic, magic) or because of a previous physical contact (contagious, or contact, magic)," or in more con- temporary terms, through association based on simi- larity or contiguity (respectively metaphoric or metonymic relations). According to Borges, "the only possible integrity" for the novel is to be found in "narrative magic." The novel should be "a rigorous scheme of attentions, echoes, and affini- ties." "Every episode in a painstaking piece of fiction," Borges writes, "prefigures something still to come."

It is not surprising that Borges supports his argument with references to the adventure novel, the detective story, and the "endless spectacular fictions made up in Hollywood." The first two, despite the primitiveness of many of their practi- tioners, offer manifold possibilities for intricate plotting, in which characters act as "functions" (much as they do in the folk tale) rather than as determiners of the action. The suppression of the psychological element in Borges may be regarded not merely as a philosophical and aesthetic reaction against "the psychologism bequeathed to us by the last century," as he puts it, but also as a reflection of a more general poetics of narrative. The emphasis on plot entails a reduction in the importance of character and necessitates a concomitant increase in embedded, structurally significant details of description which prefigure the action and thus form a sort of "secret plot," to use Borges' term.

In returning to "The Garden . . . ," one can see clearly how essential a role details play in cementing the two plots together in line with Borges' aesthetics of "anticipation" and "prefiguration." It is precisely the undercurrent of signification, the "secret plot" formed by connecting links between the two plots, which renders neither plot adequate in explaining the action and results in the disorienting "heterotopia" typical of Borges. The role of detail is most obvious on the level of imagery, where the emphasis on the circle reinforces the theory of cyclical time advanced in the metaphysical plot; as Ronald Christ has pointed out, "cyclical time is evinced in the portentous detail." On the level of plot Yu Tsun's meditation on his ancestor's labyrinth before meeting by "accident" the man who has solved its riddle—a meditation which would seem initially to be a mere "digression"—motivates the meeting with Albert, which does not in the least surprise Yu Tsun. Furthermore, as E. Rodriguez Monegal has shown, Yu Tsun's meditation actually anticipates on an intuitive level the intellectual solution later offered by Albert: "I thought of a maze of mazes, of a sinuous, ever growing maze *which would take in both past and future and would somehow involve the stars*" (italics mine). The details embodied in Albert's discussion of Ts'ui Pen's novel also serve to link the detective and metaphysical plots. In describing the novel's structure, besides the rather portentous example of the character Fang, a stranger, and a murder, Albert has recourse to an illustration based on the present situation, Yu Tsun's appearance at his house: "Sometimes the pathways of the labyrinth converge. For example, you come to this house; but in other possible pasts you are my enemy; in others my friend." And further:

> " . . . your ancestor . . . believed in an infinite series of times in a dizzily growing, ever spreading network of diverging, converging and parallel times. This web of time—the strands of which approach one another, bifurcate, intersect or ignore each other through the centuries—embraces *every* possibility. We do not exist in most of them. In some you exist and not I, while in others I do, and you do not, and in yet others both of us exist. In this one, in which chance has favored me, you have come to my gate. In another, you, crossing the garden, have found me dead. In yet another, I say these very same words, but am an error, a phantom."

Yu Tsun replies: "In all of them . . . I deeply appreciate and am grateful to you for the restoration of Ts'ui Pen's garden." Albert's response, his last words before being assassinated by Yu Tsun, seem to reveal an intuition of his death at the spy's hands: "'Not in *all*,' he murmured with a smile. 'Time is forever dividing itself toward innumerable futures and in one of them I am your enemy.'" In terms of the metaphysics of repetition, Albert's death may be interpreted as a reenactment of Ts'ui Pen's "assassination by a stranger" centuries before. Yu Tsun experiences the "pullulation" of past and future identities, a state in which he becomes an "abstract spectator" of his own life, which seems directed by a will other than his own. His last words to Albert, "The Future exists now . . . ," seem almost ironic. We are abruptly returned to the detective plot by the sudden appearance of Madden, whom Yu Tsun sees coming through the garden (as if emerging out of his vague hallucinations) to arrest him. The spy's enactment of his plan, the murder of Albert, occurs simultaneously on the level of the mundane causality of the detective plot and on that of the inscrutable causality of the metaphysical; the moment of the murder is on the borderline between the "real" and the "fantastic."

The use of two plots, of a murder mystery and a metaphysical mystery which runs imperceptibly parallel and counter to it, is motivated by Borges' desire to upset any notion of plot understood as simple chronological causality, as well as the conception of reality which underlies such a notion. The disjunction of the two plots, the impossible distance which separates the realms to which each pertains, is so startling precisely because of their apparent and less obvious parallelisms. The two plots are connected with history through the framing device and make it (a potential model for plot in general) seem as fantastic as the time of Ts'ui Pen's labyrinth. The "delay" Yu Tsun has caused becomes more significant as having been the cause of his primal reenactment of Ts'ui Pen's assassination than it was in "real" history, and the total significance of the story is caught up in the unfathomable metaphysics of repetition. As one critic temptingly formulates it: "The labyrinth and the book are one and the same. But they are also something else as Borges insinuates—the universe."

Source: Stephen Rudy, "The Garden *of* and *in* Borges' 'Garden of Forking Paths,'" in *The Structural Analysis of Narrative Texts*, edited by Andrej Kodjak, Michael J. Connolly, and Krystyna Pomorska, Slavica Publishers, Inc., 1980, pp. 132-144.

Sources

Barth, John. "The Literature of Exhaustion," in *Atlantic Monthly*, Vol. 220, No. 2, August, 1967, pp. 29-34.

Borges, Jorge Luis. *Labyrinths*, preface by Andre Maurois, edited by Donald A. Yates, and James E. Irby, New York: New Directions Books, 1964.

Fraser, John. "Jorge Luis Borges, Alive in His Labyrinth," in *Criticism*, Vol. 31, Spring, 1989, pp. 179-91.

Gonzalez-Echevarria, Roberto. "Borges and Derrida," in *Jorge Luis Borges*, edited and with an introduction by Harold Bloom, New York: Chelsea House, 1986.

Irwin, John. "A Clew to a Clue: Locked Rooms and Labyrinths in Poe and Borges," in *Raritan*, Vol. 10, Spring, 1991, pp. 40-57.

Jaen, Didier T. *Borges Esoteric Library: Metaphysics to Metafiction*, New York: Lanham, 1992.

Lindstrom, Naomi. *Jorge Luis Borges: A Study of the Short Fiction*, Boston: Twayne, 1990.

Stabb, Martin. *Jorge Luis Borges*, Twayne, 1970, p. 138.

Stoicheff, Peter. "The Chaos of Metafiction," in *Chaos and Order: Complex Dynamics in Literature and Science*, edited by N. Katherine Hayles, Chicago: University of Chicago Press, 1991, pp. 85-99.

Updike, John. "Books: The Author as Librarian," in *New Yorker*, October 31, 1965, pp. 223-46.

Waugh, Patricia. *Metafiction: The Theory and the Practice of Self-Conscious Fiction*, London: Routledge, 1988.

Weissert, Thomas P. "Representation and Bifurcation: Borges' Garden of Chaos Dynamics," in *Chaos and Order: Complex Dynamics in Literature and Science*, edited by N. Katherine Hayles. Chicago: University of Chicago Press, 1991, pp. 223-42.

Wheelock, Carter. "Borges and the 'Death' of the Text," in *Hispanic Review*, Vol. 53, 1985, pp. 151-61.

Woodall, James. *The Man in the Mirror of the Book: A Life of Jorge Luis Borges*, London: Hodder and Stoughton, 1996.

Further Reading

Bloom, Harold, editor. *Jorge Luis Borges*, New York: Chelsea House, 1986.
    A collection of important critical essays, including the chapter-length essay, "Doubles and Counterparts: 'The Garden of Forking Paths'" by Shlomith Rimmon-Kenan.

Lindstrom, Naomi. *Jorge Luis Borges: A Study of the Short Fiction*, Boston: Twayne, 1990.
    Offers an introduction to Borges, as well as an interview, selected criticism, a chronology, and a bibliography.

Sorrentino, Fernando. *Seven Conversations with Jorge Luis Borges*, translated by Clark M. Zlotchew, Troy, NY: The Whitson Publishing Company, 1982.
    A collection of seven interviews with Borges, considered to be among the best books of its kind. Includes a helpful appendix identifying personalities mentioned by Borges.

Weissert, Thomas P. "Representation and Bifurcation: Borges' Garden of Chaos Dynamics, " in *Chaos and Order: Complex Dynamics in Literature and Science*, edited by N, Katherine Hayles. Chicago: University of Chicago Press, 1991, pp. 223-43.
    Provides an interesting account of chaos and bifurcation theory in lay terms. Weissert uses the theories to demonstrate Borges' fundamental determinism and modernism, as opposed to chaotic postmodernism. A good choice for the advanced student interested in both literature and science.

Woodall, James. *The Man in the Mirror of the Book: A Life of Jorge Luis Borges*, London: Hodder and Stoughton, 1996.
    An accessible biography of Borges. Includes photographs and bibliography as well as a listing of films based on Borges' work.

Half a Day

Naguib Mahfouz

1989

Recognized as a prominent author in his own country of Egypt, Naguib Mahfouz was not widely known in the Western world until receiving the Nobel Prize for Literature in 1988. After receiving the award, he gained international recognition as one of the more important writers of the twentieth century.

In 1989 "Half a Day" was first published in Arabic as part of a short story collection entitled *The False Dawn*. In 1991 "Half a Day" was included in an English-language collection entitled *The Time and the Place*.

"Half a Day" belongs to the later phase of Mahfouz's literary career, which is characterized by a shift from social realism to a more modern, experimental mode of writing. It is a very short (5-page) allegorical tale in which the narrator begins the day as a young boy entering school for the first time, but leaves the schoolyard an old man whose life has passed in what seemed like only "half a day."

The central allegorical implications of this tale are a commentary on the human condition; an entire life span is experienced as only "half a day" in the school of life. The story also alludes to the cycle of life, whereby the narrator passes through childhood, middle age and old age in the course of one day.

Critic Rasheed El-Enany, in *Naguib Mahfouz*, has called "Half a Day" a "technical *tour de force*." El-Enany explains that "brief as it is, the

story must count as the author's most powerful rendering of the dilemma of the gulf between observable time and mnemonic time.''

Author Biography

In 1911 Mahfouz was born in Cairo, Egypt, the youngest of seven children in a lower middle-class family. His father was a strict Muslim and he was raised in a strong religious atmosphere. He earned an undergraduate degree in philosophy from the University of Fuad (now Cairo University) in 1934.

Although his first short story was published in 1932, Mahfouz did not decide to become a writer until two years after graduating from college. He also maintained a career as an Egyptian bureaucrat. His first position was in the Ministry of Waqfs, the body overseeing pious Muslim foundations.

He held many bureaucratic positions—primarily in relation to the national film industry, as director of the Censorship Office, director and chairman of the Cinema Support Organization, and counselor for Cinema Affairs to the Minister of Culture. He retired from bureaucratic work in 1971, after which he has continued to publish novels, short stories, and memoirs.

Mahfouz has traveled abroad only twice in his life: once to Yugoslavia, and once to Yemen, both on government assignment. For many years, he has been part of a close social group of men who congregate in coffeehouses in Cairo, calling themselves ''al Harafish'' (''common people'').

He has published more than thirty novels and fourteen collections of short stories. His first three novels, written between 1943 and 1945, are historical novels set in ancient Egypt. His next three novels, referred to as ''The Trilogy,'' published between 1956 and 1957, are set in lower middle-class sections of modern Cairo. This series of novels established Mahfouz as the foremost novelist in Egypt, and attracted international recognition.

In addition to novels and short stories, he has written many screenplays for the Egyptian film industry. Between 1945 and 1960, he wrote many screen adaptations of the stories of other writers. After 1960 many of his own stories were adapted to the screen by other screenwriters. In 1988 he was awarded the Nobel Prize for Literature, the first Arabic language writer to be given the prize. As a result, many of his works were translated into different languages and international interest in his work grew.

In 1994, Mahfouz was stabbed in an attack orchestrated by Islamic extremists, who had taken to heart condemnation by religious leaders based on their belief that one of his novels (first published seventeen years earlier) was blasphemous. He survived this attack, and those who orchestrated the assassination attempt were arrested and executed.

Although notoriously private about his childhood and personal life, Mahfouz published a personal memoir in 1994, entitled *Echoes of an Autobiography*. Written as a collection of vignettes, it is beautifully written and provides some insight into his life and career.

Plot Summary

As the story opens, the narrator is a young boy walking to his first day of school. The boy is delighted with the new clothes he is wearing for the occasion, but is apprehensive about going to school. As he walks along, holding onto his father's hand, he occasionally turns to ask his father why he must go; he feels that perhaps he is being sent away from home as a punishment.

Although his father reassures him, he is not convinced that ''there really was any good to be had in tearing me away from the intimacy of my home.'' At the gate to the school, the boy hesitates again, and must be gently pushed by his father to enter the schoolyard. Telling him to ''be a man,'' the father explains that ''today you truly begin life.''

Upon stepping into the yard, the boy sees the faces of the other boys and girls, but feels ''like a stranger who had lost his way.'' One boy approaches and asks the narrator who brought him to school; when he replies that it was his father, the other boy states that his own father is dead.

The narrator soon becomes one of the group of children, and the narrative voice changes from the first person singular ''I'' to alternatively speaking in the third person plural ''we.''

The narrator makes friends with some of the boys and falls in love with some of the girls. He describes the school day in a manner which is meant to be interpreted as an allegory for human life, with its ups and downs, trials and tribulations.

Naguib Mahfouz

When the bell rings to announce the end of the day, the narrator steps outside the gate, but his father is not waiting there for him as promised. He encounters a familiar middle-aged man; they greet one another and shake hands before the man moves along.

The narrator finds that the street and surroundings have completely changed since the morning. These changes are meant to be understood in allegorical terms, as representing the effect of modernization and urbanization in radically changing the face of the city within the lifetime of one man.

He is unable to cross the street because of heavy traffic. Finally, a "young lad" offers to help him across, addressing him as "Grandpa"—the little boy has passed an entire life time in what seemed like only half a day, and is now an old man at the end of his life.

Characters

The Father

It is the young boy's father who, "clutching" his hand, takes the boy to school. When the boy asks if he is being sent away from home for being a bother, his father assures him that school is not a punishment, but a "factory" which turns boys into men. As he enters the school the boy hesitates, but his father gently pushes him and tells him to "be a man."

The boy's father is an important character in both a literal and a symbolic sense. As a coming-of-age story, "Half a Day" concerns themes of fatherhood and the different stages of human life. The boy's father is seen to represent the narrator himself, at a different stage of life.

He may also symbolize God, who ushers each human being both into and out of life.

The Middle-aged Man

When the narrator leaves the school, he encounters a familiar middle-aged man. This man approaches the narrator, greeting him and shaking his hand. When the narrator—now an old man—asks how he is doing, the middle-aged man replies, "As you can see, not all that good, the Almighty be praised!" The man then shakes the narrator's hand again and continues along his way.

The Mother

The image of the boy's mother appears only once, at the beginning of the story. As he sets out for his first day of school, his mother stands at the window "watching our progress." The boy occasionally turns to look back at his mother, "as though appealing for help."

The mother is a significant part of the coming-of-age process. The father initiates this process by taking his son out of the home and away from his mother, "tearing me away from the intimacy of my home." Although he occasionally looks to his mother for comfort, the boy must separate from his mother in order to become an adult. (It is interesting to note that Mahfouz lived with his own mother until the mature age of forty-three, when he married for the first time.)

The Narrator

As the story opens, the narrator is a young boy going to his first day of school. Apprehensive about being away from home, he soon begins to fit in and enjoy his time as a member of the class.

When the bell rings to announce the end of the day, the narrator steps outside the gate. His father is not waiting there for him, and he starts to walk home by himself. He finds that the street and surroundings have completely changed, a sight that leaves him overwhelmed and disoriented.

He attempts to cross the street, but the traffic is heavy and he hesitates. Finally, a ''young lad,'' offers to help him across, addressing him as ''Grandpa''—the little boy has passed an entire life time in what seemed like only half a day, and is now an old man at the end of his life.

The Other Children

Although he at first feels like a ''stranger,'' the narrator soon becomes a member of the class. His identification with the other children is indicated in the narrative by the fluctuation between first-person singular narrative voice (''I''), and first-person plural (''We''). The children represent humanity, and their experiences are meant to be interpreted as symbolic of the human experience of life.

The Teachers

The primary teacher introduces the children to some of the wonders of life; she is also a harsh disciplinarian who frequently ''would resort to physical punishment.'' On an allegorical level, the teacher is not an individual person, but life itself, which offers many wonders and many punishments.

The Young Lad

The ''young lad'' appears in the closing lines of the story. He extends his arm to the narrator, addressing him as ''Grandpa.''

Themes

Life/The Human Condition

''Half a Day'' can only be fully understood if interpreted as an allegorical tale, in which each element is symbolic of some greater meaning. The central allegorical motif of ''Half a Day'' is that a morning spent in school is symbolic of an entire lifetime spent in the school of life.

Everything that occurs in the story represents common experiences of the human condition: birth, childhood, old age, death, the afterlife, religion, love, friendship, pain, fear, joy, learning, memory, and nostalgia, as well as the cycle of life from generation to generation.

Media Adaptations

- Mahfouz has written numerous screenplays for the Egyptian cinema. Many of his stories have been adapted to the screen, including sixteen of his novels. These films are not readily available in the United States.

Coming-of-Age

''Half a Day'' is a ''coming-of-age'' story, meaning that one of its central themes is the transition from childhood to adulthood.

The narrator, a young boy, is at first reluctant to be ''torn'' away from ''the intimacy of my home.'' As his father leads him by the hand toward school, he looks back ''as though appealing for help'' to his mother, who stands in the window, ''watching our progress.'' This scenario suggests the early stages of life.

As he matures and moves farther away from the security and intimacy of home and family, however, he symbolically looks to his mother for comfort and reassurance. When the young boy protests that he does not want to be sent away from home, his father describes the school as a place in which boys become men. At the gates of the schoolyard, the boy is still reluctant to take the first step in the transition from childhood into adulthood, but his father instructs him to ''be a man,'' telling him ''Today you truly begin life.''

Time, Memory, and Old Age

The title ''Half a Day,'' indicates the story's central concern with the human experience of time and memory. The narrator emerges from the gates of the school unaware that his entire life has passed, and that he is now no longer a young boy but an old man.

He is confused and disoriented as his surroundings are barely recognizable. It is not until a ''young lad'' addresses him as ''Grandpa'' that the narrator,

Topics for Further Study

- Mahfouz's life has spanned much of the twentieth century, and his work has been greatly influenced by the social and political upheaval in Egypt. Research the history of Egypt in the twentieth century. How have these events influenced specific themes and concerns of Mahfouz's stories?

- Recurring themes in the stories of Mahfouz include death, time, God, and the human condition. These concerns were influenced in part by his religious upbringing in an Islamic family. What are the fundamental beliefs of the religion of Islam? Which countries in the world are predominantly Islamic? How has Mahfouz's Islamic upbringing impacted the central themes and concerns of his stories?

- Westerners are generally familiar with the ancient history of Egypt. Yet what artistic and cultural styles are relevant to modern Egypt? Find out more about modern Egyptian art, music, or theater. What social and political factors have influenced modern artistic and cultural trends in Egypt?

- Mahfouz has been criticized for the portrayal of

women in his stories. Learn more about the status of women in modern Egypt. How has the role of women changed over the course of the twentieth century? How is the status of women in Egypt different from the status of women in the West?

- Mahfouz's involvement in the film industry ranged from holding a bureaucratic position in the national film censorship office, writing screenplays based on the stories of other authors, and seeing his own stories made into films. Find out more about the Egyptian film industry and Mahfouz's involvement in it. In what ways has Mahfouz influenced the Egyptian film industry? Did his experience with film impact his writing style?

- Receiving the Swedish Academy's Nobel Prize for literature in 1988 catapulted Mahfouz into the international limelight. Investigate the history of the Swedish Academy and the Nobel Prize. What is the criterion for determining the winners? When was the first prize awarded? What other writers have received Nobel Prizes?

---

as well as the reader, becomes aware that he is now an old man. In fact, the entire story can be understood as a memory of a life from the perspective of an old man.

The Cycle of Life

At an allegorical level, ''Half a Day'' is concerned with three stages of life: childhood to middle age to old age. It is also concerned with the cycle of life from generation to generation.

Each of the male characters encountered by the narrator can be interpreted as images of him at various stages in the life cycle. The first child he encounters in the school asks: ''Who brought you?''

Symbolically, this question is not about the person who brought him to the school, but gave him life—his father.

The boy then responds that his own father is dead. This exchange symbolizes the condition of every boy in relation to his father (or child in relation to both of her or his parents): that it is the parents who bring the child into the world; and that everyone's parents must eventually die.

When the narrator emerges from the gates to the schoolyard, his father is indeed not there to take him home. The implication is that his father has died.

The narrator does, however, see a middle-aged man whom he recognizes. This man is an image of both the narrator's father and the narrator himself in the middle stage of life.

Finally, the "young lad" who helps him across the street in the end of the story is both an image of himself as a youth and a reminder of his status as grandfather.

Style

Allegory

An allegory is a story with events and characters not meant to be interpreted at a literal level but at a symbolic one. Menahem Milson, in his book *Naguib Mahfouz: The Novelist-Philosopher of Cairo*, maintains that in the work of Mahfouz, "allegory is an extremely important literary mode." "Half a Day" is an allegory for life and the human condition. The story is clearly not meant to be interpreted literally, since the use of time in the narrative is completely unrealistic. The narrator enters the schoolyard a young boy and leaves it "half a day" later, only to discover that the world outside has been completely transformed and he is now the age of a grandfather. The "half a day" spent in school is thus an allegory for the way in which an entire lifetime can seem to last only "half a day."

The school represents what one might call the "school of life," as all of the events that take place there are allegorical for the human condition and the human experience of life. Because the story is an allegory, none of the characters, including the main character, are given names; they are meant to represent humanity in general, and their experiences are that of the human condition, rather than of individuals. The meaning in this story is thus derived from re-examining it in terms of its allegorical, rather than literal, implications.

Setting

As is the case in many allegorical stories, the setting of "Half a Day" is general. Mahfouz has lived in Cairo, Egypt, all of his life—and nearly all of his stories take place there—so it can be assumed that the story is set in Cairo. Yet it is told in such a way that it could take place in almost any schoolyard in any city over the course of the twentieth century.

The setting, however, is more important in terms of its allegorical meaning. The schoolyard refers to the "school of life." The events that occur there represent the experiences of an entire human life span. The gate to the schoolyard thus represents an important stage of transition in the life of the narrator. He first passes through the gate in order to make the transition from early childhood into manhood and adulthood. As the narrator's father tells him while gently pushing him through the gate, "today you truly being life."

Stepping out of the gate at the end of the "half a day" spent in school, the narrator, now and old man, is once again making the transition to the ending of his life, on his way to "home," which signifies death and the afterlife.

Narrative voice

The narrative voice of a story refers to who tells the story. In "Half a Day," the narrative voice is that of the main character, who, at the beginning, is a young boy; by the end, the narrator is an old man.

In the beginning, the story is told in the "first person singular," meaning that the narrator speaks from the perspective of an individual "I." However, this voice alters once he has entered the schoolyard, at which point it slides into a first person *plural* voice from a group perspective of "We." The narrator thus describes school as a group experience, whereby he speaks from the perspective of the common experience of all of the children.

This change in perspective is significant to the allegorical implications of the story. The story describes the experience of the human condition; therefore, the narrator's experiences in school are meant to be understood in terms of the ways in which "we," all humans, experience life, time and memory.

Historical Context

Egypt in the Twentieth Century

Mahfouz has been a witness to all of the major events in Egyptian history during his lifetime. Many of these events have had a profound effect on the subject matter, style, and political implications of his stories and novels.

In 1922 Egypt gained independence from British rule. With the establishment of Israel as a sovereign nation in 1948, Egypt, and much of the Arab world, became engaged in a series of conflicts with Israel. As soon as the Israeli state had been

Compare
&
Contrast

- **1989:** When Mahfouz's short story ''Half a Day'' was first published in Arabic in 1989, he had recently been awarded the Nobel Prize for Literature, earning him instant international recognition. By this point, however, most of his novels and short story collections were not yet available in English translation.

  Today: In the decade since he received the Nobel Prize for literature, more than half of Mahfouz's body of work has been published in English translation.

- **1922:** Egypt gains independence from British rule.

  Today: Egypt, despite many social and political upheavals, remains a sovereign state and a United States ally.

- **1948:** Israel is established as an independent state, ushering in a tumultuous period of conflicts between Egypt and Israel.

  1978: The signing of a peace treaty between Israel and Egypt initiated a new era in the relationship between the two nations.

  Today: The relationship between Israel and Egypt is improved, but still problematic.

---

formed, the surrounding Arab nations of Egypt, Syria, Iraq and Jordan attacked the new nation—a conflict that ended with Israel's victory over the four nations.

In 1952 a military coup overthrew the Egyptian monarchy. In June 1967, Egypt again suffered a loss to Israel in the Six-Day War. This defeat wounded the national pride of the people of Egypt. In 1973, under the new regime of Anwar Sadat, Egypt and Syria attacked Israel in the Yom Kippur War (launched during the Jewish high holiday); although they could not claim a victory, Egypt did regain some national pride.

In 1978, Sadat met at Camp David, Maryland, with Israeli Prime Minister Menachem Begin and United States President Jimmy Carter. This historic meeting resulted in a peace treaty between Egypt and Israel.

Arabic literature

Arabic literature includes any literature written in an Arabic language, regardless of the nationality of the author. Thus, Arabic writers have included a broad compass of nationalities, such as Egypt, India, Iran, Persia, Spain, and Syria.

The work of Mahfouz, an Egyptian, can thus be understood in the context of Arabic literary history.

The classic era of Arabic literature, mainly proverbs and poetry, was first communicated in the oral tradition and later written down in text form. Classic Arabic literature dates from the sixth century to the sixteenth century. Although this classic literature was not necessarily religious, it is categorized into two distinct periods: first before the advent of Islam in the early seventh century, and the second after the advent of Islam.

Arabic literature was virtually eliminated in the sixteenth and seventeenth centuries as most of the Arab-speaking world was conquered by other cultures.

The modern era of Arabic literature emerged in the nineteenth century, in part through contact with Western culture and literary traditions. Whereas the European short story and the modern novel had its roots in the eighteenth century, the Arabic world did not begin to develop these literary forms until the late nineteenth century.

According to *Encyclopaedia Britannica Online,* Egypt ''became the center of the renaissance'' in Arabic literature. Highly influenced by translations of French literature, the first generation of Arabic writers of the realistic short story and novel did not emerge until after World War I. Naguib

Mahfouz was one of the first to master the literary form.

The Arabic Language

The Arabic language is written and spoken in many nations and encompasses many regional and national dialects. Moreover, there have always been two distinct forms of Arabic: the written and the spoken. In developing the modern form of the realistic story, however, fiction writers in Arabic have been faced with a difficult dilemma: when and if to continue to write in classic written Arabic, and when and if to write in the spoken dialect that would realistically be used by the story's characters in their conversation.

Throughout the twentieth century, individual Arabic writers have made their own choices in this matter. Some, for instance, continued to use written Arabic in the prose sections of their stories, while utilizing the spoken dialect in the dialogue sections. In all of his works, however, Mahfouz has consistently utilized the classic written Arabic.

Children playing on a playground.

Critical Overview

Since winning the Nobel Prize for Literature in 1988, Naguib Mahfouz has become internationally acclaimed as Egypt's foremost literary figure and recognized as one of the most accomplished novelists of the twentieth century. He is also celebrated as the first Arabic language writer to receive a Nobel Prize.

While a renowned writer in the Arabic world, Mahfouz's work was unknown in the West until receiving the prize. Since then, however, over half of his books have been translated into English, for the first time making his work available to readers in the English-speaking world.

Mahfouz's body of work is generally categorized into three distinct phases: the historical/romantic, the social realist, and the modern/experimental. His first three novels, written between 1943 and 1945, represent his historical romance phase. They are set in ancient Egypt, but function as allegories for modern Egyptian politics and society.

His most celebrated novels, however, are those set in modern-day Cairo and written in a social realist style. Among these works are *Midaq Alley*, published in 1947. A series known as "The Trilogy," established his reputation as the foremost Egyptian novelist, while for the first time earning him recognition in literary circles outside of Egypt.

These novels trace three generations of an Egyptian family from just after World War I to the end of World War II. They have been translated into English in the 1990s as *Palace Walk: Cairo Trilogy I, Palace of Desire: Cairo Trilogy II,* and *Sugar Street: Cairo Trilogy III.* In his depiction of the struggles of lower middle-class Egyptians, Mahfouz has been compared to Charles Dickens and Fyodor Dostoyevski.

The third phase of Mahfouz's literary output, sometimes referred to as his modern or experimental phase, began in the 1960s when Mahfouz turned away from the realist style that had won him such critical acclaim. The watershed work which ushered in this new style was *The Thief and the Dogs*, published in 1961.

In this and later novels and stories, Mahfouz turned to the use of symbolism, experimented with such narrative techniques as stream-of-consciousness writing, and used film-style dialogue to tell his stories. He also began to explore existentialist themes, which became a central concern of much of his later work.

Rasheed El-Enany described the general response to this change in literary style in his book *Naguib Mahfouz: The Pursuit of Meaning:* "Mahfouz's sudden headlong dive into surrealist and absurdist modes of expression left his critics reeling from the impact of the surprise." Expecting a realist style of narrative that reflected the modern conditions of life in Cairo, they were not prepared for "the artistic reality badly distorted to reflect the disintegration of the society is sought to comment upon."

It was in this later period that the majority of his short story collections were published. Among his later novels of note is *Arabian Nights and Days* (1982), clearly a reference to *Arabian Nights,* a traditional Egyptian story familiar to Western readers.

Although known primarily for his achievements as a novelist, Mahfouz has also mastered the form of the short story, publishing fourteen collections of stories. As El-Enany has noted, "If Mahfouz had not written any of his novels, he would still have merited a place of high prominence in the history of modern Arabic letters on account of his short stories alone. . . ."

His first collection of short stories, *The Whisper of Madness* (1947) is generally considered unremarkable. His second collection, *God's World,* did not appear until 1963. Twelve more collections of stories followed.

Included in his collection *The Time and the Place,* "Half a Day" concerns Mahfouz's recurring existential themes of life, death, and time, as the entire life of the main character seems to last only half of one day spent in school. El-Enany has called the five-page story a *"tour de force."* He goes on to state: "Brief as it is, the story must count as the author's most powerful rendering of the dilemma of the gulf between observable time and mnemonic time."

Criticism

Liz Brent

Brent has a Ph.D. in American Culture, specializing in cinema studies, from The University of Michigan. She is a freelance writer and teaches courses in American cinema. In the following essay, she discusses the use of descriptive and figurative language in "Half a Day."

Mahfouz makes skillful use of language in this concise, economic story. Describing the narrator's journey from home to the gates of the schoolyard, Mahfouz takes advantage of both descriptive and figurative language to convey the anxiety of the young boy on his first day of school.

Rich, descriptive language is used to describe the positive elements of the little boy's experience on this momentous day. His new clothes are described with a child's attention to color: "All my clothes were new: the black shoes, the green uniform, the red tarboosh."

When he first sets out with his father, his surroundings are described as if they were a lush and abundant paradise: "We walked along a street lined with gardens; on both sides were extensive fields planted with crops, prickly pears, henna trees, and a few date palms."

By contrast, the little boy's apprehension about being taken to school is conveyed through language that evokes images of punishment, confinement, military discipline, and industrial labor. The first indication of his anxiety is expressed through a description of the first day of school as "the day on which I was to be cast into school for the first time." The phrasing to "cast" something away is more often used to describe the shedding or throwing out of something undesirable. The narrator thus feels that his parents are treating him as an undesirable person whom they wish to "cast" into the school in order to rid themselves of him.

Even when his father protests that school is not a "punishment," he describes it in terms that sound equally undesirable: "It's a factory that makes useful men out of boys." This image suggests still more negative connotations; if school is a "factory," then the boy himself is being treated as no more than a mass of raw material to be "processed" into manhood through methods of industrial labor, hardly an appealing image of the process of growing up.

The narrator's description of what is being done to him accumulates still more negative connotations: "I did not believe there was really any good to be had in tearing me away from the intimacy of

What Do I Read Next?

- *The Palace Walk: Cairo Trilogy I,* (1956) by Naguib Mahfouz, is the first novel of the acclaimed trilogy, which follows three generations of an Egyptian family. The other two novels, *Palace of Desire: Cairo Trilogy II* (1956) and *Sugar Street: Cairo Trilogy III,* (1957) complete the trilogy.

- Mahfouz's *Echoes of an Autobiography* (1994) is a memoir written as a loose collection of vignettes from the author's personal experience.

- *The Early Novels of Naguib Mahfouz* (1994), by Matti Moosa, introduces the Western reader to the most noted novels of Mahfouz. The study also places his stories in social, political and religious context of modern Egypt.

- *The Arabic Novel in Egypt, 1914-1970* (1973), written by Fatma Moussa-Mahmoud, is a concise, easy-to-read history of the Arabic novel. It provides brief overviews of the careers and work of key Arab writers.

- *The History of Egypt from Muhammed Ali to Mubarek* (1985), by P. J. Vatikiotis, is a comprehensive, authoritative history of Egypt.

- Menahem Milson's *Naguib Mahfouz: The Novelist-Philosopher of Cairo* (1988) provides close readings of the works of Mahfouz based on an analysis of their linguistic and literary sources.

- *Naguib Mahfouz: From Regional Fame to Global Recognition* (1993), edited by Michael Beard and Adnan Haydar, is a collection of articles that addresses the work of Mahfouz from the perspective of both his regional importance as an Arabic writer and his international significance.

---

my home and throwing me into this building that stood at the end of the road like some huge, high-walled fortress, exceedingly stern and grim.''

He describes the process of leaving home as ''tearing'' him away from it, a word that suggests violence and rupture. Furthermore, he perceives that he is being ''thrown'' into the school building, an image which picks up on the term ''cast,'' used earlier, to describe the experience as if he were an undesirable object being violently ''thrown'' away by his parents.

The school is then described as ''some huge, high-walled fortress.'' The image of a fortress suggests a warlike atmosphere, and evokes images of a building that is heavily guarded against anyone who wishes to escape from it. This image further builds on the child's fear that he is being ''punished,'' for the fortress sounds something like a guarded prison.

When they arrive at the gate to the courtyard, the little boy perceives that it is ''vast and crammed full of boys and girls.'' The word ''cram'' implies both that they have been violently shoved together and that they occupy a physically uncomfortable space.

Once he enters the schoolyard, the child's sense of disorientation and confusion at his new surroundings are expressed through figurative language, for he first feels ''like a stranger who had lost my way.'' The first child who speaks to him only confirms the narrator's sense that school is an ominous place; ''my father's dead,'' the boy tells him.

This line has strong implications for the rest of the story. First, the fact that this child's father is literally dead functions as an external expression of the narrator's feeling that his father has abandoned him completely, as if he were dead.

Furthermore, the death of the narrator's father is foreshadowed. When, at the end of the allegorical ''half day''—meaning the end of the narrator's life—he leaves the gates of the schoolyard, his father is not there. By this point in the story, the narrator is an old man and it can be assumed that his

> Here the story's allegorical implications become more apparent, for Mahfouz suggests that the experience of life, the human condition, is that of being cast out of a paradise of early childhood into a harsh world of struggle and pain, tempered by moments of love and joy."

father is not there to help him across the street because his father has indeed been long dead.

The mention of death also functions as a foreshadowing of his death. By the end of the "day," the narrator is an old man, and very close to the end of his life. In allegorical terms, when this story is read as a description of life and the human condition, it is a reminder that death is already lurking. Everyone who is born must eventually die.

The narrator's sense of distress at been "pushed" into the schoolyard and abandoned by his father is further expressed through use of descriptive language. He mentions that "the gate was closed, letting out a pitiable screech." The "pitiable screech" of the gate sounds like a description of a child crying.

Indeed, "some of the children burst into tears." The earlier description of the school as a "fortress" is echoed in the military style by which the children are organized, as "the men began sorting us into ranks." This military imagery evokes associations of discipline, strict authority, violence and an unshakable structure of power.

The child's sense that he is at the bottom of a hierarchical structure and that he stands under the eye of an all-knowing and unforgiving authority is expressed through his description of the architecture of the school itself, as well as the physical location of the children in that architecture: "We were formed into an intricate pattern in the great

courtyard surrounded on three sides by high buildings of several floors; from each floor we were overlooked by a long balcony roofed in wood."

The key term in this description is "overlooked"; although the narrator does not indicate actual people in the balconies who overlook the children, the implication is that authority lurks in every nook and cranny of the school, whether it is seen or not. A feeling of being overlooked by unseen eyes carries ominous undertones, for the threat of discipline and punishment hangs upon the vision of absolute authority.

Finally, the children give in to their powerlessness over their situation: "We submitted to the facts, and this submission brought a sort of contentment." The use of the word "submission" confirms the previous implications that this is a place where one has no free will over the powers that be, and that the only way to achieve "a sort of contentment" is to "submit to the facts," to give in to the will of the authorities.

Once the narrator has overcome his initial anxiety, the language that evokes images of punishment, discipline, and imprisonment disappears. He describes a rich variety of experiences in the school that culminate in the line: "We ate delicious food, took a little nap, and woke up to go on with friendship and love, play and learning."

However, these positive experiences inside the school are tempered by negative ones. The "lady," who is the schoolteacher often resorts to physical punishment. So the child's initial apprehension that school is a place of punishment is in part confirmed by his actual experience.

Furthermore, the sense of being stuck in the school remains since "the time for changing one's mind was over and gone." Here, the opening imagery describing the neighborhood of the boy's family as a paradise is echoed once again: "there was no question of ever returning to the paradise of home." The use of the term "cast" to describe the boy's experience of being forced to leave his home is given greater depth, as the children have all been cast out of the paradise of their own homes.

Here the story's allegorical implications become more apparent, for Mahfouz suggests that the experience of life, the human condition, is that of being cast out of a paradise of early childhood into a harsh world of struggle and pain, tempered by moments of love and joy. ''Nothing lay ahead of us but exertion, struggle, and perseverance. Those who were able took advantage of the opportunities for success and happiness that presented themselves amid the worries.''

The implication is that, like the children who ''submit'' to their imprisonment in the school, human beings must ''submit'' to the conditions of life, and make the best of it ''amid the worries.''

Source: Liz Brent, for *Short Stories for Students*, The Gale Group, 2000.

Rena Korb

Korb has a master's degree in English literature and creative writing and has written for a wide variety of educational publishers. In the following essay, she discusses the perception of time and the changes that the passage of time brings in ''Half a Day.''

''Half a Day,'' included in his 1989 collection of short fiction *The False Dawn*, is one of Naguib Mahfouz's final works. It was written toward the end of his long and successful writing career, which spanned much of the twentieth century. In his fiction, both novels and short stories, Mahfouz chronicled the significant political, social, and cultural changes Egypt had experienced during his lifetime, such as the rebellion against the British colonizers and the loosening of restrictions on women. Mahfouz's work often concerns itself with overarching moral and spiritual themes told through the experiences of very real people. His short stories differ from his novels in their immediate impact on the reader. As Mahfouz once said, he extensively researched his novels, but his ''short stories come straight from the heart.''

In ''Half a Day''—which derives its style from the ''sudden fiction,'' or short short stories, that a younger generation of Egyptian writers began producing in the 1970s—Mahfouz encompasses a vast span of time. He is able to do so by using the literary device of a young boy attending school for the first time who emerges at the end of the school day an old man. The half day, from sunup to sunset, represents almost an entire lifetime. The narrator in the story conflates mnemonic time—time pertaining to the memory—and spatial time, blending the passage of his life into one brief period. While the story demonstrates how quickly time can pass, it also func-

> **Against this cyclical nature of life, the young lad can also be seen as symbolic of death--as the being that will usher the old man to the next stage of existence. The young lad, like the boy's father, is taking the narrator to a new place against his will."**

tions on a larger level, focusing on Egypt as a place of transition instead of on only the aging of one man. Ahmad Muhammad 'Atiyya writes in his article ''Naguib Mahfouz and the Short Story'' that ''the short story is certainly the art of the partial, the individual and the simple, through which we are led to totalities and generalities.'' In ''Half a Day'', with only a few carefully chosen words, Mahfouz evokes the changes that Egypt has undergone throughout the course of the twentieth century.

The story is told from the point of view of a young boy who takes ''delight'' in his surroundings but is fearful of being ''cast into'' his first day of school. The physical scene that the narrator describes is idyllic; his clothes are new and colorful, and he walks hand in hand with his father ''along a street lined with gardens.'' The street is surrounded by fields filled with growing crops, themselves symbolic of the regeneration and vitality of life. The prickly pears and henna trees appeal to the senses as well, and contribute to the completeness of the boy's experience growing up in this pleasant suburb of Cairo.

The boy, however, does not want to go to school. He unfavorably compares the ''intimacy'' of home, where his mother watches for him at the window, with the ''building that stood at the end of the road like some huge, high-walled fortress, exceedingly stern and grim.'' The boy's father understands the magnitude of this day, though his son does not; he knows that this is the first step made by his son toward becoming a productive citizen, as he enters the '''factory that makes useful men out of boys.''' More optimistically, the father also tells his son, '''Today you truly begin life,''' for the boy is about to begin to learn about the world.

The boy soon comes to embrace his schooling and the intellectual, social, and spiritual growth that comes with it. Indeed, the next paragraphs reveal the development of the boy into an adult. He experiences friendship and love, and learns how to play and how to think. His transition from innocent and naive child, one who enjoys ''delicious food'' and ''first songs,'' into a more knowledgeable adolescent takes place. The boy learns to be ''watchful, at the ready, and very patient.'' More importantly, he comes to understand that life ''was not all a matter of playing and fooling around.'' He also discovers that life can bring hardship and discomfort, as epitomized by the teacher's scolding and more frequent reliance on physical punishment. He is undergoing the process of maturation, learning to work and wait for what he wants, but accepting the difficulties and the setbacks that come with life.

Further evidence of the boy's ascent to adulthood is his understanding that ''there was no question of ever returning to the paradise of home.'' The grown boy now has responsibilities, which preclude the utter bliss and carefreeness of youth. The narrator does not long for the comforts of childhood, but sets himself to the challenges of adulthood, realizing that ''[N]othing lay ahead of us but exertion, struggle, and perseverance.'' The narrator knows that some of his contemporaries manage to build contented lives for themselves, for they ''took advantage of the opportunities for success and happiness,'' but whether or not he achieves happiness with his own life is not clear.

The ringing of the bell ''announcing the passing of the day and the end of work'' symbolizes the transformation of the narrator into an old man. Instead of tolling the end of the day at school, the bell signifies the end of the narrator's participation in the world of adult work. It is at this moment that the narrator re-enters the outside world—that is, the world not consumed by the duties required of productive citizens, whether it is school or employment; he experiences a great shock. He sees the change that has overtaken the landscape of Cairo. The streets are lined with automobiles and trash, and land that once was fields is now ''taken over'' with skyscrapers. The narrator also finds the street filled with ''hordes of humanity'' instead of individuals. Among those who inhabit the world of

Cairo are conjurers, tricksters, and clowns. The negative slant with which the narrator views his surroundings is apparent as he clearly evokes a chaotic street scene, filled with sirens wailing, ''disturbing noises,'' and angry people. The narrator's disgust with what he sees is further evidenced by his words when he sees a fire engine attempting to reach a blazing fire: '''Let the fire take its pleasure in what it consumes.'''

The final paragraph of the story indicates the changes that Cairo has undergone. The beginning of the story certainly takes place prior to the 1950s (and probably earlier), which was when Egypt achieved complete freedom from British domination. This time period is indicated by the reference to the red tarboosh that the boy wears, a hat that was banned by the government of the new republic. By the end of the story, many decades have passed, during which time Egypt, and particularly Cairo as its largest urban center, underwent enormous change. Egypt became industrialized and experienced all of the problems that go along with industrialization, such as overcrowding in the cities and pollution. Mahfouz saw firsthand the effects—both positive and negative—of the move toward modernization. At the age of 12, Mahfouz moved to a suburb of Cairo known as Abbasiyya, which he later described as ''lush with greenery and had few building. Houses were small, consisting only of one storey and each surrounded by a garden, while open fields stretched as far as the horizon. . . and the silence was deep.''' In ''Half a Day,'' Mahfouz expresses his nostalgia for the old quarters of Cairo, in the days before industrialization. A comparison of Mahfouz's perception of the Abbasiyya of the 1920s with his representation of the neighborhood of the narrator's youth in ''Half a Day'' shows remarkable similarities between the two; and Abbasiyya certainly compares favorably to the chaos that comes to inhabit the area.

As the location transforms, so does the narrator, but the full extent of his aging is not revealed until the last line of the story. Unable to get across the busy street, the narrator waits a long time. Finally, a boy comes up to him and offers his arm along with these words: '''Grandpa, let me take you across.''' With this gesture, the narration makes clear the unrelenting quality of life, which forces people and places to change. This narrative twist also returns the text full circle: the story begins with a young boy clutching tight his father's hand, about to be taken to a new and unknown place where he is not eager to go; the story ends with the old man about to grab hold of a young lad's arm so the boy can take him to what has become a strange place—modern Cairo.

Against this cyclical nature of life, the young lad can also be seen as symbolic of death—as the being that will usher the old man to the next stage of existence. The young lad, like the boy's father, is taking the narrator to a new place against his will. The narrator's death is foreshadowed in the two encounters he has with other male figures. One is the boy he meets at school whose father is dead. Then, upon leaving school, the narrator encounters an acquaintance, a middle-aged man who is instantly recognizable to the narrator. The man answers the question of how he is doing with the words, "'not all that good.'" In this response, the narrator's death is symbolically foretold. The aging of the man's corporeal body is also reflected in the run-down state in which he finds the streets of Cairo. While the narrator's eventual death is a foregone conclusion, these elements further reinforce the inevitable cycle of birth and death—the cycle of change.

Source: Rena Korb, for *Short Stories for Students*, The Gale Group, 2000.

Carol Dell'Amico

Carol Dell'Amico teaches English at Rutgers, the State University of New Jersey, where she is currently working on a dissertation. The essay which follows presents "Half a Day" as a story in which there are two allegories. One allegory is argued to have universal significance and the second to refer specifically to Egyptian history.

"Half a Day" is an allegory in which a child's experiences at school symbolize a typical person's experiences of coming of age and maturation. This allegory is achieved through a multiplication and overlapping of "times." That is, the boy's narration suggests more than one unit of time (some obvious units or concepts of measure are: one minute, childhood, one light year, an average human life-span, a millennium, and so forth).

The narration about the school day engages four different times. First, it is understood to cover a school day, that is, almost the whole of the titular "half a day." Second, it can be taken to encompass a youth's entire scholastic experience and, therefore, a temporal unit of roughly twelve years (the boy's description of his school day is presented in

> And, finally, this story's amazing compression of time passing can be understood to be a representation of the way in which human psychology experiences the passage of time."

grammatical tenses that convey the passing of many years' observations, many of which specifically pertain to a person's combined years at school). Third, since the narrator meets a "middle-aged" friend upon leaving the school that day, his description also encompasses the "time" of childhood to full maturity or middle-age, which is a temporal unit of roughly forty years. Fourth, insofar as most everybody on this earth comes of age and then matures, this tale encompasses universal time (i.e. the time of global humankind). It is everybody's story. Thus, the progress of a human being from youth to middle-age is conveyed through a skillful rendering of (almost) half a day, in which (at least) four different "times" are cleverly overlapped and interwoven.

Yet, there is also that part of "Half a Day" that occurs after the boy leaves the school. In this "after school" portion of the story, the middle-aged man becomes a "Grandpa" whom a young man "gallantly" offers to escort across a busy street. Coming of age and maturation correspond to the time spent at school, and this second part of the story covers aging or growing old. This latter section also purveys the following idea: that when the boy was in school (for those forty years), a seemingly rural and rather bucolic world of "gardens," "extensive fields planted with crops" and other flora, mutated into a strange, mechanized, foreign world. This new world causes the now middle-aged narrator to come "to a startled halt" outside of the gates of the school:

> Good Lord! Where was the street lined with gardens? Where had it disappeared to? When did all these vehicles invade it? And when did all these hordes of humanity come to rest upon its surface? How did these hills of refuse come to cover its sides? And

where were the fields that bordered it? High buildings had taken over, the street surged with children, and disturbing noises shook the air.

The "disturbing" nature of this new world is perhaps best symbolized in the man's alarmed focusing on the fire engine's wail, which to him is like a shriek: "The siren of a fire engine shrieked," the reader is informed; and then again: "The fire engine's siren was shrieking at full pitch as it moved at a snail's pace. . .".

This second part of "Half a Day" adds some complexity to this allegory of life and maturation. Clearly, there is at least one additional level of meaning to take into account; namely, that the maturation of this character coincides with the urbanization and industrialization of his surroundings. While this boy has been growing up, his surroundings have moved from being largely rural ("gardens" and "fields"), to being those of a typical late-twentieth-century big city ("vehicles," "refuse," "hordes of humanity," and so on).

One thing to be said about this is that it adds a possible autobiographical dimension to the story. While Egypt may have begun to accommodate the technologies of heavy industry in the nineteenth century like most other nations, significant levels of industrialization did not occur in this country until the mid to late twentieth-century. As Naguib Mahfouz came of age and matured, so Egyptian metropolitan centers industrialized. Mahfouz is from Cairo; Cairo is Egypt's most urbanized area; Mahfouz's lifespan coincides with Egypt's urbanization and industrialization.

An easy conclusion to come to, with the above in mind (but a far too hasty and incorrect conclusion), would be that the story recounts Egypt's "coming of age," or its belated "modernization" on the heels of its already more industrially technologized global neighbors. The problem with such a conclusion is that it leaves a number of narrative details unaccounted for. For instance, why does this process of urbanization occur as a separate history? In other words, why is this process of mechanization depicted as occurring entirely separate from the story of the boy's coming of age and to maturity? Why does it occur in the second part of the story, in the "after school" and "growing old" portion? There is no mistaking, after all, the effect of having the character stop short in shock, upon leaving the school's gates, at the sight of the noisy and crowded scene before him. "Half a Day," in no uncertain terms, is cleaved into two separate parts. In a story whose first part is a bravura meshing of

disparate "times" (four, no less), why not the interweaving of one more, the time or history of industrialization? Yet, this process is very carefully set apart from the phase of maturation and is instead intertwined with the time of the man growing older. Clearly, urbanization in "Half a Day" does not pertain to coming of age or maturation, but, rather, to aging or becoming older.

A reasonable interpretation of this distinction follows from deciding that while the boy-becoming-adult in the first part of the story stands in for all of humanity, the old man in the second part stands in only for Egypt. In this light, the story has two parts so as to separate Egyptian time from global, universal time. There are, therefore, two allegories to consider: one of significance to humans in general, and another which pertains to industrialization and societies in which the particular society in question is Egypt. What this leads one to realize is that the meeting of old and young at the story's end is, in an allegorical nutshell, the story's model for Egypt in terms of its long history and its metropolitan centers in their newly urbanized guise.

The man in the second part of the story is old already, and growing older. If one considers the long stretch of Egyptian history, industrialization would not signify, as it is tends to mean in the west, the latest major signpost on a road of continuous progress over time. It would present itself, rather, as the latest culture in a long history of different cultures, or the latest way of organizing life in a long series of different regimes and societies. The territory now hosting the United Arab Republic of Egypt, already had, as far back as 3500 B.C., a society and culture as complexly organized and bureaucratically networked as any today. Moreover, after the age of the pharaohs, a number of other cultures and empires flourished on the very same soil— Mesopotamian, Roman, and Greek cultures, for example. In terms of different civilizations, cultures, or ways of life, Egypt is terribly old indeed. And, so, the old man sniffs in tired disdain, feeling, merely, "[e]xtremely irritated": "Let the fire take its pleasure in what it consumes." Far from being bowled over by the advent of vehicles and other such inventions, the old man tends to notice how this machine of speed and efficiency can only proceed at a "snail's pace" in the clogged city space. The noise and smoke that accompany urbanization and industrialization could not possibly connote, the story pointedly makes clear, coming of age or absolute progress within the context of Egyptian history. It entails, rather, the inventions and ways of life of the new cultural kid on the block—old man (Egypt) meets young (heavy industry, urbanization). ''Half a Day,'' in this way, reflects Mahfouz's most recent stance toward societal changes in Egypt. Whereas he long has been known as one to embrace all varieties of change, by the time of the writing of this story, he has begun to express selective reservations about certain types of change.

By now, six possible timescapes have been entertained: a school day; a scholastic tenure; maturation; universal time; twentieth-century metropolitan Egyptian history; and, lastly, deep Egyptian time. There are at least two more ''times'' worth considering in this story, and they are especially felt upon reading the story's final sentence: ''Grandpa, let me take you across.'' With this, the reader is suddenly imbued with a sense of the terrible brevity of a human being's life-span. The protagonist has not simply aged, his life seems almost to be over! This, when but a few hundred words before this enfeebled old creature was a fresh little boy! The surprise of this final line makes the reader feel that the human life-span is an abbreviated and paltry thing. This last frame of time is that of the vast cosmos itself. And in this timescape, the life of human beings and the march of different civilizations seem petty, brief little events indeed.

And, finally, this story's amazing compression of time passing can be understood to be a representation of the way in which human psychology experiences the passage of time. Mahfouz, certainly, was greatly impressed, during his years of literary apprenticeship, by various writers and thinkers who were exploring the vagaries of memory and temporality. Why is it, they ask, that some moments seem like an age, but sitting down and trying to remember one's childhood makes one feel as if the years lasted no more than a few minutes? The regularly ticking time of clock and calendar means very little in respect to human psychology and emotion, they averr. Or, some propose, is not the passage of time more fully felt—and the past even recaptured—if one's memory of it is vast and faithful? One of the most famous books that explores memory, and which influenced Mahfouz, was written by a Frenchman named Marcel Proust. Its title, once translated from the French, tends to be either *The Past Recaptured* or else *Remembrance of Things Past*. It is a hugely long book, in three volumes, in which the main character remembers his whole life and society in great and minute detail. In this light, Mahfouz's tale of accelerated time signifies how

most people feel about time passing. That is, unless one makes a prodigious effort to re-live and remember the past, one will feel, on the whole, that ''time flies.''

Source: Carol Dell'Amico, for *Short Stories for Students,* The Gale Group, 2000.

Sources

'Atiyya, Ahmad Muhammad. ''Naguib Mahfouz and the Short Story,'' in *Critical Perspectives on Naguib Mahfouz,* edited by Trevor Le Gassick, Three Continents Press, Washington, D.C., 1991.

Charters, Ann. Introduction to ''Half a Day'' by Naguib Mahfouz, in *The Story and Its Writer: An Introduction to Short Fiction,* 4th ed., Boston: Bedford Books of St. Martin's Press, 1995, p. 848.

El-Enany, Rasheed. *Naguib Mahfouz: The Pursuit of Meaning,* London: Routledge, 1993, pp. 195, 203, 212.

Encyclopaedia Britannica Online [database online], [cited September 1999], available from Encyclopaedia Britannica, Inc., Chicago, IL, s.v. ''Arabic literature.''

Milson, Menahem. *Naguib Mahfouz: The Novelist-Philosopher of Cairo,* New York: St. Martin's Press, 1998, pp. xiii, 82.

Further Reading

El-Enany, Rasheed. *Naguib Mahfouz: The Pursuit of Meaning,* London: Routledge, 1993.
    A reassessment of the writings of Mahfouz, updating earlier criticism of the writer. Discusses the need to categorize the stylistic phases of his literary output.

Gordon, Haim. *Naguib Mahfouz's Egypt: Existential Themes in His Writings,* New York: Greenwood Press, 1990.
    Discusses the novels of Mahfouz in terms of existential issues facing modern Egyptians. Examines his work in the cultural, political, social, and religious context of modern Egypt.

Le Gassick, Trevor, ed. *Critical Perspectives on Naguib Mahfouz,* Washington, D.C.: Three Continents Press, 1991.
    A collection of essays on the work of Mahfouz. Provides an overview of the subjects and themes of his work, and determines his contribution to Arabic literature.

Mehrez, Samia. *Egyptian Writers between History and Fiction: Essays on Mahfouz, Sonallah Ibrahim, and Gamal al-Ghitani,* Cairo: American University in Cairo Press, 1994.
    Analysis of three of the most prominent Egyptian writers of the twentieth century.

Janus

Ann Beattie

1985

"Janus" first appeared in the May 27, 1985, issue of the *New Yorker* magazine. It later appeared in the 1986 collection *Where You'll Find Me,* and has often been singled out as one of Beattie's best stories.

"Janus" is the story of a successful, yet unhappy real estate agent named Andrea. She grows attached to a cream-colored bowl, often placing the bowl in the homes of her clients when she shows the home to potential buyers. By the end of the story, readers discover that the bowl was a gift from Andrea's lover.

In "Janus," Beattie explores the emptiness of contemporary life. She is often regarded as the spokesperson of her generation, reflecting the lives of middle- and upper-middle class men and women. Beattie is often linked with other minimalist writers such as Bobbie Ann Mason and Raymond Carver.

Author Biography

In 1947 Ann Beattie was born in Washington, D.C. She grew up in a middle-class suburb and graduated near the bottom of her class in 1965. She attributed her poor academic record to a lack of interest; in an interview with Gene Lyons, she stated that she believes she was clinically depressed during her high school years.

She attended American University, where she earned a degree in English in just three years. In 1970 she received a M.A. in English from the University of Connecticut. Although she began work on a Ph.D. at the University of Connecticut, she did not complete it, dropping out after a few of her stories were published.

In 1973 Beattie published her first major short story, "Victor Blue," in *Atlantic Monthly*. In 1974 the *New Yorker* published the story "A Platonic Relationship." Beattie became a regular contributor to the *New Yorker*.

"Janus" first appeared in the May 27, 1985, issue of the *New Yorker*. It was published later in the collection *Where You'll Find Me,* and has often been singled out as one of Beattie's best stories. In her popular novels and short fiction, she continues to chronicle the lives of men and women who came of age in the 1960s and 1970s.

Anne Beattie

Plot Summary

"Janus" opens with the line: "The bowl was perfect." In the second paragraph, Beattie introduces the protagonist of the story, Andrea, a successful real-estate agent and owner of the bowl described in the first paragraph. The story is told completely from Andrea's point of view with little dialogue or action.

When she shows homes to a prospective buyer, Andrea places the bowl in a prominent place. She believes that the bowl is particularly "wonderful" because "it was both noticeable and subtle." The bowl is cream colored with a glowing glaze. Scattered across its surface are small flecks of color.

Andrea reports, "There were a few bits of color in it—tiny geometric flashes—and some of these were tinged with flecks of silver. They were as mysterious as cells seen under a microscope; it was difficult not to study them, because they shimmered, flashing for a split second, and then resumed their shape. Something about the colors and their random placement suggested motion."

At times, people who see the bowl call Andrea and want to know where the owners purchased it.

She always pretends not to have noticed the bowl. Only Andrea's husband seems unimpressed with it.

Andrea becomes convinced that the bowl is responsible for her success as a real estate agent. One day she forgets the bowl, and nearly panics in her attempt to retrieve it. She becomes obsessed and even dreams about the bowl.

Over time Andrea realizes that she is relating to the bowl as if it is a person. She knows that this is not entirely sane, yet she finds she has a deeper relationship with the bowl than with her husband.

As Andrea relates that "[s]he had first seen the bowl several years earlier, at a crafts fair she had visited half in secret, with her lover." This is the first mention that Andrea had at one point had a lover. Shortly after, he asked Andrea to make a decision: her husband or him. Andrea is unable to make such a decision, however, and her lover left her.

The story ends with Andrea gazing at the bowl's surface at night. In a line that brings the reader back to the beginning of the story, Beattie closes the story, "In its way, it was perfect: the world cut in half, deep and smoothly empty. Near the rim, even in dim light, the eye moved toward one small flash of blue, a vanishing point on the horizon."

Characters

Andrea

Andrea, the protagonist of the story, is the only character with a name. She is a successful real estate agent. Although married, Andrea appears to have little passion for either her husband or her life.

Indeed, the only thing she seems to have passion for is a cream-colored bowl; she places the bowl in a prominent place in the homes of her clients when she shows the homes to prospective buyers. Andrea begins to obsess about the bowl and credits her success in business to the bowl itself.

As time goes by, she worries about the bowl getting damaged—she even begins to dream about it. Andrea spends a good deal of time contemplating the bowl and her own relationship to it. Beattie writes in the final paragraph, ''Alone in the living room at night, she often looked at the bowl sitting on the table, still and safe, unilluminated.''

Andrea's Husband

Andrea's husband remains unnamed throughout the story. He is a stockbroker who considers himself ''fortunate to be married to a woman who had such a fine aesthetic sense and yet could also function in the real world.'' Andrea describes him as quiet and reflective, a man who does not like ironies or ambiguities.

Andrea's Lover

Andrea's lover does not appear until the closing paragraphs of the story. He buys the bowl for Andrea and then tells her that she needs to choose between him and her husband. He leaves her after Andrea refuses to make the choice.

Themes

Aesthetics

Although it might not be apparent on first reading, ''Janus'' can be perceived as Beattie's philosophy of aesthetics. Aesthetics is a branch of philosophy having to do with the nature of beauty, art, and taste as well as with the creation of art.

As a minimalist, Beattie has been derided by critics who find her prose to be flat and lacking in beauty. However, her supporters maintain that the gaps she leaves in her stories allow the reader to participate in the creation of art. In ''Janus,'' Beattie's fictional bowl bears uncanny resemblance to her own theory of the short story.

For example, in her opening lines Beattie writes: ''The bowl was perfect. Perhaps it was not what you'd select if you faced a shelf of bowls, and not the sort of thing that would inevitably attract a lot of attention at a crafts fair, yet it had real presence.'' The stories that Beattie writes are much like this, well-crafted but not flashy, the kind of stories that stay with the reader long after reading.

Like the bowl, Beattie's stories are ''subtle but noticeable—a paradox of a bowl.'' As Susan Jaret McKinstry argues in ''The Speaking Silence of Ann Beattie's Voice,'' Beattie's stories ''tell two stories at once: the open story of the objective detailed present is juxtaposed with a closed story of the subjective past, a story the speaker tries hard not tell.'' It is within this paradox that readers find the point of Beattie's story.

Beattie also layers detail in her story; in fact, some critics contend that her stories are nothing but detail. While the details may seem randomly placed, each is layered so as to propel the story forward. As T. Coraghessan Boyle notes in *The New York Times Book Review*, ''her stories are propelled not so much by event as by the accumulation of the details that build a life as surely as the tumble and drift of sediment builds shale or sandstone. Pay attention to the small things, she tells us.''

Finally, Beattie's stories—like the bowl—present a smooth surface. Beattie's critics at times seem unable to penetrate the surface of the stories. However, if one examines the stories in just the right light, one finds a marked similarity to the bowl: ''Near the rim, even in dim light, the eye moved toward the one small flash of blue, a vanishing point on the horizon.'' That is, when one looks at Beattie's stories obliquely, one is likely to find a flash, or a small epiphany, located just on the edge of the story.

In ''Janus'' Beattie seems to be answering her critics, asserting that her stories should be appreciated in the same way that readers appreciate the bowl—aesthetically pure and clean.

Love and Passion

While ''Janus'' is not a classic love story, it nonetheless is a story about love and passion. The protagonist, Andrea, shares her life with a husband, a lover, a dog, and a bowl. The dog drops out of the story early on, and it seems clear that Andrea does not have a passionate relationship with her husband.

Just as the reader questions Andrea's relationship to the bowl, Andrea herself wonders, "Could it be that she had some deeper connection with the bowl—a relationship of some kind? She corrected her thinking; how could she imagine such a thing, when she was a human being and it was a bowl. It was ridiculous. Just think of how people lived together and loved each other. . .But was that always so clear, always a relationship?"

This thought reveals that although she lives with her husband, she is not sure that she has a relationship with him. Moreover, her relationship to her lover is over. What does Andrea feel for anyone or anything other than her bowl? It is a mystery.

In the end, Andrea sits alone with her bowl. Like the Roman god Janus, the two-face guardian of doors and of beginnings and endings, the bowl marks both the beginning and the ending of the story. It may also mark the beginning and ending of Andrea's ability to feel love or passion.

Style

Symbols and Imagery

The bowl in "Janus" serves as both the primary image and symbol of the story. Indeed, the story seems to be more about the bowl than about the main character; Beattie takes great care to present the bowl in a variety of settings and light. Such careful attention to the detail of the bowl suggests that Beattie places the weight of the story on this image.

It is possible to view the bowl as a symbol for Andrea: smooth, perfect, empty. It is also possible to read the bowl as a symbol for the world that people of Andrea's (and Beattie's) generation find themselves in: "the world cut in half, deep and smoothly empty." In such a world, filled with materialism rather than spiritual wealth, people find themselves alone without close or intimate relationships. Certainly, it seems apparent that the bowl becomes the receptacle for and focus of Andrea's longings.

Finally, it is possible to view the bowl as a reminder of the lover who has passed out of Andrea's life. He has become the "vanishing point on

Topics for Further Study

• Ann Beattie, Raymond Carver, and Bobbie Ann Mason are often classified as "K-Mart realists." Read several stories by each writer and a few definitions of realism. Do you think the label "K-mart realist" fits each of these writers? Why or why not?

• Ann Beattie is often called a "minimalist." Find a definition of minimalism and read it carefully. Does the description fit Beattie's work? How is minimalism expressed in art and architecture, as well as literature? Collect pictures of minimalist art and home interiors to illustrate your answers.

• Freudian literary criticism often studies the use of phallic symbols in literature. Read a brief description of Freudian criticism and a definition of phallic symbols. What are some ways that a Freudian critic might "read" the bowl in the story?

• Janus is an allusion to a mythological character. Using a classical dictionary and/or encyclopedia, find out all you can about the Roman god Janus. Why do you think Beattie chose this title? What is the connection between the story and Janus?

the horizon," the small flash on the margins of her life. Perhaps what draws Andrea to the bowl is the statement her lover left her with: "Her lover had said that she was always too slow to know what she really loved." Now that her lover is gone, all that remains is the bowl.

Narration

Beattie tells her stories from a limited third-person perspective. Readers are told only what the main character is thinking or doing; all information is provided by the narrator. Generally, Beattie tells her stories in the present tense, giving the reader the sense that the events of the story are unfolding now.

Yet "Janus" is told in the past tense and the events of the story take place over several years. This is an important stylistic decision on Beattie's part, because the story takes on a quality that her other stories do not generally have.

Andrea does not reveal everything to the reader. It is with some surprise that the reader learns that the bowl was given to her by her former lover. This seemingly important detail is withheld from the reader until nearly the last page of the story. By holding this information until the end, Beattie forces the reader to rethink the significance of the bowl for the story and for the main character.

At the end of the story, the reader is left wondering what has happened in the intervening years. It is implied that Andrea's world has continued to shrink, until the bowl itself becomes her world, ''cut in half, deep and smoothly empty.''

Historical Context

Children of the 1960s

Born in 1947, Beattie reached adulthood during the 1960s. Although her stories are not set in the 1960s, her characters are children of the decade and therefore impacted by the cultural and historical contexts of the Vietnam War era.

Many things happened during that tumultuous time: large numbers of young people protested the Vietnam War; many experimented with drugs and free love; and the Civil Rights struggle raged in the American South.

By the 1980s many people of that generation had entered the job market and started families. Certainly, the characters of Beattie's stories were generally white, educated people. As Thomas R. Edwards summarized in a October 12, 1986, book review from *The New York Times Book Review*:

> [Ms. Beattie's] people suffer emotional and moral disconnection in a world that has yet been rather generous to them in material ways. They live comfortably enough in New York, the suburbs, the country; they work at business, finance, editing, modeling, writing, the law,; they have been to college and sometimes graduate school, and now, as they approach 40, they miss what they remember as the innocence and intimacy of student community. . . .

In short, the young liberals growing up in the 1960s became middle-aged conservatives in the 1980s. For many, this shift resulted in alienation from their past.

The Minimalist Moment

In the 1970s and 1980s, an artistic movement called minimalism emerged. As Christina Murphy reports in her book *Ann Beattie* (1986): ''Minimalism originated as a concept to designate a movement in the contemporary plastic arts that emphasized the use of small spaces as integers with the thematics of painting and sculpture.'' In minimalist art and architecture, the artist focused on ''the use of space itself as a counterpoint to line. . . .'' As used to describe art, the term ''minimalism'' was a positive term.

In literature, certain writers focused on what a story did not say as much as what it did say. Like the plastic artists, writers found themselves paring away all non-essential material in a story. They focused on the details of everyday life, rather than on large moral or ethical issues.

For some reason, minimalism came to be considered a pejorative term when applied to literature. Much of the negative criticism of minimalism resulted from a philosophical conflict over the role of literature. What should a story do and be? For supporters of the ''mimetic tradition''—that is, those critics who believed that fiction should reflect reality—minimalist stories were nothing more than surface details.

Critical Overview

Reviews of Beattie's work are often mixed; it seems as if critics either love or hate her work. Although her 1989 novel, *Picturing Will,* was both a popular and critical success, her short story collection *Where You'll Find Me*—the collection which includes ''Janus''—met with mixed reviews.

For example, Thomas Edwards, in an otherwise fairly negative review appearing in *The New York Times Book Review,* singled out ''Janus'' as being ''sufficiently open and worked out to give convenient access to the materials from which they are all made.'' He found the rest of the stories ''terse'' and less ''ample in scale and mood'' than her earlier stories.

On the other hand, Michiko Kakutani deemed the story ''a highly crafted, almost surreal meditation on the intrusion of time past into time present and on the perils of everyday life.''

Compare & Contrast

- **1980s:** In 1981 the divorce rate peaks at 5.3 divorces for every 1000 people, before falling off slightly in the next few years.

  Today: While the divorce rate drops slightly, it is still generally believed that one out of every two marriages ends in divorce. Cohabitation is a growing trend. The marriage rate continues to drop throughout the 1990s.

- **1980s:** Home mortgages reach double digits, slowing the housing market and making it very difficult for first time home owners to buy a house.

  Today: Home mortgages decline to post-World War II record low rates. Financing a house is relatively easy.

- **1980s:** Unemployment peaks at 10.8 percent in 1982, the highest since the Great Depression of the 1930s. Inflation remains high, but businesses are making a slow recovery.

  Today: The last half of the decade sees low unemployment rates, low inflation, and a booming economy. In some sectors, notably technology, worker shortages cause problems.

- **1980s:** Members of the "baby boom" generation reach adulthood and flood the job market. Seeking financial security, many families become two-wage families with both the mother and father employed.

  Today: Older members of the "baby boom" generation near retirement; as a result, worries about pensions and the social security system escalate.

A good deal of the controversy surrounding Beattie's work deals with her reputation as a minimalist writer. According to Christina Murphy in her book *Ann Beattie*, "[T]here is a persistent focus upon cutting away from fiction all that need not be there to 'tell' the story." Many critics find the bare, lean prose of minimalist writers to be flat and uninteresting. Further, those critics who take issue with minimalism argue that by reducing the exposition, minimalist writers produce limited stories without moral import.

In a famous article appearing in the *New Criterion*, Joshua Gilder attacks minimalist writers such as Beattie, Raymond Carver, Tobias Wolff, and Alice Munro, stating that writers like these "seem intent on proving the proposition that less is, indeed, less."

However, other commentators contend that these writers are the best of their generation. Minimalism requires active involvement on the part of the reader; they must read what is not said as well as what is. Readers such as Margaret Atwood, herself a noted novelist, short story writer, poet, and critic, admire Beattie's stories and novels precisely for their terse and understated style.

Although Beattie's stories have generated much critical controversy among reviewers, there are few recent scholarly studies of her work. Indeed, although "Janus" continues to be anthologized as one of Beattie's best stories, few scholars have examined the story closely.

In *The Explicator,* Philip Miller links the bowl to the Roman god Janus. According to Roman mythology, Janus is responsible for guarding both entrances and exits. The story, Miller asserts, is about beginnings and endings, and thus the title is particularly apt.

Other critics, such as Carolyn Porter in *Contemporary American Women Writers: Narrative Strategies* (1985) and Susan Jaret McKinstry in *Studies in Short Fiction* focus on the gaps Beattie inserts into her stories. These two studies, while not about "Janus" directly, help readers better understand Beattie's narrative approach.

Cover illustration of "If I Shoul Die before I Wake," showing Janus mask with girl's face facing outward in both directions.

Criticism

Diane Andrews Henningfeld

Henningfeld is an associate professor at Adrian College who writes extensively for educational publishers. In the following essay, she discusses the use of the bowl as a symbol of the main character's sexuality in "Janus."

Ann Beattie's short story, "Janus," first appeared in 1985 in the *New Yorker*. Included in her 1986 short fiction collection, *Where You'll Find Me*, the story is widely anthologized and frequently cited as one of Beattie's best works.

At first glance, the story seems much like Beattie's other stories. It is limited in character, plot, and scope, focusing on the small details of life. The prose is lean and spare, and there are empty spaces, or gaps, in what Beattie tells the reader. Such gaps require active participation on the part of the reader, who must "read" what is missing in the story.

Yet there are some very important ways that this story is different from her other stories. In the first place, "Janus" is told in past tense, rather than present. The past tense creates a sense of recollection and meditation in the story, as the narrator recalls the history of the bowl.

There are many reference to the passing of time in the story. Unlike other Beattie stories, told in the present tense and happening in the moment, "Janus" unfolds over a period of years; this is an unusual framework, given the brevity of the story.

Another difference is the emphasis placed on one object: the bowl. Images are generally important in Beattie's short stories; one riveting image can replace in just a few words what might take pages of exposition to accomplish. Nevertheless, Beattie rarely indulges in the kind of symbolic significance the bowl in this story seems to take on. As Jonathan Penner in *Book World—The Washington Post* points out, "The beloved bowl becomes a psychoanalytical symbol, odd as an archaeopteryx in Beattie's post-Freudian world."

Penner's observation paves the way for a reading that requires some understanding of the theories of Sigmund Freud, widely regarded as the father of modern psychotherapy. Although his theories have been questioned and even discredited as the basis for psychiatric treatment, they still provide an interesting and informative way to examine literature.

Literary scholars who use Freud's ideas are often called psychoanalytic critics; they are interested in examining the imagery and symbolism in a story to find ways of explaining the actions of the characters. These critics approach a story the same way a psychiatrist might approach a dream—by analyzing images for symbolic content, both the critic and the psychiatrist learn something about the character or the patient.

In many cases, the images present in stories or dreams can be called "phallic." Phallic symbols are everyday objects in a story that stand for male or female sexual organs and often represent the repressed sexual desires or fears of the characters. Analyzing the significance of phallic symbols can reveal important insights into both the characters and the meaning of the story.

Generally, objects such as towers or rockets, or any item that is taller than it is wide, often serve as male phallic symbols. Lakes, swimming pools, tunnels, and other rounded structures with openings are often used as female phallic symbols.

What Do I Read Next?

- *Park City: New and Selected Stories* (1998) is a collection of some of Beattie's best stories. The collection allows the reader to compare and contrast earlier stories with later ones.

- *Where I'm Calling From: New and Selected Stories,* (1988) is the last collection published by the late Raymond Carver.

- Bobbie Ann Mason's collection of short stories, *Shiloh and Other Stories* (1982), features tales that reflect on the materialistic and empty nature of contemporary society. Mason, like Beattie, has been labeled a ''K-mart realist'' by a number of critics.

- *The American Short Story: Short Stories from the Rea Award* (1993), edited by Michael Rea, provides students with a broad range of short stories and minimalist prose. Rea has selected stories by Anne Beattie, Charles Baxter, Raymond Carver, and Grace Paley, among others.

- *New Women and New Fiction: Short Stories Since the Sixties* is a collection of stories by contemporary women writers such as Cynthia Ozick, Toni Cade Bambara, Anne Tyler, Fay Weldon and Anne Beattie.

Another Freudian concept is that of the ''fetish.'' In anthropological terms, ''fetish'' refers to an object that the bearer regards with reverence and trust. The bearer believes that the object has magical powers that both protect its owner and lead the owner to success.

In psychology, the word fetish means, according to *The American Heritage Dictionary*: ''an object or body part whose real or fantasized presence is psychologically necessary for sexual gratification and that is an object of fixation to the extent that it may interfere with complete sexual expression.''

Using this background information, the reader can view ''Janus'' as a psychoanalytical exploration into the sexuality of the main character. The dominant image in ''Janus'' is the bowl, and Andrea's attachment to the bowl suggests that it has more than passing importance for the story.

As the story moves forward, the bowl fulfills the function of a fetish for Andrea, at least in the anthropological sense. She credits it with almost magical power and believes that it is responsible for her financial success. When one considers the bowl as a psychological fetish, however, the story grows in depth and complexity.

It is possible to read the bowl as a symbol for the female womb. In literature, the womb is often seen as a mysterious, hidden entity, and is the primary difference between men and women. When a woman is not pregnant, the womb remains small and flat, hidden in the woman's body. However, when a woman is pregnant, her womb swells to house the growing fetus and gives the woman's midsection a bowl-shaped appearance.

Thus, when Beattie describes the bowl as ''both subtle and noticeable—a paradox of a bowl,'' it can be interpreted that she is commenting on the dual nature of the womb: small and hidden in its non-pregnant state, and rounded and noticeable in its pregnant state. In addition, Beattie tells the reader that although people are drawn to the bowl, ''they always faltered when they tried to say something.''

Over the course of the story, the bowl takes on increasing significance to Andrea. She ''asked her husband to please not drop his house key in it. It was meant to be empty.'' Such a statement at least suggests Andrea's desire to remain without child. Indeed, for a woman to be successful in a career often requires a choice between having children and remaining childless. Andrea's connection of the

---

> By choosing to keep her womb empty and unilluminated, Andrea chooses a path without progeny. The tragedy of the story, however, is not only the loss of potential life, but also Andrea's failure to recognize the choice."

bowl with her own success as a real-estate agent may reflect this.

Furthermore, Beattie is explicit about the husband's response to the bowl. "When her husband first noticed the bowl, he had peered into it and smiled briefly. . . . In recent years, both of them had acquired many things to make up for all the lean years when they were graduate students, but now that they had been comfortable for quite a while, the pleasure of new possessions dwindled."

The husband also "turned away" from the bowl. Such disinterest suggests that the husband is content to ignore the bowl; like his wife, he seems to have no need for children.

Andrea's lover—the man who purchased the bowl for her—asks her to change her life, perhaps implying a fertile and productive relationship. "Why be two-faced, he asked her." Again, the comment calls attention to the dual nature of the womb.

If Andrea looks toward her husband with one face, she is looking toward a financially secure, yet essentially sterile relationship. By looking at her lover, however, Andrea opens the possibility of a different kind of life, one that includes a potentially fertile relationship.

Phillip Miller explains the significance of the title of the story by exploring the connection between the Roman deity Janus and the bowl. According to Miller, Janus is a "two-faced household god," who is also the god of beginnings and endings. Furthermore, Janus "guarded Roman entrances and exits."

Miller's point is pertinent; certainly Beattie's choice of title is deliberate. It is also possible, however, to connect the entrances and exits brought into play by the title with a woman's womb. The womb is both a place of entrance for the male sperm, and a port of exit for the about-to-be-born baby.

Andrea refuses her lover's offer but keeps the bowl, choosing a life for herself that is much like the description of the bowl in the last paragraph of the story:

Alone in the living room at night, she often looked at the bowl sitting on the table, still and safe, unilluminated. In its way, it was perfect: the world cut in half, deep and smoothly empty. Near the rim, even in the dim light, the eye moved toward one small flash of blue, a vanishing point on the horizon.

Significantly, Andrea is "alone." The bowl is "unilluminated"—that is, without light, or life. Like her womb, the bowl remains "deep and smoothly empty." Yet the bowl only represents half a world, like a womb fulfilling only one part of its dual nature. The "vanishing point on the horizon," for Andrea, is the loss of a potential new life, both for herself with her lover, and for the child she does not bear.

By choosing to keep her womb empty and unilluminated, Andrea chooses a path without progeny. The tragedy of the story, however, is not only the loss of potential life, but also Andrea's failure to recognize the choice. As Thomas R. Edwards asserts in *The New York Times Book Review* : "Andrea is not allowed fully to recognize how aptly the bowl reflects her own condition."

Without noticing, Andrea has displaced her own sexuality onto the bowl. By so doing, she can keep it perfect and undamaged. Furthermore, the displacement allows her to relate to both her husband and her lover from a distance, unencumbered by emotional or physical attachment. Thus, the bowl—a symbol for her own displaced sexuality—operates in the story as a fetish, an object she regards with increasing fascination and obsession.

As the story ends, Andrea is alone with her bowl—living in half a world, a world without emotional or physical intimacy. Beattie seems to making a comment here on the ability (or lack of ability) of people of her generation to form lasting human connections. Rather they seem better able to form relationships with things and objects, choosing a sterile path.

Source: Diane Andrews Henningfeld, for *Short Stories for Students*, The Gale Group, 2000.

Liz Brent

Brent has a Ph.D. in American Culture with a specialization in cinema studies from The University of Michigan. She is a freelance writer and teaches courses in American cinema. In the following essay, she discusses the significance of the bowl as fetish object in "Janus."

In Anne Beattie's short story, "Janus," the bowl functions as a *fetish* object for Andrea, the story's main character. The term "fetish" refers to small stone carvings of animals that are found in some cultures and are thought to have spiritual powers. *Merriam Webster Online* defines "fetish" as "an object believed to have magical power to protect or aid its owner."

More generally, *Webster* defines fetish as "a material object regarded with superstitious or extravagant trust or reverence." A fetish can also be defined as "an object of irrational reverence or obsessive devotion." (The term *fetish* also has *sexual* connotations in Freudian psychoanalytic theory, which will not be discussed here.)

Andrea's treatment of the bowl as a *fetish* is indicative of the emotional and spiritual emptiness of her life. While Andrea endows the bowl with spiritual and emotional significance and regards it with fetishistic reverence and devotion, it is, in fact, an empty vessel. The bowl's emptiness is suggestive of the overwhelming meaninglessness of Andrea's life.

While it is just an ordinary bowl that Andrea found at a flea market, it eventually takes on the role of a *fetish* as she regards it with "a superstitious or extravagant trust or reverence." Andrea's "extravagant" reverence for the bowl as an object of devotion is indicated by the first line of the story: "The bowl was perfect." Its spiritual or mystical properties for Andrea are suggested in part by her sense that it emits its own light, or glow: "Its glaze was the color of cream and seemed to glow no matter what light it was placed in."

The bowl for Andrea takes on an otherworldly quality: "The bowl was a mystery, even to her." Its mystery is connected to a sense of wonder in relation to the forces of life: "There were a few bits of color in it—tiny geometric flashes—and some of these were tinged with flecks of silver. They were as mysterious as cells seen under a microscope."

> "Andrea's fetishistic attachment to the bowl reflects the total lack of meaning in her life. Her relationships to other people become equated with her relationship to a consumer object—spiritually and emotionally empty, and devoid of all meaning."

The mystical or spiritual significance of the bowl for Andrea is further suggested by the fact that it enters into her half-waking dreams, almost as a vision or sign from a spiritual source: "In time, she dreamed of the bowl. Twice, in a waking dream— early in the morning, between sleep and a last nap before rising—she had a clear vision of it. It came into sharp focus and startled her for a moment—the same bowl she looked at every day."

As with a *fetish*, Andrea believes the bowl to have "magical power to protect and aid its owner." Andrea views the bowl as a powerful good luck charm: "She was sure that the bowl brought her luck." The bowl seems to her to be a benevolent godlike force, responsible for all of her good fortune.

As many people feel a gratitude toward God for their blessings in life, Andrea feels a gratitude toward the bowl: "She had the foolish thought that if only the bowl were an animate object she could thank it." Yet she has no method of prayer by which to show her gratitude: "It was frustrating because her involvement with the bowl contained a steady sense of unrequited good fortune."

As many people feel an obligation to God, Andrea wishes for a means by which to carry out some kind of duty in service to the bowl: "it would have been easier to respond if some sort of demand were made in return." Andrea even equates the bowl with some kind of fairy godmother, or another supernatural force, which could assign her some task in return for her good fortune: "But that only happened in fairy tales."

Out of her reverence for and devotion to the bowl, Andrea develops a fear that something bad might happen to it. Andrea therefore treats the bowl like a *fetish*, an object that possesses strong spiritual powers, but that could cause bad luck or disaster if not treated with the proper reverence. "It was clear that she would not be the one who would do anything to the bowl. The bowl was only handled by her, set safely on one surface or another; it was not very likely that anyone would break it."

Her fears of what forces could potentially destroy the bowl suggest an irrational fear of godlike retribution, in the form of lightning: "A bowl was a poor conductor of electricity: it would not be hit by lightning." Since lightning is, in Greek mythology, the means by which the god Zeus expresses his wrath, Andrea's fear that lightning may strike the bowl suggests a sense of guilt or anxiety that she may be punished by some godlike force.

Thus, Andrea regards the bowl as the source of all meaning in her life, without that her life would be unimaginable: "Yet the idea of damage persisted. She did not think beyond that—to what her life would be without the bowl. She only continued to fear that some accident would happen."

Andrea's "obsessive devotion" to it takes on an air of secrecy and deception. Originally purchased by her lover during a secret rendezvous, the bowl comes to represent not only Andrea's secret love affair, but an entire inner life—spiritual as well as emotional—which she does not share with him: "There was something within her, something real, that she never talked about."

While she occasionally feels the urge to share this part of herself with her husband, she does not do so. "There were times when she wanted to talk to her husband about the bowl. But she never talked to him about the bowl." Yet she continues to harbor a desire to share with her husband the reverence in which she holds the bowl: "she was often tempted to come right out and say that she thought that the bowl in the living room, the cream-colored bowl, was responsible for her success. But she didn't say it. She couldn't begin to explain it."

In her secrecy, Andrea harbors feelings of guilt: "Sometimes in the morning, she would look at him and feel guilty that she had such a constant secret."

While the bowl takes on many properties associated with a religious *fetish*, it also represents a pure form of "love" for Andrea—in terms of

human relationships as well as spiritual yearnings: "The bowl was just a bowl. But she did not believe that for a second. What she believed was that it was something she loved."

When she accidentally leaves the bowl behind at someone's house, she compares it to losing a friend, or even a child. "All the way home, Andrea wondered how she could have left the bowl behind. It was like leaving a friend at an outing—just walking off. Sometimes there were stories in the paper about families forgetting a child somewhere and driving to the next city. Andrea had only gone a mile down the road before she remembered."

Andrea even entertains the idea that her relationship with and love for the bowl has taken on the quality of a relationship to another human being: "Could it be that she had some deeper connection with the bowl—a relationship of some kind? She corrected her thinking: how could she imagine such a thing, when she was a human being and it was a bowl? It was ridiculous."

Andrea begins to wonder if her relationship to her husband may be no more meaningful than a relationship to an inanimate object: "Just think of how people lived together and loved each other. But was that always so clear, always a relationship? She was confused by these thoughts, but they remained in her mind."

Indeed, her fear of losing the bowl becomes equated with the fear of losing a lover: "She wondered how the situation would end. As with a lover, there was no exact scenario of how matters would come to a close. Anxiety became the operative force. It would be irrelevant if the lover rushed into someone else's arms, or wrote her a note and departed to another city."

Andrea's love for the bowl takes on the status of the *only* source of love in her life, and she comes to fear that she could not live without it: "The horror was the possibility of the disappearance. That was what mattered."

It is significant that the bowl is a *consumer* object. Andrea and her husband are financially successful. In fact, their relationship seems to be based largely on their mutual appreciation for indulging themselves in the purchase of consumer luxuries: "When her husband first noticed the bowl, he had peered into it and smiled briefly. He always urged her to buy things she liked. In recent years, both of them had acquired many things to make up for all the lean years when they were graduate students.''

Her husband's appreciation for her seems to be largely based on her ability to both earn money and spend money: ''He was a stockbroker, and sometimes told people that he was fortunate to be married to a woman who had such fine aesthetic sense and yet could also function in the real world.'' And Andrea herself understands the relationship in such terms: ''They were a lot alike, really—they had agreed on that.''

However, this relationship lacks any lasting meaning or remnant of human love: ''But now that they had been comfortable for quite a while, the pleasure of new possessions dwindled.''

Andrea's fetishistic attachment to the bowl reflects the total lack of meaning in her life. Her relationships to other people become equated with her relationship to a consumer object—spiritually and emotionally empty, and devoid of all meaning. She sees the bowl as ''the world cut in half,'' but what she finds inside the world, as inside herself, is a complete absence of meaning, ''deep and smoothly empty.''

While she lives in fear of losing the bowl, Andrea neglects her attachments to other human beings, such as her lover and her husband. The final image is of utter loneliness, emptiness and meaninglessness; a woman with nothing in the world but an empty bowl purchased at a flea market by a lover long gone: ''Time passed. Alone in the living room at night, she often looked at the bowl sitting on the table, still and safe, unilluminated.'' What she sees in the bowl is a ''flash'' of blue light, ''a vanishing point on the horizon.''

Ultimately, all the bowl has to offer her is an illusive vision that vanishes into nothingness. Like most of Beattie's stories, ''Janus'' offers no hope for redemption. We are left in a world of material luxury, where love and the spirit are devoid of all meaning, and human beings surround themselves with consumer objects.

Source: Liz Brent, Overview of ''Janus'' for *Short Stories for Students*, The Gale Group, 2000.

Sarah Madsen Hardy

Madsen Hardy has a doctorate in English literature and is a freelance writer and editor. In the following essay, she analyzes how Beattie's writing technique reflects the themes of emptiness and deception in ''Janus.''

Ann Beattie's ''Janus'' tells the story of one woman's powerful feelings for a ceramic bowl, exploring what the protagonist describes in the most personal terms as her ''relationship'' with the object. ''The bowl was just a bowl. She did not believe that for one second. What she believed was that it was something she loved,'' Beattie writes of Andrea, the discontented real-estate agent who is the story's central character. Andrea sees the bowl as a lucky charm, a secret passion, and a bulwark against the emptiness and loss in her life. She invests the bowl with imagined powers and reaches a point where she can't imagine life without it.

Readers are unlikely to have a hard time identifying the bowl as the story's most important literary symbol. Clearly the bowl is more than just a bowl. By focusing the story exclusively on an inanimate object, Beattie makes this fairly obvious. However, because Beattie reveals so little *other* than Andrea's strange and furtive feelings for the bowl, interpreting the symbolism becomes somewhat bewildering.

It is important to note that when approaching *any* piece of literature, readers must participate in making connections between characters, actions, symbols, and ideas. Yet in the case of a minimalist story like ''Janus,'' active participation is paramount, since gaps in the story are in some ways just as relevant as the words on the page. It is up to readers to do the work that Andrea is unwilling or unable to do in interpreting the connections between the significance of the bowl and the most important and troubling aspects of Andrea's life. Though Janus, for whom the story is named, is the Roman god of beginnings and endings, nothing notable begins or ends within the action of the story.

As the story closes, Beattie notes that time has passed. Andrea is still married, still using the bowl to sell real estate, and still—like the bowl— ''unilluminated.'' That is, she feels the power of the bowl's hold on her but she does not understand what it symbolizes or why, which is part of the reason that she is unable to take action to change her unsatisfying life. ''The bowl was a mystery, even to her.''

The superficial simplicity and smoothness of Beattie's prose is deceptive, belying its difficulty. Her narration is rich in detail, but information about the situation is doled out extremely selectively, and the interpretive guidance offered by the narrator is

> **By having a covert intimate relationship with the bowl that is a token of the lover's affection as well as a symbol of his absence, Andrea can maintain her passivity and continue, Janus-like, to 'have it both ways.'"**

sparse. This quality has won Beattie as many detractors as fans.

In her article "The Art of Missing," Carolyn Porter comments on Beattie's unpopularity among scholars, pointing out that many have suggested that something is *missing* in Beattie's stories. Some focus on her subject matter—the homogeneity of her white, upper-middle-class characters. These characters' problems exist only within a narrow range of experience.

Others find fault with her style—the pared-down quality that leaves it up to the reader to make all of the missing connections and figure out all of the "whys" behind the characters and their actions. Porter argues that in Beattie's most successful stories, her technique is appropriate to her subject, reflecting "the peculiar quality of [Beattie's] fictive yet familiar world—the sense that something has been lost, although no one can quite remember what."

Porter does not deny that there *is* something missing in Beattie's narration, but argues that the gaps and omissions that riddle her fiction express something true and painful about the rootless, valueless, and materialistic aspects of contemporary society. "Beattie's techniques," Porter writes, "even while producing results that often seem highly artificial, are informed by a clean aim at the real, the here and now." In other words, the form of Beattie's stories suits their content. Absence, emptiness, and loss, as well as deception and withheld information, shape Andrea's life as well as the form of the story.

Although there are hints that the bowl is somehow intimately involved in aspects of Andrea's relationships, the only concrete thing that readers learn is of Andrea's use of it as a prop for her real-estate business. It is in this capacity that we learn most about the bowl's powers.

Andrea secretly places the ordinary-yet-extraordinary looking bowl in property up for sale in order to inspire a positive feeling about the house, a "trick used to convince the buyer that the house is quite special." Though Andrea has used many different tricks in the past, the bowl is especially effective, and she attributes her success to it. The houses up for sale, trading hands as commodities through the anonymous intervention of a realtor, have been stripped of their status as centers of individual and family identity.

Andrea compares the bowl to a friend, a child, a husband, and a lover. When she places the bowl in a house, it subtly evokes a longed-for human touch, standing in for what has been lost to the house-hunters, who are, like Andrea, part of a class and generation that moves frequently. Andrea believes that the bowl helps her sell houses by making a house that is up for sale—emptied of its human life, if not its physical contents—feel like a home.

Andrea moves the bowl to various properties she is selling and then brings it back home—a place as lacking as a source of intimacy and identity as the houses Andrea sells. And the bowl serves a similar purpose in Andrea's private life as it does in her real-estate business. Just as a realtor might bring any number of homey "props" to cover up the coldness of the sales transaction, Andrea and her husband fill their home of any number of beautiful and valuable possessions to cover up the underlying dissatisfaction of their life together.

There is emptiness and secrecy in Andrea's marriage, which the bowl comes to both represent and compensate for. Her husband has encouraged Andrea to buy "things she liked" to "make up for all the lean years when they were graduate students," and appreciates her good taste. Yet he does not understand the allure of the bowl or Andrea's attachment to it. He deems it pretty, but expresses no further interest in it.

To Andrea, the bowl is more than a source of aesthetic or consumerist pleasure. She has come to see the bowl as different from all of her other possessions, reflecting a part of her private self that her husband does not recognize, "something within her now, something real, that she never talked about." How inauthentic the rest of Andrea's life must be, if a ceramic bowl is the closest thing to what is real in her innermost self.

As Andrea becomes more obsessed with the bowl—more grateful to it for her success and more anxious about some harm befalling it—she begins to see the her relationship to the bowl as something to feel guilty about, a "constant secret." Very near the end of the story—almost as an afterthought—the narrator reveals that the bowl was a gift from an ex-lover. This seems to explain a lot of the "whys" behind Andrea's fixation. The lover is now absent, and the bowl remains as a token of what is lost and a symbol of what is longed for. The bowl is a presence in Andrea's marriage, representing her secret and reminding her of what is missing.

Before leaving her, the lover accuses Andrea of being "two-faced"—Beattie's only direct reference the story's title. Janus, the Roman god of doorways, boundaries, and beginnings, faces both east and west and is represented by an icon of two faces.

"Two-faced" also implies deceptiveness—not being what one appears to be. The lover was referring to Andrea's inability to reveal their relationship and leave her husband for him, accusing her of being "too slow to know what she really loved." By having a covert intimate relationship with the bowl that is a token of the lover's affection as well as a symbol of his absence, Andrea can maintain her passivity and continue, Janus-like, to "have it both ways."

Ultimately, then, Andrea may feel such a deep connection to the bowl less because it represents the lost lover than because it reflects her own empty, passive condition. It is Andrea's own mental trick in an insecure, frightening "world full of tricks." Like Andrea, the bowl has it "both ways" and is "two-faced."

The language that Beattie uses to describe the physical qualities of the bowl reflects the bowl's simultaneous association with fulfillment and its absence. It is "a paradox of a bowl," representing the opposite qualities of emptiness and completion at once. "In its way, it was perfect, the world cut in half, deep and smoothly empty." Beattie goes on to compare it to the horizon, which, in keeping with the bowl's perfection, suggests that the bowl is complete unto itself, a whole world.

Yet it is "a world cut in half," evoking lack and loss. The outside of a bowl is smooth and round, circular, suggesting the first set of qualities—completeness, fullness, perfection—while the inside is an empty space for something that is not there. This is, after all, the purpose of a bowl, and Andrea insists that "it was meant to be empty." The same might be said of Beattie's narrative technique.

Source: Sarah Madsen Hardy, for *Short Stories for Students*, The Gale Group, 2000.

Sources

Aldridge, John A. *Talents and Technicians: Literary Chic and the New Assembly Line Fiction*, New York: Charles Scribner's Sons, 1992, pp.56-70.

Boyle, T. Coraghessan. Review of "Pictureing Will," in *The New York Times Book Review*, January 7, 1990, pp. 1, 33.

Edwards, Thomas R. *The New York Times Book Review*, October 12, 1986.

Gilder, Joshua. "Less is Less," in *New Criterion*, Vol. 1, February, 1983, pp. 78-82.

Kakutani, Michiko. Review, in *The New York Times*, October 12, 1986.

McKinstry, Susan Jaret. "The Speaking Silence of Ann Beattie's Voice," in *Studies in Short Fiction*, Vol. 24, No. 2, Spring, 1987, pp. 111-17.

Miller, Philip. "Beattie's 'Janus,'" in *The Explicator*, Vol. 46, No. 1, Fall, 1987, pp. 48-9.

Montresor, Jaye Berman, ed. *The Critical Response to Ann Beattie*, Westport, CT: Greenwood Press, 1993.

Murphy, Christina. *Ann Beattie*, New York: Twayne, 1986.

"The Hum inside the Skull—A Symposium," in *New York Times Book Review*, May 13, 1984, p. 1.

Penner, Jonathan. "Ann Beattie: The Surface of Things," in *Book World—The Washington Post*, October 19, 1986, p. 7.

Porter, Carolyn. "Ann Beattie: The Art of the Missing," in *Contemporary American Women Writers: Narrative Strategies*, edited by Catherine Rainwater and William J. Scheick, Louisville: University of Kentucky Press, 1985, pp. 9-25.

Virginia Quarterly Review, Vol. 63, Spring, 1987, p. 59.

Further Reading

Aldridge, John A. *Talents and Technicians: Literary Chic and the New Assembly Line Fiction*, New York: Charles Scribner's Sons, 1992, pp.56-70.

A highly critical view of minimalist fiction.

Montresor, Jaye Berman, ed. *The Critical Response to Ann Beattie*, Westport, CT: Greenwood Press, 1993.

A collection of critical essays on Beattie's work.

Murphy, Christina. *Ann Beattie*, New York: Twayne, 1986.

A book-length study of Beattie's work. Although it does not contain a discussion of the stories from *Where You'll Find Me*, the book nonetheless provides an excellent introduction to Beattie and provides literary and cultural contexts for her work.

Rainwater, Catherine, and William J. Scheick, eds. *Contemporary American Women Writers*, Lexington: University of Kentucky Press, 1985.

A collection of essays, photographs, and bibliographies on important contemporary women writers including Annie Dillart, Cynthia Ozick, Anne Tyler, and Toni Morrison. Also includes Carolyn Porter's essay on Ann Beattie, ''The Art of the Missing.''

The Jolly Corner

Henry James

1908

First published in the inaugural issue of *The English Review* in 1908, ''The Jolly Corner'' also appeared the following year in the definitive New York edition of James's work. The main character of the story, Spencer Brydon, is a middle-aged man who returns to his birthplace of New York City. He has lived abroad for thirty-three years, and while visiting his childhood home—situated on ''a jolly corner''— he questions if leaving the States was the best decision. He walks around the vacant house late at night, wondering about what could have been. The story reaches a climax when he believes that he is being haunted by his alter ego.

Some critics praise James's creation of a ghost story worthy of Edgar Allan Poe with ''The Jolly Corner.'' The protagonist's decision to move from his homeland echoes the lives of famous, romanticized writers who died far from home—Percy B. Shelley, Lord Byron and Margaret Fuller—and foreshadows the themes and experiences of other great expatriate writers—Gertrude Stein, James Joyce and James Baldwin.

Author Biography

Henry James was born in New York City in 1843, where he lived until his family moved to Boston during his childhood. His father, Henry James, Sr., was a renowned theologian; his brother, William

James, would become a famous philosopher and professor at Harvard.

James left the United States in 1875 to live in England. In fact, he spent most of his adult life there. His novels and short stories often focus on Americans traveling in Europe and the inevitable culture clash between the Old World and the New World.

James was very prolific, writing several novels, short stories, plays, travel reflections, and literary criticism. Much of his fiction was serialized in popular literary magazines like *The Atlantic Monthly*, *Harper's*, and *The New Review*.

After living abroad for many years, he returned to America for a visit in 1905 and recorded his impressions in the travelogue *The American Scene*. In America, he found that many of his friends and members of his family had passed away; moreover, he found the people and landscape very different than he remembered. The economic prosperity of a new industrial age had resulted in the elimination of older buildings in favor of towering skyscrapers. The social landscape had changed nearly as dramatically. "The Jolly Corner" was written shortly after James returned to England and reflects some of his impressions of the United States.

Before he died, James became an English citizen. In 1916 he received the prestigious Order of Merit from King George V for his literary accomplishments. He died in 1916.

Plot Summary

At age fifty-six, Spencer Brydon returns to New York City after spending thirty-three years of his life in Europe. When he left New York, he left behind his family and a promising business career to pursue his appreciation of art. While he is quick to remind himself that he returned merely for the practical task of looking into two pieces of property that he has inherited after the death of his brothers, he is also curious to see how his hometown has changed over the years.

He is shocked by what he finds: the monstrous skyscrapers; the crush of the crowds; the exciting bustle of the social scene; and the thriving economy. Overwhelmed by the change, Spencer feels alienated from the people around him.

While in New York, Spencer renews an acquaintance with an old friend, Alice Staverton. Spencer's family—his parents, two brothers and "favourite sister"—are dead and Alice is the only remaining person he was close to in his youth. Throughout the story, Alice accompanies Spencer as he visits his property, listening to him reminisce. Of all the people he meets in New York, only Alice has the patience and deep sense of the past necessary to understand his complex reactions and emotions.

He is especially drawn to the house on "the jolly corner"—Fifth Avenue near Washington Square—the place where he grew up. Spencer divides his days between his hotel, his eating club, and his two properties. He decides to renovate one of the properties, increasing the already lucrative rents that have supported his life in Europe. Yet although his childhood home—the house on "the jolly corner"—would be an extremely lucrative apartment, Spencer refuses to surrender it to the marketplace. Instead he employs a woman, Mrs. Muldoon, to keep the vacant house clean.

One day, Alice wonders what might have become of Spencer had he stayed in New York those thirty-three years ago. She even admits having seen a different version of Spencer in her dreams—a Spencer who had remained in New York and became a real-estate baron.

Spencer has been wondering the same thing. In fact, he becomes obsessed with what he might have been. In hindsight, his decision to leave seems foolish; his time in Europe seems a relative waste, a "selfish, frivolous, scandalous" life. He begins to walk the halls and rooms of his childhood home late at night, reflecting on the memories of his youth and bemoaning his lost potential. At times he hopes to find his "alter ego": the man he would have been had he stayed in New York all those years ago.

Alice suggests that he take up permanent residence in the house. Disconcerted by the thought, Spencer goes to the empty house and believes that his alter ego is in the house with him. Noticing that a door he had left open has been inexplicably shut, he believes that his alter ego is sitting in the room behind the closed door.

Unwilling to open the door, Spencer attempts to make his escape. As he descends the stairway, he catches a glimpse of another door that should be closed but is not. Through this open door Spencer finally faces his alter ego. The apparition, described as a ''black stranger,'' is dressed in evening wear but has a monstrous face. Shocked, Spencer collapses.

The next afternoon, Alice finds and revives Spencer. Professing her love for him, she explains that she also saw the ''black stranger'' in her dream. Instead of the revulsion at the image of an alternative Spencer, Alice felt pity for him. When she pulls Spencer to her breast, it seems that he is finally home to stay.

Characters

Spencer Brydon

A wealthy, cultured man, Spencer Brydon returns to New York City after spending thirty-three years living in Europe and pursuing an interest in art. He is overwhelmed by the changes he finds in the city.

Now fifty-six, Spencer revisits the house on the ''jolly corner'' of Manhattan where he grew up. His parents, sister, and two brothers have passed away, leaving him the sole owner of his childhood home and another property.

While Spencer oversees the renovation of one of his properties, he discovers an affinity for project management and negotiating a business deal. Surprised by his natural business acumen, he wonders what his life would have been if he had stayed in New York. Soon is obsessed with thoughts of what he has missed.

Mrs. Muldoon

Mrs. Muldoon is a cleaning woman employed to keep Spencer's childhood home clean.

Narrator

The story is told by an anonymous narrator with limited omniscience who addresses the reader as a social acquaintance. At least twice, the narrator uses the first personal pronoun ''I.'' At another point, the narrator explicitly associates with the reader, referring to the story's characters as ''our friends.''

Alice Staverton

Alice is a childhood acquaintance of Spencer's. She accompanies him on his business trips and listens to him reflect on his past. She seems to be the only person who enjoys listening to his reminiscences.

Henry James

A single, middle-aged woman, Alice seems lonely and suggests that Spencer move back to New York City for good. At the story's end, Alice confirms that she is not only very fond of Spencer but possibly in love with him.

Themes

Memory and Reminiscence

Spencer Brydon's return to New York, his friendship with Alice Staverton, and his attraction to the house of his youth illustrate his overwhelming need to analyze his past. He needs to reflect on past events in order to understand who he is now. In particular, Spencer needs to come to terms with what he could have been had he remained in New York; in that way he can accept himself and move on with his life.

Alienation and Loneliness

When Spencer left New York as a young man, he was rejecting a life in business and embracing a career in art. Upon his return, he discovers the full implications of his decision. He has he lost his family; also, New York City has irrevocably changed to the point where he hardly recognizes it. In some

Media Adaptations

• *The Jolly Corner* was made into a short movie in 1977. It was directed by Arthur Barron and starred Salome Jens as Spencer Brydon. The video is distributed by Monterry Home Video.

ways, Spencer's experience is universal: in an attempt to recapture the past, he discovers that the world he remembers does not exist anymore. As a result, he feels alienated, cut off from his past and his own identity.

The American Dream

After living abroad for so many years, Spencer is able to view the American Dream as an outside observer. As a child, Spencer grew up in a wealthy, privileged household. As an adult, Spencer has continued to live comfortably on inherited wealth. When he returns to New York, he is disgusted by the ambitious and materialistic nature of the American businessman. From his privileged position, he views the capitalistic system as one that robs its citizens of integrity and culture.

Art and Money

Spencer rejects a career in business and escapes by pursuing a career in art in Europe. Yet while Spencer vilifies the American scene as materialistic and obsessed with money, he continues to live off the profits of that world. The rents from his properties make it possible for him to travel without financial restriction and to live abroad without having to work. The story implies that the pursuit of art is inextricably linked with money; to deny the connection is hypocritical.

Gender Roles

Spencer's rejection of a business career raises questions about what it means to be a powerful man in the early twentieth century. When he leaves New York City, he seems to have left behind the opportunity to marry and have a family as well as a thriving

business career. By linking Spencer's rejection of business to his absence of family, the story implies that personal choices are related to public pressures. In a sense, Spencer's pursuit of art is a protest against one-dimensional concepts of masculinity—concepts that relate economic power to one's worth as a man.

Alice also raises questions about how women are supposed to live their lives. While she stays in Manhattan her entire life, she never marries. The reader learns little about her life apart from her relationship to Spencer. Is her final embrace of Spencer a strong assertion of her will or a late and failed capitulation to the stereotypic woman's role of passive and dutiful wife?

Transformation and Change

The story hinges on Spencer confronting his alter ego. The story's conclusion suggests Spencer and Alice will end up together and that Spencer's wandering has ended. But what has Spencer learned? It is an open question whether Spencer has accepted his past and truly been transformed.

Style

Point of View and Narration

In "The Jolly Corner," the narrator is nearly omniscient, relating exactly what Spencer sees, thinks, and feels. However, this perspective is a limited one. For example, Alice's opinions are presented by Spencer; all impressions of her character—as well as others—are presented through him.

Also, at a few points in the story the narrator addresses the reader directly, implying perhaps a collaboration between the reader and narrator. Another narrative technique utilized by James is the slightly different narrative tone used for the different sections of the story. In the second section, Spencer wanders the house alone and the narrative voice nearly becomes his point of view. In the first and third sections, the narrator is more objective in explaining not only Spencer's impressions but other characters' actions and opinions.

Setting

The story takes place around the year 1908, shortly after James visited New York City after having lived for many years in Europe. The house "on the jolly corner" is in Manhattan on Fifth

Avenue near Washington Square. On a personal level, Spencer is yearning to comprehend both the passing of his family and friends and the emergence of a new type of urban social environment. Therefore, the incredible growth of heavy industry and architectural innovation—such as the proliferation of skyscrapers—represent progress, ambition, and power: things that he left behind when he moved to Europe.

Symbol and Images

Spencer's childhood home is the most fully developed image in the story. As a symbol, the house operates on many different levels. While walking in the rooms of the house Spencer recalls the time when the building was his home. The house also symbolizes his economic circumstances; his choice to protect the building as a sacred space is enabled by his wealth, partially generated from the rents he collects on the other property. Spencer's personal quest to revisit the past are connected to the business operations he has attempted to avoid.

In Henry James' other writings, he utilizes architectural metaphors—including ''the house,'' and ''the window''—metaphorically, symbolizing the structure that organizes and communicates meaning in fiction. In the preface to his novel *The Portrait of a Lady* (1881), James describes the ideal ''house of fiction'' as having millions of windows, each representing distinct perspectives on the world.

Structure

The story is divided in three parts, each with a different narrative tone. The first introduces us to Spencer and Alice, explaining Spencer's return to New York. The second section chronicles Spencer's attempt to track down his alter ego and is characterized by dense narrative description. In the third section Alice revives Spencer and pledges her love to him.

Historical Context

Robber Barons

At the turn of the century, American industrial production greatly increased. As technological innovations facilitated large-scale agricultural production, many small farmers were put out of business. Factories—often situated in urban areas—needed a large labor force and attracted people from rural areas, the South, and immigrants from all over

Topics for Further Study

- Spencer Brydon's explorations of his childhood home are characterized by their ritual nature: he hires Mrs. Muldoon to come at an appointed hour in order to keep the house clean for his nightly visit, and he maintains a supply of candles in a drawer so that he can light his way at night. Until he faints, he is careful to cover his tracks by shutting the window shutters and returning to the hotel at a decent hour. Why all the secrecy? What do Spencer's preparations mean? What is he hiding?

- Alice Staverton is an enigmatic figure in the story. Consider Alice's behavior. Do her comments to Spencer have more than one meaning? As a reader, what additional information is needed about Alice's character? Does she adhere to the normal expectations of a woman in 1908?

- Describing his midnight walks, Spencer uses metaphors that cast him as a big game hunter and a knight holding his sword aloft. Why does Spencer choose these metaphors? What does this say about his state of mind?

the world. With so many people looking for work, companies kept wages low and conditions poor. Working people began to protest the unfairness of the economic system, organizing the Populist Party and labor unions.

The financial rewards in business were enormous. Those men that were industrious, ambitious, and lucky had a decent chance of success. A few number of men earned the title ''captain of industry,'' controlling very large companies and becoming rich. However, the concentration of this wealth took place at the expense of average workers who often worked long hours in unsafe conditions to support their families.

In response to the greed and exploitation, the Populist Movement became popular promoting working-class interests. Eventually the movement was

Compare
&
Contrast

- **1908** Between the years 1860 and 1914 New York's population increases from 850,000 to more than four million people. In 1910, the population of New York City is 4,766,9000; the population of Manhattan is reported as 2,331,000 people.

  Today: According to the United States Census Bureau, the population of New York City is 7.3 million. The 1990 census reported a population for Manhattan of 1,487,500.

- **1910** Women comprise 21% of the workforce. Approximately 25% of working women are married.

Today: Women make up approximately 45% of the workforce; almost 60% of working women are married.

- **1910** Only 8% of households have electric service.

  Today: Nearly all homes have electric service.

- **1900** Life expectancy for women is 48.3 years. For men, the figure is estimated at 46.3 years.

  Today: Approximate average life expectancy for women is 78 years of age and men 74 years.

superseded by the Progressive Era's politics of accommodation. In the early twentieth century, the Progressives attempted to break up giant corporate trusts and monopolies. Despite some anti-trust legislation, big business continued to prosper.

The focus shifted to the effects of immigration on the United States. In 1907 Congress set up the Immigration Commission to study immigration. Restrictions on immigration from China, Japan, and Korea were already being imposed by individual states and national diplomatic agreements. After World War I, strict immigration quotas were established.

United States Imperialism

As the United States became the preeminent industrial power in the world, the nation began to expand its political and economic interests to former colonies of Europe in the Pacific. In the 1890s a scholar named Frederick Jackson Turner proposed a "frontier thesis" to explain the incredible power of United States economic advancement.

According to Turner, the exploration and settlement of the Western frontier had been an inspiring challenge for a young nation. As the twentieth century began, the new frontier would become the

development of American economic influence all over the world, especially in Asia. In Samoa, Hawaii, the Philippine Islands, Cuba, Central and South America, the United States acted like an imperial power: claiming possession, backing these claims up with military force, and exercising economic influence.

Critical Overview

"The Jolly Corner" has generated much critical commentary. On one level, Spencer Brydon's experience is quite familiar and represents a painful but inevitable aspect of the human condition. Critics explore the implications of his self-doubt and insecurity as well as the meaning of the story's conclusion. Is the final scene a moment of redemption for Spencer; or, is Spencer incapable of really coming to terms with his past?

Some commentators view the story as autobiographical. Like Spencer, James left the United States (in 1875), lived in Europe for a long period of time, and returned to find America much changed. Spencer's conflict between Europe and America is subject of much of James's fiction, literary criticism, and diary entries. Moreover, Alice Staverton's name echoes James's beloved younger sister.

Spencer's alter ego represents a personal and philosophical crisis that James's father often spoke about—the "vastation." Henry James, Sr. was influenced by the moral philosopher Emmanuel Swedenborg, whose ideas explored the unmanageable energies of nature and the extremes of human consciousness. The "vastation" was a visitation by one's evil self that forced one to confront their most sensitive weakness.

One well-established view is that by facing the "black stranger," Spencer confronts Henry James's alter ego. Leon Edel, James's most meticulous and authoritative biographer, considered Spencer's conflict emblematic of whether James regarded the United States or England as the source of his fiction. In *Henry James, The Master: 1901–1916* (1972), Edel responds to early criticism of James's career, most notably that of Van Wyck Brook. In *The Pilgrimage of Henry James* (1925) Brook charged James with turning his back on the United States in an ineffective attempt to associate with the more highly esteemed, genteel class literary tradition of England.

By focusing on James's later work, and reading Spencer's crisis as a final acceptance of America, Edel recasts James's aesthetic effort as being primarily an attempt to reconcile, understand, and depict what it means to be American in an increasing international world. Edel's argument echoes earlier appraisals of James, the most notable appraisal by F. O. Matthiessen in *Henry James: The Major Phase* (1944). In these accounts, Spencer is reconciled with his alter ego.

Some critics are skeptical of Spencer's redemption at the end of the story. In *The American Henry James* (1957), Quentin Anderson views Spencer as hopelessly self-centered. In "The Beast in 'The Jolly Corner': Spencer Brydon's Ironic Rebirth" (1974), Allen Stein argues that Spencer actually sees who he will become. Stein not only sees Spencer as lacking self-awareness but an ugly human being. Instead of redeeming Spencer, Alice may simply be an enabler, shielding him from what he really is.

Alice is considered an enigmatic figure in the story. A few critics have examined the character of Alice with interesting results. In "'Doing Good by Stealth': Alice Staverton and Women's Politics in

Times Tower Building under construction on Times Square in New York City, 1904.

'The Jolly Corner'" (1992), Russell Reising views Alice as a major character. Within the context of her time, Alice seems to be an anomaly or outcast—unmarried, no children and self-supporting.

However, instead of symbolizing failed femininity, Alice is viewed by some critics as manipulative and deceptive. Some have even characterized her as an artful liar. It is a bit disconcerting, however, that despite Alice's apparent strength and independence she is so set on marriage to Spencer. Has she spent thirty-three years merely waiting for her man to come home?

Recent criticism has both emphasized Spencer's egotism and attempted to uncover the full role of Alice in Spencer's resurrection. In "A New Reading of Henry James's 'The Jolly Corner'" (1987), Daniel Mark Fogel contends that as the story ends Spencer realizes that the monstrous stranger is his alter ego. Only Alice's love will save him. In Alice's embrace and Spencer's return, Spencer saves himself from tragic fate. At the story's end, Spencer is "loving and beloved," enjoying "at last a blessed state the beauty of which the black stranger had never tasted or could never taste."

Criticism

Kendall Johnson

Johnson teaches American literature at the University of Pennsylvania where he recently received his Ph.D. In the following essay, Johnson explores the function of windows in "The Jolly Corner."

Opening a window may not seem an important event in life; after all, Brydon hired Mrs. Muldoon "for a daily hour to open windows and dust and sweep." Yet when Brydon opens the window after retreating from his alter ego, the effect is nearly magical, "a sharp rupture of his spell." By looking closely at how windows function literally and figuratively in the story, one can understand both Brydon's limitation as a hero and James's subtle criticism of the protagonist's simplistically oppositional thinking. With images of architecture and specifically of windows, James explores the boundaries between public and private, as well as individual and community.

In the 1908 preface to his New York Edition of *The Portrait of a Lady* (1881), James proposes that fiction can best be described as a house. Like a house, the plot of a story depends on a certain structure; like a comfortable home a good story is something the writer and reader share in personal ways.

Describing fiction as a house may ostensibly imply an inflexibility of form, conformity to blueprint, and hostility to individuality; however, James explains that it is up to the individual writer to make the house of fiction her or his own, carving a window into the structure, a window through which he or she can see the outside and communicate that vision to the world. For James, "the house of fiction" theoretically has potential windows to accommodate everyone's perspective.

In James's metaphor, the window is not a given fact but the product of individual will. The author's "vision" and "pressure of individual will" pierces the house of fiction with unique perspective. Every individual sees something different although watching the same material world. The "house of fiction" is theoretically moldable to any perspective. It contains not "one window" "but a million" or rather, "a number of possible windows not to be reckoned." For James, the structure of fiction is not in itself interesting. Instead, the eyes and I's behind each window and each story are the true curiosity.

James's metaphor seems particularly apt for Spencer Brydon. Following the preface's logic, one can surmise what motivates Spencer by considering the view he manages from his room. Through most of the story, the window operates as a lens to the world, emphasizing Spencer's feeling of transcendence above the vulgar, "awful modern crush" of the public life below. At night he opens the shutters, allowing the light from the street to illuminate his own private theater of nostalgia. The window is more than a transparent glass-plate but a psychological buffer to the world. The elevated point of his view is important to his world view, setting him literally over the city that he judges and condemns.

Importantly, Spencer does not feel that he is doing anything as he stands before the window feeling powerful. Effortlessly, his window acts as a lens, providing the focal point through which the disparate elements of the world are arranged for his vision.

The magisterial attitude with which Spencer surveys the world scene complements his hyperbolic self-image as a heroic knight, a big-game hunter tracking the "beast in the forest," or as "the traveller emerging from an Egyptian tomb," "assaulted" by the "outer light of the Desert." When Spencer performs his midnight vigil he characterizes his reflections as requiring the concentrated force of an exceptional individual will. This sacred routine generates his life's most concentrated tension and he finds "no pleasure so fine" as his "stalking" the alter ego.

Like the Greek hero Ulysses, Spencer has traveled the world for many years, leaving behind his Penelope in Alice Staverton. The story evokes a potentially epic melancholy, spotlighting a man whose world has passed him by while he wandered. During the night of the final showdown, Spencer chooses a self-description that makes the heroic nature of his inner conflict explicit.

Keenly aware of his alter ego's presence, he holds to the conviction "to show himself, in a word, that he wasn't afraid." While walking down the stairs he imagines himself "a physical image, an image almost worthy of an age of greater romance." The hyperbole intensifies as Spencer gauges his present showdown as unmatched by any "age of romance." By proving to himself that he is not spooked by his alter ego, Spencer envisions himself "[proceeding] downstairs with a drawn sword."

What Do I Read Next?

- Published in 1887, *The American* is James's third novel. The protagonist, Christopher Newman, is a brash, young American businessman. He travels in Europe, learning about art and European culture. Newman and Spencer offer a fascinating contrast.

- James's "In the Cage" is a short story published in 1898. It chronicles the life of an English, working-class woman who works in a telegraph booth. She reads the messages of her upper-class clientele, obsessed by their correspondence and personal intrigues.

- The novels *The House of Mirth* (1905) and *The*

Age of Innocence (1921), written by Edith Wharton, focus on the lives of upper-class American families in the Gilded Age.

- *The Souls of Black Folk*, a collection of essays by W. E. B. Dubois, cuts to the heart of social conflict in the early twentieth century. Published in 1904, the essays record his impressions of living in the North and in the South as an African-American.

- Published in 1910, *Twenty Years at Hull-House* by Jane Addams documents the poverty and exploitation of immigrants settling in the major cities of the United States.

This exaggeration foreshadows Spencer's exceptional opening of the window even as it threatens to disturb the structure of Spencer's story. His hyperbolic terms invite the reader to scrutinize Spencer and to doubt that he offers a reliable window onto the world. After all, what value does Spencer claim to hold that makes him feel so superior to the world below?

Throughout the story, Spencer considers himself brave because he has resisted the call of the New York business world. Instead he wants to find "values" other than those that depend on the "beastly rent-values" of New York. As a young man he rejected his father's advice and turned his back on business and the United States, leaving for Europe where he pursued his interest in art.

Spencer's alternative idea of "value" is hard to discern. He seems unable to explain a positive ideal behind his decisions, characterizing his thirty-year absence as "a selfish frivolous scandalous life." In order to prove himself, Spencer prepares for a series of showdowns—with the construction representative, his alter ego, and Alice's implicit request for him to stay with her in New York. Spencer's heroism is a series of confrontations through which he makes himself "stand up." His operating logic is

binary opposition, yes or no propositions that he accepts or rejects. The properties he returns to administer reflect this polarity. One is sacred, "consecrated," and the other a symbol of vulgar money interest.

Spencer's confrontational egotism saturates the image of the honorable knight. He manages to build his heroic status only by dominating someone else. His search for the alter ego runs parallel to his confrontation with the "representative of the building firm" at his other property to whom Spencer also "[stood] up." In both instances, Spencer masters a threatening adversary. His alter ego is a personification of this violent opposition: "some erect confronting presence, something planted in the middle of the place and facing him through the dusk." Spencer yearns to win, to "turn the table on the apparition," proving again that he is not scared by scaring someone else.

The broader effect of this attitude is that Spencer seems incapable of recognizing those around him, even when they are crucial to his happiness. The narrator characterizes Alice as "[listening] to everything" and as "a woman who answered intimately but who utterly didn't chatter." In these terms, Alice seems to be a mere complement to Spencer's

> This turn from physical humor into deep despair demonstrates how radically Spencer needs to shift his thinking. It is not enough that the window is open or shut, instead Spencer must entirely reconsider his method of seeing."

heroic musings. Later, he characterizes her in a static, one-dimensional fashion as "you were born to be what you are," "you're a person whom nothing can have altered." Such terms erase Alice's entire life experience and feeling through a gross generalization in contrast to which Spencer fills his own crisis with dramatic depth.

In the end, Spencer learns that life is not a series of oppositions but a vast network of decisions that prevent such easy victory. While opposing the business world has been his primary goal, he realizes in front of his fourth-floor window that the extremes are themselves related. In the end, Spencer's opposition of business and art fails as he is unable to locate a space outside of the economic space. His attempt to maintain private sanctity by holding the publicly commercial at bay is unworkable. Alice sums up the situation well when she remarks that he makes "so good a thing of [his] sky-scraper that, living in luxury on those ill-gotten gains, [he] can afford for a while to be sentimental" in the house on the jolly corner.

The plot's thickening depends on questioning the way Spencer has lived his life. As Spencer stands at the window, he realizes the full force of his isolation. The landscape has changed dramatically since he abandoned the United States and as he looks out from his fourth-floor window near dawn, the homes seem "hard-faced houses" that speak "so little to any need of his spirit." Instead of seeing a vulgar world against which he can elevate himself, he sees a "void." The void lacks any sense of proportion or measure and reflects a deeper crisis in Spencer's perspective on the world. His confu-

sion at the window represents his final inability to separate himself from the world he had believed himself to have transcended.

In perceiving the world as an "incalculable void," Spencer recognizes the emptiness at the heart of his own oppositional thinking. When there is nothing left to reject, who is Spencer? Is his art really separate from business, and if not, what is the relationship of art to business? Instead of a sacred space apart from the money-lust of the public "void," his private sanctuary is merely another "door into a room shuttered and void."

The scene at the window emphasizes the blurred relationship between these oppositions. It is not enough to open or shut the window as it was to open or shut the doors of the house while tracking the apparition. Standing at the window, Spencer's pretension to have derived a transcendent value erodes as he realizes that he is trapped not by "others" but by his own methods of establishing himself through confrontation and equating truth with the either/or polarity of ultimatum.

Spencer struggles with the scene's "large collective negation" even as dawn breaks. In opening the window, Spencer addresses the terms through which he reads the world. He will do anything to shake up the system. First he tries to make contact with those he watched from his window. In order to circumvent the vacuity of his vision, he looks on to "The empty street . . . the great lamplit vacancy" and decides it "was within call, within touch." He yearns for "some comforting common fact, some vulgar human note, the passage of a scavenger or a thief, some night-bird however base."

The condescending terms ("vulgar human note," "night-bird however base") are echoes of his binary logic and self-assured egotism, echoes resonating even in his most vulnerable moment. The policeman walking his beat, "whom [Spencer] had hitherto only sought to avoid" now desperately becomes his "friend" whom Spencer wants "to get into relation with" or "to hail" from his fourth floor.

But, despite his "choked appeal from his own open window" no "vulgar human note" appears, and Spencer continues to fall deeper into isolation. The story takes on a nearly comic note as Spencer struggles to reinvent his vision, to situate himself with a significant difference in relation to the window. Unable to connect with a human presence in the street, Spencer imagines himself clumsily "astride of the window-sill," flailing an "outstretched leg and arm'' to a ladder or scaffolding with which he can descend to the street.

With these pathetically desperate moments, James explodes Spencer's self-inflated heroism of romantic knighthood. Finally, the comedy turns gruesome as Spencer imagines throwing himself out of the window, ''uncontrollably insanely fatally [taking] his way to the street.''

This turn from physical humor into deep despair demonstrates how radically Spencer needs to shift his thinking. It is not enough that the window is open or shut, instead Spencer must entirely reconsider his method of seeing. In this line of argument, recent critics have looked at the story through different windows asking: What is Alice's window, or Mrs. Muldoon's?

Reading the story, one can glimpse shadows of these different perspectives. In Alice's acceptance of Spencer either as he is or as he might have been, she is able to locate the contradictions of life and not shirk admitting her role in the machinery of economic existence. This is not to say that Alice's window to life is without its limitations—how different might her impression of Spencer's drama be than Mrs. Muldoon's? How might Mrs. Muldoon's window reflect critiques of the economic privilege on which the story stages Alice and Spencer's reunion?

Source: Kendall Johnson, ''World View, World Void: Brydon at His Window in 'The Jolly Corner','' for *Short Stories for Students*, The Gale Group, 2000.

Barbara Hardy

While examining James's use of the idea of divided identity in ''The Jolly Corner,'' Hardy also affirms the piece as ''James's great love-story'' in the following essay.

''The Jolly Corner'' was published in 1908, after the stunning achievement of *The Ambassadors, The Wings of the Dove,* and *The Golden Bowl,* all written between 1900 and 1905. ''The Jolly Corner'' was also written while Henry James was still working on the two unfinished novels, *A Sense of the Past* and *The Ivory Tower.* The subtly packed story is probably his most original and exciting brief narrative, and its many links with other novels and stories show its density, freshness, and some of its sources of power. It relates closely to *A Sense of the Past* in its themes of historical determination and identify as well as its supernatural fantasy. It revises other earlier ghost stories, especially ''The Turn of the Screw'' and ''Owen Wingrave.'' It is rooted in the bitter symbolist tales of unlived passion, ''The Altar of the Dead'' and ''The Beast in the Jungle,'' remembering but rejecting their tragic mode. Less conspicuously, but significantly, it qualifies and develops subjects and symbols in the last great novels, especially *The Golden Bowl,* whose flaw it mends, though in the simplicity of fable.

To concentrate first on the story itself. It is a typical product of James's last period in its dominant subjects, distinct but for him inseparable: the power of individual imagination, and the conditional, constructed nature of human identity. James conceives imagination as creative, poetic in the true sense of making something new, capable of radical revision and subversion of the lived life, but at the same time he is clear that the creature which creates is created by its circumstances. He speaks with crystalline lucidity to the imagination of our own period, where we may be historically knowing, aware of the essentialist fallacy, yet paradoxically cling to a sense of creative power. Putting it another way, we know ourselves passive but feel ourselves active. James resolves the contradiction by making us aware that the process of constructing is a tentative and uncertain process, and is itself something constructed.

Nowhere is the active-passive consciousness clearer than in ''The Jolly Corner,'' whose central character, Spencer Brydon, is a James-resembling exile returning home to New York City from somewhat vaguely outlined wanderings in Europe, after thirty years. In his alarmed response to the changed and changing New York at the beginning of the century he is like the James who returned to pay a long visit in 1904 and as a consequence wrote *The American Scene,* but unlike his author, he is not committed to another departure. It is the story of a might-have-been which draws on biographical fact and converts it to fiction. Unlike Brydon, James returned to America to face his might-have-beens, and uneasily accept historical flux, but gladly confirmed and returned to his European choice and life in Rye and London. Brydon imagines and confronts the might-have-been, that *alter ego* in his haunted family home on a jolly corner in New York. Unlike James, and unlike many of the characters in James's stories, he is not an artist, though actively creative, prolific like his author in devising image and character. James imagines his imagination, conceiving it as a fine instrument for scrutinizing and speculating about the power of social circumstance.

> James chose not to end with noumenal imagery of death and resurrection and prodigious journey but firmly returns us to the phenomenal world."

Like so many of the novels and tales, the story begins with a telling title. Brydon's house is physically located on a real corner between two streets, also between demolition and conservation, past and present. It joins the over-developed row where Brydon owns another house, undistinguished between similar neighbours, and like them being converted into a high-rise apartment house, with the unnamed or unnumbered avenue which still retains the buildings and spirit of the past. The developers have their eye on his house on the jolly corner, but Brydon hangs on to it and begins to visit its empty rooms late at night. Like the apparition he meets there, he haunts and walks. The corner site is not only architecturally desirable and different, as corner properties are, but symbolically eloquent. The epithet "jolly" is typically Jamesian in its colloquial lightness, its dissonant irony as a designation of a haunted place, and its final dissolution of irony in unexpected aptness. The corner in the city turns out to have seemed sinister but to have been jolly, after all, in this grim story with a happy ending. So does the corner in the mind, a corner turned by a character in crisis, as Spencer Brydon turns or transforms his consciousness to see the self he might have been, then grasps the nature of his lived identity and dies into a new future where he is able to love. (Though not until he turns another corner, helped to revise and elucidate his experience by Alice Staverton, who is mentor as well as lover, like few women in previous fiction.) The image of the corner figures the arrival of the unexpected, a something unforeseen suddenly rounding a corner. It is an image of cornering, apt for a story where the metaphor of hunting is elaborated and varied as both the uncanny *alter ego,* who has never lived, and the living man, who is committed to history, are cornered in turn. The multifaceted suggestiveness of the corner confirms the total resonance of place, especially the

empty house and all its interior, rooms, hall, staircases, landings, doors and windows. The story is a complete exercise in the psycho-dynamics of place. The empty house is occupied and furnished for Brydon, he declares, by his past, cherished as the family home where he lived and where his parents and siblings died, valued as the place he can afford not to sell because of the other house being developed in the street of skyscrapers. When Alice lightly jokes about the way sentiment is founded on commercial success—"In short you're to make so good a thing of your sky-scraper that, living in luxury on those ill-gotten gains, you can afford for a while to be sentimental here!"—she proffers the same political metonymy as Dickens in *Great Expectations,* where a convict's cash creates a gentleman. The story doesn't dwell on this insight, casually put in with a passing smile, but it is fascinatingly articulated, totally relevant like all this artist's detail, bringing out clearly his politics of anti-essentialism. James knows that the liberal man of culture depends on the *alter ego* he rejects, which is one of several reasons why the ghost has to be seen, and in a way accepted. (James himself started his European travels on American money, and benefited from inherited rents, though unlike Brydon, he earned money too.)

The *alter ego* is the most materialist of ghosts, the American successful early twentieth-century man, builder of skyscrapers, the man of power, the man of violence, even a gangster. As an apparition he is terrifying in many ways, not least because of that power and violence, but also because of his vulnerability, since he has been maimed by violence. Like Charlotte Bronte's Rochester he is wounded in the right arm—actually the hand—and almost blinded, though the sexual suggestion is certainly not that found by some critics in *Jane Eyre.* What this story suggests are the hazards and threats of potency, not impotence, and the alternative self may endow his weaker rival with his sexual energy, one way or another. He is imagined from the inside, as having interiority, as Brydon feels first his superior power, next imagines a secret sharer, cowering and hunted, then feels a shift in the balance of power, and eventually imagines the powerfully motivated aggressiveness of the violent, inferior, jealous, unlived and unchosen identity. Like his novelist, whom he represents, and does more than represent, since he is not an artist, Brydon is brilliantly attentive to motive and passion. The *alter ego* is terrifying because of his powerful physicality, but also, like many of the best ghosts, because of his inhuman indeterminacy. (It's a quiet grim joke that he is so determined as well as indeterminate.) His immateriality is certainly not incompatible with a grossly materialized physical horror, like that of the unseen but imagined mutilated ghost in W. W. Jacobs's "The Monkey's Paw," also conjured up by passionate desire. Brydon dreads seeing the apparition's face, and its slow exposure shows he is right to fear, though James cleverly avoids crude description, successfully relying on the power of suggestion:

> the face was the face of a stranger. It came upon him nearer now, quite as one of those expanding images projected by the magic lantern of childhood; for the stranger, whoever he might be, evil, odious, blatant, vulgar, had advanced as for aggression.

He is a ghost of the mind, but his subjectivity doesn't diminish the terror of the character's and the reader's experience. There is cold comfort in thinking him a projection of the subject, since that subject is clearly established as a source from which idea emerges and grossly expands—James's precise image—into materialization.

The story is dazzlingly reflexive, with many facets: it is a fiction about self-fantasy, a ghost story about making up ghosts, a symbolist story about creating symbols from the hard surfaces of facts. It would be hard to find a more genre-conscious and style-conscious story, but like all great literature it is Janus-headed, facing life as well as art. So it conceives Spencer Brydon—and Alice Staverton, the woman in the story—perhaps as types of the artist, but certainly as imaginatively active in a broadly humane way, in a story about the hard business of loving the whole of a person, accepting the grossness of the shadow-self, accepting historical construction. It is a speculative fable pushing at the boundaries of fable, a realist narrative breaking the bounds of realism. There can be fewer more elastic reflexive narratives.

How is it narrated? Concentrating on the imagination of Spencer Brydon, his typical third-person sensitive register of consciousness, James almost completely effaces his narrator. Almost but not quite. As in *The Ambassadors*, and its great ancestor, Jane Austen's *Emma*, the reader is placed just behind the chief character's awareness, close to the dominating mind but outside it. As that last episode about the apparition's face shows, there is a tiny functional gap between character and reader, bridged by a scrupulously tentative and reticent narrator. In that passage the free indirect style shows Brydon's definition of his other self, but does not commit the story to his moral judgement, leaving room for

Alice's final intelligent and compassionate demurral, "he must have been less dreadful to me" and "He has been unhappy. . . ." The chief narrator is conspicuously and consistently provisional, his narrative threaded with "perhapses" and "possiblys," in which he frames the doubting slow step-by-step speculativeness of Brydon. Conspicuously discreet even in the company of James's restrained tellers, the chief narrator never raises his voice, but it is heard once or twice, well on in the story, addressing the reader and making a point more emphatically, though in an aptly muted tone. On one occasion, for instance, the quiet narrator repeats something he said five sentences earlier, "He had made, as I have said, to create on the premises the baseless sense of a reprieve, three absences." In the next paragraph this first-person narrative affirmation is repeated, to pick up a point made eight sentences before: "There came to him, as I say . . . the acuteness of this certainty. . . ." But this time the repetitive reminder is qualified, making the personal appearance stronger, "There came to him, as I say—but determined by an influence beyond my notation!—the acuteness of this certainty. . . ." These are the only three first-person pronouns, drawing attention to the reticence by this little neighbourly cluster, asserting rarity. The last disclaimer of authority, the topos of inexpressibility, in "beyond my influence," and the restrained cool term "notation," contribute to the functional vagueness and uncertainty that hovers over the whole narrative, making it a wonderfully blurred and opaque medium for the strange happening.

The expansive internal narrator's uncertainty meets and matches that of the reticent outer narrator. It is a presiding uncertainty, since Brydon's is the only dramatized consciousness, Alice's presence being behaviouristically presented, with her interiority done only through Brydon's reading of her behaviour. His own responses are marked from the start by the rhetoric of qualification, doubt and provisionality: we hear on the first page that his return to America has been attended by "rather unattenuated surprises," that everything was "somehow" a surprise, that the surprises "seemed" to have been given a big time-margin for play, and later, that he had "supposed" himself to allow for change, and that uncanny phenomena place him "rather" under their charm.

He is introduced by a direct speech, the complaint that everyone asks him what he thinks of "everything"—"everything" referring to the impression made by New York after an absence of thirty-three years, and we then swerve back into a long retrospective account of his first impressions and take in his visit to the house on the jolly corner, and the first stealthy intimations of its haunting. We then go back to pick up the conversation at the beginning, after ten pages of Edel's edition, ''It was a few days after this that . . . he had expressed his impatience. . . .'' The retrospect justifies the narrative compression, which lends itself to a useful summary form, with a deliberated lack of particularity. From the start, we are in a twilight zone, or even in the dark, as Brydon is to be on his wanderings through the house, with or without a candle, groping and feeling our way, as Brydon feels his. The marked stylistic feature—not confined to this story, but given particular effect in it—remains that of qualification and uncertainty: ''old association seemed to, stray'' his new-found business ability ''quite'' charmed him, ''perhaps'' charmed Alice ''perceptibly'' less, and he ''imagined'' Alice asking him if he has started to prowl round the house. His is an imagining mind, and his ''sensitive register'' is the only consciousness notated within the third-person narrative.

Alice Staverton's point of view is consistently indicated by limit, presented through the indirections of Brydon's speculative and inferential mode: ''things she didn't utter, it was clear, seemed to come and go in her mind . . .'' ''whatever her impression might have been . . . ,'', ''She appeared to imply . . . ,'' ''it perhaps produced for her. . . .'' The uncertainty is there not only in Brydon's reading of this sensitive and intelligent woman of few words, who doesn't ''chatter,'' but in nearly all his reading of experience. The hesitancy and tentativeness of his sensibility create an idiolect for the guarded observer, who has not chosen to be a man of action, and the perfect register for the imagining of a supernatural apparition and the creation of a ghost from mere potentiality. (He is a ghost even more nebulous than a post-mortem revenant, who has had a mortal existence.) Brydon's confidence at the end, when he confronts his constructed image of alternative construction, is the more marked and startling as it contrasts with his general wariness and doubt.

Until the last meeting, then, his isolated consciousness is made misty, emphasizing both the introspective and subjective experience and the traditional mistiness of apparitions, though this one is to be grossly solidified. This is a story about the invocation of a ghost, by imagination. As in *Hamlet* we begin with a question then quickly move on to another; after ''Everyone asks me what I 'think' of everything,'' Brydon explains that he is not interested in everything, only wonderingly absorbed in one question: ''What would it have made of me, what would it have made of me? I keep forever wondering . . . as if I could possibly know!'' His wondering determines the action on the jolly corner. Like Kafka's K before the castle and Alice before the looking-glass, Brydon initiates the ghost and the ghost-story. The haunting by a self-styled *alter ego* is initiated by his curiosity and desire, his creative *fiat*. In Kafka, Carroll and James the fantastic story originates in a character's urging fantasy, presented in a third-person narrative, through a subtle, free, indirect style, just right for the introspective mode and for the narrative lack of disclosure. The characters are not artists but their weird stories are thoroughly motivated: K, Alice and Brydon create their own story, urged by passionate desire for knowledge. In each case something is imagined in advance, then turns out to be authenticated by experience, with a chilling and grotesque sense of sinister but comprehensible coincidence. K says he is the land-surveyor, and after an apparent hitch, is confirmed in his imagined appointment. Alice imagines going through the looking-glass, then does. James is clearly recalling Lewis Carroll in the eerie traffic through the painting in *The Sense of the Past* and here too Ralph Pendrel imagines that his *alter ego* will show his face and he does. Brydon thinks of a ghost, and sees one.

These two entries are in the old tradition of magic: ghosts, fairies and devils have to be invoked and invited over the human threshold, as scrupulously recalled in Marlowe's *Dr Faustus* and Yeats's *Land of Heart's Desire*, but not in ''The Turn of the Screw,'' the subjectivity of whose ghosts has been extensively debated, and, I think, understandably mistaken, ever since Edmund Wilson proposed his Freudian reading. ''The Jolly Corner'' makes it clear that Brydon's ghost begins in the mind. The earlier story made its ghosts external, but Wilson and the critics who followed his reading seem to have been compelled by the very proper rational belief in the subjectivity of ghosts, so rewrote them, though with sexist implications, as projections of the governess's neurotic repression. ''The Jolly Corner'' may be read as a revision of ''The Turn of the Screw,'' in its insistence that ghosts are—or begin—inside the psyche of the ghost-seer. In this story, and in ''Owen Wingrave,'' James's ghosts and ghost-seeing are grounded in rationality.

The repressions of the hero in ''The Jolly Corner,'' unlike those of the governess and Owen

Wingrave, are cured. He is horrified by his vision, which is like the vastation experienced by James's father and his brother, William, but turns out to be the opposite of vastation, an affirmative and reconstructive vision. What it resembles, as Leon Edel points out, is a famous dream Henry James recorded, in which he was in the Galerie d'Apollon of the Louvre threatened and terrified by a "creature or presence," then turning the tables, "surpassing him for straight aggression and dire intention," hunting and routing the haunter. The "visitant" is displaced as the cause of the dreamer's fear and turns into the terrified victim. The dreamer becomes hero of the nightmare, in an unconscious allegory of creativity's conversion of dread to power.

It is fascinating that James's dream, and "The Jolly Corner," use a vastation, an experience of fear, horror, and physical loathing, in order to overcome and assimilate fear and horror, and imagine its benign visionary opposite. James also overcame his two male seniors, his father and his elder brother, in the two fantasies of the real dream and the dreaming fiction.

To do this he imagined a powerful woman, a more positive version of Maria Gostrey in *The Ambassadors*, and the women characters in the earlier great tragic stories, "The Altar of the Dead" (1895) and, closest of all, May Bartram of "The Beast in the Jungle" (1903). The central symbol of this story is significantly revised in the image-rich "Jolly Corner": "the hunted thing" and "the fanged or the antlered animal brought at last to bay," "an awful beast; whom I brought, too horribly, to bay." Reading "The Jolly Corner" with "The Beast in the Jungle" in mind brings out the relation between Brydon's confrontation with power and virility and his final embrace of Alice. The beast in the earlier story was not awful or destructive, and neither is the apparent beast in this story, though Brydon thinks he is, and needs Alice to put him right.

This is perhaps the clearest and most satisfying act of Jamesian self-revision. It is also James's most affirmative imagining of a woman character's creativity, power and fulfilment, admittedly within the compressed scope and permitted simplification of fable. ("The Jolly Corner" is James's last great story, though of the five written after it, "Crapy Cornelia," "The Bench of Desolation," and "A Round of Visits," are all thematically related and worthy companions.) Alice Staverton succeeds where May Bartram, who closely resembles her, failed. Brydon catches his beast in the jungle in the nick of

time, unlike John Marcher. John Marcher shows an advance, in his turn, on the more easily defeated and destroyed George Stransom in "The Altar of the Dead." Both Stransom and Marcher go into the making of Spencer Brydon. His story is affirmative in its accomplishment of a vision of love and—in spite of love's middle age—sexual fulfilment. Brydon tells Alice he longs to know what he would have been like had he stayed in the family house on the jolly corner of New York City, and because this is a love-story as well as a story about imagination, Brydon, unlike K and Alice in Wonderland, is supported by love, or imagination. His Alice fully understands his wonder, and wonders with him, as good lovers do, attending to the wholeness of the beloved.

So it is appropriate that though the initiation is his, it is a collaborative act which transforms metaphor into reality. Alice feels his desire and responds to his simile for the *alter ego*, said to resemble "the full-blown flower ... in the small tight bud," though pointing out that she thinks the flower would be "quite splendid, quite huge and monstrous," disagreeing with his sense of it as "quite hideous and offensive," in preparation for her revisions at the story's end. She says interestingly that he would "have had power," and to his amazement, that she must have liked him "that way," 'How should I not have liked you?' She also says she has seen the apparition, long before he does, in two dreams, and at the end says she has seen him at the moment of Brydon's dawn vision. The coincidence is acceptable both because she gives no description, pressing on our credulity with the lightest possible touch, because it completes the fable, and because—like *Jane Eyre*, where love is also redemptively telepathic—she is as obsessed as he is with what he might have been: 'my mind, my imagination, had worked so over what you might, what you mightn't have been—to show you, you see, how I've thought of you. . . .'

It is important that Alice is attracted to the powerful alternative capitalist Brydon, and that she repels his sense of the ghost as a "black stranger," repulsive and alien. It is important to attach the final embrace, and his completed declaration, echoing but changing Amerigo's "I see only you" in "I have you," to the fabulous ghost story. It is as if Brydon's dying—as he insists on calling it—fully establishes a transition from partial to whole identity. He has to recognize and accept the "black stranger," as something within his range of possible identity, his shadow self or id. The fable works in

Freudian and Jungian terms, as well as being a politically lucid fable of the constructed self by social circumstance. There is no need to see it in terms of any of the traditional systems: it is a recognition of potentiality, in unromantic and tough imagery. It is a fable of the divided self, like Conrad's *Secret Sharer* and unlike Stevenson's *Dr Jekyll and Mr Hyde*, in acknowledging the kinship of each half of a divided self. And however we systematize it, the fable is more than a fable because of its emotional trajectory: it is a particularized and dynamic love story of self-analysing passion and power. It analyses as it feels the nature of loving another self.

At the beginning the lovers seem to be on the brink, making love telepathically but on tiptoe as only James's characters can. Brydon asks Alice, 'don't you see how, without my exile, I shouldn't have been waiting till now—?,' leaving the sentence and declaration wittily unfinished on that ''now,'' to be answered by her responsive incomplete and ambiguous sentence, 'It hasn't spoiled your speaking—.' He has to wait a little longer, until he sees the self in all its potentiality and potency, and until she has proved how she ''has thought'' of him, and suffered the vision with him. Then he can speak and Alice can accept.

It is the subtle Jamesian structure of reversibility, found in *The Golden Bowl*, with its sub-text of Adam Verver giving Maggie what she is seen as giving him—protective action, silence, and cunning. ''The Jolly Corner'' is even more complex in its sub-texts because we feel that the *alter ego* and Alice each has a point of view from which the story might be told. It was not for nothing that James had pondered and experimented with shifting sensitive registers of consciousness from the beginning of his career. His shifts in voice are as interesting, if less mannered and conspicuous, as those of James Joyce. Joyce liked to show the shifts of viewpoint—Stephen, Bloom, Gerty, the Citizen, Molly, and the rest—as James had done with the Prince and the Princess in *The Golden Bowl*. One of James's most subtle formal achievements is this Escher-like reversibility or exchange, in which we feel the pressure of sub-textual potentiality stir beneath the main text. It is of course the appropriate form for a story of an *alter ego*, but it is also a good pattern for the love story.

As it is enacted, the story is Brydon's creation. It begins like *Hamlet* by moving from generality and neutrality to particularity. Brydon feels a bell

ring—as the crude language of cliché would say—when Alice says to him that he would have invented the skyscraper in his alternative American existence: ''He was to remember these words while the weeks elapsed, for the small silver ring they had sounded over his own lately most disguised and most muffled vibrations.'' The use of tense is brilliant: the avoidance of the present and slide into the future makes narrative evasive. This sentence of generalized forecast is followed by another time-shift, into a generalized past: ''It had begun to be present . . . .'' What had begun was the haunting. It started with the vagueness of that image of responsive deep vibration—another evasion there as the image circles round the unspoken object sending out vibrations—and moves on to the image of an ''odd echo'' when he laughs at Alice and the superstitious Mrs Muldoon. These suggestions and avoidances of indication work like the avoidance of personal pronouns in ''this thing'' and ''it'' at the beginning of that dialogue about the ghost in the first scene of *Hamlet*, noticed by the sharp-eyed Coleridge as preparation for the growth of an undefined something into shocking materialization. James had created the extraordinary image of ineffable suspicion when Maggie circled the pagoda and knocked on its doorless surface to hear an echo of her knock, and now recycles the method for the purposes of fantasy. There is no more subtly psychologized ghost-story, and the subtlety links James's fantasy with his realism. His ghost stories are familiarized by psychic truths, his self-analysing psychological novels make imagination strange.

The story also shows James's stylistic and structural habit of scattering innocent-seeming images over the surface, images which turn out not to be superficial but profoundly relevant, pointing the way to conclusion with the utmost delicacy, like the early adjectives of illness in *The Wings of the Dove*. Here they are imagistic suggestions of the uncanny, more or less unobtrusive on first reading: ''queernesses,'' ''ugly,'' ''monstrosities,'' ''compartment of the mind never yet penetrated,'' play their part in what James called, in the Preface to *The Tragic Muse*, the novelist's, as well as the dramatist's ''art of preparations.'' But associations cluster rapidly after that small silver bell's vibration:

> It had begun to be present to him after the first fortnight, it had broken out with the oddest abruptness, this particular wanton wonderment: it met him there—and this was the image under which he himself judged the matter, or at least, not a little, thrilled and flushed with it—very much as he might have been met

by some strange figure, some unexpected occupant, at a turn of one of the dim passages of an empty house.

This speaks for itself. Earlier steps in the building of his fantasy are described less definitely but in suggestive images which accumulate suggestion: ''begun to be present,'' ''broken out,'' ''oddest,'' ''wanton,'' ''quaint,'' ''hauntingly.'' Such images prepare for the apparition innocently and perhaps subliminally.

The process, and our awareness of process, are stepped up, and the paragraph goes on to anticipate not only haunting and oddness but the future events of opened doors, empty rooms, passages, presence, dusk, and shock:

> when he didn't indeed rather improve on it by a still intenser form: that of his opening a door behind which he would have made sure of finding nothing, a door into a room shuttered and void, and yet so coming, with a great suppressed start, on some quite erect confronting presence, something planted in the middle of the place and facing him through the dusk.

This is a summary of what is to come, with small variations. But it is an oblique summary, since it does strike us as metaphor—which it is—so the clue is buried. A little later the collaborative process is taken up, in the detail of imagery, but after Mrs Muldoon's fear of ''craping'' round the upper rooms in the ''ayvil'' hours after dark has introduced real superstition. Agreeing that he has no reason for hanging on to the family house, Brydon says in relaxed colloquial image that he hasn't ''the ghost'' of a reason, only to have Alice press the dead metaphor into appropriate life, 'Are you very sure the ''ghost'' of one doesn't, much rather, serve—?' One of the story's several important unfinished sentences makes the shift from rhetoric to reality (fiction's reality) even clearer, before Brydon replies, with the proleptic and transformative expression, ''between a glare and a grin,'' with a proleptic and transformative admission, 'Oh ghosts—of course the place must swarm with them! I should be ashamed of it if it didn't.'

After this the ghost must walk, pressed into a ''lively stir''—another anticipatory half-dead image—by speculation and curiosity and desire. In other words, James, who described himself in *Notes of a Son and Brother* as ''a man of imagination,'' makes the hero of his story a man of imagination too.

Thus metaphor becomes reality, though of course a reality in a fiction. Brydon does what artists do, and the story is about itself. But it moves as an excellent ghost-story too. James knows as well as Shakespeare (especially in *Hamlet* but in *Macbeth*

too) that a ghost should enter stealthily and startlingly. The expectation of seeing Brydon's *alter ego*, or Hamlet's father's ghost, in no way weakens the shock of the appearance. James does something else like Shakespeare in *Hamlet*: he deflects our attention after putting us on the *qui vive*. Brydon, the ghost-seer to whose mind we are so close, thinks he has got free of the haunting. He flees downstairs from the room where he supposes the ghost to be, the room whose closed door makes him (and the reader) feel the apparition as an objective presence, outside the mind, to the presence waiting in the vestibule to shock him out of consciousness. He faints and falls on the great black and white marble floor—which first made him conscious of style, a characteristic example of fine small nuance, a bonus for the care James demands and rewards. Brydon's other self is terrifying and pitiable, though Brydon himself feels only the terror, and Alice is needed for pity. Perhaps it is easier to be afraid of oneself than to pity it, since self-pity has been so unfortunately disapproved, and Alice's tenderly imagined presence demonstrates the need we all have to be loved, and the way love's pity can be gladly received.

I used to think this story's achievement was its amazing imagining of the politics of identity through psychic division, and so it is; but I have come to believe that it is also James's great love-story. Love makes the divided self whole in understanding not only the existential self but also the whole potential. Love is another word for imagination, here demonstrated in Alice's ability to be present when Brydon's bruised ego wakes to wholeness, and to complete his knowledge of the stranger whose closeness is repugnant. Alice's dream of the flower in the bud is the dream of love, what Keats called Adam's dream, brilliantly imagined by James as a dream hard to dream. The lovers wake to find the dream true, but the woman has to dream for the man, as Penelope has to do the dreaming for Odysseus. Homer and James make the stay-at-home woman a type of negative capability and wise passiveness. Both emphasize intelligence so we should not mistake the location of creativity in the woman as patronizing. Homer calls Penelope the clever one, and shows her not only as the dreamer but as the analyst of dreams, false and true. Similarly, James shows Alice always a step ahead of Brydon's intelligence, rather as Maria Gostrey knows what is in store for Strether in Paris and Woollett. James's emphasis at the beginning on Alice's integrity, her ability to stay whole in the changing and self-destroying but creative New York, makes her a type of the passionate intellect which can put up the maximum resistance to conditioning. This is why her expertise is so valuable for her lover. She has maintained her quiet but ridden the streetcars. It seems likely at the beginning that he wants to be her lover, and at the end it is certain that he is:

> ''He has a million a year . . . but he hasn't you.''

> ''And he isn't—no—he isn't *you* !'' she murmured as he drew her to his breast.

A happy ending for Jamesian lovers is rare, though his first novel, *Watch and Ward*, imagined precisely this, but much less passionately and much less intelligently. The beauty of these middle-aged happy lovers is that they are old enough to know as well as still young enough to do. In *The Ambassadors* Strether was not able to marry his mentor Maria, and though James imagined him renouncing her, it is significant that he did not imagine Strether actually loving any of the three women—Mrs Newsome, Maria, and Marie de Vionnet—who seem to solicit his love. Strether is James's earlier demonstration of a man who, like Brydon, comes to acknowledge his constructed self, to re-imagine himself as a creature of history, but the novel's sense of reality chooses to enlighten him but not to reward or establish him either in the rich lax habitat of Paris or the moral materialist habitat of Woollett, Massachusetts. Strether is torn between two social constructions, seeing both and choosing neither. Brydon is Strether more tenderly imagined, and rewarded. The story is also a revision of the happy ending ambiguously offered at the end of *The Golden Bowl*, and it is satisfying to find that in ''The Jolly Corner'' James re-imagines that novel's key symbol, and restores its wholeness, The revisionary process is oblique, and I don't suggest that there is a very close resemblance between the two, only that the link shows that James wrote his 1908 story with the earlier symbol somewhere in his mind. The bowl in ''The Jolly Corner'' is a simile for the haunting, but it is neither gilded nor cracked, and is touched to music:

> feeling the place once more in the likeness of some great glass bowl, all precious concave crystal, set delicately humming by the play of a moist finger round its edge. The concave crystal held, as it were, this mystical other world, and the indescribably fine murmur of its rim was the sigh there . . . of all the old baffled possibilities.

It is dangerous, perhaps impossible, to hold love in a golden bowl, as Blake's Book of Thel instructed James, but James wonderfully shows that it can be held in crystal. (The New York *alter ego*, not Brydon, is the billionaire.) The purely metaphorical bowl of ''The Jolly Corner,'' like Keats's urn, is fragile but as yet unbroken. It is ungilded, without duplicity, crystalline in lucidity, a medium for light and music, a good omen. It is touch-and-go whether Brydon can accept the old baffled possibilities, after they have more humanly and horribly materialized, but the crystal bowl suggests something of the sanctity of a grail, to counteract the hideousness perceived by Brydon in the encountered stranger. Without this image the encounter with that other self would be simpler and harsher, and Alice's love for the potential more startlingly strange and artistically willed.

It is appropriate that James re-imagined the crystal bowl of his last great novel, since the image of the ghost in his repulsive aspect also began in *The Golden Bowl*. Maggie images the treachery suddenly perceived on her hearth, ''evil seated . . . where she had only dreamed of good'' as a surprise meeting, not round a corner but in a corridor: ''it had met her like some bad-faced stranger surprised in one of the thick-carpeted corridors of a house of quiet.'' There is an arcane relation between the two works, as there so often is in sibling works of art: *Richard III* is intimately recalled in *Macbeth*, ''Mr Gilfil's Love Story'' in *Daniel Deronda*. So if we compare the happy endings of love, it is clear that ''The Jolly Corner'' has the simple, benign and unambiguous ending, not undermined like *The Golden Bowl* by the destructiveness and complacency of Maggie's powerful victory over a powerful sister—destructive and complacent like many victories—nor by her unattractive and patronizing articulation of the novel's truth that Charlotte has been necessary in order to build her marriage. The ''black stranger'' is necessary for Brydon's fulfilment, but the interpretation is left to the reader's intelligence. In any case he is not (the fiction of) a human being with equal rights, only (the fiction of) a piteous might-have-been like Charles Lamb's dream children and the sentimental J. M. Barrie's unborn daughter in *Dear Brutus*. He is also politically significant as these little apparitions are not. Like them, he is endowed with affective life. Unlike them, he is not sad, but angered—Brydon supposes—by being haunted and hunted, and perhaps also, we may suppose, by meeting his rival's existence. (This is where the *scriptible* story's reversibility gets into play, stirring the reader into activity.) But he is invoked in order to be understood, pitied, perhaps admired, even loved.

It is a story, like *The Golden Bowl* and *The Wings of the Dove*, about sexual power and desire.

Alice tells Brydon clearly, at the beginning of their conversation about his *alter ego*, that the man he is so curious about, the man he would have been had he not stayed cultivating his perceptions in Europe—like so many of James's characters, and perhaps just a little like James himself—would have had power. Perhaps one implication of Brydon's fear, and acceptance, of his other self, the black stranger, is his fear and acceptance of his own virility. It is also why dreaming Alice is so drawn to him, not simply for the nobler reason that she loves the whole man, potential as well as actualized. Perhaps this is why Brydon can't complete his declaration of love, leaving it as an unfinished sentence—'I shouldn't have been waiting till now—'until he has encountered his grosser self, and died, like St Paul, Martin Chuzzlewit, and other heroes of *lysis*, or sudden conversion, in order to be resurrected.

It is also why he insists, after waking into full self-consciousness from a long unconsciousness, that he has died. He is in a coma for many hours, through "a long dark day." This interval in consciousness is one of the tantalizing gaps in James, famous for constructing *lacunae* and absences in his *scriptible* stories. When Brydon calls the coma a death, the gap becomes more interesting, and when he asks, 'in my strange darkness—where was it, what was it?' more interesting still. James remembers and suggestively reverses Hamlet's image of the bourn from which no traveller returns: "He had come back from further away than any man but himself had ever travelled." The emphasis is first on return, then fleetingly, on the journey: "it was strange how with this sense what he had come back *to* seemed really the great thing, and as if his prodigious journey had been all for the sake of it." The feeling and imagery of the fantasy "The Great Good Place" (1900) feed into this solemn mood of recovery and homecoming. Brydon and the story come to rest, and the mystery of where he has been is not solved by narration, only designated in the traditional metaphor of journey, with its suggestive but secret epithet "prodigious", colloquial and technical. As so often in James, the colloquial register lightens or quietens solemnity, while permitting it. (You never catch James rhapsodizing, like Thackeray, Dickens and George Eliot.) But there is a sense of prodigies, a rite of unspecified passage. The return emphasizes the relaxation after trauma, and after vision: "It had brought him to knowledge." It is satisfying that he returns to knowledge as well as love, like Cymbeline.

There is a sense of healing and convalescence after the strains, terrors and the vision of the ravaged life. This gives a particular tone to a traditional ritual of dying into resurrection. To describe the experience in these Christian terms seems too abstract, not quite right, though Brydon does ask Alice how she managed to turn up, and bring him "literally to life" "in the name of all the benedictions" and feels "beatitude" after she replies by kissing him. The particulars of the return to love are human, not religious, in spite of this language. So too are the particulars of the return to knowledge. And it is interesting that James doesn't end the story with the rapture of knowing or the holy calm of *nostos* but, after introducing these high points, takes the lovers through a humanly particularized retrospect and discussion, and ends with their declaration and embrace. It is not exactly understatement but it is a choice of the ordinary, rather than the extraordinary, aspect of the whole experience. James chose not to end with noumenal imagery of death and resurrection and prodigious journey but firmly returns us to the phenomenal world.

The noumenal imagery is socially grounded. Perhaps one would die after a full lucid sight of historical possibility, which in this case includes a full lucid sight of the self, potential and actual. In a simpler, but not dissimilar, fable of conditioning and attempted freedom, the more pessimistic ghost-story "Owen Wingrave" (1892), the hero does die after confronting the unequivocal aggression of his militant ancestor and *alter ego*: James is revising this fable after a long interval. In *The Sense of the Past*, and the scenario-notes for its continuation, James is especially interested in the psychic strain of time-travel, and perhaps one reason for his failure to finish the novel is the sheer difficulty of sustaining the narrative of such an experience at length. Confronting an historical alternative is an experience more easily dealt with in a short story.

It is an experience from which only fictional characters can recover, and only fictional characters can experience. James imagined it, and must have come pretty close to it, as the story suggests. And not only the story. The imagining of a might-have-been in "The Jolly Corner" is backed up by the sort of thing James said to friends about his choice of the single life, where he is evidently considering unacted possibilities. For instance, he told Grace Norton that he felt happier and more powerful after he made up his mind not to marry. Not that this would be the only glance back at unlived choices. The return journey in 1904, articulated in *The American Scene,* also stirred speculative retrospect. James's sharpened experience of life-choices obviously lies behind the astonishing ghost-story, informing and forming his imaginative grasp of historical construction. He is the great anti-essentialist to emerge out of Victorian fiction into the twentieth century.

Source: Barbara Hardy, "The Jolly Corner," in *Henry James—The Shorter Fiction: Reassessments*, edited by N. H. Reeve, St. Martin's Press, Inc., 1997, pp. 190-208.

Russell J. Reising

In his historicist reading of "The Jolly Corner," Reising sees the story "not as a mirror of a stable and coherent moment in history but as a text that represents, through its own flux and contradictions, an arena of social and cultural change."

I

At the conclusion of "The Jolly Corner" Spencer Brydon recovers consciousness (after swooning at the sight of his double) in the lap of his friend, Alice Staverton. In sharp contrast to the complex and sometimes violent imagery of Brydon's experience throughout the extraordinary middle section of the tale, the mood of the brief, concluding section is mild and conciliatory. Significantly, it is Alice Staverton, not Brydon, who dominates that final scene, both physically and verbally. The barely conscious Brydon is aware, as he comes to, of his head "pillowed in extraordinary softness and faintly refreshing fragrance . . . and he finally knew that Alice Staverton had made her lap an ample and perfect cushion to him." Throughout this section Brydon and Staverton engage in a remarkably conventional and sentimental dialogue. Brydon, for example, remarks,

> 'Yes—I can only have died. You brought me literally to life. Only,' he wondered, his eyes rising to her, 'only, in the name of all benedictions, how?'

> It took her but an instant to bend her face and kiss him, and something in the manner of it, and in the way her hands clasped and locked his head while he felt the cool charity and virtue of her lips, something in all this beatitude somehow answered everything. 'And now I keep you,' she said.

> 'Oh keep me, keep me!' he pleaded while her face still hung over him: in response to which it dropped again and stayed close, clingingly close.

The tale ends with an embrace, projecting this emotionally lush and intimate final scene into an implicitly romantic future. Too sentimental? Perhaps. Staverton's clasping and locking Brydon's head as she stays clingingly close, however, jars with the cloying tone of these final lines and much of the concluding of the tale.

"The Jolly Corner" has been regarded solely and obviously as an examination of Spencer Brydon's character and crisis, and James criticism has marginalized Brydon's friend, Alice Staverton, viewing her as an appendage to the "hero" of the tale. Critics offer hope that Spencer Brydon will achieve a sense of psychic wholeness "through [this] woman's unselfish, all comprehending love," or view Staverton as Brydon's conscience, as "the integrating spirit, the principle of divine love which makes selfhood possible in the fullest sense," as a "prize" for Brydon, as an "all-forgiving, all accepting mother figure," embodying the "redemptive power of love," as an "example for the reader of the tale" (by virtue of her understanding the complex figurative reality of Brydon's vision), and as a "frame character," whose "most important function is to be sensitively aware of those muffled vibrations" of Brydon's. Such readings share the view that the tale valorizes Brydon's priorities, while Staverton is valuable primarily insofar as she validates his identity. Such readings do not take as problematic either the uncharacteristic sentimentality of the final scene or the appropriative implications of Staverton's locking and keeping Brydon.

Nonetheless, while viewing Staverton as typical of many women in James's tales—more a passive sounding-board for a man's ideas than an active participant in the narrative action—may be normative, it is not, I feel, correct and should not go unexamined. In fact, Alice Staverton's role in "The Jolly Corner," like so much of that tale, is an anomaly in James's canonical short fiction. Staverton, no less than Brydon, is situated in a complex historical and political world that, in her case, defines and constrains her options, priorities, and rhetorical strategies as a woman in turn-of-the-century United States. The historical frame of James's tale encompasses the later half of the nineteenth century (Brydon leaves the United States as a young man at about the time of the Civil War and returns just after the turn of the century), and James's representation of Staverton draws extensively on representations of women from early to late nineteenth-century Anglo-American discourses. I will also be drawing on texts even earlier than this explicit chronology (but, for the most part, coherent with the characters' plausible pre-narrative biographies) in order better to suggest popular representations of women and women's political status that would constitute the discourse of women's power informing the historical reference of James's text. Such a focus reveals James's tale not as a mirror of a stable and coherent moment in history but as a text that represents, through its own flux and contradictions, an arena of social and cultural change.

This new perspective on Staverton's role in "The Jolly Corner" can productively follow the methodological revisions called for by feminist historians and literary critics. For example, Judith Fetterley argues that "the first act of the feminist critic [explicitly of American culture, but implicitly of all cultures] must be to become a residing rather than an assenting reader" of all texts that have become sedimented with masculinist critical priorities. The historian Carroll Smith-Rosenberg defines her own revisionist project by arguing that the major limitation of traditional historiography inheres in its viewing women as only acting roles in a male script.

> It fails to look for evidence of women's reaction, of the ways women manipulated men and events to create new fields of power or to assert female autonomy. . . . [Women's historians] see history as an ongoing struggle between women and men actors for control of the script, a struggle that ultimately transforms the play, the players—even the theater itself. But if we reject the view of women as passive victims, we face the need to identify the sources of power women used to act within a world determined to limit their power, to ignore their talents, to belittle or condemn their actions.

To draw on Smith-Rosenberg's metaphor, Alice Staverton is more than a supporting actress in this tale; she is fully Brydon's cultural, if not his social and financial, equal. In three senses in particular—her actions, her imaginative boldness, and her rhetoric—she signals the complex historical dialectic marking the emergence of a new political strategy for American women. Historicizing Staverton's role throughout the tale, and particularly in the final section, helps us not only to grasp her place in the social world of the tale, but also to account for the bizarre shift in James's tone and to avoid the masculine priorities that characterize much criticism of this tale.

II

It is important to note that Staverton is remarkably like Brydon in many ways. Both characters represent a troubled response to modernity and its economic and cultural upheavals, to the shock of the new. Upon his return to New York after a thirty-three-year sojourn in Europe, Brydon stands repelled by the altered face of modern urban life and defines both himself and Staverton in opposition to

> " Alice Staverton's differences from earlier historical and literary representations of women's ideas and practices, then, can be read as marking the emergence of a new set of strategies and options for women."

modern life. He finds solace amidst modern disorder in two places: in his family home—the "jolly corner" of the title—and in Alice Staverton's flat, which he values as "a small still scene where items and shades, all delicate things, kept the sharpness of the notes of a high voice perfectly trained, and where economy hung about life like the scent of a garden." Similarly, Alice Staverton's quarters in Irving Place, roughly like the jolly corner in their seclusion and in its associations, are *her* haven from New York life. As Brydon defines her, "His old friend lived with one maid and herself dusted her relics and trimmed her lamps and polished her silver; she stood off, in the awful modern crush, when she could, but she sallied forth and did battle when the challenge was really to 'spirit,' the spirit she after all confessed to, proudly and a little shyly, as to that of the better time, that of *their* common, their quite faraway and antediluvian social period and order." Like Brydon's, Staverton's world seems a regressive one, opposing the "awful modern crush" at every crucial point. Her solitude, her quaintly anachronistic dusting of relics and trimming of lamps, and the arcane knowledge she shares with Brydon of their "ante-diluvian" past all suggest that Alice Staverton, like Brydon, is a genteel warrior against modernity.

Throughout "The Jolly Corner" the two properties Brydon owns—his high-rise apartment house and his family home—represent two conflicting sets of values in American culture, an aggressive commercial life versus one of high ideality and culture, and serve as two poles around which many of the other oppositions in the tale cluster. Brydon's two structures, that is, make concrete the essential contrast in ''The Jolly Corner'' between sentiment and traditional values, on the one hand, and industrialization and modernization in general on the other. George Santayana associated this split in American culture with what he termed the ''genteel tradition'' and he offers an architectural trope strikingly appropriate for ''The Jolly Corner'': ''This division [industry versus culture] may be found symbolized in American architecture: a neat reproduction of the colonial mansion—with some modern comforts introduced surreptitiously—stands beside the skyscraper. The American Will inhabits the skyscraper; the American Intellect inhabits the colonial mansion. The one is the sphere of the American man; the other, at least predominantly, of the American woman. The one is all aggressive enterprise; the other is all genteel tradition.'' Santayana's image (roughly contemporary with James's tale) neatly coincides with the representation in the tale of modern New York as a world split between social transformation and aggressive enterprise on the one hand, and a realm of cultural and spiritual values on the other. Brydon's high-rise parallels Santayana's skyscraper, the jolly corner his colonial mansion.

A new constellation for the family emerged along with this perceived split in American culture. Many of the terms and contradictions associated with this domestic milieu inform the terms and contradictions represented in Alice Staverton's role in ''The Jolly Corner.'' The American family responded to the emerging urban, industrial order by more systematically defining itself as a humane and consoling alternative to the world of ruthless and mechanized enterprise. This localized split, however, played off society at large in two contradictory ways—assuming an arguably new identity as what Christopher Lasch refers to as a ''haven in a heartless world,'' while at the same time mirroring the split in American culture with its own stereotyped division of labor. The Reverend Charles Burroughs articulated a version of this ideology in *An Address on Female Education, Delivered in Portsmouth, N. H., Oct. 26, 1827,* in which he communicated this vision to young women in his audience: ''It is at home, where man . . . seeks a refuge from the vexations and embarrassments of business, an enchanting repose from exertion, a relaxation from care by the interchange of affection: where some of his finest sympathies, tastes, and moral and religious feelings are formed and nourished;—where is the treasury of pure disinterested love, such as is seldom found in . . . a selfish and calculating world.''

The emotional response to the putative hostility of this ''selfish and calculating world'' was the glorification of private life and of the family, which ''represented the other side of the bourgeois perception of society as something alien, impersonal, remote, and abstract—a world from which pity and tenderness had fled in horror.''

The woman's place in this domestic matrix was complicated by her being designated as the guardian—often the virtual embodiment—of the values associated with home and the family. The genderized terms of this ideological milieu permeate even technical and economic discourses of Victorian Anglo-American culture. According to the industrialist Peter Gaskell, ''the moral influence of woman upon man's character and domestic happiness, is mainly attributable to her natural and instinctive habits. Her love, her tenderness, her affectionate solicitude for his comfort and enjoyment, her devotedness, her unwearying care, her maternal fondness, her conjugal attractions, exercise a most ennobling impression upon his nature, and do more towards making a good husband, a good father, and a useful citizen, than all the dogmas of political economy.'' Gaskell's explicit contrast of the domestic and maternal role played by women with ''all the dogmas of political economy'' provides a powerful analogue to James's vision of the ideological work of gender in late Victorian America; both imagine the realms of public and private life in tenuous opposition. According to Eli Zaretsky, in the nineteenth century, ''the housewife emerged, alongside the proletarian—the two characteristic labourers of developed capitalistic society. Her tasks extended beyond the material labour of the family to include responsibility for the 'human values' which the family was thought to preserve: love, personal happiness, domestic felicity. . . . The split in society between 'personal feelings' and 'economic production' was integrated with the sexual division of labor. Women were identified with emotional life, men with the struggle for existence.'' Of course, ''The Jolly Corner'' is about neither housewives nor proletarians, but Gaskell's and Zaretsky's remarks nevertheless illuminate Alice Staverton's status in the world of ''The Jolly Corner.'' Alice Staverton's role as guardian of human values takes the form of her quaint domesticity, her trimming of candles and polishing of lamps. It also appears in her urging Brydon to humanize the jolly corner by living in it and in her pillowing and cushioning him at the conclusion of the tale. Her role as emotional guardian is reinforced by her nearly clairvoyant reading of Brydon's feelings. She has dreams in which Brydon's alter ego appears to her, suggesting the profundity of her capacity to understand and accept.

The imagery associated with Staverton (and with the jolly corner) also situates her within the context of genteel and sacred Victorian womanhood. Harriet Beecher Stowe, for example, articulated the sanctification of the American housewife in *The Minister's Wooing* (1859): ''priestess, wife, and mother, there she ministers daily in holy works of peace, and by faith and prayer and love redeems from grossness and earthliness the common toils and wants of life.'' Magazine articles and other popular literary genres throughout the nineteenth century voiced related sentiments. As early as 1840, the *Ladies' Magazine* issued a typical panegyric on the virtues of the model woman: ''See, she sits, she walks, she speaks, she looks—unutterable things! Inspiration springs up in her very paths—it follows her footsteps. A halo of glory envelops her, and illumines her whole orbit. With her, man not only feels safe but is actually renovated. For he approaches her with an awe, in reverence, and an affection which before he knew not he possessed.'' As Ann Douglas comments, the woman was ''of value because she [was] able to work a religious transformation in man; she represents nothing finally but a state of susceptibility to very imprecisely conceived spiritual values.'' In a similar vein, Lasch argues that late-century husbands and wives escaped the dehumanizing ''world of commerce and industry'' by finding ''solace and spiritual renewal in each other's company. The woman in particular would serve, in a well-worn nineteenth-century phrase, as an . . . angel of consolation.'' Of course, poetic work such as Coventry Patmore's *The Angel in the House* and Tennyson's *The Princess* provide literary representations of the sexual division of labor characteristic of mid and late nineteenth-century Anglo-American culture as well as of the sacred aura imposed on women by male ideologues. As Carol Christ comments on these poems, ''woman possesses a purity, a self-sufficiency, a wholeness, but man, for Tennyson as for Patmore, is disjointed, never at peace.''

Such religious associations, in fact, characterize Alice Staverton's role throughout the tale. Brydon himself asserts her redemptive powers when, upon waking up in her lap, he refers to the ''mystifying grace of her appearance'' and when he asserts, ''Yes—I can only have died. You brought me literally to life. . . . only, in the name of all benedic-

tions, how?'' Brydon's other spiritualized terms for Staverton's agency—virtue, charity, and beatitude—only confirm the divine role she plays for him.

At this point one might conclude that Staverton's role in ''The Jolly Corner'' is normative—that she represents trivialized genteel femininity and that the jolly corner and a ''woman's sphere'' are roughly synonymous zones. Staverton could be seen, then, as the angel of the jolly corner (a divine and consoling alternative to the beastly specter that confronts Brydon), as an agent of the love implicitly absent from the ''chilled adolescence'' of Brydon's childhood, or as a successful May Bartram who triumphs where her predecessor had failed. These interpretive options correspond roughly to the prevailing critical assessments of Staverton's role in the tale as a divine center of love, as an image of maternal care and affection, or as a sensitive auditor for Brydon's privileged anguish. But if critics of ''The Jolly Corner'' have responded to these significant narrative details, they have tended to abstract and/or mythicize them rather than to situate them historically, and consequently they have simplified the very attitudes they attempt to elucidate.

III

While Staverton does embody a suggestive array of traits definitive of the trivialized bourgeois matron, she also strains against those conventions in a manner that marks an important departure from an earlier mode and signals the emergence of a new strategy of feminine politics. It is important to note that the narrative moments situating her within the so-called cult of domesticity tend to be either remarks made by Brydon or perspectives mirroring *his* priorities—they are not remarks made by Staverton nor are they perspectives consistent with how we see her independently of Brydon's commentary. We can, then, profitably shift our focus to Staverton's own words and actions in order to fashion our understanding of her role in the tale.

Staverton is not simply a feminine version of the male protagonist in the tale—her differences from Brydon are many and significant. In one important respect, Staverton's status as a single woman in the turn-of-the-century United States distinguishes her, though such unmarried women tended to be regarded more as problems for a male economy than as successes as New Women. According to Lasch, a rising divorce rate and a falling birth rate among ''better sorts'' in late nineteenth-century American cities constituted a national problem. While Theodore Roosevelt addressed the ''problem'' of sluggish birthrates among middle-class white women, medical science was tending to represent the unmarried woman as a significant health risk. According to Carroll Smith-Rosenberg and Charles Rosenberg, ''the maiden lady, many physicians argued, was fated to a greater incidence of both physical and emotional disease than her married sisters and to a shorter life-span. Her nervous system was placed under constant pressure, and her unfulfilled reproductive organs—especially at menopause—were prone to cancer and other degenerative ills.'' Apparently, single men were a hardier breed and immune to such internal disorders. We need, of course, to read such warnings as ideological prescription rather than ''scientific'' description; however, we can situate the supposed dangers Alice Staverton and other women like her were risking as a powerful challenge to Brydon's imagining himself in danger on a ''big-game'' hunt (a veiled allusion to Roosevelt's own ''vigorous'' pursuits?). Indicating that single women were perceived as a ''problem'' on the other side of the Atlantic, the manufacturer W. R. Greg complained of ''an enormous and increasing number of single women in the nation, a number quite disproportionate and quite abnormal . . . who, not having the natural duties and labours of wives and mothers, have to carve out artificial and painfully sought occupations for themselves; who, in place of completing, sweetening, and embellishing the existence of others, are compelled to lead an independent and incomplete existence of their own.'' To this extent, women were, paradoxically, blamed for a perceived decline in birthrates and crisis in family (and, in England, class) stability even while they were pitied as victims of recent economic and industrial transformations. Staverton's ability to weather such ideological assaults on the viability of single womanhood is at least a partial indication of her ability to withstand potentially hostile trends in public opinion while adhering to her own image of her life. Staverton's apparent physical health in the midst of traumatic urban change is even noted by Brydon when he remarks that her physical appearance ''defied you to say if she were a fair young woman who looked older through trouble, or a fine smooth older one who looked young through successful indifference.''

Staverton's strengths and inner resources as well as her adaptability to cultural and social transformation are represented directly in a variety of other ways. While distinctly ''genteel'' and refined (though, perhaps, embattled), she nonetheless operates actively within modern New York on its own terms. For example, she stands off from the modern crush when possible, but ''she sallied forth and did battle when the challenge was really to 'spirit,''' and she rides the street cars and confronts ''all the public concussions and ordeals.'' She admires both Brydon's skill in debating a construction company representative and the knowledge of building techniques he exhibits. Staverton again demonstrates a greater imaginative response to New York and to Brydon's potential when she suggests to Brydon that, had he only remained in New York, ''he would have anticipated the inventor of the sky-scraper,'' words that eventually precipitate Brydon's search for the Other self he might have become. Staverton, we realize, is capable of articulating an alternative history for Brydon, one in which she understands the kind of aggressive enterprise, invention, and complicity in a new economic and urban order that Brydon feels is only monstrous and ugly.

She also demonstrates a bolder imagination by envisioning in her dreams the grizzled self Brydon might have become had he stayed in New York. Brydon, we recall, faints away at the hideous sight of this alter ego and rejects the possibility of that Other holding any significance for his life. As Staverton attempts to reeducate Brydon concerning the identity of his Other in the final moments of the tale, her question as to why she should not have liked the ''black stranger''

> brought Spencer Brydon to his feet. 'You ''like'' that horror—?'
>
> 'I *could* have liked him. And to me,' she said, 'he was no horror. I had accepted him.'
>
> '''Accepted''—?' Brydon oddly sounded.
>
> 'Before, for the interest of his difference—yes. And as I did n't disown him, as I knew him—which you at last, confronted with him in his difference, so cruelly did n't, my dear—well, he must have been, you see, less dreadful to me.'

The important difference in this and other similar exchanges is that where Brydon polarizes his identity from that of his Other (and the jolly corner from his skyscraper), Staverton attempts to undo the imagined opposition between Brydon and the self he might have become. Both Staverton's recurring dreams of this grizzled figure and her explicit remarks about accepting him, then, suggest the extent to which she has confronted the competitive and potentially disarming forces of cultural and social transformation. Whereas Brydon rejects this vision, Staverton integrates it.

We can return to the architectural trope for Brydon's real estate for a final illustration of this point. Brydon, we remember, imagines an absolute split between the jolly corner and his soon-to-be-gentrified high rise. Staverton, however, challenges Brydon's distinction between the two worlds of the tale when she remarks to Brydon, as he is badgered by others to commercialize the jolly corner in addition to his apartments, ''In short you're to make so good a thing out of your sky-scraper, living in luxury on *those* ill-gotten gains you can afford for a while to be sentimental here!'' Staverton understands that one needs to be able to *afford* to be sentimental. Rather than representing antithetical worlds, Brydon's two properties, in Staverton's vision, are mutually constitutive of a new urban formation in which the interrelationship of culture and economics is no longer veiled or deniable but made manifest. Whereas Brydon's vision is one of unresolved and antagonistic polarities, Staverton grasps and argues for the interpenetration of the two worlds of the tale. Any self-respecting ''angel of the house'' would almost certainly fear to tread this path toward a new urban, industrial order.

In *Disorderly Conduct*, Smith-Rosenberg provides a useful historical paradigm for Staverton's divergences from an earlier domestic model. During the 1870s and 1880s, Smith-Rosenberg notes, ''a new bourgeois woman had emerged. Confident and independent, a self-created urban expert, she spearheaded bourgeois efforts to respond creatively to the new city and the new economy. In the process of working for herself and other women, she had begun to demand equality in education, in employment, and in wages. Certain of her own abilities, she began again to demand the vote, so as to implement her new social visions more effectively. In short, she had politicized gender.'' I do not intend to suggest that Alice Staverton fully embodies the traits Smith-Rosenberg attributes to this new female crusader or that she represents an unambiguous and stable image of women in turn-of-the-century United States. Staverton is in some respects too patient (she waits thirty some years for Brydon's return) and too passive (it is possible she imagines a union with Brydon as the fulfillment of her life). She does, nonetheless, represent in her actions as well as in her response to a new economic and social order some of the traits Smith-Rosenberg cites as definitive markers of this New Woman. Staverton also represents some of the historically specific options made available to women following the power and labor shortages brought on by the Civil War. Wom-

en entering public activity following the war acquired experience in techniques of industrial organization and political mobilization, and by so doing recognized not only their independence but their ability to effect social change as well.

This instrumental role is most significantly represented in Staverton's speech. Staverton's apparent lack of a decisive (or at least an unambiguous) voice may be the result of her being subordinated in a position so manifestly dictated by the male hegemony over mass culture. That we see her more than we hear her in the tale may suggest that Staverton counters the dominance both of men and of voice represented in ''The Jolly Corner'' with an array of tactics meant to preempt Brydon's own attempt to control the world through his own economic and political practice. Her problem is that Brydon simply does not comprehend any of her statements, even those of assurance, support, or acceptance, because they are articulated from a position alien to his own social, economic, and gendered perspective. However, while Staverton's direct role is limited to parts one and three of the tale, where she exists primarily as a discursive presence that confounds Brydon as much as her physical presence consoles him, she might also be understood as the precipitating agency in the narrative, motivating even the protracted and stylistically demanding account of Brydon's search for his Other in part two of ''The Jolly Corner.'' For example, after she broaches the topic of what Brydon might have become had he only stayed at home, his growing obsession with his potential alter ego produces in him a defensiveness that makes him bristle and interpret her assurances as challenges. Moreover, after she intimates that, though ''quite huge and monstrous,'' Brydon's other self would not have been entirely contemptible, Brydon asks, ''You'd have liked me that way?'' to which his friend gently responds, ''How should I not have liked you?'' Entirely missing the implied reconciliation as well as the imaginative strength in Staverton's answer, Brydon wrongly concludes, ''I see. You'd have liked me, have preferred me, a billionaire!'' Staverton immediately counters—''How should I not have liked you?'' but the point is lost on Brydon. He is incapable of comprehending the discourse of a feminine other.

''The Jolly Corner'' concludes, however, with an embrace sealing Staverton's and Brydon's apparently shared understanding of Brydon's relationship with his Other, not with a further exacerbation of their linguistic difficulties:

Then, 'He has a million a year,' he lucidly added. 'But he hasn't you.'

'And he isn't—no, he isn't— *you* !' she murmured as he drew her to his breast.

Staverton's hesitation in this final sentence, along with her many remarks earlier in the tale suggesting that Brydon's identity is not so simply separated from that of his Other, points to the likelihood that, in these final lines, she may well be lying, agreeing with Brydon not because she actually shares his perception (we know, in fact, that she does not), but because she realizes that by corroborating Brydon's interpretation she accomplishes a significant transformation of his priorities and future.

IV

How do we account for what appears to be a lie, however, in the context of the representation in ''The Jolly Corner'' of genderized political struggle? We might refer to Marlow's lie to Kurtz's intended—a lie Marlow justifies as a strategy to protect the woman from a truth too dark for her to comprehend or bear. Staverton's prevarication would reverse the gender roles—here a woman protects an aging man from a truth too horrible for him to bear—but it also secures an emotional (and perhaps financial and political) victory for her. We might also turn to another late James work for significant intertextual resonance. Alice Staverton's subtle, yet authoritative and successful, verbal ministrations can be read as a later examination of what Maggie Verver accomplishes in *The Golden Bowl*. While very different in age, both Verver and Staverton operate in linguistically subtle and strategic ways to achieve and protect their vision of their lives and futures. Both do so by lying.

Elizabeth Allen's *A Woman's Place in the Novels of Henry James* is so synthetic and so compatible with my argument that I will briefly summarize her position on Maggie Verver in order to establish Verver's relationship with her successor, Alice Staverton. Central to James's representation of women is the struggle between their existing as *signs* for male interpretation and consumption and as *selves* capable either of themselves becoming interpreters of others or of mystifying (and thereby manipulating) the process whereby men transform women into grist for their masculinist interpretive mills. A woman's function in *The Golden Bowl*, according to Allen, is ''to mediate experience for those [men] in control; to order either by representation, or by arranging existing appearances and making sense of them.'' Maggie Verver succeeds large-ly by virtue of her mastering the linguistic channels through which social (and domestic) reality is mediated and through her mastery over linguistic signs and the arrangements they are meant to signify, triumphing in controlling the delicate and, for women, potentially destructive dynamics of social *and* sexual intercourse. As Allen argues,

> if Maggie is to preserve social form and take her place within it . . . she has to function in recognisable forms, speak understandable language. The fact that this involves lying and deceit reminds us of the self-assertion that is simultaneous within this process of repair and conservation. Maggie pretends to be a fool, she pretends to be an unchallenged and unchallenging wife. . . . Her selfhood is asserted through concealment, her signification is that of opacity and mystery and she gains, if not the intimacy of being, for another, herself, at least the attention of the Prince.

Allen's description of Maggie Verver's triumphant rearrangement of the domestic relations at the conclusion of *The Golden Bowl* touches on what I regard as Alice Staverton's similarly successful transformation of Brydon at the conclusion of ''The Jolly Corner'' in a number of ways. Both Maggie and Alice confront threats to their futures, and, after coming to understandings of these crises, both privately formulate strategies for combating them. Both deploy subtle verbal manipulations of the realities they share with the other characters—they articulate and promote versions of the past and present that insure that the future unfolds according to their terms. Finally, the strategies and successes of both Maggie Verver and of Alice Staverton remain unknown to the men whose realities they were designed to disrupt. Completed just a few years after the publication of *The Golden Bowl*, ''The Jolly Corner'' can be read as James's projection of the verbal and genderized dynamics of his late novelistic work, replete with overt sexual and economic issues, into the work of his late tales, in which the characters' older ages and barely examined social and financial statuses seem to mystify, if not to suppress, explicit questions of sexual and financial power.

In addition to furthering James's analysis into discursive strategies available to women, Staverton's oblique approach to cornering Brydon has analogues in the political discourses of disenfranchised women in the nineteenth century. Speaking of the paradoxical position of middle-class women in nineteenth-century America, Ann Douglas notes that a woman's future quite literally depended ''on the willingness and ability of her male peers, increasingly absorbed in the tasks of settlement and competition, to recognize the values which their activity apparently denied.'' Although women played active roles in political and social undertakings such as anti-war pacifism and temperance movements, Douglas reminds us that ''women were more likely . . . to evince their concern by less direct and conspicuous means.'' For example, Harriet Farley, one of the editors of the *Lowell Offering*, advocated ''picniques'' over strikes as an appropriate vehicle for feminine protest against factory conditions. By way of rationalizing so delicate and arguably ineffective a strategy, Farley explained, ''To convince people, we must gain access to them: to do this we cannot assault them with opinions contrary to their own. We cannot harm them by revealing the deprivation which could suggest our rage and their danger. We must sugarcoat the proverbial pill. . . . we must 'do good by stealth.''' Alice Staverton succeeds at winning Brydon to her point of view by precisely such nonconfrontational means.

If we read (as critics have tended to read) Alice Staverton's circumvention of direct confrontation ahistorically, her goals might appear simply regressive and domestic, and her apparent complicity in enabling Brydon to reject the significance of his Other could be read as a lie that caters to Brydon's vision. However, by historicizing the complex representation of social and sexual struggle in the tale, we can also discern within this moment Alice Staverton's own deployment of the subtle political action that Farley advocates, suggested in the ''way her hands clasped and locked his head,'' in her face staying ''clingingly close'' to Brydon's, in her assertion ''And now I keep you,'' and, finally, in the likelihood that she has transformed Brydon, has ''won'' him to her vision of his past and their future. Alice Staverton gently, though effectively, closes off Brydon's private search for his true self and opens him up to her ministrations, which, in sharp contrast to those of an ''angel in the house,'' will escape domestic containment and extend into the realm of social and political organization. And, like Maggie Verver's ''lies'' in *The Golden Bowl*, Staverton's ''lie'' (as well as her clasping and locking Brydon's head) can also be regarded as thoroughly conscious, an exercise of women's historically specific political praxis calculated to generate a new social arrangement.

Ann Douglas argues that the mission of the heroine in women's historical novels in the nineteenth century ''is to free the hero from history: she rescues him paradoxically from the historical novel, which she transmutes into a domestic tale.'' ''The Jolly Corner'' begins in a complex historical world filled with the material facts of newly modernized and internally divided America and with Spencer Brydon's struggle to grasp his place in so contradictory a world. The tale ends with Staverton and Brydon falling into each others' arms, repudiating (or at least tabling) the potentially disruptive social significance of Brydon's Other, while possibly ushering in a newly feminized social order. Brydon's willingly accepting her agency in his life offers a fitting conclusion to the tale—Staverton has Brydon cornered, as it were, in the jolly corner.

This political struggle also registers in the generic flux of the tale. Section one of ''The Jolly Corner'' reads nearly like Howellsian realism, replete with amply documented urban landscapes, homely architectural detail, and an account of the characters' lives amidst a volatile urban scene. Section three, on the other hand, reads more like domestic romance, but romance with a political difference. Whatever emotional energies the final pages represent are framed within Staverton's subtly politicized operations within modern New York. It is not, then, completely accurate to argue that Staverton rescues Brydon from the historical narrative (as Douglas's model might suggest). More to the point, Staverton's words and actions initiate Brydon into a different historical experience, one that generates the generic transformations within James's tale. In this respect, Staverton's ''lie'' is not a sacrifice of the ''truth'' of Brydon's condition as much as it is a recasting of the very grounds of truth in an emerging urban order in which women are no longer subordinate figures.

V

How does one account for the contradictions characterizing Staverton's role in ''The Jolly Corner''? One might recall that the tropes situating her as the angel of the jolly corner are Brydon's, or at least come from a narrative voice representing Brydon's perspective, and that another view of Staverton emerges once we focus on *her* words and actions expressed in relatively uncontaminated narrative commentary. I have argued that the array of differences in James's text can be approached from the perspective of gender analysis and sexual politics. However, we might also note that Brydon's perspective corresponds not only to a male definition of a woman's role but to an earlier historical era as well, dating roughly from the time of his leaving the United States for Europe, even before that. Staverton's ''disorderly conduct'' happens to correspond more closely with an image of women's power and priorities roughly coincidental with the narrative present of the tale. Brydon represents his friend, then, in largely anachronistic terms. Staverton, despite some arguably arcane habits, presents herself in a grammar (of actions and words) both more contemporary and more complex. In terms of James's narrative, this difference points to the important implications of Brydon's and Staverton's respective histories. Brydon, absent from the United States for over thirty years, returns with outdated notions of cultural and social forces, of the urban landscape as well as of women's place. Like Julian West in Edward Bellamy's *Looking Backward*, Brydon confronts the present with the vocabulary of the past. Staverton, presumably as a result of her remaining in New York, embodies a variety of progressive skills and strategies. Like many a character in Howells or Dreiser, indeed, like many a realist author, Staverton is energized by the pulse of an active and changing American urban reality. In other words, James's text lies on the margins of the genre of naturalism, suggesting a close and crucial connection between one's material and historical conditions and one's ideological assumptions and conduct.

To shift briefly to a different vocabulary, Brydon's perspective corresponds roughly to what Raymond Williams terms "residual," while Staverton represents Williams's notion of "emergent" cultural forces. For Williams, any dominant cultural formation is characterized by "internal dynamic relations" and contains elements both residual of earlier forms and emergent of transformations to come. The "residual" means, in Williams's lexicon, practices and structures of feeling formed in the past but "still active in the cultural process, not only and often not at all as an element of the past, but as an effective element of the present." The emergent, on the other hand, marks "new meanings and values, new practices, new relationships and kinds of relationship [that] are continually being created," usually in "relation to the emergence and growing strength of a class." The differences inscribed within "The Jolly Corner" between Brydon and Staverton as well as between Brydon's view of Staverton and her own serf-presentation suggest a dynamic of cultural and genderized struggle analogous to that which Williams argues characterizes any cultural moment.

Two recent feminist perspectives corroborate Williams's vision. Amidst the fluidity of late nineteenth-century America, Elizabeth Allen notes, "one might expect to find change, even progress, in the role and status of women. What one does find is a confusing mix of old and new ideology, of women as somehow more than anything the example of the new nation with new freedoms, and yet at the same time more than anything the constant amidst flux, the paragon of perennial domesticity and, again, social relations." Mary Poovey offers a compatible reading of such "uneven developments" when she argues that the ideological formation of mid-Victorian England "was uneven both in the sense of being experienced differently by individuals who were positioned differently within the social formation (by sex, class, or race, for example) and in the sense of being articulated differently by the different institutions, discourses, and practices that it both constituted and was constituted by." Poovey's work also provides important insight into the difficulty of identifying the roles that women played in the emergence of feminist politics when she addresses the likelihood that women working out of the public view and "behind the scenes," as it were, were often as important as more public spokeswomen for women's rights Such is, in fact, the cultural fluidity and historical stutter represented by Alice Staverton's role.

Alice Staverton's differences from earlier historical and literary representations of women's ideas and practices, then, can be read as marking the emergence of a new set of strategies and options for women. That those options are not yet consolidated in James's text but exist in solution with an earlier, anachronistic view of Staverton suggests the troubled history of any new area of political practice. In fact, "The Jolly Corner" reinscribes similar fissures of these modern social and historical upheavals within the contradictory social, material, and architectural tropes. Nothing exists simply or self-identically in the world of "The Jolly Corner."

It is not my intent to define James as either an incipient proletarian or feminist novelist, only to suggest that his relationship to matters of social change and to women's issues are, at least in his fiction, more complicated than many critics grant. Consider Terry Eagleton in a definition of James's reactionary political significance. James's work, Eagleton asserts, "represents a desperate, devoted attempt to salvage organic significance wholly in the sealed realm of conciousness—to vanquish, by the power of such 'beautiful,' multiple yet harmoniously unifying awareness, certain real conflicts and divisions." I would comment only briefly that "The

Jolly Corner.'' represents nothing if not the omnipresence of conflicts, divisions, and contradictions.

Patricia Stubbs offers the following view on James's attitude toward women in his fiction: ''In James we meet pure ideology and an anti-feminism so subtle and fused so completely with the form and texture of the novels that it can be overlooked altogether. His hostility operates at such a sophisticated level, and enters so closely into the fabric of his thought that it becomes all pervasive yet invisible.'' Stubbs also defines three general points about women in James's fiction: (1) that they are put in impossible situations, (2) that they invariably fail, and (3) that they are ''scared of sex'' and that they ''tie themselves into knots of inhibition and self-consciousness at anything resembling a sexual encounter.'' At least in her winning some kind of victory and in her aggressive sexual overtures at the end of the story, Alice Staverton reverses each of these general truths.

Aside from a new perspective on one woman's role within one late tale, a historicized approach to ''The Jolly Corner.'' offers a challenge to these and other critical commonplaces about James and perhaps about other writers too quickly perceived as ''reactionary,'' ''sexist,'' or aloof from immediate social/cultural concerns. This is not to say, of course, that no such reactionary or sexist writers exist. However, I would suggest that, in literary texts, the difference between the uncritical expression or endorsement of a prevailing ideology and an immanent critique of such positions may be more vexed than we often grant.

Source: Russell J. Reising, '''Doing Good by Stealth': Alice Staverton and Women's Politics in 'The Jolly Corner,''' in *The Henry James Review*, Vol. 13, No. 1, Winter, 1992, pp. 50-66.

Jesse Bier

In the following essay, Bier shows how Nathaniel Hawthorne and Edgar Allan Poe provided a model and an ''anti-model,'' respectively, for ''The Jolly Corner.''

We know how much James admired and identified himself with Hawthorne. He not only wrote the first extended critical study of Hawthorne but manifestly used him as a model for his own work: the general moral orientation, including Hawthorne's concept of the Unpardonable Sin of human manipulation;

the cool cerebral style and distancing technique; the careful effects of subtlety and ambiguity; and the famous disenchantment, exemplary and then strategic for James, with the impoverished and sometimes repelling American scene.

But if James's conscious literary and psychological model was Hawthorne, he had also an antimodel or alter ego, and that was Hawthorne's opposite number, Poe. It was Poe, that is, in all his intensity and intermittent power, but whose qualities were always purchased at the cost of sensationalism and no little vulgarity, his allegories more personal and neurotic than universal, his very style a constant first-person extortion of emotion, and his chief effects not simply unelevated but meretricious. Nonetheless, in the following generation one could not practice the Gothic mode, the ghost story in particular, without having Poe in the back of one's mind—without forcefully remembering the crass and, as it were, more native American performance, the overt and even potboiling alternative to Hawthorne.

The very outline of ''The Jolly Corner'' suggests James's striving for a delicate amalgam of his two predecessors. At fifty-six years of age, Spencer Brydon, after living abroad as a dilettante for thirty-three years, returns to New York City. He picks up his American life in two ways, entreprenurially as an apartment-house builder on one of his two city properties and romantically as friend and platonic lover of Alice Staverton. In the course of his return, he senses and eventually confronts a ghost in the unreconstructed property, his family mansion. This presence is his horrific American alter ego, the money-minded, power-driven, ravaged doer and builder that the intervening years would have made dominant had he stayed home. Their mutual confrontation, together with Spencer Brydon's open love affair with Alice Staverton at the end, and his attempted reintegration of personalities form the substance and climactic action of the story.

One of the two principal sites to which the patently autobiographic hero periodically returns is Miss Staverton's house on Irving Place: the one sure and sedate resting place in New York and America's landscape, named pointedly after our first renowned tale-teller. Aside from James's literary imagery when locating the address for us—on New York's ''vast ledger-page, overgrown, fantastic, or ruled and criss-crossed lines''—the refuge is an ''antediluvian'' harbor from the ''public concus-

> In actuality the whole story has been a coming-into-being and, in the process, a recapitulation of the hero's past."

sions and ordeals'' of New York and America: it is a place indeed which Rip Van Winkle, himself an early psycho-allegorical exile and prototype, would have appreciated and sought out. For the rest of the story, after this generic signal, James adumbrates Hawthorne and Poe as his immediate models as he also shifts contextually to an architectural motif, using literature's sister art for his purpose of a continuous underlying fable.

> If he had but stayed at home he would have anticipated the inventor of the sky-scraper. If he had but stayed at home he would have discovered his genius in time to really start some new variety of awful architectural hare and run it till it burrowed in a gold mine. He was to remember these words while the weeks elapsed. . . .

Certain correspondences of ''The Jolly Corner'' to James's own career and psychology are quite recognizable. Like his protagonist, James also had left his country for over twenty years. And indeed his return home is memorialized by ''The Jolly Corner,'' drafted just after and possibly even during his American sojourn. The tale itself is rife with autobiographic correlations—

> He found all things come back to the question of what he personally might have been, how he might have led his life and ''turned out,'' if he had not so, at the outset, given it up.

> '' . . . a strange *alter ego* deep down somewhere within me . . . blighted . . . for once and for ever.''

—including sallies that come as close as they can to explicit familial and personal wishes and fears, revealing his innermost life:

> . . . since his parents and his favourite sister, to say nothing of other kin, in numbers, had run their course and met their end there.

> . . . And confessing for the first time to the intensity within him of this absurd speculation [of how he would have ''turned out''] . . . he affirmed the impotence there of any other source of interest, any other native appeal.

If we keep in mind James's deep-seated problems of sex and potency, without necessarily even going as far as orthodox Freudian views, then his full resemblance to a hero fighting for a passionate as well as esthetical reintegration of himself is strong.

The one undeniable virtue of Poe that James wished to incorporate in himself was, in fact, his alter ego's potent force. And nowhere else does he succeed better in power and immediacy, neither in the celebrated ''The Beast in the Jungle'' nor in ''The Turn of the Screw.''

> . . . the stranger, whoever he might be, evil, odious, blatant, vulgar, had advanced as for aggression, and he knew himself give ground. Then harder pressed still, sick with the force of his shock, and falling back as under the hot breath and the roused passion of a life larger than his own, a rage of personality before which his own collapsed, he felt the whole vision turn to darkness and his very feet give way.

Yet the Poe-like side of the author-hero capable at last of such impact was nonetheless derived from a real and vulgar Poe. Is it not this Poe—reciting ''The Raven'' constantly at social gatherings, a progressively corrupted and lionized model—who is stigmatized as having lost his two right-hand writing fingers, ''which were reduced to stumps.'' This was the man mutilated by vulgar American sensationalism and self-exploitation, spending too much of himself for even his qualified success or notoriety.

It seems to me that at the penultimate moment of Spencer Brydon's full view of the alter ego, James resorts to the most obvious Poetics possible in order to give us an incontrovertible sign.

> He saw, in its great grey glimmering margin, the central vagueness diminish. . . . It gloomed, it loomed, it was something, it was somebody, the prodigy of a personal presence.

This is alliterative and assonantal signaling worthy of, and plucked from, Poe himself.

But the mediating ego, the chosen self and conscious artistic model, remained Hawthorne. Probably Hawthorne's most useful distinction from Poe was the combination of style and third person point of view that provided James both the distance and control he wanted. For such effect he went on taking the risks of overqualification and spun-out syntax:

> . . . if he had formed, for his consolation, that habit, it was really not a little because of the charm of his having encountered and recognised, in the vast wilderness of the wholesale, breaking through the mere gross generalisation of wealth and force and success, a small still scene where items and shades, all delicate

things, kept the sharpness of the notes of a high voice perfectly trained, and where economy hung about like the scent of a garden.

The highly wrought and frequently inactive expression especially suited James's subject in "The Jolly Corner." It also matched his protagonist up until the very conclusion, according perfectly with a hypersophisticated Europeanized involuteness, as rendered in prepositional hesitancy:

> He nursed that sentiment, as the question stood, a little in vain, and even—at the end of he scarce knew, once more, how long—found it, as by the action on his mind of the failure of response of the outer world, sinking back to vague anguish.

The devitalized effete, a reproduction of so many Hawthornean exempla of negativity and waste, might think or at least feel very much like this. Furthermore, beyond syntactical effects of a style for once not so purely dysfunctional, James sought greater distance by using abrupt and somewhat surprising narrative obtrusions.

> There came to him, as I say—but determined by an influence beyond my notation!—the acuteness of this certainty. . . .

> When I say he "jumped" at it I feel the consonance of this term with the fact that—at the end indeed of I know not how long—he did move again, he crossed straight to the door.

Such instances represent forced Hawthornean perspective—ironically the "I" of Poe converted to cool third person intervention and auctorial control. It is a technique designed to save James from egotistic display, from that temptation of spending the private self in the intimate vulgar paroxysm of hysteria that Poe committed with regular and helpless abandon.

Might not James hold to his conscious model while he moved closer than ever to his alter ego, having the best of both in one venturesome Gothic tale and supreme psychoesthetic experiment? For one thing, he might forego the woodenness of Hawthornean allegory for the more direct symbolic imbroglio of Poe. But if power enhances subtlety, the reverse is also true, a fine subtlety of artistic complication restrains power; in the resolution of "The Jolly Corner" surrogate Hawthorne is vindicant over doppelgänger Poe. Indeed the superlative central effect of the story is the responsive terror experienced by the alter ego in confronting the protagonist!

> It made him feel, this acquired faculty, like some monstrous stealthy cat; he wondered if he would have

glared at these moments with large shining yellow eyes, and what it mightn't verily be, for the poor hard-pressed *alter ego,* to be confronted with such a type.

The extra subtlety of this brilliant complication is that the quality that the power-driven American alter ego would fear most (as *his* unknown, or as *his* missed life) would be, precisely, the unpuritanic dilettantism and spectatorship that the distancing and repudiative hero, more alien, therefore, than exile, would represent.

In any event, such a conjunction of artistic forces could happily produce both power and subtlety, directness married to complexity. Some years ago Martha Banta glimpsed the possibilities of "a new Gothicism" available to James in this literary fusion, although she left particularization to later investigators. But, indeed, for "The Jolly Corner" as for its closest analogue in our literature, Melville's "Bartleby," there is something even more compelling than this technical fusion of a new Gothicism or the cunning substratum of a writer's fable, something lower layered yet and more profound and generalizable.

What James's title, "The Jolly *Corner,*" tells us is that the protagonist seeks an ideal intersection of possibilities that are otherwise running to different directions. At a certain nexus might one not join high sensibility to an equal and opposite potency? Familiar name symbolism in James is helpful in this regard. The hero, Spencer Brydon, has spent himself but, as Bride-on, he hopes for an assumption of force, with its sexual component, at last; and Miss Staverton will provide his support.

In another sense, James's chief task is to differentiate between vulgarity and power on the one side, as he will also between effeteness and genuine sensibility on the other. He seeks a certain stasis, or means between extremes. To this end, the spectral American is portrayed, first and foremost, as the crass extremist, the success-ridden, money-oriented self, quite opposed to the conscious ego:

> . . . my perversity, . . . my refusal to agree to a "deal"—is just in the total absence of a reason. Don't you see that if I had a reason about the matter at all it would *have* to be the other way; and would then be inevitably a reason of dollars? There are no reasons here *but* of dollars. Let us therefore have none whatever—not the ghost of one.

The alter ego is the gross American type responsible for native architecture in all its dark threatening grandeur and nihilism: "Great builded voids . . . in the heart of cities . . . this large collective negation. . . .'' Still, even it the entrepreneurial sordid alter ego is at last a figure of ravagement and repulsion—''evil, odious, blatant, vulgar''—he has also been active, potently engaged—with a ''roused passion of a life larger than . . . [Brydon's] own, a rage of personality before which his own collapsed.'' He therefore represents the positivity, the sexual and social force, and even identity that might yet be separated out and seized from a congeries of materialistic, meaningless, and destructful values implicit in the whole vulgar nightmare of American life.

On the other side is the complex of effete hedonism and true sensibility from which the right set of saving qualities must also be struck, as the hero comes into his own. His climactic self-possession is linked especially to love and, before everything else, it is the quality of that love which must develop in some pronounced way. As things stand most of the time in ''The Jolly Corner,'' the unspoken love between Brydon and Miss Staverton is not only undeclared but is perilously close to unacknowledged. Their conversation shows a fastidious and faltering delicacy, a sort of highly mannered flirtatious inexpression; its indirections signal real retreats and cancellations:

> '' . . . these thirty years, a selfish frivolous scandalous life. And you see what it has made of me.''
>
> She just waited, smiling at him. ''You see what it has made of *me*.''
>
> ''Oh you're a person whom nothing can have altered. . . .'' But he pulled up for the strange pang.
>
> ''The great thing to see,'' she presently said, ''seems to me to be that it has spoiled nothing. It hasn't spoiled your being here at last. It hasn't spoiled this. It hasn't spoiled your speaking—'' She also however faltered.
>
> He wondered at everything her controlled emotion might mean.

and:

> Their eyes met for a minute while he guessed from something in hers that she divined his strange sense. But neither of them otherwise expressed it. . . . What she said however was unexpected. ''Well, *I've* seen him.''
>
> ''You—?''
>
> ''I've seen him in a dream.''
>
> ''Oh a 'dream'—!'' It let him down.
>
> ''But twice over,'' she continued. ''I saw him as I see you now.''
>
> ''You've dreamed the same dream—?''

> ''Twice over,'' she repeated. ''The very same.''
>
> This did somehow a little speak to him, as it also gratified him. ''You. dream about me at that rate?''
>
> ''Ah about *him*!'' she smiled.

Mainly, of course, it is Brydon who continues so self-absorbed that he hardly knows there is any kind of love to be acknowledged, much less spoken. Alice Staverton cannot help her own breach of all etiquette at one point when she declares: ''Oh . . . you don't care for anything but yourself.''

Actually, the career Brydon admits to having led during his expatriate mid-life, a ''selfish'' and ''scandalous'' life, was in reality only a miniscandal of self-pampering. We glimpse a long jejune career of self-involved pleasure, profoundly frivolous in its onanistic containments. It is no wonder, then, that the climax of present circumstances represents a crisis both of love and true action for Brydon, who is returning home from a long past of protracted and virtually total psychic impotence.

> Oh to have this consciousness was to *think*—and to think, Brydon knew, as he stood there, was, with the lapsing moments, not to have acted!

His shame, his ''deep abjection,'' has been his escapism not only there in the corner house but throughout his life. His meeting the alter ego therefore becomes an act of such suspenseful self-transcendence and transformation that it renders the ghost story per se the least tense element of the plot.

What the Hawthornean protagonist must do is acknowledge and overcome the practiced dispassionateness that has become lovelessness, the putative hedonism that has degenerated to inertness, the effete refinement that has become reflexive cowardice. At the same time this surrogate hero must salvage what remains worthwhile in the duplicitous ego, like the residual sensibility that makes Brydon and James recoil from American ugliness and voids. The newly discovered virtue that allows him this reconstructive and salvaging process and that authorizes vital manhood now is, finally, raw courage. It may even be the hunter's courage that is crucial. Indeed, toward the very end of ''The Jolly Corner'' Brydon, the same man who has been a quondam expatriate sportsman but never a real hunter, cries aptly, ''There's somebody—an awful beast, whom I brought, too horribly, to bay.'' In doing so, he finally loses his own worst attributes and lays courageous claim to his integrated psyche—and woman.

And so, in its furthest recesses, the story is a profound psychological romance. It is a tale of death and love, in that order, since the hero must somehow die before coming to new life and emotion. "Yes," Brydon himself says, "I can only have died—" although he attributes too much of his revival to Alice Staverton's presence when he comes to, as if she had actively brought him back rather than simply presided at his rebirth: "You brought me literally to life."

In actuality the whole story has been a coming-into-being and, in the process, a recapitulation of the hero's past. Therefore the recapitulatory effects of children's games throughout: the "playing at hide-and-seek" with the ghostly alter ego through all the rooms and corridors of the old family house, the marble floor squares of past hopscotch games fast becoming the ground of a more deadly present game, etc.

But the recapitulatory process is pushed back further yet. At Brydon's coming to, after his swooning confrontation with the ghost, James makes much of the scenic tableau—an infantile Brydon lying in Alice Staverton's "ample" lap, her madonna's face "bending . . . directly over him"—a necessary psychic as well as artistic or religious image. Stretched on the morguelike stairs of cold "black-and-white slabs," Spencer Brydon dies to a missed adult life but revives in this place "of his youth"; in his "rich return of consciousness" he experiences significantly "the most wonderful hour he had ever known," in a quick obvious resumption of birth and a deliciously "abysmally passive" infancy. The psyche has undergone the fullest regression before the man can truly claim himself. At this time, of course, undeclared romance finally becomes acknowledged, active love—"It took but an instant to bend her face and kiss him"—coincident with Brydon's courageous self-confrontation. Our only objection is, indeed, to the sentimental prolonging of the scene with which the story ends just before Brydon symbolically gets to his feet. During the extended tableau and interview the infantile and maternal motifs are a trifle too exquisite and embarrassing for modern taste:

> "Oh keep me, keep me!" he pleaded while her face still hung over him. . . .

But Brydon does progressively rise in physical and symbolic self-accomplishment.

> At this Brydon raised himself . . . sat up, steadying himself beside her there. . . .

"Ah I've come to myself now. . . ."

It is still hard for him to appreciate all that has happened. But Alice Staverton does not fail him at the end.

> " . . . So why," she strangely smiled, "shouldn't I like him?"

It brought Spencer Brydon to his feet. "You 'like' that horror—?"

> "I *could* have liked him. And to me," she said, "he was no horror. I had accepted him."

Led to welcome and accept his own vitality, he enters upon a new personal integration of alter ego and ego. In a manly synthesis of complementary qualities left over from the wrong extremes in himself, he achieves love between lust and discretion. Appropriately, it is Brydon and not Alice Staverton who has not exactly the last word but the last gesture.

> "And he isn't—no, he isn't—*you*!" she murmured as he drew her to his breast.

James's deepest wish was, on the one side, for power without vulgarity and, on the other, delicacy without death. He wanted profoundly to match force and form; to blend potency, rightfully gained after an expended courage, with subtlety and sensibility. His hero now begins to reconstruct his life as he will remodel the family house, without extreme idealizations one way or the other but maintaining his esthetic sense. Thus, Spencer Brydon wakes up to several blisses, but the primary one is "the beauty of his state."

The trouble is that the Hawthornean side remains dominant, quite overbalancing the other. The hero is, penultimately at least, too prostrated by his experience to convince us of synthesis. That is because, in my opinion, James *was* afraid of the psychological value as well as artistic power of Poe. The alter ego is not truly, finally integrated with the ego. We are certainly meant to infer so symbolically and structurally, but it is not, strictly speaking, accomplished for us. In fact there is still, after all, a kind of repudiation at the end; the alter ego has been faced and even recognized, but not absorbed:

> " . . . he isn't—no, he isn't—*you*!"

Still, wasn't the attempt singularly worth it? I believe so. And for these lower layered themes James's predecessors, Hawthorne and Poe, provided the exact model and anti-model. They gave him, in particular, the means that would mute and yet reveal the deeper psychodrama he wished to suggest even more compellingly than the writer's fable with which he started.

Source: Jesse Bier, "Henry James's 'The Jolly Corner': The Writer's Fable and the Deeper Matter," in *Arizona Quarterly*, Vol. 35, No. 4, 1979, pp. 321-34.

Sources

Anderson, Quentin. *The American Henry James*, New Brunswick: Rutgers University Press, 1957.

Brook, Van Wyck. *The Pilgrimage of Henry James*, New York: Dutton, 1925.

Edel, Leon. *Henry James, The Master: 1901–1916*, London: R. Hart Davis, 1972.

"Political and Diplomatic: The Unemployed," in *The English Review*, Vol. 1, December, 1908, pp. 161-64.

Fogel, Daniel Mark. "A New Reading of Henry James's 'The Jolly Corner,'" in *Critical Essays on Henry James: The Late Novels*, edited by James W. Gargano, Boston: Hall, 1987, pp. 190-203.

Matthiessen, F. O. *Henry James: The Major Phase*, New York: Oxford University Press, 1944.

Reising, Russell J. "'Doing Good by Stealth': Alice Staverton and Women's Politics in 'The Jolly Corner,'" in *The Henry James Review*, Vol. 13, 1992, pp. 50-66.

Stein, Allen F. "The Beast in 'The Jolly Corner': Spencer Brydon's Ironic Rebirth," in *Studies in Short Fiction*, Vol. 11, 1974, pp. 61-6.

United States Bureau of the Census. *Statistical Abstract of the United States, 1997*, 117 edition, Washington, D. C.: Government Printing Office, 1997.

Zinn, Howard. *A People's History of the United States, 1492–Present*, New York: Harper Perennial, 1995.

Further Reading

Edel, Leon, ed. *Henry James: Selected Correspondence*, Cambridge: Belknap Press of Harvard University Press, 1987, 446 p.
   These letters provide insight into James's philosophies and concerns.

The Man Who Was Almost a Man

In the mid-1930s Richard Wright drafted an early version of ''The Man Who Was Almost a Man'' as a chapter in a novel about the childhood and adolescence of a black boxer entitled *Tarbaby's Dawn*. Wright never finished the novel, but in 1940 the story appeared in *Harper's Bazaar* under the title ''Almos' a Man.''

In this period Wright was at the height of his powers, publishing his three major works, *Uncle Tom's Children, Native Son,* and *Black Boy* between 1938 and 1945. With *Native Son* he became the first African-American author to write a bestseller and gained an international reputation for his exploration of racial issues and bold, realistic style.

The final version of ''The Man Who Was Almost a Man'' was not published until 1960—the year of Wright's death—in a collection of short stories entitled *Eight Men*. While it is sometimes compared unfavorably to his early fiction, many critics praised the collection for offering a sensitive look at racial oppression.

''The Man Who Was Almost a Man'' chronicles the story of Dave, a young, African-American farm laborer struggling to assert his identity in the restrictive racist atmosphere of the rural South. Longing for a symbol of power and masculinity, Dave fantasizes that owning a gun will win him the respect he craves. After he gets a gun, he learns that he needs more than a gun to earn respect.

Richard Wright

1940

Author Biography

Wright was born on September 4, 1908, near Natchez, Mississippi. His father, an illiterate farm laborer, left the family when Wright was six. He was raised by his mother, a well-educated schoolteacher. Wright had a difficult childhood, as his mother was seriously ill; Wright and his younger brother went to live with her parents in Jackson, Mississippi, where he came under the strong influence of his grandmother's strict Seventh Day Adventism.

At the age of nineteen, Wright moved to Chicago. He became involved with a leftist literary group known as the John Reed Club and joined the Communist Party. He worked as a journalist for several leftist newspapers and published essays on Marxism and Black Nationalism as well as short stories and poetry. During this period he wrote an early version of ''The Man Who Was Almost a Man'' as part of an unfinished novel.

In 1938, after moving to New York, he published his first collection of short stories entitled *Uncle Tom's Children* . The following year he was awarded a Guggenheim grant to finish his first novel, *Native Son,* which became the first bestseller written by an African American. His autobiography, *Black Boy,* appeared in 1945 and solidified his reputation as a courageous African-American voice.

He broke with the Communist Party in 1944 and moved to France, where he lived in voluntary exile for the rest of his life. He associated with many prominent writers and intellectuals and became an outspoken critic of colonialism. He continued to publish both fiction and nonfiction books, but none had the success of his major early works. Toward the end of his life, Wright was plagued by financial and health problems. He died in Paris at age 52.

Plot Summary

The story opens as Dave, the seventeen-year-old protagonist, heads home from a day working in the fields. He fantasizes about buying a gun and knows that if he had a gun his fellow workers would no longer treat him like a boy.

He goes into the local store and asks to look at catalogues. The proprietor, Joe, questions him about what he wants to buy and shows him an old pistol he wants to sell. Dave is excited that Joe is only asking two dollars for the gun and resolves to convince his mother to let him buy it.

He brings home the catalogue and looks at it during dinner. His parents question him about it but he waits until after dinner. When his father has left the room, he asks his mother for the money he has been saving.

Dave's mother first dismisses Dave's request, calling him a fool; but when Dave suggests that he could buy the gun for his father, she reconsiders. She gives him the money and tells him to bring the gun straight to her. He buys the gun, but doesn't go home right away. Instead he plays with the gun until he knows everyone has gone to sleep. Then he leaves for work early, taking the gun with him.

His boss, Mr. Hawkins, questions Dave about why he is early and then sends him to a field to start plowing. In the field he fires the gun and its strong recoil causes him to drop it. He looks up to see Jenny, the mule pulling the plow, running across the field. When he catches up with her he sees that she is bleeding. He tries to block the bullet hole with dirt, but Jenny bleeds to death. In a panic, he buries the gun.

At the end of the day, a group of people has gathered to watch two of Hawkins' workers bury the mule. Dave's parents are among them. When Hawkins questions Dave about what happened, Dave tells what he knows is an unconvincing lie—that Jenny stabbed herself to death on the point of the plow. Dave's mother tells him to tell the truth and asks him where the gun is. His father becomes angry and shakes him and Dave starts to cry. Hawkins promises not to hurt him and Dave sobbingly confesses.

The crowd laughs at him. Hawkins tells him that he has just bought a dead mule and says that he can pay off the debt by working for him for twenty-five months. Dave's father tells him to find the gun and sell it back to Joe in order to make his first payment to Hawkins and then promises to beat him when they get home.

That night Dave continues to think about firing the gun. He wants to fire it one more time, so he sneaks out in the night and retrieves the gun from where he buried it. He fires it several times and uses up the bullets. When he passes Hawkins' house on the way home he fantasizes about firing at it in order to scare Hawkins and to repair his injured sense of masculinity.

Richard Wright

As he heads home on the same road where the story opens, he thinks despairingly about working for two years to pay off his mistake. Just then he hears the sound of a train approaching. He jumps aboard the train, heading for "somewhere where he could be a man."

Characters

Jim Hawkins

Jim Hawkins owns the large plantation where Dave works as a farm laborer. Dave is working on Hawkins's farm for the summer in order to save money for school. When Dave accidentally shoots the mule, Hawkins charges Dave fifty dollars—equal to two years labor—for the dead mule.

At the end of the story Dave longs to shoot at Hawkins's big house in order to scare him and gain a sense of power in relation to Hawkins, but he has already used up his bullets. As a wealthy white man, Hawkins represents all of the power that Dave lacks.

Joe

Joe is a white merchant in the rural community where the story takes place. He lends Dave a cata-

logue and when he learns that he wants to buy a gun, offers to sell him a revolver for two dollars.

Ma

Ma is Dave's mother. She controls the finances in the family, so Dave asks her to give him money to buy the revolver. At first she responds by calling him a fool, but she agrees when he tells her that he loves her and points out that his father has no gun. Dave is not afraid to defy his mother and finds her easy to manipulate.

Pa

See Bill Saunders

Bill Saunders

Bill Saunders is Dave's father. He is a strong, authoritative figure who questions Dave about his relationship with Hawkins and threatens to beat him after he is caught shooting the mule. However, his actions have little influence on the events of the plot.

Dave goes behind his father's back to ask his mother's permission to buy the gun. He convinces her with the argument that Pa has no gun; given the close association between guns and manhood, this implies that for all of his apparent masculinity, Pa's manhood is compromised.

Media Adaptations

- Learning in Focus made a film adaptation of "Almos' a Man" in 1976, directed by Stan Lathan, written by Leslie Lee, and produced by Dan McCann. The film was released on videotape by Coronet Films and Video in 1985.

Dave Saunders

Dave Saunders is the protagonist of the story. He is the "man who was almost a man," a seventeen-year-old black farm laborer living in a small rural community in the South. The story centers on Dave's longing for a gun and the disastrous events that ensue when his wish comes true.

Dave fantasizes that having a gun will earn him respect in the eyes of his peers and the men around him. He convinces his mother to give him money to buy a gun and then accidentally shoots a mule. Dave tries to cover up his responsibility for the animal's death, but this just exacerbates the humiliation he experiences when his role is exposed.

Despite the fact that it has led to his downfall, Dave remains fascinated with the gun and convinced of its power to make him a man. He goes out in the middle of the night to furtively shoot the gun again. Focusing on the power it makes him feel, he decides spontaneously to hop on a northbound train with nothing but the old revolver in his pocket.

Themes

Coming of Age

As the title suggests, Dave is poised between boyhood and adulthood. In various ways, all of the other figures in the story—Dave's parents, Hawkins, and the unnamed men he works with—threaten Dave's fragile sense of manhood. Dave's problem is that he is almost a man, yet his lack of social and economic power make him acutely aware that he is *not quite* one.

The story is structured around Dave's quest for a gun as a symbol of power, maturity, and manhood as well as the ironic results of attaining this wish—his further loss of pride and autonomy. However, the story's conclusion—Dave's impulsive decision to break free from the setting that belittles him by jumping on a northbound train—suggests a more successful passage toward maturity and independence.

Race and Racism

Although racial issues are not in the foreground of "The Man Who Was Almost a Man," racism and injustice are underlying themes. Dave's feeling of being disrespected results in part from a typical adolescent struggle with how he is seen by his peers and his parents.

Yet this lack of respect is more acute and poignant because of the segregated, racist culture. The social circumstances that relegate blacks to an inferior status contribute to Dave's sensitivity about being seen as nothing but a boy.

Dave's father, a physically powerful adult man, is characterized as something less than a man because he does not have a gun and because he capitulates to the white Hawkins. Thus, Wright suggests, in an atmosphere of racism Dave will never have the chance to be fully a man unless he takes action to ensure it.

Class Conflict

Dave's economic status is central to his struggle for power and respect. Although he works hard to earn money, he has none of the autonomy that comes with financial independence. On one level, his mother controls the his earnings because she wants to save it for his schooling; education is a means for Dave to escape from his limited potential as a farm laborer.

On another level, Hawkins controls Dave financially. Dave fantasizes that the gun will give him the power that he lacks as a young black farm worker, but in fact, the gun results in further entrapping him in a situation of economic exploitation.

Dave does not seem particularly conscious of his economic exploitation but his aggression toward Hawkins' property—killing Jenny, the mule, and his thinking about shooting at Hawkins' big white house—suggests that Wright understood Dave's actions as a form of class struggle.

Topics for Further Study

- Dave believes that a gun will make him a man. What are other objects that signify manhood in contemporary culture? Choose one such object and compare it to the gun in ''The Man Who Was Almost a Man.'' What do these two objects say about what it means to be a man in each time and place?

- Do some research about the economic situation of black farm laborers in the early twentieth-century South. How was the situation of such laborers similar to and different from the institution of slavery that had been abolished half a century earlier? How does this comparison enhance your understanding of the story?

- At the end of the story Dave jumps aboard a train heading north. The story takes place during a period when huge numbers of African Americans were migrating north for a variety of social and economic reasons. Do some research about this migration.

- When Wright wrote an early version of ''The Man Who Was Almost a Man'' in the mid-1930s, he was an active member of the Communist Party. Research the basic tenets of the Communist political philosophy and consider how the story reflects these ideas.

- In the 1930s many authors—both black and white—utilized dialects in their writing. Find another author who uses dialect, and compare its effect on the representation of African Americans with that in ''The Man Who Was Almost a Man.'' Why do you think Wright chose to write in dialect?

Violence

Dave's strong desire to own and fire a gun has very little to do with malice or violence. He wants the gun for the status it will bring him in the eyes of others and the feeling of power it will give him. He seems almost unaware of the physical violence that firing a gun can cause, which is demonstrated when he unintentionally shoots and kills Jenny.

After the accident, his father beats him and Hawkins has an even bigger advantage over him. This further whets his appetite to possess the gun—again, not to inflict injury, but to repair his own injured sense of self-esteem. The fact that he fires it into empty space suggests that he does not understand how to direct his rage.

Guilt and Innocence

Dave is responsible for a number of acts that are quite clearly wrong. Wright presents us with a character who desires a dangerous weapon, lies to his mother to get it, uses it to kill an innocent animal belonging to his employer, and lies again to cover up his actions. According to abstract values or objective facts, Dave appears guilty of deceit and destruction, but Wright reveals the particularities of Dave's circumstance in such a way as to question such a definition of guilt.

Wright explores Dave's motivations and thought processes, which show him as an innocent person with benign intentions. He never means to hurt anyone else, only to preserve his pride and end his own subjugation. Furthermore, Dave experiences his mistakes as so terrifying and pays for them so dearly that it is easy to see him as a victim. Wright suggests that Dave is trapped in his social and economic circumstance and that his motives are understandable and justifiable.

Style

Setting

The story is set in a rural southern community in the early years of the twentieth century. All of the events of the story take place within the space between Hawkins' large farm and Dave's modest home, including the road that connects them and the store along the way. This constricted setting suggests the limitations of Dave's options and contributes to an atmosphere of entrapment.

The two locales of farm and home suggest a duality between have and have-not, rich and poor, white and black, which is evocative of the larger segregated culture. The road is a particularly significant setting as it is a place of movement and transition where the story both begins and ends.

Narration

"The Man Who Was Almost a Man" is narrated by a third-person, omniscient narrator. That is, the story is told by a narrator who is not part of the story's action and who is able to see into the minds of the characters. In this case, the omniscient narrator has insight into Dave's consciousness, as in the first paragraph of the story, which describes Dave's private thoughts and feelings.

One of the most notable stylistic aspects of the story's narration is Wright's use of dialect—the particular grammar and pronunciation of black southern farm workers—in juxtaposition to standard literary English. When he describes thoughts as well as quoting speech, Wright uses dialect, but when he describes actions he uses standard English. He switches back and forth between these two modes of narration, creating an implicit comparison between internal and external, subjective and objective, subordinate and dominant, as in the story's first two lines, "Dave struck out across the fields, looking homeward through the paling light. Whut's the use talkin wid em niggers in the field?"

Irony

The story's structure is based on irony, which means that the outcome is the opposite of what one or more characters had expected. Irony always has to do with a difference or gap in knowledge. In this case, this gap is revealed through actions and events rather than through tone or speech.

Dave believes that buying and firing a gun will lead to manhood, respect, and autonomy. Thus it is ironic when firing the gun knocks him to the ground, causes his peers to laugh at him, his father to beat him, and Hawkins to claim control over his labor for the next two years—events deeply incongruous with what he intended and anticipated.

Symbolism

The story makes strong use of symbolism. The gun, an old Wheeler pistol, is the central symbol of the story. Dave longs for a gun, any gun, as a symbol of his manhood. He believes that people will take him seriously if he has a gun.

When this fantasy becomes a reality and Joe sells him an obsolete weapon, the respect and freedom he had hoped for turns into humiliation and entrapment. When Dave shoots the gun he is thrown to the ground by its recoil. Then he discovers that he has made the terrible mistake of killing a defenseless mule. Thus, while the idea of a gun symbolizes power for Dave, the actual gun symbolizes powerlessness.

Later, when Dave confesses and is punished, he thinks, "Nobody ever gave him anything. All he did was work. They treat me like a mule, n then they beat me." Thus, instead of being able to identify with the more powerful men in the story, Dave ends up identifying with Jenny, the defenseless mule. However, Dave still perceives the gun as symbolizing manhood and runs away rather than selling it back to Joe as he had promised.

Historical Context

Racism and Black Masculinity

The first decades of the twentieth century were difficult and violent ones for African Americans in the South. The agricultural economy was suffering, leading to poverty for poor whites and blacks; but with "Jim Crow" segregation laws, which appealed especially to poor whites, blacks were kept oppressed with limited opportunities. Moreover, African-American masculinity was threatened during the time when "The Man Who Was Almost a Man" takes place, offering a useful context for Dave's struggle for manhood and respect.

More than two thousand African Americans— the great majority being men—were lynched by angry mobs between 1890 and 1920. Historians cite economic frustrations as the primary cause for this violent phenomenon, but at the time the common excuse for lynching was the alleged rape of a white woman by a black man. Lynching victims were subjected to torture, burning, and even castration.

According to *The Oxford History of the American People,* "hundreds of lynchings were for theft, alleged insult, altercations between black tenants

Compare & Contrast

- **1930s** Spurred by the stock market crash of 1929, the Great Depression cripples the United States economy. In 1932 approximately 25% of the work force is unemployed. Social security and unemployment insurance do not yet exist to help the disenfranchised.

  Today: During the late 1990s the United States enjoys a period of strong and steady economic growth. The stock market reaches record highs and unemployment is at its lowest point since the 1960s. Welfare programs are significantly cut in many states.

- **1930s** There is a national glut of agricultural products, resulting in wheat and corn prices falling to the lowest point in American history. Under a New Deal program, the planting of staples such as grain, tobacco and sugar is reduced, fields of crops are plowed under, and surplus foods are bought and distributed to the needy by the government. The exploitative economic system of sharecropping—where black tenants work the land of white landowners—remains prevalent.

  Today: Agriculture is run like a big business and is dominated by a small number of corporations. Yet farming remains carefully regulated by the federal government. Due to developments in farm machinery, populations shifts, and reductions in cotton productions, the number of share-

croppers in the South has declined by more than 80% since 1935.

- **1930s** African Americans are oppressed by "Jim Crow" laws that enforce racial segregation in public places. The National Association for the Advancement for Colored People (NAACP) is established to fight for the civil rights of African Americans in 1909.

  Today: Decades after laws designed to ensure equal opportunity for blacks are put in place as part of the Civil Rights Movement, a disproportionate number of African Americans still live in poverty. The policy of Affirmative Action, designed to offset discrimination and increase opportunity for blacks in schools and workplaces, is struck down as unconstitutional in a number of court cases.

- **1930s** In rural areas, a family gun is a common household item. Gun control laws restricting the sale of firearms do not yet exist and guns are easily available for purchase through general stores and catalogues.

  Today: Gun control laws restrict the purchase of firearms, but there are still more than two million firearms in U.S. homes. Unfortunately, there are almost forty thousand firearm-related deaths each year.

---

and white landowners, or such trivial causes as killing a white man's cow or refusing to sell cottonseed to a white man at his price." This relates to Dave's reflection that "he was glad he had gotten out of killing the mule so easily," when he is punished for killing Jenny with two years of labor and a beating by his father.

The Great Migration

Due to the economic problems and racial violence of the South as well as new opportunities in

industrial northern states, a huge population shift among African Americans took place between the 1890s and the 1940s known as the Great Migration. The interruption of European immigration after 1914 led to a labor vacuum in the northern states; subsequently, black labor from the South was heavily recruited. In fact, Wright left the South for Chicago in 1927.

While racism, violence, and segregation existed in different forms in northern cities, they continued to represent freedom, opportunity, and new beginnings for modern African Americans. For many blacks, the move from southern farms to northern cities represented an important symbolic break from a past of slavery and oppression. Dave's flight by train at the end of the story thus reflects both the underground railroad of slavery days and the "escape" to the northern territory.

Communism and Communist Intellectuals

When Wright wrote an earlier version of the story entitled "Almos' a Man" in the mid-1930s, he had recently become involved in a circle of communist intellectuals in Chicago. The class critique implicit in "The Man Who Was Almost a Man" must therefore be understood within this ideological context. Communists espouse a radical philosophy that promotes the enlightenment of oppressed workers and the destruction of the economic system of capitalism, working toward a goal of the common ownership of resources by all workers.

In 1933 Wright joined a new club promoting both political action by communist sympathizers and the creation of radical art. Through its literary magazine this club offered him a forum where his art was taken seriously by blacks and whites alike. In the circle of communist intellectuals Wright found not only a group of artistic peers who appreciated his writing, but a framework for understanding his experiences of racial oppression in a global economic context.

"The Man Who Was Almost a Man" can be seen as part of Wright's mission to reveal the experiences and struggles of the common working person as represented by Dave and to criticize the unjust power of the capitalist as represented by Hawkins.

Critical Overview

Wright's literary reputation was established in the early 1940s when he published two critically acclaimed bestsellers, *Native Son* and *Black Boy,* in rapid succession. Though he was a prolific writer in many genres, over the decades the great majority of critical attention has focused on these two major works and, to a lesser extent, his first book of short stories, *Uncle Tom's Children,* all written before Wright turned forty.

At the height of his popularity Wright was considered the best African-American writer of his generation, but his critical reputation has since declined. In fact, recent critics view his work as uneven. In 1946 Wright left the United States to live in France. He continued to write fiction and nonfiction until his death at age fifty-two.

In 1960, when *Eight Men* appeared, Wright had fallen into relative obscurity with his earlier success sometimes attributed to his topical subject matter rather than the literary merits of his writing. Additionally, scholars may have neglected Wright because his career fell between two great high points in African-American letters—the Harlem Renaissance of the 1930s and the Black Power movement of the 1960s. However, the rise of the field of African-American studies has led to a renewed scholarly interest in Wright in recent years.

The critical reaction to *Eight Men* was tepid; most reviewers find only one or two of the eight stories up to Wright's standards. The collection contains stories written over the course of twenty-five years, representing a wide range in style and subject matter. Some critics praise the greater subtlety and sympathy evidenced in the collection's representations of race relations, suggesting that Wright's exile led to a more humanistic and philosophical outlook.

Yet most critics prefer the older stories, including "The Man Who Was Almost a Man." These stories are considered similar to his major early works.

In *New Republic,* Irving Howe asserts that "these stories do give evidence of Wright's literary restlessness, his wish to keep learning and experimenting, his often clumsy efforts to break out of the naturalism which was his first and, I think, necessary mode of expression. . . . I think he went astray whenever he abandoned naturalism entirely."

While Howe perceives *Eight Men* as successful in his naturalistic stories, *Commonweal's* Richard Gillman condemns the book as "dismaying stale and dated."

An early critic of Wright, James Baldwin provided a positive review of the short fiction collection. He asserted that Wright, had he not died, would have been on the edge of a new artistic breakthrough, "acquiring a new tone, and a less uncertain aesthetic distance, and a new depth."

Baldwin also praised the older stories: ''perhaps it is odd, but they did not make me think of the 1930s or even, particularly, of Negroes. They made me think of human loss and helplessness.''

In an unfavorable review, W. G. Rogers of the *Saturday Review* maintains that only one story, ''The Man Who Went to Chicago,'' ''shows Wright at his realistic, bludgeoning, blunt best.''

Regarding Wright's direct style, Gloria Bramwell compares ''The Man Who Lived Underground,'' to Ralph Ellison's 1952 classic *Invisible Man* in a way that may sum up Wright's status on the literary scene:

> ''Today Americans are more sophisticated and more likely to approve Ellison's action as he strips society's pretensions bare, laughs at it and at himself, and mocks its attempts to destroy him. Wright was never far removed enough to do more than suffer and articulate that suffering incompletely . . . but powerfully enough to touch us. And he is merciless in the presentation of that suffering . . . It fascinated, it horrified, it aroused, it even repelled, but its force was undeniable. It has the hypnotic force of nightmares from which we cannot wake voluntarily. . . . He articulated as no other an American nightmare. That he could not waken out of it himself is our loss.''

Pack mule being loaded with flour.

Criticism

Sarah Madsen Hardy

Madsen Hardy has a doctorate in English literature and is a freelance writer and editor. In the following essay, she discusses the significance of the gun as a symbol of manhood in ''The Man Who Was Almost a Man.''

''Shucks, a man oughta hava little gun aftah he done worked hard all day,'' muses Dave, the protagonist of Richard Wright's short story ''The Man Who Was Almost a Man.'' A man ought to have a little gun. Throughout the story, Dave, who is almost but not quite a man, never wavers in this conviction that a gun will make the difference and signal the manhood to which he aspires.

In this sense, Dave provides an interpretation of the significance of the gun, the story's central literary symbol. Armed with a gun, Dave believes that he will no longer be scared. He will be powerful and respected. However, through both plot and

narration Wright is careful to show that Dave is naive and misguided in this belief.

For one, Dave is childish in his strategy for getting a gun. ''Mebbe Ma will lemme buy one when she gits mah pay from ol man Hawkins,'' Dave speculates, sounding every bit a boy as he resolves, ''Ahma beg her t gimme some money.'' He is childish when he tries to solve the problems that ensue after his mishandling of the old revolver, attempting to plug the bullet hole he has shot in the mule's side with dirt and telling a ''story he knew nobody believed'' about how she died.

The story is crushingly sad. Dave makes a bid for more respect only to inspire shame and humiliation. He ends up further entrapped in a situation that made him feel diminished—something less than a man and also, perhaps, less than a person. The symbol of manhood in which Dave has invested so much—both financially and emotionally—fails him. This would seem to be proof that a gun does not make a man after all.

Is Wright really debunking the idea that a gun can make the difference between being almost and fully a man? Even after it leads to Dave's humiliation and financial ruin, the obsolete weapon has an almost magical power in his eyes and holds a power

What Do I Read Next?

- *Uncle Tom's Children* (1938), Wright's first and best-known collection of short stories, explores the legacy of slavery and the psychology of oppression among blacks of the deep South.

- *Native Son* (1940), Wright's most celebrated work, was the first novel by an African American to become a bestseller. It tells the controversial story of a young black man's anger and rebellion.

- *Autobiography of an Ex-Colored Man* (1912), offers an insightful portrait of African-American identity and race relations at the turn of the century. Its author, James Weldon Johnson, is considered an important precursor to Wright.

- *Invisible Man* (1952), written by Ralph Ellison,

was a best-selling novel and a National Book Award winner. This landmark novel offers a powerful account of a black man's struggle as he migrates to a northern city.

- *Go Tell It on the Mountain* (1953), a semi-autobiographical classic by James Baldwin, tells of a minister's son's search for identity in 1935 Harlem.

- *Makes Me Want to Holler* (1994), an autobiography about growing up black and male in the 1970s by *Washington Post* reporter Nathan McCall, describes his experiences with violence, prison, and the education system.

---

that he cannot give up. At the end of the story Dave holds it in his hand almost like a charm as he jumps aboard a passing train and leaves his family, his past, his mistake, and his debt behind.

The story's abrupt ending, when Dave spontaneously flees, offers a reprieve from the suffocating fate he seemed to have brought down on himself. I am interested in how the gun and its exhilarating effect—which is, on the one hand, central to Dave's folly—ends up, on the other, empowering Dave to make a move that is a truer assertion of independence, if a desperate one.

The main events of the story expose Dave's ideas about the gun as completely wrong. Every result Dave had wished for is ironically reversed. But it does not seem to me that Wright's intention is to completely dismantle Dave's fantasy that the gun will bring him some kind of desperately needed power to transform himself.

The idea that a gun symbolizes power is so prevalent it may seem barely worth stating. Yet since Wright seems to be saying that in a way Dave is wrong and in a way he is right in his belief that a gun makes a man, thinking about the different kinds

of power it represents is important for understanding the meaning behind Wright's deceptively simple symbolism.

To begin on a most literal level, a gun gives its carrier power through the threat of physical violence. After all, the South was not safe for young black men in the 1920s when the story is set. Thousands of black men were summarily executed by mobs of whites for petty or unproven crimes in a practice called lynching. In fact, in the unfinished novel of which Wright originally conceived the story as a part, the protagonist hears word that a laborer in the next county has been lynched shortly before the events that make up ''The Man Who Was Almost a Man'' begin.

However, it is significant that in the version Wright did publish there is no mention of lynching and no other imminent sense of physical danger for Dave. He seems to have no concept of the practical use of a gun at all. He never refers to needing a gun to defend himself or wanting to shoot someone out of a sense of anger, vengeance, or justice. He doesn't want to use the gun so much as he wants to *possess* it.

"Lawd, ef Ah only had tha pretty one! He could almost feel the slickness of the weapon with his fingers. If he had a gun like that he would polish it and keep it shining so it would never rust. N Ah'd keep it loaded, by Gawd!'' Rather than being either criminal or revolutionary, his attitude toward the gun is somewhere between consumerist and erotic longing.

This brings us to the next interpretation of the kind of power a gun represents. The most familiar symbolic meaning of a gun, popularized through a method of interpretation called psychoanalysis, is that it represents the phallus or the male sex organ. This interpretation is useful because it directly connects guns to the idea of manhood. To have a gun is to have a phallus—the embodiment of manhood. Isn't this exactly what Dave is after?

The next question is this: If Dave isn't interested in the practice of physical violence, what kind of power does the gun provide as a phallic symbol? According to psychoanalysis, the phallus doesn't have to do with anatomical parts or sex per se so much as it has to do the status and authority associated with masculinity. The phallus represents power of the father within the male-dominated family and, by extension, the male-dominated society. Actual fathers may or may not have the patriarchal power that is associated with fathers in general.

Thus, it is significant that the plot pivots on the fact that Dave's father does *not* have a gun. His father *does* appear to be an authoritative figure at the dinner table when he asks Dave gruffly how his work is going, but Dave knows to go to his mother for the two dollars he needs to buy the gun. When he first approaches his mother she calls him a fool. It is only when he reminds her, "Pa ain got no gun. We needa gun in the house,'' and tells her he loves her that she agrees to give him the money to buy it and bring it back to his father.

Notice that despite his father's masculine manner, he lacks the power associated with manhood that Dave has identified as crucial: "Shucks. A man oughta hava little gun aftah he done worked hard all day.'' Dave's father works hard but he doesn't have a gun and neither does he have the power to make household financial decisions. It is Dave's mother who keeps "a slender wad of bills'' stowed in the top of her stocking.

In this case, the phallic power that Dave seeks is not modeled on what his father has but on what he lacks. Therefore, let me suggest that the allure of the

> ❞❞ ... it is the white storekeeper Joe and the white landowner Hawkins who determine the value of guns and mules and labor. It is through association with exactly these more subtle forms of power that the gun represents true or full manhood for Dave."

gun does not, as one might suppose, have to do with Dave becoming a man like his father but instead with his sense that the conditions of his father's life prevent even him from being fully a man.

Dave's father is presumably a farm laborer; so is Dave. His father earns his money through manual labor and he asserts his authority through the threat of beatings. He is, therefore, physically powerful. However, his father lacks access to some other order of power that Dave knows exists, even if he does not have the tools to describe quite what it is. His father lacks the power connected to the catalogue, money, and, of course, the gun—which, in the story, serves as an *object of economic exchange* more than an object of physical violence.

Dave's world is not only male-dominated, it is divided by racial and economic forms of dominance according to which the father is divested of some important forms of phallic power. Dave's mother holds the family purse strings, but it is the white storekeeper Joe and the white landowner Hawkins who determine the value of guns and mules and labor. It is through association with exactly these more subtle forms of power that the gun represents true or full manhood for Dave.

Dave's father represents the rural southern life, physical labor, and passive compliance with the white power structure that echo conditions of slavery under which his own father's generation suffered. Dave lacks the tools to analyze his father's conditions of oppression or his own but he does have a sense, as he trudges from Hawkins' field to his humble home, that as long as he walks the same path as his father he will remain in some ways profoundly powerless.

By keeping the gun and hopping aboard a northbound train, he at least opens up the possibility of a new kind of manhood in the future. With this impulsive act, Dave becomes part of a historic migration of African Americans seeking new beginnings and economic opportunities in the booming industries of northern cities.

For Wright, the son of a Mississippi farm laborer who sought his fortune in Chicago, the figure of the rural southern father fails to offer an acceptable model of manhood, leaving sons to face a future of ''almost manhood'' or to take a chance on an unknown future and pay the painful price of leaving the past—with ties of community and family—behind.

Source: Sarah Madsen Hardy, ''Gun Power'' for *Short Stories for Students*, The Gale Group, 2000.

Charles Hannon

In the following essay, Hannon discusses the exploitation of African Americans in ''The Man Who Was Almost a Man'' in the context of the exploitation of temporary faculty at universities.

In response to an early draft of this essay, a reader at *College Literature* made the point that ''adjuncts have always existed; until the 1970s they were typically faculty wives''; the reader went on to ask, ''has adjunct exploitation only recently become an issue because there are more men in the ranks?'' The reader's insight helped me to see the historically ''feminized'' position of adjunct faculty, and to recognize the underpaid and underacknowledged labor of temporary teachers and staff as an effect of structural sexism in American institutions. The reader caused me to question whether my criticisms of the academic hierarchy were the result of an unconsciously perceived threat to my own ''masculinity,'' since masculinity, as a gender construct, historically has been tied to income security. By extension, I am compelled to consider whether my response to low-status employment is conditioned by the loss of white male privilege, real or imaginary, in the wake of much-needed affirmative action programs in higher education. But this reader overlooked my argument that the widespread replacement of retired faculty with temporary, full-

time, non-tenure-line appointments represents a threat to tenure, academic freedom, long-term program development, and the faculty-administered university department that was not posed in the past by the use of adjunct faculty. The trend toward temporary staffing threatens to add a class barrier to the ideological divisions that, as Gerald Graff has demonstrated, already obstruct communication and problem solving among department faculty. Faculty on two- or three-year appointments do not have a stake, and often have no voice, in departmental matters such as hiring, promotion, and tenure decisions, curriculum reform, undergraduate major requirements, and graduate program development. Yet often, these are the faculty with the most experience in how other university departments address these issues, and to shut them out as a matter of policy is injurious to them and their departments. This is an issue of class blindness, because what temporary faculty often perceive as dysfunction in a department, many of their seniors consider the normal order of business: non-tenure-line faculty are apprentices, the argument goes, training for a future position which will provide them the full rights and privileges of academic citizenship. This stance is supported by a pervasive fiction of merit, which implies that temporary faculty who do not advance to tenure-track positions simply do not work hard enough, or teach or publish well enough to succeed. Faculty who hold such attitudes and express them in the profession's journals and newsletters often do so despite evidence to the contrary in their own departments. In some cases, departmental policy serves to elide this evidence by foreclosing opportunities for adjunct and temporary faculty to receive official recognition, let alone reward, for their publications and successful teaching records.

If some faculty are unable to recognize the causes and long-term effects of labor exploitation in their departments, students are similarly conditioned to rationalize economic, racial, and gender inequities in literary texts as the result of differing degrees of ability and individual incentive. In my experience teaching Wright's ''The Man Who Was Almost A Man'' for instance, students focus on the theme of immaturity in Dave Saunders, and resist tying this theme to the exploitative economic conditions which infantilize both him and his father. Wright's story (written in 1936, published as ''Almos' A Man'' in *Harper's Bazaar* in 1940, and as ''The Man Who Was Almost A Man'' in the posthumous *Eight Men* [1961]), is about a black tenant family working for a white landowner, Mr.

Hawkins. The story opens with an ambiguous insult to seventeen-year-old Dave Saunders's masculinity, which Dave thinks would be redressed were he to possess a gun: "a man oughta hava little gun aftah he done worked hard all day." Wright clearly develops the gun as a phallic symbol which will substitute for his and his father's appropriated "manhood," itself a metaphor for economic security and self-sufficiency. When the story opens, Dave walks from the fields to the general store, traditionally the site of exploitation for tenant farmers and sharecroppers (both black and white), and he asks Joe, the white store manager, if he can borrow the Sears catalogue, the symbol of Hawkins's control over the commodities available to his tenants. Joe hands over the catalogue, and confirms that Dave's "manhood" has been appropriated by the exploitative economic system when he tells Dave, "If you wanna buy a gun, why don't you buy one from me? I gotta gun to sell." At home Dave thumbs through the catalogue's pornographically glossy pictures of guns; the story moves quickly between Dave's interior thoughts and the narrator's commentary, and both use sexually charged language to represent the weapon's potency as a phallic symbol: "Lawd, ef Ah only had tha pretty one! He could almost feel the slickness of the weapon with his fingers. If he had a gun like that he would polish it and keep it shining so it would never rust. Ah'd keep it loaded, by Gawd!" After supper, Dave offers his mother an opportunity to retrieve the family phallus: "with the open catalogue in his palms," Dave approaches his mother, raises the book, and says, "Ma, Gawd knows Ah wans one of these." His mother resists, but ultimately acquiesces when Dave reminds her that without a gun, her husband also feels emasculated. She hands Dave the cash and says, "Lawd knows yuh don need no gun. But yer pa does."

First-year students rarely want to pursue these connections between masculinity, race, and economic exploitation, because for them Wright's story is a simple tale of immaturity and the consequences of irresponsible behavior. In this, their stance is curiously like James Baldwin's, who wrote that this and one other story in *Eight Men* ("The Man Who Saw the Flood") "did not make me think of the 1930s, or even, particularly, of Negroes. They made me think of human loss and helplessness." Of course, both Baldwin and my students are correct: Dave does use the gun irresponsibly. He carelessly shoots Mr. Hawkins's mule Jenny and then makes up a preposterous story about the mule's going wild and falling backward upon the plow. But when I

> **"** Driving down worker morale in all three labor contexts (the Depression South, and today's academic and private sectors) is the implicit charge (implicit too in my students' criticisms of Dave Saunders) that contingent workers either 'prefer or choose temporary work,' or 'possess serious characterological flaws that prevent their employment in full-time, 'real' jobs.'"

suggest that Wright inserts this plot into a larger discussion of race, class, and gender inequity—for instance, that Dave articulates a specifically racial rage while "looking at Jim Hawkins' big white house" and fantasizing about taking a "shot at tha house. Ah'd like to scare ole man Hawkins jusa little"; or that Jenny's death is symbolic of Dave's betrayal of his mother, or of the treatment of women workers generally under Depression-era labor structures—students prefer to revert to the fictions of merit and equal opportunity in a "free market" economy, and to assert that Hawkins's treatment of Dave, his demand of two dollars a month for the next twenty-five months, is a perfectly fair resolution to the story of Dave's incompetence.

It is difficult for some students to perceive the invidiousness of Dave's situation because, for laudable reasons, they have trained themselves to occupy a race- and class-neutral stance toward both literature and work. From this position, Dave's two-year indenture to Mr. Hawkins is not an effect of race or class discrimination, but rather a matter of Dave's compensating for the economic injury his own irresponsible behavior has caused Mr. Hawkins. Here again, students' belief in the self-determined, concrete individual serves to elide historical difference, to make the utter instability of Dave's economic position invisible. Since we continue to teach that "apprentice" years of industry are rewarded under the American system with promotion and greater economic autonomy, it is difficult for students to see that under the debt-driven agricultural system of the postbellum South, Dave's two-year encumbrance would likely translate into lifelong servitude. This delusion has a long history in America: despite successive years of crop liens and store credit, late nineteenth- and early twentieth-century southern farm workers were told, and often believed, that if they worked hard they could climb the "agricultural ladder" out of indenture and into the small (or large) landowner class. Paul Mertz, in the *Encyclopedia of Southern Culture*, writes that "these persistent views were a major impediment to efforts to reduce rural poverty." Other impediments included the unchallenged power of landowners who could set terms of employment unilaterally, and the job insecurity of farm workers, which parallels that of today's contingent workers closely enough to merit quoting at length from Mertz's description:

> They worked under year-to-year verbal agreements that left landlords free to dispense with their services at settling time. With a great surplus of unskilled labor at hand, planters usually felt little need to hold dissatisfied or unwanted tenants. Most landless farmers were highly mobile, moving as often as every year or two. This transience was socially and economically wasteful; it deprived tenants of any role in their communities and reinforced illiteracy by preventing regular schooling for their children. It destroyed incentives to maintain farm property and contributed greatly to soil erosion.

Analogies to academic piecework here are clear: without tenure protections, temporary and adjunct faculty, especially those who appear dissatisfied by agitating for better working conditions, can be released at any time; moving from one adjunct position or instructorship to another, they incur large debts and are discouraged from being active in civic events; and the lack of a clear reward system diminishes the chance they will spend "free" time contributing to programs for the long-term health of their institutions or local communities. In the private sector, the endless drive for short-term profits at the expense of long-range planning and corporate "citizenship" leads to similar consequences. Driving down worker morale in all three labor contexts (the Depression South, and today's academic and private sectors) is the implicit charge (implicit too in my students' criticisms of Dave Saunders) that contingent workers either "prefer or choose temporary work," or "possess serious characterological

flaws that prevent their employment in full-time, 'real' jobs."

The reluctance of some to address issues of economic inequity stems from our national habit of romanticizing exploitative situations as moments of opportunity. My students have indulged in this habit in responding to the final lines of Wright's story: after Dave climbs atop a moving train, he feels "his pocket; the gun was still there. Ahead the long rails were glinting in the moonlight, stretching away, away to somewhere, somewhere where he could be a man. . . ." When I raise the issue of modernist irony, and suggest that Wright is using it to emphasize the futility of Dave's attempt to escape problems deriving from his low economic status, I find I can convince only about a third of my students. Most will read these lines as Yoshinobu Hakutani does, in the context of other powerful images of freedom in American history and culture. Hakutani writes that "just as the Mississippi was to Huck and Jim a symbol of escape, independence, and freedom, modes of transportation such as trains, trucks, and planes appear frequently in Wright's work." This reading overlooks the fact that such symbols rarely lead to full, self-sufficient lives in Wright's novels and stories, and that in his own life, Wright found this kind of release only by escaping America's oppressive racial climate altogether. A similar desire to see opportunity in low-status positions accounts for the widespread acceptance of the temporary help industry's public relations claims that contingent employment is beneficial for the worker since it provides "greater scheduling flexibility, varied and satisfying work experiences, skill acquisition and development, access to permanent employment opportunities, and a cornucopia of other supposed monetary and non-monetary rewards." While some of these benefits are real, people who cite them to justify exploitative arrangements ignore the fact that they can just as well be provided by meaningful full-time (permanent) positions.

In academia, the same litany of alleged benefits of contingent employment is recited by apologists for the present trend toward contract employment as an alternative to tenure. David Helfand, for instance, faults tenure for rewarding "those with a desire for the security of lifetime employment, rather than those less averse to risks, who might be better suited to pioneering work on the frontier of knowledge and to inspirational teaching of the young." I agree that the current tenure system has rewarded some undeserving professors while punishing many innovative adjunct and junior faculty; the answer, however, is not a wholesale conversion to a system based upon five-year renewable contracts, unless these carry strong protections for academic freedom, and unless the renewal process can somehow be removed from university politics. With the continued overproduction of Ph.D.'s, it is unlikely that universities will negotiate 5-year contracts that include salary increases and rewards for teaching and scholarly merit. It is more likely that deans, like the banks to whom a landowner in Wright's (or Faulkner's) own time inevitably would have owed mortgage payments, will take the first opportunity to foreclose upon prior contractual arrangements, and replace long-term workers with cheaper, more itinerant labor. To return to Wright's story, when Dave Saunders alights from his train to seek employment, he likely will find only short-term, day-wage work, since by the late 1930s many southern landowners were accepting payments from the New Deal's set-aside programs, releasing their "share" workers and re-employing them merely on a piecemeal basis during planting and harvest months (an early version of today's "planned staffing"). . . .

Source: Charles Hannon, "Teaching the Conflicts as a Temporary Instructor," in *College Literature*, Vol. 24, No. 2, June, 1997, pp. 126-41.

John E. Loftis

Taking the deer hunt from William Faulkner's story "The Old People" as a model of the literary tradition of a hunt as a boy's initiation into manhood, Loftis shows how the conventions are subverted in Dave's killing of the mule.

For a people living in a new and unsettled land, variations on the archetype of the young hero who achieves manhood by hunting and slaying a wild beast came early and naturally as a literary theme. American writers have consistently dramatized the threat of the wilderness as an element in their heroes' *rites du passage*. The courageous and determined Natty Bumpo, the Deerslayer, is still an All-American hero and a model for the heroes of later generations. Captain Ahab, equally courageous in his madness, is perhaps the archetype in its demonic or perverted form. Modern writers continue the tradition: Hemingway with Francis Macomber and Faulkner with, particularly, Ike McCaslin. In Ameri-

can literature, however, the hunt is a European and thus white tradition, and its heroic and mythic dimensions hardly seem available to black American writers—unless used ironically to underscore the gulf between the chivalrous white hero and the black field hand or urban outcast. But when deftly handled, this problematic theme becomes an artistic asset for the black writer: the hunt can embody the hero's maturation at the same time that its parodic implications dramatize the disparity between black and white possibilities of growth and development in American society. The initiation story can thus criticize the society within which it occurs in a uniquely effective way, as it does in Richard Wright's "The Man Who Was Almost a Man."

To clarify the precise nature of Wright's parody of the hunt tradition, I would like to compare it with Faulkner's story of Ike McCaslin's initiation in "The Old People." I am not arguing here that Wright is directly parodying Faulkner or that there is any direct connection at all between the two stories, but for several reasons, Faulkner's story is a useful and logical one to represent the normative, mainstream pattern of the hunt in American literature in a comparison with Wright. First, the stories are contemporaneous: Faulkner's story was first published in *Harper's Magazine* in September 1940; Wright's had appeared only nine months earlier, in January 1940, in *Harper's Bazaar*. In addition, the thematic and geographical similarities between the two stories invite comparison, while the ethnic and cultural differences between the authors and the stories suggest new areas of interpretation, especially for Wright's story. Most important, Faulkner's story offers a double initiation where the successful hunt itself serves almost as a preliminary to the more important, more mysterious initiation of the vision of the ancestor-buck. Because he is reaching beyond the simple hunt-as-initiation, Faulkner relies particularly heavily on the tradition itself to inform his initial hunt with meaning and thus becomes especially representative of that tradition.

Initiations occur within personal, social, and literary contexts, and Wright's parody of the hunt-as-initiation exploits the differences between those contexts for his hero, a seventeen-year-old black field hand, and the pattern as it develops for most white heroes, like Ike McCaslin. The fact of initiation is, of course, a partial creation of individual identity, and identity is closely bound to names and

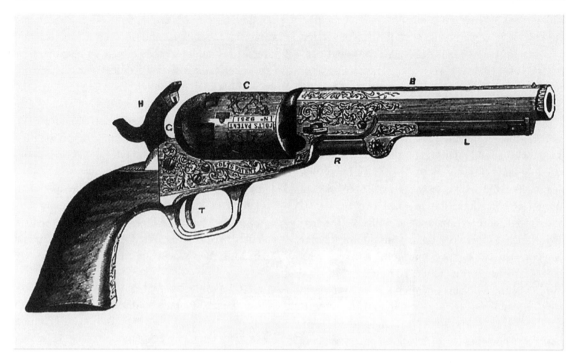

The original gun called the Colt's Revolver.

naming. Fenimore Cooper's Deerslayer, for example, receives his name from his prowess as a hunter, although his initiation involves the killing of a man, not just an animal. In "the Old People," Ike McCaslin's name is not only a given, it is a part of a larger web of identity with implications for larger meanings in the story. His father, Carothers McCaslin, was an old man when Ike was born, and his present guardian is his cousin McCaslin Edmonds. As these interlocking names suggest, a great deal of the story investigates Ike's hereditary background to establish his relationship to the white, black, and Indian communities of which he is a part. His initiation, then, solidifies a complex of relationships to family, community, and heritage.

Dave, on the other hand, has only his given name as the story opens. He has family—mother, father, brother—but neither their given names nor the family name is provided until late in the story. And when we finally learn that Dave's surname is Saunders, the fact is presented not just as information but as something significant that Dave has earned and has had to assert, to claim. After successfully firing his pistol and just before hopping the freight train out of Mississippi, Dave looks at Jim Hawkins' "big white house" and thinks to himself,

"Lawd, ef Ah had just one mo bullet Ah'd taka shot at tha house. Ah'd like t scare ol man Hawkins jusa little . . . Jusa enough t let im know Dave Saunders is a man"; his assertion of his name is identical with his assertion of his manhood. Only now that he has mastered the pistol that had caused his apparent disaster, just before the ultimate assertion of abandoning his family and immediate social setting, can Dave rightfully claim the identity that is associated with his own name. Dave must earn that which is a complex given for Ike McCaslin.

Second, the relationship of each protagonist to guns points to an important distinction between their situations. Guns are a natural part of Ike's life. He grows up among hunters, and he is given his first small rifle as soon as he is "big enough to walk alone from the house to the blacksmithshop and then to carry a gun." Ike is taught to shoot small game, and then, when he is ten, when he can count his name in two numbers, he is taken on the big game hunts in the wilderness. It is part of Ike's heritage to own guns and to use them to prove his manhood.

For Dave, however, the gun is at first only a dream. His desire for a gun and his equating ownership of the gun with manhood seem almost pathetic. He envisions it as the great equalizer: "One of these days he was going to get a gun and practice shooting, then they [the other field hands] couldn't talk to him as though he were a little boy" (Wright). Dave's attempts to get money from his mother to buy the gun reveal that he is in fact still a child; he whines, wheedles, and begs, and his mother responds as if he were a child. As he approaches her, he "shyly" raises the catalogue that he has opened to the page of pistols:

> "Ma, Gawd knows Ah wans one of these."
>
> "One of whut?" she asked, not raising her eyes.
>
> "One of these," he said again, not daring even to point. . . .
>
> "Get outta here! Don yuh talk t me bout no gun! Yuh a fool!" . . .
>
> "But yuh promised me one—"
>
> "Ah don care whut Ah promised! Yuh ain nothing but a boy yit!" (Wright)

Dave's final argument is that the gun is really for his father (suggesting perhaps a tacit association in his culture also between manhood and owning a gun). To this his mother finally relents, telling Dave, "Yuh bring it straight back t me, yuh hear? It be fer Pa." In a literal sense, Dave never receives permission to own a gun. Although he keeps the gun and takes it with him when he leaves, his family and immediate social environment do not allow for him what was so natural for Ike McCaslin.

Finally, while Ike McCaslin has a teacher and guide, Dave lacks not only that but even adult male models for defining adulthood. Ike has had Sam Fathers, whose very name suggests his relationship to Ike, to teach him to hunt and to become a man. When Sam abandons the farm and goes to live in the Big Bottom, Ike is only momentarily confused. He recalls that Sam had already told him, "I done taught you all there is of this settled country. . . . You can hunt it good as I can now" (Faulkner). He realizes that Sam's leaving is "not only temporary but that the exigencies of his maturing, of that for which Sam had been training him all his life some day to dedicate himself, required it" (Faulkner). When Ike shoots his first deer, Sam Fathers is standing just behind him, and it is Sam who ritually slits the deer's throat and marks Ike's face with the steaming blood to signal his achieved manhood.

> " Wright's child-man, unlike Faulkner's, lacks the familial and cultural mechanisms and personal supports that make growing up a natural journey with identifiable ritual milestones. Dave, quite the contrary, finds barriers and dead ends at every crucial turn."

Dave has no adult black males to guide him or even to serve as models that could allow him to define manhood. He is surrounded daily by anonymous black field hands; he lives in a matriarchal family; and his larger social setting is obviously dominated by white men, Joe at the store and especially Jim Hawkins, his employer. His father is virtually a phantom figure in the story, appearing at supper where he asks Dave what he is reading and again in the scene when Dave is being brought to account for the mule he killed. In that scene Dave's father promises to beat him, but he offers no support for Dave or resistance to Jim Hawkins about the settlement for the mule. We have been told that Dave's father does not own a gun, and Dave's mother assents to Dave's claim that he should own one. Inadequate as the gun is as a symbol of manhood, the absence of the gun perhaps suggests that Dave's father does not, can not serve as Dave's model of manhood. If anything, Dave's adults are threats and exploiters, virtually the opposite of the guides with which Ike McCaslin is so abundantly supplied.

These three factors, then, provide the context in which we must read the crucial scenes of killing animals. Ike's initiation through hunting is fairly straightforward. He is nervous, of course, but he has Sam Fathers at his side to instruct and guide him through the critical moments. When the buck appears, Sam says, "Now, . . . shoot quick, and slow"

(Faulkner), and when Ike, who will never actually remember the shot, runs excitedly to the buck, Sam warns him not to approach from the front. Sam also slits the buck's throat and marks Ike's face, signifying his manhood. Ike still has in store another and perhaps more important initiation, but that Faulkner opens the story with this hunt scene suggests both its importance and its traditional meaningfulness as a literary device.

If Ike's initiation is both traditional and serious, Dave's is both unique and funny. Dave has not gone out that morning to hunt; he has sneaked his gun along into the field he is supposed to plow for his boss, Jim Hawkins. The gun is hidden, and Dave must maneuver himself into a place where he can try to fire it. To be sure he is safe, he plows "two whole rows before he decide[s] to take out the gun" (Wright). He then looks around carefully, unstraps the gun from his leg, and proudly displays it to the mule: "Know whut this is, Jenny? Naw, yuh wouldn know! Yuhs jusa ol mule! Anyhow, this is a gun, n it kin shoot, by Gawd!" (Wright). He further warns Jenny: "When Ah pull this ol trigger, Ah don wan yuh t runnacka fool now!" (Wright). In fact, he is telling Jenny what he himself really needs to know, and he warns her not to behave in essentially the way that he himself will after he fires the pistol.

The shot itself is a disaster. Dave moves away from Jenny, holds "the gun far out from him at arm's length, and turn[s] his head" (Wright), unconvincingly telling himself that he is not afraid. "The gun felt loose in his fingers; he waved it wildly for a moment. Then he shut his eyes and tightened his forefinger. Bloom!" (Wright). The gun is as much in control of Dave as Dave is of the gun in this scene, and his reaction to the shot, even before he realizes that he has shot Jenny, is childishly funny:

> A report half deafened him and he thought his right hand was torn from his arm . . . and he found himself on his knees, squeezing his fingers hard between his legs. His hand was numb; he jammed it into his mouth, trying to warm it, trying to stop the pain. The gun lay at his feet. He did not quite know what had happened. He stood up and stared at the gun as though it were a living thing. He gritted his teeth and kicked the gun. Yuh almos broke mah arm! (Wright)

Unlike Ike's superficially similar confusion caused by the intensity of his experience, Dave's confusion is funny because it results from his overreaching his abilities and reveals the disparity between what he believes he is and what he actually is.

Yet, to his horror, Dave discovers that he too has shot an animal, Jim Hawkins' mule Jenny. The grim humor continues as the panic-stricken Dave chases the bleeding mule "for half a mile, trying to catch her" (Wright), merely managing to make a bad situation even worse. When he does catch Jenny, he futilely tries to stop the bleeding by plugging the bullet hole with "handfuls of damp black earth" (Wright). She escapes his grasp again, and Dave catches her only when she stops and kneels to the ground, "her front knees slopping in blood" (Wright).

If Ike is justifiably proud of his hunting success, Dave is not and tries his feeble best to disguise his. He hides the pistol and concocts an absurd story about Jenny's suddenly acting peculiar and falling on the point of the plow. Try as he will, Dave cannot convince Jim Hawkins or the other field hands that he is telling the truth, and when his mother appears and asks him, "Dave, whut yuh do wid the gun?" (Wright), his story collapses completely. "All the crowd was laughing now" (Wright), and Dave's humiliation is complete.

If Ike McCaslin's killing the deer is his transition into manhood, so in a different sense Dave's killing the mule is his; Ike's is a conscious act that marks a normal stage of development, while Dave's is a childish error that means nothing in itself but forces the development that Dave could not otherwise achieve. His rejection of his bondage to Jim Hawkins to pay for the mule motivates Dave to return to the hidden gun and to assert his manhood by successfully firing it. This success in turn provides the confidence he needs to reject his childhood, turn his back on his family, and board the freight train headed "away, away to somewhere, somewhere where he could be a man . . ." (Wright).

Dave's initiation by shooting an animal, then, is a parody, not specifically of Faulkner or of "The Old People," but of the tradition that informs Faulkner's version of the hunt with much of its significance. Wright's child-man, unlike Faulkner's, lacks the familial and cultural mechanisms and personal supports that make growing up a natural journey with identifiable ritual milestones. Dave, quite the contrary, finds barriers and dead ends at every crucial turn. If Ike's deer has symbolic significance, so does Dave's mule. First, it is a domestic, not a wild, animal, and Dave's domestic situation, his family and immediate social setting must be eliminated before he can mature. Second, Jenny is short for Jennifer which derives from Guinevere which in turn derives from the Welsh "gwen," white. Dave's society is one dominated by whites who refuse to allow any black male to truly mature, and Dave must symbolically kill this domination before he is free to grow up. If Ike's initiation is within a tradition, Dave's lies outside that or any other tradition. Wright's solution to the artistic problem of presenting a unique initiation where the traditional motifs not only will not work but in some ways represent the very obstacles that keep them from working is to parody the tradition itself. Far from the "crude and careless," "technically unpolished" writer he is sometimes labelled, Wright in fact succeeds in a sophisticated manipulation, parody, of a complex literary tradition, the hunt, to embody his vision. Through this parody Wright shapes a convincing and moving account of the black experience of growing up in the rural South in the second quarter of the twentieth century.

Source: John E. Loftis, "Domestic Prey: Richard Wright's Parody of the Hunt Tradition in 'The Man Who Was Almost a Man,'" in *Studies In Short Fiction*, Vol. 23, No. 4, Fall, 1986, pp. 437-42.

Sources

Baldwin, James. "Alas, Poor Richard: 'Eight Men,'" in *Dial*, 1961, pp. 188-99.

Bramell, Gloria. "Articulated Nightmare," in *Midstream*, Vol. 8, No. 2, Spring, 1961, pp. 110-12.

Gillman, Richard. "The Immediate Misfortunes of Widespread Literacy," in *Commonweal*, Vol. 74, No. 5, April 28, 1961, pp.130-31.

Howe, Irving. *The New Republic*, Vol. 144, No. 7. February 13, 1961, pp. 17-18.

Rogers, W. G. Review, in *Saturday Review*, Vol. 44, No. 65, January 21, 1961.

Further Reading

Fabre, Michel. *The Unfinished Quest of Richard Wright*, New York: Morrow, 1973.

> A comprehensive biography of Wright that covers a great deal of material not found in either of his autobiographies. Fabre views the various political and artistic stages of Wright's life as a series of partially successful struggles.

Kostelanetz, Richard. *Politics in the African-American Novel: James Weldon Johnson, W. E. B. DuBois, Richard Wright and Ralph Ellison*, Greenwood Publishing, 1991.

> A study interpreting the novels of Wright and three other major African-American writers in terms of political ideas.

Wright, Ellen, and Michel Fabre, eds. *The Richard Wright Reader*, New York: Harper & Row, 1978.

> A wide selection of Wright's writings including some of his important nonfiction essays on race, writing, and politics.

Wright, Richard. *Black Boy: A Record of Childhood and Youth*, New York: Harper, 1945.

> Widely considered a classic, Wright's autobiography describes his southern upbringing, his move North, his beginnings as a writer, and his involvement with the Communist party.

One Day in the Life of Ivan Denisovich

Alexandr Solzhenitsyn

1962

The publication of "One Day in the Life of Ivan Denisovich" in 1962 in the leading Soviet intellectual magazine *Novy Mir* (*New World*), was a significant victory for dissident artists in the Soviet Union. This short story about a single day in the life of a "zek" (a political prisoner) in the Soviet "Gulag" (work camps) brought its author, Alexandr Solzhenitsyn, almost immediate notoriety in the Soviet Union and throughout the world.

Unfortunately, with the fall of Soviet Premier Nikita Khrushchev in 1964 and a resumption of hard-line attitudes, Solzhenitsyn's outspoken writings were banished and much of his writing circulated in Samisdat (self-published format). He was awarded the Nobel Prize for Literature in 1970, and most critics still regard "One Day in the Life of Ivan Denisovich" as the most realistic and evocative depiction of life in a Stalinist prison camp. In fact, Solzhenitzyn drew from his own personal experience as a prisoner in the camps under Stalin.

Today "One Day in the Life of Ivan Denisovich" is still admired for its succinct and stark depiction of the cruelty and degradation of prison life during that time. Its publication opened the door for further revelations and explorations of Gulag life by other authors. The major themes of the story are human survival and human dignity in the face of human cruelty and absurdity.

Author Biography

Alexandr Isayevich Solzhenitsyn was born in Kislovodsk, Russia, on December 11, 1918. His father died in a hunting accident before his birth, and his mother, the daughter of a wealthy landowner, struggled to support the family on her meager wages as a typist.

Between 1939 and 1941 Solzhenitsyn studied philosophy, literature, mathematics, and language; in 1941 he received a degree in mathematics and physics from the University of Rostov. During World War II he served as commander of a Soviet Army artillery unit and was twice decorated for bravery.

In 1945 he wrote a letter criticizing Stalin, which fell into the hands of authorities; as a result, he was arrested and sentenced to eight years for anti-Soviet activities. In 1946 he went to Butyrki Prison and worked in construction; from 1947 to 1950 he worked at Marfino Prison as a mathematician on technological projects; from 1950 to 1953 he was sent to the Ekibastuz labor camp, Kazakhstan, where he worked as a mason and carpenter.

In 1953 he was released from prison—but still in internal exile, which limited his movement and activities—and became a mathematics teacher in Kok-Terek, Kazakhstan. During this period he began work on his poetry, plays, and novels.

Freed from internal exile, he moved to Riazan, Russia. He taught physics and astronomy and continued to write. With the thaw in Soviet censorship during Khrushchev's regime, friends encouraged Solzhenitsyn to submit his novel concerning the struggles of a political prisoner to the Russian literary journal *Novy Mir.*

"One Day in the Life of Ivan Denisovich" ("Odin den iz zhizni Ivana Denis-ovicha") was published in 1962 and resulted in almost immediate success. When Khrushchev was ousted by radical hard-liners, Solzhenitsyn fell from favor. His struggles with the Soviet establishment escalated with the banning of his writing and with personal and public harassment.

He received the Nobel Prize for Literature in 1970. Between 1964 and 1968, he wrote *The Gulag Archipelago,* a massive chronicle of Soviet slave labor camps. While he was smuggling it to Paris for publication in 1973 the Soviets arrested him, stripped him of citizenship, and exiled him to the West in 1974.

He settled in Cavendish, Vermont, and resumed his writing career—although not before first offending liberal American intellectuals by making widely publicized remarks about the decay of spiritual life in the United States, remarks which earned him such labels as "authoritarian" from some quarters.

Solzhenitsyn has been married three times and has three children and one stepchild. With the advent of *glasnost* in the mid-1980s and the collapse of the Communist Soviet Union, Solzhenitsyn had his citizenship restored in 1990. His return from exile in 1994 was marked by a nationwide train ride. He has continued his writing and has been active in Russian politics.

Plot Summary

An inmate in a Siberian prison camp, Ivan Denisovich Shukhov awakes in the dark and cold of early morning. Feeling sick, he lingers too long in his bunk. He is caught by a guard and is ordered to wash the guardroom floor; this is a light sentence, considering he could have received ten days in solitary confinement. He finds a way of washing the floor with minimal effort, which is the only way a "zek"— a political prisoner—survives in the Soviet labor camps.

When finished, he rushes to the mess hall—a prisoner never misses food if he can help it. Then he runs to the infirmary, but he is too late: they already have filled their daily quota of two sick people.

The day begins in earnest for Shukhov. The prisoners are lined up in fives by the guards and are counted and recounted. They are forced to march through the subzero cold to their work camps where, with inadequate tools and mismanaged work planning, they are given their day's assignments.

Things look up for Shukhov when his work squad is sent to the unfinished power station. If they had been sent to the ironically named "Socialist Way of Life Village" they would have had unbearable work. Tiurin, Shukov's squad leader, has managed a good assignment.

Pavlo, Tiurin's able assistant, works to keep the men moving. Some other members of Shukov's team include: Fetiukov, a lazy, uncouth, unlikable man; Alyosha, the pious Baptist; Buinovsky, a

Alexander Solzhenitsyn

former naval officer; the old Senka; and Kilgas, the joking Lett, who works with Shukhov as a mason.

The morning is occupied with organizing the area for the afternoon's labor. Some zeks try to get an old, broken-down stove operational; others haul work materials. Having scrounged some felt from another sector of the work site, they tack up the windows, giving them some protection from the freezing temperatures. Guardrails on the stairways are ripped down in order to build mortar troughs. Shukhov procures his hidden trowel—a zek learns that he must hide things to make his work easier.

At lunch, Shukhov manages to steal an extra bowl of oatmeal. In the afternoon, the masonry work on the wall finally begins. Shukhov and Kilgas work with efficient speed. The whole team works hauling bricks and mortar. Only the unpopular Fetiukov is slacking. They work to the last minute, and then the labor is done for the day.

The guards notice that a zek is missing. The lines are counted and recounted. Finally they find the man, a Moravian, who had fallen asleep near a stove. He is beaten and cursed. The column begins its journey back to camp.

Halfway back, they discover that another column is also returning late to camp. In spite of the

cold and their exhausted bodies, they begin a race to see who will get to camp first. First back will be first to the food. Shukhov's column wins. He even smuggles in a bit of hacksaw blade that might make a nice little tool for mending shoes.

Always thinking of ways to survive, Shukhov does a number of favors for Tsezar, one of the intellectual prisoners, who receives many parcels of food from the outside. Shukhov is rewarded for his efforts with some extra food. Every bite counts.

Lying in bed, Shukhov, mutters a prayer of thanks. The pious Alyosha overhears him and uses the opportunity to discuss religion. Shukhov's religion is that of the common man—a believer in God's existence but cynical about life. He does not have Alyosha's fervent faith and patience. Alyosha bears his suffering as the will of God; Shukhov believes he suffers for his own nation's failure in time of war.

Shukhov reflects on his day:

> [He] went to sleep fully content. He'd had many strokes of luck that day: they hadn't put him in the cells; they hadn't sent his squad to the settlement; he'd swiped a bowl of kasha at dinner; the squad leader had fixed the rates well; he'd built a wall and enjoyed doing it; he'd smuggled that bit of hacksaw blade through; he'd earned a favor from Tsezar that evening; he'd bought that tobacco. And he hadn't fallen ill. He'd gotten over it. A day without a dark cloud. Almost a happy day. There were three thousand six hundred and fifty-three days like that in his stretch. From the first clang of the rail to the last clang of the rail. Three thousand six hundred and fifty-three days. The three extra days were for leap years. (Excerpt from ''One Day in the Life of Ivan Denisovich,'' translated by Ralph Parker)

In perspective, it was for Ivan Denisovich ''an almost happy day.''

Characters

Alyosha

Alyosha is a prisoner noted for his strong religious faith. His is able to endure the camp experience because of his faith in Christ. He begins each day with prayer and reads aloud from the New Testament, two-thirds of which he has transcribed into a little notebook that he keeps hidden in his bunk area. The other men view the arctic Gulag camp as a frozen hell—Alyosha, conversely, sees the creation of God, and is therefore always willing to work hard.

Buinovsky

Buinovsky is an ex-naval man. He is not yet used to the camps and still maintains the pride and dignity of an officer. He barks orders at the others as if he was in command, and quotes the legal code to the guards. As a result, he spends much time in the confinement cells. The system appears to be slowly breaking his will.

Ivan Denisovich

See Ivan Denisovich Shukhov

Fetiukov

Fetiukov is considered the bottom man in group 104; also, he represents what the system can do to a man. Shukhov describes him as the kind of man "who would steal potatoes from your stew." He is the kind who would stare at men smoking, hoping for a cigarette butt, and fish tobacco out of spittoons. Lazy, he would dump out mortar from the wheelbarrow in order to make it less heavy.

Kilgas

Kilgas is an easy-going Latvian who works well with Shukhov. The pudgy-faced Kilgas is always good for a joke.

Tsesar Markovich

Tsesar Markovich is considered the intellectual of group 104. He manages to get regular parcels from home and wrangles the "cushion job" of working in the heated camp office while the rest of the group work outside in sub-zero temperatures. A man of Greek, Jewish, and possibly Gypsy background, he is oblivious to the suffering around him as he discusses Russian cinema in the confines of a warm office.

Pavlo

Pavlo is Tiurin's assistant squad leader. A pleasant, plump-faced Ukrainian and former military man, he oversees the squad during Tiurin's absence.

Senka

Senka is an old zek. An unfortunate fellow, he endured the torture and floggings in Buchenwald only to be sent to Stalin's prison camp system. His

Media Adaptations

- "One Day in the Life of Ivan Denisovich" was adapted into a film directed by Casper Wrede (1971). The film stars Tom Courtenay, Alfred Burke, James Maxwell, and Espen Skjonberg. It is distributed in VHS and videodisc formats from Sony Video Software and Image Entertainment.

- There is a three-cassette (300 minutes) unabridged recording of "One Day" read by Frank Miller, from Recorded Books of Charlotte, Maryland.

- http://www.almaz.com/nobel/literature/ Solzhenitsyn.html This site, the Nobel Prize Archive page, gives information and link sites to Solzhenitsyn.

deafness makes him oblivious to his surroundings, thereby buffering some of the misery of camp life.

Ivan Denisovich Shukhov

Ivan Denisovich Shukhov is a prisoner in the Gulag Archipelago serving a ten-year sentence for political crimes. Camp life has not destroyed him— he has never taken a bribe or allowed himself to sink to the low levels of morality.

A married man with children, Shukhov comes from the modest village of Temgenova and still retains a peasant's sense of moral order: God exists, but men and the Church are corrupt.

The character of Shukhov is one of an honest survivor. Hardened by the camps, he has not lost his dignity. He may steal food, but he would never steal another man's food. When he borrows tobacco from other zeks, he always returns it when his supply comes in. Survival requires a quick eye and some risk taking—a stolen plate, a hidden trowel, a bit of smuggled metal, a favor here, a simple task there. For a guard, he will do as much as he has to, but no more. For his squad leader, Tiurin, and for himself, however, he will work hard.

Andrei Prokofievich Tiurin

Andrei Prokofievich Tiurin is the squad leader of Ivan Denisovich's group. Not only does he organize the work parties, but he is also responsible for relating to camp officials—sometimes inaccurately—the amount of work done by his group. A seemingly decent man, he does what he needs to do in order to survive.

Tiurin is a Kulak, a member of the wealthy peasant class persecuted by Stalin. Once a decorated ''Red Army Man,'' he was discharged when it was discovered that his family's social status made him ''an enemy of the people.'' As Shukhov says of squad leaders: ''A good one will give you a second life, a bad one will put you in the coffin.'' He considers Tiurin to be a good one.

Kolya Vdovushkin

Kolya Vdovushkin is a medical assistant who knows little about medicine. Instead, he writes poetry during work hours. Kolya is an example of how a class system emerged within the camp itself, a system that protects some of the prisoners so that they may develop their talents.

Lieutenant Volkovoi

Lieutenant Volkovoi is the security chief in the gulag. Unpopular with the prisoners as well as the guards, he is even hated and feared by the commandant.

Themes

Survival

From the moment Shukhov wakes up until the moment he goes to sleep, only one thing is foremost on his mind: survival. The theme of surviving the deprivations of a Soviet work camp is the driving force of the story. Some survive by wit; some by luck. Some survive by sinking into inhumanity—becoming thieves, scavengers, and stool-pigeons. Several men will not survive the camps, but Shukhov is determined to not be one of them.

The men that will survive will become acquainted with the unwritten laws of the camp: do as much for the guards as you need, no more; always share your parcels with the right people—like your squad leader; watch out for your tools and hide them if you need to; obey—do not fight the authorities; don't hurry.

Survival and Food

Because survival is one of the most important issues of camp life, food takes on a special importance throughout the story. Every bit of bread and piece of meat becomes a cherished symbol of life. Every meal of oatmeal, thin stew, or bread ration is the vehicle one needs to reach the end of the day. If you get a bit of sausage in a parcel eat it slowly and chew it thoroughly—get every last drop of fat out of it. If you can swipe an extra bowl of oatmeal from the mess room orderlies, do so. Food (and tobacco) act as a means of exchange. Men trade with it, steal it, and will even kill for it.

Survival and God

Surviving the camps is not only a physical ordeal, it is also a spiritual trial. Solzhenitsyn would agree with the biblical quotation, ''Men do not live by bread alone, but by every word that proceeds out of the mouth of God.'' Just as men need bread to physically survive, so also they need a sustaining spiritual vision.

This theme can is illustrated at the morning meal—when the Ukrainian prisoners cross themselves—as well as the theological discussions of Shukhov and Alyosha. Alyosha represents a strict religious nature: reading scripture, praying, seeing not sorrow but God's joy, aiding others in their work. Even though there is plenty of cynicism, as in Shukhov's recounting of the sins of his local Orthodox priest, it is faith that keeps the men going.

The Human Condition: Suffering

Suffering has always been a theme of Russian literature—one only need think of Dostoyevsky's works. ''One Day'' depicts a life of beatings, food deprivation, and wet and cold weather.

Suffering is related to the spiritual theme: Alyosha quotes the Bible in the beginning of the tale, ''If you suffer, it must not be for murder, theft, . . . but as a Christian . . . to the honor of God,'' and ends the tale by quoting the Apostle Paul's prison epistles.

The Human Condition: Cruelty

Camp life is very cruel. The pressures of the camp and the lack of any human restraint on cruelty make the prison a hothouse of violence and abuse. For instance, the character Volkovoi is especially illustrative of human sin and cruelty. His power

Topics for Further Study

- Life in a work camp has a way of bringing out the essential character of human beings. How was this true in relation to Shukhov, Alyosha, Fetiukov, Tsezar, and Tiurin?

- Investigate "prison writings" from different cultures. Do they differ from era to era, culture to culture? Determine their impact on literature and history.

- The concentration camp is an invention of the twentieth century and has been used by the Soviets, the Chinese, the Nazis, and to a degree by the Americans in the incarceration of Japanese-Americans during World War II. Investi-

gate the concept of the concentration camp. Compare and contrast the various purposes and severity of such camps.

- Since "One Day" is almost devoid of political statements, how was Solzhenitsyn able to convey his political opinions in the story?

- Unlike the devout Alyosha, Shukhov is portrayed as a man of limited religious faith. Faith in God is an important theme in Solzhenitsyn's writings. What techniques does he use in "One Day" to communicate his ideas about Christian faith?

---

allows him to whip and torment prisoners with impunity. Volkovoi can make irrational demands—like stripping men down to their shirts in subfreezing cold—and the men must obey.

The Human Condition: Government and Absurdity

There is a strange absurdity to camp life. Ridiculous rules are put in place by the government. For example, men must take off their hats in subfreezing cold when passing guards. Limitations are made on the number of sick people allowed in any given day. Work is declared to be a form of medicine. Bribery is commonplace. Paperwork is full of lies. Men are expected to work without tools. Cold ground is to be drilled without thawing it first with fire. This is not the same as human cruelty—it's human stupidity. Ironically, the worst work site in the camp is the "Socialist Way of Life Village."

The Human Condition: Dignity

In spite of the horrid nature of camp life, human dignity is never lost. Though starving, Shukhov still balks at eating fisheyes and men still clean the fishbones from their table as an act of politeness. Men like Kilgas continue to make jokes and

Buinovsky reprimands men for their lack of dignity. Shukhov still finds joy in a job well done. Men share with those who have less. Alyosha still prays. Though you can treat men like dogs, you cannot take away their human dignity.

Style

Point of View

The point of view is that of an omniscient, third-person narrator. The story is told in a linear manner: from task to task, place to place, and from conversation to conversation. The author utilizes the speeches of various characters to make his point, but because the narrator is indicating which speeches are important, the reader is forced to listen carefully to the characters in order to understand their perspectives.

Narration and Language

Written in Russian, with a number of Ukrainian words thrown in, the story is easily comprehensible because of its direct, clear style. The conversations are simple and generally colloquial. The use of prison camp words like "zek," "Gulag," and "article 58," lend historical accuracy. The street language used by guards and prisoners realistically depicts the rough atmosphere of a prison. The humor is often ironic and understated.

Setting

The location is a Siberian prison camp during the post-World War II Stalinist era. As the title suggests, all the action of "One Day in the Life of Ivan Denisovich" takes place in a single day, from early morning to lights out. It follows a somewhat classical Aristotelian "unity of time, place, and action" in that the entire story remains focused on the central characters, in a specific location, and in a fixed time period.

Christian Realism

Solzhenitsyn is writing in the tradition of Christian Realism—a prophetic expression of truth in a redeeming spiritual framework. It is important to note that this it is not Socialist Realism, which was the ideologically acceptable method of writing in Russia at that time: full of happy endings and socially well-adjusted workers. Socialist Realism used literature as a form of propaganda.

Solzhenitsyn's narrative style was influenced by the American writer John Dos Passos and the Russian classics of Leo Tolstoy, Fyodor Dostoyevsky, Nikolay Gogol, and Aleksandr Pushkin. Also it is informed by his prophetic vision of the author as truth-giver: his is a tragic vision with a gleam of religious hope. Through the chronicling of events, the reader is drawn to see the message of the author. The events of Shukhov's day make the reader understand the life of a "zek."

Historical Context

"One Day in the Life of Ivan Denisovich" takes place in the context of the post-World War II Soviet Union. The Communist Revolution of 1917 had resulted in the overthrow of the Czar. The communist system that replaced Czarist Russia was even more totalitarian in nature than its predecessor. The planning and misplanning of the centrally organized economy resulted in constant shortages and production problems. Lenin gave great power to the inter-

nal security forces and began the use of work camp labor as a means of augmenting production.

After the death of Lenin, Stalin solidified his power and dominated the Soviet Union between 1924 and 1953. His government engaged in ethnic and religious purges, persecutions and harassment, and planned catastrophes like the famine in the Ukraine. Millions of people died during his violent and tyrannical regime.

The Gulag Archipelago was a system of prison camps spread throughout the Soviet Union. Gulag is an acronym for *Glanoe upravlenie ispravigtelno-trudovykh lagerei,* the administrative title for the work camps. A paranoid and cruel man, Stalin sent millions to the camps—some for ludicrous and meaningless reasons.

Stalin trusted no one except one man: Adolf Hitler. Ironically, Hitler betrayed him when the German leader attacked the Soviet Union in September 1941. Unfortunately Stalin's war with Germany allowed him to establish an alliance with the West as well as garner the support of intellectuals worldwide. With Stalin's death in 1953, and the subsequent de-Stalinization during the Khrushchev years, writers like Alexandr Solzhenitsyn were more able to express themselves.

The Cold War represented an intense competition between the United States and the Soviet Union. The race to explore space was generated by the launching of the Soviet satellite Sputnik, while tensions were raised worldwide by the advancement and spread of communism. The Cuban Missile crisis of 1962 generated real fears of Soviet power and expansionism.

In spite of this, the era of Khrushchev reflected a general thawing of the Stalinist attitudes. At the Twentieth Congress of the Party in 1956, Khrushchev delivered his "secret speech" that acknowledged some of the immense crimes of Stalin—a significant moment in Soviet history. Solzhenitsyn was later to remark about this speech: "I knew that my enemy Stalin had fallen, and I was on the way up."

The thaw began to impact the Soviet literary intelligentsia. *Novy Mir*, a literary magazine, was influenced by "liberal" ideas and in 1962 published "One Day in the Life of Ivan Denisovich." The story met with immediate success.

As Solzhenitsyn points out in the *Gulag Archipelago*, the forced labor camps were not an excep-

Compare & Contrast

- **1960s:** The Soviet Union and the United States are in the midst of the Cold War, a period of arms escalation and suspicion between the two superpowers. With the Soviet aid to Fidel Castro in Cuba, the United States fears communist forces and nuclear weapons stationed close to American soil. This tension resulted in the Cuban Missile Crisis in 1962; in the end, the Soviets were forced to remove missiles from Cuba.

  Today: Relations between the United States and a democratic Russia are friendly, despite some disagreement over recent actions in Serbia and Kosovo. Since the 1960s the two nuclear powers have signed several treaties regulating the proliferation of nuclear weapons and testing. Although Cuba remains a communist country, there are signs that it is adopting capitalist values.

- **1960s:** Under the leadership of Nikita Khruschev, censorship laws relax and writers are less hesitant to write and publish in the Soviet Union. After Khruschev's ouster in 1964, hard-liners assumed power and put into place harsh censorship laws.

  Today: Under the leadership of Boris Yeltsin, Russia became a free society with censorship laws similar to those of the United States. Authors such as Solzhenitsyn can publish with little or no fear of reprisal from the Russian government.

- **1960s:** The system of Soviet prison camps, known as the Gulag Archipelago, is filled with political dissidents, enemies of the State, criminals, and others that had somehow fallen into disfavor. These prisoners provide vital services: building infrastructure such as roads, bridges, factories, and dams. Conditions are harsh, and many prisoners die.

  Today: The Gulag system is no longer used in Russia. With the open policy, media is better able to monitor the criminal justice system, thereby stemming abuses; moreover, citizens can protest and publicize unfair sentences and treatment.

---

tion to the Soviet system, but an integral mechanism of the Soviet society. Without forced labor, much of the road building, dikes, canals, and public works could not have been built. In some ways, the era of glasnost (openness) and perestroika (restructuring), the dismantling of the Soviet Union into its representative states, the acceptance of democratic principles, and even the acceptance of a market economy, reflect an admission that the Soviet Socialist experiment was a failure.

Critical Overview

"One Day in the Life of Ivan Denisovich" garnered immediate critical and popular success. It was even reported that the Soviet Premier, Nikita Khrushchev, read and personally advanced its publication.

Breaking the taboo subject of Stalin's crimes in the heavily censored Soviet Union, however, was like cutting the rope on a catapult. It propelled Solzhenitsyn into the limelight of a whole generation of readers and writers who had been waiting for someone to broach the topic of Stalinism.

As Leopold Labedz described it: "the novel was a literary as well as a political bombshell; it received an enthusiastic reception on the part of liberal writers, a cautious one from the fence sitters, and it infuriated the die-hards." Yet in a sense, the hard-liners were right: Solzhenitsyn meant trouble for them. By opening the door for anti-Stalinism, writers began to openly publish and publicly discuss anti-communist ideas.

The critical acclaim "One Day in the Life of Ivan Denisovich" garnered was not only for its content, but also for what Solzhenitsyn's story said about Socialist Realism—a literary style that propa-

Russian slave laborers building the "Stalin Canal" under arctic conditions.

gated communist ideals. The publication of "One Day" meant freedom in regard to literary style as well as content.

As the political direction of Solzhenitsyn's writings became clear, the controversies concerning his writings intensified. He polarized both sides: in one sense, he was the radical upsetting the "conservative" communist nomenklatura (the people of power and knowledge). On the other side, the liberal Russians—modernists and avant-garde writers—found his traditionalist philosophy troublesome in its defense of non-westernized Russian culture, Orthodox religion, and patriotism.

Having attained almost immediate popular success, he gained even more moral advantage from the persecutions that followed. He found it impossible to publish anything in the Soviet Union. His writings were banned, and he was forced to publish in Samisdat (underground publication). He smuggled out his novels *First Circle, Cancer Ward,* and the *Gulag Archipelago* for publication abroad.

In the West, Solzhenitsyn was initially lauded by the media, readers, and political figures. While he was still a persecuted figure in the Soviet Union, his novels were popular in the West and received generally favorable reviews.

After his exile and especially after his lecture at a Harvard commencement, it became clear that he was not in any sense a Western liberal. In fact, his views were considered almost authoritarian.

His acceptance in the United States became increasingly polarized by national politics. American liberals castigated him for his anti-democratic values, rigorous orthodoxy, authoritarianism, and for his condemnation of what he saw as the excesses of American legalism, as well as sexual depravity and moral bankruptcy. Conservatives tended to view him as a prophetic ally in the battle against communism and Western moral decline.

At first hailed as a successor to the traditions of Leo Tolstoy, Anton Chekhov and Fyodor Dostoyevsky, Solzhenitsyn's stature has since dimmed slightly. However, he is still viewed as a writer of the first rank and his position is considered important as a "writer-prophet"—the artist who challenges the moral failures of a society.

In spite of the controversies regarding Solzhenitsyn's politics and controversial opinions, "One Day in the Life of Ivan Denisovich" has had almost continual positive critical acceptance in Western educational circles. Its dark themes of suffering and human perseverance in the face of evil have made it a popular text for high school and college English courses.

Criticism

James Sauer

Sauer has taught poetry and drama at Eastern College in Pennsylvania. In the following essay, he examines Solzhenitsyn's "One Day in the Life of Ivan Denisovich" and asserts that it is an "essentially Christian picture."

"One Day in the Life of Ivan Denisovich" presents a stark and concise indictment of the communist Soviet system. Unlike Solzhenitsyn's sprawling novels *First Circle, Cancer Ward,* or *August 1914,* "One Day in the Life of Ivan Denisovich" presents the essential human story of survival in a hostile government-sponsored hell. It is the fictional preface to the non-fictional *Gulag Archipelago.*

In "One Day" we have a stylized rendition of single day in the life of a "zek"—a political prisoner in Stalin's work camps. In the Gulag we have an edited anecdotal history of hundreds of political prisoners, what one critic called "fictionalized history," meaning it is not absolute history in a scientific sense, but the artistic portrayal of historical human life.

After a while, it ceases to matter whether it was twenty-five million, thirty-five million, or forty-five million that died during Stalin's regime. Whatever the number, it was evil—and Solzhenitsyn presented a vision against it. Both texts are witnesses to the tragic suffering of the Russian people. Both have been literary weapons in a war against human tyranny.

There is no escaping that "One Day" represents a biographical testament to Solzhenitsyn's life. Writers tend to write what they know; Solzhenitsyn used his life in the camps as the grist for his writing. But we engage in what C. S. Lewis called the "personal heresy"—the tendency to read literature as merely regurgitated autobiography—if we think that his art is just the reworking of his own memories. Solzhenitsyn's story was not about the traumatic psychology of one man. "One Day" embodies the collective autobiography of an entire generation of men and women swept up in the Soviet police state.

Marxist-Leninism was pathological and inefficient. Stalinism was applied Marxism-Leninism—applied unrelentingly to the backs of the Russian people. Tiurin, Shukhov's squad leader, tells the story of how he was stripped of his freedom because of his economic class and the his ancestry.

Many men were sent to the camps for having escaped from the Germans, like the "luckless" Senka—as if returning to one's fatherland was a crime. Solzhenitsyn himself was arrested for a thought crime expressed in a letter. "One Day in the Life of Ivan Denisovich" is a memorial to a point in history when the absurdity of George Orwell's *1984* took on flesh and dwelt among us.

Solzhenitsyn can easily be classified: he is an anti-communist. His is not a scholarly dissection of economic theory, but a living witness against a system that put men to death through Five-Year Plans. He is a prophet: like a man bearing witness to a sleeping generation while fires rage around, he awakens them to the memories of an incendiary holocaust.

He is also an artist: his vocation gives him a sense of calling, as he described it in his Nobel Lecture, "to save the world with beauty." And yet the beauty he presented is the sad beauty of human struggle.

He is a traditionalist: he loves the common sense of the common people, their ways, their lives, and their proverbs. He is a Russian: his is an old value system and he loves his country. He is learned, but simple. He is civilized, but coarse. He is a representative of the paradoxes that are Russia.

At the same time, "One Day in the Life of Ivan Denisovich" has a surprisingly modern voice. It is not a novel of refined Victorian sensibility. Its language is the language of the street. It also has the rough vices and virtues of human life about it. There are ambiguities in the workcamp. During periods of survival, issues of rectitude are sometimes stretched.

The State would not understand truth. If you tell it the truth you will be punished. When you are cold, you steal the cloth needed to cover the open windows. Honest men become honest thieves. But this is not the moral relativism of the West, full of decadence and unsure of absolutes. It is the history of men having a nightmare only to wake up and find it real. Solzhenitsyn's modern ambiguities are the recognition of what men can do to other men when they have "forgotten God."

What Do I Read Next?

- In *Darkness at Noon* (1940), Arthur Koestler chronicles the story of an innocent man purged by the Communist Party who, nevertheless, continues to believe in the Revolution. Koestler presents a fictionalized indictment of the Stalinist methods of forced confessions, show trials, and legal murder.

- The novel *1984* was written in 1948 and represented George Orwell's insightful analysis of the trend in ideological governmental control of our lives and thought through the beneficent image of "Big Brother." Life under totalitarian control is one large work camp.

- George Orwell's other totalitarian tale, *Animal Farm* (1945), is especially noteworthy for its satiric attack on Stalin. A socialist himself, Or-well uses the parable of farm animals revolting against the oppressing farmer only to be put under the tyranny of their fellow animals, the pigs, who proclaim that "All animals are equal, but some animals are more equal than others."

- Solzhenitsyn's three-volume *Gulag Archipelago* is a magnum opus of anecdotal history of the Soviet Gulag work camps. His treatment spans the camps from the time of Lenin to Brezhnev. Published: Volume I (1973), Volume II (1974), Volume III (1976).

- *Against All Hope* (1986) by Armando Valladares offers an ugly picture of humiliation, torture, and murder in Fidel Castro's Gulag system a little over a hundred miles from the American coast.

The opening pages of Michael Scammel's biography of Solzhenitsyn contains a quote from the author Octavio Paz that summarizes Solzhenitsyn's paradoxical voice:

"Solzhenitsyn speaks from another tradition and this, for me, is impressive; his voice is not modern, but ancient. It is an ancientness tempered in the modern world. His ancientness is that of the old Russian Christianity, but it is a Christianity that has passed through the central experience of our century—the de-humanization of the totalitarian concentration camps—and has emerged intact and strengthened. If history is the testing ground, Solzhenitsyn has passed the test. His example is not intellectual or political or even, in the current sense of the word, moral. We have to use an even older word, a word that still retains a religious overtone—a hint of death and sacrifice: witness. In a century of false testimonies, a writer becomes the witness to man."

The constrictions of Soviet society made it difficult for authors to write openly against it. This created a problem for the artists. Subconsciously, the artist must not say too much for fear of reprisal; but not say too little, for fear of having no art. This self-imposed censorship of the author created a form that allowed facts to speak for themselves.

Even the minor editing required to make "One Day in the Life of Ivan Denisovich" politically correct for publication in *Novy Mir* may have contributed to its literary power. Solzhenitsyn was forced not to tell, but to show. His natural tendency to pontificate was channeled into framing a story that would communicate in and of itself.

The pictures he created in "One Day" were like those of his prose poems. The picture was the picture of man oppressed, but not broken; of a man suffering, but not in despair; a man crucified, but rising again. It was an essentially Christian picture, transformed into the dimensions of a Russian icon: Ivan Denisovich Shukhov.

Source: James Sauer, "Overview of 'One Day in the Life of Ivan Denisovich,'" in *Short Stories for Students,* The Gale Group, 2000.

Frederik Pohl

Pohl has published many science fiction books and has edited several collections of short science fiction. In the following excerpt, he contends that instead of being censored and kept away from young people, "One Day in the Life of Ivan Denisovich" should be read by them as an important account of life in the Soviet Union.

"One Day in the Life of Ivan Denisovich" is the first and most famous novel written by Aleksandr Solzhenitsyn, who is not only a Nobel laureate but very possibly—there are no more than a handful who could challenge him—the 20th Century's greatest and most courageous writer.

It is the business of literature to tell us truths about ourselves and the world we live in, and in that way to give us understanding about what life is really like. This is an accomplishment of great value, because without it we can never really mature as human beings.

That is what "Ivan Denisovich" does for us. It tells us the story of one man—a single human being, whose story nevertheless is the story of many millions of other human beings—who has committed no fault, but through the evil caprice of a tyrant has been condemned to the terrible ordeal of life in a Soviet prison camp. Ivan Denisovich Shukhov has been stripped of everything. He has lost his wife, his children and his freedom. He owns nothing but the ragged clothes he wears and the crust of bread he has hidden in his mattress, and he is condemned to labor long hours in the deadly cold of a Russian winter, at the mercy of sadistic guards and "trusties" among his fellow prisoners . . . and yet he still remains human, and even decent. The novel is not a cheerful story, because the truth is not always cheerful. But it is a noble one.

And yet "One Day in the Life of Ivan Denisovich" has an unexpected distinction, for it is also one of the thirty-three books that those who would sanitize America's school libraries are most avid to suppress.

To learn that fact is to look into the naked face of madness.

What can the censors be thinking of? What child could be harmed, in what improbable way, by reading this splendid novel? Is it, for example, obscene?

But of course it is not; there is not a salacious passage, or even the hint of one, anywhere in the book. It does, to be sure, contain a few individual words—I have been able to count less than a dozen of them in the whole novel—which most of us

The constrictions of Soviet society made it difficult for authors to write openly against it. This created a problem for the artists. Subconsciously, the artist must not say too much for fear of reprisal; but not say too little, for fear of having no art. This self-imposed censorship of the author created a form that allowed facts to speak for themselves."

would prefer not to hear from the lips of our children. Most of us also realize, though, however much we may regret it, that none of our children will grow up without having encountered those words many times, in many places, perhaps even starting with the casual conversation of their littlest schoolmates. I do not believe that there is even one child, anywhere in the world, who will have learned any of those words through the reading of Solzhenitsyn's novel—but what a child may well learn from this book is the extent to which even decent people may be driven to crudeness in both speech and actions when they are being systematically dehumanized by brutes, and that is a lesson well worth having.

There are those, too, who do not wish to "spoil childhood" by acquainting the young with the more distasteful facts of human life. That's understandable. We would like to see our children happy and untroubled, because we love them. But children must grow, and to grow they must learn the bad things as well as the good: If we don't allow that, if in some unimaginable way we were possibly able to *prevent* that, all we could achieve would be to keep them childish forever. It is, I think, far better for children to learn what evil is from books than to put them in the position of learning it in some far more damaging way from real life later on.

> "It is, I think, far better for children to learn what evil is from books than to put them in the position of learning it in some far more damaging way from real life later on."

When Solzhenitsyn wrote "One Day in the Life of Ivan Denisovich" the very process of writing it was an act of conscience. His reason for writing the novel was simply that he could not live with himself if he didn't. Solzhenitsyn could not have seen any real possibility of getting the book published before the world, so that others could know the truth he had to tell; books containing far less hurtful truths had been suppressed in his country for forty years. More than that, he certainly knew that the mere act of writing it, if discovered, would mean his immediate arrest. That would at least send him back to those same degrading prison camps, if indeed it didn't cost him his life.

That "Ivan Denisovich" was published at all was almost an accident. It happened because Nikita Khrushchev, then the ruler of the Soviet Union, had his own political reasons for wanting at least some of the truths about the Stalin regime made public at last. It took courage for Solzhenitsyn to write it. It took courage for his first editor, Alexander Tvardovsky, to attempt to get it past the censors so that he could publish it in his magazine. It even took courage for Nikita Khrushchev to order that it be permitted, since Khrushchev himself had been a part of Stalin's bureaucracy and thus was not without guilt of his own for some of its evils.

It does not take nearly as much courage for any of us to allow the book to be read by our children—and I hope that we will find at least that much courage, all over this country of ours that has made dedication to freedom of speech and writing a part of its most sacred and fundamental law.

Source: Frederik Pohl, "'One Day in the Life of Ivan Denisovich,'" in *Censored Books: Critical Viewpoints,* Nicholas J. Karolides, Lee Burress, John M. Kean, eds., The Scarecrow Press, Inc., 1993, pp. 395–97.

Alfred Cismaru

In the following excerpt, Cismaru discusses Solzhenitsyn's depiction of food and scenes of eating in "One Day in the Life of Ivan Denisovich."

The year 1983 marks the twentieth anniversary of Alexander Solzhenitsyn's "One Day in the Life of Ivan Denisovich." Although this important work has benefited from numerous critical comments abroad, in this country there have been only cursory exegeses. With the hindsight of two decades it may be profitable to look at it again. Because the theme of physical survival is at the core of "One Day in the Life of Ivan Denisovich," and because, so far, its importance has been eclipsed by critics in favor of that of spiritual victory, this essay will emphasize Solzhenitsyn's concern with food collection, ingestion, digestion, and with body preservation in general.

Those who know Solzhenitsyn are aware of the fact that he is a hearty eater, a gourmet and perhaps even a gourmand. But this is not the main reason for his preoccupation with food as a requirement for survival. Men who have experienced the gulag, or indeed any imposed confinement, know that more than the rigors of climate, more than the forced marches and forced labor and the beatings and the spiritual deprivations, the incarcerated notes first and foremost the quasi-absence of food and the poor quality of that which is available. One need not go so far as Freud and proclaim that the mouth is the sexual organ *par excellence*, that eating is essentially a sexual act, in order to acquiesce in the centrality of food ingestion in man's daily routine. Moreover, no sort of spiritual well-being or preservation is possible for long on a starvation diet. It is this truism, more than Solzhenitsyn's own culinary concerns, that made him devote many a passage in "One Day in the Life of Ivan Denisovich" to the art of eating in prison.

Kuzyomin, the brigade foreman in the camp, a person with a twelve-year experience in the *modus vivendi* required by the gulag, has a formula for survival, one which he shares liberally with the others: "Here, fellows, *taiga* is the law." A Russian word meaning "virgin Siberian forest," *taiga* implies the law of the beasts of the jungle, the law that recognizes that only the fittest survive, and that fitness is the result of adequate food intake. No wonder, then, that the problems of hunger and diet are introduced as soon as the novel begins, in the description of the so-called breakfast shoved in front of the prisoners.

Ivan Denisovich Shukhov, with the accumulated tact of eight years of incarceration, looks upon eating as an artful endeavor whose gestures are meticulously performed, as befits the discipline of the artist:

> The only good thing about camp gruel was it was usually hot, but what Shukhov had was now quite cold. Even so, he ate it slow and careful like he always did. Mustn't hurry now, even if the roof caught fire. . . .
>
> The fish was mostly bones. The flesh was boiled off except for bits on the tails and the heads. Not leaving a single scale or speck of flesh on the skeleton, Shukhov crunched and sucked the bones and spit them out on the table. He didn't leave anything—not even the gills or the tail. He ate the eyes too when they were still in place.

Though Shukhov must be a beast, Solzhenitsyn adds, ''But when they'd [the eyes] come off and were floating around in the bowl on their own he didn't eat them.'' This line asserts not so much a minimal awareness of the fact that even in the jungle there are traces of morality and ethics, as it points to the necessity that ingestion must maintain certain standards which would not conflict with proper digestion. Should nausea and vomiting result from certain unappetizing foods, or from their unappetizing presentation, the calories taken in would be lost, at least partially. In his careful survival scheme Shukhov realizes that he cannot afford this risk.

Eating, then, is no longer an elemental activity, deriving from instinct and being pursued casually. It is a strategy replete with well-formulated tactics designed to afford the undernourished the best chances of retaining a viable body. More importantly, it becomes, without the here's knowledge, a religious ritual which is approached with respect and quasi-reverence. Thus, during lunch, the process of chewing every mouthful is described minutely. Shukhov's hands, lips, tongue, taste buds and facial muscles participate in unison, slowly and deliberately, for the ultimate enjoyment of swallowing and digesting. Every single trace of food is scraped from the bowl with a piece of bread saved until last for this purpose. When Shukhov has finished, the bowl looks as if it has been washed and dried by the most thorough of hands.

Prior to lunch on the same day, Shukhov has been able, through astute maneuvering and well-planned tactics, to secure from the kitchen staff a few extra bowls of food for his brigade. He thus becomes entitled to a second helping. Therefore he eats his first portion even more slowly, trying not to feel as partially full as he does normally. Having conditioned his stomach to the proper introduction

> Shukhov's spirit, then, reduced by imprisonment to instinct, acts in order to attain measurable and immediate results: the maximum caloric intake to maintain physical viability, which allows him to work and avoid the ire of the other prisoners and the camp authorities."

of the second ration, he proceeds to eat his mush with the acute pleasure of one who becomes sexually aroused again soon after experiencing climax. All his senses are now at play and extreme concentration is required in order for him to reach yet another gourmet's orgasm.

There is nothing mechanical in his approach. He is quite unlike prisoner K-123 at whom he looks from time to time, and about whom he concludes to himself: ''He ate his mush, but there was no taste in his mouth. It was wasted on him.'' On the contrary, Shukhov knows that to be content requires intent, and to reach perfect satisfaction requires the most elaborate premeditation. Since the body is a whole, it must participate wholly in the process of ingestion. Above all the brain must be engaged in picking up the food, introducing it into the mouth, chewing and swallowing it. No distractions are possible. Shukhov cannot understand why prisoner K-123 talks with another prisoner about a film he had seen a long time ago while eating his gruel. Activities extraneous to eating, while eating, can only diminish the benefits derived from food. Since it is a sexual sacrament, ingestion demands total bodily and spiritual involvement, without which the inadequate quantity and the poor quality of the food fail to contribute to the orgasmic satisfaction sought. And, significantly, such satisfaction, once gained, gives rise to a general feeling of well-being and to an optimistic view of life and the future, not unlike post-coital euphoria. On one occasion, after eating,

Shukhov is described as not having "a grudge in the world now—about how long his sentence was, about how long their day was, about that Sunday they would not get off. All he thought now was: 'We'll get through! We'll get through it all! And God grant, it'll all come to an end.'"

Post-meal euphoria is, however, like post-coital fulfillment, short-lived. Soon reality sneaks back, and at times, in order to avoid it, the hero's thoughts revert to the past, before his incarceration. But even recollections of family and friends pale before those having to do with food:

> In the camp he often remembered how he used to eat in the village—potatoes by the panful and pots of kasha, and in the early days before that, great hunks of meat. And they swilled enough milk to make their bellies burst. But he understood in the camps this was all wrong. You had to eat with all your thoughts on the food, like he was nibbling off these little bits now, and turn them over on your tongue, and roll them over in your mouth—and then it tasted so good, this soggy black bread.

When it is come by easily, affluence provides less pleasure than scarcity which is well managed and calculatingly appropriated. Of course, Shukhov does not see the sour-grapes attitude involved in such reasoning. His need to think that he is making a go of camp life is so great that he has succeeded in conditioning himself psychologically to feelings and thoughts that make survival possible. Yet, at the same time, it may be concluded that this is all the more to his credit because the gulag affords no other means of overcoming starvation and death.

In fact, starvation in the gulag is not merely punishment for sins committed against the State; it is above all a way of having the prisoners compensate the State, a way of controlling and rendering more efficient their labor which enhances the economic well-being of the State. That is why the slave-labor force of the camp is divided into brigades and why the collective work of the brigade is considered rather than that of an individual prisoner. Each has to do his share of work, or else all members of the brigade have their rations cut or diminished:

> In the camp they had these [brigades] to make the prisoners keep each other on their toes. . . . It was like this—either you all get something extra or you all starved. ("You're not pulling your weight, you swine, and I've got to go hungry because of you. So work, you bastard!")

Each *beast* in the camp must contribute, then, to the maintenance of survival based on food allotments, which in turn are based on the amount of daily work.

Not meeting a work quota even for one day involves a cut in rations. If the *beast* is not properly fed one day, the work quota cannot be met the next, which means that a vicious circle is created, leading to slow death by starvation. Hence *beast* pushes *beast* to do his best, the collective survival of all depending on the efforts of each. The gulag strips the person of even his most individualistic traits, and at the end of the tunnel, if ever one gets there, is a spoonful of mush.

The camp's currency is, of course, food. The State gets the work it wants done for the food it gives the prisoners; the authorities are bribed with food in parcels sent by relatives to the gulag; when a theft is committed food is always involved directly or indirectly. The emperor of the camp is the chief cook. He disposes of the food as he sees fit and puts on the airs of a French chef at a fancy resort. He controls innumerable assistants, acts pompously and authoritatively, yet all he actually does is boil water and groats, preparing a meal that any Boy Scout could fix over a campfire.

The importance of nourishment is presented with most vigor however in the oft-repeated or alluded to question of whether those who clear off the tables should lick the other prisoners' bowls thereby providing themselves with extra food. Kuzyomin's code forbids this, for it makes one dependent on scraps, and the humiliation of the act of licking is bound to strip one of any vestige of human dignity. Self-respect, though required for spiritual preservation, may be at odds with the caloric intake necessitated by the body. Shukhov is unable to choose easily: "And the worst thing was that if there was something left in the bowls you started to lick them. You couldn't help it." His concern for moral and esthetic standards conflicts with his appetite which is spurred by the continuous hunger within. But there is no transcendental reality in the gulag; there is no hereafter with its notions of reward and punishment. There is only the stark presence of starvation, the pain in the stomach emanating in the limbs and in the throat, the need to fill the void with something solid, with anything that will ease the hurt and make for life, or the semblance of life. There is nothing beyond the natural limits of the physical world here and now, and, within the confines of the camp, life is its own reward.

In addition, Kuzyomin's code may be wrong with reference to licking the bowls, reasons Shukhov, because it is wrong when it forbids a prisoner to spy on another prisoner. The code maintains that a stool pigeon cannot survive, but Shukhov's observation proves otherwise. He remarks: "About the secret spying he [Kuzyomin], of course, exaggerated. Exactly those [the stool pigeons] do survive." In the jungle there is no room for the niceties of principle, and those who live by the laws of the outside die inside. If Shukhov ultimately resists the temptation to lick the bowls, it is for the same practical reason that he would not eat the eyes of a fish floating in a soup: fear that physical repulsion would induce nausea and vomiting. The law of the *taiga* cannot be mellowed or modified, and Shukhov can only accept that part of it which helps physical survival. Kuzyomin cannot have it both ways; Shukhov will not even try, for the risk is personal annihilation.

In fact, the more one is confined in the gulag, the more animalistic his reaction to food becomes. For example, sniffing turns out to be the most efficient sensory mode for detecting the presence and the sort of food. When one of the prisoners, Caesar Markovich, receives a parcel from home, he need not unpack the contents in order for Shukhov to know exactly what they are:

> Like all the others he had the eyes of a hawk, and in a flash they ran over the things Caesar had laid out on the bed and on the locker. But though he still hadn't taken the paper off them or opened the bags, Shukhov couldn't help telling by . . . a sniff of the nose that Caesar had gotten sausage, canned milk, a large smoked fish, fatback, crackers with one kind of smell and cookies with another, and about four pounds of lump sugar. And then there was butter, cigarettes, and pipe tobacco.

Shukhov's sense of smell is so precise that he can distinguish "crackers with one kind of smell" from cookies with another. In the gulag, the human being-become-beast develops the instincts of the latter, and, in time, uses them with the same degree of accuracy.

Finally, the sacramental quality that food has for the incarcerated is shown poignantly in a discussion the hero has with the prisoner Alyoshka. The latter, a devout believer in the Baptist Church and a practitioner of its codes, talks to Shukhov in an attempt to convert him to Christianity. His speech, replete with vocabulary that might be effective outside, is powerless in the confines of the camp. Where physical survival is paramount, it is useless to invoke the might of the spirit, the immortality of the soul, and the purity of Paradise. Evangelical

metaphors, likewise, are ill-placed in the atmosphere of the gulag, and the miracle of moving mountains means little to someone whose every moment of continued existence is in itself a miracle. And so Alyoskha fails; but, significantly, when he refers to the daily bread in the Lord's Prayer, Shukhov properly asks: "You mean that ration [the daily one hundred gram bread allotment per man] we get?" Obviously, if that is all a person can hope for, or is permitted to ask of God, then, Shukhov reasons, there is not much point in prayer.

Shukhov's spirit, then, reduced by imprisonment to instinct, acts in order to attain measurable and immediate results: the maximum caloric intake to maintain physical viability, which allows him to work and avoid the ire of the other prisoners and the camp authorities. One can stay alive this way, and one can count the days that pass and those that remain in one's sentence. We meet Shukhov for only one day. We do not know if he will survive until he is released, or indeed if he will be released—the Soviet courts can renew a sentence if they so seem advisable. Still, we may conclude that his chances of self-preservation are good. After all, the law of the *taiga* may have its shortcomings (Shukhov recognizes these himself), but it is a natural law, one that ought to work. Man's responsibility to his body may be secondary under normal conditions; within the narrow limitations of the gulag it becomes primordial.

Source: Alfred Cismaru, "The Importance of Food in 'One Day in the Life of Ivan Denisovich,'" in *San Jose Studies,* Vol. 9, No. 1, Winter, 1983, pp. 99-105.

Robert L. Yarup

When this article was published, Yarup was affiliated with Indiana University of Pennsylvania. In the following excerpt, he examines Solzhenitsyn's use of sensory imagery—particularly that of sound and taste—in "One Day in the Life of Ivan Denisovich."

Much in the manner of Macbeth's offstage murder of his kinsman, sound or the lack of it in the opening section of "One Day in the Life of Ivan Denisovich" forces attention on the meaning of the hammering and the significance it has for Denisovich as it beckons his consciousness to awaken to the fact of Soviet domination and oppression. In fact the five basic sense perceptions play a distinct part in the opening section to dramatize the novel's underlying theme and to underscore the omnipresent conflict between body and spirit that manifests itself at every turn of Denisovich's day. The parallel is clear: primitive sense perception dramatizes man's instinct for freedom. Indeed, the agonizing cry of man's unquenchable need for freedom is antithetically heard in the emblematic and "ringing" Soviet hammer.

The Soviet dissection of the human personality, however, is the dominant motif as each sense registers a negative sensation. Sound or the lack of it is reiterated in all three paragraphs. In the first it becomes fused with feeling, both physical and mental. The sound of repression, "The ringing noise" of "a hammer pounding on a rail," comes "through the windowpanes covered with ice" and thus is immediately associated with the "cold," a burden from which Denisovich is never released. Contrarily, while the effect has infinitesimal ramifications for Shukhov, the anonymous bellman of oppression, who "didn't feel like going on banging," can nonchalantly rid himself of the "seventeen and a half below" temperature.

In the second paragraph, "the sound stopped and it was pitch black." The effect of the blackness increases the awareness of bondage. The ears strain without accompanying sight. The intensity of the shrill sound of "ringing" in an atmosphere of ice is replaced with a psychological chain. The idea pervades. Nothing breaks its terrifying grip. Within this vacuum, the blackness is given analogous meaning: "just like in the middle of the night when Shukhov had to get up to go to the latrine." Shukhov is compelled biologically to relieve himself, and, as if to reinforce this meaning of compulsion, Solzhenitsyn then focuses on the "three yellow beams [which] fell on the window" from the compound lights. The image of prison bars, Shukhov's biological compulsion, and the blackness thus fills the vacuum with realization which the hammering sounds.

In the final paragraph silence continues as consciousness beyond awareness of bondage has not yet awakened: "He didn't know"; "nobody'd come"; "And you couldn't hear the orderlies hoisting the latrine tank." As the sound, sight, and feeling of enslavement is absorbed into the body, its stench is likewise registered by the residue of man's biological waste. The odor must be all encompassing, for there are two hundred men in the barracks, and the "twenty-gallon" tank is filled to capacity. The stench becomes as much a part of Denisovich as the air he breathes.

Of the five senses, taste is omitted. Does the absence of that sense which accompanies man's most essential physical need demand explication, or is it sufficient to note that "You couldn't help" licking the bowls in the morning?

Thus in the opening three paragraphs, Solzhenitsyn dramatizes how the most primitive, physical aspects of man are subjugated to Soviet domination. His body is dissected into parts, and there seems less than little difference between the labor camp inmate and his counterpart emerging from the Ice Age. And yet he does emerge with an instinct towards freedom. The "stars" are obscured by the compound lights, the words of Peter and Paul are hidden away in Alyoshka's notebook; "It's the law of the jungle here, . . . But even here [man] can live." And if the reader steps back and sees the panoramic view of man emerging from darkness into the light of the "red sunrise" and understands the spiritual message of Peter and Paul which frames Denisovich's day, he will also perceive Solzhenitsyn hammering out his theme of man's irrepressible instinct for freedom.

Source: Robert L. Yarup, "Solzhenitsyn's 'One Day in the Life of Ivan Denisovich'," in *The Explicator,* Vol. 40, No. 3, Spring, 1982, pp. 61–3.

Gleb Zekulin

When this article was published, Zekulin was affiliated with McGill University. In the following excerpt, he provides an overview of the plot, style, and themes of "One Day in the Life of Ivan Denisovich."

It is little over a year since A. Solzhenitsyn's first story 'One Day in the Life of Ivan Denisovich' was published in the Soviet Union. It made history there and, for a time, became the most discussed book in the west as well. This interest, both in the USSR and the west, was mainly 'sensational' and due to the exposure of what Tvardovski in his foreword calls euphemistically 'the unhealthy symptoms in our development which are linked with the period of the personality cult'. The literary value of the story was discussed very little. . . .

[The story] is a mine of information, much more so than the well-known 'Notes from the House of the Dead' by Dostoyevski which treats in a not dissimilar artistic manner the same theme—life in a prison camp—and to which it has often been compared. Firstly, we find an almost minute-by-minute time-table of a camp inmate's long day. We are given detailed descriptions of what he wears and eats, what tricks he uses to protect himself against cold, hunger and the senseless cruelty of his fellow-prisoners and, especially, of his guards. Further, we are acquainted with the organization of the camp, the layout of the compound and of the building-site where the prisoners work, the system of guarding them inside the camp, during their daily march to work and back, and while they work. Then, the work itself is described thoroughly. In brief: having read the story, we know how the prisoner lives, what he does and thinks, we know what punishment he can receive and for what, and even what would happen to him if he escaped.

A comparatively large proportion of space is devoted to the portrayal of Ivan Denisovich Shukhov and his fellow-inmates. The mass of the prisoners are divided into 'good ones', i.e. all those whom the author calls 'donkey-workers' (*rabotyagy*), and 'bad ones', i.e. those who managed to find for themselves by hook, but largely by crook, a 'cushy job' as an orderly, cook or minor clerk, to avoid manual work and increase their chances of survival. A whole range of means is reported by which such a position of relative security can be obtained: from morally unimpeachable ones, like possession of a specific skill or smartness or just sheer luck, to the morally bad ones, like exaggerated servility or bribes, or—worst of all—denunciation of fellow-prisoners to the camp authorities. Thus, the 'bad ones' who collaborate with the camp authorities are subdivided into two groups on the simple criterion of whether they do this under duress or of their own free will.

The 'good ones' are also subdivided into the group of the 'better' and the 'not-so-good'. This subdivision is much more subtle and reflects, to some extent, those values which enter into the Soviet code of ethics: thus, the man who helps his fellow-prisoners in any way (e.g. the brigade leader Tyurin) or who pulls his weight conscientiously in the work (e.g. the brigade member Klyovshin) belongs to the first group. (A curious and rather unexpected detail which, in all probability, also reflects an attitude common in the Soviet Union outside the camps but, this time, is opposed to the 'official line', is the possibly unconscious unwillingness on the part of the author to put the non-Russians into the group of the 'better ones'; for instance, the two Estonians who help others and work conscientiously, etc., etc., and possess in addition other moral and civic virtues, are neverthe-

> **Thus in the opening three paragraphs, Solzhenitsyn dramatizes how the most primitive, physical aspects of man are subjugated to Soviet domination."**

less classified as 'not-so-good ones'. Is it that Solzhenitsyn, like his nineteenth century predecessors, still views non-Russians as incapable of entirely pure, unselfish and noble motivations? This explanation seems to be fortified by Solzhenitsyn's other nineteenth century traits, as will be shown later.)

The guards and warders in the camp and the soldiers who escort the prisoners to outside work and guard them there are shown in much less detail. Both groups are clearly enough the prisoners' enemies. But the soldiers of the escort are hated only as representatives of the authorities, of 'them,' while the camp guards are hated with a frightening intensity (e.g. the secret police officer Volkovoi who, not long before, carried a whip which he used freely on prisoners, mainly those incarcerated in single cells of the BUR, this 'prison within the prison' and the only solid stone building on the camp site).

'One Day . . .' provides the reader with direct information on other matters, less detailed but no less revealing. For example, the few remarks about the 'free men' (*volniye*) living near the construction site and for whom the prisoners have built houses and a cinema, show that their life is not so very much easier than that of the prisoners: their food is bad, very inadequate and rationed (the year in which the action takes place is 1951); they are apt to steal at the site not only the materials and the tools which belong to the government (therefore, perhaps, in their minds, to nobody or even to 'themselves') and which, for this reason, have to be guarded day and night, but even, incomprehensibly, the bowls from which the prisoners eat.

From incidental references to kolkhoz life we learn (in addition to more familiar matters) of a farm on which no able-bodied men remain; instead, with the connivance of the farm's authorities, they travel

" Probably the most striking feature of the stories is the calm and detachment of presentation. The emotional stress which the subject-matter itself created must have been tremendous, but it never appears on the surface."

across the country, sometimes even by air, earning big money by smearing with the help of three pseudo-artistic stencils carpet patterns on old bed sheets or any old piece of fabric.

There is in the story a wealth of indirect information as well. Perhaps the most interesting is a short survey of Soviet history from a peculiar though not unique angle: the generations of camp inmates. From 1930 to 1951 the flow of prisoners never diminished. The first prisoners, victims of the collectivization drive, were serving their first term when in 1935, after Kirov's assassination, a new wave was sent to the camps, followed by that of the Great Purge which started in 1937. They were serving their second term when, after the war began, the soldiers who managed to break out of German encirclements and get back to their lines began to arrive, and continued to arrive until the end of the war. And those of them who survived were serving their third term in 1951 and 'breaking in' new prisoners—actors, students, Baptists, Heroes of the Soviet Union, naval officers, directors of industry and bureaucrats, old men, middle-aged men and almost children—who came in a continuous stream to the camps with uniform sentences, now expediently increased to 25 years.

The question of people's attitude to work as treated in 'One Day . . .', in relation to the place of work in the official Soviet scale of values, deserves a short study in itself. . . . The 'big scene' in the story is the prisoners' work on building a wall. At first glance this scene is the apotheosis of work, a song of praise to work (and, incidentally, the story's

only 'redemption' theme). But, seen more closely, it becomes quite plain that Shukhov and his brigade do not work for the work's sake but in order to erect as quickly as possible a shield against the killing frost and to receive a bigger ration of bread. Their enthusiasm has no other basis. Among his mates Shukhov is the only one who pays attention to the quality of the work (and even he slips a little towards the end of the scene), and the pride of work well done is a particular feature of his own character, not the general attitude. . . .

The two stories, 'One Day . . .' and 'Matryona's Household', are not sketches (a genre which has been very popular in the Soviet Union since the early 1930s, and the artistic purpose of which is to draw attention to some external feature of life in general, some topical matter of public importance), but works of art, the purpose of which is to expose a problem (external or internal) which attracts or worries the author personally and which, in this opinion, deserves or needs his comments or his attempt at a solution. As works of art the two stories are based on the author's knowledge, understanding and interpretation of life, in this case, on facts and happenings which he has actually experienced. (In 'One Day . . .' he identifies himself with his characters and three or four times, when speaking about them, he uses the personal pronoun '*we*'; 'Matryona's Household' is narrated in the first person.) The descriptive and narrative method he selects is 'direct' and 'objective': he represents life as it would be seen and understood by any 'normal' person, that is, by people who neither possess any special knowledge, skill or understanding, nor have any extraordinary sensitivity, emotionality or mental or spiritual deformity. This method is usually called realism. The specific facts of life narrated and analysed in this cool and detached, direct way acquire through the author's sincere and impassioned moral and intellectual *engagement* (usually called in such cases compassion) an intensity and sharpness which give them the qualities of universality and authenticity.

The problem which excites and worries Solzhenitsyn in these two stories is a familiar one to Russian literature, namely that of the Russian peasant. His approach to this problem, his comment upon it and—perhaps, it would be right to say—his attempt to solve it, is traditional for Russian literature (particularly that of the nineteenth century). His Russian peasant, as exemplified by Shukhov and by Matryona, is seen with all his faults; and at the same time he is idealized as he was by Grigorovich,

Turgenev, Nekrasov, Lev Tolstoy *et al.* This idealization, for lack of other moral or social qualities present in the Russian peasantry, has to concentrate on two intangibles which can be neither proved nor disproved. These are patience and love of work.

The patience of the Russian peasant was for a long time a favourite theme with Russian writers who liked to see the peasant as the conscious 'bearer of the cross', the martyr suffering willingly and hoping for reward only in the other world. It is difficult to understand this view of the Russian peasant, which was shared even by such exponents of the peculiar brand of peasant socialism as Chernyshevski and the Populists, or by such clear-headed and rational thinkers as Herzen. 'Pure idealizers', while sympathizing deeply with the peasants, admiring them boundlessly, glorifying their Christian virtue and condemning morally those who seemed to be responsible for these shameful conditions, were content to leave things more or less as they were. 'Progressive idealizers' thought to see the answer simply in overthrowing tsarism and transferring power to other hands; they hardly began to think of how, in practice, this would affect the peasants; they were only sure that their action would relieve the peasants of their undeserved martyrdom.

The notion of the Russian peasant as a mute and always patient sufferer became so widespread (it is the cornerstone of a myth known the world over under the name of 'the Russian Soul') that it does not seem to have occurred to writers (and politicians, too) to look for other inherent characteristics, possibly more specific, to explain his condition (such as inability or unwillingness to think of the common good or far ahead, or to feel as a member of an organization of fellow human beings—characteristics to be found more readily in the masses of all races and nationalities than patience and readiness to suffer).

The Russian peasant's love of work was, again traditionally, elevated by writers of both the nineteenth and twentieth centuries to the level of a moral quality, and that, through a peculiar logic, for the very reason that in real life the opposite is the case. We are told that the peasant is lazy, indolent, fond of dodging work and, when forced to work, doing it in the most perfunctory manner. And, in the opinion of 'idealizers', the peasant is right in being as he actually is, because he is forced to do the work which is of no benefit or no interest to him. Let him work as he wants—they suggest—and he will pro-

duce miracles of cleverness, skill and artistry, and all this by intuition or inspiration, without training or preparation.

The curious fact that Solzhenitsyn continues the traditional idealization of the Russian peasants seems to suggest that the conditions of their life today are not basically different from those a of century ago. 'Matryona's Household' indicates that even the peasants' material condition has not changed appreciably. In so far as this is the case, its implications as regards the Soviet regime can scarcely be exaggerated.

The artistic merits of 'One Day ...' and 'Matryona's Household' are very considerable. Not only is there sincerity and passion (which, in this case, is indignation at the way peasants, human beings, are being treated), without which a work of art is flat and unconvincing, but also great craftsmanship, ability to narrate a story and remarkable skill in doing so.

Probably the most striking feature of the stories is the calm and detachment of presentation. The emotional stress which the subject-matter itself created must have been tremendous, but it never appears on the surface. 'Internally', this is because Solzhenitsyn is concerned with more than the immediate subject-matter, which is only the outer skin of his ideas and ideals. 'Externally', he achieves this composure firstly, by careful selection of facts, secondly, by strict control over his vocabulary and use of language.

The facts selected for representation are in both stories ordinary—life, external, commonplace facts, like, in the case of Shukhov, getting-up, having breakfast, going to work, working, returning, having supper, spending a few leisurely moments and going to bed; in the case of Matryona, their range is deepened (but not extended) by her hopes, dreams and memories. Never is there resort to emotional colouring, hyperbole or cheap sensationalism (which, with the subject-matter on hand, would be an easy slip to make for a lesser and less disciplined writer). The impact on the reader is achieved through his realization of how and why these commonplace facts of life are different from anything we know in our own life.

The description and narrative are conducted in a language which is cool and placid, simple and matter-of-fact. The type of language used is almost colloquial; it turns into slang or dialect in the dialogues, which are employed sparingly and only in order to emphasize or clarify the narrative or the description. The vocabulary is that of an educated Russian well versed in his national literature. There is no intentional play with words, no attempt to achieve special 'artistic' effects by means of words, though Solzhenitsyn does create a great number of new words, mainly descriptive, mostly by an unusual method of noun-formation; but all his neologisms are perfectly understandable without special philological knowledge and are very effective.

Source: Gleb Zekulin, ''Solzhenitsyn's Four Stories,'' in *Soviet Studies,* Vol. XVI, No. 1, July, 1964, pp. 45–62.

Sources

Labedz, Leopold, ed. *Solzhenitsyn: A Documentary Record*, Bloomington: Indiana Press, 1973, 320 p.

Scammell, Michael. *Solzhenitsyn: A Biography*, New York: Norton, 1984, 1051 p.

Further Reading

Barker, Francis. *Solzhenitsyn: Politics and Form*, New York: Harper and Row, 1977, 112 p.
    Scholarly analysis of the political function of Solzhenitsyn's writings. It shows how Solzhenitsyn's later writings moved him from democratic values to traditional Russian authoritarianism.

Bjorkegren, Hans. *Alexandr Solzhenitsyn: A Biography*, New York: Third Press, 1972, 186 p.
    A dated, but readable biography of Solzhenitsyn. Gives a good chronology of controversy over ''One Day in the Life of Ivan Denisovich.''

Ericson, Edward E., Jr. *Solzhenitsyn: The Moral Vision*, Grand Rapids, MI: Eerdmans, 1980, 239 p.
    A survey of Solzhenitsyn's works using the theme of moral and religious vision.

Labedz, Leopold, ed. *Solzhenitsyn: A Documentary Record*, Bloomington: Indiana Press, 1973, 320 p.
    Collection of letters, speeches, pronouncements and notes by the participants in Solzhenitsyn's literary life and the Soviet establishment which sought to suppress him.

Nielsen, Niels C., Jr. *Solzhenitsyn's Religion*, New York: Thomas Nelson, 1975, 164 p.
    An analysis of Solzhenitsyn's literary faith, with special emphasis on the Orthodox Church.

Scammell, Michael. *Solzhenitsyn: A Biography*, New York: Norton, 1984, 1051 p.
    A thorough biography of Solzhenitsyn. Scammell offers a critical analysis that sees the greatness of the writer, as well as displaying his personal weaknesses.

Solzhenitsyn, Alexandr. *The Oak and the Calf*, New York: Harper and Row, 1979.
    Solzhenitsyn's memoir of literary life in the Soviet Union. It contains a kind of personal account of his emergence as a writer, the petty politics of writers, and of the censorial powers of the Soviets.

Solzhenitsyn: A Pictorial Autobiography, New York: Farrar, Straus, and Giroux, 1974, 95 p.
    A dated but entertaining overview of the man, providing a visual feeling of his life and times.

A Spinster's Tale

Peter Taylor
1940

First published in the *Southern Review* in 1940, Peter Taylor wrote ''A Spinster's Tale'' while he was still an undergraduate at Kenyon College. A rich and complex story, ''A Spinster's Tale'' touches on Taylor's recurring themes: family dynamics, gender conflicts, and, most importantly, life in the American South in the early twentieth century.

''A Spinster's Tale'' is considered one of Taylor's finest short stories and is often praised for its honest depiction of growing up in the America South. Yet because it was published so early in Taylor's career, some critics believe that the story tends to be overlooked in favor of his later works.

Author Biography

In 1917 Peter Taylor was born in Trenton, Tennessee. His mother, Katherine, was a daughter of Tennessee Governor Robert Taylor; his father, Matthew, was descended from a prominent western Tennessee family. Not surprisingly, much of Taylor's short fiction, including ''A Spinster's Tale,'' depicts the lives of upper-middle-class residents of Tennessee.

Taylor's fiction reflects the changing environment of the American South. Southern culture revered tradition, but it was nonetheless changing rapidly during Taylor's youth: new, modern cities

were replacing the largely rural landscape of the past, the established roles of men and women seemed to be destabilizing, and African Americans were challenging laws of racial separatism. Taylor's fiction reflects all of these subjects, though sometimes in only the most indirect way.

Taylor spent a year in England after high school and then returned to America. He attended several colleges in the late 1930s. His story, "A Spinster's Tale," was his first story to appear in a major literary journal, the *Southern Review*, edited by Cleanth Brooks and Robert Penn Warren.

By the late 1940s, Taylor was teaching and writing fiction. He published his first book of stories in 1948.

Through the 1950s and 1960s, Taylor published regularly in the *New Yorker*. He was a visiting professor at Harvard and received an O. Henry prize for short story excellence. In 1969 Taylor's *Collected Stories* was published. In 1986 he won the prestigious PEN/Faulkner Award for his short fiction collection *The Old Forest*.

His only novel, *A Summons to Memphis*, won the Pulitzer Prize in 1987. A year later, Taylor was a founding member of a new group called the Fellowship of Southern Writers, which was dedicated to promoting Southern literary efforts. He died in 1994.

Plot Summary

The first line of "A Spinster's Tale" reveals several important facts: "My brother would often get drunk when I was a little girl, but that put a different sort of fear into me from what Mr. Speed did." The author reveals (as the story's title also suggests) that his narrator is older now, that drinking played an important role in her family life, and that there is a menacing character named Mr. Speed.

The narrator, Elizabeth (named after her late mother), discusses her vague obsession with Mr. Speed, the town drunk. Elizabeth's father dismisses him as a "rascal," yet Elizabeth suggests that she will eventually confront Mr. Speed.

Elizabeth reveals some of her fears when she stands before a mirror, craving escape, whispering "away, away," until she bursts into tears. She then sees Mr. Speed "walking like a cripple" down the street. Elizabeth remembers her late mother and tries to forget about Mr. Speed.

One evening, Elizabeth stays awake until her brother returns home. He offers her candy, but she reenters her bedroom. He follows and she smells the "cheap whiskey" on his breath. Crying and hugging him, she exclaims, "I'm always lonely." The narrator recounts:

> He kept his face turned away from me and finally spoke, out of the corner of his mouth, I thought, "I'll come home earlier some afternoons and we'll talk and play."
>
> "Tomorrow."
>
> When I had said this distinctly, I fell away from him back on the bed. He stood up and looked at me curiously, as though in some way repelled by my settling so comfortably in the covers. And I could see his eighteen-year-old head cocked to one side as though trying to see my face in the dark. He leaned over me, and I smelled his whiskey breath. It was not repugnant to me. It was blended with the odor he always had. I thought he was going to strike me. (Excerpt from "A Spinster's Tale")

Later Elizabeth confesses "something like a longing for my brother to strike me," and she wishes that she had said to him languidly, 'Oh Brother,' (as if we had in common some unmentionable trouble." But Elizabeth then says "I would not let myself reflect further on my feelings for my brother—my desire for him to strike me and my delight in his natural odor"; she wants to be "completely settled with Mr. Speed first."

Her brother comes home early the next day and Elizabeth acknowledges to herself that she has "come to accept (Mr. Speed's) existence as a natural part of my life." Sure enough, Mr. Speed appears, and Elizabeth's brother even helps him retrieve his hat, which is blown off by the wind. "Mr. Speed is very ugly, brother," Elizabeth says, but he responds "You'll get used to him, for all his ugliness."

One afternoon her brother and his friends stop by the house. One of the boys, only a year older than Elizabeth, asks her why she doesn't wear her hair up as young women did at that time. Elizabeth blushes at this remark and bursts into the closed parlor where her father and uncles had been visiting, not heeding the boy's pleas to leave the doors shut. Later, Elizabeth is glad that "I was a bold, or at least naughty, little girl."

She is then lightheartedly accused of "flirting" with the youngest visiting boy and told "if you spend your time in such pursuits you'll only bring upon yourself and upon the young men about Nashville great unhappiness."

At this moment, Mr. Speed appears. Elizabeth tries to express her fear of Mr. Speed to her father, who tells her that she must shut her eyes against some things then says "'After all ... you're a young lady now.'"

At the story's climax, Mr. Speed runs onto Elizabeth's porch to escape the rain. The maid mistakes him for Elizabeth's father and opens the front door for him. After he drunkenly enters the house, Elizabeth stares at him while the servant begs her to run upstairs to safety.

Part of Elizabeth longed "to hide my face from this in my own mother's bosom," but another part wants to "deal with Mr. Speed, however wrongly, myself." Elizabeth phones for the police, who come and take Mr. Speed away. "I was frightened by the thought of the cruelty which I found I was capable of, a cruelty which seemed inextricably mixed with what I had called courage."

Elizabeth's father is angry when he learns that she called the police. That was the last time she ever saw Mr. Speed, but even in her old age Elizabeth is still clearly affected by him. The story ends: "It was only the other night that I dreamed I was a little girl on Church Street again and that there was a drunk horse in our yard."

Characters

Betsy
See Elizabeth

Brother
Elizabeth's brother is intelligent and kind. In one scene with incestuous overtones, Elizabeth hugs her brother in her bedroom, crying but also wishing that he would strike her. He tells Elizabeth that she will get used to Mr. Speed "for all his ugliness."

Elizabeth
The narrator of the story, Elizabeth is an elderly spinster recalling her adolescent years. As a youth she lived with her brother and father in a comfortable, large house. She is also repulsed by, but strangely obsessed with, the town drunk, Mr. Speed.

Various critical readings exist regarding Elizabeth: first, she is searching for a feminine maternal presence in her life; second, that the grotesque Mr. Speed introduces the harshness of adult life to young Elizabeth; third, Elizabeth's only view of sexuality comes from intimidating male figures. All of these readings, and others, imply that the events of these critical years cause Elizabeth to become a spinster later in life.

Father
A widower, Elizabeth's father is an important male presence; she feels affection for him yet connects him with the grotesque Mr. Speed. In the end, Elizabeth's father is displeased with his daughter's decision to turn Mr. Speed over to the police.

Lucy
Lucy is the African-American housekeeper at Elizabeth's house. She also appears at the critical moment of the story's conclusion, pleading with Elizabeth to stay away from Mr. Speed. Elizabeth defies Lucy and chooses to confront him, suggesting that perhaps Mr. Speed and Lucy represent opposite emotions, such as security and fear.

Narrator
See Elizabeth

Old Speed
See Mr. Speed

Mr. Speed
Although he never speaks an entire sentence, Mr. Speed is nonetheless a critical character in this story. He intimidates and repulses the young Elizabeth, and she is alarmed to find similarities between Mr. Speed and her brother and father. The story's climax occurs when he bursts into Elizabeth's house. She calls the police, and he is arrested.

Mr. Speed may represent many things to Elizabeth, among them masculinity, the consequences of alcoholism, and the deterioration of Southern society. Even his name suggests that he "speeds" Elizabeth's maturation or "speeds" her toward some unpleasant sexual initiation or toward spinsterhood.

Themes

Growth and Development
That Elizabeth recalls so vividly the events recorded in "A Spinster's Tale"—in particular her discovery of Mr. Speed as well as her ultimate

Topics for Further Study

- Watch the 1942 Orson Welles film *The Magnificent Ambersons* or read John Cheever's short story "The Fourth Alarm." These two works, like "A Spinster's Tale," make references to the advent of automobiles and to the general themes of changing technology and changing times. Compare and contrast how each work addresses changes in society or technology.

- View D. W. Griffith's 1915 film *The Birth of a Nation* or the classic 1939 film *Gone With the Wind.* How do these films depict the South? How do these films depict women and African Americans? What similarities are there between the character Scarlett O'Hara, in *Gone With the Wind* and Elizabeth in "A Spinster's Tale"? What are the major differences?

- Read Maya Angelou's *I Know Why the Caged Bird Sings,* a nonfiction memoir of growing up in Arkansas from an African American perspective. Compare some of Angelou's experiences with Elizabeth's. Despite their racial differences, are there any similarities between Elizabeth and Angelou?

confrontation with him—indicates that these are pivotal moments in her youth. It can also be inferred that these events affected Elizabeth for the rest of her life.

Coming to terms with her family—including her late mother—as she is growing up seems to be Elizabeth's unspoken mission throughout this story. She recalls suggestive, ambiguous scenes with her brother (in her bedroom when she pleads loneliness, then wishes he would strike her) and father (when he tells Elizabeth to close her eyes to Mr. Speed) that describe her attempts to understand them.

When Elizabeth reports Mr. Speed to the police, it seems her father's disapproval of this act is as important as the act itself. It suggests (along with Elizabeth's spinsterhood) that growing up was con-

fusing for Elizabeth, and these events may have stunted her, sexually and socially, for life.

Sex Roles

One way to read "A Spinster's Tale" is to view it as Elizabeth's unsuccessful search for a proper female role model. A young girl raised in a house of men, it is apparent from her odd dreams and her vivid descriptions of Mr. Speed's drunkenness that Elizabeth is fearful of masculinity— especially in light of her own budding femininity. However, she has a strong attachment to her father and brother— who both drink, (although considerably less than Mr. Speed does)—and is concerned how alcohol affects them.

She also seeks an answer to the crucial question: what is the appropriate way for a young woman to act in a male-dominated household? At times she is coquettish, even alluring (the bedroom scene with her brother); or cute and defiant (when she bursts into the parlor and "flirts" with a young boy); or assertive (threatening to report the family cook to the police); and finally, sometimes powerless and scared (revealing her loneliness and her fear of Mr. Speed).

Nonetheless, Elizabeth's final act—reporting Mr. Speed to the police—seems to be her most significant one. Because Elizabeth has become a spinster, this final action, reveals that Elizabeth never learned how to act appropriately in her father's eyes.

A feminist reading of "A Spinster's Tale" might even suggest that since women are expected to be silent and demure, Elizabeth's ability to assert authority made her unattractive to men, who expect women to act in a more subservient way.

Sex

Several critics have noted the importance of sexual issues in "A Spinster's Tale." Given Elizabeth's confusion over masculinity, it is not surprising that at different times she seems both attracted and repelled by sexuality. This is consistent with the passive-aggressive nature of her behavior.

Mr. Speed represents negative male attributes: he is ugly, clumsy, and forceful. Furthermore, Taylor highlights the prominence of his cane, which could be perceived as a phallic symbol. Elizabeth's ultimate fate as a spinster suggests that she never was able to fully discard her fearful view of masculinity—or perhaps her fear of sex—since her mother died after giving birth to a stillborn child, directly linking both sex and birth to death.

Still, throughout the story there are times when Elizabeth is attracted to men. For example, Elizabeth seems sexually assertive when she bursts into the parlor and is then accused of ''flirting.'' Some critics have pointed out the importance of doorways in this story, which could be seen as a simulation of the sexual act of penetration.

More disturbing are the incestuous overtones in the scene with her brother in the bedroom. Elizabeth's desire to be struck could be viewed as a desire for some form of sexual contact; however, since in her youthful confusion she cannot discriminate between sexual violence and gentleness, or family love and sexual love, she seeks to combine them. Taylor's details—the way he describes Elizabeth's hair, up or down, or her speech, as languid or fearful—also support a reading of Elizabeth as conflicted over sexual matters.

Style

Setting

Peter Taylor's fiction is set in the American South. His ''A Spinster's Tale'' is set in Nashville, where the Taylor family lived for several years. Another autobiographical aspect is socio-economic status; Taylor's and Elizabeth's families are wealthy and privileged. Elizabeth's home is comfortable and staffed with several ''Negro'' servants and cooks. The use of the word ''Negro'' provides insight into the setting, as well as the era, since this is what African Americans were commonly called in the early part of the twentieth century.

At that time, discriminatory practices limited opportunities for African Americans in the South. One of the few jobs available was as domestic help. Racial segregation is obvious when Elizabeth reveals that her father's secretary lives in an area she casually refers to as ''nigger town.'' This indicates how widespread views of racial inferiority were, as does Mr. Speed's constant refrain ''nigger, nigger,'' during the story's climax.

Point of View

Since ''A Spinster's Tale'' is told exclusively from Elizabeth's point of view, it can be assumed that these events have affected her in a profound way and that she might not be aware of certain motivations. Therefore we cannot depend on Elizabeth to explain certain events objectively.

For example, many critics have noted that the scene in which she hugs and cries to her drunk brother in her bedroom appears to have certain sexual overtones. (''I stood straight in my white nightgown with my black hair hanging over my shoulders. . . . I beckoned to him.'') Yet Elizabeth, even in her old age, (which is when the story is being told) can't be relied upon to point out such suggestive facts. So what she does not reveal, and does not remember, should be examined as closely as what she does.

Symbolism and Imagery

Taylor's symbolism and imagery may be the richest, most revealing aspect of ''A Spinster's Tale.'' For example, Mr. Speed's role in the story is symbolic. Some critics suggest that he represents a grotesque exaggeration of Elizabeth's brother and father, a personification of her fears of male sexuality and masculinity. Others read the story from a Freudian psychological standpoint and perceive phallic symbols in Mr. Speed's walking cane, which Taylor makes references to several times.

Alcohol is also a symbol that links Elizabeth's father and brother with Mr. Speed. Early in the story Elizabeth recalls her mother telling her son that she would rather see him in his grave than see him drunk. When the men are drunk, they become belligerent and unmanageable. Some critics also link the loosened inhibitions that alcohol consumption causes with possible sexual abuse in ''A Spinster's Tale''.

Imagery is also important in ''A Spinster's Tale.'' Specifically, Taylor makes many references to light and warmth, which often precede important scenes which depict either fear or escape. Early in the story, Elizabeth sets some logs in the hearth on fire and watches the flames until her face gets hot. Then she looks into the mirror, seeking to disappear into it. Soon afterwards, Mr. Speed makes an appearance.

Several references are made to Elizabeth's mother. These references are often made at frightening moments for her. Since her mother is dead it appears Elizabeth sorely misses the security of her mother.

One final important technique Taylor uses to convey important symbols is dream memories. Elizabeth's dreams (of a drunken horse, of men flocking to see a girl with big hands, who hides them under her skirt) also convey a fear of sexuality and masculinity. The large hands in the dream may be her father's, representing the possibility of his having sexually abused Elizabeth. The hands under her skirt may be her own, as Elizabeth is confused and blames herself for the abuse.

Historical Context

"A Spinster's Tale" is told in a very complex way. Even though it is apparent that the events in the story take place around 1914 or so—the Spanish-American War of the late 1890s is still a fresh memory to Elizabeth's father and "the possibilities of a general war" are referred to, foreshadowing World War I—the story is told much later. Elizabeth is telling the story as an elderly spinster, many years after the events of the story.

With that in mind, it is clear that Taylor is interested in exploring the time when the events of the story take place, rather than when Elizabeth is actually recalling them. The main theme of the story—Elizabeth's exploration of her family and her attempts to make sense of what the town drunk, Mr. Speed, means to her—are rather timeless themes. However, as is the case with most of Taylor's fiction, the American South is featured prominently; from a historical perspective, this is important in several ways.

Racial Attitudes

With the story set fifty years before the Civil Rights movement, "A Spinster's Tale" provides insight into the racially segregated South of the first half of the twentieth century. This can be seen in the abundance of "Negro" (the accepted term for African Americans at the time) domestic servants. Often deprived of the opportunities to work challenging, lucrative jobs, many black women and men worked as servants. Lucy, the family servant, is the most visible black character in the story.

In the early part of the twentieth century, when the events in "A Spinster's Tale" take place, most African Americans resided in Southern states such as Tennessee. Yet, it is clear that none live in Elizabeth's middle- to upper-class neighborhood. Elizabeth even makes reference to "nigger town," which tells us not only of the racial separation that kept the races apart, but also the casual way in which a young girl would use what has today become an offensive racial slur.

Mr. Speed also repeats the word "nigger" during the story's climax. This passing reference shows how deeply ingrained certain racial attitudes were, when "A Spinster's Tale" takes place, and even when Taylor published it, in 1940.

The Automobile

"A Spinster's Tale" is also historically specific in its vague references to what Elizabeth calls a "horseless carriage." This is a reference to an early model automobile. Its novelty is evident by the way the automobile is discussed: when it is revealed that someone owns such a "machine," it is considered an event to ride in it. The car is not used just to get from one place to another, simply driving in it is adventurous enough.

Taylor also provides us with additional insight into the types of profound questions the advent of the automobile raised. Elizabeth recalls that automobile owners had to proceed with some tact, because they were often "uncertain of our family's prejudices regarding machines." As is the case with many inventions throughout history, as the automobiles garnered more and more attention, some people felt obliged to oppose the impact that it might have on society. The automobile could have offended Elizabeth's father—it does not, and several of the boys eventually go for a ride. This fairly minor scene is a fascinating glimpse into a world without the traffic jams, red lights, and highway accidents which are viewed as so common today.

Southern Life

Taylor often focuses on the changes that occurred in Southern life over the decades of the early twentieth century, specifically in the changing lifestyles and forgotten traditions that resulted from the rapid urbanization of the region. Such changes are not so evident in "A Spinster's Tale," though some critics have spotted it. For example, Mr. Speed may represent the utter breakdown of civilized society, and the refusal of Elizabeth's brother and father to see this acknowledges their complicity in this breakdown.

There are also suggestions of a cultural clash in the parlor scene when Elizabeth's uncles are por-

Compare & Contrast

- **1914:** At the time the story is set, the American South is strictly segregated. African Americans are denied opportunities to work challenging, lucrative jobs; as a result, many work as servants.

  Today: As a result of the Civil Rights Movement of the 1950s, many discriminatory laws and customs are challenged and eliminated. For example, laws that support segregation no longer exist; African Americans have every legal right and opportunity to pursue jobs and housing.

- **1914:** The automobile is a rare sight outside of major cities. Yet with the growing popularity of automobile travel, people are able to move around faster and more efficiently.

  Today: Automobiles have become prevalent in

American society. With the car culture comes the traffic jams, red lights, suburban sprawl, and highway accidents.

- **1914:** American culture dictates that women marry and have children; because Elizabeth never marries, she is considered strange and outside of the norm. In general, to be a spinster is something to be avoided.

  Today: Many traditional values do not carry the social stigma they once did. For example, the marriage rate has dropped consistently throughout the decade; cohabitation is accepted and even encouraged. The concept of spinsterhood is considered archaic and outdated.

---

trayed as somewhat tactless, accepting "with-the-greatest-of-pleasure what really had not been an invitation at all" to ride in the car. This suggests that Elizabeth's uncles, in their fascination with the automobile, are not as refined as the machine's owners.

"I thought how awkward all of the members of my own family appeared on occasions that called for grace," Elizabeth reports, again suggesting that while her family is wealthy, they lack a certain style. This signifies their position as a traditional family tied to the past, facing the future with a mixture of uncertainty and clumsy wonder.

Critical Overview

In 1948 the great American author, Robert Penn Warren, wrote an introduction to *A Long Fourth, and Other Stories,* Taylor's first collection of short fiction. In the essay, Warren places "A Spinster's Tale" within the context of Taylor's fiction, high-

lighting both the importance of family as well as the presence of a first person narrator.

Taylor's best work, Warren writes, employs "a natural style, one based on conversation and the family tale, with the echo of the spoken word, with the texture of some narrator's mind."

In a review in the *New York Times Book Review* that same year, the reviewer also lauds Taylor's short fiction, commenting that "A Spinster's Tale" mirrors "the deterioration of family life . . . through a girl's developing neurosis. . . ."

In a lengthy essay which appeared in the *Sewanee Review* in 1962, the writer and critic Ashley Brown found in Taylor's first collection of stories "the thematic unity of (James Joyce's) *Dubliners:* childhood, youth, marriage, and maturity. . . ."

Brown also explores the "dissolution of the family" theme in "A Spinster's Tale," and notes that Elizabeth's plight is that of "a motherless child . . . misplaced in a masculine household. Her gentle father and her amiably drunken brother and her uncles cannot replace the balance lost by the death of her mother. The equilibrium of this family, where

Two drunken men passed out on a sidewalk.

old-fashioned courtly manners still prevail . . . is deceptive, simply because the masculine courtesy has no true challenge from the other sex, and Elizabeth, being young, is discouraged by this masculine indirection.''

Brown views Mr. Speed as a symbol of ''the breakdown of civilized behavior,'' which the men in the story choose not to acknowledge. ''Thus Mr. Speed becomes to Elizabeth the symbol of brutality and indifference which she finds in all men.''

By the 1970s, some critics began to view Taylor's work as skilled, but limited in scope; they

suggested that the Southern themes he is so concerned with have been explored by too many other writers. One critic wrote, ''[E]nough of the eccentric or incestuous families tending to their faded houses and lives.''

But critic Jan Pinkerton countered such criticism, contending that there are important universal themes in Taylor's short fiction, which transcend strictly Southern interpretations. Pinkerton uses ''A Spinster's Tale'' to illustrate the fact that Taylor's work is not bound to the South, writing that the story ''is a tale of frigidity and of the inevitability of spinsterhood, a subject, incidentally, that has been more frequently associated with New England than the South. Region, in other words, is secondary here. . . .''

Pinkerton, in a later essay published in *Kansas Quarterly,* focuses specifically on "A Spinster's Tale," acknowledging that some of the themes in the story may no longer be considered noteworthy, and that critics "reject as outdated" certain aspects of the story which may be associated with "Victorian" fiction from a century earlier.

Nonetheless, Pinkerton finds aspects of "A Spinster's Tale" not only relevant, but also "modern," particularly the way Elizabeth's assertiveness is discouraged. "Her feminine lifestyle . . . can be preserved not by ignoring or avoiding the dreaded opposite lifestyle, but by learning how to defend against it."

She later asks rhetorically: "So do we have here . . . the story of the rise of a no longer fearful, but rather, fear-inducing female?" By applying what could be viewed as a feminist reading to "A Spinster's Tale," Pinkerton is hoping to preserve the story's relevance for an age when women in general are more assertive, and to perhaps illustrate the changes that have occurred only in recent years.

Still, Pinkerton acknowledges that this story "despite skillful telling, may well be headed for oblivion."

Critics continue to interpret "A Spinster's Tale" from a psychological point of view. In 1988, Roland Sodowsky and Gargi Roysircar Sodowsky, using models set forth by the prominent psychologists Sigmund Freud and Alfred Adler, are able to interpret Elizabeth two distinct ways: she may be seen as trapped by sexual fears and the constraints of a relationship between child and parent; or alternatively, she can be perceived as controlling her role in her family.

These separate readings suggest a basic difficulty in interpreting "A Spinster's Tale": is Elizabeth a victim of her various problems or does she conquer them?

The author has stated that "A Spinster's Tale" is one of his favorite stories. It "may be one of my best," Taylor stated in a 1973 interview, "but I hate to admit it. It was written right at the beginning, and no one likes to think he hasn't gotten better."

Criticism

Tom Deignan

Deignan has been a teaching assistant in American Cultural Studies at Bowling Green State University. In the following essay, he argues that sexual conflict is the primary theme of "A Spinster's Tale."

Critics tend to focus on the sexual themes in Peter Taylor's "A Spinster's Tale," especially as it relates to the budding femininity of young Elizabeth. This discussion seems pertinent when the reader learns that Elizabeth grew up without a mother, has a difficult time with men, and never marries.

It is clear that Elizabeth loves her father and brother, but at the same time she seems to fear certain aspects of their personalities; specifically, she is concerned with similarities between her father and brother and the repugnant Mr. Speed. "As their voices grew louder and merrier, my courage slackened," Elizabeth recalls. "It was then I first put into words the thought that in my brother and father I saw something of Mr. Speed. And I knew it was more than a taste for whiskey they had in common."

Such comments, when combined with other aspects of "A Spinster's Tale"—Elizabeth's growth into a young women, her irrational fear of Mr. Speed (who, some critics note, is associated with several sexual symbols, such as the phallic cane), and her curious desire to be struck by her brother— make it clear that sexual conflict is one of the major themes of this work.

It is also possible that not only is such a conflict *the* most important theme in "A Spinster's Tale," but that something much more horrific has taken place. Perhaps "A Spinster's Tale" is a tragedy about a father's sexual abuse of his young daughter, who is vigorously attempting to repress her memory of these acts.

Such an interpretation may seem far-fetched. Elizabeth's father, after all, may be clumsy at times, but he seems to be a likable character, hardly one to commit such an awful crime. And yet, the very aspect of the story which makes any sexual reading so uncomfortable—Elizabeth's youth—may begin to point in the direction of repressed molestation. Such a reading makes Elizabeth's resulting spinsterhood and her inability to connect with men much more dramatic and painful.

What Do I Read Next?

- Considered a masterpiece, *The Diary of Anne Frank* is an actual diary written by a young Jewish girl before she was taken away by the Nazis during World War II. Some of the more memorable passages in the diary are about the difficulties of growing up and dealing with family members.

- William Faulkner's *The Sound and the Fury* (1929) depicts the changing landscape of the American South in the early 1900s.

- *Conversations with Peter Taylor*, published in 1987, is a collection of interviews with the author

of ''A Spinster's Tale.'' These pieces provide insight into Taylor's thought processes as an artist. Also, *Parting the Curtains* (1994) is a book of interviews with many Southern writers, including Taylor, Eleanor Ross, Shelby Foote, Maya Angelou, Pat Conroy, and William Styron.

- There are many studies of Taylor's life and work, including most recently, *Critical Essays on Peter Taylor* (1993). Another critical study, *Southern Accents: The Fiction of Peter Taylor,* written by Catherine Clark Graham, was published in 1994.

Early in the story, Elizabeth makes an important distinction: her brother's drinking frightens her, yet ''those nights put a scaredness into me that was clearly distinguishable from the terror that Mr. Speed instilled by stumbling past our house. . . .'' So Mr. Speed, for an unknown reason, is clearly more threatening than her brother.

Elizabeth then notes that ''by allowing him the 'Mr.''' she seeks to ''humanize and soften the monster that was forever passing our house. . . .'' In this way, Elizabeth both eases her fear of Speed, and transforms him into a deformed authority figure.

The next sentence is important: ''My father would point him out through the wide parlor window. . . .'' Elizabeth later notes that her father, while drinking with her brother and uncles, would refer to Mr. Speed ''in a blustering tone of merry tolerance: 'There goes Old Speed, again. That rascal!''' Elizabeth is annoyed at her father's ''tolerance,'' and prepares for the ''inevitable day when I should have to speak of (Mr. Speed) to someone.''

Elizabeth reveals that it is her father who first points Mr. Speed out to her, that she doesn't care for his tolerance of Mr. Speed's behavior, and that Mr. Speed represents something profoundly unsettling to her. This could be an indication that Elizabeth has shifted her mixture of love and loathing—which her

father's sexual violation has inspired—onto Mr. Speed. This may begin to explain her intense fear of him. His ugliness symbolizes and personifies Elizabeth's repressed knowledge of her father's acts. This may be one reason she uses the authoritative ''Mr.'' to refer to Speed.

It also may explain the curious scene before the mirror, when Elizabeth craves to be taken ''A-way-a-way. . . .'' Here, the sexual and emotional confusion caused by her father's sexual violation has overwhelmed her. And whom does Elizabeth see at that moment, gazing out the window? ''I beheld Mr. Speed,'' she reports. He was walking, ''cursing the trees as he passed them, giving each a lick with his heavy walking cane.'' Elizabeth is scared, her ''breath came short, and I clasped the black bow at the neck of my middy blouse.''

Many important elements suggest that Elizabeth is repressing sexual abuse: her confused desire for escape but inability to articulate why, the presence of the hateful Mr. Speed and his phallic cane, her inexplicable movement to cover up her blouse. Also, it seems that Elizabeth's defenses—denial and repression—are starting to crack.

Indeed, it is important to note that Elizabeth is maturing constantly throughout the story. (She notes at one point, ''my legs had got too long this summer to stretch out straight on the settee.'') Thus, she may only now be becoming aware of the unacceptable nature of her sexual relationship with her father; her behavior suggests that she is confused. After all this is her father, a man she is supposed to love unconditionally, regardless of what he might be doing to her. That he seems a loving father can only complicate things more—for Elizabeth, as well as for the reader.

Elizabeth's ambivalence is clearly illustrated in the bedroom scene with her brother. He is drunk, suggesting a loss of inhibition. Elizabeth's mother despised drinking, as Elizabeth does. Furthermore, it is drinking that initially raises questions about Mr. Speed's relation to her father and brother. As the most persistent drunk in the story, Mr. Speed embodies the least inhibited, most threatening potential of men—such as a sexual relationship with one's own daughter.

In the bedroom scene, Elizabeth wakes up when her brother comes home drunk. She ''smiled at him and beckoned,'' as he stumbles up the stairs. Twice, Elizabeth notes (as she does always with Mr. Speed) the redness of her brother's face. ''I stood in my white nightgown,'' Elizabeth says, ''with my black hair hanging over my shoulders. . . .''

He asks if she's ''been reading something you shouldn't,'' before she throws her arms around him, confessing, ''I'm always lonely.'' The scene is quite tender up to this point, as Elizabeth's brother attempts to conceal his drunkenness and offers to play with her the next day.

Then he ''stood up and looked at me curiously, as though in some way repelled by my settling so comfortable in the covers.'' Elizabeth's demands seem to have shaken her brother, which matches a pattern through the story: when Elizabeth is assertive, she is encouraged to be more passive.

This can suggest any number of things. Regarding the thesis of this essay, perhaps Elizabeth, at this moment, believes acting in a sexual way with family members is somewhat normal. She even says that she smells her brother's whiskey, but that it ''was not repugnant to me.'' She then expresses a desire to be struck and wishes she had indicated to her brother ''that we had in common some unmentionable trouble.''

Many critics have written of the ''incestuous overtones'' of this scene. It appears her brother's

> **And yet, the very aspect of the story which makes any sexual reading so uncomfortable--Elizabeth's youth--may begin to point in the direction of repressed molestation."**

look of shock has jolted Elizabeth into realizing such sexual behavior around family members is not appropriate. And yet, she cannot deny her love (sexual or otherwise) for her brother. Indicating her intense confusion, Elizabeth simply combines affection and punishment. She wants contact with her brother but seems, on some level, to comprehend the forbidden nature of such behavior.

For Elizabeth, getting hit by her brother at that point would be not only a way to express love, but also a punishment for her feelings. That she desires to share an ''unmentionable trouble'' with her brother suggests not only that something intense is being repressed, but also that Elizabeth is perhaps starting to comprehend the roots of her confusion—her father's violation of her and her brother's silent complicity.

Indeed, later she admits that she ''had come to accept (Mr. Speed's) existence as a natural part of my life.'' Since Mr. Speed represents a displaced awareness of Elizabeth's father's sexual violation, this may be one of the saddest lines in the entire story. Elizabeth has resigned herself to living with this horrible abuse. And her brother is not innocent either, for he also says of Mr. Speed: ''You'll get used to him, for all his ugliness.''

It is additionally important to note that Elizabeth shares her mother's name; moreover, she maintains that ''from day to day, I began to take my place as a mistress in our motherless household.'' This suggests that Elizabeth seems to have become a sort of surrogate mother/wife in this house. As the sole female family member in the house, perhaps her father viewed his desire for her as almost normal— especially now that his wife (and natural sex partner) is dead.

Elizabeth's own warm (warmth is a key image) affection for her mother can be seen, then, not only as affection for a lost mother, but also a desire for protection from her father that is no longer available. ''I remembered only the warmth of the cheek and the comfort of that moment,'' Elizabeth says recalling her mother. This is contrasted with the perverted love of her father.

Also, it should be noted that after pleading to the mirror for escape, then seeing Mr. Speed, ''a sudden inexplicable memory of my mother's cheek and a vision of her'' strikes Elizabeth. At moments when she is forced to confront her father's abuse, symbolized by Mr. Speed, Elizabeth always seems to call upon an image of her mother to delay confrontation.

Elizabeth's dreams also suggest serious sexual violations; in one dream, some men come to see a girl with big hands and the girl decides to hide them under her skirt. The big hands may, in fact, be Elizabeth's father's, but guilt and confusion forces Elizabeth to blame herself for the violation. Thus, she believes the hands under her skirt are the girl's own.

Yet Elizabeth does not fear her father. In a critical scene near the end of the story, she runs to her father, with other family members in the room, proclaiming of Mr. Speed ''I'm afraid of him. . . . He's always drunk!'' Elizabeth then confides that she ''was eager to tell (her father) just exactly how fearful I was of Mr. Speed's coming into our house.'' This scene could be viewed as a confrontation. Again, if Mr. Speed represents her own father's deviant sexuality, than Elizabeth is, in a sense, proclaiming her displeasure at the situation. She no longer wants her father to treat her in such unnatural ways.

Her father cuts her off, telling her she ''had no business watching Mr. Speed, that I must shut my eyes to some things. 'After all,' he said . . . 'you're a young lady now.''' Elizabeth's father is, in effect, issuing an order here: don't confront this issue (Mr. Speed/sexual violation), repress it.

So Elizabeth's assertiveness has been quashed, and she is now ''accustomed to thinking that there was something in my brother's and in my father's natures that was fully in sympathy with the very brutality of (Mr. Speed's) drunkenness.'' In refusing to hear her concerns about Mr. Speed, both her brother and father refuse to face up to Elizabeth's abuse.

Elizabeth is a bold girl and because she is growing older and more aware, she will continue to explore ways to confront this issue. Her confidence grows during the scene with the kitchen help (which also foreshadows the story's climax) when Elizabeth, at the height of her assertiveness, threatens to call the police. She realizes the power in this threat, and decides that she will use this same threat against Mr. Speed when he comes into the house.

Again, this climactic scene fits a pattern found throughout ''A Spinster's Tale.'' Mr. Speed breaks though the doorway violently. (Many entrances through doorways occur in this story, and many critics have suggested a possible link to the act of sexual penetration.) References are yet again made to his red face and his cane, and Elizabeth realizes that perhaps ''it was the last time I ever experienced the inconsolable desperation of childhood.''

However, even as she leaves childhood behind with this final overt violation, Elizabeth longs ''to hide my face away from this in my own mother's bosom.'' Yet another part of her ''was making me deal with Mr. Speed . . . myself.'' Indeed, she has called the police station, asserted herself, and, symbolically anyway, confronted her father's mistreatment of her.

It is no surprise, then, that Elizabeth's father is displeased. In his world, acknowledgment of such heinous acts amounts to bad behavior. Elizabeth has confronted her father, and indeed, he has sealed off the doorway, suggesting perhaps an end to his sexual abuse of her.

The fact that Elizabeth becomes a spinster is significant. In dealing with the effects of a lost, abused childhood, perhaps the following passage provides a terrible, conclusive insight. '''What ever did happen to Speed's old-maid sister?' my uncle the doctor said. 'She's still with him,' Father said.''

As an old maid herself, the terrible actions and memories that Mr. Speed represents have remained with Elizabeth and always will. ''It was only the other night that I dreamed I was a little girl . . . again and that there was a drunk horse in our yard,'' the story's last line reads.

As they have throughout the story, such dream images prove the fact that Elizabeth is still haunted by the scary, violent images of her childhood.

Source: Tom Deignan, ''Overview of 'A Spinster's Tale,''' in *Short Stories for Students*, The Gale Group, 2000.

Roland Sodowsky and Gargi Roysircar Sodowsky

At the time this article was published, Gargi Roysircar Sodowsky was a pre-doctoral Intern in Counseling Psychology at Iowa State University, and Roland Sodowsky was Associate Professor of English at Sul Ross State University, Alpine, Texas. In the following excerpt, the critics present two differing psychological interpretations of Betsy.

Several critics have noted the depth and richness of the characters in Peter Taylor's work, a complexity which makes his stories particularly apt for psychological interpretation. An especially good example is "A Spinster's Tale," in which the protagonist, Betsy, may be seen from a Freudian point of view as being trapped by the forces of parent-child relationships and sexual fears or from an Adlerian point of view as choosing and controlling the unsocial direction of her life.

Set in an upper-class home in Nashville around 1900, "Spinster's Tale" is narrated by an unmarried woman named Elizabeth who recalls events beginning with her mother's death and ending about a year later, shortly after her fourteenth birthday. Her mother has died a few days after bearing a stillborn child. Elizabeth, called Betsy by her eighteen-year-old brother, lives with her father, brother, and several servants. During a moment of grief one afternoon about six months after her mother's death, the girl observes an old man passing the house, red-faced, drunk, stumbling and cursing. Seeing this man, Mr. Speed, causes her to become "dry-eyed in my fright" and to remember vividly the burial of the stillborn infant and a few minutes spent with her mother just before her death. Betsy recognizes Mr. Speed as a "permanent and formidable figure in my life which I would be called upon to deal with," and thereafter she observes him from the parlor window each time he passes, even though the sight of him makes her teeth chatter. Much of the rest of the story consists of variations of this basic pattern in which the terrified girl watches the old man, anticipating the day when he will come to her door.

In one variation, Betsy stands at the door of her bedroom late at night while her drunken brother, whom she intuits as a less menacing version of Mr. Speed, climbs the stairs. With apparent incestuous intent, she entices him into her bedroom. Thinking about the encounter later, she wishes she had made him aware of "some unmentionable trouble" they have in common. In another variation, she learns the unwelcome lesson that her brother and Mr. Speed

> "Betsy is not the victim of causality, but rather the pilot of her dreams and of the direction of her life as well. In her own terms, she has achieved 'equal superiority' over Mr. Speed, her brother, and therefore all men."

are more alike than she had thought. In another, just after the girl's father and uncles jokingly accuse her of flirting with a boy, Mr. Speed appears outside and she becomes hysterical.

In the final variation, Mr. Speed, caught in a rainstorm, actually enters the house, frightening both Betsy and Lucy, a maid. After letting him in, the maid flees up the stairs, but Betsy calls the police. The old man tries to leave but falls from the porch and is knocked unconscious. The police find him thus a few minutes later and take him away.

"Spinster's Tale" is replete with objects and actions for which, in his discussion of dream symbols in *The Interpretation of Dreams* [in *The Basic Writings of Sigmund Freud*, trans. and ed. A. A. Brill, 1938], Sigmund Freud assigns various sexual meanings. A study of Betsy's reactions to these symbols suggests that despite the lonely girl's desperate attempts to deal with the phenomena these symbols represent, she cannot adjust to them. Instead, she projects her unacceptable, frightening sexual impulses to external dangers. Thus she fears maleness and male sexuality and thereby copes projectively and unconsciously with her fears, although in a deviant manner.

Except for a flashback to the burial of the stillborn infant, the girl is never seen outside the house, which she repeatedly describes as "shadowy," the dream-like setting thus making an interpretation in Freudian terms especially appropriate. Although her father, brother, and the servants also occupy the house, she persistently calls it "my house," "my door," to which Mr. Speed will eventually come, reminding one of Freud's symbolization of persons as male organs, of the house as body, doors as apertures, and rooms as female; churches too are equated with the vagina, and Betsy's house is on Church Street. Mr. Speed carries a top coat, a later version of the cloak, one of Freud's phallic symbols, and a heavy walking cane, also phallic, with which he beats the trees or pokes at the "soft sod along the sidewalk." When the March wind blows off his hat, another male genital symbol, it rolls across the lawn toward the house. And when he finally does come to the door, he raps on it with his cane. Once inside, however, he throws the cane on the floor in an apparent gesture of defeat.

Betsy unconsciously defends herself, displacing her guilty, fearful attraction for Mr. Speed upon her brother, a safer target. She remembers her brother in terms of phallic images. He shows her "a box of cigarettes which a girl had given him"; he chases after and returns Mr. Speed's hat, thus identifying himself more closely in Betsy's eyes with the old man; in her white nightgown, symbolizing chastity, she watches her brother from her bedroom doorway as he comes up the stairs, stumbling like Mr. Speed, "putting his white forefinger to his red face"; after he has climbed the stairs, an act symbolizing coitus, and entered her room, she remembers "something like a longing for my brother to strike me," but since he does not and therefore does not symbolically enter her, she presumably has failed to cope with her fears.

She also remembers the box, a female symbol, containing the stillborn infant when it is buried, and she associates it in a rapid sequence of images with Mr. Speed, who apparently epitomizes maleness, with her last moments with her mother, and with her mother's death, which her "memory did not dwell upon." When Mr. Speed finally enters the house, one assumes Betsy cannot help but react as she does. The maid Lucy, who could be but is not Betsy's surrogate mother, pleads with Betsy to climb the stairs, that is, to perform, in Freudian terms, a symbolic coital act. Instead, she reacts unconsciously, circling defensively behind Mr. Speed to telephone the police, thereby repressing her desire for the male "invasion." A few minutes later Mr. Speed's "limp body" is taken away.

Betsy sees herself as having acted with a mixture of cruelty and courage, and instead of being fearful of or attracted to Mr. Speed, she both despises and pities the old man lying unconscious in the mud. In the last paragraph the narrator says,

". . . my hatred of what he had stood for in my eyes has never left me . . . not a week has passed but that he has been brought to my mind by one thing or another." The child Betsy may appear to have been victorious, but in Freudian terms the adult Elizabeth is the regressing victim of the girl's failure to overcome her terror.

An Adlerian point of view leads to a different conclusion. According to Alfred Adler [in *The Individual Psychology of Alfred Adler: A Systematic Presentation in Selections from His Writings*, ed. H. L. Ansbacher and R. R. Ansbacher, 1956], the biological and environmental "givens"—for example, Betsy's plain looks, adolescent stirrings, and isolation in a discouraging male world—are recreated by a person with her "private logic" to attain "success": "Experiences, traumata, and sexual developmental mechanisms cannot yield an explanation, but the perspective in which they are regarded . . . which subordinates all life to the final goal, can do so." In *Superiority and Social Interest* [1965] Adler sees the neurotic as striving toward a goal of superiority in order to overcome past and current feelings of inferiority. Rather than reacting automatically to events which determine her to be a spinster, Betsy is actively carving out her niche in the world, a niche that in her eyes is inferior to none. Betsy's fear of heterosexual intimacy, for example, may express the direction she is taking to attain her goal of superiority over men.

From this point of view, the incidents from her puberty that the narrator recalls are important not in themselves but because she remembers them and because of the way the girl Betsy chooses to respond to them. In *Individual Psychology* Adler says, "There are no chance memories. Out of the incalculable number of impressions which meet an individual, he chooses to remember only those which he feels, however darkly, to have a bearing on his situation." The narrator's selective *re*-collection of pubescent experiences mirrors her present biases and view of life, and, as the story's title suggests ("A Spinster's Tale"), her reconstruction of events does not necessarily correspond to the historical truth. The purposeful delving into the past has the power of repetitive rehearsals or of a self-fulfilling prophecy, expressing the narrator's intention of continuing with the symbolic, spinster-like life of her youth. These memories, Adler says, a person " . . . repeats to himself . . . to keep him concentrated on his goal, and to prepare him by means of past experiences, so that he will meet the future with an already tested style of action."

When Betsy is frightened by Mr. Speed, her ultimate symbol of maleness, for example, she construes the image of her dead mother, whom she remembers as wan, smiling, gentle, and religious—the opposite of the stumbling drunk. By symbiotically escaping into this idealized memory, Betsy sidesteps a social problem—confrontation with the old man and thereby with males in general—thus avoiding possible defeat or humiliation in a relationship. In choosing "not to dwell upon" the memory of her mother's death, Betsy thus denies it, as well as the challenges of adolescence, i.e. the stepping toward new freedom and adult responsibilities. Betsy calls her memories of her mother "sudden and inexplicable" but they are neither: they manifest her preference for nonexistence, passivity, and social withdrawal. After seeing Mr. Speed the first time, Betsy stands "cold and silent," a metaphorical and literal expression of her chosen life style.

Betsy recalls that her mother severely condemned drinking before her death, an attitude not shared by her brother or by her father, who has toddies with her uncles every Saturday afternoon. Her father calls "Old Speed" a "rascal" with "merry tolerance," but simultaneously warns her brother of the consequences of drinking by using Mr. Speed as a bad example. Betsy cannot identify with her father's contradictory attitude and the well-defined masculine pattern he establishes in the house. She wonders whether he ever thinks of her mother, since he never mentions her. She seems to accuse him of indifference, saying " . . . in a year I had forgotten how he treated her when she had been alive." Unable to establish satisfactory alliances with her brother or father, she replaces the human tendency for *gemeinschaftsgefühl* with an attitude of distrust and poor regard for her surviving family members and, ultimately, the world at large.

The development of this attitude appears clearly in the sibling rivalry between Betsy and her brother. Sober, he teases her mercilessly. Drunk, he tries to make her a conspirator by offering the passive, watchful girl candy, but she sees him as "giggling," "bouncing," and "silly" and refuses to compromise the attitude about drinking that she has adopted from her mother. Rudolf Dreikurs, the popularizer of Adler in the United States, says [in *Psychodynamics, Psychotherapy, and Counseling*, 1967] such sibling differences indicate competition and the development of different personalities. Betsy, feeling intellectually ignored by her father and class-valedictorian brother, sees her brother as the "boss" and herself as inadequate. To compete with her brother's ruling style, she chooses the feminine avoiding style, a typical example of familial confrontation between two Adlerian types. She requests, for example, her father and brother "not to talk about war, which seemed to [her father] a natural enough request for a young lady to make." While father and son argue on a vast diversity of male-oriented topics, Betsy quietly observes her brother or slips away because she finds the contentious dialogue unbearable.

Dreikurs points out that where one sibling succeeds, a competing sibling gives up; and where the sibling fails (the brother's intemperance, for example), the competitor moves in, thus finding a place and significance in the family. Betsy's behavior fits this pattern. Adler says a woman feels equal to a man she perceives as superior if she can experience herself in her "masculine protest" to be "equally superior" to him. This striving for compensatory superiority reflects an exaggerated perception of male power and recognition such as Betsy sees in her small world on Church Street. Not being brave enough to confront them, Betsy resorts to what Adler calls "depreciation tendency" (the neurotic's tendency to enhance self-esteem by disparaging others) in order to maneuver her brother and Mr. Speed, to sneak into power struggles with them, and to inflict sly revenge in their weak moments. Betsy's nearly incestuous encounter with her brother, for example, in which she appears uncharacteristically confident and well-rehearsed, may be an attempt to compromise him and thus gain a "victory" and revenge. Her desire for him to strike her could be seen as her search for confirmation of suspected male violence and cruelty.

Betsy has long been preparing for the "eventuality" to settle completely with Mr. Speed. The narrator recalls, "And the sort of preparation that I had been able to make [was] the clearance of all restraints and inhibitions regarding Mr. Speed in my own mind and in my relationship with my world. . . ." The "restraints" and "inhibitions" that Betsy rids herself of are the foundations of Adler's *gemeinschaftsgefühl* . Instead of giving the drunk Mr. Speed shelter in her house from the rain, Betsy, in a tone of pretended innocence, calls the police. She is keenly aware that she deals with Mr. Speed, "however wrongly," all by herself, that is, unsocially. Her father's curt remark, "I regret that the bluecoats were called," underscores the disparity in father and daughter's life attitudes.

The passive-aggressive Betsy begins to find her place and power in her family by her success in hurting others through her one-upmanship games. She discovers a way to supervise her father's household staff by snooping around, springing out upon the unsuspecting servants, and intimidating them by threatening to call her father or the police. The narrator recalls, "In this way, from day to day, I began to take my place as mistress in our motherless household."

Betsy's life-style is that of a cautious, contriving busybody. Even in her nightly dreams she allows no mysteries or loose ends and "pieces together" these dreams into a "form of logic." The fearful Betsy grows into the controlling Betsy who says, "I would complete an unfinished dream and wouldn't know in the morning what part I dreamed and what part pieced together." In one such dream a "big" Betsy, in control of everything, watches "little" Betsy "trembling and weeping." Betsy then makes a "very considerable discovery" about herself—that instead of being fearful she can be feared. Betsy is not the victim of causality, but rather the pilot of her dreams and of the direction of her life as well. In her own terms, she has achieved "equal superiority" over Mr. Speed, her brother, and therefore all men. Just as the pubescent Betsy pieces together her dreams into patterns which suit her, the adult narrator continues to piece together her life in ways that, according to her private logic, reveal her to be superior and successful.

That "A Spinster's Tale" can sustain two such disparate interpretations of its protagonist demonstrates, we feel, the profundity of Taylor's characterization. We see in the story the dynamics of familial relationships, and little else, either shaping a girl and the woman to be or being used by the girl to shape the woman she chooses to be. The ambiguity in Taylor's fine story is satisfying, like truth.

Source: Roland Sodowsky and Gargi Roysircar Sodowsky, "Determined Failure, Self-Styled Success: Two Views of Betsy in Peter Taylor's 'Spinster's Tale,'" in *Studies in Short Fiction*, Vol. 25, No. 1, Winter, 1988, pp. 49–54.

Jan Pinkerton

In the following excerpt, Pinkerton offers a new interpretation of "A Spinster's Tale."

I

Egon Schwartz, demonstrating how the vagaries of Hermann Hesse's reputation have depended on place and time [in "Hermann Hesse, The American Youth Movement, and Problems of Literary Evaluation," *PMLA*, Vol. 85, 1970], suggests that literary scholarship, even when presuming to be value-free, is constantly reflecting its temporal situation, that it "is replete with unreflected values and engages in indirect evaluation all the time." The example of Hesse, that belatedly acclaimed guru, is surely dramatic; yet, beyond even the unknown-today, adulated-tomorrow (or vice versa) stereotype, there are many other, more subtle, manifestations of temporal influence on literary scholarship and evaluation.

I shall speak of two. There is, first of all, the simple matter of subject matter. Critics have not sufficiently acknowledged the important role that "subject" plays in determining the literature that they praise or, more subtly, that they choose to write about. Secondly, there is the critical urge toward consistency, an urge which denies the established author the right to "minor" efforts. The tendency of literary scholarship is to deal with the totality of a man's work, and thus an unimportant work by a nevertheless important writer is often given special attention and even unmerited praise. A leveling effect results: a leveling, in this case, upward.

In order to illustrate these temporal influences on literary criticism, I should like to build a demonstration case around a story that has been generally undiscussed, even though the author is a respected American contemporary (although not sufficiently "established" to require the investigation of the entire canon): Peter Taylor's "A Spinster's Tale." The story is undiscussed probably because it is woefully old-fashioned—old-fashioned in subject matter, which constitutes an objection that critics are not likely to admit as an objection. I should like to formulate a hypothetical rehabilitation of the story—the sort of rehabilitation that would become necessary if Taylor were to be given establishment status. We must first look at the problem of his out-of-date subject matter and then see how, in conformity with the practice of contemporary critics, the story might be redeemed. The redemption would involve upward leveling, to bring all of the writer's work to "classic" status—a process that takes place constantly in literary journals.

II

Taylor's "A Spinster's Tale" deals with female fear of the male, and immediately we see the problem of subject matter; what is appropriate for *Clarissa* or for Victorian novels seems totally quaint today. A topic far more current, in fact, is male fear of the female, although "the new chastity," which women's lib has been accused of promoting, might represent a topic even newer in fashion. It is true, nevertheless, that such sexually fearful Victorian heroines as Gwendolen Harleth, Isabel Archer, and Sue Bridehead are simply not appropriate for reincarnation by a contemporary writer.

So how do we react to a fairly recent story (1940) that focuses on old-fashioned female trembling before the male? The tale, briefly, is of a motherless girl's obsession with what she considers a brutal masculine world. Although she lives with her father and brother, the exemplification of masculinity to her is a drunken Mr. Speed, whom she sees frequently passing by her house; she watches from the safety of her parlor, but she is nevertheless terrified and is convinced that someday she will have to deal with him personally. She begins, then, at the age of thirteen, to prepare herself for an inevitable confrontation with masculinity, and her preparation consists of hardening herself, of making herself cold and formidable. One day Mr. Speed drunkenly stumbles to her steps, and instead of taking pity on his helplessness—as her father or brother would have done—she calls the police and has him taken away, after which she never sees him again. She has conquered her fears of the male world through the assumption of a cruel authority, and, knowing now how to deal with frightening situations, she will obviously lead a life henceforth of both sternness and sterility.

There seems little, then, that is ''modern'' about this story. Female frigidity, as we have suggested, is no longer considered a noteworthy topic for fiction, and critics will reject as outdated a topic in a contemporary writer that they will admire in a Victorian. Not that they will reject it specifically for that reason; there are still too many critical absolutes that preclude judgments based on subject matter. Yet these judgments are made, if only unconsciously. As a further example, critics today would be likely to find naive—and therefore ''popular''—a contemporary story exalting war or praising those who die for their country. Such topics are staples of literature of other eras, but at the moment, in America, this kind of expression is not encouraged. We do give heed, in other words, to the specifics of subject matter.

So what can we do with ''A Spinster's Tale'' ? Let us say that we wish to bestow true establishment status on Taylor and that therefore we must find relevance in this story, as we must in the whole canon. If the heroine's sexual problem is no longer

> " Her feminine life style, as she sees it, can be preserved not by ignoring or avoiding the dreaded opposite life style, but by learning how to defend against it. The battle of the sexes--the rigid distinguishing of roles and the resultant impasses and irreconcilabilities--is shown in full force in this story."

relevant, then there are other ways in which we can deal with this story. We can look for other, perhaps more subtle, nuances that do not seem quite so distant from our sensibilities. It is patronizing, perhaps, to do so, but the practice is nevertheless standard; it is a version of the old search for universals in human nature—or, to be more accurate, for the particular concepts that are accepted as universal at a particular time. Let us turn this story, then, into a hunting ground for the concepts that happen to please us; literary criticism has rarely done otherwise.

III

For an initial example of the story's ''modernness,'' we can point to its case-history approach. Contemporary readers are sufficiently clinically oriented to respond to a story of how-she-got-that-way; the title indicates what she is—a spinster—and the narrative documents the process. The heroine first becomes aware of Mr. Speed, for instance, only after her mother dies, when she can no longer withdraw into feminine protection against the opposite sex. And we see that she had been taught already to think of the opposite sex with less than charity; one recollection of the mother is her words to her son who had come home drunk: ''Son, I'd rather see you in your grave.'' Moreover, the mother had died after a stillbirth; her death, then, is associated with her sexual function, or with what might be considered male imposition on the female.

The mother had been defeated by the male world, for in succumbing to an illness connected with or exacerbated by childbearing, she had clearly not been able to deal with masculine imposition. That is one matter that the daughter would learn. She knew intuitively, in fact, that "Mr. Speed was a permanent and formidable figure in my life which I would be called upon to deal with." Her main tie to the masculine world had been her older brother, but in him, too, as he develops into manhood, she sees what she must defend against. She realizes that "in my brother and father I saw something of Mr. Speed. And I knew that it was more than a taste for whiskey they had in common."

So, as she grows up, she prepares herself. She ventures into the servants' and men's bathrooms, finding even a fascination in filth and in "wet shaving brushes and leather straps and red rubber bands." She assumes a more domineering role in the household than previously and manages to fire the cook completely on her own. And her fears now diminish: "I could no longer be frightened by my brother with a mention of runaway horses"; she has long associated runaway animals with Mr. Speed, with drunkenness, and with masculinity, but now she feels that she can deal with them. She has grown up, become "mature"—but her maturity, her womanhood, is formidable and cruel.

We have traced, then, the case history of a spinster. But we have also found a psychological matter more "modern" than sexual hysteria—an insight into the connection between fear and cruelty; this is a subject highly congenial to current discussion. The girl's father, we realize, has no fear of Mr. Speed, and he never would have taken the step of calling the police, an action which apparently resulted in drastic consequences for Mr. Speed. She, however, acted from fear, and her deed was one of personal cruelty and what might be called—since Mr. Speed's civil liberties were undoubtedly curtailed or suspended—"political" repression. She admits, "I was frightened by the thought of the cruelty which I found I was capable of," and yet, "my hatred and fear of what he had stood for in my eyes has never left me." Here, in the connection made between fear and cruelty and between fear and repression, is an insight which appeals to readers today; we always delight in the expression of one of our very own "universals." The story, then, is "relevant" after all.

There are further insights that come close to the sexual problems of the girl and yet approach con-temporary issues as well. If, as seems true today, the distinction between male and female roles has been diminished, this story, on the other hand, shows the roles in their full flowering—which is a cause, of course, of the heroine's problems. In this story of how-she-got-that-way, her fears of the male result from the great gulf she has been taught to observe between masculine and feminine values and behavior, and from the widely differing roles that are assigned as a result of this gulf. Her father speaks of "Old Speed" to her brother in terms of a bad example, and to her uncles in terms of amusement; yet in her mind, "these designations were equally awful, both spoken in tones that were foreign to my father's manner of addressing me." Her father, in other words, speaks to people in terms of their roles; and his manner toward men, even though it varies from person to person, is far different from his manner toward women. At another time her father discusses the possible coming of war and recalls the troops that gathered before the Spanish-American conflict—"hundreds of men in the Union Depot." The girl reacts as we might expect:

> Thinking of all those men there, that close together, was something like meeting Mr. Speed in the front hall. I asked my father not to talk about war, which seemed to him a natural enough request for a young lady to make.

She feels threatened by the thought of such unmitigated masculinity, but her request to her father is considered natural for much more general reasons—because it is inappropriate for ladies to be exposed to anything serious or unpleasant. The great distinction in sexual roles is seen as axiomatic at this time and in this society, and the story tells the consequences.

Indeed she begins to conceive her role *vis-à-vis* men even more drastically. She feels that she must actively learn to handle situations involving masculinity. Her feminine life style, as she sees it, can be preserved not by ignoring or avoiding the dreaded opposite life style, but by learning how to defend against it. The battle of the sexes—the rigid distinguishing of roles and the resultant impasses and irreconcilabilities—is shown in full force in this story.

So do we have here—as a final "modernism"—the story of the rise of a no longer fearful but, rather, fear-inducing female? Does this story coincide with a point in a psychological model that indicates the shift from female fears of the male to male fears of the female? Has not the heroine come to resemble the formidable and threatening woman that is found in much current literature? Might not

Taylor's exemplum of how-she-got-that-way be considered an historical landmark on the road to how-*he*-got-that-way?

All these interpretations are perhaps too facile—and patronizing—in the attempt to fit a story to currently fashionable notions. For the story ends, after all, with the heroine obviously on the path to spinsterhood. The story has approached a seemingly modern subject, but the final sentence nevertheless seems rather dated: ''It was only the other night that I dreamed I was a little girl on Church Street again and that there was a drunk horse in our yard.'' This makes a neat symbolic summary of the story, but the symbol is quaint; the dream and the drunken horse are too patently Freudian, too out-of-date for a contemporary society that has rejected Freud's dicta on women and that finds female fear of the male a little preposterous.

So have readers unconsciously evaluated this story on the basis of its subject matter? Is it true that Henry James, because he was born seventy-five years earlier than Peter Taylor, can say things that Taylor cannot? Must Taylor automatically find a different topic? The answer is, in part, yes. This story, despite skillful telling, may well be headed for oblivion, even though a certain recognition for it has been granted the author. There are many reasons for the burying of thousands of stories published in our periodicals of the last quarter-century, but—our critical absolutes notwithstanding—an important reason is the vagaries of our taste in subject matter and in treatment.

Source: Jan Pinkerton, ''The Vagaries of Taste and Peter Taylor's 'A Spinster's Tale,''' in *Kansas Quarterly,* Vol. 9, No. 2, Spring, 1977, pp. 81–5.

Sources

Brown, Ashley. ''The Early Fiction of Peter Taylor,'' in *The Sewanee Review*, Vol. LXX, No. 4, Autumn, 1962, pp. 588-602.

Creekmore, Hubert. Review in *The New York Times Book Review*, March 21, 1948, pp. 6.

Pinkerton, Jan. ''The Non-Regionalism of Peter Taylor,'' in *The Georgia Review*, Vol. 24, No. 4, Winter, 1970, pp. 432-40.

———. ''The Vagaries of Taste and Peter Taylor's 'A Spinster's Tale,''' in *Kansas Quarterly*, Vol. 9, No. 2, 1977, pp. 81–85.

Robison, James Curry. ''The Early Period,'' in *Peter Taylor: A Study of the Short Fiction*, Twayne, 1988, pp. 19–31.

Sodowsky, Roland, and Gargi Roysircar Sodowsky. ''Determined Failure, Self-styled Success: Two Views of Betsy in Peter Taylor's 'Spinster's Tale,''' in *Studies in Short Fiction*, Vol. 25, No. 1, Winter, 1988, pp. 49–54.

Warren, Robert Penn. Introduction to *A Long Fourth, and Other Stories*, Harcourt Brace Jovanovich, 1948, pp. vii-x.

Further Reading

Brown, Ashley. ''The Early Fiction of Peter Taylor,'' in *The Sewanee Review*, Vol. LXX, No. 4, Autumn, 1962, pp. 588-602.
   Brown perceives Mr. Speed as a symbol of both Elizabeth's fear of men and the breakdown of civilized behavior, and considers family dissolution as a key theme in ''A Spinster's Tale.''

Creekmore, Hubert. Review in *The New York Times Book Review*, March 21, 1948, pp. 6.
   An early review praising Taylor's first collection, particularly his depiction of the deterioration of urban family life.

Pinkerton, Jan. ''The Non-Regionalism of Peter Taylor,'' *The Georgia Review*, Vol. 24, No. 4, Winter, 1970, pp. 432-40.
   Pinkerton argues that Taylor's story possesses universal themes that transcend its Southern setting.

Robison, James Curry. ''The Early Period,'' in *Peter Taylor: A Study of the Short Fiction*, Twayne, 1988, pp. 19–31.
   Robison focuses on the character of Betsy in ''A Spinster's Tale'' and her rejection of sex, death, and the passage of time. He also examines the relationship between narrative technique and theme in the story.

Warren, Robert Penn. Introduction to *A Long Fourth, and Other Stories*, Harcourt Brace Jovanovich, 1948, pp. vii-x.
   Warren praises Taylor's first collection, maintaining that ''A Spinster's Tale'' is a superior example of Taylor's attempt to depict Southern family life through a first-person narrator.

The Stationmaster

Alexander Pushkin

1830

Originally published anonymously, ''The Stationmaster'' (1830), is perhaps the finest short story by the ''father of Russian literature,'' Alexander Pushkin. One of the *Tales of the Late Ivan Petrovich Belkin*, the story chronicles the tragic story of a humble stationmaster and his beautiful runaway daughter.

''The Stationmaster'' is considered influential for its concise, plain style, a hallmark of Pushkin's writing. The story is told in chronological order, with a clear beginning, middle, and end and addresses themes such as familial vs. romantic love, moral corruption, the conflict between social classes, and the ambiguity of human existence.

Author Biography

Pushkin's stature in the history of Russian literature is unparalleled; in fact, he is variously called Russia's ''national poet'' and ''the father of Russian literature.'' While critics suggest that Pushkin's relative obscurity outside of Russia is due, in part, to his particular use of language, which is not easily translatable, other masters of Russian literature, such as Leo Tolstoy and Fyodor Dostoevsky acknowledged their great debt to the achievements of Pushkin.

Born May 26 (June 6, modern calendar), 1799, into an aristocratic family, Pushkin was raised in a literary environment. He traced his lineage back six hundred years, including his maternal great-grandfather Hannibal, a black slave bought by Peter the Great in Turkey and brought back to Russia. Both his father, Sergei, and his uncle, Vasily, were writers, and the young Pushkin had free access to his father's extensive library, which contained a large collection of French literature.

At the age of twelve, Pushkin was sent to school at Tsarskoe Selo near St. Petersburg. There, under the supervision of progressive educators, he developed his literary talents and cultivated friendships with students who would later participate in the Decembrist rebellion. In 1817 he finished school and was appointed to the Ministry of Foreign Affairs.

After the defeat of Napoleon in 1812 republican sympathies became widespread among Russian intellectuals. Secret societies were formed, such as the Union of Welfare, to bring about an end to autocracy and serfdom. Living primarily in St. Petersburg, Pushkin was a member of "the Green Lamp," the literary branch of the Union of Welfare. His reputation as a writer led to his being exiled by Czar Alexander I for allegedly spreading anti-government and atheistic ideas.

In 1826 Pushkin wrote to Czar Nicholas I asking for an end to his exile. The Czar's consent was conditional; Nicholas insisted that he would personally censor all of Pushkin's writings.

In May the writer became engaged to Natalya Nikolaevna Goncharova. The great cholera epidemic of 1830 delayed their marriage, forcing Pushkin to live at his father's estate in the village of Boldino.

During this time he composed five *Small Tragedies*, the long poem *A House in Kolomna*, and the collection of short stories, *The Tales of the Late Ivan Petrovich Belkin*, which includes "The Stationmaster."

Pushkin and Natalya married in 1831. In 1836 he challenged a French officer to a duel because of rumors that the officer was having an affair with Pushkin's wife. The duel was averted when the officer married Natalya's sister, but the rumors persisted. Pushkin was killed in a duel with his brother-in-law at the age of thirty-seven. Despite his untimely death, Pushkin's legacy makes him the most cherished writer of the Russian literary tradition.

Alexander Pushkin

Plot Summary

Prologue

"The Stationmaster" opens with the narrator, A.G.N., frustrated with the stationmaster as he travels on his journey. In early nineteenth-century Russia travelers used horses provided by post-stations to go from one town to another, along post-roads. The stationmaster was responsible for the administration of road permits (required of all travelers) and the horses travelers would use.

The narrator becomes more sympathetic, insisting that the stationmaster is "a veritable martyr of the fourteenth class." This alludes to the institution known as the Table of Ranks, which, in Czarist Russia, established an order of social ranking among all government workers, including the military. The fourteenth class was the lowest of the ranks in the Table. The narrator appeals to his "reader's conscience" by offering examples of situations in which a stationmaster is a victim of circumstances, subject to verbal and physical abuse.

Part II

The narrator discusses a stationmaster he had come to know along his travels. On a hot day he is caught in a spring shower, arriving at a station "along a route that has since been abandoned." Hoping for dry clothes and some tea, the narrator is greeted by the stationmaster and his beautiful fourteen-year-old daughter, Dunia. The stationmaster is described as "a man about fifty years of age, still fresh and agile."

As the stationmaster copies out the traveler's order for fresh horses, the narrator passes the time observing a series of pictures depicting the Biblical parable of the Prodigal Son. The narrator enjoys a drink and conversation with the stationmaster and Dunia as if they were old friends. As he reluctantly leaves the station, he asks Dunia for a kiss, and she consents.

Part III

Years pass before the narrator has a chance to return to the station; he speculates what has happened to the stationmaster and Dunia during those intervening years. When he arrives again at the station, he recognizes the pictures depicting the parable of the Prodigal Son, but both the station and stationmaster are in a state of neglect.

When the narrator asks about Dunia, the stationmaster tells him how one winter evening "a slim young hussar" (a cavalry officer) arrived at his station in an angry mood. When greeted by Dunia, the young officer's anger quickly dissipated. When the horses were readied for the traveler, he suddenly fell ill, insisting he would not be able to travel on. The stationmaster offered the officer his bed and Dunia attended him until a doctor could arrive the following day.

The doctor arrived and the officer spoke to him in German (which the stationmaster could not understand). The doctor then told the stationmaster that the young officer would need more rest. Then both the officer and the doctor enjoyed dinner and a bottle of wine. After another day passed, the hussar was fully recovered, and offered Dunia a ride in his carriage to church. When Dunia hesitated, her father encouraged her to accept his offer, "His Honor's not a wolf; he won't eat you: go ahead, ride with him as far as the church."

Later the poor stationmaster could not understand how he could have permitted Dunia to go off with the hussar; what had blinded him? what had deprived him of reason? Half an hour had scarcely passed when his heart began to ache and ache, and anxiety overwhelmed him to such a degree that he could no longer resist setting out for the church himself. He could see as he approached the church that the congregation was already dispersing, but Dunia was neither in the churchyard nor on the porch. He hurried into the church: the priest was leaving the altar, the sexton extinguishing the candles, and two old women still praying in a corner; but Dunia was not there. Her poor father could hardly bring himself to ask the sexton if she had been to mass. She had not, the sexton replied. The stationmaster went home more dead than alive. (Excerpt from "The Stationmaster," translated by Paul Debreczeny.)

Falling ill at the loss of his daughter, the stationmaster was treated by the same physician who had seen the hussar, who told him that the officer had not truly been sick. Using the travel documents to determine the identity and destination of the hussar, the stationmaster set off for Petersburg, telling himself, "I shall bring my lost sheep home." When at last he tracks down Captain Minskii, the officer apologizes to the stationmaster but refuses to return Dunia to her father, sending him out to the street.

After a few days the stationmaster returned to Minskii's lodgings but was refused entry. After attending a service at the Church of All the Afflicted, he recognizes the young officer traveling by in a carriage. Following the carriage, the stationmaster arrives at a three-story building and discovers that Dunia lives on the second floor.

Forcing his way into the apartment, the stationmaster sees his daughter seated beside Captain Minskii. When she recognizes her father, Dunia faints and falls to the floor. Angered, the hussar throws the stationmaster out of the apartment. The stationmaster concludes his story, telling the narrator that he has received no news of his daughter's fate.

Part IV

Years pass, but the narrator cannot forget the stationmaster or Dunia. Traveling nearby on an autumn day, he discovers that the station has been abolished and that the stationmaster has passed away. As he is led to the stationmaster's grave by a little boy, he is told that a wealthy young lady (whom the narrator seems to presume is Dunia), traveling with three children, had come to visit the stationmaster in the summer. When she was shown his grave, she "threw herself on the grave and lay there for a long time." Having learned this, the narrator leaves the town satisfied.

Characters

A. G. N.

See Narrator

Dunia

The stationmaster's daughter, Dunia breaks her father's heart by running off to St. Petersburg with the wealthy young Captain Minskii.

The narrator is struck by her youthful beauty the first time he meets her. When he requests a kiss, she consents. She keeps her father's house in order, performing all the domestic duties earlier taken care of by her late mother. She is so lovely that ladies would give her presents and gentlemen would seek excuses to linger about the station to gaze at her.

When Minskii arrives, she attends to him when he feigns sickness. She hesitates to accept his offer of a ride to church but eventually accepts at her father's urging. During the ride, she is persuaded to run off with Minskii. When her father finds her in St. Petersburg, she looks more beautiful than ever as she plays with the curls of Minskii's hair.

The narrator believes her to be the wealthy woman who arrives with three children, a dog, and a servant to mourn at the stationmaster's grave.

Dunja

See Dunia

Minskii

Minskii is the "slim young hussar" who seduces the stationmaster's daughter, Dunia. ("Hussar" is a military term denoting light cavalry.) When he arrives one winter evening, he threatens to strike the old stationmaster when he is told that no horses are available. Yet when he sees Dunia, his temperament quickly changes. Making himself at home, he settles into a pleasant conversation with them. When the horses are prepared for him, he suddenly falls ill and insists that he is unable to travel.

After spending the night in the stationmaster's bed, he is visited by a doctor. The next day he feels better and he offers Dunia a ride to church on his way to St. Petersburg.

When the stationmaster later tracks him down in town, Minskii apologizes but refuses to send Dunia back home. He then hands the stationmaster some money and sends him out into the street. Later, he again throws the stationmaster out in the street

Media Adaptations

- A German film version of "The Stationmaster," entitled *Der Postmeister*, was made in 1940 by Wein Films.

---

when Dunia is startled to see her father in her apartment.

Minskij

See Minskii

Minsky

See Minskii

Narrator

The Narrator, also known as Titular Councillor A. G. N., meets the stationmaster and his daughter, Dunia, while traveling. In the time that passes between his first encounter with them and the time of the story, he is promoted in rank. He becomes interested in their lives, claiming that he "would rather talk with them than with some official of the sixth class traveling on government business."

Attracted to Dunia, he kisses her after their first meeting. When he returns years later, he is sad to learn that Dunia has left and he sympathetically listens to the stationmaster's story. On his third visit he learns that the old man has passed away. When he visits the stationmaster's grave, he is comforted to learn that a wealthy young lady (whom he presumes to be Dunia) has recently mourned at the grave as well.

Postmaster

See Samson Vyrin

Avdotia Samsonovna

See Dunia

Stationmaster

See Samson Vyrin

Titular Councillor A. G. N.
See Narrator

Samson Vyrin

The elderly manager of a posting station, Vyrin loses his teenage daughter to the wealthy Captain Minskii. When the narrator first meets the station-master, he is "a man about fifty years of age, still fresh and agile, in a long green coat with three medals on faded ribbons." He is proud of his daughter, Dunia, and relies on her to fulfill the domestic duties once performed by his late wife.

When the narrator returns, Vyrin is an unkempt, hunchbacked, "feeble old man." He relates how Captain Minskii violated his hospitality. He follows Minskii and Dunia to St. Petersburg, where he stays with an old friend from the army. When he finds Minskii, he is turned away and given money, which he throws away in disgust.

When Dunia sees him again she faints. After Minskii again sends him away, his army friend encourages him to file a complaint. He does not and returns home, where he gradually drinks himself to death.

Themes

Class Conflict

Much of the conflict in "The Stationmaster" involves the inequality between social classes. The prologue alludes to the Table of Ranks that established an order of social ranking among all government workers. The stationmaster is in the fourteenth class, the lowest rank in the Table. The narrator tells us that he would rather talk with a stationmaster "than with some official of the sixth class traveling on government business."

He tells the reader of his frustration that a stationmaster would give away to a higher-ranking official horses that had been prepared for him. The narrator asks, "what would become of us if the rule convenient to all, 'Let rank yield to rank,' were to be replaced by some other, such as 'Let mind yield to mind'? What arguments would arise?" While the narrator dismisses his question in favor of practicality, the reader is left to ask the question in the context of the story.

The young hussar, who "steals" Dunia away from her father is an officer, and, therefore, of a higher rank than the stationmaster (who was an enlisted man). In deference, the stationmaster allows the officer to use his bed while he fakes illness. When the stationmaster comes to town and tries to speak with Captain Minskii about his daughter, he is obstructed by the officer's servants. He tries to gain access to Minskii by asking an orderly, who was cleaning the officer's boots, to "announce to His Honor that an old soldier begged to see him."

While we are told how a stationmaster may be called upon at any hour, the orderly informs him that Minskii "never received anybody before eleven o'clock." When he finally confronts Minskii at eleven in the morning, the officer meets him wearing his sleeping attire, hands him money, and sends him out the door. The stationmaster is encouraged by a friend to file a complaint against the officer; after much thought, he decides against it.

Wealth and Poverty

Closely related to the theme of class conflict is that of wealth and poverty. The station is described as "humble but neat." The pictures illustrating the parable of the Prodigal Son at the station show an old man giving a young man a bag of money. After spending the money wastefully, the young man is destitute. He then returns to his father, who welcomes him back.

While Captain Minskii stays at the stationmaster's, he pays the physician a handsome amount and invites him to stay for dinner as if he were in his own home. The next day he pays the stationmaster "generously" for "his bed and board." Later in the story, when the stationmaster confronts Minskii about Dunia, the young hussar shoves money in the stationmaster's coat sleeve before sending him out in the street. When the stationmaster throws the money away in disgust—then second-guesses himself—a well-dressed young man snatches up the money before it can be retrieved by the old man.

Moral Corruption

The theme of moral corruption in integral to "The Stationmaster." The pictures of the parable of the Prodigal Son tell a story of moral corruption and redemption. The narrator calls Dunia a "little coquette" when she notices his attraction to her beauty. She is on her way to church when she decides to run away with Captain Minskii. The stationmaster tells the narrator that Dunia "is not the first, nor shall she be the last to be seduced by some rake passing through, to be kept for a while and then discarded."

He perceives his daughter as corrupted and Minskii as the corrupter. However, when the narrator is informed that the stationmaster is dead, he is told the cause is "a glass or two too many." While the stationmaster's pleasure in rum and its effect on his conversation are humorous earlier in the story, the loss of Dunia leads to his abuse of alcohol and to his own moral corruption and ultimate ruin.

Style

Point of View

"The Stationmaster" is told from the point of view of the narrator. Although the story is one of *The Tales of the Late Ivan Petrovich Belkin*, the preface to the collection names Titular Councillor A.G.N. as the source of "The Stationmaster," leaving Belkin (apparently) the editor. Although Pushkin is the author of the short story, he effectively removes himself from identification with the narrator's voice.

The story begins with a prologue discussing negative stereotypes of stationmasters as rude and offensive bureaucrats who hinder the traveler on his journey. The narrator plays on these generalizations only to question them, appealing to his "reader's conscience" by offering examples of situations in which a stationmaster is a victim of circumstances and subject to verbal and physical abuse. But the narrator quickly shifts from these generalizations to the story of a specific stationmaster he once knew.

The next section of the story describes the narrator's first meeting with the stationmaster and his only meeting with the stationmaster's daughter, Dunia. While the point of view remains the narrator's, his language is now fully involved with the narrative. The narrator quotes both of the other characters, but any psychological observations are based entirely on the narrator's own perceptions.

When the narrator returns to the station to find that Dunia has left her father, the point of view shifts to that of the stationmaster, who tells the narrator the circumstances of her departure. But the stationmaster's point of view holds for only a paragraph; that is when the narrator takes over the stationmaster's narrative. Some critics have cited Pushkin's dislike of writing in dialect as a reason for this shift (a difference one may detect only if reading the story in the original Russian: the stationmaster,

Topics for Further Study

- Research the social order in Russia under the reign of Czar Nicholas I. How is this hierarchical order depicted in "The Stationmaster"?

- Discuss the character of Dunia in the context of recent advances in women's rights. How would her actions be viewed today?

- Research the role of the military in early nineteenth-century Russia. Determine how this affects the relationship of the young hussar and the stationmaster.

being of a lower rank than the narrator, uses language differently).

This shift back to the narrator's voice also allows for psychological analysis of both the stationmaster and Dunia. Still, the narrator's perspective of these events does not differ radically from that of the stationmaster (despite, or perhaps because of, his having kissed Dunia).

When the narrator returns to learn the fate of the stationmaster, the point of view switches to that of the red-haired boy. He describes the arrival of the wealthy lady, presumably Dunia (although the narrator never states this), who mourns over the grave of the stationmaster. The point of view returns to that of the narrator for the last sentence of the story, which merely states his satisfaction with the boy's description and leaves many questions unanswered.

Setting

The setting of "The Stationmaster" is a crucial aspect of the story. The station itself is "along a route that has since been abandoned," in the Russian village of P. When the stationmaster goes to rescue his daughter from Captain Minskii, he goes to the city of Petersburg, a thriving metropolis familiar to any of Pushkin's readers.

The differences in locale are less subtle than the differences in seasons. The initial visit occurs in the spring. When the narrator returns we are not told of the season, but the stationmaster tells him that Minskii arrived in the winter. The narrator returns a final time in the fall and is told by the boy that the wealthy lady visited the stationmaster's grave in the summer.

While the narrator initially tells us that he met the stationmaster and Dunia in 1816, the only indication given by the narrator of time's passing is "years went by," while the stationmaster tells him "almost three years" had passed since he last saw his daughter. The setting of the story is, then, roughly contemporary with its publication, 1830.

Realism

Pushkin is often considered the father of Russian literary realism. The realistic style of "The Stationmaster" is evident in the linear flow of the narrative. Each episode follows the last sequentially. There is a clear beginning, middle, and end, and they follow each other in that order. Likewise, the attention to detail conveys a clear representation of the story's reality, in conformity with what may be viewed as "normal" reality. The characters are not of a heroic aristocracy from times long gone; "real" people, like the characters in "The Stationmaster," could be encountered in Russia at the time the story was written. The ambiguity of the story's conclusion is similar to that of "real" life.

Irony

Irony—an indirect presentation of a paradox, or of an ideal situation or circumstance in contrast to the actual—is a key stylistic element of the story. Dramatic irony, in which the irony is inherent in the situation, but unknown to the characters, is evident when Dunia returns wealthy, not destitute, to her "prodigal" father.

The story of the stationmaster and Dunia is an ironic reversal of the parable of the Prodigal Son, as depicted in the series of pictures on the walls of the station. Some scholars have noted inconsistencies in the number of years which pass according to the story, concluding that this may be a form of Romantic irony which forces the reader into awareness of the story as a piece of fiction despite its realism.

Historical Context

"The Stationmaster" was published in 1830—a year of great revolutionary conflict throughout Europe. In France Charles X was deposed by revolutionaries on July 29 after a six-year reign. The Bourbon duc d'Orleans was then declared "citizen king" by the French Liberals. He would reign until 1848 as Louis Philippe.

Inspired by the French example, Belgian revolutionaries demanded independence from the Netherlands and forced Dutch troops out of Brussels in early October. Belgium was recognized as an independent nation-state by the end of December.

Russia was not immune to the revolutionary fever sweeping Europe. In 1830 Polish nationalists formed a union with Lithuania and declared independence from Russia. The rebellion was subsequently put down with the Russian victory at Warsaw in September, 1831.

In Russia Czar Nicholas I, a member of the Romanov dynasty, became ruler on December 14, 1825. That date marks the Decembrist rebellion in St. Petersburg, when a group of young army officers led 3,000 troops in an attempt to take advantage of the death of Emperor Alexander I. After Alexander I defeated Napoleon in 1812, republican and constitutional ideologies began circulating among Russian intellectuals, fostered by secret societies such as the Union of Welfare (of which Pushkin was a member).

In 1822 Pushkin published his *Observations of Russian History of the Eighteenth Century*, which addressed the peasant problem, i.e. Russia's reliance on the medieval system of serfdom (a form of slavery). Pushkin claimed that the problem must be resolved in one of two ways: either by spontaneous uprising or by gradual enlightenment; he claimed to support the latter.

The Decembrists sought to abolish autocracy in the absence (or interim) of a Czar and to replace that form of government with a constitutional monarchy or republic. But Nicholas I assumed the title of Czar and administered oaths of loyalty to the Senate and State Council before the troops had gathered. Troops loyal to the Czar surrounded the rebels, putting a bloody end to the rebellion.

The rebellion was the first armed, open attempt to topple autocracy and abolish serfdom in Russia. Pushkin was in exile at the time of the Decembrist rebellion, but he was sympathetic to their struggle. He wrote to Decembrist leaders in his "Letter to Siberia," "Your sorrowful work will not pass away."

Compare & Contrast

- **1830s:** After the death of Emperor Alexander, his brother Nicholas is made Czar of Russia. An armed uprising of young army officers and troops numbering nearly 3,000 men gathers in St. Petersburg to demand a republican government. Known as the Decembrist revolution, troops loyal to Nicholas quelled the uprising.

  Today: The Russian political system is by no means stable. Communist radicals threaten to topple the democratically elected President, Boris Yeltsin. Economic problems add to the political instability.

- **1830:** Cholera sweeps across Russia and spreads to the rest of Europe, killing millions of people. By the end of the year the disease kills 900,000 Russians.

  Today: Cholera is very rare. Diagnosis and treatment for such airborne diseases has greatly improved, but the threat remains with the danger of germ warfare or a hybrid of existing contagions.

- **1830s:** In Russia travelers use horses provided by post-stations to go from one town to another along post-roads. The stationmaster is responsible for the administration of road permits (required of all travelers) and horses.

  Today: Russia has all forms of modern transportation, with a comprehensive and reasonably priced train system. The job of stationmaster does not exist and horses were replaced by autos long ago.

But revolution was not the only crisis facing the Russia of Czar Nicholas I. In 1830 a cholera outbreak swept across Russia. In some areas crop failure lead to famine and quarantine efforts lead to rioting. By the end of 1830 cholera had claimed the lives of 900,000 Russians. The disease would spread, eventually killing several million people across Europe.

Despite these social crises, the reign of Nicholas I is considered the golden age of Russian literature. Despite strict censorship (Nicholas I was Pushkin's personal censor), writers such as Pushkin, Nikolay Gogol, Fyodor Dostoevsky, and Leo Tolstoy produced numerous masterpieces during this era.

Critical Overview

Critics have praised "The Stationmaster" as a masterpiece of the short story genre. Generally regarded as the "father of Russian literature," Pushkin was a great innovator in many mediums,
including poetry, drama, and the novel, in addition to the short story. The Realist school of Russian literature owes much to Pushkin, and "The Stationmaster" exemplifies a realistic depiction of Russian life in the time of the author.

Analysis of the story really began in 1919, when M. O. Gershenzon became the first critic to analyze the symbolic significance of the pictures depicting the Biblical parable of the Prodigal Son. While he may not have been the first to notice the parallels between the pictures and the story itself, Gershenzon was the first to speculate on the affect the pictures may have had on the story's characters.

Gershenzon contends that the stationmaster allowed the pictures to dictate his understanding of Dunia's departure. Rather than being happy for his daughter, who has found not only love, but also wealth, the stationmaster instead sees Dunia as an embodiment of the Prodigal Son. This is why he follows the couple to St. Petersburg. The stationmaster's belief in the story of the Prodigal Son clouds his judgment, Gershenzon insists, forcing him to see things not as they are, and deceiving himself into despair.

Map of Russia and Siberia.

Willis Konick agrees with Gershenzon regarding the importance of the Prodigal Son pictures, but suggests that Gershenzon perhaps overstates Dunia's happiness. The point of the story, Konick argues, is that sin does not necessarily lead to catastrophe and a moral slip does not always result in a fall.

Walter Vickery, in his book-length study *Alexander Pushkin,* shares this view of the story, calling it "a rebuttal of the sentimentalist fallacy that poor girls are by nature innocent, that they are ensnared and deceived by rich men, and that the results of their seduction or abduction are bound to be catastrophic."

Konick also stresses the emotional effect the story has on the narrator, who is as important to the story as the stationmaster and Dunia. While Konick is interested in how the narrator becomes involved emotionally, Paul Debreczeny, in *The Other Pushkin*, asserts that the narrator "stands for eighteenth-century and early-nineteenth-century sentimentalism."

Whereas Konick notices—but does not question—the narrator's emotional involvement, Debreczeny maintains that the narrator's point of view is "narrow," incapable of seeing that "Dunia

is running away from a suffocatingly close relationship with her father as well as from the boredom and poverty of provincial life." While Vickery insists that the element of parody must not be overemphasized, and that emphasis should be placed on the story's "clear and concise" style, "with no attempt at psychological analysis and very few comments from the narrator," Debreczeny shows how the narrator's sympathetic view of the stationmaster's story "is at times obstructed by a ludicrous presentation."

Debreczeny points to the narrator's penchant for literary allusion, breaking into quotation when recalling Dunia's kiss or comparing the stationmaster's wiping of tears to a character in a ballad, as examples of his "ludicrous presentation." This refusal to comply with the narrator's perspective allows Debreczeny to question the narrator's notion of "poor" Dunia. Instead of viewing her as a victim, subject to the seduction of the hussar, Debreczeny insists, "there is something attractive in her daring. Against all odds, she makes a dash for a better life."

However, he cautions, not all of the details of her life are clarified by the story's conclusion. Most critics assume that Dunia has married the young officer. This is, Debreczeny notes, "despite the scarce evidence of the text." The officer may not have married her because of her lower social status, not uncommon for the times. Perhaps, he speculates, she is merely a "kept woman" with children; "her future is uncertain: otherwise, as a married woman, she would have come to make it up with her father much sooner. . . ."

Debreczeny maintains that this uncertainty of the story is its virtue: "Ambiguity—a result of the author's identification with all sides—is a concomitant of Pushkin's highest artistic achievements."

Richard Gregg offers a different perspective in his essay, "A Scapegoat for All Seasons." He shows how the hussar fits the stereotype of the storybook hero, while the stationmaster represents the direct opposite—a contemporary "counterhero." Gregg uses Northrop Frye's myth-criticism method to show how the story may fit into an "archetypal" tragic pattern. He notes that the only outdoor scene in the story occurs in autumn, and that (in Frye's archetypal system) autumn corresponds with tragedy.

Gregg sees in the title of the story the ambivalence, or double nature, of the tragic hero who falls from greatness due to the error of pride. He views the stationmaster as a mythical scapegoat figure, a hero who suffers for the pleasure of others.

Despite the lack of Pushkin criticism in English (due in part, his critics suggest, to his particularly untranslatable use of the Russian language), the criticism addressing "The Stationmaster" in English displays a wide variety of reading perspectives and interpretive strategies.

Criticism

David Kilpatrick

Kilpatrick is a freelance writer and editor. In the following essay, he examines Pushkin's use of irony in the story.

Early in his literary career, Alexander Pushkin was sent into exile by Czar Alexander I for allegedly spreading anti-government and atheistic ideas with his "revolutionary verse." Pushkin was a member of "the Green Lamp," the literary wing of the Union of Welfare secret society.

The Union of Welfare (as well as other political secret societies) was formed in the wake of Napoleon's defeat in 1812. Russian intellectuals began to call for political reform in the form of either a constitutional monarchy or a republic, and for an end to the repulsive institution of serfdom. Czar Alexander I was unwilling to give up power and to allow Russia to modernize.

While he was in exile, Pushkin received word of the Decembrist rebellion in 1825. The death of Czar Alexander I left the nation in a state of crisis: which of the dead monarch's brothers would become Czar? Led by a group of young officers, many of whom were involved in political secret societies (such as the Union of Welfare), 3,000 troops gathered on December 14, 1825, in St. Petersburg, calling for an end to autocracy and serfdom.

Yet Nicholas I had already taken the oath of office. When the revolutionaries gathered in the Senate Square, they were met by loyalist troops who put a quick and bloody end to their attempt at reform. Pushkin had established friendships with many of the Decembrist leaders, some from his school days. He wrote to them, in his *Letter to Siberia*, "Your sorrowful work will not pass away."

With this introduction to political power, Czar Nicholas I began a regime marked by conservatism and based on the Divine Right of the Czar. In May, 1826, Pushkin wrote to the Czar requesting release from exile. Nicholas I consented in September, under the condition that he would act as Pushkin's personal censor.

How, then, could Pushkin ensure that his friends' "sorrowful work" would endure? What could he, with the Czar as his censor, write that could promote their progressive cause without endangering his life?

In the midst of the cholera epidemic which swept across Russia in 1830 (claiming 900,000 Russian lives that year), Pushkin spent September through December at his father's estate in Boldino. Recently engaged to Natalya Nikolaevna Goncharova, Pushkin enjoyed four months of seclusion that proved to be the most productive, creative period of his life. It was in these circumstances that "The Stationmaster" was composed.

What Do I Read Next?

- The historical drama *Boris Godunov* (1831) was Pushkin's attempt to shatter the conventions of dramatic literature.

- *Eugene Onegin* (1833), a verse-novel, is perhaps Pushkin's most famous work. The hero of the title refuses the love of a country girl, only to fall in love with her after she marries another.

- Fyodor Dostoevsky's *Notes From the Underground* (1864) describes the isolation of a hyperconscious modern man.

- Leo Tolstoy's *The Death of Ivan Ilyich* (1886) details the reactions of family members, friends, and colleagues to the death of a Russian judge.

The story begins with a quote from the poet Viazemskii (a friend of Pushkin's), calling a stationmaster a ''despot,'' or a tyrant. The narrator then asks, ''Who has not cursed stationmasters?— who has not quarreled with them frequently?'' The stationmaster was responsible for providing a traveler with a permit and horses for a journey along post-roads, which linked towns in early nineteenth-century Russia.

Just as he conveys the frustration of the traveler waiting for fresh horses, the narrator shifts from this negative tone to a more sympathetic one and insists that the stationmaster is ''a veritable martyr of the fourteenth class.''

This alludes to the institution known as the Table of Ranks (created by Peter the Great) that established an order of social ranking among all government workers, based on and including the ranks of the military. The fourteenth class was the lowest of the ranks in the Table.

The narrator tells us he is appealing to his ''reader's conscience'' by offering examples of situations in which the stationmaster is a helpless victim of circumstance, subject to verbal and physical abuse. This appeal to conscience also invites the reader to question the victimization of others based on rank and class.

Having shifted the reader's perception of stationmasters from tyrants to martyrs, the narrator leaves behind generalizations to focus on the story

of a particular stationmaster whom he had met in his travels. Yet just as he tells us the time and place (May 1816) when he met this stationmaster, he recalls that he himself was ''of low rank at the time'' and that he used to become upset, ''being young and hotheaded,'' when forced to yield his appointed horses to someone of a higher rank.

The narrator dismisses his frustration with the social order as youthful impracticality: ''Indeed what would become of us if the rule convenient to all, 'Let rank yield to rank,' were to be replaced by some other, such as 'Let mind yield to mind'? What arguments would arise?'' With Czar Nicholas I as his personal censor, how much could Pushkin argue with this notion?

If the reader focuses on the question of rank, as the narrator suggests, ''The Stationmaster'' becomes a critical commentary on the social structure of Pushkin's Russia. After all, each rank yields to a higher rank until the Czar, who yields only to God. This ironic quality of the story—in which the surface meaning conceals a deeper, contrary meaning—is what makes it a masterpiece of short fiction. It is a further irony that censorship encouraged Pushkin's literary genius.

The unfair advantages of social class are illustrated when the stationmaster tells the narrator his story of how he lost his daughter. The young hussar is an officer, whereas the stationmaster was an enlisted man. Despite his youth, the officer is prepared to whip the old man.

When the officer feigns illness, the stationmaster gives the young officer his bed. When the stationmaster goes to St. Petersburg to bring home his "lost sheep," his access to both Captain Minskii and Dunia is obstructed by servants. When the stationmaster tries to retrieve the money Minskii had given him, a well-dressed young man snatches up the money and races off in a cab. All of these situations arouse the reader's sympathy and appeal to the "reader's conscience."

This appeal to the reader's conscience is effective because of the narrator's point of view. The narrative voice is not omniscient. When the narrator kisses Dunia all objectivity is lost. Some critics have noted the emotional effect the stationmaster's story has on the narrator, but have not reflected on the fact that the narrator participates in the narrative. The narrator identifies with the stationmaster's despair, maintaining his point of view as he narrates, calling Dunia "poor" despite her wealth in St. Petersburg.

Paul Debreczeny, in his *The Other Pushkin*, emphasizes the over-sentimentality of the narrator. Debreczeny argues that the narrator's "narrow point of view" prevents him from seeing that Dunia "is running away from a suffocatingly close relationship with her father as well as from the boredom and poverty of provincial life."

This interpretation stresses another level of irony and allows the reader to see not only sympathy for the poverty-stricken or the low in rank, but to recognize the necessity for the overcoming of such conditions. For Debreczeny, Dunia is not a victim but a hero: "there is something attractive in her daring. Against all odds, she makes a dash for a better life."

The emphasis on the stationmaster's sorrow, emphasized not only through the narrator's point of view but also in most criticism of the story, obscures Dunia's decisive action (an almost misogynist refusal to see her as anything but a victim). Indeed, as J. Thomas Shaw notes in his essay "'The Stationmaster' and the Parable," "We are never allowed to share her consciousness."

Many critics, following the lead of M. O. Gershenzon, have analyzed the story as a parody or reversal of the Biblical parable of the Prodigal Son. Shaw suggests that "the narrator himself feels and

> " An awareness of the ambiguities of the story and a suspension of the reader's rush to a complete conclusion opens up to the truly tragic aspect of 'The Stationmaster.'"

reacts to the return of the 'prodigal' as the older brother in the parable should have felt and reacted."

However, such an idealization of and identification with the narrator's point of view obscures the textual evidence that suggests that the kiss the narrator and Dunia share is anything but sibling innocence.

Debreczeny notes that in "The Stationmaster" "most questions are answered and most details conscientiously followed up ... but there is one question that is asked twice, yet left conspicuously unanswered to the very end." He points out that most critics assume that when Dunia returns home, she is married, "despite the scarce evidence of the text." He suggests that perhaps Minskii does not marry Dunia, for "it was by no means unusual for nineteenth-century noblemen to refuse to marry mistresses who were not of their own social status."

Debreczeny insists that Dunia's fate is uncertain; this "Ambiguity—a result of the author's identification with all sides—is a concomitant of Pushkin's highest artistic achievements."

However, the ambiguity of Dunia's condition extends beyond the question of her marital status. This is, of course, a question of point of view. We learn of Dunia's return not from an omniscient narrator, but from the "red-haired, one-eyed little boy in tatters." Because point of view is crucial here, isn't the description of the boy's visual impairment essential?

Critics have often noted that Pushkin's great contribution to Russian literature is his precise use of the language. The Russian word he uses to describe the boy is *krivoy*, which has no direct equivalent in English, but may be translated as either one-eyed or (perhaps more accurately) cross-eyed.

This boy never directly states that the "wonderful lady" is Dunia. He is poverty-stricken, "in tatters," and he mentions, twice, that "she gave me a silver five-kopeck piece—such a nice lady!" While the narrator is satisfied with the boy's point of view, should we accept his visually impaired perspective? Perhaps the boy's story is merely a (successful) attempt to extract money from the narrator.

Thus, while Debreczeny is correct in noting the absence of textual evidence to support the view that Dunia was happily married to Minskii, we must also acknowledge the absence of evidence to support the view that it was Dunia who visited the graveyard.

An awareness of the ambiguities of the story and a suspension of the reader's rush to a complete conclusion opens up to the truly tragic aspect of "The Stationmaster." If the author identifies "with all sides," what about Captain Minskii?

What do we know of the young hussar? The stationmaster, under the influence of rum, told the narrator of the officer's rash behavior. Still, why would he not welcome the stationmaster, who not only is the father of his beloved Dunia, but gave him his very bed and welcomed him earlier into his home? Why did Dunia faint at the sight of her father? Why would Minskii throw the stationmaster out again when Dunia sees him? If the stationmaster was such a loving father, why would she run away?

The narrator calls Dunia a "little coquette" who seemed "like a woman who has seen the world." How did she attain such experience living in her father's house? We know that the stationmaster later drinks himself to death, but what indication is there that he was not alcoholic when Dunia lived with him? Perhaps the greatest irony of the story may be that the stationmaster was a tyrant after all.

Only an omniscient perspective could resolve these ambiguities, but the reader is denied such a view. We are left with the tragic sense of not knowing what really happened. Of course, "The Stationmaster" is a work of fiction; the story did not "really" happen. Pushkin's use of irony leaves us with questions, though he provides the appearance of answers.

Such a narrative strategy was a necessity given Pushkin's desire for the survival of his friends' "sorrowful work." Likewise, reflection on familial vs. romantic love is appropriate for one awaiting marriage, and such a tragic worldview understandable for a story written in a time of epidemic. The ambiguities of the story leave us to consider the tragic limitations of humanity.

Source: David Kilpatrick, "Tragic Ambiguity in Pushkin's 'The Stationmaster,'" for *Short Stories for Students,* The Gale Group, 2000.

Paul Debreczeny

In the following excerpt, Debreczeny gives an overview of Pushkin's "The Stationmaster," focusing on Pushkin's use of parody, sentimental imagery, and poetical devices.

"The Stationmaster," by far the most successful of Belkin's tales, is narrated by Titular Councillor A.G.N. Older than Belkin, he claims to have, "in the course of twenty years, traversed Russia in all directions" at the time of the telling—a claim incongruous with other information given on the same page. He informs us that in 1816—the time of his first meeting with the stationmaster—he was of low rank and was "young and hotheaded," which implies that he had just begun his career. We know, on the other hand, that Belkin retired in 1823, and that the *Tales* represented his first literary efforts, written probably no later than 1824 or 1825. A.G.N., therefore, could not have been traveling around on business for more than seven or eight years before he told his tale. By this incongruity—in line with the many others in *The Tales of Belkin*—Pushkin may have wished to remind the reader that his narrators are playful fabrications, not to be taken too seriously. . . .

The tale that follows is, at least at first glance, in keeping with the prologue. When A.G.N. first visits the hero of the tale, the stationmaster Samson Vyrin, he meets a hale and hearty man, the doting father of a fourteen-year-old daughter, Dunia, a pretty and coquettish girl, who willingly gives A.G.N. a farewell kiss when he asks for it. When A.G.N. visits Vyrin again some years later, the stationmaster is alone, depressed, and old-looking. He tells A.G.N. the story of his daughter. Dunia had always been good at calming travelers who were angry because of a lack of horses. On one occasion a young hussar officer named Minskii came to the station, demanded horses, and was ready to raise his whip when he heard there were none; but Dunia's appearance on the scene produced its usual effect. Minskii enjoyed waiting in Dunia's company, and when horses became available, he declared that he was ill. He was put to bed and stayed at Vyrin's house for a couple of days.

It was a Sunday when Minskii was at last able to continue his journey; he offered to drive Dunia as far as the village church. Dunia never came back; her father learned from the coach driver that she had gone on with Minskii. Vyrin fell sick with grief, and when he recovered he went to St. Petersburg, aware that this had been Minskii's destination. There he found Minskii; the young man assured him that Dunia was happy and gave him some money. But this encounter with Minskii did not satisfy the old man: he wished to see Dunia in person just once more. He succeeded in finding her apartment, forced his way in past a protesting maid, and saw her sitting close to Minskii, who was visiting with her. When she caught sight of her father she fainted, and Minskii angrily pushed the old man out of the apartment. Vyrin returned home and had been living by himself ever since, obviously drinking a great deal. It is clear to A.G.N. that he expects Dunia to be abandoned by Minskii and to end up on the street.

Some more years pass, and A.G.N. comes to visit Vyrin's station once more. The post had been abolished; A.G.N. is told that Vyrin is dead. He visits his grave and hears from a village boy that an elegant lady, traveling in a coach-and-six with three children, had also been seeking Vyrin; and when she heard of his death she went to the cemetery and lay prostrate on his grave for a long time.

Some of the sentimental imagery introduced in the prologue is carried over into the narrative. The image of a stationmaster's "poor abode," mentioned in the first paragraph, recurs in connection with Vyrin, who lives in a "humble but neat dwelling." This image is, once more, borrowed from Zhukovskii, who advised that "the whole universe, with all its joys, should be contained in the unpretentious dwelling where one loves and reflects." [V. A. Zhukovskii, *Sobraine Sochinenii*, 1959–60] Vyrin and his daughter create the impression of domestic bliss, of the kind depicted by V. Karlgof in

> "Is Dunia married, then, or not? Some critics have assumed she is, despite the scarce evidence of the text. Yet she could equally well still be a kept woman."

his sentimental idyll "The Stationmaster" (1826)—another target of Pushkin's parody. It is this tranquil family happiness that the cruel young hussar sets out to destroy.

A.G.N. strives to touch the reader's heart at every step. On his second visit, not only does he exclaim about how much Samson had aged (the "laconic" Belkin, one would suppose, would be content with that much), but he enters into detail about the man's "gray hair, the deep furrows lining his face, which had not been shaven for a long time, [and] his hunched back." Not satisfied even with this forceful image, A.G.N. repeats what he has already stated in other words, that Vyrin had become a "feeble old man". Further, Vyrin does not simply put up the sick Minskii (for which there should have been facilities at a wayside station), but yields him his very own bed, which makes the young man's ingratitude appear even more heinous. A civil servant, low-ranking as he may have been, should have nevertheless been able to go to the city by coach, but A.G.N. makes Vyrin take to the road on foot, in order, presumably, to make even more of a martyr of him. Phrases like "his heart began to ache and ache," he was "more dead than alive," "tears welled up in his eyes," "tears welled up in his eyes once more," "with an inexpressible leap of the heart," and "a few seconds of painful anticipation" put added emphasis on emotions that should already be clear from the situation. When the sorrowful old man goes to religious services, it is, naturally, to the Church of All the Afflicted (Tserkov' Vsekh Skorbiashchikh.) A.G.N., like Karamzin, often addresses the reader, asks rhetorical questions, bursts into exclamations, uses anaphora to achieve poetic effects, and—what brings him even nearer to the early sentimentalists—favors archaic forms such as *tokmo* (''only''), *stol'* (''so''), *sii* (''these''), and *koi* (''which,''). Miss K.I.T. succeeded in stamping her sentimental style on ''The Blizzard'' and on ''The Squire's Daughter'' only occasionally; A.G.N.'s stylistic presence, though not exclusive, is felt throughout ''The Stationmaster.''

Like Burmin in ''The Blizzard'' and Silvio and the Count in ''The Shot,'' Samson Vyrin is given an opportunity to tell his own story up to a point. His speech abounds in colloquialisms, often substandard. But, as we have seen, Pushkin did not like to burden his prose with class speech: after a dozen or so sentences the stationmaster ceases to speak in first person, letting A.G.N. tell the rest of the story for him. He takes over again only after the conclusion of the St. Petersburg episode, in order to lament his daughter's fate. Consequently his narrative, except for dialogues quoted directly, is not given in his style. But often where his style is not maintained, his point of view is. For example, when Minskii slips ''something'' into the cuff of Samson's sleeve, this is clearly his own, and not an omniscient narrator's, perception of what happened. His point of view is all the more easily maintained because A.G.N. is fully in sympathy with Samson, describing him as his ''friend,'' as the ''warmhearted stationmaster,'' and as ''the poor stationmaster.'' Minskii is no less of a ''deceiver'' in A.G.N.'s eyes than he is in Vyrin's. And, what also emphasizes his closeness to the indigent stationmaster, A.G.N. worries about the seven rubles it cost him to make a detour in order to accomplish his last visit.

As we have seen, in ''The Shot'' Pushkin fully exploited the technique of frustrating expectations to great effect. At first sight exactly the opposite seems to be happening in ''The Stationmaster'': A.G.N. seems to fulfill each and every expectation he raises. The theme of the beating of stationmasters, introduced in the prologue, is taken up by Vyrin as he describes how Dunia used to calm angry gentlemen; and Minskii raises his whip at Vyrin, only to lower it again as he beholds Dunia. The general rule is that gentlemen pretend they want a meal in order to stay with Dunia a little longer; the individual scene presented to us shows Minkii pretending to be ill with the same purpose in mind. We see Dunia sewing a dress before Minskii's arrival; it is her physical attractiveness that will make a lasting impression on the young hussar. She sees A.G.N. to his carriage and gives him a kiss, which prepares the reader for the second occasion she walks to a carriage—this time in order to get in and ride away for good. When ladies give kerchiefs and earrings to Dunia, she is placed dangerously within the reach of all the wealth that passes by the station; and indeed we shall see her in St. Petersburg, decked out in the latest finery, with her fingers glittering with rings. ''The pots of balsam'' are sketched in as symbols of a cheerful household in the first scene, only to be mentioned for their conspicuous absence in the second. Minskii's generous payment for his room and board is a prelude to the scene in which he gives money to the old man in an attempt to compensate him for his daughter. The bed that Vyrin yields to the seducer is the same bed he himself takes to later, sick in earnest. If the story begins with a spring shower, a big storm will play havoc with the lives of the characters; if Vyrin feels instinctively restless after his daughter has gone to church, there is good reason for it; and if A.G.N. is full of forebodings while approaching the station for his second visit, we can safely predict some tragic development in the plot. There is no detail given in this story that does not fit into a pattern or is not followed up in some way.

If A.G.N. is such a trustworthy fulfiller of expectations, can we believe that he would place a set of images in the center of the story's symbolic structure without assigning those images prognostic function? Yet this is precisely what happens. These central images are a set of pictures on the stationmaster's wall depicting the parable of the Prodigal Son; their function is to reverse the pattern of fulfilled expectations.

The first quality that strikes us as we read the description of these pictures is their divergence from the Biblical text. Here are the relevant passages from Luke 15 and ''The Stationmaster'' ; expressions in the tale that conspicuously deviate from the Biblical text are italicized: . . .

Luke 15

11 And he said, There was a man who had two sons;

12 And the younger of them said to his father, Father, give me the share of property that falls to me. And he divided his living between them.

13 Not many days later, the younger son gathered all he had and took his journey into a far country, and there he squandered his property in loose living.

14 And when he had spent everything, a great famine arose in that country, and he began to be in want.

15 So he went and joined himself to one of the citizens of that country, who sent him into his fields to feed swine.

16 And he would gladly have fed on the pods that the swine ate; and no one gave him anything.

17 But when he came to himself he said, How many of my father's hired servants have bread enough and to spare, but I perish here with hunger!

18 I will arise and go to my father, and I will say to him, Father, I have sinned against heaven and before you;

19 I am no longer worthy to be called your son; treat me as one of your hired servants.

20 And he arose and came to his father. But while he was yet at a distance, his father saw him and had compassion, and ran and embraced him and kissed him.

21 And the son said to him: Father, I have sinned against heaven and before you; I am no longer worthy to be called your son.

22 But the father said to his servants, Bring quickly the best robe, and put it on him; and put a ring on his hand, and shoes on his feet;

23 And bring the fatted calf and kill it, and let us eat and make merry;

24 For this my son was dead, and is alive again; he was lost, and is found. And they began to make merry.

25 Now his elder son was in the field; and as he came and drew near to the house, he heard music and dancing.

26 And he called one of the servants and asked what this meant.

''The Stationmaster''

In the first [picture], a *venerable* old man, in *nightcap and dressing gown,* was bidding farewell to a *restless* youth who was *hastily* accepting his blessing and a *bag of money.*

The second one depicted the young man's lewd behavior in *vivid colors*: he was seated at a table, surrounded by *false friends* and *shameless women.*

Farther on, the ruined youth, in rags and with *a three-cornered hat* on his head, was tending swine and sharing their meal; *deep sorrow* and *repentance* were reflected in his features.

The last picture showed his return to his father: the *warmhearted* old man, in the same *nightcap and dressing gown,* was running forward to meet him; the Prodigal Son was on his knees; in the background the cook was killing the fatted calf, and the elder brother was asking the servants about the cause of all the rejoicing. . . .

This is the morality that suits A.G.N.'s sentimental attitudes best. He clearly is very favorably impressed by the pictures, for he attempts to heighten their effect by the epithets he chooses in describing them. The simple Biblical phrase ''there was a man'' is transformed into a ''venerable old man''; the Prodigal Son, instead of simply asking for his share, is ''restless'' and receives his money ''hastily''; later ''deep sorrow and repentance'' are reflected on his face, which is the same kind of overstatement of emotions that we have seen A.G.N. make elsewhere in the story; the Biblical father, just like Vyrin, is a ''warmhearted old man''; and all this is depicted in ''vivid colors.''

Indeed, at times the reader cannot be sure just what was in pictures and what was read into them by A.G.N.: one can credit a painter's brush with suggesting the looseness of women, but how can the falseness of friends, sitting by a table, be indicated in a picture? . . .

As he arrives for his second visit, A.G.N. emphasizes that he ''immediately recognized the pictures illustrating the parable of the Prodigal Son.'' This repeated emphasis lends the pictures the kind of premonitory meaning that the reader of romantic literature was used to. . . . A.G.N.'s general trustworthiness is a further enticement to the reader to accept the pictures as portentous. So many signs have been followed up, so many expectations have been fulfilled in the story, that the reader cannot doubt the outcome of the plot: it is only too natural that Dunia, the Prodigal Daughter, should come on hard times in St. Petersburg and return to her father, repentant.

Several details, in accord with the pictures themselves, seem to point to such a denouement. Encouraging his daughter to take a ride with Minskii, Vyrin says, ''His Honor's not a wolf; he won't eat you,'' which prepares us for the old man's later declaration, ''I shall bring my lost sheep home.'' This detail refers the reader back to Luke 15, for the parable of the Prodigal Son immediately follows— indeed elucidates—that of the lost sheep. In both parables, the dear ones that have been lost are found. Further, when Samson Vyrin begs Minskii, ''You have had your fun with her; do not ruin her needlessly,'' we are reminded of the false friends and shameless lovers of the parable and do not doubt for a moment that Dunia will indeed end up on the street. Indeed, the old man explicitly says as much. ''Anything can happen,'' he predicts. ''She is not the first, nor will she be the last, to be seduced by some rake passing through, to be kept for a while and then discarded. There are many of them in Petersburg, of these foolish young ones: today attired in satin and velvet, but tomorrow, verily I say, sweeping the streets with the riffraff of the alehouse.'' Sweeping the streets with the riffraff, Dunia would of course remember her aging father and come home.

In sympathy with Vyrin and sharing his view of the world, A.G.N. also accepts his friend's interpretation of the pictures. . . .

Indeed convention—not only of sentimentalism, but eventually also of romanticism—demanded that the victim of seduction perish. Baratynskii's Eda, in the verse tale bearing her name (1826), pines away after her hussar leaves, and even Pushkin's own Water-Nymph throws herself in the Dnieper after her Prince tells her he is marrying someone else. The stationmaster's exclamation ''Oh, Dunia, Dunia!'' echoes both Karamzin's ''Oh, Liza, Liza!'' and Baratynskii's ''Oh, Eda, Eda!''

But in this instance A.G.N. lets his reader down. In all likelihood he does not do this by design: rather, his own expectations have been frustrated. Try as he might, he cannot fit life into the mold of *petit bourgeois* morality. The analogy between the parable of the Prodigal Son (as perceived by a Philistine) and Dunia's fate proves to be false. In fact the parallels only serve to draw attention to the contrasts: unlike the Biblical father, the stationmaster himself encourages his daughter to ride away with Minskii; Dunia takes no bag of money from her father; she runs away from poverty rather than recklessly abandoning a life of contentment; the father, rather than the child, appears to sue for favors at another man's doorstep; and Dunia, even if she wished to return, would have no home to come back to, for it is her father, rather than she, who ends up in dissipation. The details that reverse the parable in the most subtle manner are items of clothing: in the picture it is the father who is in nightcap and dressing gown—that is, wearing the symbols of domestic comfort and stability—but in the story we see Minskii receiving the stationmaster in just such garments. Moreover, in the parable (though, admittedly, this is not mentioned in the description of the pictures) the father orders his servants to put a ring on his repentant son's hand, but in the story it is through Minskii's generosity that Dunia's fingers glitter with rings.

Pushkin's manipulation of his narrator is most successful in ''The Stationmaster'' because A.G.N.'s narrow point of view is never ostensibly abandoned, yet vistas open to a broader understanding of life. This creates a dual perspective, reminiscent of that in *Poltava*. Like Mazepa, the characters in ''The Stationmaster'' are susceptible of different interpretations: some critics see Vyrin as a poor old man, a victim of corrupting social forces that have taken away his last comfort in life, his beloved daughter; others see Dunia as a justified and successful rebel against social and moral stagnation.

Despite the narrator's naive overstatement of his case, a sympathetic appraisal of Samson Vyrin is indeed achieved, for he is undoubtedly the victim of a cruel personal and social destiny. . . .

Dunia is running away from a suffocatingly close relationship with her father as well as from the boredom and poverty of provincial life. The description in the epigraph—''Despot of the posting station'' —may well imply, as one critic suggests, Vyrin's emotional tyranny over his daughter. Moreover, the fact that Pushkin insisted on restoring Vyrin's original first name, ''Samson,'' after it had been misprinted as ''Simeon'' in the first edition, indicates that he wanted Vyrin to be associated with a Biblical hero who had been deprived of is power by a woman. . . . With this in mind, we are not so surprised to hear that Vyrin would sooner see his daughter in the grave than in Minskii's arms.

Whether or not Dunia's elopement can be justified, she certainly feels guilty about it: although she is going voluntarily, she cries all through the first two stages of the journey; she faints when she beholds her father in her apartment; and she lies prostrate on his grave for a long time. All these details make us judge her conduct less harshly. Besides, there is something attractive in her daring. Against all odds, she makes a dash for a better life. What she takes is a calculated risk: she might very well end up as her father expects—as Katia Maslova was to do in Tolstoi's *Resurrection* (1899)—but she throws a challenge to fate. In his 1829 lyric ''Reminiscences of Tsarskoe Selo'' Pushkin had likened himself to a Prodigal Son; there is no doubt he felt kinship with Vyrin's Prodigal Daughter.

But it is not only the author's divided sympathies that leave the story open to various interpretations. If the parable of the Prodigal Son were fully reversed—if we saw Dunia happily married at the end—the issues would be much clearer. In that case we could simply say that the stationmaster and his friend A.G.N. applied the wrong set of moral standards to life and were deceived. But in fact the final outcome is not the exact opposite to A.G.N.'s expectations: it is neither their confirmation nor their full reversal, for we are not told whether Dunia is married or not.

This is a story, as we have seen, in which most questions are answered and most details conscientiously followed up—either in a straight line or reversed—but there is one question that is asked twice, yet left conspicuously unanswered to the very end. Approaching Vyrin's house for the second time, A.G.N. says: ''I remembered the old stationmaster's daughter, and the thought of seeing her again gave me joy. I told myself that the old stationmaster might well have been replaced, and that Dunia was likely to have married.'' Having roused Vyrin from sleep and asked how his daughter was doing, A.G.N. receives an uncertain answer, to which he rejoins: ''So she's married, is she?'' If A.G.N. were true to himself, he would answer this question in no uncertain terms; but in the end all the information we are given is this: '''A wonderful lady,' replied the urchin; 'she was traveling in a coach-and-six with three little masters, a nurse, and a black pug.''' Is Dunia married, then, or not? Some critics have assumed she is, despite the scarce evidence of the text. Yet she could equally well still be a kept woman. If she is, she is certainly kept well; and the fact that she has had three children indicates that her position must be fairly secure. But it was by no means unusual for nineteenth-century noblemen to refuse to marry mistresses who were not of their own social status. . . . Thus in my own view Dunia's fate is still in the balance. She is not sweeping the street with the alehouse riffraff; nor has she come back, as the Prodigal Daughter, to sue at her father's door. But her future is uncertain: otherwise, as a married woman, she would have come to make it up with her father much sooner. . . .

Having experienced difficulties with an omniscient mode of narration, Pushkin turned to the use of imaginary narrators chiefly with parody and stylistic experiment in mind. Four of Belkin's five tales reflect—to varying degrees—his parodic design. But in the fifth he transcended parody and, putting a conventional technique to a novel use, created one of the masterpieces of nineteenth-century Russian prose.

Source: Paul Debreczeny, '''Belkin' and 'Goriukhino,''' in *The Other Pushkin: A Study of Alexander Pushkin's Prose Fiction,* Stanford University Press, 1983, pp. 56–137.

J. Thomas Shaw

In the following excerpt, Shaw contends that although Pushkin's ''The Stationmaster'' is an adaptation of the New Testament parable, there is a basic contrast of style and tone. Shaw also studies the role of the narrator and the narrative structure of the story.

The narrative technique of the Parable of the Prodigal Son, like that of the other New Testament parables, is quite different from that of ''The Stationmaster.'' The parables of Jesus as quoted in Luke and the other synoptic Gospels are in third-person, omniscient-narrator form. Their basic style is simple, direct, succinct, and unambiguous; they are homely in subject and setting, and devoid of the ''literary.'' In them, the narrator is not a participant in the story told. In the Parable of the Prodigal Son, which has more conversation than perhaps any other biblical parable, the mode of narration and the mode of speech of all the characters is basically the same; the speech of the different characters is differentiated by what they say, rather than by a different manner of speaking. The words of the father and each of the two sons fit into the one style of the parable.

''The Stationmaster'' presents a basic contrast in style with the biblical accounts of the parables. All is seen through the consciousness of a first-person narrator, whose own mode of writing is quite different from the passages in which the Stationmaster is quoted directly. ''The Stationmaster,'' like the other *Tales of Belkin (Povesti Belkina),* is quite short and concise; nevertheless, it is many times as long as even the longest New Testament parable. The story proper in ''The Stationmaster'' consists of the narrator's account of what he himself saw and heard during three successive visits to the poststation. Three of the scenes directly relating to the Parable of the Prodigal Son are presented during his recountal of the second visit, and the fourth such scene, in the third visit. Of the four scenes relating to the parable, the narrator participates directly only in the last one. The narrator's mode of narration, instead of being simple and direct, shows qualities of empathy and ironic detachment. The detachment of the story is increased by the use of distancing literary allusions. . . . There is complexity of attitude and response in ''The Stationmaster'' that is

Cornet Wilkin of the 11th Hussars, wearing an elaborately decorated uniform.

quite different from the simple, terse, immediate directness of the third-person narrative technique that Jesus used in the New Testament parables.

"The Stationmaster" is, along with "The Shot" ("Vystrel"), one of the two of the *Tales of Belkin* told in the first person by a narrator. One of the most characteristic qualities of the *Tales of Belkin* is the way they use artistic distance and give a multiple illumination to the events narrated "The Stationmaster" is said to have been told to Belkin by titular councillor A. G. N., who can be considered as directly representing the first person of the narrator. Belkin is to be considered as having revised the

"anecdotes," shaping them into stories, and the "publisher A. P." (that is, Pushkin himself) to have supplied the titles, epigraphs, and specifically literary allusions.

The role of the narrator in the story is of such importance that his characterization must be studied in some detail. At the time of telling the story, his rank of titular councillor is "ninth class" in the Table of Ranks, while Vyrin has the fourteenth (or lowest) rank, that of collegiate registrar. (Vyrin's past as an enlisted soldier suggests that he is of peasant origin, and that he has been given, upon retirement from the army, a civilian post with a promotion to the lowest civilian rank—one that was supposed to protect him from corporal punishment. Pushkin's own rank during his government service from 1817 through 1824 was collegiate secretary, "tenth class.") The narrator has been promoted since he paid his first visit to Vyrin's station in 1816, though his rank even then was well above Vyrin's. Minskij, at the time of his visit, has a military rank of *rotmistr* (captain), "eighth class." By 1816 the narrator had already been in government service long enough to have become accustomed to the way those of lower rank were treated (and mistreated), though he professes to see no practical alternative to *chin china pochitaj* ("observe precedence of rank"). His age in 1816 is suggested to be about twenty-six, so that he is young enough both to be Dunja's older brother and to appear to be a whole generation younger than the Stationmaster, who is about fifty. The time of the telling the story is suggested as being approximately a decade later.

The mode of narration in "The Stationmaster" shows two sharply contradictory characteristics as regards the Stationmaster and his daughter Dunja: sympathetic involvement in their life, character, and fate; and objective, even ironic, detachment. Sympathetic involvement is directly expressed or clearly implied a number of times. In the introduction the narrator says that he will tell of a particular stationmaster whose "memory is precious to me." At the end of the first visit, his haste has been forgotten: "The horses had long been ready, but I did not want to part from the stationmaster and his daughter." Before the second visit, he has "sad forebodings" that perhaps the Stationmaster has been replaced and Dunja has married. At the end of this visit, during which he learns of Dunja's elopement and the old man's vain effort to bring her back, he says that the Stationmaster's "tears moved me deeply," and adds that "after taking leave of him, it was a long time before I could forget the old Stationmaster, and for a long time I thought of poor Dunja." His interest in them is emphasized by the fact that the last visit requires special arrangements and expenditures to find out about the Stationmaster, "my friend" (*o moem prijatele*). Once there, he is not satisfied after learning of the death of Vyrin until he learns about Dunja at the end of the story.

The narrator's mixture of involvement and detachment is particularly pronounced regarding Dunja. He warmly remembers her kiss at the end of the first visit: "I can count up a great many kisses 'Since first I chose this occupation,' but not one has left

> **What the narrator has understood is that the old Stationmaster's fears for Dunja's fate have not come to pass but that she has nevertheless found it within herself to return to ask her father's blessing."**

behind such a long, such a pleasant recollection." But, as Vinogradov points out, the specifically literary allusions of the story are distancing, and to classify kissing as an "occupation" is hardly enhancing. [V. V. Vinogradov, *Stil' Pushkina*] The kiss is remembered at the beginning of the third visit, when he sees the "portals where poor Dunja kissed me once upon a time." We have noted above how he specifically thought of Dunja before and after the second visit and how, in the third visit, he is not satisfied until he learns of Dunja's visit. Along with the expressions of empathy, there is a characterization that shows her ability to take care of herself, to note and make use of the impression she makes on others (including the narrator), to induce people to do what she wishes. The story shows her utilizing this ability to protect her father from the bad temper and even the whips of travelers. Her name Dunja (Avdot'ja, Evdokija) suggests her ability to arouse "favor, kindness, good will." We are never allowed to share her consciousness. We are told that her conversation is lively, but her speech is directly quoted only once. However, this quotation gives the story's basic characterization of her: she tells her children to "sit still" while she visits the graveyard; and she tells the young boy who offers to guide her, "I know the way myself." Thus the term "poor Dunja," is either the Stationmaster's consciousness, which is given ironic illumination in the story, or the narrator echoing the Stationmaster, with multilevel irony. But, curiously enough, the light irony hardly lessens her appeal.

There is similarly a mixture of empathy and irony toward the Stationmaster, beginning with his name. His surname comes from *vyr'* or *vir* ("whirlpool"), but more particularly from the folk expressions containing it. One is *s viru i s bolotu* ("from no one knows where, the dregs of society," Ushakov), a double-edged allusion to his low birth and rank in the government service. The other has multilevel application to both Vyrin and Dunja, *poshsol v mir, a popal v vir* ("into temptation," Dal'). Vyrin's given name, Samson, alludes to the Old Testament story of the man who lost his strength and eventually his life because of a weakness for a woman, with the sharp distinction that Samson Vyrin's death brings destruction unto no Philistines. There is artistic distancing in the use of a literary allusion with regard to him. He is seen "picturesquely" wiping away tears, like Terent'ich in Dmitriev's ballad "Karikatura." In that ballad, the "zealous" and faithful servant contrasts with both the master's wife, who kept a den of thieves during her husband's long absence and was taken away by the police, and with the returned husband, a cavalry sergeant major, who quickly manages to find solace with another wife. Detachment, as well as empathy, is shown in the narrator's words about Vyrin's tears: " . . . these tears were partly aroused by the punch, five glasses of which he drained during the narrative. . . ." There is considerable distancing in the way Vyrin's words and attitude about Dunja are conveyed. On the first visit, upon being asked whether Dunja is his daughter, "'My daughter, sir,' he answered with a *rather self-complacent air.*" (Italics mine.) His hurt puzzlement at her decision to leave him is self-centered: ". . . didn't *I* love my Dunja, didn't *I* cherish my child, didn't *she* have the good life here?" (Italics mine.) In that every instance of the term "poor Dunja" has an ironic component, the four different uses of the same adjective with regard to the Stationmaster are suspect (the last of them occurs in Scene II, quoted above). Nevertheless, the characterization of Vyrin is appealing in its humanity, while sentimentality is completely avoided through the use of irony and the rather detached point of view.

In the structure of "The Stationmaster" the first three of the scenes corresponding to the Parable of the Prodigal Son are recounted to the narrator during his second visit, and he retells them (quoting the third of them directly in the Stationmaster's words). The narrative of the fourth scene—the return of Dunja—is a small boy's directly quoted account, interspersed with the observations and reactions of the narrator.

Dunja, who did not wish to be *returned*, returns voluntarily. She has to ask about her father—which shows that she had not known about his death—but she knows, without asking, where his grave would be. Through the eyes of the small boy we see how she went to the grave, "lay down on it and lay there a long time," showing grief in the peasants' way [N. Ja. Berkovskij, *Stat'i o literature*, GIXL, 1962], and then gave money to the priest for prayers and departed. The narrator's reaction—first of vexation that he has "squandered" the seven rubles for the trip (when he learns about the Stationmaster's death but not about Dunja), and then, upon learning of her visit to the grave, of no longer regretting the seven rubles—suggests a "recognition" on his part and a reaction to that recognition. In the context of the story, Dunja returns, like the Prodigal Son, for reconciliation with her father and for his blessing. In the mature Pushkin's world, real and fictional, one must go home again; even the heroine of *Poltava* returns home, in madness. Though Dunja did not return barefoot or in rags, she returned. The final "picture" of the Prodigal Son kneeling before his father is balanced by the scene where she lies on her father's grave.

The Parable of the Prodigal Son has not just two main characters in the father's household—father and son—but also a third, the older brother who reacts with hurt jealousy when he learns how his father has received his prodigal brother. The fourth German picture shows in the background the older brother inquiring of servants what is happening and this figure suggests the rest of the parable. In the relatively short Gospel parable, there is a recounting no fewer than four times of the reception of the prodigal son by the father: in the objective narrative, in the servant's words to the older brother, in the older brother's angry refusal to join in the festivities, and in the father's conciliatory words to the older son. But in "The Stationmaster" there is only one account of the "prodigal's" return. In the final passage of the story the narrator asks the boy what has happened, and then through the boy's words the narrator visualizes the scene of the daughter visiting her father's grave. And the narrator has a "recognition" that leaves him rejoicing.

What the narrator has understood is that the old Stationmaster's fears for Dunja's fate have not come to pass but that she has nevertheless found it within herself to return to ask her father's blessing. This understanding makes him content, not only with his memory of her but also that of his "friend" the Stationmaster, who provides the title of the story and its main focus. In terms of the biblical text and the German picture of the return of the Prodigal, the little boy has played the role of the "servant" who tells the ''older brother'' what happened. And the unaccepting, jealous blood brother of the Gospel parable has been replaced by one who accepts the return of the ''prodigal'' daughter with disinterested and unselfish rejoicing. Her ''brother,'' then, is one who accepts and understands as a brother should. This brotherly attitude can combine compassion and the objective acceptance of human frailties and mixed motivations (as indicated by the artistic distancing and the play of irony in the story).

The story ends with the narrator's ''recognition'' that Dunja returned for reconciliation with her father. The further recognition available to the reader is that the narrator himself feels and reacts to the return of the ''prodigal'' as the older brother in the parable should have felt and reacted. Thus, in this adaptation and application of the parable, he plays the role of the older brother, but a quite different one—not the ''real'' one, but the kind of brother the desirability of whose existence is the main point of the parable. . . .

''The Stationmaster'' presents both in content and in form a complex, sophisticated, and integrated adaptation and application of the New Testament parable. This adaptation and application leads, however, to a prose literary form quite different from the New Testament parable, especially in style and tone, largely through the technique of first-person narration and through the role of the narrator in the story. . . .

Source: J. Thomas Shaw, ''Pushkin's 'The Stationmaster' and the New Testament Parable,'' in *Slavic and East-European Journal,* Vol. 21, No. 1, Spring, 1977, pp. 3–29.

Richard Gregg

In the following excerpt, Gregg examines the unity and narrative structure of each story in The Tales of the Late Ivan Pertrovich Belkin, *particularly with regard to the story ''The Stationmaster'' and the tragic character of Vyrin.*

Pushkin's *Tales of the Late Ivan Petrovich Belkin* are five in number, and four of them (''The Shot,'' ''The Blizzard,'' ''The Stationmaster,'' and ''The Lady-Peasant'') belong to the same literary species. The narrative features binding this quartet of stories together are, in the main, conventional. Each relates—among other things—the story of a young

man who, having won the affections of a beautiful woman, overcomes some obstacle (or series of obstacles) which threatens their union, thereby paving the way to, or consolidating, a *mariage d'amour* at the end of the tale. All of which is to say that embedded in each is one of the oldest of all plots, the ''successful courtship.''

But these tales share resemblances that go beyond such broad fictional stereotypes; and it is on the less conventional (and less obvious) points of similarity that I wish to dwell at greater length. From the time that man first became aware of those differences in station, wealth, and natural endowments which separate one individual from another, storytellers—especially tellers of love stories—have preferred to draw their protagonists from the ranks of the fortunate. Thus the typical lover-hero of the older fictional forms (the short story, the romance, the legend, etc.) has through the ages been young, handsome, nobly born, and—at the end of the narrative at least—materially well off. Moreover, until the advent of the picaresque novel it was axiomatic that these ''external'' attributes were the counterparts of moral qualities without which the hero would be no hero. ''Handsome is,'' after all, ''as handsome does.''

Now insofar as their outer attributes are concerned, Pushkin's suitors conform perfectly to the familiar mold; for Count *** (''The Shot''), Burmin (''The Blizzard''), Minsky (''The Stationmaster''), and Berestov (''The Lady-Peasant'') are without exception young, handsome, wealthy, and wellborn. Morally speaking, however, they diverge somewhat from the traditional norm. For each is endowed with a touch or more of patrician presumption, which has nothing to do with virtue and is, at times, opposed to it.

In ''The Shot'' (''Vystrel''), for instance, a tincture of this attitude colors the scene where Count ***, the perfect, hence blasé, gentleman, shows his aristocratic indifference to life itself by munching cherries as Silvio takes deadly aim. In ''The Blizzard'' (''Metel'') this attitude is less pleasantly apparent in Burmin's wild and wanton caprice of marrying an unknown bride without her consent. And in ''The Stationmaster'' (''Stantsionnyi smotritel'') Minsky's abduction of Dunia is a similar perversion of the young gentleman's ''right'' to sow his wild oats. Finally, in ''The Lady-Peasant'' (''Baryshniakrest'ianka''), though young Berestov,

"Autumn, we have seen, is the season of 'The Stationmaster,' the season of tragedy. Because the tragic <u>mythos</u> (like the ironic one) cannot, by definition, coincide with a 'successful courtship' a hybrid narrative might, again, be expected."

like the Count, is essentially likable, it cannot be denied that his aloof manners before the daughters of the local gentry and the not-quite-proper advances he makes to "Akulina" in the woods are examples not of *noblesse oblige* but of its antonym, *noblesse permet*.

In endowing his young lovers with a certain sense of privilege or license Pushkin is not so much breaking with an old-fashioned fictional model as conforming to a more recent one. For, as the examples of Tom Jones, Squire B., and Peregrine Pickle suggest, a streak of frivolity or highhandedness can be found in many an eighteenth-century lover-hero. It is noteworthy, however, that whereas Fielding, Richardson, and Smollett uphold conventional morality by punishing or purging their errant heroes, Pushkin rewards the presumption of his noblemen with outrageous good fortune. Thus it is precisely the Count's lordly indifference to life which prompts Silvio, temporarily at least, to spare it. Had Burmin not indulged in a "criminal" (the word is his) whim at a wayside church he would never have ended up enjoying the affections of the beautiful and wealthy Masha. And if Minsky had not acted with the heartlessness of a Lovelace, he would never have made the charming Dunia his wife. Though the comic spirit of "The Lady-Peasant" tends to dissolve such ironies into uncritical laughter, it is a fact that the wooing of Liza—a venture which brings profit or pleasure to all concerned—begins with the liberties which a young nobleman tries to take with a "peasant girl" in the woods. In short, if crime does not quite pay in *The Tales of Belkin*, it is certain that the common peccadillo of its four gentlemen suitors, a touch or more of aristocratic fecklessness, is nobly rewarded by the author.

But the most unusual feature shared by these stories remains to be mentioned—namely, the presence, alongside the gentleman "hero," of a second "hero." In the first three tales the identity of this person is obvious. In the last it is, for reasons that will be discussed in due time, less so. But in all four his self-fulfillment and that of the gentleman suitor are mutually exclusive goals. For this reason I shall, provisionally, call him the "counterhero."

In contradistinction to Pushkin's broadly stereotyped gentlemen suitors his counterheroes are a very mixed lot. The first (Silvio) is an ex-officer of mature years; the second (Vladimir) is a young subaltern and petty land-owner; the third (Vyrin) is a middle-aged widower and *chinovnik* of the lowest grade. Yet despite these differences they share certain attributes which bring them together and oppose them to their more fortunate adversaries. In the first place, whereas the latter possess both wealth and status, the former have little of either. Thus, despite his bravado and barracks-room popularity, the shabby and obscurely foreign Silvio is no social match for the Count. Similarly, Vladimir, unlike Burmin, is too poor and obscure to sue openly for Masha's hand. As for Vyrin, his plebeian birth places him wholly beyond the social pale.

The unusual and sometimes unmerited good luck of Pushkin's gentlemen suitors has been noted. The opposite is true of his counterheroes. Silvio, who is early eclipsed by the brilliant Count and is later forced to swallow public insult without requital, and ultimately perishes in a futile campaign abroad, is not, to say the least, the darling of fortune. Before Vladimir is killed in 1812 he is the victim of an almost unbelievably calamitous convergence of circumstances—the wedding, a blizzard, the caprice of a chance intruder. Vyrin's downfall, too, is largely precipitated by bad luck—the unpredictable machinations of a young libertine.

It was further noted that, viewed as a product of literary history, Pushkin's gentlemen suitors are an amalgam of traditional stereotypes—the storybook hero plus a tincture of the eighteenth-century rake. In direct contrast, the counterheroes are distinctly contemporary (i.e., Sentimental or Romantic) in conception. Thus the brooding, mysterious, and vengeful Silvio derives from the satanic hero popularized by ''Monk'' Lewis, Maturin, and Byron. Vladimir, the poor, persevering young suitor who is accepted by Masha, but rejected by her parents, recalls the hero of *La Nouvelle Héloïse*. (Saint Preux is, in fact, named in the story.) And Vyrin, the patriarch whose white hairs are mocked by cruel youth, steps out of a Diderot *comédie larmoyante* or a sentimental painting by Greuze.

To sum up then: each of the four stories portrays a rich, handsome, happy-go-lucky nobleman, based on traditional fictional models, and a beautiful woman whose love he is trying to secure; in each story this union is threatened by the existence of an impecunious and socially inferior man, based on a Sentimental or Romantic stereotype; and in each the ''scapegrace'' suitor triumphs, while his ''scapegoat'' adversary is defeated and dies. . . .

Evidence that a number of items are similar is not *ipso facto* proof that they are *unified*. Unity inheres only when the group as a whole is seen to possess a definable ''shape.'' When perceived in the context of this shape, the items, though similar and coordinate, will be seen to play different—that is, functionally diversified—roles. The basic structural similarities binding these four tales have been shown. We must now ask whether, taken together, they make an organic whole.

A clue to the answer is provided by the number of stories we are dealing with. Among the great quaternary patterns present in nature (e.g., the lunar phases, the points of the compass, the times of day) none is more fundamental to our experience than that of the four seasons. Whether, as some have argued, Western literature itself is an outgrowth of seasonal rites celebrated by primitive man need not be debated here. Proof that the seasonal cycle is deeply rooted in the creative ''mind of Europe'' is supplied by the great number of artists, literary and other, who have through the ages drawn on it for inspiration. In *The Tales of Belkin* Pushkin joins their number.

Although none of our four stories encloses a single season, a specific time of year may be said to dominate each. . . .

As for ''The Stationmaster,'' although the narrator makes several seasonal references in the course of the tale, only once is an outdoor scene fully

evoked. Near the end of the story, having learned that Vyrin's old station has recently been shut down, he goes to the nearby village to make inquiries: ''This occurred in autumn. Grayish clouds covered the sky; a cold wind blew from the reaped fields, carrying off the red and yellow leaves from the trees which we met on the way.'' A moment later, apprised of his friend's death, he has a small boy lead him to Vyrin's grave: ''We arrived at the cemetery, a bare unenclosed place sown with wooden crosses and not shaded by a single small tree. Never had I seen such a sad cemetery.'' It is while the narrator is taking in this desolate scene that his small guide tells how a ''beautiful lady'' (Dunia) had recently visited the same sad spot and had prostrated herself at the stationmaster's grave for some time before leaving. In this autumnal mood and autumnal setting the story ends. . . .

Each of the four stories is, then, colored—or at least ''tinted''—by one of the four seasons: ''The Shot'' by early summer, ''The Blizzard'' by winter, ''The Stationmaster '' by autumn, and ''The Lady-Peasant'' by spring. And we need only join the seasonal epithet to the narrative moment which it frames to see that the former harmonizes with the latter. We may thus speak of the *summer* fullness of the Count's happily preserved marriage, the *wintry* despair of Vladimir, hopelessly lost in the blizzard, the *autumnal* melancholy that suffuses Vyrin's burial place, and the *spring* freshness of Liza's early morning escapade. But beyond this rather obvious consonance of narrative moment with seasonal milieu, one can recognize two larger patterns—one defined by the relation of the season in question to the total narrative structure of its particular story, the other defined by the relation of the sum of all the seasons to the quartet of tales taken as a whole.

An invaluable tool for clarifying these relationships is supplied by the eminent literary theorist, Northrop Frye. In the third part of his seminal *Anatomy of Criticism*, entitled ''Archetypal Criticism: Theory of Myths,'' Frye argues that all narratives are reducible to the four archetypal *mythoi* of romance, tragedy, irony (or satire), and comedy. [*Anatomy of Criticism: Four Essays* , 1968] Concerning the specific narrative features assigned to each of these *mythoi* more will be said later. Of immediate relevance is Frye's association of each *mythos* with a particular season of the year: romance with summer, tragedy with autumn, irony with winter, and comedy with spring. . . .

Autumn, we have seen, is the season of "The Stationmaster," the season of tragedy. Because the tragic *mythos* (like the ironic one) cannot, by definition, coincide with a "successful courtship" a hybrid narrative might, again, be expected. What in fact we find is a tale with two unequal facets: one—which is "happy" and plays a subordinate role—reflects Minsky's love affair with Dunia; the other—which is melancholy and plays a dominant role—describes Vyrin's reaction to these events.

That Vyrin's fate is in the popular sense "tragic" is plain enough: brokenhearted at his daughter's supposed ruin, he takes to drink and dies. That his career imitates the tragic curve in the narrow literary sense needs, perhaps, some amplification. Like the tragic hero of antiquity Vyrin is, as the story opens, at the top of fortune's wheel: a happy bemedaled patriarch, boasting to strangers of his daughter's virtues. Then, briefly but fatally, he reveals the classic symptoms of *hubris*—rashness and arrogance. Flattered by his passing acquaintance with a "gentleman," he imprudently accepts his offer to drive Dunia to Mass unaccompanied, brushes aside her doubts with a rebuke, and watches the two depart—never to return. His downfall thus stems from that peculiar combination of impersonal fate (*moira*) and individual error (*hamartia*) which, typically, lays the tragic hero low. And while he never attains the ultimate moment of high tragedy, insight into his own error, there is in the final pictures of the helpless suppliant in the streets of St. Petersburg and the lachrymose drunk in the dilapidated stationhouse more than enough pathos to confer the tragic title on his destiny. . . .

Our seasonal cycle is now complete: four stories with a common narrative core, each colored by one of the four seasons, and each modified (or reinforced) by the *mythos* associated with that season. Seen as a whole, moreover, their overall design is clear: starting with the moral simplicities of romance, where noblemen are good and lucky, and their enemies evil and ill-tarred, Pushkin has taken us through the darker and more complex seasons of irony and tragedy, where the victors are not always right, nor their victims necessarily wicked, to bring us out into the reconciling brightness of spring, where scapegoats turn out to be chimeras and every mouth is found to have a silver spoon in it. . . .

Source: Richard Gregg, "A Scapegoat for All Seasons: The Unity and the Shape of *The Tales of Belkin*," in *The Slavic Review,* Vol. 30, No. 4, December, 1971, pp. 748–61.

Sources

Bloom, Harold, ed. *Alexander Pushkin*, Chelsea House, 1987.

Brasol, Boris. *The Mighty Three: Pushkin, Gogol, Dostoievsky: A Critical Trilogy*, William Farquhar Payson, 1934.

Cross, S. H., and Ernest J. Simmons, eds. *Centennial Essays for Pushkin*, Russell & Russell, 1937.

Debreczeny, Paul. "'Belkin' and 'Goriukhino,'" in *The Other Pushkin: A Study of Alexander Pushkin's Prose Fiction*, Stanford University Press, 1983, pp. 56–137.

Gregg, Richard. "A Scapegoat for All Seasons: The Unity and Shape of *The Tales of Belkin*," in *The Slavic Review*, Vol. 30, No. 4, December, 1971, pp. 748–61.

Konick, Willis. "Categorical Dreams and Compliant Reality: The Role of the Narrator in *The Tales of Belkin*," in *Canadian American Slavic Studies*, Vol. 11, pp. 75–90.

Simmons, Ernest J. *Pushkin*, Cambridge: Harvard University Press, 1937.

Vickery, Walter N. *Alexander Pushkin*, Boston: Twayne, 1992.

Further Reading

Bloom, Harold, ed. *Alexander Pushkin*, Chelsea House, 1987.
    Collection of modern critical approaches to Pushkin.

Brasol, Boris. *The Mighty Three: Pushkin, Gogol, Dostoievsky: A Critical Trilogy*, William Farquhar Payson, 1934.
    Studies of Pushkin and two of his literary descendants.

Cross, S. H., and Ernest J. Simmons, eds. *Centennial Essays for Pushkin*, Russell & Russell, 1937.
    Essays addressing various aspects of Pushkin's life and literature.

Simmons, Ernest J. *Pushkin*, Cambridge: Harvard University Press, 1937.
    Authoritative biography by a noted Pushkin scholar.

Vickery, Walter N. *Alexander Pushkin*, Boston: Twayne, 1992.
    Comprehensive book-length study of Pushkin's life and works. His brief discussion of "The Stationmaster" emphasizes Pushkin's clear, concise style.

Two Kinds

Amy Tan

1989

"Two Kinds" is the last story in the second of four sections of Amy Tan's immensely successful first book, *The Joy Luck Club*. Tan intended the book to be read as a loose collection of interrelated stories, but it is often referred to as a novel. Several of the stories appeared in periodicals separately, many of them in *Atlantic Monthly*, which purchased the serial rights to the book prior to its publication. "Two Kinds" was initially published in the *Atlantic* in February 1989, one month before the book was released.

Like all the stories in the book, "Two Kinds" is concerned with the complex relationships between mothers and daughters. In particular, Tan's subject is the distance between mothers who were born in China before the communist revolution and thus have been cut off from their native culture for decades, and their American born daughters who must negotiate the twin burdens of their Chinese ancestry and American expectations for success.

In this story, the narrator, Jing-mei, resists her overbearing mother's desire to make her into a musical prodigy in order to compete with one of her friend's daughters. The narrator recalls these events after a period of more than twenty years and still struggles to understand her mother's motivations.

"Two Kinds" contains all the elements that won Tan the well-deserved praise she received for her first book. It shows off her keen ear for the fractured English of the older generation (Tan was

trained as a linguist, after all), and her sharp eye for detail in recreating the domestic scenery of mothers and daughters, especially in her descriptions of food and clothing.

Author Biography

Amy Tan was born in 1952 in Oakland, California, to Daisy and John Tan. Her Chinese name, An-mei, means "Blessing from America," and she is the only daughter in the Tan family. Her parents' experiences as immigrants became the basis of her fiction.

When her father and her older brother died of brain tumors within eight months of each other, Tan's world changed. Her mother returned to her old Chinese beliefs and religious practices and became convinced that the family's house in Santa Clara was cursed. Consequently, she packed up her remaining son and daughter and took them on a rambling tour of the East Coast and Europe. Eventually they settled in Montreux, where Amy attended and graduated from high school.

A rebellious teenager, Tan chafed at her mother's insistence that she attend a conservative Baptist college in Oregon and she quickly transferred to San Jose City College and then to San Jose State. She further disappointed her mother by changing her major from pre-med to English and linguistics.

By this time, she was married to a tax lawyer and drifting toward a doctoral degree when she decided to pursue other interests. After a couple of false starts she found considerable success as a freelance business writer.

After a period of introspection and a new interest in her mother's life and stories from China, Tan began writing fiction. She found support in a San Francisco writer's group and found an agent after publishing only one story. Her first book, *The Joy Luck Club* , of which "Two Kinds" is a part, was an astonishing success, and is often credited with sparking the public's interest in Asian American literature. Since then she has written two more novels, two, children's books, and several essays. She lives and works in San Francisco, where she still meets regularly with her writing group.

Plot Summary

In the story "Two Kinds," the narrator is a Chinese American girl who is locked in a struggle over her identity with her Chinese immigrant mother, who believes "that you could be anything you wanted to be in America." This particular struggle invokes the mother's attempt to mold her daughter, Jing-mei, into a musical prodigy so that she will be able to brag to her friend Lindo Jong, whose daughter is a precocious chess champion.

The idea for piano lessons comes from television and popular magazines. The narrator and her mother watch Shirley Temple movies and try to imagine her as a child star. They even go so far as to get her hair styled to make her look like the blond, curly-haired Temple. The mother also reads countless "stories about remarkable children" in the magazines she brings home from people whose houses she cleans.

The mother's vague ambitions for her daughter take shape one night when they are both watching the Ed Sullivan Show (a long-running and popular variety show in the 1960s). There they see "a little Chinese girl, about nine years old, with a Peter Pan haircut," playing a piano solo in a fluffy white dress.

Sure enough, just three days after the watching the show, the narrator's mother has already arranged to trade housecleaning for piano lessons with Mr. Chong, the retired piano teacher in the building. A fierce struggle ensues between the mother's desire to make her daughter into a prodigy (more to satisfy her own ego), and the daughter's resistance to her mother's efforts to make her into someone she is not.

The narrator's strategy is one of quiet and passive resistance. She lies about her practice time and does only what she has to do during her lessons. Subsequently, her mother has no idea how poor and undisciplined a musician she is. At her piano recital, her awful, unpracticed playing embarrasses herself as well as her mother.

Much to the Jing-mei's shock, however, her mother insists that the piano lessons continue. With her mother literally dragging her to the bench to practice, the narrator says that she wishes she weren't her mother's daughter, that she wishes she had been one of the babies her mother abandoned long ago in China.

Such a cruel and hurtful statement silences her mother and ends the piano lessons for good. Many years later, the mother offers to give the piano to her daughter, now in her thirties, who interprets it as a kind of peace offering, though she still does not fully understand her mother's motivations.

Characters

Mr. Chong

Mr. Chong—also known as Old Chong—is Jing-mei's deaf and partially blind piano teacher. When she realizes that he can't hear the music, she stops trying to hit the right notes; when she sees that he can't read fast enough to follow the sheet music, she just keeps up the rhythm and he is pleased. At her disastrous recital he is the only one who cheers enthusiastically.

Father

The narrator's father makes only a token appearance in the story. He is not involved in the mother-daughter struggle over piano lessons. He does attend the recital; in fact, the narrator can't tell if he is horrified or silently amused at her performance.

Jing-mei

Jing-mei is a rebellious child caught between two cultures: the Chinese culture that prevails in her mother's home; and the American one that prevails everywhere else. She resists her mother's attempts at discipline and resents the pressures of high achievement that immigrant parents typically place on their children.

She also understands that her mother is using her to win a competition with her friend Lindo Jong; both women brag about whose daughter is more talented. She is resolved to be true to herself and not take part in such a competition. Refusing to practice the piano, she tells her mother that she wishes she were dead, like the babies she knows her mother was forced to abandon when she fled China. She regrets saying such hurtful things later.

Lindo Jong

Also called Auntie Lindo, she is married to Uncle Tin and is the mother of Waverly, the preco-

Amy Tan

cious chess prodigy who is the narrator's rival. Lindo goads the narrator's mother into bragging about her daughter's dubious musical talent.

Waverly Jong

"Chinatown's Littlest Chinese Chess Champion," Waverly Jong is Auntie Lindo's daughter. She and the narrator have grown-up together and have long been competing with one another.

Mother

The narrator's mother is a Chinese immigrant who wants her daughter to have the best of both worlds: Chinese tradition and American opportunity. Like many mothers, however, she has a tendency to try to make her daughter into her own image rather than allow her to develop into her own person.

The mother's hopes for her daughter's future belies her own tragic past, however. Like Tan's own mother, the mother in "Two Kinds" was forced to leave her three children behind when she fled an abusive marriage in her native China. By the end of the story, Jing-mei better understands her mother's sacrifices and motivations.

Old Chong

See Mr. Chong

Media Adaptations

- "Two Kinds" is a part of the film version of *The Joy Luck Club.* Tan wrote the screenplay (with Ronald Bass) for this adaptation of her novel. The film was released in 1993 and directed by Wayne Wang. It was released on videocassette in 1994 and is available from Buena Vista Home Video.

- "Two Kinds" also appears in the (abridged) audiocassette version of the book, available from Dove Books Audio and narrated by the author.

Themes

American Dream

Anthropologists and other scholars who study the immigrant experience in America have long noted that the American dream exerts a powerful influence on new arrivals in the country. These scholars have also pointed out the burden of these dreams usually falls more heavily upon the shoulders of American-born children of immigrants.

Often immigrant parents are willing to sacrifice everything, including careers, family, and property, to pursue new lives in America. Realizing that they may not achieve the American dream of material success and social acceptance, they tend to transfer those ambitions to their children.

The narrator's mother in "Two Kinds," for example, insists that "you could be anything you wanted to be in America." She ticks off the possibilities to her daughter: "You could open a restaurant. You could work for the government and get good retirement. You could buy a house with almost no money down. You could become rich. You could become instantly famous."

While such pressures on the second-generation of immigrant families is common to all ethnic groups in America, the mother in "Two Kinds" and other Chinese American women of her generation were particularly interested in their daughters' success. The women of Jing-mei's (and Tan's) mother's generation grew up in rigidly patriarchal China and were expected to be subservient and silent even in America. Though they feared the effects of liberal American culture on their daughters, they also wished to live vicariously through them and pressured them to succeed in ways they could not have imagined.

As critic E. D. Huntley puts it, these "mothers have borne daughters, and invested in them all of the hopes and dreams that have propelled the older generation across an ocean to America. To give those daughters the best that the New World can offer the mothers have sacrificed their youth and their homeland."

The problem arises, however, when the daughters want to make choices of their own. As Huntley maintains, "the daughters see in their mothers not nurturing angels, only stern disciplinarians, domineering and possessive women who refuse to relinquish any maternal control."

Identity

When Jing-mei's mother says to her daughter in the opening paragraph of "Two Kinds," "you could be anything you wanted to be in America," she really means that her daughter could be anything her mother decided she could be. There are many aspects to the cultural and generational gap that separates Jing-mei from her mother (and the other mothers and daughter in *The Joy Luck Club*), but the one featured in the story entitled "Two Kinds" is the question of identity.

For Jing-mei's mother identity is not problematic; even in California she identifies herself as a Chinese wife and mother. She also strives to maintain Chinese traditions and beliefs in her new culture. Her intersections with American cultural are transitory and superficial and do not require her to reconsider or reconfigure her identity.

Since most of her contact with American culture is through the popular media like magazines and television, she can be a passive and uncritical receptor of new ideas. It's not so simple for her daughter, however, who has to move across cultural boundaries and obstacles that her mother cannot begin to appreciate.

Writing about generational differences in *The Joy Luck Club* as a whole, Walter Shear observes that in each story "the focus is either on a mother, who figures out her world, or on the daughters, who seem caught in a sophisticated cultural trap, knowing possibilities rather than answers, puzzling over the realities that seem to be surrounding them and trying to find their place in an ambivalent world.''

The mother-daughter struggle over identity in ''Two Kinds'' is less about who Jing-mei will turn out to be, prodigy or not, and more about their different beliefs about the nature and mechanisms of identity. Jing-mei's mother, for whom destiny and biology were synonymous with identity, believes fiercely but naively that she can invent her daughter's identity.

For Jing-mei, identity is not something put on or invented, it's something essential and individual. The mother and daughter have completely opposite understandings of identity and individuality, making their conflicts inevitable. As the narrator says later in the story, ''Unlike my mother, I did not believe I could be anything I wanted to be. I could only be me.''

Style

Memoir

All the stories in *The Joy Luck Club* are interlocking personal narratives in different voices. Because the narrators appear as characters in each other's stories, as well as tell their own stories, Tan does not have to fully develop the narrator's voice in each story. Nevertheless, the stories can stand alone, and ''Two Kinds'' was published separately; therefore it is possible to discuss the narrative technique utilized in the story.

In ''Two Kinds'' the perspective moves back and forth between the adult and the child. In this way, Tan tells the story through the child's innocent view and the adult's experienced eyes. This allows readers to make judgments of their own, to add their own interpretations of the mother-daughter struggle.

This literary device also invites readers to think about the way memory itself functions, how we use events in the past to help make sense of our present. Literary critic Ben Xu explains that ''it is not just that we have 'images,' 'pictures,' and 'views' of ourselves in memory, but that we also have 'stories' and narratives to tell about the past which both shape and convey our sense of self. Our sense of what has happened to us is entailed not in actual happening but in meaningful happenings, and the

Topics for Further Study

- What does Jing-mei expect will happen at the recital? Does she plan to give the kind of performance that she gives? Why or why not?

- Why is the narrator's mother so fixated on making her daughter into some kind of prodigy? Besides the competition with Lindo Jong, what larger cultural forces may be encouraging her to think this way?

- At the end of the story the narrator notices that the piece of music that she struggled with as a child (''Pleading Child'') has a companion piece, ''Contented Child.'' She realizes that they are ''two halves of the same song.'' Explain how this can be understood as a metaphor for the story.

- A recurring theme in Tan's work is the difficulty of assimilation into American society for many immigrants. Research your own family history and, if possible, gather stories from your family history. What problems did your family encounter as they assimilated into American culture? What traditions have survived the assimilation process?

meanings of our past experience . . . are constructs produced in much the same way that narrative is produced.''

In other words memory is a two-way street; it shapes the story as much as the story makes the memory. In Xu's words, ''memory is not just a narrative, even though it does have to take a narrative form; it is more importantly an experiential relation between the past and the present, projecting a future as well.''

Talk Story

While American daughters like Jing-mei employ personal narrative as a way of telling stories, the Chinese mothers in Tan's stories find it more difficult to talk about themselves. The specific and innovative strategy that Tan uses to voice the mother's experiences is borrowed from Chinese folk tradition, the talk story.

E. D. Huntley defines talk story as ''a narrative strategy for those characters whose ties to Chinese tradition remain strong.'' It allows these characters to ''draw on traditional oral forms to shape their stories and to disguise the urgency and seriousness with which they are attempting to transmit to their daughters the remnants of a culture that is fading even from their own lives.''

This means that the mothers, ''who have been socialized into silence for most of their lives,'' learn to ''reconfigure the events of these lives into acceptable public utterances: painful experiences are recast in the language of folk tale; cautionary reminders become gnomic phrases; real life takes on the contours of myth.'' Because this indirect means is the only way Jing-mei's mother can interpret and express her experiences, she is shocked into silence when her daughter speaks directly about the daughters she abandoned in China years earlier.

Historical Context

Chinese Immigration to America

San Francisco was (and still is) one of the largest Chinese American communities in the United States. When immigrant groups settle in one area and create extensive social and economic structures, these areas are called enclaves. By the time the mothers in *The Joy Luck Club* (and Tan's own parents) arrived in California, there was a large and thriving Chinese American enclave.

The first wave of Chinese immigrants to the United States occurred in the latter half of the nineteenth century. Until the passage of the Chinese Exclusion Act of 1882, which was designed to limit the numbers of Chinese entering the country and prevented those already here from becoming citizens, as many as 30,000 a year arrived in the United States from mainland China.

These immigrants were almost exclusively male and ''only the hardest, dirtiest, most menial jobs were open to them,'' according to social historian Thomas Sowell. They built most of the railroad across the Sierra and took on the dangerous jobs of strikebreakers in the mines. Nonetheless, they maintained strong social ties and were able to establish economic structures such as mutual aid societies and credit unions.

When the Chinese Exclusion act was finally repealed in 1943, more women arrived from China and the sex imbalance (and seedy reputation) of Chinatowns improved. The population of Chinese Americans began to rise and by 1950 it was higher than its earlier peak in 1890. These children, like Jing-mei in ''Two Kinds'' were often expected to make significant strides up the American social and economic ladder.

Although they escaped the anti-Chinese laws and overt prejudice that faced earlier generations, they still encountered a whole range of difficulties associated with biculturalism: ''cultural dislocation; the problems and challenges of integrating two cultures; intergenerational struggles within immigrant families; the conflict between acculturation and adherence to an ancestral tradition, and between assimilation and parochialism,'' in Huntley's words.

Asian American Literature

The conflicts and tensions associated with biculturalism are a recurring theme of Asian American literature. Tan's unique contribution to the literature is the articulation of the Chinese American woman's voice. Critics and social historians have noted that Chinese women are acculturated to silence and are unlikely to speak or write publicly about private experience.

Chinese American women writers, in Huntley's estimation, ''have been largely but inadvertently responsible for the new and sudden popularity of Asian American writing, a development made even more startling because Chinese woman were an almost invisible minority in American society until the early 1950s.''

Following the lead of Maxine Hong Kingston, Tan developed literary and narrative techniques like the use of the talk story that allowed the individual experiences of the older generation of women to be expressed in mythic and symbolic terms. Tan's other major contribution to the genre is the use of many narrators in a single text, a device that Hong Kingston had already introduced American readers to in *The Woman Warrior: Memoirs of a Girlhood Among Ghosts*.

Despite her identification with other Asian American writers and the subject matter of her work, Tan is reluctant to be seen as a writer of ethnic American literature. In an interview in on-line magazine *Salon*, Tan explained her position. ''Placing on writers the responsibility to represent a culture is an onerous burden. Someone who writes fiction is not necessarily writing a depiction of any generalized group, they're writing a very specific story.'' Nevertheless, the commercial and critical success of Tan's work is often credited with sparking a new interest among publishers and readers in Asian American writing.

Critical Overview

Early reviews of Tan's *The Joy Luck Club*, often mistakenly called a novel, were generally positive. Writing for the *New York Times Book Review*, Orville Schell praises Tan's grasp of the Chinese American experience and says that Tan ''has a wonderful eye for what is telling, a fine ear for dialog, a deep empathy for her subject matter and a guilelessly straightforward way of writing.'' The stories, he claims, ''sing with a rare fidelity and beauty.''

In a review in *Time* magazine, John Skow maintains that ''the author writes with both inside and outside knowing, and her novel rings clearly, like a fine porcelain bowl.''

Some reviewers were less impressed with Tan's narrative structure, however. Writing in *New York* magazine, Rhoda Koenig finds the book ''lively and bright but not terribly deep,'' and notes that ''some of the stories resolve themselves too neatly and cozily.'' She concedes, however, that ''one cannot help being charmed . . . by the sharpness of the observation.''

Similarly, Carole Angier in *New Statesman and Society* asserts that the book is ''over-schematic,'' that ''in the end it gives you indigestion, as if you've eaten too any Chinese fortune cookies, or read too many American Mother's Day cards.''

In the decade since its publication, Tan's collection of stories has remained a critical and commercial success. Its popular success has helped open the doors of the publishing industry to other Asian American authors. Though it remains too soon to tell how literary history will assess the stories in *The Joy Luck Club*, the book has already received a great deal of attention in critical journals and has been the subject of numerous master's theses and doctoral dissertations in recent years.

E. D. Huntley contends that the ''proliferation of scholarly examinations . . . points to the literary and cultural value of Tan's work.'' She goes on to assert that ''Tan has already earned herself a berth in the canon of contemporary American literature,'' and that ''Tan's novels have proven both their literary staying power as well as their broad appeal to a wide readership.''

Criticism

Elisabeth Piedmont-Marton

Elisabeth Piedmont-Marton teaches American literature and writing classes at Southwestern University in Georgetown, Texas, and she writes frequently about the modern short story. In this essay she discusses power, matriarchy, and domestic space in ''Two Kinds.''

When Jing-mei's mother shouts at her daughter and demands her complete obedience toward the end of Tan's short story, ''Two Kinds,'' she is defending her power over the only territory to which she can lay claim, the domestic sphere. Cut off from her native China by distance and political upheaval, yet distanced from surrounding American culture by language and other cultural barriers, the mother in the story makes a fortress of her home and uses it as a base of operations for deploying her matriarchal power over the life and destiny of her child.

Because her daughter has absorbed American ideas about individuality and self-determination, she has different expectations about gender and domestic space. In short, she is more likely to expect the household to be the site of nurturing instead of coercion, a place where her singularity is celebrated rather than bent to external standards of conformity.

The rise of the women's novel in nineteenth century American literature was accompanied by the idea of women's sphere. Though some used the notion of a specified female territory—both literal and figurative—as an argument for excluding woman from public life, many readers of popular women's literature eagerly embraced a world view that celebrated their domestic lives.

Domestic fiction did more than depict the lives of housewives, however, as feminist critics have pointed out; in fact, it helped carve out an autonomous realm where women could exert influence on their lives and on the lives of their loved ones.

Generally speaking, the form this influence took was the opposite of the means of influence that

Example of a child playing a piano.

prevailed in the masculine sphere. Women's sphere was characterized by moderation, moral certainty, piety, and above all, nurturing. It was the duty of every woman to keep the pressures and vulgarities of the outside (masculine) world from crossing the threshold into the haven of the home.

This is the tradition of women's literature within and against which Tan places her stories of mothers and daughters. In "Two Kinds" the domestic space is most certainly in the mother's control. Her dominance over the space is so complete, in fact, that the narrator barely mentions that her father also lives there.

Unlike traditional domestic space in American literature, Jing-mei's mother uses her realm not as a refuge from the machinations of the larger world, but as a kind of home base from which to interpret that world and launch her attacks on it. She gathers information assiduously, collecting magazines from other people's homes and studying them diligently, "searching for stories about remarkable children."

She also learns from television, and becomes fixated on the image of the little Chinese girl performing on the Ed Sullivan Show. The narrator describes how her mother "seemed entranced by the music, a frenzied little piano piece with a mesmerizing quality, which alternated between quick, playful passages and teasing, lilting ones."

In this image, Jing-mei's mother has found the ideal model for her daughter: exceptional but not unattainably remarkable. "Just like you," she says to her daughter, "Not the best." The difference between the girl on television and the girl in the living room watching television is merely effort. Jing-mei could be the girl on television if only she would try.

The mother exercises matriarchal power in the domestic space that she controls. But unlike traditional uses of domestic space in the American women's novel, the mother is not interested in excluding influences from the outside or public world. Unfortunately, since she lacks cultural fluency in American ways, she does not have the critical apparatus to evaluate or interpret the messages she receives. As a consequence, she accepts with neither skepticism nor cynicism that "you could be anything you wanted to be in America."

According to Jing-mei, her mother has a whole litany of things "you" could become in America. The "you," of course, refers to her daughter; the mother has no faith or interest in exploring new public identities for herself. Obsessed with infinite

What Do I Read Next?

- *The Woman Warrior* (1976) is Maxine Hong Kingston's memoir of her bicultural childhood. Tan cites it as an influence on her fiction.

- Another story that inspired Tan is Louise Erdrich's

Love Medicine (1984). The novel chronicles the story of two Native American families.

- Gus Lee's *China Boy* (1991) is a semi-autobiographical novel.

---

possibilities of improvement, the mother (and her reluctant daughter) "watch Shirley's [Temple] old movies on TV as though they were training films." Jing-mei confesses that in the beginning she was "just as excited" as her mother at the prospect of becoming a prodigy.

Yet soon the atmosphere in the domestic sphere becomes less nurturing and more coercive. The mother would "present tests" on multiplication, world capitals, and Bible passages. These kinds of objective measurements of a child's worth do not typically belong in women's sphere, where cooperation and sacrifice are privileged over competition and mastery.

Thus, the mother has wielded the only power she has, matriarchal authority largely derived from Chinese culture, in the only space she controls, the household. The problem is that in America the child cannot be contained in the household, the matriarchal authority is not absolute. Jing-mei soon begins to resist.

Because her mother's power within the domestic space is impossible to challenge directly, Jing-mei discovers that passive resistance, or negative power, will thwart her mother's plans. After too many evenings trying to meet the challenges, she says: "[something] inside of me began to die. I hated the tests, the raised hopes and failed expectations."

Failure brings a new revelation as well, that she has the power to resist. She looks in the mirror and sees "what seemed to be the prodigy side of [her]." She is surprised to discover that " the girl looking back at [her] was angry, powerful." In an instant, Jing-mei devises a rudimentary strategy against her

mother's coercive practices: "I had new thoughts, willful thoughts—or rather, thoughts filled with lots of won'ts. I won't let her change me, I promised myself. I won't be who I'm not."

For a while, the narrator thinks that her desultory and distracted performances on the tests have made her mother give up hope on making her into a prodigy. But then they see the Chinese girl playing piano on the *Ed Sullivan Show*. The mother forms a new plan and the daughter redoubles her efforts to resist it.

The mother's plan is to make her daughter into a musical prodigy so that she herself can compete with other women in her social world, specifically with Lindo Jong, whose daughter Waverly is "Chinatown's Littlest Chinese Chess Champion." Meanwhile, Jing-mei vows "not to be anybody different" and daydreams about "being somewhere else, about being someone else."

The mother's objective has less to do with securing her daughter's future than it does with her own desire for status within a matriarchal and domestic social structure of Chinese American women. Jing-mei is well aware of her mother's self-interested motives and is "determined to put an end to her foolish pride."

Jing-mei's performance at the talent show certainly does end her mother's boasting about her superior musical abilities, but it also humiliates Jing-mei herself. Suddenly aware that the struggle over piano virtuosity had larger stakes than just thwarting her mother's wishes, Jing-mei feels like the "whole world" is watching as she embarrasses herself and her family. After the show she is "dev-

> So when her mother tries to assert her power over her daughter's sense of self, the daughter has only one defensive strategy left to her: to reject her matrilineal heritage altogether and to destabilize her mother's source of power...."

astated'' by the look on her mother's face, ''a quiet, blank look that said she had lost everything.''

Certainly the mother has lost her bid to compete with Lindo Jong and her attempt to raise her status in her world, but she is not ready to surrender all her authority yet. Just three days after the ''talent-show fiasco'' the mother tries to command Jing-mei to resume her piano practice. Emboldened by her ability to exercise negative power, the daughter refuses. She reasons to herself: ''I didn't have to do what my mother said anymore. I wasn't her slave. This wasn't China.'' But the mother persists, asserting her will upon her daughter's body by dragging her to the piano bench.

As if her physical dominance were not enough to prove her authority over the domestic space, the mother makes a move toward appropriating the daughter's identity. By demanding total obedience, she erases her daughter's sense of self. For the Americanized Jing-mei, identity is not something destined or something achieved. It's not a *thing* at all. Jing-mei ''did not believe I could be anything I wanted to be, I could only be me.''

In other words, identity is synonymous with individuality—it's part of a person's singular essence. So when her mother tries to assert her power over her daughter's sense of self, the daughter has only one defensive strategy left to her: to reject her matrilineal heritage altogether and to destabilize her mother's source of power by saying that she wishes she were not her daughter and by reminding her mother of the two children she abandoned in China years before.

The narrator reveals more than twenty years later that this incident did permanently alter the relationship between her and her mother. They ''never talked about the disaster at the piano bench or [her] terrible declarations afterward.'' Yet the mother's power over domestic space, though diminished, is never completely overthrown. The mother's offer to give Jing-mei the piano for her thirtieth birthday is a gesture of forgiveness certainly, but it can also be seen as a colonizing gesture, a way of exporting her influence into her daughter's domestic space.

As an adult, and after her mother's death, Jing-mei seems more open to her mother's influence and respectful of her matriarchal authority. By packing up her mother's Chinese silk dresses and hand-knit sweaters in bright colors and deciding to take them home with her, she assents to her mother's ongoing presence in her life and stakes a claim on the domestic space in her own world by letting her mother share it.

Source: Elisabeth Piedmont-Marton, for *Short Stories for Students*, The Gale Group, 2000.

Liz Brent

Brent has a Ph.D. in American Culture with a specialization in American cinema from The University of Michigan. She is a freelance writer/editor and film critic and teaches courses in American cinema. In the following essay, she discusses the mother-daughter relationship in ''Two Kinds.''

The central struggle in Amy Tan's story ''Two Kinds'' is a battle of wills between the narrator, a young Chinese American girl, and her mother, a Chinese immigrant. ''Two Kinds'' is a coming-of-age story, in which the narrator, Jing-mei, struggles to forge her own sense of identity in the face of her strong-willed mother's dream that she become a ''prodigy.'' Jing-mei is caught between her Chinese mother's traditional ideas about how to raise a daughter, and her own development as a Chinese American girl straddling two cultures.

Like many immigrants to the United States, Jing-mei's mother has created idealized visions of her adopted country as a land of opportunity where all dreams may be realized. The first line of the story introduces this central idea: ''My mother believed you could be anything you wanted to be in America.'' This vision of America as a place where the streets are paved with gold is further described in the opening paragraph:

> You could open a restaurant. You could work for the government and get good retirement. You could buy a house with almost no money down. You could become rich. You could become instantly famous.

The tone of this opening paragraph introduces an element of irony in the narrator's attitude toward her mother's vision of America as a place where "you could become anything you wanted to be." Everything sounds too simple and too easily achieved. Yet the narrator does not paint a picture of her mother as ignorant or silly. The story indicates that America is a symbol of hope and optimism in the life of a woman who has suffered numerous tragedies in the form of great personal and financial loss, and yet refuses to give up her dreams:

> America was where all my mother's hopes lay. She had come here in 1949 after losing everything in China: her mother and father, her family home, her first husband, and two daughters, twin baby girls. But she never looked back with regret. There were so many ways for things to get better.

Her mother's American dreams, then, function as a symbol of hope for a brighter future for her daughter.

Having absorbed idealized visions of the "American Dream" from television and other forms of mass media, Jing-mei's mother manages to fabricate a seemingly endless supply of success fantasies for her daughter. Each new inspiration about the nature of her daughter's destiny to become a "prodigy" is sparked by what she sees on television, reads in women's magazines or reads about in such mass-market publications as *Ripley's Believe-it-or-Not*.

Her first attempt to turn Jing-mei into a "prodigy" is derived from television movies. "My mother thought I could be a Chinese Shirley Temple," explains the narrator. "We'd watch Shirley's old movies on TV as though they were training films." Later, her mother's determination to make her daughter a musical prodigy is inspired by a Chinese girl she sees performing on the *Ed Sullivan Show*.

Through this process, Jing-mei's mother demands that she "try on" a variety of identities: from "Chinese Shirley Temple," to child genius, to piano virtuoso. Jing-mei at first absorbs her mother's dreams in which one may simply decide to be a prodigy, and then pick and choose which type of prodigy to be as if it were as easy as trying on clothes in a store or changing the TV channel.

> " Through playing both 'Pleading Child' and 'Perfectly Contented' again as an adult, Jing-mei reaches a sort of epiphany, or moment of insight and personal revelation."

I pictured the prodigy part of me as many different images, trying each one on for size. I was a dainty ballerina girl standing by the curtains, waiting to hear the right music that would send me floating on my tiptoes. I was like the Christ child lifted out of the straw manger, crying with holy indignity. I was Cinderella stepping from her pumpkin carriage with sparkly cartoon music filling the air.

Yet Jing-mei soon finds that her mother's determination that she becomes a prodigy threatens to stifle her own sense of who she is. Ironically, it is out of defiance against her mother that she ultimately does forge her own sense of personal identity.

Jing-mei's sense of failure to embody her mother's hopes and dreams is at first distressful to her: "I hated the tests, the raised hopes and failed expectations." When she looks in the mirror one night, she sees only her mother's vision of her as a failure and a disappointment:

> I looked in the mirror above the bathroom sink and when I saw only my face staring back—and that it would always be this ordinary face—I began to cry. Such a sad, ugly girl!

The face Jing-mei first sees in the mirror is the face of who she is in her mother's eyes. "Trying to scratch out the face in the mirror" symbolizes her attempt to erase or obliterate her mother's image of her as a failure. Through this acknowledgment to herself that she is not the person her mother wants her to be, she begins to glimpse an image of her own definition of herself emerging from the mirror.

> And then I saw what seemed to be the prodigy side of me—because I had never seen that face before. I looked at my reflection, blinking so I could see more clearly. The girl staring back at me was angry, powerful. This girl and I were the same. I had new thoughts, willful thoughts, or rather thoughts filled with lots of won'ts.

Through this insight, Jing-mei for the first time articulates her determination to live by her own self-definition, rather than those ill-fitting ''selves'' her mother continues to impose upon her: ''I won't let her change me, I promised myself. I won't be what I'm not.'' As the story progresses, Jing-mei becomes more and more openly defiant against her mother's wishes. One night, she bursts out at her mother:

> ''Why don't you like me the way I am? I'm not a genius! I can't play the piano. And even if I could, I wouldn't go on TV for a million dollars!'' I cried.

Later, when her mother insists that she continue to attend piano lessons, after she has made it clear that the piano is not her calling, Jing-mei further strengthens her resolve not to conform to her mother's wishes. This is also an important moment in the development of Jing-mei's *cultural* identity. For the first time, she articulates her resistance to her mother in terms of the cultural gap between her mother's traditional Chinese ideas about daughters being obedient and her own perspective as a strong-willed Chinese American girl.

> And then I decided. I didn't have to do what my mother said anymore. I wasn't her slave. This wasn't China. I had listened to her before and look what happened. She was the stupid one.

When her mother continues to insist that she attend her piano lesson, Jing-mei becomes openly defiant. Through this assertion of her own will against her mother's, Jing-mei strengthens her sense of personal identity in opposition to her mother. Jing-mei begins to sense the emergence of her true, inner self.

> ''No!'' I said, and I now felt stronger, as if my true self had finally emerged. So this was what had been inside me all along.

With this moment of self-assertion, Jing-mei releases a floodgate of protest against her mother's attempts to mold her in the shape of her own hopes and dreams. Along with this, Jing-mei protests against the unwritten message her mother has given that she is not all right the way she is.

> ''You want me to be someone I'm not!'' I sobbed. ''I'll never be the kind of daughter you want me to be!''

Her mother's response is expressive of her traditional Chinese ideas about mother-daughter relationships.

> ''Only two kinds of daughters,'' she shouted in Chinese. ''Those who are obedient and those who follow their own mind! Only one kind of daughter can live in this house. Obedient daughter!''

She says this in Chinese, emphasizing that it is a perspective that comes from her Chinese background, and marking the cultural gap between Chinese immigrant mother and Chinese American daughter. For Jing-mei, defining herself in relationship with her mother is also a way of expressing her attitude as a child raised in America, a Chinese American daughter who follows her ''own mind,'' not the ''obedient'' Chinese daughter her mother wants her to be.

> ''Then I wish I wasn't your daughter! I wish you weren't my mother,'' I shouted.

Jing-mei describes this release of anger toward her mother as a cathartic experience, in which she is relieved of the burden of her unexpressed anger toward her mother and her own negative feelings about herself.

> It felt like worms and toads and slimy things crawling out of my chest, but it also felt good, as if this awful side of me had surfaced, at last.

The ''worms and toads and slimy things'' crawling out from Jing-mei's chest symbolize the anger and other dark, negative feelings that have been penned up deep inside her until this moment.

Although this incident of confrontation between mother and daughter is never again mentioned directly, the older Jing-mei is able to reconcile these dichotomies in her sense of self when, twenty years later, after her mother's death, she is sorting through her mother's belongings.

Jing-mei first comes across items that she remembers in a negative light—symbolic of her mother's relentless habit of imposing upon her things she didn't like. ''The sweaters she had knitted in yellow, pink, bright orange—all the colors I hated—I put those in moth-proof boxes.''

However, Jing-mei stumbles upon some items from her mother's past in China that she ultimately values enough to keep. Her mother's old Chinese silk dresses come to symbolize a positive element of Jing-mei's Chinese heritage.

> I found some old Chinese silk dresses, the kind with little slits up the sides. I rubbed the old silk against my skin, then wrapped them in tissue and decided to take them home with me.

In choosing to keep these items, Jing-mei symbolically chooses to maintain and preserve certain elements of her Chinese heritage, handed down through her mother. In sorting through her mother's things, Jing-mei symbolically maintains her individual identity as she continues to reject certain things her mother tried to impose upon her (the sweaters), while seeing other items with new eyes (the silk dresses).

Jing-mei next comes upon the piano sheet music she had once refused to learn. As a child, she had failed to learn a song called "Pleading Child." This song title symbolically refers to her own position as a child, silently "pleading" with her mother not to force her into an identity not of her own choosing.

Yet, when she rediscovers this sheet music still on her mother's piano, she finds another title: "Perfectly Contented." This title suggests a sense of stability and happiness. Through playing both "Pleading Child" and "Perfectly Contented" again as an adult, Jing-mei reaches a sort of epiphany, or moment of insight and personal revelation.

In the closing line of the story, she finds that she "realized they were two halves of the same song." The idea of her negative associations with being a "pleading child" in youth are reconciled with the positive associations of being at least closer to a state of being "perfectly contented," refers to Jing-mei's adult perspective that her childhood self and her grown-up self represent "two halves" of the same person, and "two halves" of the same identity—the Chinese and the American.

Likewise, the story's title, "Two Kinds," refers to the story's central concern with the mother and daughter as two different kinds of people, yet members of the same family, and the same cultural heritage.

Source: Liz Brent, for *Short Stories for Students*, The Gale Group, 2000.

Kate Bernheimer

Kate Bernheimer received her M.F.A. in fiction writing from the University of Arizona and is the author of Mirror, Mirror on the Wall: Women Writers Explore Their Favorite Fairy Tales *(Anchor Books, 1998). In this essay she discusses the mother-daughter bind and how it hinges on notions of abandonment and identity.*

"I wish I were dead," the protagonist and narrator of Amy Tan's "Two Kinds," the young Jing-mei, yells at her mother, watching her blow away in response like a leaf, "thin, brittle, lifeless." In this moment Jing-mei's empty battle for self has been

Shirley Temple as a child.

won, though the victory is also a death, symbolized by her mother disappearance from the scene. The crisis between Jing-mei and her mother in Amy Tan's "Two Kinds" is grave and of a classic type of interest to psychoanalytic theorists: the peculiar love/hate entwinement between mother and daughter which hinges on ideas of identity and abandonment. In this story, the tug of war over Jing-mei's identity is essentially tragic; for either one to give in will mean a loss for both. Should Jing-mei bend to the fierce will of her mother and become something she feels she is not (prodigy), she must abandon her sense of her own unique identity, which is itself inchoate and unstable. Likewise, for Jing-mei's mother to give up on Jing-mei's potential, she believes she will enact abandonment, as she feels it her duty as a newly Americanized mother to mold Jing-mei to perfection, or leave Jing-mei for naught. This maternal drama is intensified since Jing-mei's mother herself harbors enormous guilt about abandonment, having lost two daughters already. By telling her mother she wishes she were dead like her sisters, Jing-mei defines herself as separate from her mother; she claims her identity, but she abandons her mother to the horrors of her past. In "Two Kinds" the psychic struggle of a daughter's separation from the mother in order to define herself is played out in a series of threats and losses.

> "Only in her thirties, at story's conclusion, does Jing-mei realize that perhaps, the war over her self-definition was one contained largely within herself, that perhaps her mother had not in fact truly abandoned her."

Exploring the crisis in a daughter's identity, Tan offers Jing-mei, the stubborn yet insecure daughter of a peculiarly strong-willed mother. Defined largely by what she is not rather than by what is for her mother, Jing-mei remains nearly paralyzed for much of the story, incapable of acting in any direction at all. Trapped between her mother's trance of Jing-mei as the emerging, perfected American daughter, and her own muted and flawed sense of identity, Jing-mei can only sabotage herself and her mother's desires for her. The plot of the story, in which Jing-mei fails to acquire musical ability, serves to dramatize the story's real drama: many kinds of abandonment, the result of Jing-mei's shaky identity. In her failure to achieve, Jing-mei abandons both herself and her mother. In refusing to become, she empties herself of all hope, she obliterates the hope of her strong-armed mother, and she forces her mother to abandon her as well.

Abandonment is not only a symbol for a mother-daughter crisis, however, in Tan's work. It has real historical value. Jing-mei's mother had two other daughters whom she had to abandon in Kweilin, China, during the Chinese Revolution. Set against that event, the mother-daughter tangle that comprises "Two Kinds" is intensified. The constant threat of abandonment remains intrinsic to the mother-daughter bond. According to prevailing psychoanalytic views, a daughter's growing sense of identity, of difference from the mother, hinges on that exact threat. Neither Jing-mei nor her mother can get over such actual losses. Tan also presents this story as a reminder that the bond between mother and daughter transcends time, has a forever meaning. The identification of both characters with each other via the concept of abandonment further fuses them together, making their imminent separation even more harsh.

"Abandonment represents the insuperable trauma inflicted by the discovery—doubtless a precocious one and for that very reason impossible to work out—of the existence of a *not-I*," French psychoanalyst Julia Kristeva writes, in an essay exploring the tenuous nature of the mother-daughter bind. "Two Kinds" finds Jing-mei at exactly this precocious juncture in her life, in which abandonment is not only *represented* by the existence of an other, but personified by it in the form of her two abandoned sisters. Both mother and daughter remain acutely aware of these phantom girls. This has an affect on Jing-mei's ability to have a sense of identity separate from her mother and her presumed-dead sisters. First, Jing-mei knows that her mother "lost everything in China." Yet if her mother lost "everything," that must make Jing-mei nothing. In fact she frequently tells herself she is nothing, will be nothing, nothing will become of her. On the other hand, sensitized to her mother's loss, Jing-mei is nevertheless too young to know that her mother will not similarly abandon her. That her mother "never looked back" does not bode well for a daughter who seems never to please a mother enough.

Earlier in the cycle of stories in which "Two Kinds" appears, Jing-mei states "I was not one of those babies" and, imagining her mother going to retrieve them, laments "now my mother's left me forever." Here one sees how intricately entwined Jing-mei's sense of identity is to her mother being present, loving her as much as the other daughters whom she lost, whom Jing-mei will never be. For Jing-mei, the two sisters in China are like a phantom limb, constantly reminding her of Kristeva's "not-I." This lack of identity is further fueled by an intense, almost primitive fear of her mother's potential abandonment. This fear echoes throughout the story and is expressed in Jing-mei's visceral response to her mother's attempts to sculpt her into something she is not. If she could become perfect, she muses, "my mother would adore me." If she is adored for something she is not — perfect — she will not be abandoned. However, this insecure child suffers from peculiar self-hatred. Knowing she is not perfect, and in fact thinking herself "ugly," she is fated to be left. For Jing-mei, a failure to be a beautiful prodigy will surely result in the loss of her mother's love. She designs exactly this occurrence, in fact.

The plot of the story, which follows Jing-mei's despondent incapability to please her mother, is a vehicle through which Tan represents Jing-mei's insecure notion of self, the story's true tragedy. A feeling of security, let alone perfection, continuously eludes Jing-mei largely because of her own refusal to try. Influenced by—but misunderstanding through exaggeration—the American notion of individualism Jing-mei believes she can only be herself. This concept, however, is of little use to this child of little identity, a girl who lives in fear of losing and who believes herself a failure from the start. As she only has a limited, and even negative sense of self, her self-image is a very unhappy one. At first she tries, but upon doing poorly at one of their early prodigy sessions, Jing-mei sees her "mother's disappointed face again," and states "something inside of me began to die." Her sense of identity is so fragile that it cannot survive even this small abandonment of hope from her mother. "Maybe I never really gave myself a fair chance," she admits, but she is not so sure that is the case. She appears to believe that she can only deserve love for what she *is*; however, she defines herself only for what she *is not*. Therefore she will get no loves at all, she will lose the mother's affection. She is not the little Chinese girl on the television, she is not Shirley Temple (only resembles "Negro Chinese" her mother exclaims at a failed perm), she is not her chess-maniac cousin. Though Jing-mei's mother is indeed disappointed, she remains full of hope and desire. It is rather Jing-mei's disappointment *in herself*, her perception of the failure of identity, that Tan foregrounds most distinctly. The question that haunts Jing-mei most throughout the years is not why her mother was disappointed, but rather "Why had she given up hope?" It is Jing-mei's fragile identity, her fears, that this story is about.

Tan offers Jing-mei one small attempt at feeling better. Early in the story, at the start of the short-lived mother-daughter conspiracy to sculpt Jing-mei's identity, Jing-mei looks in the mirror and at first sees a "sad, ugly girl." This enrages her. She proceeds to rage against the image, trying to "scratch out the face in the mirror." But after a moment something better shines through. Recognizing the power of a daughter's anger, Tan allows Jing-mei a moment of clarity that foreshadows the story's calming end. "This girl and I are the same," she thinks calmly. Here, Jing-mei expresses a nascent sense of identity, one full of power and rage, which separates her from her mother. Her mother, one scene earlier, had nearly lost hope. But here Jing-mei recognizes that though she fears abandonment by her mother, she also desires such separation, because it frees her to be herself. Yet this strength and serenity cannot last. It is not strong enough to compete with the anxieties Jing-mei feels in the face of her mother's constantly dissipating pleasure in her daughter. "Why can't you like me the way I am," she soon plaintively asks. Finally, disavowing any hope of happy union in herself or with her mother, Jing-mei enacts a symbolic suicide of sorts: she stops trying to achieve. This represents that she stops trying to become. Jing-mei gives up hope of being loved by her mother, of having an identity they both can embrace. For her this is the equivalent of being dead.

This harrowing, precocious childhood realization has grave consequences for Jing-mei only alluded to in this story. Jing mei remarks that she eventually drops out of college, among other failures. Yet the story's true tragedy is contained within its obsession with the mother-daughter identity bind. In fact it is a double bind: the child Jing-mei cannot be what her mother wants and therefore, she decides, she must not be wanted. Likewise, as the child Jing-mei believes she can only be herself, and does not yet know who she is, she must therefore be nothing. This thwarts her development into a productive, self-defined adult. Projecting her anxieties onto her mother in youth, she ends up essentially blaming her mother all the way through early adulthood for her trauma (she states near the end of the story "I never found a way to ask her how *she had hoped for something so large that failure was inevitable*" [emphasis added]). Tan's fragile Jing-mei floats a long time, identity-less, abandoned to her worries. Kristeva describes this as "the [girl] child's unstable identity," which when faced by the mother, gets "frozen within the drive of intensities that disturb it."

Only in her thirties, at story's conclusion, does Jing-mei realize that perhaps, the war over her self-definition was one contained largely within herself, that perhaps her mother had not in fact truly abandoned her. Receiving as a gift the piano on which she failed to prove her genius, Jing-mei finds the musical score for a piece she performed quite poorly at a recital. This horrible recital had been one of the nails in the coffin of her mother's desires for her greatness. The piece as she remembers it was called

''Pleading Child.'' This is the child she remembers being—pleading with her mother to let her be herself, to leave her alone without abandoning her truly. Yet, turning the page, Jing-mei realizes the song has a second part, ''Contented Child.'' She finds a sense of calm while playing it. The story ends with an eerie note of stability, Jing-mei finding melancholy pleasure in the recognition of ''Two halves of the same song,'' or the song of herself. ''I am large, I contain multitudes,'' the great American poet Walt Whitman wrote in his seminal tribute to American individualism, ''Song of Myself.'' The piano is a gift from her mother, who has not left her after all. In playing the song, Jing-mei is embracing the two sides of herself. She finally leaves behind that selfish dread of losing her mother's love, which had kept her from being. ''Identity,'' Kristeva writes, ''emerges only at the end of this process when narcissistic shimmering draws to a close,'' that is, when one is able to recognize that ''firm identity remains a fiction.'' In the end, Tan does not abandon Jing-mei to her daughterly fears.

Source: Kate Bernheimer, for *Short Stories for Students*, The Gale Group, 2000.

Sources

Angier, Carole. Review, in *New Statesman and Society*, June 30, 1989, p. 35.

Huntley, E. D. *Amy Tan: A Critical Companion*, Westport, CT: Greenwood Press, 1998.

Koenig, Rhoda. Review, in *New York*, March 20, 1989, p. 82.

Kristeva, Julia. ''The Meaning of Grief,'' in *Black Sun: Depression and Melancholia,* New York: Columbia University Press, 1989.

Schell, Orville. ''Your Mother is in Your Bones,'' in *The New York Times Book Review*, March 19, 1989, pp. 3, 28.

Shear, Walter. ''Generational Differences and the Diaspora in *The Joy Luck Club*,'' in *Critique*, Vol. 34, No. 3, Spring 1993, pp. 193-99.

Skow, John. ''Tiger Ladies in *The Joy Luck Club*,'' in *Time*, March 27, 1989, p. 98.

Sowell, Thomas. *Ethnic America: A History*, New York: Basic Books, Inc., 1981, pp. 133-54.

Xu, Ben. ''Memory and the Ethnic Self: Reading Amy Tan's *The Joy Luck Club*,'' in *MELUS*, Vol. 19, No. 1, pp. 3-16.

Further Reading

Kim, Elaine. *Asian American Literature: An Introduction to the Writings and Their Social Context*, Philadelphia: Temple University Press, 1982.
    An influential and ground-breaking study, this remains an essential work in the field and provides an excellent introduction to major authors and critical issues.

Victory Over Japan

Ellen Gilchrist

1984

The title story of Gilchrist's second collection of short fiction, "Victory Over Japan" (1984) is a first-person narrative that chronicles the adventures of a young girl named Rhoda Manning during the final days of World War II. This is the first of three stories in the "Rhoda" section of the book; the other two stories deal with Rhoda as a willful adolescent determined to lose her virginity and as a thirty-four year-old divorcee adjusting to declining fortunes.

Gilchrist's work is praised for its "deceptively simple" style, for the richness and eccentricity of her Southern female characters, and for the engaging quality of her prose. The story challenges gender stereotypes and explores the dynamics of power and victimization.

Author Biography

A Southern writer often compared to Bobbie Ann Mason, Carson McCullers, and Tennessee Williams, Ellen Gilchrist was born in Vicksburg, Mississippi in 1935. In early adolescence, her father's duties with the Army Corps of Engineers caused the family to move around the country during World War II. At the age of nineteen, Gilchrist dropped out of school and ran away to marry the first of her four husbands. Her education was not resumed for sever-

al years; in 1967, at the age of thirty-two, she earned a B.A. from Millsaps College.

Gilchrist's writing career did not begin until she was forty with a stint as a contributing editor for a New Orleans newspaper. She joined poet Jim Whitehead's writing class at the University of Arkansas in Fayetteville. According to Gilchrist, the easy mix of social classes and the comfortable relationships between university professors and the members of the local community provided a welcome change from the pretensions and limitations of the upper class society she left behind in New Orleans. The constraints of that life are recurring themes in her fiction.

Gilchrist has published several collections of short stories, five novels, two books of poetry, and a collection of her journal entries. She has also authored a play based on the stories of one of her former teachers at Millsaps College, Eudora Welty.

In the mid-1980s, Gilchrist was heard regularly on National Public Radio's *Morning Edition,* reading selections from her journals. Her work has appeared in a wide variety of periodicals and she has won numerous awards for both poetry and fiction, including the American Book Award for *Victory Over Japan.*

Plot Summary

In "Victory Over Japan," third-grader Rhoda Manning recounts a series of incidents that occurred at school and at home during the final months of World War II. As the story opens, a fellow classmate named Billy Monday has been bitten by a pet squirrel and must undergo a series of painful rabies shots. The daily ritual, in which the child is escorted from the classroom by his mother and the school principal, Mr. Harmon, turns the shy boy into the center of attention.

Rhoda's curiosity and her desire to capitalize on the sensational aspects of Billy's experience make her determined to interview Billy for the school newspaper. She had previously scored a journalistic coup with her revelation that Mr. Harmon had suffered shell shock during World War I; she was, she bragged, the only third-grader whose story was published that year.

Rhoda's initial overtures to Billy are rejected by her perceptive teacher, Mrs. Jansma, who tries to

protect the boy from further victimization. In an effort to secure the exclusive interview and, at the same time, score points with her mother, Rhoda shrewdly chooses the unpopular child as her partner in a PTA-sponsored competitive paper drive in support of the war effort. Rhoda describes the incident:

> When I got home that afternoon I told my mother I had volunteered to let Billy be my partner. She was so proud of me she made me some cookies even though I was supposed to be on a diet. I took the cookies and a pillow and climbed up into my treehouse to read a book. I was getting to be more like my mother every day. My mother was a saint. She fed hoboes and played the organ at early communion even if she was sick and gave away her ration stamps to anyone that needed them. She had only had one pair of shoes the whole war. I was getting more like her every day. I was the only one in the third grade that would have picked Billy Monday to help with a paper drive. He probably couldn't even pick up a stack of papers. He probably couldn't even help pull the wagon. I bet this is the happiest day of her life, I was thinking. (Excerpt from "Victory Over Japan")

Although Billy refuses to go to the doors of any of the houses on their route, the pair do very well collecting paper. At their teacher's urging the pair go out on one last trip before dark. This time Billy accompanies Rhoda to the door of a brick house on a corner, where a man invites them to take whatever they can carry from a stack of newspapers and magazines in the basement. Billy discovers that the magazines are pornographic; in fact, many of them are filled with pictures of naked children.

Shocked, Billy and Rhoda leave the man's basement and throw the magazines into a culvert. Rhoda swears Billy to secrecy. Although Rhoda intended to tell her mother about the magazines, she never quite gets around to it until she thinks she sees the man driving by in a car. Imagining herself as the man's next victim, she races home to report the entire story to her mother.

Mrs. Manning is listening to news of the bombing of Hiroshima and Nagasaki and the subsequent Japanese surrender on the radio. For the Manning family, this means, of course, that Rhoda's father will be coming home; rather than being overjoyed, Rhoda has mixed feelings about this news. Her father, when he was on the scene, frequently threatened Rhoda with physical violence and suggested to Rhoda's mother that she "hit her with a broom. Hit her with a table. Hit her with a chair."

Rhoda consoles herself with the thought that her father will not be home for days and falls asleep dreaming of finishing off both the Japanese and the man in the brick house with bombs, brooms, chairs, and tables.

Characters

Bad man
See Man in the Brick House

Mr. Harmon
Mr. Harmon is the principal of Horace Mann Elementary School. He acts as an escort for Billy Monday on his daily trips to the doctor for rabies shots.

Mrs. Jansma
Mrs. Jansma is Rhoda's third grade teacher. She rescues Billy Monday from Rhoda's attempt to capitalize on the boy's misfortune and comforts him afterwards.

Kenniman
Father Kenniman is an Episcopal minister. While Mr. Manning is away at war, he frequently stops in for a drink with Ariane Manning, Rhoda's mother. He regularly offers advice on how to handle Rhoda and his suggestions are far more gentle than her father's harsh recommendations.

Letitia
Rhoda Manning's best friend, Letitia, shares her fondness for chasing boys at recess, but habitually reminds Rhoda of her superior social standing.

Man in the Brick House
The man in the brick house is Rhoda Manning's description of the unnamed character who invites her and Billy Monday to take a stack of pornographic magazines to their school's paper drive. Several months later, Rhoda thinks she sees him driving by and watching her while she walks home from school.

Ariane Manning
Ariane Manning is Rhoda's mother and is described as "a saint" who makes regular sacrifices for the war effort. The story strongly suggests that Ariane is involved with her minister while her husband is away at war. This, however, is lost on Rhoda, who proudly reports that it is just like her mother "to be best friends with a minister." Rhoda's

Ellen Gilchrist

mother also acts as a buffer between Rhoda and her abusive father.

Rhoda Manning
Rhoda Manning, a recurring character in Gilchrist's fiction, is the protagonist of "Victory Over Japan." In the story, she appears as a third-grader narrating her experiences during the closing months of World War II. Although she aspires to be like her saintly mother, Rhoda's actions are far more self-serving than self-sacrificing. She attempts, for example, to befriend the victim of an animal bite, not out of genuine concern for the boy, but in order to obtain an exclusive interview for the school newspaper and to impress her mother with her apparent generosity. Rhoda is a rebel and a rule-breaker and hardly fits the stereotypical role of a little girl in the 1940s. She is determined never to become a victim—of an animal bite, of a potential child molester, of her potentially abusive father, or even of the Japanese. Her aggressive, proactive stance toward these threats is contrary to the notion of the passive female usually associated with this time period.

Minister
See Father Kenniman

Momma

See Ariane Manning

Billy Monday

Billy Monday is a shy third-grader who was bitten by his brother's squirrel and has to undergo a series of painful rabies shots. The experience makes him the unwilling center of attention in a classroom full of students who previously ignored him. According to Rhoda, Billy is "a small washed-out-looking boy" who talks to no one and who is barely able to read. Billy's meek acceptance of the daily ritual of the rabies shots marks him as one of the story's victims. As Rhoda explains, "[e]very day we waited to see if he would throw a fit but he never did. He just put his books away and left the room with his head hanging down on his chest and Mr. Harmon and his mother guiding him along between them like a boat." The passive demeanor of Billy is contrasted with the active resistance of Rhoda, who swears she would take her chances with rabies before she would allow herself to be led away to such an ordeal for fourteen straight days.

Themes

Victims and Victimization

The theme of victimization is integral to "Victory Over Japan." For example, Billy Monday is the victim of a squirrel bite and the painful rabies shots that follow. Rhoda is quick to exploit Billy's tragedy. Pretending to befriend the unpopular child, she hopes to exploit his situation in an effort to enhance her own reputation both as a budding journalist and as a "good" daughter. She had, after all, been the only third-grader to have a story published in the school newspaper by capitalizing on the victim status of the school's principal, Mr. Harmon, who suffered shell shock during World War I. She hopes to do the same with Billy.

When Billy and Rhoda discover the child pornography, Rhoda sees the children in the pictures primarily as prey: "They looked like earthworms, all naked like that. They looked like something might fly down and eat them. It made me sick to think about it. . . ." A few months later when Rhoda thinks she has spotted the man whose basement contained the offensive material, she fears that she herself will become his next victim.

Racing home to tell her mother about the man, Rhoda is confronted with the news that Japan has been devastated by an American nuclear attack— the potential victimizers have themselves become victims of an atom bomb. As Rhoda ponders her violent father's return from the war, she falls asleep and dreams of bombing Japan as well as the "bad man" in the brick house; they will be her victims, not the other way around.

Violence and Cruelty

The themes of violence and cruelty are directly related the issue of victimization in the story. Billy correctly perceives Rhoda as a threat when she approaches him at recess offering him a forbidden cinnamon toothpick. His vulnerability brings out Rhoda's mean streak, although she resists the temptation to act on that impulse: "Part of me wanted to give him a shove and see if he would roll. I touched him on the shoulder instead," Rhoda reports. Her teacher, Mrs. Jansma, also senses Rhoda's true intentions towards Billy and rescues him just as he is starting to cry.

The man in the brick house poses a very real threat to both Rhoda and Billy. Later that summer, Rhoda imagines the possible violence this sexual predator might visit upon her: "He might grab me and put me in the car and take me off and kill me." Yet the reader soon learns that the more likely threat to Rhoda comes not from this stranger, but from her own father, whose return from the war is imminent in the wake of America's violent victory over its enemy Japan.

Sex Roles

The character of Rhoda challenges conventional gender stereotypes. Rebellious and even outrageous, she chases boys and shows off her underpants. It is Rhoda who plays the part of the schoolyard bully, preying on a much weaker male. While she claims that she wants to emulate her sainted, self-sacrificing mother, Rhoda's fantasies of violent retribution against her enemies, both personal and political, suggest that her true role model is her aggressive father.

Style

Point of View

"Victory Over Japan" is narrated in the first person by Rhoda Manning, a third-grade girl. Like many of Gilchrist's female characters, Rhoda is completely self-absorbed, which makes her version of the events she recounts entirely subjective.

Style

Allowing her characters to speak for themselves is typical of Gilchrist's fiction and "Victory Over Japan" is no exception. Since Rhoda is a child when she recounts these events, it is natural that her narrative voice will be that of a young child. But critics have commented that this style marks many of Gilchrist's stories even when the narrator is an adult woman. According to Dean Flower, "The distinctive trait of Gilchrist's colloquial style is its deliberate naiveté: short sentences, simple phrasing, lists. At moments this voice can sound like children's storytelling."

Structure

Like many of Gilchrist's stories, Rhoda's tale is gossipy, even amusing at points. An unexpected violent ending is a Gilchrist trademark; in "Victory Over Japan," the violence is a threat rather than an actual event, but nonetheless the reader realizes that for all of Rhoda's blustery insistence on her own invincibility, she is apparently a victim or a potential victim of abuse.

Setting

The geographical setting of "Victory Over Japan" is Seymour, Indiana. This Midwestern setting, with such homey details as treehouses, children on the playground, and the PTA-sponsored paper drive, evokes the idealized nostalgia of small-town American life. This idyllic vision contrasts with the suggestions of violence that emerge in the story.

However, since Gilchrist was born and raised in the South and lived (and continues to live) there as an adult, she thinks of herself as a Southern writer and is characterized that way by critics. Her character Rhoda also remains a Southerner. Indeed, the other Rhoda stories in both this collection and the earlier one feature Rhoda in various Southern locales like New Orleans and Franklin, Kentucky.

The temporal setting for the events in "Victory Over Japan"—the final months of World War II—adds to the sense of potential violence that underlies the story. The Allied Forces, which included those of the United States, achieved victory in Europe with the surrender of Germany on May 7, 1945 (VE Day). The war in the Pacific continued until the United States dropped the atomic bomb on the

Topics for Further Study

- Research the contribution women and children made to the war effort during World War II. What types of scrap materials, besides paper, did children collect? What consumer commodities were rationed and how did Americans compensate for these shortages?

- Read another of Gilchrist's "Rhoda" stories, either in the collection *Victory over Japan* or in another of her books. How does the character change over time?

- Read one of Gilchrist's "Miss Crystal" stories, either in the collection *Victory over Japan* or in another of her books. How do Rhoda and Miss Crystal compare as characters?

Japanese cities of Hiroshima on August 6 and Nagasaki on August 9; the Japanese surrendered the following day (VJ Day). It is this news that commands the attention of the adults in Rhoda's life when she attempts to tell her mother about the "bad man."

Historical Context

International Warfare

During the 1980s civil war raged in several Latin American countries—often with at least a hint of U.S. involvement—most notably in Nicaragua and El Salvador. There were at least two instances of limited wars involving superpowers: the British invasion of the Falkland Islands in May, 1982, and the American invasion of Grenada in October, 1983.

However, the most volatile area of the world during those years was the Mideast, where Iran and Iraq engaged in constant warfare. Lebanon became the site of numerous conflicts between the Israelis and the Palestinians, and terrorist attacks against the U.S. presence in Lebanon occurred during this time. In April, 1983, the U.S. Embassy in Beirut was bombed and sixty-three people were killed; later that year, a suicide attack on the U.S. Marine barracks resulted in 241 deaths.

Child Abuse and Pornography

Child abuse became the focus of enormous media attention and public concern in the 1980s. This was the result of not only an increase in the number of abuse and neglect cases, but also an increased reporting of such incidents due to new laws which mandated that teachers and other professionals report all suspected cases of child abuse.

Prominent cases involving sexual abuse of children outside the home, such as those involving the McMartin Preschool, the Boy Scouts of America, and various clergymen, received national attention in the media. It also led to an intense campaign to educate youngsters on potential dangers.

Another national debate involved the issue of pornography. Various conservative groups joined forces with some feminist leaders to condemn pornography on the basis of its possible link to violence against women and children. While child pornography was universally condemned, restrictions on adult material were considered by many to be forbidden under the provisions of the First Amendment.

Critical Overview

The collection *Victory Over Japan: A Book of Stories* won the American Book Award for fiction in 1985. In general, the book was favorably received and commercially successful.

Critics invariably focus on Gilchrist's female characters and their unique narrative voices. Commentator Dean Flowers maintains that her colloquial style is deliberately naive; at times, he remarks, ''this voice can sound like children's storytelling.'' While occasionally, as in ''Victory Over Japan,'' the narrator actually is a child, Flower finds this voice appropriate even for adult narrators, since ''the style admirably suits the frustrated-child mentality of most Gilchrist characters.'' These child-women are variously characterized by critics as spoiled, willful, unpredictable, and racy. Lowry, for instance, describes Rhoda as ''redheaded and a hellion.''

Gilchrist's surprise endings are praised by Flower, who says her stories typically seem like ''the most marvelous gossip you ever heard'' until the reader is faced with the sadness and anger of the final paragraphs. On the other hand, Beverly Lowry finds fault with these abrupt changes in tone. ''Miss Gilchrist seems to have her difficulties with endings,'' Lowry writes, ''Sometimes the last paragraph seems tacked on, like a patch placed slapdash on a leaking inner tube.''

Most critics seem to agree that the unity Gilchrist achieves by featuring the same characters in different stories is both pleasant and effective. ''Because many of the stories are connected in ways both obvious and subtle, you feel as though you are reading a novel; at the end you have that satisfied, contented feeling only a good novel can give,'' writes Jonathan Yardley in the *Washington Post*.

Yet when Gilchrist has ventured into the longer form, the reviews have not been positive. Yardley himself claims that her second book, the novel *The Annunciation* (1983), is ''flabby, narcissistic, sophomoric.''

Criticism

Suzanne Dewsbury

Dewsbury has taught English and American Studies at Wayne State University. In the following essay, she explores Rhoda's efforts to defy gender stereotypes and avoid victimization—efforts that in the end are futile.

Although Ellen Gilchrist's writings include poetry, novels, and even a screenplay, she is most recognized as a master of short fiction, specifically short stories that feature Southern females chafing against their confining culture. Many of her characters, including Rhoda Manning, Nora Jane Whittington, and Crystal Manning (Rhoda's cousin), appear in several stories at different ages and in varying circumstances.

For example, Rhoda appears in the first three stories of Gilchrist's second short story collection, *Victory Over Japan*. The ''Rhoda'' section includes ''Victory Over Japan,'' featuring an eight-year-old Rhoda during the spring and summer of 1945; ''Music,'' in which Rhoda as a rebellious young teenager experiments with smoking and sex; and ''The Lower Garden District Free Gravity Mule Blight or Rhoda, a Fable,'' which catches up with Rhoda at the age of thirty-four, when she is in the process of a divorce.

Although all three of these incarnations of Rhoda have plenty to say for themselves, it is only the first who is permitted to tell her own story in her own words. Rhoda also appeared in several stories at various ages in Gilchrist's first short story collection, *In the Land of Dreamy Dreams.*

Gilchrist's characters are variously described as willful, brash, outspoken, and outrageous; Rhoda, even at the age of eight, exhibits all those traits. Although she is a Brownie Scout in ''Victory Over Japan,'' Rhoda otherwise defies gender stereotypes. She is neither sweet nor innocent—she recounts without shame her normal routine at recess: chasing boys with her best friend Letitia and hanging upside down on the monkey bars in order to show off her underpants. She is opportunistic and devoted to enhancing her reputation at any cost.

She is a bit of a bully to her shy classmate, Billy Monday. The boy's unfortunate encounter with a potentially rabid squirrel provides Rhoda with a chance to get a second story published in her school's newspaper. Her first story exposed her principal's experience with shell shock during the First World War.

When she tries to get an exclusive interview with Billy, the young victim becomes visibly upset; perhaps he senses the predatory nature of her overtures to him. Her teacher recognizes the threat Rhoda poses and rescues Billy just as he collapses into tears.

It is perhaps the backdrop of World War II that emboldens Rhoda. For the most part, the men are away at war and the women are preoccupied with the war effort. Rhoda seems, at least temporarily, unfettered by normal social constraints.

The males who remain on the domestic scene appear to be victims of one sort or another, prompting Rhoda to exploit their condition even more. The language that she uses to describe both Billy and Mr. Harmon emphasizes their vulnerability.

For example, Mr. Harmon, wearing casual clothes for the school paper drive, ''looked more

Double mushroom cloud rising over Nagasaki, August 8, 1945, from second atomic bomb.

shell-shocked than ever'' to Rhoda who had never seen him in anything but a gray suit.

Billy is compared to a bug in Rhoda's descriptions—first a roly-poly, then a spider. As he tries to protect himself, Billy answers her prying questions with ''I don't know,'' while ''his head was starting to slip down onto his chest. He was rolling up like a ball.''

Rhoda persists and Billy shrinks into himself even more: ''He had pulled his legs up on the bench. Now his chin was so far down into his chest I could barely hear him talk. Part of me wanted to give him a shove and see if he would roll.'' When Mrs. Jansma intervenes, Billy clings to the teacher ''like a spider,'' according to Rhoda.

The young boys in the pornographic pictures are described in a similar fashion. Although the magazines contain photos of both boys and girls, it is the males that Rhoda focuses on—she is, of course, interested because she's never seen a boy naked before, but she is also morbidly fascinated by their vulnerability and assigns them the same victim status she has given to Billy and Mr. Harmon.

What Do I Read Next?

- *In the Land of Dreamy Dreams* (1981) is Gilchrist's first collection of short stories. Rhoda Manning makes several appearances at various ages.

- *Net of Jewels* is a 1992 novel featuring Rhoda Manning as a college student and young adult.

- *Rhoda: A Life in Stories* is a 1995 collection that brings together all of the Rhoda short stories from earlier collections plus two new ones.

- Published in 1987, *Falling Through Space: The Journals of Ellen Gilchrist* features several of the journal entries read by Gilchrist in her regular appearances on National Public Radio's *Morning Edition*.

- *Shiloh, and Other Stories* is a collection of short fiction written by Bobbie Ann Mason and published in 1982. A Southern writer, Mason shares with Gilchrist many stylistic elements and thematic concerns.

As she walks home, she thinks about the little boys in the picture. "They looked like earthworms, all naked like that," she thinks, "They looked like something might fly down and eat them. It made me sick to think about it."

Rarely does she think of herself as a victim. If she were Billy, she would kill the squirrel by cutting its head off, she tells him. If she were faced with fourteen painful rabies shots, she would run away. The threat posed by animals, like the squirrel that bit Billy, does give her a moment of reflection. "I was thinking about the Livingstons' bulldog," she recalls, "I'd had some close calls with it lately."

Throughout most of the story, Rhoda is in charge. For example, she quickly assumes control at the paper drive. So sure that Billy is too weak to be of much real help, Rhoda pulls the wagon; moreover, she approaches the homeowners asking for papers, since Billy says he would prefer to wait on the sidewalk.

On their final stop of the day, Billy finally does the talking and it is he who discovers the contents of the magazines the man has invited them to take. Still, it is Rhoda who insists on a hasty retreat from the basement and swears Billy to secrecy.

Only when she thinks she sees the man on the street does Rhoda's bravado begin to crumble.

Suddenly she begins to imagine herself as a potential victim, describing the events of an August afternoon:

> I had been to the swimming pool and I thought I saw the man from the brick house drive by in a car. I was pretty sure it was him. As he turned the corner, he looked at me. *He looked right at my face.* I stood very still, my heart pounding inside my chest, my hands as cold and wet as a frog, the smell of swimming pool chlorine rising from my skin. What if he found out where I lived? What if he followed me home and killed me to keep me from telling on him? I was terrified. (Excerpt from ''Victory Over Japan'')

Rhoda describes him as about the same age as her father, a fact that makes him immediately suspect. Why, after all, is he not away at war with all the other men of fighting age? The connection becomes more concrete when the reader discovers that both ''the bad man'' and her father are sources of physical danger to Rhoda. The end of the war means her father will be coming home, Rhoda realizes, and she is uncertain how she feels about that.

Before he left for the war, he was always yelling at her mother to discipline Rhoda. ''Hit her with a broom. Hit her with a table. Hit her with a chair,'' her father would shout. This is in direct contrast to the minister's gentle advice to Rhoda's mother concerning her child's discipline problems, advice that had more to do with correcting the possible psychological problems behind the behavior than with physically punishing the misdeeds.

Suddenly the reader begins to understand the source of Rhoda's aggressive ways. Although she deludes herself (and perhaps her preoccupied mother as well) that she is becoming more and more like the generous, self-sacrificing Ariane with each passing day, the final two paragraphs of the story suggest that her father is the parent Rhoda most emulates.

Overjoyed that America has "dropped the biggest bomb in the world on Japan," Rhoda lapses into a dreamy slumber in which she imagines herself bombing both the Japanese and the man in the brick house. Thus, Gilchrist brings together the violence of war and the violence of child abuse in Rhoda's dream. In the same language that Rhoda's father had used regarding her, Rhoda dreams of destroying her enemies, both foreign and domestic: "Hit 'em with a table, I was yelling. Hit 'em with a broom. Hit 'em with a bomb. Hit 'em with a chair."

Some critics, notably Beverly Lowry, have criticized Gilchrist's abrupt, often violent, endings, but the fact that they differ in tone from the rest of the stories adds considerably to their sobering, even shocking effect.

Dean Flower and others are convinced that the jarring effect Gilchrist achieves in her stories' closing passages is deliberate, and not the result of some failing on the part of the author, as Lowry suggests.

Gilchrist is, Flower claims in his review of the short story collection, "ostensibly a comic writer, and can be relied on for hilariously funny moments, but at heart all these tales are grim." "Victory Over Japan" is certainly no exception.

Source: Suzanne Dewsbury, "Overview of 'Victory over Japan,'" in *Short Stories for Students*, The Gale Group, 2000.

James Sauer

Sauer is a professor of English at Eastern College in Philadelphia. In the following essay, he discusses the major themes of Gilchrist's story.

Ellen Gilchrist has developed her engaging voice as a writer by using a low-keyed, half-humorous, amoral tone. Her stark, down-home style holds

> "Suddenly the reader begins to understand the source of Rhoda's aggressive ways. . . . the final two paragraphs of the story suggest that her father is the parent Rhoda most emulates."

our interest. In "Victory Over Japan" we are carried along not by expansive epic, but by straight storytelling, a bit of wit, and eye-opening concluding images.

Gilchrist's humor can be sarcastic, as it is when Rhoda's teacher thanks her for "comforting" Billy Monday, whom Rhoda has reduced to tears; or satirical in its implication of adult hypocrisy, as instanced when Rhoda's mom prepares for a "visit" from the Episcopal priest. Our mind's eye is drawn to her mother's legs as she applies liquid hose, our suspicions confirmed by the off-hand childish remark, "He'd been coming by a lot since daddy was overseas. That was just like my mother. To be best friends with a minister." Sexuality is ever-present in this world, but the child cannot recognize it.

It is this innocent reflection through the voice of a child that provides the dynamic vehicle, jumping from topic to topic, observing, but not seeing, being central to the action, while actions move all around her. Rhoda is the know-it-all American kid who in fact knows but little of reality. Her perception of reality is filtered through Book-of-the-Month Club readings and speeches by shell-shocked old World War I veterans, through overheard conversations and a precocious imagination.

Like all of us, Rhoda is piecing together bits of reality trying to make sense of a world at war and of a family separated by oceans. Often a brat but never dull, Rhoda is growing up and will soon join in the empty human lives of the "spoiled, willful yet captivating women" who inhabit Gilchrist's fictional world. "Victory Over Japan" allows us a glimpse of Rhoda's psychological development.

> **Gilchrist transfers this methodology of solving the world's problems to Rhoda's childish vision. A sweeping annihilation offers itself as the solution to the problems that confront her."**

Gilchrist writes in the tradition of the mildly depressed, emotionally dissipated, morally worn-out South. Like many a literary Southerner, her voice offers a lilting emptiness, which in some ways is an echo of the jaded voice of mid-America. The South is a parable of our national exhaustion.

Yet in spite of this, we also feel a connection to Gilchrist's characters and settings. Her evocative use of references to Americana throughout the short story link us to the familiar. Her allusions to our cultural framework act as a means for calling forth the stock responses and memories of American life. We feel nostalgia for sensate objects: cinnamon toothpicks, coonskin caps, the beating of chalky erasers for the teacher, treehouses, basements full of newspapers tied up neatly with string as if sloppy newspapers were a crime.

She evokes a bygone era of innocence, an American pastoral already passing away at the time she describes. Yet the American dream is an illusion that also has its dark underside. The innocent child or nation is father to the ''wised-up'' adolescent of empire. Rhoda and America are both changing.

Throughout the story these two worlds of innocence and dark worldliness are kept psychologically distinct, interacting at various moments for contrast and revelation. Gilchrist's writing leaps back and forth between contrasting concepts and images: the ideal of living happily with a pet balanced against a boy undergoing painful treatment for the bite of a rabid squirrel; the safe orderly world of public school and its reassuring teachers against the hidden world of doctors who strap you down and stick you with needles. Paper drives with their light suburban feel of civilized productivity and frugality support a war effort that drops bombs on people and destroys lives.

World events balance against personal events; the sublime and the trivial are related. Violence in the world parallels conflict in the soul. Nations are destroyed; the innocence of little girls is lost. All reality is two-sided. Our memories may choose to recall only the sweet images of girls in their little Brownie suits; we repress the sick awakenings of our imaginations to pornography in somebody's basement.

The loss of innocence, the rites of passage into adulthood, the glimpses of sexual awareness, are the central creative and destructive powers in human life. Gilchrist has used the merger of events, themes, feelings, and conflicts to bring the personal sexual catastrophe and the world war catastrophe together. The evil that men do reaches out into the mind of the child.

This American pastoral ends for two children as they look at the pictures of child and adult pornography in a man's basement. (Never mind that the tale offers no explanation of why the man is nonsensically giving his pornography away for the paper drive. We suspend our disbelief for the purpose of the shock.) Rhoda and Billy Monday feel real evil and its presence in the world, hidden in the dark, in the depths of a basement, in the subterranean depths of mankind's dark side.

The children flee, but the pornography is now in their wagon. They can't escape; it will follow them forever. It is in their minds, awakening the dormant sexual darkness. They cast it away into the bushes as if to rid themselves of its taint. They swear to each other never to reveal what they found.

Later in the story, the man reappears in Rhoda's life as he drives by and stares at her. Rhoda cannot escape the knowledge of his eyes. ''He looked right at my face.'' The man will always be looking.

Gilchrist's characters are broken creatures sliding from the world of Southern gentility into an American muck. Rhoda is no exception. What seems to be missing in this world of hostile and malignant men is any sense of redemption. Gilchrist's light storytelling techniques reflect the sorry sadness of Southern tragedy.

By contrast one thinks of Harper Lee's novel *To Kill a Mockingbird*. In that book, Jem and Scout, two children, also provide the narrative viewpoint. As in Gilchrist's writings, there is a sense of the tragic structure of Southern life, of things not appearing as they are, of hidden evils. In Harper Lee's work, however, we have a greater sense of resolution—the villain falls on his knife (or does he?), and reclusive hero Boo Radley is left alone. A Southern tragedy finds a Southern solution.

In Ellen Gilchrist's world, there is less of a sense of finality; the evil pornographic man is always lurking. The best our little Rhoda can do is to wish that the world were not as it is.

Beverly Lowry has commented: "Gilchrist seems to have her difficulties with endings. Sometimes the last paragraph seems tacked on, like a patch placed slapdash on a leaking inner tube." Some might find it so with "Victory Over Japan." There is a purposed strangeness to the ending; but it is a strangeness which ties the themes together. The violence of the ending serves to bring the two worlds of adult and child together in an explosive and apocalyptic conclusion.

The symbol for that conclusion is the atomic bomb. Today we understand that the Bomb is dangerous. The Bomb is our collective phobia. We worry about nuclear holocaust, nuclear accidents, nuclear proliferation, nuclear terrorism, and nuclear waste. What we often fail to remember is that the initial use of the atomic bomb offered not a problem, but a solution. It solved the problem of the continuing war with Japan by vaporizing large numbers of Japanese. However horrendous the killing of thousands of Japanese, the general response of the American people was one of triumph and relief. The war was over.

Gilchrist transfers this methodology of solving the world's problems to Rhoda's childish vision. A sweeping annihilation offers itself as the solution to the problems that confront her. Press this button, throw that switch, and your problems will disappear. With the Bomb, Rhoda can eliminate the war, the evil man with the child pornography, and a distant unloving father whom she is really not sure she wants to come home.

The psychological explosion within cleanses the world outside. Problems and people are vaporized. Her psychological overload is solved by the release of the dark side. With the pure selfishness of a child she offers up her wish fulfillment: destroy the enemy. Blast him. She has become like the rest of us, like the adult world around her. The quick

solution is the human solution. Rhoda has started to grow up.

Source: James Sauer, "Overview of 'Victory over Japan,'" in *Short Stories for Students,* The Gale Group, 2000.

Doreen Fowler

In the following excerpt, Fowler analyzes the characters of Rhoda, Nora Jane, and Crystal, contending that they "are not only willful, they are also warmhearted, brave, and generous."

In one of the stories in Ellen Gilchrist's *Victory Over Japan.* a wealthy woman barricades herself in her bedroom and combs through newspapers and magazines cutting out words and gluing them to the walls, the chair, the bed. It is, she says, "her work"—"I have to find the words, when I find the right words I will expose them. You'll see. I will have it all out in the open where everyone can see. Then they will not be able to deny it. Then everyone will know." When a friend comes to visit, she whispers urgently, "Bring me words."

For Southern author Ellen Gilchrist too, words are important. In her new collection of stories, *Victory Over Japan* she too is looking for the right words, to set it all down just right and so then perhaps to make some sense of the diverse and bizarre shapes human existence can take. For the most part, the stories in this collection revolve around the lives of three very similar Southern women: Rhoda, Nora Jane and Crystal. Above all, what these women have in common is an awesome and seemingly undeterrable willfulness. When, for example, Rhoda, an adolescent of 14, determines to take a train to St. Louis to offer her virginity to her reluctant Jewish boyfriend and her mother attempts to stop her, Rhoda seems to go mad. Blind with rage, she screams, "'I'm going to kill you . . . I really am,' and she thought for a moment that she would kill her, but then she noticed her grandmother's Limoges hot chocolate pot . . . and threw it all the way across the room and smashed it into a wall beside a framed print of 'The Blue Boy.'" Equally formidable is Nora Jane Whittington, a self-taught anarchist who, to get enough money to go to San Francisco to join her lover, disguises herself as a Dominican nun and robs a bar in the Irish Channel section of New Orleans. And nothing stands in the way either of beautiful, wealthy, notorious Crystal Manning. In the climactic final story of the collection, Crystal has a showdown with her archrival, her brother, who arranges African safaris in Texas for

A view of Nagasaki in the aftermath of the atomic bomb blast.

people who do not have the time to go to Africa. Using her brother's custom-made Mercedes like a tank, Crystal rams it repeatedly into a pen holding his prized imported antelopes and frees them, then makes good her own getaway in his smoking Mercedes.

But Gilchrist's women are not only willful, they are also warmhearted, brave and generous. Crystal Manning, a born crusader, campaigns obsessively against the selling of young boys in whorehouses; Nora Jane demonstrates soldierly calm when during an earthquake she is trapped on a collapsing bridge; and the third-grader Rhoda chooses for her paper-drive-partner Billy Monday, a classmate who has been bitten by a rabid squirrel and has to have 13 shots in the stomach.

Multifaceted and unpredictable, Gilchrist's Southern belles elude easy classification. But Traceleen, Crystal's black maid, comes closest to assessing accurately all of the members of this sisterhood when she says, ''Some people just meant to be more trouble than other people. Demand more, cause more trouble and cause more goodness. Got to study them, so we see how things are made to happen.'' In *Victory Over Japan,* Gilchrist takes Traceleen's advice seriously and, with resounding success, ''studies them.''

Source: Doreen Fowler, in a review of ''Victory over Japan,'' in *America,* Vol. 152, No. 16, April 27, 1985, p. 351.

Dean Flower

In the following excerpt, Flower assesses the colloquial style of Gilchrist's story, suggesting that her narrative form is appropriate for the characters and themes in the stories.

Ellen Gilchrist's stories are charming and funny, instantly engaging, deceptively simple. With the appearance last fall of her second collection [*Victory Over Japan*] it has become clear that her voice is unique. Another woman, you say, to compete with Bobbie Ann Mason, Alice Adams, Ann Beattie, Alice Munro, Ella Leffland, and (name your favorite) all the rest? Amazingly, yes. And another Southerner besides. Gilchrist now lives in Fayetteville, Arkansas, but her stories range from Indiana and Kentucky on down through Memphis and Jackson to New Orleans, taking side trips to Pensacola and Texas, out to Berkeley and back to Virginia. Her characters are mostly affluent girls and women from families well-rooted in Southern traditions (collapsing, of course) and richly aware of the privileges money can buy. Most of them are busy causing trouble, and getting themselves into it.

"Music," the second of three stories about the youth, adolescence, and marriage of Rhoda Manning, describes the determined way in which a fourteen-year-old loses her virginity. "The Double Happiness Bun" tells how the nineteen-year-old Norah Jane robs a New Orleans bar, steals a car, and gets herself pregnant. Naturally for a Gilchrist character, her baby has *two* fathers. In a sequence of stories about the restless life of Crystal Weiss, the heroine gets her older brother's new Mercedes smashed and then wreaks havoc on his soak-the-rich business, a game ranch in Texas. These quite extravagant actions are all kept credible and even sympathetic by Gilchrist's skillful handling of voice. Here is how "Music" begins:

> Rhoda was fourteen years old the summer her father dragged her off to Clay County, Kentucky, to make her stop smoking and acting like a movie star. She was fourteen years old, a holy and terrible age, and her desire for beauty and romance drove her all day long and pursued her if she slept.

If is a charming touch. Whether in the first person or the third, Gilchrist always gets her characters vividly on the page by letting them talk. The author remains detached, paring her fingernails. "The Gauzy Edge of Paradise" begins, "The only reason Lanier and I went to the coast to begin with was to lose weight." Another voice starts out, in "DeDe's Talking, It's Her Turn," "The groom's mother's garden. You've never seen such roses," followed by a list. Four of the stories about Crystal come from the voice of Traceleen, a black woman who tries to care for this flamboyantly unhappy family. Traceleen is a perfect choice for narrator because she foreshortens things so decisively: "He was marrying this girl, her daddy was said to be the richest man in Memphis," Traceleen explains. "The Weisses were real excited about it. As much money as they got I guess they figure they can use some more." Greatly to the author's credit, she does not strain to differentiate the language of Traceleen from anyone else's, rich or poor, black or white. Traceleen is no fool in any case: "That's the kind of man Miss Crystal goes for," she tells us. "I don't know why she ever married Mr. Manny to begin with. They not each other's type. It's a mismatch. Anybody could see that."

The distinctive trait of Gilchrist's colloquial style is its deliberate naiveté: short sentences, simple phrasing, lists. At moments this voice can sound like children's storytelling: "Nora Jane Whittington was going to have a baby." Or, "Lady Margaret Sarpie felt terrible." But the style admirably suits the frustrated-child mentality of most of Gilchrist

> For the most part, the stories in this collection revolve around the lives of three very similar Southern women: Rhoda, Nora Jane and Crystal. Above all, what these women have in common is an awesome and seemingly undeterrable willfulness."

characters. Freed of linguistic entanglements, one dashes headlong through these stories, sometimes as if they were just the most marvelous gossip you ever heard, only to come up short against the sadness and anger and self-defeating pride of these vigorously unselfconscious people. Gilchrist has a strong impulse to tie her stories together, in sequences of three, four, and five episodes about a single figure, and with very suggestive non-chronological loops to hint at the fateful patterns of these lives. She is ostensibly a comic writer, and can be relied on for hilariously funny moments, but at heart all these tales are grim. Traceleen has an apt comment on this phenomenon: "Sometimes I start telling a story that's sad and the first thing anybody says is how come? How come they went and did that way? Nobody says how come when you tell a funny story. They're too busy laughing." Gilchrist's unique art is to tell such funny stories *and* get you to ask how come.

Source: Dean Flower, in a review of "Victory over Japan," in *The Hudson Review,* Vol. XXXVIII, No. 2, Summer, 1985, pp. 313–14.

Beverly Lowry

In the following excerpt, Lowry provides an overview of the female characters in "Victory over Japan," praising Gilchrist's portrayal of racy Southern women.

Ellen Gilchrist is a very nervy writer. That fact ought, first off, to be given its due. Nerve won't suffice to get a tightrope walker across the wire, but

> The distinctive trait of Gilchrist's colloquial style is its deliberate naivete: short sentences, simple phrasing, lists. . . . But the style admirably suits the frustrated-child mentality of most of Gilchrist characters."

it provides the initial boost: without nerve, no circus. In the same way, nerve urges a fiction writer to go ahead and shoot whatever moon it is he has been given to aim at, without caution or respect for current fashion, a boon for the reader to be sure.

In her new collection of stories, *Victory Over Japan,* Miss Gilchrist once again demonstrates not only her willingness to take risks, but her generosity as a writer as well. Without much authorial manicuring or explanation, she allows her characters to emerge whole, in full possession of their considerable stores of eccentricities and passion. A Gilchrist story typically begins with the central character—almost always a woman—out on some limb. The limb will be of a spindly tree, say a blossoming crape myrtle, and the woman on it, who will have grown up as somebody's daughter, will once have been better off than she is now: richer, thinner, younger . . . in short, will once have had more power in her world. She does not, however, cling to the branch, since nothing in her life has taught her that clinging ever did anybody any good, but is perched there, commenting on the view, trying to think of a way down that will neither scare small children nor tear the lace from her French underwear.

Miss Gilchrist's first collection of stories, *In the Land of Dreamy Dreams,* was published in 1981 by the University of Arkansas Press, an event still noted in those short lists of authors made famous by university press books. The book was widely noted and well received. Miss Gilchrist, as a result, was given a fair amount of literary publicity when she signed on with Little, Brown, which has published two other books, her novel *The Annunciation* and now, this new collection. Those who loved *In the*

Land of Dreamy Dreams will not be disappointed. Many of the same characters reappear, including the bravehearted and tenacious Nora Jane Whittington who, "nineteen years old, a self-taught anarchist and quick change artist," dressed as a Dominican nun and robbed a bar in the Irish Channel section of New Orleans to get enough money to go meet her boyfriend in San Francisco. Often new characters show up with old names. A Dudley, for instance, crops up here and there, usually as a father. A land surveyor whizzes through, wearing various hats, as does an aristocratic Mr. Leland. Rhoda and Crystal Manning have the same last name, though it's not clear they are kin. These crossovers are neither distracting nor accidental. Like Nora Jane, Ellen Gilchrist is only changing costumes, and she can "do wonderful tricks with her voice."

The stories in *Victory Over Japan* are divided into four sections: "Rhoda," "Crazy, Crazy, Now Showing Everywhere," "Nora Jane" and "Crystal." Rhoda also appeared in *In the Land of Dreamy Dreams.* In the new collection, she is variously 8 years old on a World War II scrap paper drive with a boy who's been bitten by a rabid squirrel; 14, with a passion for cigarettes; and 34, divorced and "poorer than she was accustomed to being." Newly acquired poverty is a constant with Gilchrist characters. And as another character in another story says, "Being poor wasn't working out. Being poor and living in a shotgun apartment wasn't working out. It was terrible." Like many other of Miss Gilchrist's women, Rhoda is redheaded and a hellion. At whatever age, poor or not, she manages to raise Cain.

The stories are wonderful to tell aloud. In "The Gauzy Edge of Paradise," two friends, Lanier and Diane, both 29 years old, go down to the Mississippi coast to loss weight. Diane speaks: "This trip to the coast was a Major Diet. We'd been at it five days, taking Escatrol, reading poetry out loud to keep ourselves in a spiritual frame of mind, exercising morning, night and noon." When Diane's cousin Sandor, who "had a nervous breakdown trying to be a movie star," appears, there goes the diet. As Sandor says, "The trouble with getting drunk with your cousins" is that "they tell everything you did." The three end up losing not pounds but all their money, and their amphetamines as well.

Nora Jane Whittington, by the way, does get to San Francisco, only to find her boyfriend gone hopelessly California. Nora Jane, however, manages to have her adventures, including one on the Golden Gate Bridge during an earthquake, in which

Nora Jane sings songs in different voices for a car full of terrified children, "Walt Disney and 'Jesus Christ Superstar' and Janis Joplin and the Rolling Stones and . . . some Broadway musicals." Nora Jane is different from other Gilchrist heroines in that she is strictly New South, an altogether modern and lovable punk kid.

Like LaGrande Magruder in *In the Land of Dreamy Dreams,* Crystal Manning may be the queen creation of *Victory Over Japan.* Crystal is one of a brand of Southern women who have not been well written about, the once rich, very bright and hard-drinking girls who, despite having to borrow the money to pay for the dress, have made their debuts and still wear silk next to their skin, one way or another. Anyone who has read the biographies of Zelda Fitzgerald and Martha Mitchell will have a speaking acquaintance with these women. Tennessee Williams's heroines—Maggie the Cat, from "Cat on a Hot Tin Roof" and especially Blanche du Bois in "A Streetcar Named Desire"—long to be what Crystal Manning already is, but Maggie is bitter and Blanche too weird. Regina, in Lillian Hellman's "The Little Foxes," comes out plain mean. And none of these characters have what is perhaps Crystal's essential element, her dark and crackling sense of humor, which can be vicious in any direction, including her own. Reynolds Price has written about women like Crystal from time to time, as does Alice Adams, but Ellen Gilchrist's racy females probably take the cake.

There are problems with a few of these stories. Miss Gilchrist seems to have her difficulties with endings. Sometimes the last paragraph seems tacked on, like a patch placed slapdash on a leaking inner tube. And her point of view within a story sometimes conveniently wanders—in order to explain something or give yet another reaction to the central character. It is jarring.

But this is a writer who does not play it safe and so the risks and misses are bound to be there. The pay-off is definitely worth the ride. *Victory Over Japan* belongs beside *In the Land of Dreamy Dreams,* not as sequel but complement. If we're lucky there will be yet another, with yet more overlapping tales, of Rhoda at 50 and Nora Jane in a new wig; of new and old versions of Lady Margaret Sarpie and

> A Gilchrist story typically begins with the central character--almost always a woman--out on some limb. . . . She does not, however, cling to the branch, since nothing in her life has taught her that clinging ever did anybody any good. . . ."

Devoie and of King Mallison and Crystal. As one character says, "Who could stay away from anything Crystal Manning is up to?"

Most of us wouldn't want to try.

Source: Beverly Lowry, "Redheaded Hellions in the Crape Myrtle," in *The New York Times Book Review,* September 23, 1984, p. 18.

Sources

Flower, Dean. "Fiction Chronicle," in *The Hudson Review,* Vol. XXXVIII, No. 2, Summer, 1985, pp. 301-14.

Lowry, Beverly. "Redheaded Hellions in the Crape Myrtle," in *The New York Times Book Review,* September 23, 1984, p. 18.

Yardley, Jonathan. "Knockout 'Victory': The Best Stories Yet from Ellen Gilchrist," in *The Washington Post,* September 12, 1984, pp. B1, B10.

Further Reading

Seabrook, John. Review, in *The Christian Science Monitor,* December 7, 1984, p. 38.
    Seabrook provides a mixed review.

The Wall

Jean-Paul Sartre

1937

"The Wall," first published in 1937 and collected in the volume *The Wall and Other Stories* (1939), is the best known of Jean-Paul Sartre's five short stories. Written prior to Sartre's activism in political causes, "The Wall" was Sartre's personal response to the Spanish Civil War; he wrote it during a period when he felt hopeless about the growing forces of fascism in Spain. The story also outlines Sartre's philosophy of existentialism. "The Wall," along with Sartre's existentialist novel *Nausea*, helped solidify Sartre's literary reputation.

In "The Wall," Sartre chronicles the story of a political prisoner condemned to execution by fascist officers. The knowledge of his death prompts the protagonist to give up on life before he is even killed. At the time of its publication, *The Wall and Other Stories* sparked some debate because of the negative content—including graphic sexuality and foul language—of the stories. Critics since have argued that these elements lend credibility to Sartre's philosophical ideas.

Throughout his long career as a writer and philosopher, Sartre produced numerous texts, yet he never again returned to the short fiction format. Critics have paid remarkably little attention to "The Wall." Interested scholars, however, have generally responded enthusiastically. "The Wall," however, remains important to the Sartre scholar as well as the general reader because of its deft exploration of Sartre's philosophies as well as its sheer narrative

force. It is a story to be appreciated on multiple levels.

Author Biography

Jean-Paul Sartre was born in Paris in 1905. His father died when he was only a year old, and shortly afterward he and his mother went to live with his grandfather. He recalled his childhood in his autobiography Les Mots, in particular the passion for literature that his tough grandfather instilled in him.

By the time Sartre finished high school, he wanted to pursue a career as a writer; unfortunately, his stepfather insisted he become a teacher. He attended L'Ecole Normale Superieur as a philosophy student. There he met Simone de Beauvoir, with whom he maintained a lifelong personal and professional relationship. A writer as well, she had a deep influence on all of Sartre's future work and ideas.

During the 1930s, Sartre taught philosophy at a preparatory school for high school students. He also went to Berlin to study the philosophy of Edmund Husserl. Sartre's early philosophical works, such as *Psychology of the Imagination* and *Transcendence of the Ego*, reflect the influence of Husserl's ideas about phenomenology-a method of analyzing the structure of consciousness.

In 1939, Sartre published a collection of five short stories entitled *The Wall and Other Stories*. In these works, Sartre explores his philosophical ideas of ''bad faith,'' or what happens when people deny moral responsibility for their behavior. Bad faith involves lying to oneself, not taking action, or having no real sense of purpose in life.

Sartre served in the French army during World War II. He was taken prisoner by the Germans and held captive for nine months. While imprisoned, he began writing his major philosophical work, *Being and Nothingness*, which outlines the concept of existentialism.

After he escaped from the prison camp, he returned to his teaching job in occupied France. Along with other French intellectuals, he formed a short-lived resistance group. He also wrote articles for underground newspapers as well as the play *The Flies*, which contained a strong anti-Nazi message. In 1945, he quit teaching and founded a leftist journal called *Modern Times*. By this time, he was well known for his philosophical ideas.

Throughout the 1950s and 1960s, Sartre became a Marxist and participated in political demonstrations that condemned capitalism and Western democratic institutions. In 1964, Sartre was awarded the Nobel Prize for Literature, but he rejected it on political grounds. He supported the Cuban Revolution and a paralyzing uprising of Parisian students in 1968.

By 1977, however, Sartre had forsaken Marxism. He died of a lung ailment on April 15, 1980. Today, Sartre is best known for his philosophical writings and is regarded as one of the most important influences on twentieth century literature and philosophy.

Plot Summary

The story opens with the narrator, Pablo Ibbieta, attending his own trial. He has been captured by the Falangists and is being tried as an opponent and war criminal along with several of his compatriots. When Pablo goes on trial, the judges demand to know the location of his colleague, Ramon Gris. Pablo claims that he does not know Ramon's whereabouts.

While awaiting the verdict, Pablo shares his cell with two other men: Tom, a member of the International Brigades; and Juan, whose only crime is having an anarchist brother. Pablo and Tom believe that they will be executed, but that Juan will be set free. However, they are informed that all three men will be executed the following morning.

Juan stops protesting his innocence; shocked, he just sits down and turns gray. Tom tries to comfort him but is rebuffed. Tom begins to talk about his experiences in the International Brigades. Pablo realizes that Tom is simply talking to avoid thinking about death.

A Belgian doctor and two guards come to the cell to wait with the men until the morning. Pablo stares at a lamp, but then suddenly comes to, feeling as if he was being crushed under an enormous weight. The doctor asks Pablo if he is cold. Pablo realizes that he is not cold at all, though he should be. When he touches his hair and shirt, he realizes he is sweating.

Juan dreads his execution, but Pablo hardly thinks about that anymore. Pablo feels irritated with

Jean-Paul Sartre

Tom's constant talking. Tom urinates on himself without realizing it.

Pablo tries to think about something other than death. He thinks about his past life, but none of it seems important to him anymore. The doctor offers to give a message to the men's loved ones. Nevertheless, he feels utterly alone. In fact, he has begun the process of disconnecting from the world and himself in preparation for his imminent execution.

When the time for the executions arrive, Juan starts shouting that he doesn't want to die. As he cries, Tom points out that daylight is almost breaking. Soon, the men hear shots fired in the courtyard. Then the soldiers come and take Juan and Tom away, but they leave Pablo in the cell for an hour. Pablo wants to scream, but he is determined to remain calm and "decent."

Finally, soldiers take him to a room. Officers try to intimidate him, which Pablo finds absurd and amusing. Once again, they question him about the whereabouts of Ramon Gris. They offer him a deal: give up Ramon and he will be allowed to go free. Pablo decides not to tell.

Later he decides to lie to them and tells them that Ramon is hiding in the cemetery. Thirty minutes later, one of the officers comes back. He orders

the guard to take Pablo to the courtyard and assigns his case to a regular, not military, tribunal. Pablo does not understand why he is not going to be shot right away. He spends the rest of the day with his fellow prisoners.

That evening he sees a baker he knows. The baker tells him that the Falangists captured Ramon. Apparently, Ramon left his safehouse due to an argument and went to hide in the cemetery. The Falangists found him in the gravediggers' shack, just as Pablo told them. Pablo passes out. When he comes to he is sitting on the ground. He is laughing so hard that tears come to his eyes.

Characters

Ramon Gris

Ramon Gris is an anarchist and colleague of Pablo's. The Falangists attempt to get Pablo to tell them Ramon's location. Pablo unwittingly tells the Falangists where Ramon is, allowing the Falangists to kill him.

Pablo Ibbietta

Pablo is the narrator and protagonist of the story. He has been condemned to death for his anarchist activities on behalf of Spain's Republicans during the Spanish Civil War. He deals with his impending death by detaching himself from life. He feels alienated from his own body, from the other condemned men who share his cell, and from his own past.

Pablo has the opportunity to save his own life when the officers ask him to give up the location of a fellow anarchist, Ramon Gris. Pablo chooses not to expose Pablo's hiding place, but instead hopes to make fools of the officers by giving them a random location, thereby sending them on a wild goose chase. However, it turns out that Pablo's "joke" causes Ramon's death, for Ramon ends up at that location by chance. Thus, Pablo's life is spared but he now bears the responsibility for a friend's death.

Juan Mirbal

Juan Mirbal is a young Spanish man whose brother is an important anarchist. Although Juan has committed no crime, he is sentenced to death. Juan protests that he has done nothing wrong. When he realizes his cause is hopeless, he is fearful of his impending execution. He cries when the men come to bring him to the courtyard.

Tom Steinbock

Tom Steinbock is an Irishman fighting on behalf of the Republicans. A member of the International Brigades, he has killed at least six men. Like Pablo, Tom is alienated from his own body, even urinating on himself and not feeling it. However, he tries to converse with the other men and come to a common understanding or solace. Tom acknowledges that he will die in the morning, but he cannot truly understand it. By the time the morning of his execution arrives, Tom has accepted his own death.

Themes

Death

Death is one of the most important themes in "The Wall." When he is sentenced to death, Pablo looks at life in a completely new way. The people that had once meant so much to him no longer matter. He also views his remaining few hours as the beginning of his death. He even comes to the conclusion that death is not natural, for people lead their lives under the presumption that they will continue to live; as he puts it, people maintain "the illusion of being eternal."

While in his cell, Pablo also takes the opportunity to think about how others react to the inevitability of death. He compares how Tom and Juan deal with their impending executions: Juan is fearful of death and afraid of suffering; Tom tries to imagine what being shot will be like, but he cannot conceive it because he envisions himself as an eyewitness to his own death.

When Pablo is brought in front of the Falangist officers again in the morning, he finds their attempts to intimidate him ridiculous. They fail to realize that their extraordinary power has been overshadowed by the ultimate power of death; they hold no threat to a man condemned to die.

Alienation

Presented in the theories of the philosophers G. W. F. Hegel and Karl Marx, alienation is described as a state of divided selfhood in which a person is distanced from his or her true being. Pablo experiences a sense of alienation once he finds out he is condemned to death. The first indication of this

Media Adaptations

- "The Wall" was adapted into a movie in France in 1967.

change in perception comes when he realizes that, instead of being cold in the drafty cell, he is actually sweating. He runs his fingers through his hair, surprised to find it stiff with sweat. He reflects that he must have been sweating for the past hours, yet he "had felt nothing."

Later he comes to view it almost as if it was someone else's body; "it was no longer I," he thinks. As the hours pass, Pablo also grows alienated from his consciousness, which includes the people and ideals that he once found of the utmost importance. He finds that nothing matters to him anymore, not the anarchist movement, not freedom, not his girlfriend. Pablo feels increasingly "inhuman," a state that again denotes his alienation from the other men that surround him, from society, and from his own former self.

War

Another important theme in "The Wall" is war. When the story takes place, Spain is in the midst of a brutal civil war. Spanish forces that favor a republican form of government are fighting against the fascist Falangists. While the story does not depict any of the fighting that is going on, it does highlight some of the significant aspects of a war-torn region.

For instance, unjust tribunals, which may dispense arbitrary and extreme punishments, are characteristic in times of war. While some of the prisoners attending the same trial as Pablo are accused of real crimes, such as sabotaging munitions, others, like Juan, seem to be guilty only by association to friends and family. The baker Garcia sums up this state of affairs after his arrest, also seemingly for having committed no crime: "They arrest everybody who doesn't think the way they do."

Topics for Further Study

- Look at paintings depicting elements of the Spanish Civil War, such as Pablo Picasso's *Guernica*, Joan Miro's *Black and Red* series, or Robert Motherwell's *Elegy to the Spanish Republic*. What do these works of art say about the Spanish Civil War? Is their message similar or different from the views expressed in "The Wall"?

- Many noted Spaniards died during the war, including the poets Federico Garcia Lorca and Miguel Hernandez. Read the works of some Spanish writers from the 1930s. How do these writers depict Spain at that time? What were their views on the Spanish Civil War?

- Find accounts of the Spanish Civil War in magazines and newspapers from the 1930s. Does Sartre's portrayal of the war seem accurate? Why or why not?

- Investigate Sartre's philosophy of existentialism. Then use what you have learned to analyze "The Wall" from an existentialist point of view.

- Read another fictionalized account of the Spanish Civil War, such as Andre Malraux's *Man's Hope* or Ernest Hemingway's *For Whom the Bell Tolls*. Compare that work to "The Wall."

Existentialism

A basic understanding of existentialism—an extremely complicated philosophical school of thought that Sartre explored in depth in *Being and Nothingness*—informs any reading of "The Wall." Existentialism is the term coined by Sartre to describe his perception of human existence. His form of existentialism is more properly called atheistic existentialism, and its followers believe that the individual is alone in a godless universe and that the basic human condition is one of suffering and loneliness.

Sartre believed that humans yearned for wholeness and meaning; without it, they live in a state of anguish and futility. Existentialism, however, does not hold that there is no hope for humankind. Because there are no fixed values, individuals can shape themselves and their characters through their own free will, that is, by making choices or by taking action; in essence, humans can create their own values. A person who asserts himself can derive meaning from life by becoming self-defining by his own decisions and actions.

Pablo, Juan, and Tom all exhibit certain characteristics of men suffering an existential crisis, but they face it differently. Juan denies what is sure to happen and refuses to walk to his execution; in forcing the guards to carry him out to the courtyard, he is passively putting his fate in the hands of others. Tom attempts to face his death with honesty and honor. Pablo's sense of alienation from his cellmates as well as from himself indicate his difficulties at creating his own life.

At the end of the story, Pablo chooses to assert his own being by sending the soldiers on what he believes to be a wild goose chase—searching for Ramon Gris. Ironically, he accurately pinpoints Ramon's location, thus his inability to live his life honestly results in a new creation of himself—the murderer of his friend Ramon.

In Sartre's eyes, Pablo bears the responsibility for Ramon's death; as the critic Kevin W. Sweeney writes in *Mosaic*, "Pablo believes that it is within his power to extend or retract his responsibility. . . . he thinks that he can rebuild the 'foundation' of his being, to choose what he will be responsible for."

When faced with the choice of Ramon's life or his, Pablo does not truly make a choice. Instead, he creates an alternate scheme for viewing the decision, one that allows him to avoid deciding whether he or Ramon will live; but as the events demonstrate, such a project is an impossibility.

Style

Narrator and Point of View

Pablo is the narrator of "The Wall." He tells his story from the first-person point of view; readers see and perceive of events through Pablo's consciousness. It is Pablo who decides when to share specific information, such as the fact that he does know where Ramon Gris is hiding.

In addition, Pablo also acts as interpreter. He presumes at times to know what the other men are thinking. When he sees Tom touch the bench, he states that Tom is touching death itself, but clearly he cannot know this to be true.

At times, Pablo appears to be an unreliable narrator. Not only does he hide the information about Ramon Gris at the man's first mention, but he poses unsatisfactory explanations about why he decides to keep Ramon's secret. He merely ascribes his behavior to stubbornness while at the same time asserting that Ramon's life is no more important than his own.

At the end of the story, he does not truly share his reaction to Ramon's death. Instead, he relates that he laughed so hard that tears came to his eyes and ends the story. This abrupt termination—almost like death—leaves readers to wonder whether he had any idea that Ramon might indeed be hiding in the cemetery.

Symbolism

The primary symbol in the story is the wall itself. On the most basic level, the wall symbolizes imminent death; the accused men will be lined up and shot in front of it the next morning. While visualizing his own execution, Tom imagines that he will want to push himself back against the wall as if he could somehow break it down and thus escape the bullets.

Pablo's clearest vision of the wall is in a dream. In this dream, the soldiers are dragging him toward the wall as he begs them not to kill him. This is his only honest statement about his lack of apathy toward his own death. Thus, for Pablo, the wall also stands for his inner fears, ones that he is suppressing from himself.

The wall also represents his alienation from the world. In a sense, he is placing both a wall around him—and creating a wall within him—as he perceives of his body functioning independently of his senses.

Historical Context

Political Instability in Spain

Since the 1800s Spain has experienced several years of economic and political instability. Economically, Spain has lagged behind other western European countries. Politically, the country has been unstable, experiencing violent strikes, assassinations, military plots, and separatist movements throughout the early 1900s. The disorder only grew worse after World War I, when a Spanish general known as Primo established himself as a military dictator.

Primo lost power in 1930; but the Spanish monarchy—led by King Alfonso XIII—had lost the country's respect through his initial support of Primo's dictatorship. In 1931, the king abdicated and Spain became a republic. The new government enacted measures that lessened the power of the Catholic Church and increased conditions for workers. Such sweeping reforms angered Spanish conservatives. Along with their Catholic allies, they united with the fascist Falange (meaning Phalanx) Party. The Falange wanted to preserve the power of the army, landowners, and the church.

In February 1936 a Popular Front government that included Socialists and Communists won a major election. The Popular Front was vehemently opposed to fascism. The new government jailed prominent fascists, and the Falange responded with terrorism. After a Falange leader was assassinated in the summer, the Spanish Civil War began.

The Spanish Civil War

The Spanish Civil War pitted the Nationalist (fascist) rebels, led by General Francisco Franco, against the Loyalists, or Republicans. This aggression captured the attention of many foreign powers: Germany and Italy, led by fascist dictators, sent the Nationalists weapons, advisers, and soldiers; the Soviet government supported the Republicans.

Approximately 70,000 antifascist volunteers from Great Britain, France, the United States, and other nations fought with the Republican Army and served as medical staff. These men and women became known as the International Brigades. By the time the Spanish Civil War ended, about half of them had died.

France and England feared that the Spanish Civil War might spread to the rest of Europe. In September 1936 the French government suggested

Compare & Contrast

- **1930s:** Spain's government experiences a complete upheaval. After King Alfonso abdicates the throne in 1931, the country becomes a republic. The democratic government, however, is challenged by the Falange Party, or the Nationalists. This struggle for power leads to the Spanish Civil War, which lasts from 1936-1939. Eventually the fascist forces win the civil war and establish a dictatorship.

  Today: Spain remains a democratic government with a parliamentary monarchy. At least seven major political parties (or party coalitions) participate in the government. Several extremist political groups continue to exist, such as the First of October Antifascist Resistance Group, which uses terrorism to oppose the government.

- **1930s:** The 1930s was a decade filled with international aggression and war: Japan invades China in 1931, Italy invades Ethiopia in 1935, and the Spanish Civil War lasts from 1936 through 1939. Under Adolf Hitler, Germany annexes Austria and the Sudetenland in Czechoslovakia. Germany also attacks Poland in 1939, the action that starts World War II.

  Today: Fighting erupts between Muslim Croatians and Bosnian Serbs in the former Yugoslavia. Ireland also experiences violent conflict as the Irish Republican Army and the Protestants battle. Many other regional conflicts threaten international security.

- **1930s:** After several devastating years of civil war, Spain's economy is in shambles. Many years pass before the economy recovers.

  Today: Spain is one of the leading economic powers of Western Europe and a member of the European Economic Community.

- **1930s:** France, like many other European nations, attempts to keep out of international affairs. The government refuses to get involved in the Spanish Civil War or in Italy's invasion and takeover of Ethiopia. Only Germany's aggression in Poland draws France into action and war.

  Today: In the 1990s the French government makes major military contributions to multinational peacekeeping operations in Lebanon and Bosnia. France also participates in the international coalition against Iraq during the Persian Gulf War.

---

that a nonintervention committee meet. This committee agreed to a policy of nonintervention in Spain, which included a blockade to halt the flow of volunteers and supplies to both sides. Germany and Italy did not participate in the agreement and continued to support Franco's forces.

As radical groups came to control the Republican forces, many Spaniards and foreigners came to see the Spanish Civil War as a struggle between fascists and communists. Franco's forces eventually prevailed in 1939.

Franco set up a fascist government that gave him unlimited power. The government permitted the Falange Party to be the only political party in the country, abolished free elections and most civil rights. This victory intensified a feeling of helplessness in the face of fascism for several Western countries.

France and the Spanish Civil War

Only three months after France's general election of 1936, the Spanish Civil War broke out. Despite appeals from Spain, the new leader of the French government, Leon Blum, reluctantly refused to lend support. Many French citizens were afraid that helping the Republican forces might lead the country into war with Italy and Germany, both under fascist rulers who actively supported Franco. Later, Blum also stated that he believed involvement in Spain might lead France into its own civil war, for the French people were deeply divided over the issue.

French Writers and the Spanish Civil War

In *What Is Literature?*, Sartre described the way in which world events of the 1930s—the depression, the rise of Nazism, the war in China—opened the eyes of French writers and intellectuals. The war in Spain jolted many out of their previous state of apathy—which is what occurred with Sartre—as well as energized those who were already politically active. Writers and intellectuals increasingly felt an awareness of history, a change that profoundly affected the literature of the period.

French intellectuals struggled to confront the chaos of the political and social realities surrounding them, and writers increasingly used their work to explore the time in which they lived. Andre Malraux's *Man's Hope*, for instance, which chronicled the first nine months of the Spanish Civil War, was published while the war was still taking place. Many writers, including Malraux, went to Spain to serve in some capacity. French writers also organized the International Congress of Antifascist Writers held in Madrid and Valencia in 1937.

Critical Overview

When "The Wall" was first published in *La Nouvelle Revue Francaise* in 1937, it introduced Sartre to the French literary world. According to one scholar, Sartre's publisher arranged the publication because he wanted to see if the public would favorably receive a novel Sartre had written, *Nausea* . The public, in fact, embraced both of these works, which quickly established Sartre's literary reputation.

Two years later "The Wall" was selected as the title story for Sartre's only collection of short fiction. Of his fiction, it has been his most popular work over the decades, yet critical reception has been slight as the short stories have been overshadowed by Sartre's writings in other genres.

From the time of its publication, critics and scholars perceived the stories in the collection as merely vehicles for Sartre's philosophical ideas. The renowned French writer, Albert Camus, did not cite the story specifically in his review of the

collection published in the *Alger Republicain* . His views on Sartre's view of man, however, aptly reflect Pablo's situation: Man is "alone, enclosed in this liberty. It is a liberty that exists only in time, for death inflicts on it a swift and dizzying denial. His condition is absurd. He will go no further, and the miracles of those mornings when life begins anew have lost all meaning for him."

Some early critics found the subject matter of the collection problematic. The other four stories featured an impotent man; a bourgeoisie who finds refuge in a fascist organization; a man who attempts to commit a heinous crime to escape his mediocrity; and a young woman desperately trying to share her insane husband's world. Critics objected to Sartre's portrayal of deviant characters and graphic sexuality, his negative outlook, and use of obscene language. Camus denied these charges: Sartre's aim, he writes, "is to show that the most perverse of creatures acts, reacts, and describes himself in exactly the same way as the most ordinary."

Camus' overall analysis of Sartre's collection was overwhelmingly positive: "A great writer always brings his own world and its message. M. Sartre's brings us to nothingness, but also to lucidity. And the image he perpetuates through his characters, of a man seated amid the ruins of his life, is a good illustration of the greatness and truth of his work."

The collection was not published in America until 1948. Several American reviewers offered similar criticisms to their French counterparts, noting the disgust that Sartre seemed to display for humanity. A review in the *New Yorker* asserted that the "only remotely normal people involved are to be found in the title piece." Other commentators, such as the *San Francisco Chronicle*'s Vance Bourjaily, found the stories to be "uniformly excellent."

Many critics fault the story's ending. Maurice Cranston wrote in 1962 that "The Wall" was actually the "least characteristic of [Sartre's] works" because of the "ironical twist" at the end, but some scholars, such as Alexander J. Argyros, dispute this analysis. Others insist on analyzing Sartre's political position on the political events in Spain.

Sartre later recalled that at the time he wrote the story he was "simply in a state of total revolt against the fact of Spanish fascism." Sartre's long-time companion, Simone de Beauvoir, remembers that the events in Spain were the first to shake the two of them from their intellectual isolation and left them feeling ''hopeless and desolate.''

Overall, many scholars consider Sartre's short stories as excellent vehicles to explore his philosophical theories. While most critics find that Sartre's philosophical arguments are the most important elements in his short fiction, a few scholars have analyzed these stories, including ''The Wall,'' on a narrative level, combining the actual structure of the story with the existential experience of existing.

Criticism

Rena Korb

Korb has a master's degree in English literature and creative writing and has written for a wide variety of educational publishers. In the following essay, she compares the reactions of the three condemned men to their imminent execution.

In the 1930s, Jean-Paul Sartre had already published his first major work, a philosophical treatise entitled *Imagination* as well as several critical articles on literary figures such as Jean Giradoux, Albert Camus, and William Faulkner. However, his publication of the novel *Nausea* and the short-story collection *The Wall and Other Stories* established his reputation as a literary figure.

''The Wall'' is set in a Falangist prison during the Spanish Civil War. The narrator of the story, Pablo Ibbieta, relates the last night of his life. Along with two other men, he has been sentenced to death by a military tribunal.

Prior to the publication of this story, Sartre had demonstrated none of his later tendency toward political activities and statements. Unlike many other French intellectuals, Sartre took no part in one of the great political battles of the decade: the Spanish Civil War. While the war was still going on, and as thousands of volunteers from France, Britain, and the United States poured into Spain to support the Republicans, a former student came to Sartre. He wanted Sartre's help in joining the International Brigades.

Although the young man never went to the war-torn country, Sartre was deeply affected by the experience. As he later said, ''I was very disturbed because, on the one hand, I felt he didn't have sufficient military or even biological preparation to survive the bad times and, on the other hand, I

couldn't deny a man the right to fight.'' As Sartre continued to muse over the situations that such a young man might face, he came up with the basic premise for ''The Wall,'' which he defines as a meditation on death.

At the time Sartre wrote the story, in late 1936 or early 1937, Spain's fate had already been decided by the Falangists' victory. Sartre's political pessimism informed his writing of the story. He later acknowledged at a press conference that since ''we were operating in the context of the Spanish defeat I found myself more sensitive to the absurdity of these deaths than to the positive elements that might emerge from a struggle against fascism.''

In the execution of the innocent Juan, Mary Jean Green, writing in *Fiction in the Historical Present, French Writers and the Thirties*, sees Sartre's ''severe indictment of fascist policy.'' Indeed, the story opens with a tribunal so brief that it comes as a surprise when a guard tells the prisoners, '''that was the trial.'''

The atmosphere reflects the unreality and the lack of order seen in the trial—where men are sentenced to death after the briefest of questioning. Even the major who announces the execution orders appears ''exasperated'' with the confusion as he was expecting to find three Basques in the cell. He then retires to leave the three men to await the morning, and their deaths, in the cold, drafty cell.

Each of the condemned men reacts differently. Juan, knowing he has committed no crime but not understanding that logic and fairness no longer matter, denies his fate. ''That's not possible,'' he says when the guard reads his execution statement. '''Not me.''' Juan also is ''terribly afraid of suffering''; his focusing on the pain is another method of denial.

As a last defense against the situation, Juan collapses when the soldiers come to take him to the courtyard. ''He was not unconscious;'' Pablo notes, ''his eyes were wide open and tears were rolling down his cheeks.'' Juan's refusal to take action is his way of denying responsibility for his own life and places him, in Sartrean terms, in a position of ''bad faith''—that is, choosing passivity as a way of escaping the self.

Unlike Juan, Tom accepts his responsibility—both for the actions that have led him to this situation—and for dealing with his upcoming death. He does avoid the thought of death through a

What Do I Read Next?

- Ernest Hemingway's *For Whom the Bell Tolls,* first published in 1940, is the story of an American teacher fighting in the Spanish Civil War. The novel chronicles the tumultuous events of a seventy-two hour period.

- Sartre's *Nausea* (American translation, 1949) uses the "found" journal of Roquentin to explore one man's metaphysical search for his place in the world.

- Sartre's short story collection, *The Wall and Other Stories,* presents five stories that explore aspects of Sartre's philosophy.

- Stephen Crane's Civil War novel, *The Red Badge of Courage* (1893), depicts the violent experiences of a young soldier. Crane's writing style challenges the reader to judge Henry's responses to his experiences.

---

number of tactics—conversing, exercising, comforting Juan—yet he also acknowledges to Pablo that "'something's going to happen to us that I don't understand.'" He talks about his perception of what the execution will be like; he sees his executioners standing in a line before him, shouldering their weapons, and he imagines himself trying to push against the wall as if he can break through it.

"'I say to myself, afterwards, there won't be anything. But I don't really understand what that means . . . there's something wrong. I see my own corpse. That's not hard, but it's *I* who see it, with *my* eyes. I'll have to get to the point where I think—where I think I won't see anymore. I won't hear anything more, and the world will go on for the others. We're not made to think that way, Pablo.'"

Pablo thinks that Tom is "certainly talking to keep from thinking." In a sense, Pablo is correct. For in refusing to understand how he can imagine viewing his own death, Tom is able to avoid the death itself. In another sense, Pablo is incorrect. For Tom gives voice to what is uppermost in both men's mind: the inability to truly continue living when one's death is foretold.

For his part, Pablo believes that his life is already over. He begins to distance himself emotionally from his life, wanting to undergo what will happen with objectivity. He realizes that he has lived life under "the illusion of being eternal," but that the knowledge of death means that he no longer truly lives. In fact, he feels that he is "dying alive." He begins to feel alienated from his own body, which he comes to view as some sort of "enormous vermin." His body sweats despite the cold air and it trembles, yet Pablo senses neither warmth nor coldness.

As the evening progresses, Pablo tries to disassociate himself from his former life by allowing himself no feelings for his friends, his girlfriend—everything that was once important to him. "I had spent my time writing checks on eternity," Pablo thinks, "and had understood nothing." His rejection of his own past, which he sees as a "goddamned lie," demonstrates the inability he has to foresee his own death. "I took everything as seriously as if I had been immortal," he realizes. However, his diatribe takes on more of a tone of bitterness than acceptance when he notes that "death had taken the charm out of everything."

Along with the alienation from his own body, Pablo wants to distance himself from the other men. Such a project contrasts sharply with his earlier behavior when the men were still awaiting sentencing. Then, Pablo's hold on life expressed itself in his belief in the ties that connect a person to others. Though he agreed with Tom that they were going to die, he still welcomed the chance to form a relationship with the Irishman. He even preferred their cell to the one he had been in for the past five days because he "had been alone, and that gets to be

> Others, however, find in the ending an expression of Sartre's philosophical ideas of the meaninglessness of life and its absurdity."

irritating." Whereas before he found Tom to be a "good talker," now he only wants to be alone.

This detachment project is not possible, however, for Pablo realizes that Tom and Juan are suffering in a similar way. Tom even urinates on himself, and when Pablo points this out, Tom angrily replies, "I can't be . . . I don't feel anything." Pablo also recognizes his own physical condition in them: the gray faces, the sweaty skin; of Tom he says, "we were both alike and worse than mirrors for each other."

Additionally, all three men believe that the Belgian doctor is the only person truly alive. "He had the gestures of a living person, the interests of a living person; he was shivering in this cellar the way living people shiver . . . We, on the other hand, didn't feel our bodies anymore . . . I looked at the Belgian, . . . able to plan for tomorrow. We were like three shadows deprived of blood; we were watching him and sucking his life like vampires." Juan even bites the doctor's hand, which finally convinces the doctor "that we were not men like himself."

For all that Pablo tries to set himself apart from Tom and Juan, this is not a valid possibility. He even recognizes in himself the conscious decision to try not to think about the next day, "about death," though he criticized Tom for this same attempt. Tom, on the other hand, comes to accept the inevitable. Pablo describes Tom looking at a bench "with a sort of smile, with surprise, even. He reached out his hand and touched the wood cautiously, . . . then he drew his hand back hurriedly, and shivered." Pablo realizes that it "was *his own death* Tom had just touched on the bench."

Pablo, meanwhile, sticks to the mode of looking at his life as utterly changed by his death. "[I]f they had come and told me I could go home quietly," he says, "that my life would be saved, it would have left me cold." He believes that even if he were given a reprieve, his future life would be changed irrevocably by the realization that he is not immortal.

Then Pablo is given the chance for a reprieve. The Falangists want his colleague Ramon Gris, and they offer Pablo his life in return for telling them his friend's hiding place. Pablo, who had lied earlier when he said he didn't know Ramon's whereabouts, wants to understand his own refusal to give up his friend even to save his own life. "[H]is life was no more valuable than mine," Pablo realizes. In fact, he has come to believe that "No life is of any value."

Yet because of his project of the past night—disassociating himself from his past, which includes any emotional ties—he cannot admit to himself that his reason for not giving up Ramon stems from loyalty. To do so would mean that his mechanism for facing death has been taken away from him. Instead, he convinces himself that he will not give up Ramon out of stubbornness.

He decides to send the Falangists on a wild goose chase and he tells them a lie about where Ramon is hiding. He does not explain why he does this, except to allude to a "malicious" streak and his disgust for the Falangist officers' lack of understanding of the "pettiness" of their actions—the pettiness of living when one's death is inevitable.

Pablo, thinking Ramon is hiding at his cousin's house, is thus surprised to find out that the men actually found Gris at the cemetery, where he had gone after disagreeing with his cousin. When Pablo learns this, he sits down on the ground and laughs and laughs. This ending has led many critics to denigrate it as a trick ending or an O. Henry ending.

Others, however, find in the ending an expression of Sartre's philosophical ideas of the meaninglessness of life and its absurdity. Sartre himself explained his ending thirty years later: Pablo "tries to react by an individual action because he thinks it's a farce. It is because he plays with forces he does not understand that he lets loose against himself the forces of the absurd. It is not the result of an absurd 'destiny' that drags men along. . . . It is the result of inadequate knowledge . . . about the real actions to take. He has obtained this result through a childish act."

Pablo only ends in confusion, mirroring in fact, the confusion at the Falangist prison. "The laugh/cry," writes Kevin Sweeney in his article for *Mosaic*, "marks Pablo's awareness of both the failure of his project of detachment and his responsibility for Gris's death. This achievement of insight underscores Sartre's thesis that there are moral boundaries to human existence and that one of these limits is the responsibility for one's actions. . . . Pablo's flash of insight is Sartre's emphatic pronouncement that responsibility for one's actions is a condition of human existence, a condition from which one cannot escape.''

Source: Rena Korb, for *Short Stories for Students*, The Gale Group, 2000.

Mary Jean Green

In the essay below, Green asserts that "the Spanish setting of 'Le Mur' serves as a pretext for the evocation of more universal philosophical problems."

If Drieu uses the war in Spain as an appropriate denouement for his character's life and as a vantage point from which to analyze the European political situation, Jean-Paul Sartre uses it to illustrate the metaphysical absurdity of the human condition. The first written and the first published (in the *Nouvelle Revue Francaise* of July 1937) of the three works discussed in this chapter, ''Le Mur'' nevertheless reveals a more pessimistic outlook about life and politics than the work of either Malraux or Drieu. Sartre had uncannily anticipated the sense of despair that was to attack all of these writers by the end of the decade. In ''Le Mur,'' in opposition to *L'Espoir*, the reality of the Spanish Civil War does not play a major role in determining characters or plot. Even more so than in *Gilles*, the Spanish setting of ''Le Mur'' serves as a pretext for the evocation of more universal philosophical problems.

The story reveals, nevertheless, a clear political position. As Sartre later explained, at the time of the composition of ''Le Mur,'' he was ''simply in a state of total revolt against the fact of Spanish fascism.'' Simone de Beauvoir has recorded that the Spanish Civil War was the first political event of the 1930s that succeeded in shaking Sartre and herself from their intellectual isolation: ''For the first time in our lives, because the fate of Spain concerned us so deeply, indignation per se was no longer a sufficient outlet for us: our political impotence, far from furnishing us with an alibi, left us feeling hopeless and desolate.'' Although many of their closest friends, Paul Nizan being a prime example, were actively engaged in the great political battles of the time, Sartre and de Beauvoir had been content to let the left-wing ideals that they shared impose

> When 'Le Mur' was turned into a film in 1967, Sartre saw this theme—'the horror of death inflicted on man by man'—as the aspect of the story with the greatest continuing political relevance."

themselves on reality without their own active help. The success of the Falangist generals in Spain provided one of the first real challenges to the validity of their stance of passive onlookers. While de Beauvoir seems to have maintained an early optimism, Sartre, by his own account, had foreseen the Falangist victory in Spain almost from the first. This political pessimism informs his story, as he was later to admit: ''Since at that time we were operating in the context of the Spanish defeat [''Le Mur,'' was written in late 1936 or in early 1937 at the latest] I found myself much more sensitive to the absurdity of these deaths than to the positive elements that might emerge from a struggle against fascism, etc.''

There is a certain political protest in the story of three men condemned to death after a summary interrogation by a Falangist committee. The questioning of the prisoners takes place in the opening pages and is so brief that it comes as a shock when the guard informs them afterwards, ''C'etait le jugement'' [You have been sentenced (translation mine)]. The few bits of information exchanged seem to bear no relationship to the death sentences later read out in the cell. Two of the three men have, at least, been fighting on the Republican side: Tom Steinbock is an Irish volunteer in the International Brigades, and the narrator, Pablo Ibbieta, is an anarchist militant. The youngest of the three, however, is totally innocent. His only ''crime'' is in being the brother of a known anarchist. Nevertheless he is condemned to be shot with the others, a fate that he finds impossible to accept. While Tom and Pablo maintain a façade of stoic resignation, Juan protests, sobs, bites the hand of the doctor, and finally, in a state of total nervous collapse, he must be carried out to his execution by the guards. Although the narrator resists any temptation to sentimentalize over Juan, this cold-blooded execution of an innocent teenage boy cannot help but represent a severe indictment of fascist policy and thus takes up a privileged theme of the antifascist work of Malraux, Bernanos, and others. When ''Le Mur'' was turned into a film in 1967, Sartre saw this theme—''the horror of death inflicted on man by man''—as the aspect of the story with the greatest continuing political relevance.

The fate of young Juan is also the anecdotal point of departure for the story. Sartre had been asked by a former student who had experienced some problems in his personal life (de Beauvoir identifies him as Jacques-Laurent Bost) to arrange with Malraux for his passage to Spain as a volunteer. Although Malraux ultimately resolved the situation with great good sense by convincing the young man that he would be less than useless to the Spanish army until he learned how to handle a weapon, Sartre had found himself torn between his commitment to the Spanish Republican cause and his fear for the student's fate: ''I was very disturbed because, on the one hand, I felt he didn't have sufficient military or even biological preparation to survive the bad times and, on the other hand, I couldn't deny a man the right to fight.'' Sartre's meditation on the possible reactions to the situations the young man might have to confront gave birth to ''Le Mur,'' which, Sartre claims, is not at all the philosophical study of the absurd that many readers have seen in it but simply a meditation on death.

Whichever of these definitions of the main theme the reader finds more appropriate, it is obvious that Sartre's central concern goes far beyond the Spanish Civil War, which serves as its point of departure. Sartre's first works of fiction, like those of the writers who share his existentialist outlook (for example, Malraux's *Les Conquerants* and *La Voie royale*, Camus's *L'Etranger*), begin by confronting the fundamental problem of human mortality. Only when human life is measured against the fact of its inevitable finitude can its real meaning be considered. Such a confrontation with death can take place only in a situation where the protagonist finds himself condemned—by illness (Garine in *Les Conquerants*), by a mortal wound (Perken in *La Voie royale*) or by a death sentence imposed by other men (Meursault in *L'Etranger* and Pablo in ''Le Mur''). The progressive dissolution of all those elements that have seemed to provide life's mean-

ing is in ''Le Mur,'' as in Sartre's previous fictional work, *La Nausee*, an introduction to the absurd.

During the night on which Pablo awaits his execution, he devotes every mental faculty to the effort of understanding the idea of death, but it remains beyond his grasp. As his companion Tom says: ''On a tout le temps l'impression que ca y est, qu'on va comprendre et puis ca glisse, ca vous echappe et ca retombe. Je me dis: apres, il n'y aura plus rien. Mais je ne comprends pas ce que ca veut dire'' [you always have the impression that it's all right, that you're going to understand and then it slips, it escapes you and fades away. I tell myself there will be nothing afterwards. But I don't understand what it means]. A consciousness cannot imagine its ceasing to be conscious.

In the course of the night Pablo becomes alienated from his physical body, which, he realizes, is separate from his consciousness of it: ''Il suait et tremblait tout seul, et je ne le reconnaissais plus. J'etais oblige de le toucher et de le regarder pour savoir ce qu'il devenait, comme si c'avait ete le corps d'un autre'' [it sweated and trembled by itself and I didn't recognize it any more. I had to touch it and look at it to find out what was happening, as if it were the body of someone else]. In a characteristically Sartrean image, he sees himself as attached to a ''vermine enorme'' [an enormous vermin]. As he is alienated from his own physical reality, he is even further removed from the physical presence of the others who share his cell, none of whom he finds particularly sympathetic. He is, however, forced to recognize the extent to which the other bodies—described in terms of excretory odors, sweat, and soft flab— nevertheless resemble his own, and he sees that his own anguish is experienced in similar fashion by his companion: ''Nous etions pareils et pires que des miroirs l'un pour l'autre'' [We were alike and worse than mirrors of each other]. This realization of a shared human condition does not therefore create a Malrucian fraternity; it simply makes Tom's presence even more intolerable and increases Pablo's feeling of solitude.

The confrontation with death forces Pablo to regard his past life in a new light. He marvels at his ability to have taken his activities seriously, but he did so because he lived as though he were eternal; now that he has definitively lost this illusion of eternity, nothing retains its former importance. He becomes progressively indifferent to his happy memories, to his love for his mistress, Concha, to his political ideals, and even to his friendship with

Ramon Gris—in order to protect whom he is nevertheless about to die. Even his spontaneous emotions of resentment toward the Belgian doctor, who provides a graphic illustration of the hostile presence of the Other, are submerged by an overwhelming feeling of indifference.

The story ends with a clever Sartrean twist, which seems to underline the notion of the fundamental meaninglessness of life. After his two companions have been taken off to be shot, Pablo is once again questioned about the whereabouts of his friend Ramon. In the light of his newfound perception of the absurdity of existence, the seriousness with which his captors take their political activity appears ridiculous: ''Leurs petites activites me paraissaient choquantes et burlesques; je n'arrivais plus a me mettre a leur place, il me semblait qu'ils etaient fous'' [Their little activities seemed shocking and burlesque to me; I couldn't put myself in their place, I thought they were insane]. He can only imagine them as future corpses: ''Ces deux types chamarres avec leurs cravaches et leurs bottes, c'etaient tout de meme des hommes qui allaient mourir. Un peu plus tard que moi, mais pas beaucoup plus'' [These men dolled up with their riding crops and boots were still going to die. A little later than I, but not too much]. He even tells one of the Falangists to shave off his mustache: ''Je trouvais drole qu'il laissat de son vivant les poils envahir sa figure'' [I thought it funny that he would let hair invade his face while he was still alive]. Overcome by the feeling that all this is a giant farce, Pablo cannot resist making fun of the overly serious Falangists by sending them off on a wild goose chase to a cemetery he knows is far from his friend's actual whereabouts. As chance would have it, Ramon Gris has, in the meantime, changed his hiding place, and he is shot by the Falangists in precisely the spot Pablo had indicated.

While many readers have interpreted this ending as a striking evidence of the absurdity of life, Sartre—at least the Sartre of thirty years later—sees Pablo's act and its consequences quite differently: ''He tries to react by an individual action because he thinks it's a farce. It is because he tries to play with forces he does not understand that he lets loose against himself the forces of the absurd. It is not the result of an absurd 'destiny' that drags men along. . . . It is the result of inadequate knowledge . . . about the real actions to take. He has obtained this result through a childish act.'' Whether or not the conclusion is a new revelation of the absurd, it fails to add a positive dimension to Pablo's experience. Since the

story is a first-person narrative written in the past tense (the *passe simple*), it is clear that the narrator has continued to live. Sartre does not feel called upon to explain how he has managed to construct a life on the basis of the devastating philosophical conclusions to which the experience described has led him.

Strangely enough, Malraux creates a strikingly similar situation in *L'Espoir*, featuring a minor character named Moreno, who is a friend of the doomed liberal, Hernandez. Almost on the eve of the Toledo debacle, Moreno and Hernandez spend an evening together in a Toledo cafe. Moreno, a Marxist army officer who had been captured and condemned to death by the Falangists in the first days of the war, has just managed to escape. Like Sartre's Pablo, he finds his experience has profoundly altered his outlook on life, totally obliterating his former ideals: '''Je ne crois plus a rien de ce a quoi j'ai cru,' dit Moreno, 'a rien''' [''I no longer believe in all I used to believe,'' Moreno said. ''I believe in nothing now'']. His long imprisonment under sentence of death has taught him about the finality of death. Hernandez later reiterates this understanding in classic Malrucian terminology, in a phrase that Sartre, too, would take to quoting: ''La tragedie de la mort est en ceci qu'elle transforme la vie en destin, qu'a partir d'elle rien ne peut plus etre compense'' [The tragedy of death is that it transforms life into destiny, that from then on nothing can be compensated for (translation mine)]. The image that Moreno retains from his imprisonment is the sound of clinking pennies (''sous''), which had echoed through his prison, as each prisoner had wagered on his chances of survival. The coins evidence the arbitrary nature of human existence and point to the vanity of human effort, which can at any moment be annihilated by death. Thus, like Pablo on his liberation, Moreno sees the frenetic activity of the Toledo soldiers as a vain *comedie*.

Hernandez, however, as disillusioned as he has become, cannot accept this nihilistic vision. Although human progress has proven itself to be slow and painful, he feels there are still some positive results: ''On attend tout de la liberte, tout de suite, et il faut beaucoup de morts pour faire avancer l'homme d'un centimetre. . . . Et quand meme le monde a change depuis Charles Quint. Parce que les hommes ont voulu qu'il change, malgre les sous—peut-etre en n'ignorant pas que les sous existent quelque part'' [one expects everything all at once from 'freedom,' but for man to progress a bare half inch a great many men must die. . . . Yet the world has moved on since then [the time of Charles the Fifth]. Because men wanted it to move on, despite the pennies—perhaps even with full awareness that those pennies were waiting for them in the background.]. Hernandez sets in opposition to Moreno's vision of meaninglessness the meaning inherent in the fraternal effort of the Toledo militias. His statements take on deeper resonance as they are borne out by the scenes in the final section of the novel, where the long, painful struggle of the Spanish peasants sums up the efforts of "triumphant human will." Malraux in *L'Espoir* cannot allow Moreno's nihilism to remain unchallenged.

When Hernandez himself is about to be executed, he thinks of Moreno's experience, and he, too, feels a sensation of absurdity before his Falangist interrogators, a sensation quite similar to that felt by Pablo: "Que les vivants employaient leur temps a des choses absurdes"[How living people waste time over futilities!]. Like Pablo, he begins to see everyone around him as a future corpse: "Quand l'homme serait mort, le cou serait plus long. Et il mourrait tout comme un autre" [the long neck which would look still longer when the man was dead. And he'd die the usual sort of death.]. Also like Pablo, he must witness the condemnation of an innocent man who struggles against his fate, in this case a streetcar conductor whose jacket, worn shiny at the shoulder by the strap of his money pouch, leads the Falangists to believe that he has been carrying a rifle. Unlike Sartre's Juan, however, Malraux's conductor dies bravely, raising his fist in the Republican salute as he is about to be executed and inspiring others to do the same. The execution scene, which Hernandez at first perceives as absurd, takes on a new seriousness as the humble little man with his raised fist defies his executioners and comes to embody the force of humanity defying its destiny: "Il est enfonce dans son innocence comme un pieu dans la terre, il les regarde avec une haine pesante et absolue qui est deja de l'autre monde" [The little man gazed at them, stolid in his innocence as a stake rooted in the soil, and gave them a look of undying, elemental hatred that had already something of the other world in its intensity].

Moreno, too, survives his despair and goes on to find a new meaning in life. Reappearing in a Madrid cafe in the midst of the bombing, he sums up the hopeless determination of the soldiers and people of Madrid, who pursue their effort in the face of death and defeat. Like the aviator Scali, he has discovered the fraternity of men who have accepted the fact of their death in combat: "Il y a une fraternite qui ne se trouve que de l'autre cote de la mort" [There's a fraternity which is only to be found—beyond the grave]. Moving beyond solitude and beyond the absurdity of the human condition, he has found that new values can emerge from despair.

In "Le Mur," Sartre's Pablo does not go beyond his vivid perception of life's absurdity in the way that the characters in Malraux's later novels are almost all able to do. Surprisingly, however, when in 1940 he was faced with an experience of defeat and imprisonment in his own life, Sartre himself was immediately able to rise to the occasion. As a prisoner of war, he had his first experience with the direct communication of the theater when he wrote an optimistic Christmas play for his fellow prisoners. And he soon returned to Paris full of determination to participate in the Resistance—at a time when most Frenchmen were still despairing over the invasion. In an exchange of roles impossible to predict on the basis of their 1937 Spanish Civil War fiction, an enthusiastic Sartre was in 1941 trying to convince a recalcitrant Malraux of the necessity of creating a writers' resistance network. The lesson Sartre had learned from his own experience in a fascist prison was formulated by the protagonist of his Resistance play *Le Mouches*: "La vie humaine commence de l'autre cote du desespoir"[Human life begins on the far side of despair]. It comes very close to the last statement of Malraux's Moreno. The Spanish Civil War confronted Malraux and Sartre in different ways and at different moments in their personal trajectories. Thus despite the evident similarity of their concerns, they tend to draw different philosophical conclusions from it.

Source: Mary Jean Green, "The Fiction of the Spanish Civil War: 'Le Mur,'" in *Fiction in the Historical Present: French Writers and the Thirties*, University Press of New England, 1986, pp. 243-51.

Kevin W. Sweeney

In the essay below, Sweeny finds "The Wall" more than just a story about fear and death; he asserts that the story "needs to be seen as a developed, philosophical argument."

Despite the lingering "old quarrel between philosophy and poetry" over the suitability of presenting a philosophical investigation in literary form (Plato's *Republic* 607 B), philosophers regularly use literary genres to present their ideas. Jean-Paul Sartre's short story "The Wall" is an example of such a philosophical project. In the story Sartre offers a counter-example to one of Husserl's views and an illustration supporting his own alternative position. Sartre's particular project is easy to overlook given the vivid, extended descriptions of the central characters' terrified reactions to the prospect of their execution. Critics routinely interpret the story as a phenomenological account of the emotional state of terror in the face of death. They refer to ''The Wall'' as a story whose ''real subject is fear,'' and as a ''classic treatment of the central existentialist motif of confrontation with death'' which closes with an ''O. Henry'' ending. As I will argue, however, ''The Wall'' needs to be seen as a developed, philosophical argument.

The philosophical character of the story stands out more clearly if close attention is paid to the integrity of the work's four-part structure. In the first section Sartre sets out the central ethical issue; the second section contrasts the protagonist's actions with those of his two companions; the third shows the predicament that results from those actions; finally, the fourth section reveals the consequences of the protagonist's choice and draws a conclusion. If one were to concentrate primarily on the anguished behavior of the main characters, the integrity of the structure might go unobserved. The ending would most likely be seen as a literary device for reducing the tension built up by the prisoners' terror in the middle sections, rather than a resolution of the themes of commitment and psychological escape on which Sartre bases his criticism of Husserl.

The integrity of the story's structure and the story's identity as a philosophical enterprise are more clearly visible if one realizes that Sartre has used some examples from Kant's essay, ''On A Supposed Right To Lie From Altruistic Motives.'' Seen in the context of Kant's examples, instances of lying in ''The Wall''—both to others (the theme of commitment) and to self (psychological escape and self-deception)—are foregrounded and show the development of Sartre's thesis.

Kant's essay is a reply to an attack by Benjamin Constant on his position that one has a duty always to tell the truth. In criticizing Kant's position, Constant poses the following situation of moral choice. (Situations of this general sort I will refer to as ''Constant situations.'') You are entertaining a friend in your home. A murderer intent on killing this friend comes to the door and asks you whether or not the friend is there, threatening to kill him. On the assumption that the murderer forces you either to lie

> **" In telling the soldiers to go to the cemetery he has acted in ignorance and has blundered like the unsuspecting animal he most dreaded becoming. Pablo's laugh/cry is an acknowledgment of his failure and, given Sartre's view on the cognitive character of emotions, a sign of awareness of his self-deception."**

or tell the truth, what ought you to do? Constant argues that anyone in such a position has the right to lie to the murderer. The murderer has no right to the truth; hence, one has no duty to reveal where the friend is. Constant chides Kant that his prohibition against lying would require one to tell the murderer the truth, a consequence of the position Constant finds ethically outrageous.

In the opening section of ''The Wall'' Sartre introduces this same general form of moral predicament—a Constant situation. Set during the Spanish Civil War, the story opens with Pablo Ibbieta, the protagonist and narrator, and two other men (young Juan Mirbal and Tom Steinbock, a volunteer in the International Brigade) being brought before a Falangist military tribunal. They face charges of complicity with the Republican side, an offense punishable by death. The last of the three to face the four-man court, Pablo is asked:

''Where's Ramon Gris?''

''I don't know.''

''You hid him in your house from the 6th to the 19th.'' ''No.''

Ramon Gris is Pablo's friend and, as Pablo later admits, an asset to the Republican cause. Although he denies knowing where Gris is, Pablo is lying. Later, in the third section, he reveals: ''Of course I knew where Gris was; he was hiding with his cousins four kilometers from the city.'' Pablo lies to the court from an altruistic motive. Knowing that the Falangists want Gris' life, he lies to protect his friend and political ally.

It is not apparent to the reader at this point of the story that Pablo is lying. The narrator says neither whether Pablo is lying or telling the truth; nor does he indicate what Pablo's motives are in answering the questions. This lack of narratorial context is augmented by the judges who neither challenge nor react to what Pablo tells them.

The ambiguity of Pablo's exchange is contrasted with Tom's straightforward trial. The International Brigade volunteer faces the court fully aware that the judges know both who he is and what his role in the fighting has been. ''They asked Tom,'' Pablo relates, ''if it were true he was in the International Brigade; Tom couldn't tell them otherwise because of the papers they found in his coat.'' As the narrator implies, Tom is in no position to bluff his way free. He tells the truth, knowing that the court has found his identity papers. This narrator-supplied confirmation of veracity is lacking in Pablo's case.

Juan's situation is different from that of Tom's truthful reply and Pablo's prevarication. Juan believes that his being brought before the tribunal is a mistake. He believes that the soldiers have confused him with his brother Jose. ''My brother Jose is the anarchist,'' he pleads, ''you know he isn't here any more. I don't belong to any party. I never had anything to do with politics. . . . I haven't done anything. I don't want to pay for someone else.'' All he needs do, he believes, is to tell the soldiers of their mistake. Unlike Pablo he is quite willing to inform on the person for whom he believes the soldiers are looking. Nevertheless, Juan's pleading is to no avail. The reader later learns that the Falangists have sentenced him to death even though as Tom says, they ''don't have a thing against him.''

Led to a cell, the three prisoners learn that they have been sentenced to be executed the next morning. This common sentence and the short and indifferent treatment by the tribunal tend to blur the differences among the three prisoners' behavior. In the second section the similar symptoms of terror exhibited by the men also create the impression of a certain uniformity. And it is this similarity which is responsible for the view that ''The Wall'' is concerned with the common physiological and psycho-

logical responses to a terrifying event. But the main concern of the story is not to dramatize terror. Rather, Sartre analyzes each character's moral choice in response to his predicament. He presents three different models of how individuals choose to confront an extreme situation.

Sartre offers a preview of these moral choices in the different ways that each of the men reacts to the court in the first section. In the next section each of the three men takes an attitude toward his death much like the one he adopts toward the court. Tom eventually confronts the fact of his approaching death, just as he recognized that he could not bluff his way out of the tribunal's charge; Juan, believing that the court has mistaken him for his brother, continues to deny his fate; and Pablo pursues a strategy of deceiving himself just as he sought to deceive the tribunal. Tom is the model of acceptance; Juan of rejection; and Pablo, the curious combination of both acceptance and denial, is the model of self-deception. Of the three prisoners Pablo receives Sartre's major attention. The other two characters serve to put Pablo's situation in perspective, and after so doing, at the end of the second section, they are eliminated.

In the second section of ''The Wall'' the psychological condition of the prisoners is presented and developed so as to provide the necessary context for assessing their moral attitudes and choices. Sartre wishes to set out the psychological conditions under which Tom, Juan and Pablo act, as well as to show in what sense the prisoners' behavior is peculiarly moral. To see what philosophical values Sartre attaches to their respective actions and attitudes, it will be helpful to analyze the prisoners's behavior in terms of his contemporary philosophical works. In ''The Transcendence of the Ego'' (1936) and *The Emotions* (1939) Sartre not only develops his own theories on the emotions and consciousness, but also criticizes Husserl's position on transcendental subjectivity. These same topics appear in ''The Wall.''

Spending the night in the cell, a coal cellar of a former hospital, awaiting execution, all three men exhibit similar symptoms of terror, appearing ''alike and worse than mirrors of each other.'' A Belgian doctor spends the night in their cell recording their ''almost pathological state of terror.'' He notes their chills and tremblings, their facial distortions and gray coloring, the profuse sweating, the involuntary urinating, and the despondent lethargy alternating with violent reactions to slight irritations.

Although such emotional responses might seem to be merely involuntary reactions, Sartre in *The Emotions* urges a theory according to which such emotional behavior indicates the presence of a conscious, cognitive attitude. Sartre claims that an emotion is ''a certain way of apprehending the world.'' Rather than being merely an affective state, an emotion is a form of consciousness, one frequently unreflective, whose purpose is to bring about a ''transformation of the world.'' Sartre describes this transformational character of emotion in the following passage: ''When the paths traced out become too difficult, or when we see no path, we can no longer live in so urgent and difficult a world. All the ways are barred. However, we must act. So we try to change the world, that is, to live as if the connection between things and their potentialities were not ruled by deterministic processes, but by magic. Let it be clearly understood that this is not a game; we are *driven against a wall*, and we throw ourselves into this new attitude with all the strength we can muster'' (emphasis mine). When a person, is driven against a ''wall,'' his fear is a magical attempt to alter the predicament confronting him. In emotional behavior, one consciously—although one may not reflectively be aware of so doing—acknowledges and transforms the relationship between consciousness and the threatening situation. One of Sartre's examples of such an emotion is the fear exhibited by someone who faints when charged by a ferocious beast. Certainly fainting is not an effective way of eluding the danger; yet it is, says Sartre, ''a behavior of escape.'' With the magical act of fainting the person eliminates the dangerous beast ''by eliminating consciousness.'' In summarizing his view, Sartre states, ''the true meaning of fear is apparent: it is a consciousness which, through magical behavior, aims at denying an object of the external world, and which will go so far as to annihilate itself in order to annihilate the object with it.''

Seen in the context of Sartre's theory of emotions, the prisoners' terror is indicative of a consciousness of their predicament. Yet, despite their similar display of terror, each prisoner adopts a different magical attitude toward his execution. Juan takes up a number of magical defensive postures. At first he moralizes about the injustice of his sentence and in so doing denies the prospect of its being carried out. Confronted with the death sentence, he exclaims: ''That's not possible . . . I didn't do anything.'' He cannot be in mortal peril, he is convinced, since he refuses to accept that he is the

one the soldiers want. Yet the ''misunderstanding'' continues, and gradually Juan becomes absorbed in self-pity. ''I could see,'' says Pablo, ''he was pitying himself; he wasn't thinking about death.'' The posture of self-pity alternates with ''a terrible fear of suffering.'' By focusing on the pain, he avoids confronting the thought of his extinction. If the execution will be painful, at least one has to be alive to suffer from the bullets. Dreading the pain of the bullets is less terrifying than facing the thought of not existing at all.

In all of Juan's ways of magically dealing with death Pablo notices that he ''made more noise than we did, but he was less touched: he was like a sick man who defends himself against his illness by fever. It's much more serious when there isn't any fever.'' Juan's final defense and ''escape'' is to collapse in terror on being taken from the cell to face the firing squad.

Unlike Juan, who denies any political allegiance, Tom accepts responsibility for his role in the fighting, telling Pablo that he has ''knocked off six [of the enemy] since the beginning of August.'' His first reaction to the prospect of dying is to talk, conversation being a way to avoid thinking about death. Pablo sees that ''he didn't realize the situation and I could tell he didn't *want* to realize it.'' Yet his bodily reactions belie this tactic of avoidance. He then tries calisthenics and the comforting of Juan as ways to avoid the thought of dying. Ultimately, however, these ploys fail and the thought of his death becomes inescapable. Yet he makes a last effort to distance himself from the thought of dying. His death, he blurts out to Pablo, is incomprehensible: ''Something is going to happen to us that I can't understand. . . . I see my corpse; that's not hard but *I'm* the one who sees it with *my* eyes. I've got to think . . . think that I won't see anything anymore and the world will go on for the others. We aren't made to think that, Pablo.'' Tom's implicit argument is that one cannot imagine oneself being dead since imagining oneself dead requires an inconsistent state of affairs: someone at the same time both actively imagining something and being the inanimate object of the imaginative activity. The argument, however, is specious. It takes a distorted view of the activity of imagining; it conflates the subject of the activity with the imaginary, mental object, and it runs together the present time of the act with the future time of the imagined event.

That Tom is using a specious argument to escape considering his imminent death is suggested by an event that occurs later that night. Pablo notices that Tom "had begun to stare at the bench with a sort of smile, he looked amazed. He put out his hand and touched the wood cautiously as if he were afraid of breaking something, then drew back his hand quickly and shuddered . . . It was *his* death which Tom had just touched on the bench." This glimmering of awareness of his own mortal condition, this coming to terms with his own fate, places Tom in a sympathetic light. Of the three prisoners, he seems, from Sartre's point of view, to be the most authentic: struggling with his fear, accepting responsibility for his past, and confronting the prospect of his death as best he can.

Pablo, on the other hand, takes quite a different attitude toward his extinction. He sets himself the project of disassociating himself from all ties to his past (his memories, values, and attachments) in order, as he says, "to die cleanly." Yet despite this disassociation, Pablo still maintains some ties to his former way of life. At the time of his trial Pablo accepts his Anarchist past; he tenaciously guards the secret of Gris's hiding place. Unlike Juan, he accepts the connection between his sentence and his former life. His continuing to maintain the secret of Gris's whereabouts is evidence that he has not abandoned all his past allegiances. Thus with his decision to disassociate himself from all that has taken place there arises a bifurcation in his character: he both acknowledges his past and denies it.

The project of disassociation is brought on by his facing "the wall" of approaching death. As Sartre would have it, Pablo's project is an instance of magical behavior. In reminiscing about his past, he disparagingly notes his previous tendency to take "everything as seriously as if I were immortal. . . . I had spent my time counterfeiting eternity. I had understood nothing." He had lived, he muses, without fully realizing his mortal condition. His lack of understanding blinds him to his commitments and makes his former way of life seem futile. With his terror he has transformed the positive attachment he had felt toward his former way of life into one of nihilistic rejection. In his emotional state he has changed his relationship to himself and the world he lives in. One can see this in the attitude he takes toward Concha, the woman he loves. "Last night," he says to himself, "I would have given an arm to see her again for five minutes. . . . Now I had no more desire to see her, I had nothing to say to her." Disillusioned, he comments about his life: "'It's a damned lie.' It was worth nothing because it was finished. . . . death has disenchanted everything."

Pablo's calling his past life a "lie" is significant. He thinks that he has deceived himself by his past unsuspecting attitude toward his pleasures, projects and goals. His rejection of his past marks a split for him between what he sees as his former, deceptive life and a present, more honest, conscious self. That he might again be deceiving himself with his project of disengagement does not enter his mind.

Pablo's project of separating himself from his past is an emotional remedy for the anguish he feels in anticipating the firing squad. If he can face death free of his past, he will, he thinks, be free from the terror he feels so acutely. He says: "I clung to nothing, in a way I was calm." He is also motivated by his desire to be fully conscious of all his remaining moments of life, especially the moment of execution. By separating himself from his past attitudes and values, he will then be able to face the firing squad fully conscious, rather than unexpectedly suffering his death like a slaughtered animal. He does not want to be groggy with sleep and oblivious to what is happening to him: "I didn't want to die like an animal, I wanted to understand."

Pablo's desire for understanding is quite a different project from Tom's quest for understanding *qua* comprehension. For Pablo, to understand is to be aware and to realize the significance of all that takes place around him. His desire for understanding and for separation from his past express themselves in his taking an attitude similar in important respects to the Husserlian *epoche*. Although he has no philosophical motive behind his project, Pablo does believe that only if he adopts the attitude of a pure observing ego will he be able to witness what happens to him objectively. In taking such a stance he believes that he will no longer perceive his surroundings in his former, natural way, colored by his emotional associations, but will instead observe them with objectivity.

The resemblance between Pablo's disengaged understanding and the Husserlian project of *epoche* is intended to make a point similar to the one Sartre makes in "The Transcendence of the Ego." In that work, Sartre takes issue with Husserl's position that conscious experience requires the existence of a transcendental subject "behind" consciousness. Husserl's argument for transcendental subjectivity depends upon the phenomenological technique of *epoche* —the bracketing or setting aside of one's natural attitude toward the existence of things in the world so as to reduce the objects of one's experience to a presentation of phenomena. This reduction, according to Husserl, allows one to perceive the world objectively. Given this objective, reduced state of the world of experience, Husserl reasons that in order for consciousness to be able to perceive the various phenomena as unified objects, there must be a unifying agent in consciousness which makes possible one's perception of ordinary things in the world. This unifying agent Husserl identifies with a transcendental subject.

Sartre rejects both Husserl's derivation of a transcendental ego and the role *epoche* plays in the derivation. Rather than being *transcendental* (an active, conscious subject manipulating immediate experience into a world), the ego, Sartre holds, is only *transcendent* (an entity not identical with a particular phenomenon but known from a number of phenomena). The ego, Sartre says, ''is the spontaneous transcendent unification of our states and our actions.'' In being transcendent the ego is like any other object in the world that has an existence independent of immediate experience. By holding there to be a transcendental ego, Husserl, according to Sartre, conflates consciousness with the subject of experience. His mistake is in identifying the conscious subject with an object having the power to unify experience. The transcendent character of the world, not any transcendental, conscious subject, ensures the unity of the things we experience.

Husserl employs the *epoche* in order to separate the subject of consciousness from the world of experience, thereby isolating the subject so as to show its transcendental nature. Repudiating Husserl's theory, Sartre holds that the ego exists in the world and cannot extricate itself. There are various ways of perceiving the world but none of them separates the self from the world, however much one might be convinced that such a separation is possible. Sartre says of Husserl's view of the ego: ''Unfortunately, as long as the I remains a structure of absolute consciousness, one will still be able to reproach phenomenology for being an escapist doctrine, for again pulling a part of man out of the world and, in that way, turning our attention from the real problems.'' Husserl's account of *epoche*, Sartre holds, is actually an escapist theory.

Sartre claims that in his theory of *epoche*, Husserl has also misdescribed an extraordinary, but actual, project of consciousness. There is something like what Husserl labels an ''*epoche*,'' but as a project bent on separating consciousness from the world of its predicament it is doomed to failure. Far from being ''an intellectual method, an erudite

procedure,'' Sartre views the project of *epoche* as induced by ''an anxiety which is imposed on us and which we cannot avoid.''

In ''The Wall'' Sartre puts forward an account of how such a project of disengagement might come about and the possible consequences of such a futile attempt to separate oneself from the world. In the guise of Pablo's project of ''staying clean,'' Husserl's *epoche* is presented and reworked so that instead of being part of a philosophical method it is a magical project consciously undertaken in order to deal with a predicament.

Pablo's attempt at disengagement is made to seem credible by devices in the story that encourage the reader to distinguish Pablo in his role as protagonist from his role as narrator. Certain information that the narrator reports is information to which Pablo the prisoner does not have access. Tom, we are told, touches ''his death'' on the bench, yet he never tells Pablo about this experience. All that occurs in the story is presented from Pablo's point of view—but it is a variable point of view. At times, as in his observations about Tom and Juan, Pablo seems omniscient; at other times, especially when he reflects about himself, he is ignorant or fallible. For example, he says about himself: ''Only I would have liked to understand the reasons for my conduct.'' Pablo's lack of self-knowledge alternating with his acute insight into others' characters tends to divide Pablo as narrator from Pablo the prisoner. That the tale should be told from the point of view of one whom—until the end of the story—the reader believes to be doomed, also encourages this division. Thus, Pablo's status as both narrator and condemned prisoner lends credence to his project of disengaging himself as conscious subject (a role compatible with being an omniscient observer) from his past identity (the role responsible for his being the condemned man).

His project of disengagement is frustrated, however, by a tie that he cannot sever. Remarking on the calm that sets in after he has adopted his attitude of *epoche*, he says: ''But it was a horrible calm—because of my body; my body, I saw with its eyes, I heard with its ears, but it was no longer me, it sweated and trembled by itself and I didn't recognize it anymore.'' His description of the ''horrible calm'' he feels is faintly reminiscent of Tom's voicing his incomprehensibility of his death. However, whereas Tom balked at imagining his body not being animate, Pablo is aghast that his body exists and behaves independently of his conscious ego.

The involuntary reactions of his body infringe on the detached integrity of his consciousness, and he rejects his body as an integral part of his being. Yet the tie still holds between his conscious self and what he considers a bothersome attachment. ''Everything that came from my body,'' he says, ''was all cockeyed. Most of the time it was quiet and I felt no more than a sort of weight, a filthy presence against me; I had the impression of being tied to an enormous vermin.'' His body is something from which he cannot escape. He can try to banish his emotional attachments and his values, and he can steel himself so that on seeing Juan weep he will be able to resist pitying himself and others, but he cannot break free from his body. The existence of his body as a constituent of his being is something that in his *epoche* he cannot deny, however much he struggles to achieve an independence from its effects on his state of mind.

In his desire for understanding, Pablo has ignored what for Sartre is a natural source of understanding—his emotions. Immediate awareness is not the only mode of consciousness: Emotion, he says, ''is a mode of existence of consciousness, one of the ways in which it *understands* (in the Heideggerian sense of *Verstehen*) its 'being-in-the-world'.'' In rejecting the terrified responses of his body, Pablo rejects the tie that holds him to his predicament; but in so doing he also rejects a form of understanding. He has deceived himself as to the true nature of his project. His desire is not for dispassionate understanding or awareness; it is for escape.

In the second section Sartre has presented three ways in which an individual might deal with ''a wall'' against which he has been driven. According to Sartre's theory of emotions such actions are conscious and take on the character of moral attitudes for which the agent is responsible. For Tom and Juan the moral implications of their decisions are clear: Tom deals authentically with his fate, whereas Juan by collapsing seeks to abandon responsibility for his actions. But in Pablo's project of disengagement Sartre presents the interesting situation of one who both accepts and denies his predicament. Yet it is not clear at the end of the second section what the moral implications of his actions are. The reader is still not certain that Pablo has lied to the Falangists, although enough about his past is presented to suggest it.

When dawn finally comes, Tom and Juan are taken out to be shot. Pablo, however, is once more interrogated by the soldiers about Gris. He now realizes that the night he spent in the coal cellar has been psychological torture bent on breaking his will and forcing him to reveal where Gris is. Seeing through his captors' ''shocking and burlesqued'' behavior, he says: ''I almost felt like laughing. It takes a lot to intimidate a man who is going to die. . . .'' The soldiers offer Pablo his life in exchange for his telling them where Gris is hiding. But Pablo continues to lie, insisting that he does not know where Gris is. The offer of his life for information about Gris is a shift in the basic Constant situation confronting Pablo. Instead of simply having the predicament of choosing to lie or tell the truth, he now has the choice of his life for Gris's.

Locked in a laundry room to consider the Falangist's offer, Pablo ponders his refusal to inform on his friend. Given his project of detachment his allegiance to Gris should be something that he abandons just as he professes to abandon his tie to Concha. His resistance to telling the soldiers what they want to know puzzles him. He questions himself: ''Only I would have liked to understand the reasons for my conduct. I would rather die than give up Gris. Why? I didn't like Ramon Gris any more. My friendship for him had died a little while before dawn at the same time as my love for Concha, at the same time as my desire to live.'' Pablo attempts to explain his resistance to inform on Gris as being due to obstinacy. Yet this is rather lame conjecture. The thought of being obstinate pops into his mind; he accepts it as if he could make himself have whatever motives he imagines. His off-hand way of arriving at this explanation casts suspicion on its being some deep insight. His puzzlement as to his motive contrasts sharply with his perspicacious seeing through his captors' schemes and his understanding of his companions' emotional responses.

Initially the reader might suppose that Pablo is correct in his judgment, given his past success in perceiving others' motives and plans. But in so doing the reader would be taken in by the narrator's authoritative point of view. Pablo is not infallible; later in the story his sense of understanding will be severely challenged. His deliberations should be seen as an attempt to reconcile a conflict between his misconstrued project of escape and his commitment to Gris. Since he cannot ''stay clean'' and at the same time preserve this commitment, he achieves a self-serving consistency by deceiving himself into believing that his loyalty is actually stubbornness. His explanation provides a motive which is consistent with his ''staying clean,'' since he views his obstinacy as a spontaneous quirk rather than as the expression of an established character trait.

The soldiers return in a while. Convinced that he is "clean," Pablo fancies the soldiers as so many players in a farce. He responds to their questions by inventing a scenario for himself and the soldiers to act out. He tells them that Gris is hiding in the cemetery. He wants to get the soldiers to search the cemetery and make fools of themselves. "I represented," he says, "the situation to myself as if I had been someone else: This prisoner obstinately playing the hero, these grim falangistas with their moustaches and their men in uniform running among the graves; it was irresistibly funny." What Pablo tells the soldiers is as much a lie as his previous disclaimer about Gris's hiding place. Not believing Gris to be in the cemetery, he gleefully anticipates the satisfaction he will receive from their futile expedition.

As if responding to his cue, the soldiers set off for the cemetery. Prepared for his imminent execution, Pablo waits the soldiers' return, gloating over his imagined victory. But when the soldiers do return, no execution order is given. Instead, he is sent out into the hospital yard to join some other prisoners. Disoriented by such an unexpected turn of events, he wanders around the yard in a daze. While earlier he had struggled to maintain a clarity of mind, he is now confused and oblivious to his surroundings. He does not understand why he has been spared and does not realize (until the baker Garcia tells him) that the soldiers have found Gris in the cemetery—precisely where he told them to look. Pablo's project of understanding has come crashing down. He had undertaken the task of detaching himself from the impinging world of his expected execution in order to perceive and understand all that took place around him during his last hours alive. He had felt confident in his detachment. Although he had taken, as he says, a "malicious" delight in sending the soldiers off on what he believed was a futile expedition, his detachment was preserved by his imagining the situation as if he had been "someone else." Confronting his captors, he had endeavored to maintain the removed stance of the "transcendental" observer and manipulator of events. Yet with his reprieve, he is thrown into confusion, his "transcendental" project exploded.

With the soldiers finding Gris in the cemetery, Sartre has introduced an elaboration on the Constant situation. This sort of situation is presented and discussed by Kant in his essay. There he presents the following example, intending to show that one can be held culpable if one lies in a Constant situation. I refer to the example as "K-1": "But if you had lied, and said he was not at home when he had really gone out without your knowing it, and if the murderer had then met him as he went away and murdered him, you might justly be accused as the cause of his death."

As a situation in which the decision-maker is claimed to be responsible for the friend's death, Kant's example highlights Sartre's similar assessment of Pablo's actions. In comparing K-1 to the situation of Gris's capture, it is well to keep in mind that the decision-maker in K-1 and Pablo both lie. Even though Pablo and the decision-maker say what happens to be true, both believe what they say to be false and both intend what they say to deceive their inquisitors. In K-1 it is due to what the decision-maker says that the murderer finds his victim. This connection needs to be stressed in order for the congruence of the two situations to be seen.

If in a purported K-1 situation there is at most a tenuous or non-existent connection between what the decision-maker says and the murderer's finding his victim, then one has a different moral situation. Such a similar sort of situation is assumed by Garcia the baker in his account of how the soldiers found Gris. I will refer to this variation on K-1 as a "Garcia situation." In a Garcia situation nothing that the decision-maker says is causally responsible for the murderer finding the friend. The murderer stumbles on him by chance, or because he happens to look in a place (e.g. a cemetery) that is a likely hiding place. According to Garcia, that the soldiers found Gris is entirely his own fault; Gris chose to hide in the cemetery. "Of course," Garcia says [they "the soldiers] went by there this morning, that was sure to happen." In the Garcia situation, Sartre offers a case in which the decision-maker is not responsible for the death; it is a case that contrasts with the one in which Pablo plays a role and for which he is in Sartre's view morally responsible.

Kant uses his example to argue that if one departs from the duty always to tell the truth one can be held responsible for unforeseeable consequences of one's actions. He states in the article: "Therefore, whoever tells a lie, however well intentioned he might be, must answer for the consequences, however unforeseeable they were. . . ." While Sartre neither shared Kant's view on truth telling, nor subscribes to Kant's de-ontological ethical system, he is interested in the issue of responsibility for one's actions, responsibility that extends even to unforeseeable consequences of one's actions. And just as Kant claims that the decision-maker is responsible for the friend's death in K-1, so Sartre—by his use of Kant's example (and as his later theory of strict responsibility in *Being and Nothingness* confirms)—implies that Pablo is responsible for Gris's capture.

In *Being and Nothingness* Sartre holds that everyone is absolutely responsible for what happens to him or her. This responsibility is a consequence of what Sartre holds is a conscious being's radical freedom. I am responsible for, in fact I choose, all that I do not stop from happening to me. He says: ''For lack of getting out of it [a situation] I have *chosen* it.'' And in a most significant passage for ''The Wall,'' Sartre says: ''the most terrible situation of war, the worst tortures do not create a non-human state of things; there is no non-human situation. It is only through fear, flight and recourse to magical types of conduct that I shall decide on the non-human, but this decision is human, and I shall carry the entire responsibility for it.'' Non-human situations would be those in which we would not be held morally responsible for our behavior. Likely candidates might be battles, tortures, or the terrifying psychological predicament that the three prisoners face. However, Sartre insists that all such situations are ''human'' ones and that magical attempts to escape such situations are also actions for which we are responsible.

In Sartre's view, Pablo is responsible for Gris's capture. His magical escape instigated the scenario that led the soldiers to Gris. Believing himself ''clean,'' Pablo thinks that he can act with impugnity. However, he is mistaken. ''I am responsible,'' says Sartre in *Being and Nothingness,* ''for everything, in fact, except for my very responsibility, for I am not the foundation of my being.'' But Pablo believes that it is within his power to extend or retract his responsibility. A major fault with Pablo's magical project is that he thinks that he can rebuild the ''foundation'' of his being, to choose what he will be responsible for. And, ultimately, Sartre's criticism of Husserl is that the project of *epoche* lends credence to the idea that one can select the moral foundation of one's being. Pablo's selective responsibility is illustrated by his deliberations on whether to inform on Gris. He ponders: ''. . . I could save my skin and give up Gris and I refused to do it. I found that somehow comic; it was obstinacy.'' Pablo rationalizes that his refusal is due to a quirk rather than a choice based on a commitment: ''Undoubt-

edly I thought highly of him [Gris]: he was tough. But it was not for this reason that I consented to die in his place; his life had no more value than mine; no life had value. They were going to slap a man up against a wall and shoot him till he died, whether it was I or Gris or somebody else made no difference.'' Since both lives are worthless, he thinks, there is no rational basis for preferring one over the other. The matter is decided by his obstinacy rather than by his deliberated choice. He realizes that he faces a choice, but he is self-deceived in thinking that he need not choose.

By presenting the consequences of Pablo's self-deceived project of *epoche*, Sartre has attempted to show the folly of such an endeavor. Pablo's project functions as a counter-example to Husserl's thesis that use of the *epoche* allows one both to perceive the world objectively and to witness the separated, transcendental nature of the self. For Sartre, Pablo's ''escape'' is an example of a plausible interpretation of *epoche*. Pablo undertakes his magical project in order to free himself from the distortion of emotional reaction and to observe all that happens to him objectively. Instead of awareness, however, all he ends up with is confusion. He is aware of neither his commitments nor his motives for his behavior. Instead of being the detached author of events, he becomes the manipulated one.

In the final section Pablo, dazed and confused, hears Garcia's interpretation of Gris's capture. His reaction to the account indicates that he realizes the truth about what has happened. ''Everything began to spin,'' he says, ''and I found myself sitting on the ground: I laughed so hard I cried.'' His outburst belies his earlier denial of any commitment to Gris; it reveals to him that his explanation of his motive as being due to obstinacy is a sham. His reaction is out of character for someone who has rejected as worthless his own and his comrade's life and is simply acting out of stubbornness.

Pablo's laugh/cry marks, I believe, a flash of insight—not only about Gris's capture but also about there being certain moral boundaries of his life. The confusion of wandering in the yard has been replaced by an understanding: not a detached state of understanding such as he longed for during the vigil in the cell, but a comprehension about his own deception. Perceiving his causal role in Gris's capture makes him aware that what had earlier seemed to him to be the very expression of his detached state of ''staying clean''— his sending the soldiers on an expedition to the cemetery—was in fact an action with telling consequences for his previous and continuing commitments.

That Pablo's outburst is a stroke of insight rather than a reaction of ironic surprise is not obvious, given the brevity of the incident. Described in the last sentence of the story, his response has very little context within which to fix its meaning. As an ending to the story, the laugh/cry certainly functions as a release of the tension built up over the course of the story. However, by limiting the interpretation of the ending to a device for the release of tension, one ignores the ending's status as a resolution of the point of this didactic story. Given Sartre's use of Kant's example, the ending serves as Pablo's final understanding of the moral repercussions of his project to "stay clean."

Interpreting the ending as insight is corroborated if one notices Sartre's similar use of the laugh/cry in his contemporary novel *Nausea*. In the novel Sartre provides more textual background with which to gauge the meaning of the outburst. Roquentin, the narrator and protagonist, during the course of the book develops an awareness of "the meaning of 'existence'"; he sees "existence" as an incontrovertible, brute fact which in its "frightful, obscene nakedness" is "the very paste of things"—not something convenient for use but something independent of human manipulation. While dining in a restaurant, he gazes around at the other diners, and breaks into a laugh/cry. The provocation for his reaction is a fantasy he has had. He muses:

> What a comedy! All these people sitting there, looking serious, eating. . . . Each one of them has his little personal difficulty which keeps him from noticing that he exists . . . but I know I exist and that they exist. And if I knew how to convince people I'd go and sit down next to that handsome white-haired gentleman and explain to him just what existence means. I burst out laughing at the thought of the face he would make. . . .I'd like to stop but I can't; I laugh until I cry.

There are a number of significant similarities between the laugh/cry in *Nausea* and in "The Wall." In the novel, the laugh/cry marks both the collapse of Roquentin's fantasy of explaining "existence" to the white-haired gentleman and an acknowledgment of the ridiculousness of such a project. It also indicates a shift from Roquentin's noticing the diners' "seriousness" to his reflexive realization of the futility of his extraordinary attempt at explanation. His reaction is more than a response to something overwhelmingly funny; it expresses an achievement of understanding: he sees the "seriousness" of the diners as a blindness to

their own "existence." But as Roquentin later remarks, "nothing that exists can be comic," so the laugh turns to a cry. In recognizing the diners' incomprehension as well as the senselessness of his own remedial response, Roquentin signals his understanding of existence.

In "The Wall" similar conditions precede Pablo's laugh/cry. First, there is the failure of his fantasized scenario. Upon hearing Garcia's tale, Pablo realizes that his fantasy with the soldiers has vaporized. He sees now who has been made to look foolish. Previously brought to the brink of laughter by what he claimed was the soldiers' "seriousness" in their roles as captors, Pablo now sees his own attitude and behavior as having been reality-denying. Whereas he had thought that it was the soldiers who did not realize their participation in some low form of comedy, Pablo now sees that he has been the one acting out the farce. Faced with this failure and reversal, he perceives that his other fantasized project has also failed—he has not "stayed clean." His attempt to sever the ties between his present state of consciousness and his past identity has failed. In telling the soldiers to go to the cemetery he has acted in ignorance and has blundered like the unsuspecting animal he most dreaded becoming. Pablo's laugh/cry is an acknowledgment of his failure and, given Sartre's view on the cognitive character of emotions, a sign of awareness of his self-deception.

The laugh/cry marks Pablo's awareness of both the failure of his project of detachment and his responsibility for Gris's death. This achievement of insight underscores Sartre's thesis that there are moral boundaries to human existence and that one of these limits is the responsibility for one's actions. Husserl's view of transcendental subjectivity, by separating the self from the world, challenges Sartre's view. Sartre seeks to argue against Husserl by presenting through his use of Kant's example a counter-example to Husserl's view. Pablo's flash of insight is Sartre's emphatic pronouncement that responsibility for one's actions is a condition of human existence, a condition from which one cannot escape.

Source: Kevin W. Sweeney, "Lying to the Murderer: Sartre's Use of Kant in 'The Wall,'" in *Mosaic*, Vol. XVIII, No. 2, Spring, 1985, pp. 1-16.

Rebecca E. Pitts

Pitts finds in the following essay evidence that despite Sartre's conviction of the isolation of indi-

viduals, ''The Wall'' conveys ''a greater truth'' about the solidarity of man.

I

It has now and then been noted that in the work of Jean-Paul Sartre ''The Wall'' holds a singularly privileged position. First published in 1939, this short story compresses into one vividly rendered situation nearly all the major themes with which Sartre the existentialist philosopher and ''engaged'' writer has later been concerned. It is thus a veritable epiphany of Sartrean man's predicament in an absurd universe; and as Walter Kaufmann points out in his *Existentialism from Dostoevsky to Sartre*, it is the best introduction to the ''heart of Sartre's thought'' not only because of its classic treatment of the ''central existentialist motif of confrontation with death,'' but because it contains other important themes to be found in such later works as *Les mains sales* (*Dirty Hands*) and *Les morts sans sepulture* (*The Victors*). In these plays, Kaufmann continues, ''man's highest value is integrity, and Sartre goes out of his way to point up its utter independence of social utility.''

The theme of ''The Wall'' is indeed integrity—solitary integrity. For the Sartrean hero is the solitary hero—ignorant, up against the wall of annihilation, and ''compelled,'' in his anguish, to choose (and to choose ''freely'') those values that define for him exactly what it means to be a human being. But from the casual comment quoted above it is not altogether clear how Kaufmann has interpreted ''The Wall.'' Another allusion five pages later, however, leaves no doubt that this critic regards the protagonist, Pablo Ibbieta, as an authentic ''hero''—a man of honor and courage who survives his ordeal only because he is saved by an absurd coincidence. ''Even in guilt and failure,'' says Kaufmann, ''man can retain his integrity (witness 'The Wall') and defy the world,'' But although this seems to be the reading that most critics have given the story, there are two other possible interpretations—one of them more consonant, as I hope to show, with Sartre's moral seriousness and attitude of anguished responsibility.

It should be borne in mind that the man who wrote ''The Wall'' was not merely the still immature philosopher of the later 1930s but a creative artist in the high tide of his young maturity. This is important, since Sartre the creative writer has always been greater (at least for many readers) and more faithful to experience than Sartre the philosopher, and not even the philosopher can be accused

of moral shallowness and frivolity, least of all where heroism is at stake. In any case ''The Wall'' is a haunting and powerful story, deeply imagined in its realism and its astonishing situation—a situation that is both completely credible and yet so frighteningly ambiguous that it calls into question the very meaning of human selfhood and the nature of the universe.

During the Spanish Civil War Pablo Ibbieta, the fictional narrator, is condemned to death and spends the night with two companions—facing the emptiness and pointlessness of existence in the light of summary execution against the ''wall'' at dawn. The condemned are Juan Mirbal, a lad under twenty, who turns out to be rat-like in the ferocity of his cowardice; Tom Steinbock, a talkative Irishman who is something of a sentimentalist; and the protagonist Pablo, a rather brave ''tough.'' Pablo has led the hard, unreflective life of the average sensual man, but under the pressure of this night of waiting he evinces more than average powers of perception and introspection.

As a purely technical performance the story gains several advantages from Sartre's choice of Ibbieta as narrator as well as protagonist. In the first place, the sheer fact that a man condemned to die has ''lived to tell the tale'' adds an extra spice of interest to the reader's alertness; it focuses attention, from the beginning, on the element of *situation*. Besides, to have told Ibbieta's story in the third person would have been to rob it of much of its credibility: the narrator vouches, somehow, for every observed detail, including the reasons for his conduct and the changes in his feeling and attitude; the effect is therefore not that Sartre imagined the story but that he heard it from ''Ibbieta.'' Then, too, since the narrative focus is always scenic, ''The Wall'' gains much in precision and economy from the personal qualities of the narrator. Detached, hard, scornful of his cellmates, Ibbieta sees the symptoms of disintegration in Mirbal and Steinbock (and himself) with a cool objectivity that would have been impossible to the others.

During the night's vigil love, friendship, the very meaning of the Loyalist cause itself—all are emptied of significance for Pablo; and when in the morning he is offered his freedom if he will only betray the whereabouts of Ramon Gris, a comrade he has greatly admired and respected, he spends the quarter-hour of respite given him in the linen-room in a baffled self-inquiry as to *why* he will not betray Ramon. (He takes it for granted—though he sees no reason why not—that he will not be a squealer.) When the time comes, however, he is preoccupied with malicious amusement at the total situation: the prisoner determined to be a hero, however meaningless the role may be; the meaningless causes to which he and his enemies are alike committed; the silly bustling and self-importance of little creatures who are all, sooner or later, going to die. Out of an idle desire to send his enemies on a wild-goose chase he directs them to the cemetery—not to the place at the home of relatives where Ramon is supposed to be hiding. But after a day's waiting in a state of idiotic emptiness he discovers the reason why he has not been executed: all unwittingly, but with deadly accuracy none the less, he has sent the Fascist soldiers to the very place where his comrade has in the last two days concealed himself. At this point he collapses in a fit of wild, hysterical laughter.

Quite rightly, therefore, ''The Wall'' has been called a metaphysical problem story, since the situation presented is a kind of paradigm of reality itself and permits a wide variety of philosophical explanations. The thing *could* have happened in this way, the reader feels: in fact, given these people in this situation, it almost ''had to happen,'' as Garcia the baker observes at the end of the story. But why? What does it mean? What does it suggest about the nature of reality? These questions are deceptively easy to answer if the story is regarded as a straightforward presentation of Sartrean themes. On the one hand we find the ''absurd'' world—a world in which anything may happen, even the cruelest coincidence, and in which the void has finally made itself visible; on the other, solitary man—about to die, hoping to die decently, but foiled in his purpose by a bitter trick of chance. Thus at first thought Sartre seems to be telling us something about the universe and the common human predicament, but not about his protagonist—except insofar as we may feel that overnight Pablo is transformed into an existential hero. But once the implications of the situation and imagery are more fully reflected on, we find that beneath the obvious irony of the denouement has suggested, obliquely yet devastatingly, an intensely *moral* condemnation of his protagonist.

If the dramatic situation has seldom been adequately dealt with in critical comment, the reason is fairly clear. Sartre's philosophy has had a powerful and fascinating effect on our time; and the reader can easily see that ''The Wall'' somehow embodies this philosopher's concepts of ''integrity'' and the ''absurd,'' as well as the idea that the values we live

> ''But Pablo did not himself break through or over-pass the wall of silly egoistic pride; and the reality he could not face was forced upon him, as if in this situation the wall was tunneled-under by unconscious drives.''

by, and the persons we are, are always created by a kind of forward-looking, future-oriented attitude. It is therefore easy to assume that this is the story of a brave man who is cut off from life and his fellows by the wall of imminent death, but who maintains his integrity (since integrity does not depend on social utility) in state of that absurd coincidence which transforms him, objectively, into a squealer.

Yet such an assumption ignores, as we shall see, certain basic principles of existentialist theatre and fiction. For what really counts in existentialist writing, at least according to one spokesman, Jacques Guicharnaud, is not the reason for an act *but the act itself*—''its present significance and the significance it gives to the characters and the world.'' It might be added that what counts *in real life*, also, is the act and its meaning—not its reasons, motives, and causes.

In this essay I am chiefly concerned with the significance of Pablo's act in the situation he is actually in. A word is in order here, however, concerning the imagery of ''The Wall''—that subtle aura of linguistic suggestion which lends its own re-inforcement to the theme. It is interesting to note that Sartre seems to have derived the symbol of the ''wall'' itself from Dostoevsky's *Notes from Underground*. As far as the ''underground man'' is concerned, the term ''wall'' comes to mean various hated aspects of the world—the laws of nature and mathematics, the deductions of science—at which he puts out his tongue in impotent derision. For Pablo, similarly, the ''wall'' is not merely the physical wall against which he is going to be shot but a number of other things—primarily, no doubt, an abrupt and inconceivable certainty of death, beyond which thought cannot penetrate and which separates him ineluctably from living men. It also means, I think, the hard wall of the ego and its limited consciousness—its narrow personal interest and absorbed concern with its own separate projects—all of which serves as a barrier between man and the universe, between man and man, between man and his own real being.

Taken alone, these suggestions would scarcely indicate that Pablo is an ''underground man,'' although something like this may be what Sartre means. Equally significant, I think, is the interesting constellation of ''insect'' and ''vermin'' images in ''The Wall''—those metaphors for the body and for other people which echo and intensify the dominant transformation theme in the reveries of the man from underground. At one point in ''Notes from Underground,'' Dostoevsky's spiteful hero tells us that he ''could not even become an insect''; elsewhere, that he could be ''neither a rascal nor an honest man, neither a hero nor an insect.'' This transformation image is later to haunt the black meditations of Raskolnikov and Svidrigailov in *Crime and Punishment*; the change is ultimately achieved by the hero of Kafka's *Metamorphosis*. Taken in context, the images of vermin in ''The Wall'' probably suggest Pablo's degradation to an infra-human level of the spirit.

Thus in more than one way ''The Wall'' may be regarded as a kind of trap. To begin with (if I may use at this point Denis de Rougemont's celebrated definition of a genuine poem), it is a ''calculated trap for meditation.'' Also, apparently, it is another kind of trap for those unwary readers (preoccupied, like Kaufmann, with what they already know about Sartre) who have ignored much of the story's imagery and underestimated the significance of the *situation* in which the protagonist is caught. And finally, if I have understood the author's intention aright—if ''The Wall'' is meant to be an image of solitary man's total responsibility in an absurd world—then the very realism and power with which the image is presented may have proved to be a trap for Sartre himself. By a beautiful paradox, in other words, the objective meaning of ''The Wall,'' as literary form, is perhaps a good deal deeper than the author intended it to be.

II

Be this as it may, Sartre's own creative intention is of the utmost importance, and to understand it we may need to review his well-known but highly paradoxical conception of man's ''total responsibility'' in a world that is stigmatized as purely ''absurd.'' Throughout his philosophical career Sartre has always denied that the universe has any ultimate ground or origin—divine or otherwise. In other words it is simply a brute, inexplicable fact; it is simply *there*, the product of irrational energies that are milling around for no reason. And yet, in spite of the assumed groundlessness of existence, Sartre places at the center of his thought an *obligation*—to find one's genuine self, or rather to create it out of nothing.

He is not, to be sure, very fond of Heidegger's word ''authenticity,'' doubtless because the term denotes the kind of authority which a document (or a personality) derives from its origin. Nor does he often use Camus' convenient phrase, ''the absurd.'' But it would seem that for Sartre, as for Camus, the absurd lies in the fact that man desires meaning even though the universe is meaningless—indeed, that man himself is meaningless unless he is creating his own meaning and values. Consequently what Sartre means by finding (or creating) one's genuine self bears no relation to any quest for the Atman, or the ''apex of the soul,'' or any other version of an ideal self that is waiting to be realized. In fact, in spite of a self-evident contradiction in the very words, Sartre has stated with a remorseless effort at self-consistency that humanity has no common essence; in other words, ''human nature'' does not exist.

To say that ''all'' men are free and thus condemned to choose their own values—to create their own essence and nature—is of course to say something very definite indeed about a common human essence. But Sartre is passionately affirming that no human being is finally subject to (no human being can be labeled as an example of) any over-riding abstraction masking as a universal law. He is thus committed to a radical pluralism of ends, in other words to a *summum bonum* consisting of empty freedom—the most freedom possible for every individual—the only limitation being that no one by his own freedom shall infringe on the freedom of others. Out of such commitments Sartre's most famous dictum is naturally derived; that existence precedes and governs essence. In other words a man does not act as a hero, or a coward, because some antecedent pattern of his nature has determined his choices prior to all choice, or even prior to his latest choice. On the contrary, as one character says to another in *No Exit*, ''You are no more than the sum of your acts.'' That is to say, your *essence* is created by the succession of your choices.

The heart of this theory of freedom and decision is that each man's role in the universe is to create values—to choose ends—and to commit himself freely to the ends and values he has chosen. Thus only does he create himself; and, simultaneously, only by the acts and decisions involved in the process does he reveal what kind of person he has by now become. (Only in this fluid, changeable sense can the word "essence" be understood in "Existence preceded essence.") And although Sartre uses the words "authentic" and "unauthentic" very seldom, he makes the distinction in other terms. The unfree man, the man of "bad faith," is unauthentic because he makes himself into what *he* is by means of those values and future projects which he chooses restlessly, halfheartedly, or dully and unclearly. On the contrary, the free man chooses *his* values and future goals and projects *as the situation demands*, committing himself to them with clear understanding and a firm and undivided will—but only *until the situation radically changes*.

Logically, in this absurd universe, there would seem to be no imperative obligation binding upon everyone alike, not even the obligation to be authentic. At this point, however, the moral tensions involved in Sartre's position become quite clear. It is perfectly plain that one profound motive in his total view is the need to assert the individual's freedom in the face of an increasingly totalitarian world situation. When man is everywhere confined by rigid walls of coercion (mechanized technology and mass conformity), freedom is very largely definable as the freedom to secede—to secede from the oppressive "we" of all the collectivities. But the danger here is obviously that of seceding from the human race itself, particularly when one has already jettisoned the notion of a common human nature. Sartre has always been acutely aware of this danger. He bases his present involvement in politics and his sympathy with Marxism on the *world* "situation" and his long-range concern for individual freedom.

Yet in spite of his awareness and world-concern, Sartre's essential thought has confronted the lonely ego with an obligation to create values for which there is no justification either in the cosmos or in human association and inter-personal relationships. For the cosmos is meaningless and absurd; and, for each ego, other people would seem to exist—at least a great deal of Sartre's writing has implied something like this—only insofar as they are part of the ego's personal forward-looking "projects." In the late 1930s Sartre was therefore faced

with the fact that despite his metaphysical nihilism he was intensely concerned with human values in a more or less traditional sense; that these values were everywhere threatened by the upsurge of something dark and subhuman and destructive of freedom, which he was later to call the "reign of the animal;" and that for him there was absolutely nothing to *justify* his choice of another set of values. Out of this recognition, as the following sentences suggest, came his doctrine of the total responsibility of each solitary ego for the survival of these groundless human values: "My freedom is the unique foundation of values. And since I am the being by virtue of whom values exist, nothing—absolutely nothing—can justify me in adopting this or that value or scale of values."

The exemplary choice is therefore the one that in any situation upholds the human image and refuses the sub-human. That the choice will change with the situation goes without saying. It also goes without saying that very few people are capable of authentic (human) decision—a fact upon which many existential thinkers have dwelt at length. Yet when a burst of hysterical laughter breaks through the wall of Pablo's self-control, we are reminded rather obviously that Sartre is—and was when he wrote this story—the philosopher of the solitary ego in an absurd world. Is he dramatizing here the absurdity of the cosmos or, somehow, the failure of his hero?

III

Never, in all his philosophical and political writing, has Sartre taken the "logical" step from the metaphysical isolation of the individual, as he sees it, to the view that the individual has no moral responsibility. Yet at least one critical study implies that Sartre is expressing an attitude in "The Wall" which is fundamentally irresponsible and nihilistic:

> But there is a distinction between Pablo and the others condemned to death. Life seems meaningless to him when confronted by the *wall*—by the fact of death; but he refuses to betray Ramon. Why? He calls it stubbornness, but it is more than that. Within the limited span of his existence from now until the time that he will be stood against the wall and shot, he has conceived of a condition which he calls, by implication, dying like a human being ("I didn't want to die like an animal"). . . . Pablo's intention (his choice) is to become hard—to die well. It no longer matters what the doctor represents or what he tells the policemen about Ramon Gris. He does not attempt either to save or to betray his former friend. *That his words betray Ramon is pure coincidence, therefore a subject for laughter, not rage or remorse.* [Italics mine]

Actually, Ramon has ceased to exist for Pablo, since he no longer figures in Pablo's future.

Actually, then, ''The Wall'' is an exemplification of Sartre's best-known philosophical statement: that ''existence precedes and commands essence.'' For Pablo to have retained his feelings for Ramon, or for him to have pitied Juan, for him even to have felt pity for himself, would have meant his accepting the view that life was meaningful beyond the *wall*, in terms of something outside his own existence.

This is a fairly accurate account of Pablo's own attitude. But in saying that Sartre's story ''exemplifies'' the philosopher's best known idea, the authors of this confusing (and very confused) comment seem to assume that Sartre endorses, or at least condones, a course of conduct which is immorally egocentric. The confusion, like the assumption, may be seen in the shift in symbolic meaning given to the ''wall'': first it means ''the fact of death''; second, obviously, the ego's ''own existence.'' It is true that Pablo intended (or chose) to ''die decently''; it is also true that he was focused wholly on his own existence. But to assume that Sartre understands the meaning of this situation as Pablo does is to ignore the profound though quiet irony in the events that are reported.

In other words, beneath Pablo's surface intention to ''die decently'' the actual events indicate his failure to execute any aspect of this decision. In the first place, it is obvious that his final intention is not, in point of fact, carried out. He does *not* ''die decently.'' Moreover, he is going to go on living very indecently, since in the eyes of the Fascists, at first (and the situation cannot be hidden forever from the Loyalists), he will always be a squealer—a greater coward than Tom or Juan. But even more significant is the fact that he has failed in carrying out his earlier and more human project: ''I didn't want to die like an animal. *I wanted to understand.*'' It is of course true that no one can ''understand'' death. But in the linen-room Pablo is given a chance to understand what it means *not* to be an animal: that is, he has a chance to see that his project of dying like a man, if that is what he meant, is inevitably linked with *not betraying Ramon Gris*. But somehow or other, ''It seemed more ludicrous than . . . anything else; it was stubbornness''—this refusal to betray Gris; and Pablo fails to see any connection between such a refusal and being a human being.

All this suggests that Sartre is pointing indirectly toward an authentic decision which Pablo did not make but should have made. (Such oblique pointing was his method, for example, in *No Exit*: all three characters in that play are monstrous failures, but through their eternal failure one gets a vision of what ought to have been.) To understand Sartrean fiction or drama, moreover, we must first look not at any psychological analysis it happens to contain, but at the *situation*: it is the act itself that is important, not its discernible reasons, causes, or motives; and to understand the act is to see its meaning in this particular situation, and the meaning it ultimately confers on the characters and on reality itself. (These are not startlingly new dramatic principles: Shakespeare must have understood them very well. What is probably new in the existentialist theater is the abrupt and unexpected quality of some of the actions.) At any rate, ''The Wall'' is dramatic in this sense and we are primarily interested in *what* Pablo has done—not why he has done it, or why he thinks he has done it.

It is astonishing how simple it all is when we take this approach. Argument dies away. What Pablo has done is to talk, and thus betray Ramon Gris to the Fascists. It is true that when he sent the soldiers to the cemetery he thought he was telling a lie and expected to be shot within half an hour. It is true that in sending his enemies on a wild-goose chase he thought, at least, that he was mocking at their silly pretensions and his own. (For who will not, in the end, be found in a cemetery?) None of this is important. It is not important whether he talked because he hoped to gain an extra half-hour of life, or simply because he was unstrung with sleeplessness, hunger, and anxiety. It is certainly not important that he wanted to ''die decently'' and that he was proud of being ''hard-headed.'' What is important is that in this situation (where it was his life or Ramon's) he opened his mouth and sent Ramon to his death. This and this alone is the fundamental meaning of his act.

In this situation, moreover, Pablo ought to have made a resolute, lucid, and single-minded decision not to betray Ramon Gris. Only as long as he had no other choice except *how to die*, could a decision to ''die decently'' mean simply ''to be hard.'' But as soon as he had a chance to live (by betraying a friend and comrade), the new situation required not a casual assumption that he would not betray Ramon, but a responsible and careful consideration of everything involved, including the one-to-a-thousand chance that a stray remark, like a stray bullet, might have fatal consequences. But in the linen-room all he does is to question the ''ludicrous'' fact that he does not intend to save his own skin by betraying a comrade.

But if betrayal is the meaning of Pablo's *act* in this situation, what must we say about the man himself? Sartre's morality is clearly more profound than some of his critics have supposed it; but at this point one is tempted to sympathize with his confused and weary protagonist, upon whose shoulders the burden of total responsibility has been so cruelly placed. In actual fact, just how guilty is Pablo? He was completely unaware that Gris had changed his hiding-place. Moreover, there can be no doubt that if the soldiers had not found Gris in the cemetery, they would have returned to Pablo on the double; he would not have lasted another thirty minutes, as he knew very well. Surely then, one thinks, if this far more probable outcome had taken place, it would be impossible to speak of betrayal.

But on this question it is difficult to misunderstand Sartre's position. As a human being endowed with freedom Pablo is guilty and responsible. He may have been *disclosed* as a squealer only by means of an absurd coincidence, but the act of self-creation had already taken place. He may have surrendered overtly to the sub-human in the act of speech itself—that uniquely human act; but this surrender had been made inevitable by that moment in the linen-room when, *in failing to decide at all*, he made his crucial decision. In other words Pablo obviously did not make at that time the one authentic decision his situation called for—the unwavering decision to die like a man, in loyalty not only to another man, but (more importantly, for Sartre) to what Sartre calls "the human." If he had done so, *he would have kept his mouth shut later.* Coincidence is always possible, as many a true and tragic story has made clear.

Neither Sartre nor anyone else can ever justify by appeals to reason and logic any obligatory, non-egoistic act—including loyalty and responsibility to others. It is therefore not surprising that in the linen-room the desperately harried and only half-conscious Pablo could think of no *reason* why he should die instead of Gris. Apparently, too, Sartre does not wish his readers to attach undue importance to the loyalist cause as such (it was too mixed in character to be, for all men, the perfect cause of freedom); thus in showing that Pablo himself had lost all political faith as well as personal feeling, Sartre is presenting for our contemplation a naked intuition of value—groundless as all values ultimately are, at least for Sartrean thought. Pablo himself acknowledges this intuition even as he distorts and evades it by calling it "ludicrous . . . stubbornness." And it is evident from the way he

tells his story that in his own clouded fashion he is aware that he has betrayed it—betrayed it, somehow, by the subconscious cowardice of his "vermin" body. How else explain his defensive allusions to what he had been through? "They figured that sooner or later people's nerves wear out. . . . I felt very weak."

It is part of Sartre's value as a philosopher that he looks so steadily at the void and yet refuses to make the logical deduction of naturalism: he sees that man is *not* just an animal, and he will not permit him to ride the waves of Nature with an animal's indifference. Meanwhile, from quite another point of view, it is part of Sartre's power as an artist that he feels so keenly and renders so vividly the predicament of men who have already lost (exhausted and confronted with death) all sense of life's reality and value, but who are compelled to decide whether they will live like animals, or die like men in the affirmation of what it means to be human. Yet he is a realistic writer. It is therefore not astonishing that his subject-matter in "The Wall" is not the decision of an authentic man. It is rather the confusion and degradation of an unauthentic man who has failed to decide clearly what he meant by that ambiguous cry: "I didn't want to die like an animal."

Of course no one ever decided clearly and firmly to *live* like an animal—to become an "insect" or a bit of "vermin." But all the same, in failing to make the hard yet necessary decision to die like a man, Pablo has created (and revealed) a "vermin" essence. The metamorphosis is finally complete. What now emerges is a figure that has haunted prophetic minds from Dostoievsky and Nietzsche to Orwell and Sartre—that was spawned in uncounted thousands in the cities and concentration camps of Occupied Europe, that will return in uncounted thousands when the plague returns—the Underground Man of the twentieth century.

Much of Sartre's mature ethical attitude was forged, in action, during the tense and desperate period of the Occupation. "The Wall," of course, was written one or two years before the fall of France; but for people who were at all aware of events and their meaning the revolt of Franco and his Fascists was already casting over Western civilization an unmistakable warning that the plague had spread and would spread further. For a young artist and philosopher in those years it was not enough to read Heidegger, to plumb the metaphysical abyss, to "open up the depths of existence" while merely reading a book. It was also necessary to explore—to try the implications (for action and experience) of the most desperate thoughts. ''The Wall'' is thus a penetrating investigation of certain questions that must have been crucial for this metaphysical nihilist who is by no means a moral nihilist—who hates, in fact, the moral and political evils that threaten all men. If the universe does not sustain man, to what extent will man himself sustain the human project? Will the line hold? How much can man—this forlorn and solitary nothingness that he seems to be—how much can he be trusted?

Thus behind the quietly terrible irony of ''The Wall'' the same theme burns that burns more hopefully in the follow-in passage from *What is Literature?* Here is an eloquent tribute to the heroes of the Resistance, in whose silent and solitary re-invention of the human Sartre's anguished ethic of ''total responsibility'' seems to have received its finest witness. But although written nearly a decade later than ''The Wall'' (1947), this piece of rhetoric depends for much of its power upon the imagery of the great story:

> But, on the other hand, most of the resisters, though beaten, burned, blinded, and broken, *did not speak.* They broke the circle of Evil and re-affirmed the human—for themselves, for us, and for their very torturers. They did it without witness, without help, without hope, often even without faith. For them it was not a matter of believing in man but of wanting to. Everything conspired to discourage them: so many indications everywhere about them, those faces bent over them, that misery within them. Everything concurred in making them believe that they were only insects, that man is the impossible dream of spies and squealers, and that they would awaken as vermin like everybody else.
>
> This man had to be invented with their martyrized flesh, *with their hunted thoughts which were already betraying them*—invented on the basis of nothing, for nothing, in absolute gratuitousness. For it is within the human that one can distinguish means and ends, values and preferences, but they were still at the creation of the world and they had only to decide in sovereign fashion whether there would be anything more than the reign of the animal within it. They remained silent, and man was born of their silence . . .

IV

It is quite possible that the event related in ''The Wall'' was an actual occurrence—a legend of the International Brigade that came to Sartre by word of mouth. If so, like a good many less sophisticated narrators of such haunting tales, he may have intended at first merely to show his readers how bravado and loose, irresponsible talk could lead inadvertently to a comrade's death. More profound-

ly, however, as a maturing existentialist facing Fascism and the oncoming World War, he needed to show that *not to make the authentic decision* is inevitably to make the unauthentic one.

This is always true, as a certain amount of honest self-examination will reveal to anyone; and it is true regardless of how the event turns out. It is likewise true that there is never any radical discontinuity between the moral quality of a decision and the moral quality of the *act* which flows from it. In other words Pablo's act of speaking would have been a morally degraded act even if Ramon Gris had not been found and killed. But within the limits of the story's action there was only one way for Sartre to objectify this fateful moral continuity between an unauthentic inward decision and the act which follows in its wake. Thus whether he invented the tale out of whole cloth or seized on an actual event to serve his purpose, Sartre had to introduce a leap of visible, ironic meaning across the gulf of chance.

Here we come to our final question about the meaning of Pablo's act. We have examined it for its significance in the dramatic situation; we have examined the significance it gives to the character who acted. And in spite of those critics who have misunderstood the story because of their prior assumptions about Sartre, we have found evidence in Sartre's own writing to support the view that those meanings are, respectively, betrayal and degradation. But what light, if any, is shed by this act—or rather by the dénouement that reveals its nature—upon the ultimate character of reality?

In any plot constructed, as this one is, along lines more or less Aristotelian, the final reversal and recognition should constitute a genuine epiphany of the total action and its meaning. To focus upon this particular denouement is to find it rich yet baffling—like reality itself in its multiple suggestiveness and susceptibility to diverse readings. Thus we perceive upon reflection that Sartre has constructed here (or found ready to his hand in actuality) a coincidence that symbolizes subtly yet clearly his own belief that onto the screen of meaningless Nature (the *en soi*, as he calls it), man the creator (the *pour soi*) merely ''projects'' his own groundless and subjective sense of meaning.

In popular speech we take a somewhat paradoxical attitude toward the term ''coincidence.'' On the one hand we rightly assume that it denotes the product of pure chance—of chance, that is, in a sense in which even a determinist might use the word. In other words the events involved may all be causally determined, but the fact that they coincide to form a certain situational pattern cannot be causally related to the antecedent situational pattern in any intelligible way. Obviously in this sense, except for events that fall together as a result of human planning or the purposeful encounters of animals, a good deal of what happens with some degree of simultaneity might be said to happen by coincidence. But the fact is that we rarely use the word unless the events that fall together (either simultaneously or in a meaningful series that cannot be causally related) seem to form a pattern too significant to be ignored.

In actual usage, then, we mean by "coincidence" a kind of correspondence between certain events that cannot be causally related—an acausal *fitness* that, in spite of the absence of causality or human purpose, seems to illuminate the final situation with meaning. Yet the notion of "meaning" remains opaque. Often this is unimportant, since the coincidence is too trivial for the meaning to matter one way or another. In certain cases, however, which are either deeply ironic or startlingly significant in some other way, the problem of meaning can hardly be overlooked. For by definition both causality and purpose are excluded; yet only causality or purpose can be invoked to give intelligible meaning. Causality alone can explain *how* an event has happened. And if any "why" is conceivable to a finite mind, only purpose in some sense can explain *why*. (Language itself suggests that "purpose" and "meaning" are practically identical.)

In the denouement of "The Wall" the reader feels both elements with paradoxical force: ironic significance and brute unintelligibility. So great is the element of ironic appropriateness that if one has understood the story as a whole it seems almost incredible that there should *not* be a purposeful connection between Pablo's words and Ramon's hiding-place. On first reading, to be sure, what creates a shock of surprise is the gulf between Pablo's assumption that he will not betray Ramon and what actually happens. But on closer reading and reflection one sees that it was inevitable, given his failure in the linen-room to make the authentic choice, that Pablo should be sub-human later in his dull, malicious amusement and self-centered indifference to Ramon's fate. This has meaning—the deepening meaning of moral blindness and a clouded sense of reality; thus it would hardly have been our key if Pablo had "ratted" consciously rather than unconsciously. Yet in spite of this moral appropriateness, the event itself remains unintelligible. Un-

less we attribute it to some form of cosmic meaning or purpose (as Sartre vehemently would not), it is impossible to explain or find objective significance *in the sheer fact that the coincidence occurred*—in the raw, improbable fact, that is, that Pablo's words sped home with such deadly accuracy.

A quasi-causal explanation for the event is that when two minds are caught in similar predicaments they very reasonably may follow a grimly similar train of thought. But what happens here, be it noted, is even on this theory no less a genuine "coincidence." It is true that Pablo's nocturnal meditations on death might well have led him to think about the cemetery. The idea comes to him with explosive suddenness when he is exhausted and on the verge of hysteria ("I felt like laughing, but I restrained myself because I was afraid that if I started, I wouldn't be able to stop"); but although there is no evidence that it had occurred to him before, it is a perfectly natural consequence of what he has already thought and felt. Ramon Gris, on the other hand, was in a different situation. There is no reason to suppose that Ramon had been thinking about death. He was a brave man in a tight spot, looking for a practical hideout. His reasons for choosing the cemetery had to do with survival possibilities, not with any contemplation of the graves themselves. Thus Ramon's choice of the cemetery as a place to stay alive in is quite unrelated to Pablo's thought of it as the place of death—*if such a thought was indeed the reason for the latter's spontaneous but deadly shot in the dark*. This theory leaves unexplained the fact that Pablo's words match Ramon's whereabouts. In the world of events, that is to say, which can be causally explained, and of actions that derive their meaning from conscious human purpose, this event has no more meaning than any stray bullet against which a responsible officer ought to take precautions for the safety of his men.

If my analysis of the moral significance of "The Wall" is at all adequate, it would seem that Sartre meant the objective betrayal of Ramon Gris as a disclosure of Pablo's inner betrayal of the human. (There is a vivid hint of this intention in the rat that darts out as Pablo goes to his talk with the officers.) Metaphysically, however, the denouement is an epiphany in a further sense: it becomes an image of Sartre's uncompromising view that meanings are not discovered in extra-human reality but projected by man onto the meaningless external world. It is like Sartre's universe, in other words—at once meaningless yet potentially meaningful to the subjectivity of the observer. Or we might compare it to a Rorschach test in its demand that the reader (or for that matter, Pablo) project upon it his own awareness of significance. On Sartre's terms there is no intelligible relation between Pablo's inner failure and the fact that his stupid words hit the mark; but again, as in the linen-room scene, our moralist is appealing not to the nature of things but to a naked and groundless intuition of value. If we have understood Pablo's failure we project upon the denouement that sense of ironic fitness which in my opinion the author meant for it to evoke. If not, we see it as a piece of absurd chance.

V

And there the matter might rest, if Sartre's evident intention could exhaust the meaning of "The Wall." But in the formal structure of the story, and the sensitive accuracy of his description of Pablo's experiences in the death cell and later, the artist has powerfully (though unwittingly, to be sure) suggested a very different interpretation. No doubt because, as a creator, he is subliminally aware of certain realities he cannot accept as a thinker, Sartre has symbolized here not only man's inescapably solitary ego but that profound and inescapable link with others which is equally man's destiny. And instead of the meaningless world of Sartrean thought he conveys to the reflective reader a suspicion that the universe *may* be expressive of stern and sometimes fateful meanings.

One reason why Sartre has fallen into this trap of his own making is to be found in the very nature of literary form. The structure of a literary work is calculated to evoke an intuition of the work's meaning—and not merely the *work's* meaning: significant form has metaphysical implications and points to the world as the writer sees it. Thus if he wants to express a vision of an irrational or meaningless world, the writer must avoid any conclusion that flows meaningfully from what goes before it—a fact which the dramatists of the absurd and the "Anti-Story" writers seem to understand very well. In this connection one recalls Aristotle's argument (*Poetics* XXIV, 10) that if what is irrational or highly improbable is ever used by a writer, it should either lie outside the action altogether (as in the antecedent circumstances of the *Oedipus*) or else appear so early in the plot, and be so cunningly veiled and succeeded by probabilities, that the reader forgets the absurd link in the chain of events. As the denouement approaches, Aristotle implies, events must seem increasingly probable, so that the catastrophe carries great conviction.

This argument makes good aesthetic sense (for everyone but the most recalcitrant absurdist) simply because experience itself is "probable." But no one who has reflected long on the power of "The Wall" is going to argue Aristotle's point against it. For Sartre has so thoroughly prepared us for his "coincidence" (although it surprises us) that we agree quite literally with Garcia the baker that it "had to happen." This reaction may be instructively compared with the one we would have if Pablo were liberated by an earthquake, or rescued by Loyalist troops. And the upshot is that the denouement has much of the same power and look of cosmic irony as does the revelation of destiny (so often miscalled fatalism) in the *Oedipus*. If so devastating an irony seems inevitable, it is as though the universe itself had spoken—as though what happened were somehow a touch of stern reproof from the *rerum natura*, a revelation from the inner depths of Being.

This brings us to a second, but closely interrelated, reason for the story's curious contradiction of everything the author believes: the psychological accuracy and realism with which Pablo's inner states are described. Pablo is depicted as obviously in a state of dissociation accompanied by a regression of libido into the "unconscious." He loathes his "vermin-body" as if it were wholly alien to himself and finds everything in his past (and in his present situation) shadowy and unreal. Shock and repressed terror can easily explain this dissociated condition: *repressed* terror, because he is brave and tough, and pride is a powerful censor; shock, because he is facing the starkness of death as a vital creature still full of zest and desire. (And although he is exhausted and sleepless throughout the story, he has not been physically injured in any way.) Therefore all this former libido—all this primitive will to live—does not perish. It simply "regresses"; that is, it drops out of conscious awareness to a level where it can activate (and enlist in the interest of sheer animal survival) his subliminal vital intelligence. In connection with subliminal activation it will be recalled that he has been questioned about Ramon Gris just before he is condemned to death, and this fact too may well drop out of consciousness to serve the same cunning vital purpose.

This seems to be a classically favorable situation for the occurrence of "unconscious" extrasensory knowledge or perception—a spontaneous flash of clairvoyance, perhaps, or telepathy. For there is general agreement that states of dissociation—voluntary or involuntary, normal or pathological—are favorable to the extra-sensory faculties; and that telepathic communication between minds frequently depends on some powerful bond between the persons—whether of permanent relationship or temporary interest. And meanwhile, in his extremity, Ramon Gris has been thinking of Pablo: how often or how fleetingly does not matter—what matters is the conjunction of their vital interests. "I would have hidden at Ibbieta's," Garcia quotes him as saying (for he had hidden there before), "but since they've got him I'll go hide in the cemetery." No wonder Pablo in the linen-room feels "a strange sort of cheerfulness": this is how a man would feel if some connection had been made and he suddenly "knew" (without having to face it) the way out of his predicament—a way, that is, which would satisfy his vital desire and at the same time get past the censor at the gate of consciousness.

It is difficult to believe that Sartre did not intend to suggest this interpretation of his story. Yet it seems impossible to believe that he did intend it. It is well known that he has categorically rejected the hypothesis of the "unconscious": everything which a depth-psychologist of any school would explain in terms of that marvelously purposeful (and sometimes incredibly creative) inner self Sartre would explain as sheer spontaneity. And as for ESP, a closely related topic, he would undoubtedly reject such para-normal means of knowledge as completely incredible and illusory. This is a perfectly logical position for an avowed phenomenologist to take; it is even more consistent with his basic view of the isolated ego confronting a meaningless world. In fact, although some parapsychologists and many Freudian psychiatrists may call themselves naturalists, no purely naturalistic thinker is going to be comfortable with any explanation based on ESP, at least if he pursues with any rigor the implications of his world outlook.

Yet I believe that if we knew "The Wall" to be a faithful record of someone's actual experience (as it might well be), we should all be forced to choose, regardless of our theological and philosophical differences on other points, between two basic interpretations of the "coincidence" involved. Either what happened to Pablo is a strange case of blind chance in the external world—an event on which we merely project our sense of his inner moral degradation; or it is truly—indeed *literally*—a revelation from the depths of things. To elect the first alternative does not require a Sartrean vision of reality. Neither Christians, agnostics, nor "atheists" are as such committed to belief or disbelief in paranormal cognition, or the unconscious either, for that matter.

Yet the empirical evidence in favor of both is massive and impressive; so that more than a half century of experiment, in this country and abroad, as well as personal experience (the mystery of certain dreams, to cite only the least remarkable factor), has forced more or less unwilling belief on countless minds.

For the benefit of those who believe (or would like to believe) in a spiritual reality transcending the confines of time, space, and causality, the evidence of ESP research suggests a universe quite different from Sartre's picture of it. Hopeless schizophrenics are usually more telepathically receptive than normal people, at least according to Jan Ehrenwald, a psychiatrist who has investigated the subject pretty thoroughly. Lovers seem exceptionally open to telepathic communication with one another; and the verdict of the laboratories at Duke and elsewhere is that experimenters usually get positive results in proportion to their shared interest in the experiments. Moreover, the intensity of extra-sensory experience is quite independent of space—of the distance between the subjects; and perhaps of time as well—since in several well-documented cases a message has been received *before* it was (at least consciously) sent.

Although the saints, mystics, and yogins of every religion are said to be exceptionally telepathic and clairvoyant, it seems clear that in the majority of these mysterious manifestations of ESP faculties there is nothing strikingly "spiritual." For in their periods of dissociation (from momentary absent-mindedness and hypnagogic drifting, to mediumistic weakness, states of exhaustion or senility, and the chronic deliriums of schizophrenia) quite ordinary people seem strangely open to accidental invasions from other minds. And in the concentrated concerns and loves of their waking consciousness some of them, at least, seem strangely able to get through to others. People are normally separated from one another by a hard, protective wall of ego. But if the above-mentioned evidence is valid, one conclusion seems almost unavoidable. There must be some literal truth behind Donne's great phrase, "No man is an island"—behind even the great *Tat tuam asi* ("That art thou") which rings through all the Upanishads. In other words there must be some more or less impersonal psychic matrix where under certain conditions the mind of one person may touch the mind of another. The implications here for any genuine ethic of human solidarity stagger the imagination.

''The Wall'' seems to be a startling symbolic image of precisely this kind of human solidarity. Why not, Pablo had asked himself, betray Gris? The true answer (which he could not hear because his hard ego could not pay attention to it) seems to have come at the very moment of the question. *Because he is here, he is part of you, part of your life, he trusts you, he touches you even now in the depths of your being.* ''That art Thou.'' But Pablo did not himself break through or over-pass the wall of silly egoistic pride; and the reality he could not face was forced upon him, as if in this situation the wall was tunneled-under by unconscious drives. Had he died, silent, in willed loyalty to what was human in his relationship to Gris, he might have seen—in the lucid moment before death—the fathomless nature of his solidarity with friend and enemy alike. The reality that is in fact revealed to him has become a scourge: knowledge of the depths of his animal will to go on living.

Sartre would reject this view of his story and of human solidarity. But he has spoken so deeply to our time because his world of walled-in egos is the world we seem for the most part to be living in. In such a world, he tells us, the seeker for authentic being must strive (and strive *alone*) to bring to light his own *me*—a quest even Sartre admits is hopeless. And though he never says so, I suspect he knows why it is hopeless. In *No Exit*, for example, his true subject is the relation—*in this world*—of one ego-consciousness to another. Here the hard, predatory ''Look of the Other'' is the one essential impact of any personality upon another; and yet these totally unauthentic beings are driven again and again to impale themselves upon that look, seeking self-knowledge and deepened being there because they can never find it in themselves.

We recognize a frightful truth in *No Exit*. Hell is the only perfect image for a world of isolated, alienated egos, who continue to need one another desperately and yet can never achieve a genuine ''I and thou'' relationship. Yet it was Sartre who invented this image, who found it out, who gave it its true name. In *No Exit* there is of course no exit from this perversion of true Being: this is the eternal human condition. But ''The Wall'' is an even greater and more significant work because it was written, I believe, out of a deeper concern for the undefaced human image. Like all tragedy, it suggests the author's ideal only by means of failure and defeat. But it also conveys the greater truth which Sartre has always rejected.

Source: Rebecca E. Pitts, '''The Wall': Sartre's Metaphysical Trap,'' in *Hartford Studies in Literature*, Vol. VI, No. 1, 1974, pp. 29-54.

Sources

Argyros, Alexander J. ''The Sense of Ending: Sartre's 'The Wall,''' in *Modern Language Studies*, 1988, Summer, pp. 46-52.

Bourjaily, Vance. *The San Francisco Chronicle*, December 19, 1948, p. 12.

Camus, Albert. *Lyrical and Critical Essays*, translated by Ellen Conroy Kennedy, New York: Alfred A. Knopf, 1969.

Cranston, Maurice. *Jean-Paul Sartre*, New York: Grove Press, 1962.

The New Yorker, December 18, 1948, p. 107.

Further Reading

Gerassi, John. *Jean-Paul Sartre, Conscience of His Century: Protestant or Protester?* Chicago: University of Chicago Press, 1989.
    The first volume of a two-volume set covers Sartre's early life. It is the only authorized biography of Sartre.

Mangini-Gonzalez, Shirley. *Memories of Resistance: Women's Voice From the Spanish Civil War*, New Haven, CT: Yale University Press, 1995.
    This well-researched book explores women's role in the Spanish Civil War.

Palmer, Donald. *Sartre for Beginners*, New York: Writers and Readers Publishing, Inc., 1995.
    This book provides an accessible yet sophisticated introduction to the life and works of Jean-Paul Sartre. It includes a glossary, bibliography, and biographical section.

Sartre, Jean-Paul. *Being and Nothingness*, New York: Washington Square Press, 1992.
    Sartre outlines his philosophy of existentialism.

———. *The Philosophy of Jean-Paul Sartre,* edited by Robert Denoon Cumming, New York: Vintage Books, 1968.
    A collection of Sartre's major philosophical works, drawing on texts from throughout his career.

Thomas, Hugh. *The Spanish Civil War*, New York: Simon & Schuster, 1994.
    Provides a detailed and vivid account of the war years.

Glossary of Literary Terms

A

Aestheticism: A literary and artistic movement of the nineteenth century. Followers of the movement believed that art should not be mixed with social, political, or moral teaching. The statement "art for art's sake" is a good summary of aestheticism. The movement had its roots in France, but it gained widespread importance in England in the last half of the nineteenth century, where it helped change the Victorian practice of including moral lessons in literature. Edgar Allan Poe is one of the best-known American "aesthetes."

Allegory: A narrative technique in which characters representing things or abstract ideas are used to convey a message or teach a lesson. Allegory is typically used to teach moral, ethical, or religious lessons but is sometimes used for satiric or political purposes. Many fairy tales are allegories.

Allusion: A reference to a familiar literary or historical person or event, used to make an idea more easily understood. Joyce Carol Oates's story "Where Are You Going, Where Have You Been?" exhibits several allusions to popular music.

Analogy: A comparison of two things made to explain something unfamiliar through its similarities to something familiar, or to prove one point based on the acceptance of another. Similes and metaphors are types of analogies.

Antagonist: The major character in a narrative or drama who works against the hero or protagonist. The Misfit in Flannery O'Connor's story "A Good Man Is Hard to Find" serves as the antagonist for the Grandmother.

Anthology: A collection of similar works of literature, art, or music. Zora Neale Hurston's "The Eatonville Anthology" is a collection of stories that take place in the same town.

Anthropomorphism: The presentation of animals or objects in human shape or with human characteristics. The term is derived from the Greek word for "human form." The fur necklet in Katherine Mansfield's story "Miss Brill" has anthropomorphic characteristics.

Anti-hero: A central character in a work of literature who lacks traditional heroic qualities such as courage, physical prowess, and fortitude. Anti-heroes typically distrust conventional values and are unable to commit themselves to any ideals. They generally feel helpless in a world over which they have no control. Anti-heroes usually accept, and often celebrate, their positions as social outcasts. A well-known anti-hero is Walter Mitty in James Thurber's story "The Secret Life of Walter Mitty."

Archetype: The word archetype is commonly used to describe an original pattern or model from which all other things of the same kind are made. Archetypes are the literary images that grow out of the "collective unconscious,'' a theory proposed by psychologist Carl Jung. They appear in literature as incidents and plots that repeat basic patterns of life. They may also appear as stereotyped characters. The ''schlemiel'' of Yiddish literature is an archetype.

Autobiography: A narrative in which an individual tells his or her life story. Examples include Benjamin Franklin's *Autobiography* and Amy Hempel's story ''In the Cemetery Where Al Jolson Is Buried,'' which has autobiographical characteristics even though it is a work of fiction.

Avant-garde: A literary term that describes new writing that rejects traditional approaches to literature in favor of innovations in style or content. Twentieth-century examples of the literary *avant-garde* include the modernists and the minimalists.

B

Belles-lettres: A French term meaning ''fine letters'' or ''beautiful writing.'' It is often used as a synonym for literature, typically referring to imaginative and artistic rather than scientific or expository writing. Current usage sometimes restricts the meaning to light or humorous writing and appreciative essays about literature. Lewis Carroll's *Alice in Wonderland* epitomizes the realm of belles-lettres.

Bildungsroman: A German word meaning ''novel of development.'' The *bildungsroman* is a study of the maturation of a youthful character, typically brought about through a series of social or sexual encounters that lead to self-awareness. J. D. Salinger's *Catcher in the Rye* is a *bildungsroman*, and Doris Lessing's story ''Through the Tunnel'' exhibits characteristics of a *bildungsroman* as well.

Black Aesthetic Movement: A period of artistic and literary development among African Americans in the 1960s and early 1970s. This was the first major African-American artistic movement since the Harlem Renaissance and was closely paralleled by the civil rights and black power movements. The black aesthetic writers attempted to produce works of art that would be meaningful to the black masses. Key figures in black aesthetics included one of its founders, poet and playwright Amiri Baraka, formerly known as LeRoi Jones; poet and essayist Haki R. Madhubuti, formerly Don L. Lee; poet and playwright Sonia Sanchez; and dramatist Ed Bullins. Works representative of the Black Aesthetic Movement include Amiri Baraka's play *Dutchman*, a 1964 Obie award-winner.

Black Humor: Writing that places grotesque elements side by side with humorous ones in an attempt to shock the reader, forcing him or her to laugh at the horrifying reality of a disordered world. ''Lamb to the Slaughter,'' by Roald Dahl, in which a placid housewife murders her husband and serves the murder weapon to the investigating policemen, is an example of black humor.

C

Catharsis: The release or purging of unwanted emotions—specifically fear and pity—brought about by exposure to art. The term was first used by the Greek philosopher Aristotle in his *Poetics* to refer to the desired effect of tragedy on spectators.

Character: Broadly speaking, a person in a literary work. The actions of characters are what constitute the plot of a story, novel, or poem. There are numerous types of characters, ranging from simple, stereotypical figures to intricate, multifaceted ones. ''Characterization'' is the process by which an author creates vivid, believable characters in a work of art. This may be done in a variety of ways, including (1) direct description of the character by the narrator; (2) the direct presentation of the speech, thoughts, or actions of the character; and (3) the responses of other characters to the character. The term ''character'' also refers to a form originated by the ancient Greek writer Theophrastus that later became popular in the seventeenth and eighteenth centuries. It is a short essay or sketch of a person who prominently displays a specific attribute or quality, such as miserliness or ambition. ''Miss Brill,'' a story by Katherine Mansfield, is an example of a character sketch.

Classical: In its strictest definition in literary criticism, classicism refers to works of ancient Greek or Roman literature. The term may also be used to describe a literary work of recognized importance (a ''classic'') from any time period or literature that exhibits the traits of classicism. Examples of later works and authors now described as classical include French literature of the seventeenth century, Western novels of the nineteenth century, and American fiction of the mid-nineteenth century such as that written by James Fenimore Cooper and Mark Twain.

Climax: The turning point in a narrative, the moment when the conflict is at its most intense. Typically, the structure of stories, novels, and plays is one of rising action, in which tension builds to the climax, followed by falling action, in which tension lessens as the story moves to its conclusion.

Comedy: One of two major types of drama, the other being tragedy. Its aim is to amuse, and it typically ends happily. Comedy assumes many forms, such as farce and burlesque, and uses a variety of techniques, from parody to satire. In a restricted sense the term comedy refers only to dramatic presentations, but in general usage it is commonly applied to nondramatic works as well.

Comic Relief: The use of humor to lighten the mood of a serious or tragic story, especially in plays. The technique is very common in Elizabethan works, and can be an integral part of the plot or simply a brief event designed to break the tension of the scene.

Conflict: The conflict in a work of fiction is the issue to be resolved in the story. It usually occurs between two characters, the protagonist and the antagonist, or between the protagonist and society or the protagonist and himself or herself. The conflict in Washington Irving's story "The Devil and Tom Walker" is that the Devil wants Tom Walker's soul but Tom does not want to go to hell.

Criticism: The systematic study and evaluation of literary works, usually based on a specific method or set of principles. An important part of literary studies since ancient times, the practice of criticism has given rise to numerous theories, methods, and "schools," sometimes producing conflicting, even contradictory, interpretations of literature in general as well as of individual works. Even such basic issues as what constitutes a poem or a novel have been the subject of much criticism over the centuries. Seminal texts of literary criticism include Plato's *Republic,* Aristotle's *Poetics,* Sir Philip Sidney's *The Defence of Poesie,* and John Dryden's *Of Dramatic Poesie.* Contemporary schools of criticism include deconstruction, feminist, psychoanalytic, poststructuralist, new historicist, postcolonialist, and reader-response.

D

Deconstruction: A method of literary criticism characterized by multiple conflicting interpretations of a given work. Deconstructionists consider the impact of the language of a work and suggest that the true meaning of the work is not necessarily the meaning that the author intended.

Deduction: The process of reaching a conclusion through reasoning from general premises to a specific premise. Arthur Conan Doyle's character Sherlock Holmes often used deductive reasoning to solve mysteries.

Denotation: The definition of a word, apart from the impressions or feelings it creates in the reader. The word "apartheid" denotes a political and economic policy of segregation by race, but its connotations—oppression, slavery, inequality—are numerous.

Denouement: A French word meaning "the unknotting." In literature, it denotes the resolution of conflict in fiction or drama. The *denouement* follows the climax and provides an outcome to the primary plot situation as well as an explanation of secondary plot complications. A well-known example of *denouement* is the last scene of the play *As You Like It* by William Shakespeare, in which couples are married, an evildoer repents, the identities of two disguised characters are revealed, and a ruler is restored to power. Also known as "falling action."

Detective Story: A narrative about the solution of a mystery or the identification of a criminal. The conventions of the detective story include the detective's scrupulous use of logic in solving the mystery; incompetent or ineffectual police; a suspect who appears guilty at first but is later proved innocent; and the detective's friend or confidant—often the narrator—whose slowness in interpreting clues emphasizes by contrast the detective's brilliance. Edgar Allan Poe's "Murders in the Rue Morgue" is commonly regarded as the earliest example of this type of story. Other practitioners are Arthur Conan Doyle, Dashiell Hammett, and Agatha Christie.

Dialogue: Dialogue is conversation between people in a literary work. In its most restricted sense, it refers specifically to the speech of characters in a drama. As a specific literary genre, a "dialogue" is a composition in which characters debate an issue or idea.

Didactic: A term used to describe works of literature that aim to teach a moral, religious, political, or practical lesson. Although didactic elements are often found in artistically pleasing works, the term "didactic" usually refers to literature in which the message is more important than the form. The term may also be used to criticize a work that the critic finds "overly didactic," that is, heavy-handed in its delivery of a lesson. An example of didactic literature is John Bunyan's *Pilgrim's Progress.*

Dramatic Irony: Occurs when the reader of a work of literature knows something that a character in the work itself does not know. The irony is in the contrast between the intended meaning of the statements or actions of a character and the additional information understood by the audience.

Dystopia: An imaginary place in a work of fiction where the characters lead dehumanized, fearful lives. **George Orwell's** *Nineteen Eighty-four,* and Margaret Atwood's *Handmaid's Tale* portray versions of dystopia.

E

Edwardian: Describes cultural conventions identified with the period of the reign of Edward VII of England (1901-1910). Writers of the Edwardian Age typically displayed a strong reaction against the propriety and conservatism of the Victorian Age. Their work often exhibits distrust of authority in religion, politics, and art and expresses strong doubts about the soundness of conventional values. Writers of this era include E. M. Forster, H. G. Wells, and Joseph Conrad.

Empathy: A sense of shared experience, including emotional and physical feelings, with someone or something other than oneself. Empathy is often used to describe the response of a reader to a literary character.

Epilogue: A concluding statement or section of a literary work. In dramas, particularly those of the seventeenth and eighteenth centuries, the epilogue is a closing speech, often in verse, delivered by an actor at the end of a play and spoken directly to the audience.

Epiphany: A sudden revelation of truth inspired by a seemingly trivial incident. The term was widely used by James Joyce in his critical writings, and the stories in Joyce's *Dubliners* are commonly called ''epiphanies.''

Epistolary Novel: A novel in the form of letters. The form was particularly popular in the eighteenth century. The form can also be applied to short stories, as in Edwidge Danticat's ''Children of the Sea.''

Epithet: A word or phrase, often disparaging or abusive, that expresses a character trait of someone or something. ''The Napoleon of crime'' is an epithet applied to Professor Moriarty, arch-rival of Sherlock Holmes in Arthur Conan Doyle's series of detective stories.

Existentialism: A predominantly twentieth-century philosophy concerned with the nature and perception of human existence. There are two major strains of existentialist thought: atheistic and Christian. Followers of atheistic existentialism believe that the individual is alone in a godless universe and that the basic human condition is one of suffering and loneliness. Nevertheless, because there are no fixed values, individuals can create their own characters—indeed, they can shape themselves—through the exercise of free will. The atheistic strain culminates in and is popularly associated with the works of Jean-Paul Sartre. The Christian existentialists, on the other hand, believe that only in God may people find freedom from life's anguish. The two strains hold certain beliefs in common: that existence cannot be fully understood or described through empirical effort; that anguish is a universal element of life; that individuals must bear responsibility for their actions; and that there is no common standard of behavior or perception for religious and ethical matters. Existentialist thought figures prominently in the works of such authors as Franz Kafka, Fyodor Dostoyevsky, and Albert Camus.

Expatriatism: The practice of leaving one's country to live for an extended period in another country. Literary expatriates include Irish author James Joyce who moved to Italy and France, American writers James Baldwin, Ernest Hemingway, Gertrude Stein, and F. Scott Fitzgerald who lived and wrote in Paris, and Polish novelist Joseph Conrad in England.

Exposition: Writing intended to explain the nature of an idea, thing, or theme. Expository writing is often combined with description, narration, or argument.

Expressionism: An indistinct literary term, originally used to describe an early twentieth-century school of German painting. The term applies to almost any mode of unconventional, highly subjective writing that distorts reality in some way. Advocates of Expressionism include Federico Garcia Lorca, Eugene O'Neill, Franz Kafka, and James Joyce.

F

Fable: A prose or verse narrative intended to convey a moral. Animals or inanimate objects with human characteristics often serve as characters in fables. A famous fable is Aesop's "The Tortoise and the Hare."

Fantasy: A literary form related to mythology and folklore. Fantasy literature is typically set in non-existent realms and features supernatural beings. Notable examples of literature with elements of fantasy are Gabriel Garcia Marquez's story "The Handsomest Drowned Man in the World" and Ursula K. LeGuin's "The Ones Who Walk Away from Omelas."

Farce: A type of comedy characterized by broad humor, outlandish incidents, and often vulgar subject matter. Much of the comedy in film and television could more accurately be described as farce.

Fiction: Any story that is the product of imagination rather than a documentation of fact. Characters and events in such narratives may be based in real life but their ultimate form and configuration is a creation of the author.

Figurative Language: A technique in which an author uses figures of speech such as hyperbole, irony, metaphor, or simile for a particular effect. Figurative language is the opposite of literal language, in which every word is truthful, accurate, and free of exaggeration or embellishment.

Flashback: A device used in literature to present action that occurred before the beginning of the story. Flashbacks are often introduced as the dreams or recollections of one or more characters.

Foil: A character in a work of literature whose physical or psychological qualities contrast strongly with, and therefore highlight, the corresponding qualities of another character. In his Sherlock Holmes stories, Arthur Conan Doyle portrayed Dr. Watson as a man of normal habits and intelligence, making him a foil for the eccentric and unusually perceptive Sherlock Holmes.

Folklore: Traditions and myths preserved in a culture or group of people. Typically, these are passed on by word of mouth in various forms—such as legends, songs, and proverbs—or preserved in customs and ceremonies. Washington Irving, in "The Devil and Tom Walker" and many of his other stories, incorporates many elements of the folklore of New England and Germany.

Folktale: A story originating in oral tradition. Folktales fall into a variety of categories, including legends, ghost stories, fairy tales, fables, and anecdotes based on historical figures and events.

Foreshadowing: A device used in literature to create expectation or to set up an explanation of later developments. Edgar Allan Poe uses foreshadowing to create suspense in "The Fall of the House of Usher" when the narrator comments on the crumbling state of disrepair in which he finds the house.

G

Genre: A category of literary work. Genre may refer to both the content of a given work—tragedy, comedy, horror, science fiction—and to its form, such as poetry, novel, or drama.

Gilded Age: A period in American history during the 1870s and after characterized by political corruption and materialism. A number of important novels of social and political criticism were written during this time. Henry James and Kate Chopin are two writers who were prominent during the Gilded Age.

Gothicism: In literature, works characterized by a taste for medieval or morbid characters and situations. A gothic novel prominently features elements of horror, the supernatural, gloom, and violence: clanking chains, terror, ghosts, medieval castles, and unexplained phenomena. The term "gothic novel" is also applied to novels that lack elements of the traditional Gothic setting but that create a similar atmosphere of terror or dread. The term can also be applied to stories, plays, and poems. Mary Shelley's *Frankenstein* and Joyce Carol Oates's *Bellefleur* are both gothic novels.

Grotesque: In literature, a work that is characterized by exaggeration, deformity, freakishness, and disorder. The grotesque often includes an element of comic absurdity. Examples of the grotesque can be found in the works of Edgar Allan Poe, Flannery O'Connor, Joseph Heller, and Shirley Jackson.

H

Harlem Renaissance: The Harlem Renaissance of the 1920s is generally considered the first significant movement of black writers and artists in the United States. During this period, new and established black writers, many of whom lived in the region of New York City known as Harlem, published more fiction and poetry than ever before, the first influential black literary journals were established, and black authors and artists received their first widespread recognition and serious critical appraisal. Among the major writers associated with this period are Countee Cullen, Langston Hughes, Arna Bontemps, and Zora Neale Hurston.

Hero/Heroine: The principal sympathetic character in a literary work. Heroes and heroines typically exhibit admirable traits: idealism, courage, and integrity, for example. Famous heroes and heroines of literature include Charles Dickens's Oliver Twist, Margaret Mitchell's Scarlett O'Hara, and the anonymous narrator in Ralph Ellison's *Invisible Man*.

Hyperbole: Deliberate exaggeration used to achieve an effect. In William Shakespeare's *Macbeth,* Lady Macbeth hyperbolizes when she says, "All the perfumes of Arabia could not sweeten this little hand."

I

Image: A concrete representation of an object or sensory experience. Typically, such a representation helps evoke the feelings associated with the object or experience itself. Images are either "literal" or "figurative." Literal images are especially concrete and involve little or no extension of the obvious meaning of the words used to express them. Figurative images do not follow the literal meaning of the words exactly. Images in literature are usually visual, but the term "image" can also refer to the representation of any sensory experience.

Imagery: The array of images in a literary work. Also used to convey the author's overall use of figurative language in a work.

In medias res: A Latin term meaning "in the middle of things." It refers to the technique of beginning a story at its midpoint and then using various flashback devices to reveal previous action. This technique originated in such epics as Virgil's *Aeneid*.

Interior Monologue: A narrative technique in which characters' thoughts are revealed in a way that appears to be uncontrolled by the author. The interior monologue typically aims to reveal the inner self of a character. It portrays emotional experiences as they occur at both a conscious and unconscious level. One of the best-known interior monologues in English is the Molly Bloom section at the close of James Joyce's *Ulysses*. Katherine Anne Porter's "The Jilting of Granny Weatherall" is also told in the form of an interior monologue.

Irony: In literary criticism, the effect of language in which the intended meaning is the opposite of what is stated. The title of Jonathan Swift's "A Modest Proposal" is ironic because what Swift proposes in this essay is cannibalism—hardly "modest."

J

Jargon: Language that is used or understood only by a select group of people. Jargon may refer to terminology used in a certain profession, such as computer jargon, or it may refer to any nonsensical language that is not understood by most people. Anthony Burgess's *A Clockwork Orange* and James Thurber's "The Secret Life of Walter Mitty" both use jargon.

K

Knickerbocker Group: An indistinct group of New York writers of the first half of the nineteenth century. Members of the group were linked only by location and a common theme: New York life. Two famous members of the Knickerbocker Group were Washington Irving and William Cullen Bryant. The group's name derives from Irving's *Knickerbocker's History of New York*.

L

Literal Language: An author uses literal language when he or she writes without exaggerating or embellishing the subject matter and without any tools of figurative language. To say "He ran very quickly down the street" is to use literal language, whereas to say "He ran like a hare down the street" would be using figurative language.

Literature: Literature is broadly defined as any written or spoken material, but the term most often refers to creative works. Literature includes poetry, drama, fiction, and many kinds of nonfiction writing, as well as oral, dramatic, and broadcast compositions not necessarily preserved in a written format, such as films and television programs.

Lost Generation: A term first used by Gertrude Stein to describe the post-World War I generation of American writers: men and women haunted by a sense of betrayal and emptiness brought about by the destructiveness of the war. The term is commonly applied to Hart Crane, Ernest Hemingway, F. Scott Fitzgerald, and others.

M

Magic Realism: A form of literature that incorporates fantasy elements or supernatural occurrences into the narrative and accepts them as truth. Gabriel Garcia Marquez and Laura Esquivel are two writers known for their works of magic realism.

Metaphor: A figure of speech that expresses an idea through the image of another object. Metaphors suggest the essence of the first object by identifying it with certain qualities of the second object. An example is "But soft, what light through yonder window breaks?/ It is the east, and Juliet is the sun" in William Shakespeare's *Romeo and Juliet*. Here, Juliet, the first object, is identified with qualities of the second object, the sun.

Minimalism: A literary style characterized by spare, simple prose with few elaborations. In minimalism, the main theme of the work is often never discussed directly. Amy Hempel and Ernest Hemingway are two writers known for their works of minimalism.

Modernism: Modern literary practices. Also, the principles of a literary school that lasted from roughly the beginning of the twentieth century until the end of World War II. Modernism is defined by its rejection of the literary conventions of the nineteenth century and by its opposition to conventional morality, taste, traditions, and economic values. Many writers are associated with the concepts of modernism, including Albert Camus, D. H. Lawrence, Ernest Hemingway, William Faulkner, Eugene O'Neill, and James Joyce.

Monologue: A composition, written or oral, by a single individual. More specifically, a speech given by a single individual in a drama or other public entertainment. It has no set length, although it is usually several or more lines long. "I Stand Here Ironing" by Tillie Olsen is an example of a story written in the form of a monologue.

Mood: The prevailing emotions of a work or of the author in his or her creation of the work. The mood of a work is not always what might be expected based on its subject matter.

Motif: A theme, character type, image, metaphor, or other verbal element that recurs throughout a single work of literature or occurs in a number of different works over a period of time. For example, the color white in Herman Melville's *Moby Dick* is a "specific" *motif*, while the trials of star-crossed lovers is a "conventional" *motif* from the literature of all periods.

N

Narration: The telling of a series of events, real or invented. A narration may be either a simple narrative, in which the events are recounted chronologically, or a narrative with a plot, in which the account is given in a style reflecting the author's artistic concept of the story. Narration is sometimes used as a synonym for "storyline."

Narrative: A verse or prose accounting of an event or sequence of events, real or invented. The term is also used as an adjective in the sense "method of narration." For example, in literary criticism, the expression "narrative technique" usually refers to the way the author structures and presents his or her story. Different narrative forms include diaries, travelogues, novels, ballads, epics, short stories, and other fictional forms.

Narrator: The teller of a story. The narrator may be the author or a character in the story through whom the author speaks. Huckleberry Finn is the narrator of Mark Twain's *The Adventures of Huckleberry Finn*.

Novella: An Italian term meaning "story." This term has been especially used to describe fourteenth-century Italian tales, but it also refers to modern short novels. Modern novellas include Leo Tolstoy's *The Death of Ivan Ilich*, Fyodor Dostoyevsky's *Notes from the Underground*, and Joseph Conrad's *Heart of Darkness*.

O

Oedipus Complex: A son's romantic obsession with his mother. The phrase is derived from the story of the ancient Theban hero Oedipus, who unknowingly killed his father and married his mother, and was popularized by Sigmund Freud's theory of psychoanalysis. Literary occurrences of the Oedipus complex include Sophocles' *Oedipus Rex* and D. H. Lawrence's "The Rocking-Horse Winner."

Onomatopoeia: The use of words whose sounds express or suggest their meaning. In its simplest sense, onomatopoeia may be represented by words that mimic the sounds they denote such as "hiss" or "meow." At a more subtle level, the pattern and rhythm of sounds and rhymes of a line or poem may be onomatopoeic.

Oral Tradition: A process by which songs, ballads, folklore, and other material are transmitted by word of mouth. The tradition of oral transmission predates the written record systems of literate society.

Oral transmission preserves material sometimes over generations, although often with variations. Memory plays a large part in the recitation and preservation of orally transmitted material. Native American myths and legends, and African folktales told by plantation slaves are examples of orally transmitted literature.

P

Parable: A story intended to teach a moral lesson or answer an ethical question. Examples of parables are the stories told by Jesus Christ in the New Testament, notably ''The Prodigal Son,'' but parables also are used in Sufism, rabbinic literature, Hasidism, and Zen Buddhism. Isaac Bashevis Singer's story ''Gimpel the Fool'' exhibits characteristics of a parable.

Paradox: A statement that appears illogical or contradictory at first, but may actually point to an underlying truth. A literary example of a paradox is George Orwell's statement ''All animals are equal, but some animals are more equal than others'' in *Animal Farm*.

Parody: In literature, this term refers to an imitation of a serious literary work or the signature style of a particular author in a ridiculous manner. A typical parody adopts the style of the original and applies it to an inappropriate subject for humorous effect. Parody is a form of satire and could be considered the literary equivalent of a caricature or cartoon. Henry Fielding's *Shamela* is a parody of Samuel Richardson's *Pamela*.

Persona: A Latin term meaning ''mask.'' Personae are the characters in a fictional work of literature. The persona generally functions as a mask through which the author tells a story in a voice other than his or her own. A persona is usually either a character in a story who acts as a narrator or an ''implied author,'' a voice created by the author to act as the narrator for himself or herself. The persona in Charlotte Perkins Gilman's story ''The Yellow Wallpaper'' is the unnamed young mother experiencing a mental breakdown.

Personification: A figure of speech that gives human qualities to abstract ideas, animals, and inanimate objects. To say that ''the sun is smiling'' is to personify the sun.

Plot: The pattern of events in a narrative or drama. In its simplest sense, the plot guides the author in composing the work and helps the reader follow the work. Typically, plots exhibit causality and unity and have a beginning, a middle, and an end. Sometimes, however, a plot may consist of a series of disconnected events, in which case it is known as an ''episodic plot.''

Poetic Justice: An outcome in a literary work, not necessarily a poem, in which the good are rewarded and the evil are punished, especially in ways that particularly fit their virtues or crimes. For example, a murderer may himself be murdered, or a thief will find himself penniless.

Poetic License: Distortions of fact and literary convention made by a writer—not always a poet— for the sake of the effect gained. Poetic license is closely related to the concept of ''artistic freedom.'' An author exercises poetic license by saying that a pile of money ''reaches as high as a mountain'' when the pile is actually only a foot or two high.

Point of View: The narrative perspective from which a literary work is presented to the reader. There are four traditional points of view. The ''third person omniscient'' gives the reader a ''godlike'' perspective, unrestricted by time or place, from which to see actions and look into the minds of characters. This allows the author to comment openly on characters and events in the work. The ''third person'' point of view presents the events of the story from outside of any single character's perception, much like the omniscient point of view, but the reader must understand the action as it takes place and without any special insight into characters' minds or motivations. The ''first person'' or ''personal'' point of view relates events as they are perceived by a single character. The main character ''tells'' the story and may offer opinions about the action and characters which differ from those of the author. Much less common than omniscient, third person, and first person is the ''second person'' point of view, wherein the author tells the story as if it is happening to the reader. James Thurber employs the omniscient point of view in his short story ''The Secret Life of Walter Mitty.'' Ernest Hemingway's ''A Clean, Well-Lighted Place'' is a short story told from the third person point of view. Mark Twain's novel *Huckleberry Finn* is presented from the first person viewpoint. Jay McInerney's *Bright Lights, Big City* is an example of a novel which uses the second person point of view.

Pornography: Writing intended to provoke feelings of lust in the reader. Such works are often condemned by critics and teachers, but those which can be shown to have literary value are viewed less harshly. Literary works that have been described as pornographic include D. H. Lawrence's *Lady Chatterley's Lover* and James Joyce's *Ulysses.*

Post-Aesthetic Movement: An artistic response made by African Americans to the black aesthetic movement of the 1960s and early 1970s. Writers since that time have adopted a somewhat different tone in their work, with less emphasis placed on the disparity between black and white in the United States. In the words of post-aesthetic authors such as Toni Morrison, John Edgar Wideman, and Kristin Hunter, African Americans are portrayed as looking inward for answers to their own questions, rather than always looking to the outside world. Two well-known examples of works produced as part of the post-aesthetic movement are the Pulitzer Prize-winning novels *The Color Purple* by Alice Walker and *Beloved* by Toni Morrison.

Postmodernism: Writing from the 1960s forward characterized by experimentation and application of modernist elements, which include existentialism and alienation. Postmodernists have gone a step further in the rejection of tradition begun with the modernists by also rejecting traditional forms, preferring the anti-novel over the novel and the anti-hero over the hero. Postmodern writers include Thomas Pynchon, Margaret Drabble, and Gabriel Garcia Marquez.

Prologue: An introductory section of a literary work. It often contains information establishing the situation of the characters or presents information about the setting, time period, or action. In drama, the prologue is spoken by a chorus or by one of the principal characters.

Prose: A literary medium that attempts to mirror the language of everyday speech. It is distinguished from poetry by its use of unmetered, unrhymed language consisting of logically related sentences. Prose is usually grouped into paragraphs that form a cohesive whole such as an essay or a novel. The term is sometimes used to mean an author's general writing.

Protagonist: The central character of a story who serves as a focus for its themes and incidents and as the principal rationale for its development. The protagonist is sometimes referred to in discussions of modern literature as the hero or anti-hero. Well-known protagonists are Hamlet in William Shakespeare's *Hamlet* and Jay Gatsby in F. Scott Fitzgerald's *The Great Gatsby.*

R

Realism: A nineteenth-century European literary movement that sought to portray familiar characters, situations, and settings in a realistic manner. This was done primarily by using an objective narrative point of view and through the buildup of accurate detail. The standard for success of any realistic work depends on how faithfully it transfers common experience into fictional forms. The realistic method may be altered or extended, as in stream of consciousness writing, to record highly subjective experience. Contemporary authors who often write in a realistic way include Nadine Gordimer and Grace Paley.

Resolution: The portion of a story following the climax, in which the conflict is resolved. The resolution of Jane Austen's *Northanger Abbey* is neatly summed up in the following sentence: "Henry and Catherine were married, the bells rang and everybody smiled."

Rising Action: The part of a drama where the plot becomes increasingly complicated. Rising action leads up to the climax, or turning point, of a drama. The final "chase scene" of an action film is generally the rising action which culminates in the film's climax.

Roman a clef: A French phrase meaning "novel with a key." It refers to a narrative in which real persons are portrayed under fictitious names. Jack Kerouac, for example, portrayed various his friends under fictitious names in the novel *On the Road.* D. H. Lawrence based "The Rocking-Horse Winner" on a family he knew.

Romanticism: This term has two widely accepted meanings. In historical criticism, it refers to a European intellectual and artistic movement of the late eighteenth and early nineteenth centuries that sought greater freedom of personal expression than that allowed by the strict rules of literary form and logic of the eighteenth-century neoclassicists. The Romantics preferred emotional and imaginative expression to rational analysis. They considered the individual to be at the center of all experience and so placed him or her at the center of their art. The Romantics believed that the creative imagination reveals nobler truths—unique feelings and attitudes—than those that could be discovered by logic or by scientific examination. "Romanticism" is also used as a general term to refer to a type of sensibility found in all periods of literary history and usually considered to be in opposition to the principles of classicism. In this sense, Romanticism signifies any work or philosophy in which the exotic or dreamlike figure strongly, or that is devoted to individualistic expression, self-analysis, or a pursuit of a higher realm of knowledge than can be discovered by human reason. Prominent Romantics include Jean-Jacques Rousseau, William Wordsworth, John Keats, Lord Byron, and Johann Wolfgang von Goethe.

S

Satire: A work that uses ridicule, humor, and wit to criticize and provoke change in human nature and institutions. Voltaire's novella *Candide* and Jonathan Swift's essay ''A Modest Proposal'' are both satires. Flannery O'Connor's portrayal of the family in ''A Good Man Is Hard to Find'' is a satire of a modern, Southern, American family.

Science Fiction: A type of narrative based upon real or imagined scientific theories and technology. Science fiction is often peopled with alien creatures and set on other planets or in different dimensions. Popular writers of science fiction are Isaac Asimov, Karel Capek, Ray Bradbury, and Ursula K. Le Guin.

Setting: The time, place, and culture in which the action of a narrative takes place. The elements of setting may include geographic location, characters's physical and mental environments, prevailing cultural attitudes, or the historical time in which the action takes place.

Short Story: A fictional prose narrative shorter and more focused than a novella. The short story usually deals with a single episode and often a single character. The ''tone,'' the author's attitude toward his or her subject and audience, is uniform throughout. The short story frequently also lacks *denouement*, ending instead at its climax.

Signifying Monkey: A popular trickster figure in black folklore, with hundreds of tales about this character documented since the 19th century. Henry Louis Gates Jr. examines the history of the signifying monkey in *The Signifying Monkey: Towards a Theory of Afro-American Literary Criticism,* published in 1988.

Simile: A comparison, usually using ''like'' or ''as,''of two essentially dissimilar things, as in ''coffee as cold as ice'' or ''He sounded like a broken record.'' The title of Ernest Hemingway's ''Hills Like White Elephants'' contains a simile.

Social Realism: The Socialist Realism school of literary theory was proposed by Maxim Gorky and established as a dogma by the first Soviet Congress of Writers. It demanded adherence to a communist worldview in works of literature. Its doctrines required an objective viewpoint comprehensible to the working classes and themes of social struggle featuring strong proletarian heroes. Gabriel Garcia Marquez's stories exhibit some characteristics of Socialist Realism.

Stereotype: A stereotype was originally the name for a duplication made during the printing process; this led to its modern definition as a person or thing that is (or is assumed to be) the same as all others of its type. Common stereotypical characters include the absent-minded professor, the nagging wife, the troublemaking teenager, and the kindhearted grandmother.

Stream of Consciousness: A narrative technique for rendering the inward experience of a character. This technique is designed to give the impression of an ever-changing series of thoughts, emotions, images, and memories in the spontaneous and seemingly illogical order that they occur in life. The textbook example of stream of consciousness is the last section of James Joyce's *Ulysses.*

Structure: The form taken by a piece of literature. The structure may be made obvious for ease of understanding, as in nonfiction works, or may obscured for artistic purposes, as in some poetry or seemingly ''unstructured'' prose.

Style: A writer's distinctive manner of arranging words to suit his or her ideas and purpose in writing. The unique imprint of the author's personality upon his or her writing, style is the product of an author's way of arranging ideas and his or her use of diction, different sentence structures, rhythm, figures of speech, rhetorical principles, and other elements of composition.

Suspense: A literary device in which the author maintains the audience's attention through the build-up of events, the outcome of which will soon be revealed. Suspense in William Shakespeare's *Hamlet* is sustained throughout by the question of whether or not the Prince will achieve what he has been instructed to do and of what he intends to do.

Symbol: Something that suggests or stands for something else without losing its original identity. In literature, symbols combine their literal meaning with the suggestion of an abstract concept. Literary symbols are of two types: those that carry complex associations of meaning no matter what their contexts, and those that derive their suggestive meaning from their functions in specific literary works. Examples of symbols are sunshine suggesting happiness, rain suggesting sorrow, and storm clouds suggesting despair.

T

Tale: A story told by a narrator with a simple plot and little character development. Tales are usually relatively short and often carry a simple message. Examples of tales can be found in the works of Saki, Anton Chekhov, Guy de Maupassant, and O. Henry.

Tall Tale: A humorous tale told in a straightforward, credible tone but relating absolutely impossible events or feats of the characters. Such tales were commonly told of frontier adventures during the settlement of the west in the United States. Literary use of tall tales can be found in Washington Irving's *History of New York,* Mark Twain's *Life on the Mississippi,* and in the German R. F. Raspe's *Baron Munchausen's Narratives of His Marvellous Travels and Campaigns in Russia.*

Theme: The main point of a work of literature. The term is used interchangeably with thesis. Many works have multiple themes. One of the themes of Nathaniel Hawthorne's ''Young Goodman Brown'' is loss of faith.

Tone: The author's attitude toward his or her audience may be deduced from the tone of the work. A formal tone may create distance or convey politeness, while an informal tone may encourage a friendly, intimate, or intrusive feeling in the reader. The author's attitude toward his or her subject matter may also be deduced from the tone of the words he or she uses in discussing it. The tone of John F. Kennedy's speech which included the appeal to ''ask not what your country can do for you'' was intended to instill feelings of camaraderie and national pride in listeners.

Tragedy: A drama in prose or poetry about a noble, courageous hero of excellent character who, because of some tragic character flaw, brings ruin upon him- or herself. Tragedy treats its subjects in a dignified and serious manner, using poetic language to help evoke pity and fear and bring about catharsis, a purging of these emotions. The tragic form was practiced extensively by the ancient Greeks. The classical form of tragedy was revived in the sixteenth century; it flourished especially on the Elizabethan stage. In modern times, dramatists have attempted to adapt the form to the needs of modern society by drawing their heroes from the ranks of ordinary men and women and defining the nobility of these heroes in terms of spirit rather than exalted social standing. Some contemporary works that are thought of as tragedies include *The Great Gatsby* by F. Scott Fitzgerald, and *The Sound and the Fury* by William Faulkner.

Tragic Flaw: In a tragedy, the quality within the hero or heroine which leads to his or her downfall. Examples of the tragic flaw include Othello's jealousy and Hamlet's indecisiveness, although most great tragedies defy such simple interpretation.

U

Utopia: A fictional perfect place, such as ''paradise'' or ''heaven.'' An early literary utopia was described in Plato's *Republic,* and in modern literature, Ursula K. Le Guin depicts a utopia in ''The Ones Who Walk Away from Omelas.''

V

Victorian: Refers broadly to the reign of Queen Victoria of England (1837-1901) and to anything with qualities typical of that era. For example, the qualities of smug narrow-mindedness, bourgeois materialism, faith in social progress, and priggish morality are often considered Victorian. In literature, the Victorian Period was the great age of the English novel, and the latter part of the era saw the rise of movements such as decadence and symbolism.

Cumulative Author/Title Index

Nationality/Ethnicity Index

Danish

Dinesen, Isak
The Ring: V6
Sorrow-Acre: V3

Egyptian

Mahfouz, Naguib
Half a Day: V9

English

Bates, H. E.
The Daffodil Sky: V7
Bowen, Elizabeth
The Demon Lover: V5
Carter, Angela
The Bloody Chamber: V4
Clarke, Arthur C.
The Star: V4
Conrad, Joseph
The Secret Sharer: V1
Eliot, George
The Lifted Veil: V8
Far, Sui Sin
Mrs. Spring Fragrance: V4
Galsworthy, John
The Japanese Quince: V3
Jacobs, W. W.
The Monkey's Paw: V2
Kipling, Rudyard
Mrs. Bathurst: V8
Lawrence, D. H.
Odour of Chrysanthemums: V6
The Rocking-Horse Winner: V2
Lessing, Doris
Through the Tunnel: V1
Orwell, George
Shooting an Elephant: V4
Saki,
The Open Window: V1
Wells, H. G.
The Door in the Wall: V3
Woolf, Virginia
The New Dress: V4

Eurasian

Far, Sui Sin
Mrs. Spring Fragrance: V4

French

Camus, Albert
The Guest: V4
Flaubert, Gustave
A Simple Heart: V6
Maupassant, Guy de
The Necklace: V4
Merimee, Prosper
Mateo Falcone: V8

Sartre, Jean-Paul
The Wall: V9

German

Mann, Thomas
Death in Venice: V9
Disorder and Early Sorrow: V4

Haitian

Danticat, Edwidge
Children of the Sea: V1

Indian

Mistry, Rohinton
Swimming Lessons: V6
Mukherjee, Bharati
The Management of Grief: V7
Narayan, R. K.
A Horse and Two Goats: V5

Irish

Bowen, Elizabeth
The Demon Lover: V5
Joyce, James
Araby: V1
The Dead: V6
O'Connor, Frank
Guests of the Nation: V5
O'Flaherty, Liam
The Wave: V5
Wilde, Oscar
The Canterville Ghost: V7

Japanese

Mishima, Yukio
Swaddling Clothes: V5
Naoya, Shiga
Han's Crime: V5

Jewish

Berriault, Gina
The Stone Boy: V7
Kafka, Franz
A Hunger Artist: V7
In the Penal Colony: V3

Jewish American

Ozick, Cynthia
The Shawl: V3
Paley, Grace
*A Conversation with My
Father*: V3
Singer, Isaac Bashevis
Gimpel the Fool: V2

Stein, Gertrude
Melanctha: V5

Jewish-American

Malamud, Bernard
The Magic Barrel: V8

Native American

Silko, Leslie Marmon
*The Man to Send Rain
Clouds*: V8
Yellow Woman: V4

New Zealander

Mansfield, Katherine
The Garden Party: V8
Miss Brill: V2

Nigerian

Achebe, Chinua
Vengeful Creditor: V3

Polish

Conrad, Joseph
The Secret Sharer: V1
Singer, Isaac Bashevis
Gimpel the Fool: V2

Russian

Chekhov, Anton
The Lady with the Pet Dog: V5
Dostoevsky, Fyodor
The Grand Inquisitor: V8
Gogol, Nikolai
The Overcoat: V7
Nabokov, Vladimir
A Guide to Berlin: V6
Pushkin, Alexander
The Stationmaster: V9
Solzhenitsyn, Alexandr
*One Day in the Life of Ivan
Denisovich*: V9
Tolstoy, Leo
The Death of Ivan Ilych: V5

Scottish

Doyle, Arthur Conan
The Red-Headed League: V2

South African

Gordimer, Nadine
The Train from Rhodesia: V2

Subject/Theme Index